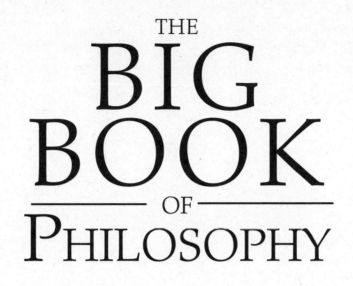

THE
BIG
BOOK
— OF —
PHILOSOPHY

# About the Author

**Naomi Zack** received her Ph.D. from Columbia University, NY, and has taught at the University at Albany, State University of New York. She is currently Professor of Philosophy at the University of Oregon in Eugene. Her recent publications include: *Inclusive Feminism* (2005), *Thinking about Race* (2006), and *Ethics for Disaster* (2009).

# THE
# BIG
# BOOK
## — OF —
# PHILOSOPHY

Naomi Zack

## FALL RIVER PRESS

New York

## FALL RIVER PRESS

New York

An Imprint of Sterling Publishing
387 Park Avenue South
New York, NY 10016

ISBN 978-1-4351-3826-1

For information about custom editions, special sales,
and premium and corporate purchases,
please contact Sterling Special Sales at 800-805-5489
or specialsales@sterlingpublishing.com.

Manufactured in the United States of America

2  4  6  8  10  9  7  5  3  1

www.sterlingpublishing.com

# Contents

# Introduction

What do we really know? What is real? Does life have a meaning? Do you have free will? These are just a few philosophical questions, there are hundreds more. They are called "philosophical questions" because they can't be answered once and for all and have occupied philosophers for almost three thousand years. You don't have to be a philosopher to ask questions like these, although you may feel like one if you read this book!

*The Handy Philosophy Answer Book* has hundreds of entries about specific philosophers and their ideas. Each entry begins with a question about the philosopher, school of thought or time period, which goes to the heart of his, her, or its importance, followed by an answer, which is also a short overview of the main ideas in the chapter. And each section within an entry also begins with a key question. This answer is followed by further questions, and answers. Each question and answer can be read independently, or as part of its broader context.

But you don't have to read the whole book to answer a question about a philosopher or an idea. If you go to the index and look up a name or a subject, you will know what page to find it on. The main part of the book, a Who's Who and What's What in Philosophy, is divided into ten historical chapters, from ancient philosophy to the present day. The table of contents, index, and glossary, can all be used as guides to the chapters.

If you don't know what a philosophical word or idea means, you can find the answer in the glossary, a series of explanations and definitions of key terms, historical periods, schools of thought, and other "isms" in philosophy.

Philosophy is largely a matter of philosophers' opinions and they rarely agree, but they do respect each other's expert opinions. (This book is written by a professor of philosophy.) The bibliography contains a list of sources for the different philosophers, periods of philosophy, main subjects, and other reference material.

You can use this book in different ways. If you want to learn the history of philosophy, you can read through the chapters in order. If you are interested in building a philosophical vocabulary, you can begin with the Glossary, first. If you are just interested in a particular period or school of thought, you can concentrate on that.

If you are interested in all of this material as an introduction to philosophy, or to refresh what you already know, you should read the whole book from cover to cover (at least once) and then track down the material in the bibliography that further interests you.

If you are still interested after you have done all that (that is, if the philosophy bug really bites into you), it might be a good idea to take a philosophy course if you are a student, or enroll in one at a local college, if your formal student days are behind you. A good part of philosophy lies in live conversation, so it's important to find a context where you can talk to others who share your interests in this subject. If you are not enrolled in a course, there may be a philosophy club that meets regularly where you live, or you could look for such a group on the Internet.

—Naomi Zack, Ph.D.

# Acknowledgments

I thank Ed D'Angelo, Ph.D., for his editorial advice, consulting, copyediting, and proofreading for the first draft of this book manuscript. Ed is a Supervising Librarian at a large branch library in Brooklyn, New York, where, since 2003, he has led a philosophy discussion group for the public. He is the author of *Barbarians at the Gates of the Public Library: How Postmodern Consumer Capitalism Threatens Democracy, Civil Education and the Public Good* (2006).

I am immensely grateful to Kevin Hile, Managing Editor at VIP, for all of his work and assistance in revising, copyediting, fact checking, and proofreading the manuscript, as well as seeing it through production. Without Kevin's patience, diligence, and professionalism, this book would not have been completed and neither would it have been useful to the reader.

Last, but also first, I am indebted to Roger Jänecke, Publisher, for his vision of a *Handy Philosophy Answer Book* for Visible Ink Press!

Given all of the conscientious and expert help I have had with this project, all and any remaining errors and sources of confusion are wholly my own.

Naomi Zack, Ph.D.
Eugene, Oregon

# THE BASICS

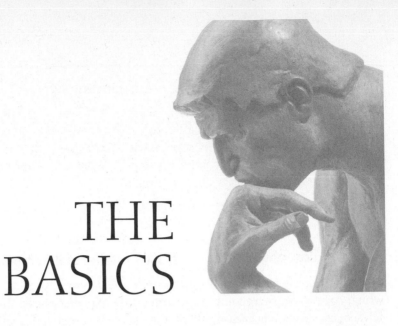

## What is **philosophy**?

Philosophy is the activity of seeking wisdom. In Greek, which was the first language of Western philosophy, "philosophy" means love of wisdom. One loves wisdom by trying to figure out what it is. There are many ways human beings seek wisdom, including art, religion, and lived experience. Philosophy is distinct because it seeks wisdom through the systematic use of reason.

Philosophers focus on ideas, the meaning of ideas, and beliefs by *analyzing* them. They break them down into their parts and then build them back up again and combine them in new ways. In addition to analysis, philosophers reflect on what goes on in the mind and the world; they seek wisdom through intuitions of whole structures of thought or experience.

## **When** did philosophy **begin**?

In the West, the scientific aspect of philosophy, or abstract general thought about the natural and human worlds, began in ancient Greece in the seventh century B.C.E., with inquiry about the earth and the cosmos by the so-called Pre-Socratic philosophers, many of whom continued to flourish in Socrates' time. Between the Pre-Socratics and Socrates, the Sophists were the first to focus on the human world, although their methods were adversarial and perhaps unethical. They were paid for their arguments, without concern about their truth or the justice of what they were arguing for. With Socrates' activities in the fifth century B.C.E., and his student Plato's dramatization of Socrates' style of discourse in written dialogues in the fourth century B.C.E., the true humanistic side of philosophy was founded. The two big subjects of the natural world and the human world endured as the concerns of philosophers, well after the physical and social sciences branched out on their own. These subjects are also perennial in ordinary life.

## Of what use is philosophy?

Philosophy is the only way to come close to answers to important questions that no amount of observation can resolve. For example, philosophy strives to answer questions such as: "What is the right thing to do if there are 10 people in a lifeboat that can only hold six safely?" "What is the meaning of life?" "Can we prove that God does or does not exist?"

## How is philosophy different from other intellectual pursuits?

Generally, the kind of wisdom philosophers love consists of answers to questions, which have to be worked out in the mind instead of discovered through microscopes, telescopes, surveys, or measurement. For example, a sociologist will study what people believe, but a philosopher will ask if those beliefs are true or justified by what is true.

Because philosophical questions cannot be answered with facts, their answers are largely a matter of opinion. But the opinions are special, because reasons are always given for them. Still—and this is what some people find so enjoyable about philosophy—much of philosophical activity is a conversation or dialogue between and among philosophers. And they almost never agree!

## Why is philosophy important?

Philosophical study of the natural world gave rise to the physical sciences of our day: physics, astronomy, geology, biology, and chemistry. Although other cultures (for example, China), have had distinctive sciences and technology, Western technology, as a product of Western science, has had global predominance in the modern period.

Philosophical study of the human world gave rise to the social sciences of psychology, history, political science, sociology, and anthropology, as well as linguistics and cognitive science. Of course, many theoretical ideas about the world remain in philosophy as metaphysics, and many human questions are still only considered in philosophy, insofar as it is part of the humanities. These human questions are of universal interest across cultures and in ordinary, practical, daily life.

## Does philosophy only deal with the big questions about life and the universe?

Not all philosophical work is about important questions. Some of it may seem absurd to non-philosophers. For example, how is the mind connected to the body? Most of us know that if we want to raise our right arm and we are not paralyzed, it is the easiest thing in the world to do—we just decide to do it and the arm goes up. But ever since the work of the seventeenth-century philosopher René Descartes (1596–1650),

As children, we often ask lots of questions of our elders about the nature of our world and the universe. Many of us seem to lose that interest as adults, but these are still central questions about the meaning of our lives that philosophers strive to answer (iStock).

philosophers have argued passionately among themselves about the right way to describe the connection between the mind and the body.

## What have been the **two main subjects** of **Western philosophy**?

Western Philosophy has always had two main subjects: the natural world and the human world. The natural world includes nature, physical reality, and the cosmos. The human world includes human beings, their values, experience, minds, ethics, societies, government, cultures, and human nature itself.

Philosophy of course occurs in all cultures and daily life; but Western Philosophy is a distinct way of thinking that consists of hypotheses and generalizations about what philosophers believe is important in the natural and human worlds. Western philosophers have not been focused on stories of the origins of peoples nor on events in time, like historians, and neither are they focused on individual lives, like biographers. Instead, they have sought to view events and lives in general and abstract ways that can tell us what is true of categories or kinds of events, and individual lives.

## What does **philosophy** have to do with **ordinary life**?

Everyone at some time thinks about general matters that do not have easy answers: "Is there a higher purpose to life?" "Is there life after death?" "What is the most impor-

3

**Where does God fit in?**

**P**hilosophers have viewed God as part of the natural world or the human world, or present in both or neither in the natural world nor the human world.

tant thing in a human life?" "Do I have free will?" Young children naturally ask "why" questions that drive their parents into philosophical answers, whether they realize it or not.

## What is the **connection** between **religion and philosophy**?

Both philosophy and religion address the issue of God, though philosophy does not concern itself exclusively with God as religion does. Philosophy tends to concentrate more on the "ideas" in religion. Depending on the extent and power of religious ideas in the cultures in which they lived, philosophers have had different degrees of relation to theology. For example, when the Catholic Church was the dominant institution in Europe during the medieval period, philosophers such as Thomas Aquinas (c. 1225–1274) devoted most of their work to questions related to God.

Ancient Greek philosophers, who were later known as "pagans," were less interested in religion, and by the eighteenth century Enlightenment, much of philosophy was secular. This secularization of philosophy was partly the result of David Hume's (1711–1776) skeptical writings about both the practice of religion and the existence of God. Nineteenth and twentieth century philosophers developed the field as a form of secular inquiry that does not require religious commitment.

## What are these **various specializations** and **subfields** of philosophy?

Various specializations of philosophy and their subject matters include:

Ethics: how human beings ought to behave in matters involving human well-being or harm.

Philosophy of science: answers to questions of what science is, how science progresses, and the nature of scientific truth.

Social and political philosophy: accounts of how society and government work as institutions, what their purposes should be, how they came into being as institutions and how their problems can be fixed.

Epistemology: answers to questions about what knowledge is, how we know that something is true, and the relation between sense perception and abstract truths.

Metaphysics: the most general questions and answers about the nature of reality, what physical things are, what relations exist between different kinds of things, and the connections between the mind and the world.

Philosophy of mind: how the mind works, whether it is dependent on the brain, how it is connected to the body, the nature of memory and personal identity.

Aesthetics: the study of art toward an understanding of what beauty is and how artworks are different from natural things and other man-made objects.

Ancient philosophy: the birth of Western philosophy from about 800 B.C.E. to 400 C.E.; it is composed mostly of Greek and Roman thought before Christianity.

Medieval philosophy: The development of philosophical thought, from about 400 C.E. until the Renaissance in the 1300s in Europe in which Christianity, provided the dominant world view and organizing principle for daily life.

Modern philosophy: the foundations of contemporary philosophy from the 1600s through the 1800s.

Nineteenth century philosophy: The "classical period" of modern philosophy, in which Friedrich Hegel, Immanuel Kant, and John Stuart Mill wrote.

Analytic philosophy: style of professional philosophy, which is abstract and technical, that developed during the twentieth century.

Post-modern philosophy: school of thought that, in the second half of the twentieth century, consisted of reactions against many of the shared assumptions held by philosophers over the centuries.

### Do philosophers from the different subfields cooperate and get along?

After post-modernism, many philosophical subfields split within themselves when interest in continental philosophy (from France and Germany) introduced existentialism, phenomenology, and deconstruction to the field. Academic philosophers became embattled in their own culture wars. Empiricist or mainstream philosophers defended both their traditional methods and established canon against approaches that were more centered on human existence and experience and cultural criticism.

### Did **philosophy lead to** the other **sciences** all at once?

No, until the end of the seventeenth century, the physical sciences were called "Natural Philosophy"; until the nineteenth century, there were no social sciences and their work was done in philosophy.

### What's the **difference** between the **practice of philosophy** and the **subject of philosophy**?

Besides being an activity, philosophy is also a field of study, like psychology, history, biology, or literature. When philosophy is studied as a subject, a lot of what's studied is the history of philosophy in the form of writings by past philosophers. At the beginning of the twenty-first century, philosophy is mainly an academic discipline, which branches off into specializations and subfields. As a practice, the activities of academic philosophers consist of college teaching and the writing of scholarly texts, which are contributions and additions to the field of philosophy as a body of knowledge that can be studied.

### How is **philosophy related** to **other fields**?

Philosophy is now a subject in the humanities within the college curriculum. Its primary purpose is to study and develop systematic habits of thought that will enable students to recognize and evaluate their own life choices and understand the society in which they live. Because so much of philosophy focuses on ideas, beliefs, and values, it is rather easily connected to literature and projects in contemporary cultural criticism and analysis in other fields. Toward the end of the twentieth century, philosophers began to apply their work to other fields, for example via medical ethics and business ethics. The relevance of philosophy also increased as philosophers added feminism, environmental issues, and questions about social justice to their curricula.

### Did the study of some of the **sciences** get their **start in philosophy**?

Yes. Until the end of the seventeenth century, the physical sciences were called "Natural Philosophy," and until the nineteenth century there were no social sciences. Social science work was done under the name of philosophy. Many sciences have their roots in philosophical debates. Western science began with the Pre-Socratics in the seventh century B.C.E. The Pre-Socratics were the first Westerners in recorded history to think about the world using reason instead of myth. Much later, Western science got another big boost from Isaac Newton (1643–1727), who practiced what was then called "natural philosophy" and persists to this day as "physics."

Chemistry also got its start through philosophical inquiry by Newton's contemporary Robert Boyle (1627–1691). In the early twentieth century, the philosopher William James (1842–1910) founded the science of psychology. And in the middle of

The sciences that we have today—everything from astronomy and chemistry to physics and psychology—have their origins in philosophy (iStock).

the twentieth century, Noam Chomsky (1928–) combined philosophy with linguistics to get the new field of cognitive science started.

There are similar origins in the social sciences: ideals of government and forms of government—topics now falling into the category of political science—were first theorized by philosophers such as Plato (c. 428–c. 348 B.C.E.), Aristotle (384–322 B.C.E.), Thomas Aquinas (c. 1225–1274), Thomas Hobbes (1588–1679), John Locke (1632–1704), and John Stuart Mill (1806–1873). Karl Marx (1818–1883), who is credited with developing the theoretical foundation of communism and socialism, modified the ideas of philosopher Georg Wilhelm Friedrich Hegel (1770–1831).

The first systematic historian was a philosopher, Giovanni Battista (Giambattista) Vico (also Vigo; 1668–1744), as was the first sociologist, the philosophical positivist Auguste Comte (full name, Isidore Marie Auguste François Xavier Comte; 1798–1857); and the philosopher Immanuel Kant (1724–1804) is usually credited with having founded anthropology.

In the twentieth century, social movements have received valuable inspiration from the work of philosophers: for instance, the women's movement from Simone de Beauvoir (1908–1986), the civil rights movement from W.E.B. Du Bois (1868–1963), the animal rights movement from Peter Singer (1946–), and the environmental preservation movement from Arne Naess (1912–2009), who introduced the term "deep ecology."

## Is **philosophy only** found in the **West**?

No. As individual intellectual tendencies and cultural traditions, philosophy has been present in all human societies since the beginning of recorded history and probably farther back than that. In the United States and Europe, philosophy, as an intellectual profession practiced by academics, developed as an official part of the higher education curriculum during the twentieth century. But many societies, particularly those that are still peopled by the original or indigenous inhabitants of a place, have maintained their philosophies through oral traditions. Oral traditions in African philosophy and Native American philosophy often deal with questions about time, space, origins, and ethics.

There are also well-developed textual traditions, going back at least as far as Socrates, in Indian philosophy, Japanese philosophy, and Chinese philosophy (collectively called Asian philosophy or Eastern philosophy). These systems of thought are increasingly part of standard philosophy curricula in the United States, as are comparative philosophy, African-American philosophy, and Latin American philosophy.

## Is philosophy just the beliefs and theories of **individual philosophers**?

No, philosophy is a broad and messy subject. It can be divided into individual philosophers, subjects that two or more philosophers have emphasized, historical periods of time, and even places such as Greece, France, Germany, England, China, Africa, India, Latin America, and the United States. The chapters in this book take a chronological approach, identifying major themes within important time periods.

## Has there been much **progress in philosophy**?

Philosophy progresses in two ways. First, philosophical work mirrors the concerns of its historical time. For example, in the seventeenth century, when modern nations were forming, philosophers like John Locke (1632–1704) and Thomas Hobbes (1588–1679) wrote about the origins of modern, democratic government. In the twentieth century, philosophers have applied ethics to new choices made possible by modern medicine. The second form of progress in philosophy consists of the growth of philosophical thought over time. This progression of philosophy is largely a conversation among philosophers, who in one way or another are in dialogue with their historical predecessors, as well as their peers.

### What **kinds of jobs** do philosophers have?

Since about 1940, most professional philosophers have been employed as teachers in colleges and universities. They also advance the discipline of philosophy by publishing books and articles.

### Does philosophy have anything to do with **ordinary life**, today?

Yes! Philosophy has a *lot* to do with our daily lives. But, depending on the reader's interests, some parts of it will seem more relevant than others. And some parts of philosophy are more abstract than others.

# ANCIENT PHILOSOPHY

### Why did **philosophy start** in ancient **Greece**?

The ancient Greeks had a broad democratic cultural tradition that encouraged individual independence of mind, the questioning of authority, and disagreement among peers.

The sea-faring, trading, and warring nature of the ancient Greeks was conducive to the development of intellectual cosmopolitanism among the privileged classes in this slave-owning society. From the Pre-Socratics on, Greek philosophers were not merely thinkers, but also men of action, capable of leadership and civic involvement. Moreover, the Greeks were warlike and valued the virtues of combat, such as courage and honor. When it came to polite interaction, they did not hesitate to voice disagreement, a trait conducive to philosophical debate, as well.

### What was **Greek wisdom**?

Although Western philosophers have always turned to ancient Greece as the source of philosophy as they know it, the ancient Greeks themselves had a view of wisdom that was broader than philosophy. The so-called "Seven Wise Men of Greece," who flourished between c. 620 to 650 B.C.E., included only one philosopher: Thales of Miletus. (The other wise men were statesman and politicians or practical leaders of men.) The sayings associated with the Seven Wise Men of Greece are:

- Thales of Miletus: "To bring surety brings ruin."
- Solon of Athens: "Nothing in excess."
- Chilon of Sparta: "Know thyself."
- Bias of Priene: "Too many workers spoil the work."
- Cleobulus of Lindos: "Moderation is impeccable."
- Pittacus of Mytilene: "Know thine opportunity."
- Periander of Corinth: "Forethought in all things."

11

# GREEK PRE-SOCRATICS

### Who were the Pre-Socratics?

The Pre-Socratics (the term simply means those philosophers who came before Socrates) came from outlying Greek city-states located on islands far from Athens, which was the cultural center of ancient Greece. Their ideas circulated widely among Greek intellectuals all over the civilized Western world. In chronological order, the main Pre-Socratics were: Thales (c. 624–c. 546 B.C.E.), Anaximander (c. 610–c. 546 B.C.E.), Anaximenes of Miletus (580–500 B.C.E.), Pythagoras (c. 575–495 B.C.E.), Heraclitus (535–475 B.C.E.), Anaxagoras (c. 500–428 B.C.E.), Parmenides (n.d.), Zeno of Elea (c. 490–430 B.C.E.), Empedocles (c. 490–430 B.C.E.), Leucippus (n.d.), and Democratus (c. 460–c. 370 B.C.E.). They were well-educated men who had enough leisure time to ponder deep questions.

### What are the main Pre-Socratic texts?

There are no surviving texts of the Pre-Socratics, and very little is known about their lives. What *is* known comes to us from the writings of other philosophers, beginning with Plato (c. 428–c. 348 B.C.E.) and Aristotle (384–322 B.C.E.), their contemporaries, and especially Aristotle's student Theophrastus (371–c. 287 B.C.E.). For example, the writings of Heraclitus (535–475 B.C.E.) consist of "fragments," and there are only 450 enduring lines from Empedocles (c. 490–430 B.C.E.). Because we have no primary sources, we can't be certain how much of what is related about the Pre-Socratics is skewed by the biases of their interpreters.

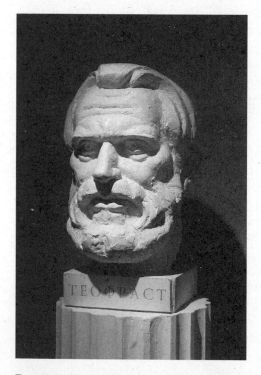

The writings of Theophrastus, one of Aristotle's students, helped philosophers learn about the Pre-Socratics (iStock).

### What was new about the thinking of the PreSocratics?

The Pre-Socratics looked for natural explanations of natural facts and events, instead of relying on mythological accounts of the actions of the gods to explain the nature of our existence. Because of this approach, the Pre-Socratics can be regarded as the first Western scientists, even though, today, many of their theories sound quaint compared to contemporary science.

## What were the **main ideas** of the **Pre-Socratics**?

Thales (c. 624–c. 545 B.C.E.), Anaximander (c. 610–545 B.C.E.), and Anaximenes (c. 580–500 B.C.E.), who were all from the city of Miletus, thought that the natural world was made up of one kind of material, such as water, the "unbounded," or air. (The "unbounded" probably meant something like what we mean by something that is infinite.) Pythagoras thought that everything was made up of number. This did not mean that everything was based on mathematics, as we might think, but rather that numbers themselves were real things that existed in everything else that existed. Heraclitus (c. 540–480 B.C.E.) noted that the world and things in it are constantly in flux, and he claimed that change was more important than what the world was made up of. Parmenides (c. 515–450 B.C.E.), on the other hand, thought that change requires that things come into existence from non-being, and for that reason he believed that change was not possible or real. Heraclitus and other Milesians held that the real stuff or substance that makes up the world cannot change, so that to account for change there has to be a number of substances making up the world. Empedocles (c. 495–435 B.C.E.) built on this idea to posit the four elements: earth, wind, water, and fire. Anaxagoras (c. 500–428 B.C.E.) thought there were more than four basic elements— perhaps as many as an infinite number. Democratus (c. 460–371 B.C.E.) posited that everything is made up of atoms.

## What did the **dialogue** between the **Pre-Socratics reveal** about their philosophy?

The philosophy of the Pre-Socratics can be viewed as one big intellectual conversation. We can see the historical development of their ideas and a kind of progress in their thinking over time if we consider them in (more or less) chronological order. A pattern was thus developed as each generation of students carefully examined and criticized the ideas of their teachers, as well as the rivals of their teachers. Ever since the Pre-Socratics, philosophers have thought about the ideas of their predecessors and tried to perfect or disprove them.

## What was **Thales' contribution** as the **first philosopher** in **Western history**?

It's not the content of Thales' (c. 624–c. 545 B.C.E.) thought that proved to be so important, but rather his willingness to boldly think about the whole of physical existence. Thales' home was Miletus, which had strong ties to Egypt. Like the Egyptians, he believed that the earth floated on water and that water or moisture was the primary substance or stuff of the world. Aristotle thought that Thales had been impressed by the importance of water and fluids for life generally. Indeed, Thales seems to have thought that life is present in every part of the universe and that it was divine; hence, he is said to have remarked, "Everything is full of gods." Thales' most striking and novel insight was that the movements and qualities of water could be used to explain the behavior of living things, as well as natural events. The behavior of water was, in

13

that way, a primary moving principle (a primary moving principle was a thing that was responsible for the movement of all other things), at the same time that water was held to be the primary "stuff" of the universe.

## What **other accomplishments** are attributed to **Thales**?

Thales visited Mesopotamia and Egypt and studied astronomy. He predicted the solar eclipse during a battle between the Lydeans and the Persians in 585 B.C.E. (A legend has it that he changed the course of the Halys River so that King Croesus could cross it). He is said to have been able to measure the height of the pyramids and distances at sea. His practical studies in engineering may have resulted in his creation of axioms, or abstract first principles, of the field of geometry. Thales was highly regarded for his wisdom.

## How did **Anaximander** seek to **revise Thales' philosophy**?

Anaximander (c. 610–545 B.C.E.) was interested in the idea of what was hot and dry; this was supposed by him to be opposed to Thales' idea of water, which was cold and wet. He reasoned that water could not be the primary substance out of which everything else was made because the primary substance must be the cause of all the others. Since water is wet and often cold, it cannot be the source of anything that is hot and dry. Therefore, Anaximander reasoned, the primary substance must be something different from both water and things that are hot and dry.

Anaximander called his primary substance, which cannot be perceived—only things that are cold and wet or hot and dry can be perceived—*apeiron,* or that which is eternal and causes other things to change, but does not change itself. Apeiron, in other words, is that thing which can't be perceived itself but which is the origin of all things hot and cold, wet and dry, and for how these things change—it is responsible for everything in the world as we can and do perceive it.

According to Anaximander, we see the Sun, Moon, and stars through holes in a cold, wet vapor that encloses Earth. On Earth, wet and dry have formed land and sea, and living things are the result of the Sun's effect on moisture. All life started in the sea, according to Anaximander, a theory that actually anticipates the theory of evolution.

### How did **Anaximenes revise** the theories of **Anaximander**?

Anaximenes (c. 580–500 B.C.E.), who followed Anaximander in the Ionian school founded by Thales, believed that the primary substance of the universe was air. Air could itself change from hot to cold and back, so with air as the primary substance it was no longer necessary to explain how the primary substance caused the separate perceptible substances. Air could either expand or contract: expanded air became fire; contracted air became the denser materials of wind, cloud, water, earth, and stone. In many religious traditions, including Hindu yoga, life itself is breath. The ancient Greeks strongly held this association, going back to the eighth century B.C.E., but Anaximenes was the first to give it formal expression.

### Why was **Pythagoras important**?

Pythagoras (c. 570–495 B.C.E.) is credited with inventing the word "Philosophia." He was born in Samos but settled in Croton, where he founded a brotherhood that was a school, a way of life, and a set of religious and political beliefs. Pythagoras discovered that the musical interval marked by the four fixed strings on seven-string lyres could be explained by ratios of the numbers 1, 2, 3, and 4. This was an important realization that forms the basis of the concept of harmony in

Most people think of Pythagoras in terms of his contributions to mathematics, but few realize that his work has also been important to philosophy (iStock).

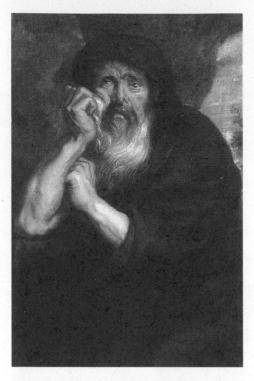

Heraclitus thought that the essence of life was an inconclusive battle of opposites (Art Archive)

music. Pythagoras went on to explain how number systems correspond to natural phenomena such as the movement of celestial bodies. Pythagoras' insight about mathematics is relevant today, because mathematics is the language of modern physics.

Pythagoras and his followers also had a great interest in numerology and theories of the mystical significance of numbers. They embraced music as the spiritual side of number and believed that the right practices—in daily habits and diet, as well as playing musical instruments—could enable them to hear the music of the stars and planets. They were strict vegetarians, except for a prohibition against eating fava beans.

## Why did **Heraclitus disagree** with **Pythagoras** about the **essence of life**?

Heraclitus (c. 540–480 B.C.E.) thought that the essence of life was an inconclusive battle of opposites. The *logos,* or rational ruling principle of the cosmos, which takes on the form of fire and is equal to soul or life, is a constant; within the logos, the strife of individual beings brings constant change.

## For what is **Heraclitus** still **famous**?

Heraclitus is the author of the saying, "You cannot step into the same river twice." He meant that human life and circumstances are in constant flux, like a river.

## What did **Parmenides** and his **Eleatic school** believe?

Parmenides of Elea (c. 515-450 B.C.E.), together with his two pupils, Zeno (c. 490–c. 430 B.C.E.) and Mellisus of Samos (fl. 440 B.C.E.), formed the Eleatic school. Parmenides had the compelling idea of uniting the ultimate primary substance of everything with our perceived reality that seems to be composed of many different things. He argued forcefully that reality is an undifferentiated whole that is unmoving and unchanging. Parmenides dismissed change and the many different things that human beings ordinarily experience as mere appearance and illusion.

16

## Why did the Pythagorians avoid fava beans?

**M**any reasons have been given for why the Pythagorians avoided fava beans: a belief that fava beans contain the souls of the dead; the resemblance of the seed in the bean to a human embryo, so that eating them would be like cannibalism; fava beans seem to have the shape of testicles or the gates of hell; they evoke oligarchy or rule by wealth because they were commonly used to draw lots; and they allow part of the soul to escape in causing "wind" or gas

Fava beans were the only beans available in Europe before the discovery of the Americas. Modern research has shown that some Mediterranean populations are deficient in G6PD enzyme, and one-fifth of those with the deficiency suffer kidney damage if they eat fava beans. On the other hand, young fava beans contain Levadopa, which in controlled doses can be an effective treatment for Parkinson's disease.

## What exactly was **Parmendides' reasoning** in his claims about **the One**?

Parmenides first assumed that reality, or what does not change, is One thing only. Given this, anything that is not that one thing is not real. Because something that is not real cannot have an effect on what is real, nothing can divide the One. The One, by definition, cannot move or change. Since the One is the only thing that is real, what we perceive as moving and changing is not real.

Parmenides' student Zeno of Elea (c 490–c. 430 B.C.E.) defended the idea that reality is One and immobile and unchanging by showing how positing its movement and change results in absurdities. He is famous for his paradoxes. Mellisus of Samos (fl. 440 B.C.E.) added that the One is unbounded, or in our terms, infinite, and insisted that there could not be empty space.

## What did **philosophers after Parmenides** assert about the **nature of appearance**?

Before Plato, there were several attempts by philosophers to rescue the reality of changing, moving components of our ordinary experience from Parmenides' claim that the only thing that is real is the One, which does not change. These philosophers who came after Parmenides tried to establish the reality of things that move or change, or in other words, they wanted to reassert common sense against Parmenides' mysterious claim that the world we think is real is not real, because it is not the One. Plato returned to Parmenides' ideas as a foundation for a more elaborate distinction between appearance and unperceived reality, although for Plato the unperceived One

17

was in fact many. Aristotle provided the most successful defense of common sense and of the reality of appearance by insisting that the world of appearance was real.

## What was the **reaction** of Pre-Socratic philosophers **to Parmenides' monism**?

Several philosophers after Parmenides felt he was oversimplifying things and offered more complex explanations of the nature of reality. Although these attempts did not always convince their contemporary audiences, they were greatly appreciated later on in the history of philosophy.

## What was **Empedocles'** idea about the **four elements**

The Sicilian poet-philosopher Empedocles (c. 495–435 B.C.E.) posited the four-element theory: fire, air, water, and earth are the four things from which everything else is made. Ordinary things like cats and rivers are but temporary recombinations of these elements. Also, the source of motion for these elements is love and strife, love bringing them together, strife separating them.

## What was **Anaxagoras'** idea about the **Mind**?

Anaxagoras of Clazoenae (c. 500–428 B.C.E.) believed that the first cause of motion was Mind, which is separate from everything else. Mind created the things in the world by starting a vortex in which different kinds of matter separated out.

Empedocles as depicted by Italian artist Luca Signorelli (Art Archive).

Democratus appears on a 1967 Greek drachma note (BigStock).

### Who first came up with the concept of atoms?

Democratus (c. 460–371 B.C.E.)—a student of Leucippus (fl. 450–420) who opposed Parmenides and Zeno (c. 490–c. 430 B.C.E.) by saying that empty space is real—said that existence is made up of a very large number of things that cannot be cut apart. He called these things *a-tomos* or atoms. Atoms are in motion within infinite space. They collide, and their movement creates a vortex; out of that, different kinds of things result. The only real qualities that we can perceive are size and shape, because the atoms have that, but everything else available to the senses is an illusion. Democratus was the originator of what became the modern theory of atoms.

# THE SOPHISTS

### Who were the Sophists?

In the fifth and early fourth centuries B.C.E. in Greece the Sophists were the solution to increasing litigiousness and education. If you can imagine a professional who is a cross between a lawyer and a self-help coach, that would be a good description of a Sophist. The Sophists put on public exhibitions for pay to teach Greek citizens how to succeed in their public and civic lives. They were constantly "on tour," and some became very famous. Intellectually, the Sophists were a cross between pragmatists (in the common sense use of this term, not the philosophical one) and relativists. In our day, a pragmatist is someone practical who is motivated by results, rather than "high-falutin" principles or abstract theories. And a relativist is someone who believes that

19

there are no absolute truths or universal values, but simply what seems to be the case for individuals, and what they desire.

## Why were the **Sophists important** philosophically?

The Sophists do not have an august reputation, and their successors in ancient times, particularly Plato, had little praise for their contributions to philosophy. However, that assessment may not be altogether fair. Unlike the Pre-Socratics, who concentrated on the natural, non-human world, the Sophists were interested in human nature and human affairs. The Sophists were the first humanists in Western philosophy. We should also keep in mind that much of their thought was opposed to the timeless wisdom prized by Plato, and much of how they were characterized comes from Plato.

The Sophists were public intellectuals who popularized existing knowledge and wisdom, with some original modification. The subjects they addressed included: grammar, theory of language, ethics, political philosophy and doctrines, religion, ideas about the gods, human nature and the origins of humankind, literary criticism, mathematics, and last but not least, speculations about the natural world that had been developed by the Pre-Socratics.

## What were the **important ideas** of the **Sophists**?

First and foremost, the Sophists were in revolt against the Pre-Socratic idea that there is some ultimate reality that is unlike what we perceive and experience in the ordinary world, but in some sense causes what we do perceive and experience. The Sophists elevated the importance of the world that appeared to exist for human beings, or as the twentieth century philosopher Jürgen Habermas (b. 1929–) famously called it, "the lifeworld" (although Edmund Husserl [1859–1938] originated the term). They all thought that virtue can be taught, which meant that anyone could participate in government, regardless of their wealth or social class. In that sense, the Sophists enabled ancient Greek democracy.

The Sophists insisted that moral beliefs should have rational reasons and be capable of defense in rational argument. In Sophistic treatments of morality, human nature was often opposed to society or convention, and the Sophists were on the side of nature.

Finally, it should be noted that the Sophists practiced in an oral tradition, which Socrates was to bring to a level of elegant perfection that no single philosopher or school has equaled in the millennia since his death.

## What was **Protagoras famous** for?

Protagoras of Abdera in Thrace (c. 490–420 B.C.E.) was the most acclaimed of all the Sophists. Plato wrote that he was the first Sophist to call himself a Sophist. He trained young men for politics and was friends with the statesman Pericles (c. 495–429 B.C.E.), who asked him to write a constitution for the new colony of Thuri. He was a productive writer, and his works included "On Truth," "On the Gods," and "Antilogic," none of which have survived to this day. Protagoras was the author of the humanistic credo "Man is the measure of all things, of all things that are, that they are and of things that are not that they are not."

Protagoras held that the soul is nothing above or beyond a person's perceptions. His relativism was based on the different perceptual experiences of different individuals; for instance, what is cold to one person may seem warm to another. And he extended the relativism of individual experience to large groups in claiming that "whatever is just to a city is just for that city so long as it seems so."

However, although all perceptions and ideas of justice are true, according to Protagoras, he thought that some were better than others. He felt that it was the job of the Sophist to change people's minds so that they had better ideas about what was just and beautiful. The better perceptions and ideas were those that had better consequences. In other words, the Sophists taught their "clients" how to succeed.

## What did **Gorgias** say about **thought versus existence**?

Gorgias of Leontini in Sicily (c. 485–380 B.C.E.) taught the art of persuasion for success in politics. His surviving treatise "Of That Which Is Not; or, On Nature" claims that nothing truly is. Although, even if anything *were* to exist, it could not be comprehended by man; and even if it *could* be comprehended, it could not be communicated. Just because we have a thought about something does not mean that thing exists. Thoughts do not entail the existence of what is thought, or else humans could not think about, for instance, imaginary animals. Or in other words, not everything we think about exists or is real. Therefore, Gorgias concluded, if anything exists, it cannot be thought. The same gap between thoughts and things occurs between words and things and between the thoughts of different human beings.

### Does **Gorgias' conclusion** that whatever is **real cannot be thought** make sense?

No, there is a gap in his reasoning. Just because thinking about a thing is no guarantee that the thing exists, does not mean that none of our thoughts are thoughts about what exists.

### What did **Hippias contribute** to **learning**?

The Sophist Hippias of Ellis (c. 460 B.C.E.) made a lot of money in his travels. He was polymathic (widely knowledgeable), and wrote poems, plays, histories, and speeches, as well as discussions of literature, astronomy, geometry, arithmetic, the arts, ethics, and mnemonics. He made an important mathematical discovery of the curve used to trisect an angle, the *quadratrix*. He argued against Pre-Socratic posits of hidden reality and advocated self-sufficiency as a virtue. In conflicts between nature and convention, he is said to have advocated following nature. This meant that if he felt like doing something, and there was a rule against it, he was in favor of doing that thing and breaking the rule.

### What did **Prodicus** tell his audiences?

Prodicus of Ceos (c. 465–415 B.C.E.) said that Empedocles' four elements of earth, wind, fire, and water were divine (a doctrine that the playwright Aristophanes (c. 446–386) made fun of in *The Birds*). He also thought that whatever was necessary to human beings was considered holy, which was not a traditional view of religion in ancient Greece.

Prodicus argued that there is no absolute good, because what is good for one man is not necessarily good for another, a doctrine that supported relativism. In his discussions of language, Prodicus tried to show how no two words can have the same meaning. He also disagreed with Democratus (c. 460–371 B.C.E.), who had said that there could be different names for the same thing.

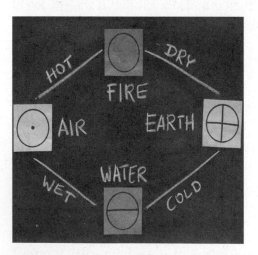

Some ancient Sophists believed the world was composed of four elements, and some considered them to be divine in nature (iStock).

### What did **Thrasymachus** think about the concept of **justice**?

Thrasymachus of Bithynia (fl. 427 B.C.E.) is known mainly as a character in Plato's *Republic,* whom Socrates trounces in preliminary attempts to define justice. Thrasymachus asserted that justice is no more than what benefits those in power, and that it is therefore of no use to those

## How did Prodicus make his living?

**P**rodicus (b. 460B.C.E.), a Sophist, was an ambassador for his home city of Ceos. He traveled widely and became rich from his exhibitions. One of his specialties was distinguishing between synonyms, and Socrates claimed in Plato's *Protagoras* and *Meno* to have been his student. Prodicus had two versions of his talks: the one-drachma lecture and the 50-drachma lecture. Socrates joked that he would have been more learned about words if he'd been able to afford the 50-drachma lecture. The one-drachma lecture had much larger audiences, but, according to Aristotle, Prodicus sometimes gave the larger audiences a bargain by "slipping in the 50-drachma lecture for them." If Aristotle's story is true, scholarly commentators have overlooked the possibility that the Sophists invented modern sales techniques.

who are ruled by them. In real life, Thrasymachus is believed to have traveled and taught throughout Greece, besides being famous in Athens. In a speech he wrote for a member of the assembly, he advocated for Greek unity and efficiency in government.

# SOCRATES

### Did **Socrates really exist**?

Socrates of Athens (460–399 B.C.E.) was both a real historical person and the main character in Plato's dialogues. In both modes, he perfected the methods of the Sophist's in rhetoric, argument, and dialogue, but as a character in Plato's later dialogues he appears mainly as a mouthpiece for Plato's abstract philosophy.

While there is some controversy about how much concerning Socrates, the philosopher, was invented by Plato, there is stable agreement about certain facts of his life. All agree that Socrates lived the principles he taught, the most famous being, "The unexamined life is not worth living." Socrates' father, Sophroniscus, was a stonecutter from Alopeke; and his mother, Phaenarete, was a midwife. Socrates himself was fond of referring to his philosophical manner of discourse as a form of midwifery. In Plato's *Meno,* he uses this role to extract mathematical truths from a slave boy as proof of the presence of innate ideas in the soul, which are first acquired in a divine realm before birth.

Sophroniscus was friends with Athenian general and statesman Aristides the Just (530–468 B.C.E.), which helped Socrates become connected throughout his life with the leadership class of Athens. He served ably and courageously as a *hoplite* (infantry-

A statue of Socrates is located at the Academy of Athens in Greece (iStock).

man) in the Peloponnesian War (431–404 B.C.E.). When he became absorbed in philosophical activities, however, he became poor. Socrates' wife, Xantippe, was depicted as a shrew in later writings about him, but he cared for his young sons, and asked his friends to provide for their (Socratic) education after his death.

Socrates was condemned to death for "not believing in the gods the state believes in, and introducing different new divine powers; and also for corrupting the young," according to the indictments related in Plato's *Apology* and Xenophon's *Apology*. He died peacefully by his own hand, drinking a cup of hemlock in preference to the escape arranged by his friends, which would have resulted in a life of exile. He refused exile because it was dishonorable and because he had voluntarily lived in Athens and accepted its laws throughout his life. To desert his city so as to avoid death would be disloyal in his mind. Socrates said he did not fear death, because he knew nothing about it. If there were no afterlife, dying would be like falling asleep, and if there were an afterlife it would enable a higher stage of discourse—it would be heaven. Another interpretation is that Socrates did not have much to lose by dying—he was already an old man.

## What are the **Socratic paradoxes**?

Socrates provided resolutions to claims that appeared to contradict common sense. Here are two examples.

> Paradox 1: No one desires evil but many have evil goals or are bad themselves. This is because those who pursue evil do not know that it is evil. That is, the source of evil is ignorance.

> Paradox 2: It is better to be the victim of injustice than the perpetrator. This is because being just is a primary virtue and a quality of all of the other virtues. Attaining virtue is the main purpose of life, as well as a path to happiness. Happiness as the result of being just is thus an inner matter that is independent of external circumstances.

## What is **Socratic irony**?

In both real life and Plato's dialogues, Socrates liked to draw his audience into debate by presenting himself as knowing nothing. The oracle at Delphi had said that there was no man wiser than Socrates, although Socrates himself always said that he knew nothing. (The fact that he *knew* he knew nothing is said to have set him apart from everyone else.)

Socrates would begin a dialogue by flattering his interlocutors about their intelligence or virtue. If they were willing to converse with him a process of careful questioning followed. From such "interrogation" it would emerge that the person he was talking to knew very little about the subject in which he was supposed to be an expert. In saying at the outset that he himself knew nothing, Socrates had nothing to lose, whereas his interlocutors would either be personally humiliated or unmasked as hypocrites or charlatans.

## What are some key **events** for which **Socrates** is often **remembered**?

Although Plato imports the character of Socrates into almost all of his dialogues, the early dialogues are considered to present a more accurate picture of the historical Socrates, who left no writings of his own. At one time, Socrates studied natural philosophy with Archelaus, who was a pupil of Anaxagoras (c. 500–428 B.C.E.). But by the time he took up philosophy in earnest Socrates' main interests were in ethics. Unlike many Athenians, he claimed not to understand how ethics derived from religion.

In Plato's *Euthyphro,* Socrates encounters the eponymous priest on the way to his own trial and asks him what piety is. Euthyphro responds that piety is what the gods love. Socrates asks him if piety is good because the gods love it, or if the gods love it because it is good. If something is good because the gods love it, then we need to know which gods to follow, because the gods often disagree. But if the gods love something because it is already good, then there must be a standard of goodness, or in this case, piety, which is separate from the gods. That means that the gods are not in themselves the source of morality. Euthyphro, of course, has no answer to this dilemma, and scurries away from Socrates.

In the *Apology,* Socrates taunts and baits the young prosecutor Meletus in a display of dialectic that is exactly what he is on trial for. He relates how he began talking to the experts in the arts and government to seek wisdom, but found that apart from their high birth, wealth, or respected positions, these experts knew less than he. Socrates swears that he has always served Athens, first as a soldier and then as a citizen concerned for the virtue of its youth. He avows his own belief in the approved gods and denies that he ever tried to introduce new gods.

The jury of 450 convict him with a majority of 30. Socrates has the right to make an alternative proposal to the death sentence. Voluntary exile would be an appropriate alternative, but instead Socrates suggests that he be given free meals in the Prytaneum for the rest of his life, in place of some charioteer (the charioteers were champion chariot drivers who had high status as popular heroes, as well as athletes.) The charioteers, Socrates says, only make people feel good, while he directly attends to

Socrates' death is depicted in this 1876 engraving. He was convicted in a trial for not having the correct belief in the gods and for "corrupting the young" (iStock).

their well-being. He also proposes first a fine of one mina, and then, at the insistence of his friends, 30 minae (still an absurdly small sum against a sentence of death). The court is not moved by Socrates' counter proposal and the death sentence stands.

In the introduction to Plato's *Republic,* Socrates sets up the purpose of this utopian work, by talking to a group of friends about the nature of justice. Here, Thrasymachus says that justice is whatever serves those in power. Socrates follows with a description of the psychology of a just person, but this does not answer the question of what justice itself is. Socrates then suggests that justice in individuals is difficult to define, but that insofar as the state is the individual "writ large," it might be easier to understand what makes a state just and answer the question in that way. The *Republic* proper is Plato's description of a just state.

## What is the **Socratic method**?

The Socratic method has two main parts. First, a question is asked about a difficult subject. Second, the answer is followed up with another question, and a dialogue follows. Socrates often asked difficult questions of people who were considered wise and competent, and when their answers were not satisfactory, Socrates asked more questions.

More generally, and without the questioner intending to make a fool of the person of whom he asks a question, the Socratic method is a way of teaching that involves an ongoing conversation about a subject between a teacher and student.

### What is **Aristophanes'** comedy *The Clouds* and how does it relate to **Socrates**?

Aristophanes' comedy *The Clouds* (423 B.C.E.) is considered a satire of Socrates and other intellectuals of the day. In the story, Strepsiades is an Athenian who has been plunged into debt by his spoiled, extravagant son, Pheidippides. Socrates appears, suspended in air, and asks Strepsiades to remove his clothes before entering his "Thinkery."

Socrates proceeds to relate his discoveries, which include the distance a flea can jump and determining if a gnat is whistling or farting. He insists that a vortex, and not Zeus, is the cause of rain. The play continues with absurdities such as Socrates stealing from a nearby wrestling school to feed his students, and insults to the audience in the course of a debate about new and old logic. At the end, Stepsiades' son, who has been schooled in the Thinkery, tells Stepsiades that it would be morally right for him to beat both his father and his mother. The outraged Stepsiades sets the Thinkery on fire and viciously beats up Socrates and his students.

Some believed that *The Clouds* contributed to the slander against Socrates that led to his trial and death sentence. But Socrates is said to have appeared on stage after the first performance and waved to the audience. And in Plato's *Symposium,* Socrates and Aristophanes are depicted drinking together and conversing in friendship.

# PLATO

### What do we know for sure about **Plato's life**?

Although Plato (427–347 B.C.E.) is perhaps the most influential and highly revered philosopher in the Western tradition, and thousands of philosophical careers have been based on his ideas, little is known about his life, with certainty. This is partly because there was a convention in Plato's time that philosophers writing about their contemporaries not mention them by name. Nevertheless, there is agreement on some broad facts about Plato's life. Plato, for instance, was present at Socrates' trial and began his own philosophical works about 15 or 20 years later. Plato was the scion of a politically well-placed, rich aristocratic family who were anti-democrats. At first, Plato envisioned a political career for himself, but after the democrats gained power and Socrates was sentenced to death, he prudently avoided politics.

Plato served in military campaigns in the war against Sparta and was probably in the cavalry. In the 380s B.C.E., he traveled to Egypt and Syracuse in Sicily. Plato went to Syracuse three times as guest of the tyrant Dionysius the Elder, and then of his son Dionysius the Younger. Both father and son were thought to be interested in Plato's ideas about government, but the results of Plato's involvement in Sicilian statecraft are usually referred to as "disastrous." Plato never married, and when he died at the age of 81 he was relatively poor.

## What was **Plato's Academy**?

A Roman statue of Plato. The Romans admired the Greeks and adapted much Greek culture to their own (iStock).

Sometime between the early 380's and 367 B.C.E., Plato founded The Academy in Athens, where he lived. Plato's Academy provided higher education to sons of the aristocracy. It was different from Isocrates' (c. 436–c. 393 B.C.E.) school, which formalized the teachings of the Sophists in politics and rhetoric for the practical aim of training lawyers. Plato's students, on the other hand, were taught mathematics, astronomy, and philosophy. Aristotle entered the Academy when he was 17, and in his early twenties added the subject of rhetoric to the curriculum.

Plato's academy was probably cofounded by Theatetus (417–369 B.C.E., after whom Plato named a dialogue) and Eudoxus (c. 408–c. 347 B.C.E.), astronomer and mathematician. Lectures were given to seated students who took notes. There were probably never more than 100 students in attendance at a time, and it is not certain that Plato himself lectured there.

## What was **Plato's metaphysical theory of forms**?

Plato's major contribution to philosophy was his metaphysical theory of forms. Plato's forms were divine objects, known by the mind through thought. The practice of such thought was believed to provide the best life. The forms, like the primary substance of the Pre-Socratics, were responsible for all of the things experienced by human beings and for the very existence and qualities of human beings, animals, natural objects, and man-made objects. Indeed, the entire world of existence was held to be made up of copies of the forms. Even ideas, such as beauty, truth, and justice, had forms. Although to Plato it was viewing the mind's representations of the forms, not the actual forms themselves, that mattered. The forms were unchanging, perfect, and divine. Everything that humans could think, perceive, or imagine, and the existing objects of thoughts and perceptions, were but imperfect copies of the forms.

## What were **Plato's dialogues**?

Plato's surviving written works span a period of about 50 years. He wrote in the form of elegant, dramatic, and poetic dialogues, which scholars usually divide into different periods. The *Apology, Charmides, Crito, Eupyphro, Hippias Minor, Ion, Laches,* and *Protagoras* (taken alphabetically) are considered his "early" works. The middle works are the *Phaedo, Symposium, Republic,* and *Phaedrus* (believed to have been written in that order), and these were followed by later works of the *Sophist, Statesman,* and *Philebus*. Plato's *Timaeus* may fall somewhere either in the middle or late writings. His *Letters,* numbered *I* through *XIII,* were written toward the end of his life. Only *Letters III, VII, VIII,* and *XIII* are unquestionably genuine, as is his will.

There were no printing presses in Plato's day and no book stores or libraries in Athens at the time he wrote. His dialogues probably reached their audiences through oral performances, and it is likely that Plato himself enacted the role of Socrates.

## What were **Plato's main ideas** as presented and developed in his **early dialogues**?

The early dialogues are very argumentative, and they display the Socratic method. Socrates is the main character, who begins by asking a question. Conclusions are not reached so much as questions are raised and clarified. The subject is morality, beginning with shared values such as piety or justice and then demonstrating how little is really known about them.

In the *Meno,* Socrates plies his questions toward the more positive end of showing how knowledge is innate in the soul. Meno is an uneducated slave boy from whom Socrates extracts knowledge of geometry through a series of skillful questions. Socrates concludes that because the soul acquired knowledge before birth, what we know is not learned, but *recollected*.

## What **topics** are addressed in **Plato's middle works**?

Plato's doctrine of immortality is taken up in the *Phaedo, Republic,* and *Phaedrus*. Plato thought that the human soul survives the death of the body. However, the soul's memories of its life are washed clean in the River Lethe; the soul then returns as the soul of another person to live a new life from birth. Also in these works, Plato develops his notion of forms, first introducing them in the *Phaedo* and going on to define them as eternal, changeless, and immaterial. The relationship between real things to the forms is one of participation. A particular cat that might be your pet, for instance, is a cat because it participates with the form of a cat. While your cat might squint or cough up fur balls, the ideal form cat would not be subject to such irregularities. However, not only neutral and beautiful things have their forms, but everything does. That is, bad cat eyesight and fur balls would also have forms in which they participate. In other words, there is the *idea or form* of a cat that includes all that makes a cat a cat, and then there is the *appearance* of your particular pet.

## How does Plato define a **"just city"** in his **Republic**?

In the *Republic,* Plato's theory of forms reaches its full development as he presents a (to him) utopian way of life. In order to understand justice in the individual, he sets out to describe a just city (the individual "writ large"). The main political principle of

## What is Plato's simile of the cave?

Plato introduces the simile of the cave in the *Republic* to convey the power of the experience of forms and describe their importance. It is his metaphysics in a poetic nutshell. Imagine a cave where prisoners are chained to the wall and the only objects they can see are shadows of things carried behind a fire in back of them. If a prisoner is freed, he will first encounter the objects in the cave whose shadows he has seen before. If he ascends out of the cave, imagine his amazement when he sees these objects, and the rest of the world, in full sunlight. Imagine also how his fellow prisoners might react if he attempts to relate what he has seen to them. The cave represents normal existence and perception, and the objects in sunlight are the world of the forms.

justice is a kind of division of labor that is mirrored in the tri-part division of the human being, or soul, into body, emotions and spirit, and reason. (For Plato, what we experience as the body belonged to the realm of mere appearance.) Just as human beings are happiest when their reason rules, it is necessary that the ideal city be ruled by those in whom reason is most perfect: namely, philosopher kings and queens.

Below the rulers are a guardian class of police and soldiers, who correspond to the spirited part of an individual soul, and at the bottom are the mechanics, servants and farmers, who are like the appetites, or an individual's physical body.

To ensure that the rulers love and serve their city above all else, Plato suggests that the family be abolished. In his social structure, men and women do not have to base their lives on their biological reproductive roles. Private property is unnecessary, too, as are monogamous sexual relationships or traditional marriage. The smartest, healthiest, and altogether best boys and girls will be specially trained, beginning with a simple diet, plain living conditions, and exercise in the open air.

Because the poets lie and teach impiety, there will be no literature in the new curriculum. In young adulthood, the young rulers will be taught mathematics and philosophy. At the age of 35, they will be sent out into the world for 15 years to serve the community as lower administrators, police, and soldiers. At the age of 50, they will be ready to rule, all the more so because it will be against their desire to devote the rest of their lives to study of the forms. (Plato, like many since him, believed that those who do not wish to rule are the very ones who should rule.)

## What did Plato mean by the **divided line**?

What Plato meant by the divided line is explained by Socrates in the *Republic:*

Now take a line which has been cut into two unequal parts and divide each of them again in the same proportion, and suppose the two main divisions to answer, one to the visible and the other to the intelligible, and then compare the subdivisions in respect of their clearness and want of clearness, and you will find that the first section in the sphere of the visible consists of images. And by images I mean, in the first place, shadows, and in the second place, reflections in water and in solid, smooth and polished bodies and the like: Do you understand?

What Socrates hoped his listeners would understand was that what they saw through sight was less clear and further from the truth than what they were able to "see" in their "mind's eye" or understanding.

## Did **Plato change his philosophy** as he grew older?

Plato became more conservative in his outlook and more attentive to existing social values and traditions as he aged. The city of the *Republic* would have required a revolution to set up. In the later *Laws,* Plato becomes less revolutionary and describes a "second-best" city in which there are traditional families and rulers are elected, rather than specially bred.

In the *Parmenides* Plato offers a series of criticisms to his earlier theory of forms, which he is apparently unable to answer and which are later taken up by Aristotle. The most famous of these is the "third man argument." Suppose we discover a form that accounts for what makes similar things similar. For example, every cat is different, but all cats share the same catness because they participate in the cat form. Now, if we compare this form with any one thing that participates in it—in this case, compare your cat with the cat form—the form and the participating thing will have similarities that make it necessary to posit a second form. If we then make comparisons of the cat to the second form, a third form will need to be posited, and on and on and on to an infinite regress. That is, Plato was aware of the theoretical problems with his theory of forms.

## Did **Plato change** his philosophical **theory of forms**?

In the *Philebus,* one of his later works, instead of equating the good life with contemplation of the forms, Plato acknowledges that pleasure seems to be an important component of what is good. He then explains how goodness consists of proportion, beauty, and truth, and argues that intelligence is better than pleasure because it is closer to those three. This was a new, more down-to-earth theory of the good life for Plato because it suggested that the best life for a human being was a life of enjoyment of what seemed to be real, rather than a life dedicated to contemplating the forms.

31

## What was **Plato**'s view of **love**?

Plato had two theories on love: one "Platonic" and the other not. In the *Phadreus* he describes the development of passion between a mature man and a beautiful boy. The man's love for the particular beautiful person grows into a love of beauty in general. That general love of beautiful things becomes a love of the beauty in laws, and its final form is a love of beauty in thought, or the form of beauty. (It should be remembered that the ancient Greeks prized what we would call homosexual [and possibly pederastic] relationships between beautiful youths and wiser older men. The older man was the lover, the youth the beloved.) In Plato's version of such unions, their highest form was thus chastity, or what came to be called "Platonic love."

In Plato's *Symposium*, Socrates credits Diotima with what he knows about love. Diotima has told him that love or Eros is a spirit, the child of Need and Resource (or Lack and Plenty), who was conceived at Aphrodite's (the goddess of beauty) birth:

> So love was born to love the beautiful.... As the son of Resource and Need, it has been his fate to be always in need; nor is he delicate and lovely as most of us believe, but harsh and arid, barefoot and homeless, sleeping on the naked earth, in doorways, or in the very streets beneath the stars of heaven, and always partaking of his mother's poverty. But, secondly, he brings his father's resourcefulness to his designs upon the beautiful and the good, for he is gallant, impetuous, and energetic, a mighty hunter, and a master of device and artifice—at once desirous and full of wisdom, a lifelong seeker after truth, an adept in sorcery, enchantment, and seduction.

The playwright Aristophanes is present at this discussion, and he gives an account of why love is so important to human beings. In the beginning, humans had three types that were each composed of two people conjoined in a spherical shape: female and female; male and male; male and female. These creatures were very strong and tried to storm Heaven itself. The gods did not want to destroy them, but something had to be done. Zeus' solution was to weaken them by cutting each of the beings in half. The result is that every human being is in search of their missing half. Men and women who were conjoined as hermaphrodites seek each other, Lesbians seek other women to complete themselves, and men who were joined to men are attracted to other men. Both Diotima and Aristophanes' explanations of love clearly involve sexual consummation and are not "Platonic."

# ARISTOTLE

## What was **Aristotle's main contribution** to Western philosophy?

Aristotle (384–322 B.C.E.) curbed the strain of intellectual mysticism that had been inaugurated by Parmenides (c. 515–450 B.C.E.) and he formalized common sense in ways that checked the speculative excesses of his teacher, Plato (c. 428–c. 348 B.C.E.). This enabled a solid foundation for empiricism, or knowledge based on sensory observation and direct experience. Aristotle accomplished his task via encyclopedic accounts of the existing knowledge of his day, assessments of that knowledge, and developments of it into new areas, using new methods of thought. He was a rare combination of a highly well-informed and diligent scholar and an original thinker. Like his nineteenth century successor Georg Wilhelm Friedrich Hegel (1770–1831), Aristotle was capable of "thinking the whole world." But unlike Hegel, he thought of the whole world not as an abstract and speculative theorist would but as an ordinary person would, if he or she could do that.

## What is known about **Aristotle's life**?

Aristotle of Stagira (384–322 B.C.E.), also known as The Stagirite, was the son of Nichomachus, who was the Macedonian King Amyntas II's court physician. Aristotle's career was shaped by this relationship with his scientific father. When Aristotle was 17, he enrolled in Plato's Academy in Athens. After Plato died in 347 B.C.E. and the Academy's curriculum changed toward the mathematical and speculative interests of its new head, Speusippus (407–339 B.C.E.), Aristotle left for Assos, which was then under the leadership of Hermias, a former slave who rose to the position of ruler that his master had held. Aristotle married Hermias' niece, Pythias, in 345 B.C.E., and after Hermias died, he traveled to Lesvos.

The island of Lesvos, in the northeastern Aegean Sea, had a great diversity of marine creatures and contemporary mammals, as well as many ancient fossils. Aristotle pursued his biological research on the taxonomy of living beings there. In 343 B.C.E., King Philip of Macedonia invited Aristotle to serve as tutor to his son, Alexander, who was to become Alexander the Great. In 335 B.C.E., Aristotle returned to Athens. He founded a school, the Lyceum, in a grove dedicated to Apollo Lyceus outside of the city. At the Lyceum, Aristotle lectured and directed research. He also constructed and stocked the first great library in ancient times. The walkway under a colonnade, or "peripatos," was the source of the name "Perapatetics" that was given to the members of the Lyceum.

After the death of his wife, Pythias, Aristotle lived with and had a son with Herphyllis. Their son was named after Aristotle's father, Nichomachus, after

A statue of Aristotle is located at a park named in his honor in Stagira, Halkidiki, Greece (iStock).

## What survives of Aristotle's work?

After Aristotle left the Lyceum, many of his books and dialogues were never seen again, and other works of his were hidden in a vault for two centuries. Indeed, until the European Renaissance, Aristotle's writings suffered a pattern of loss and rediscovery. A good part of Aristotle's existing corpus may have been reconstructed by his students from lecture notes they took, or compiled years later by Aristotelians consulting secondary sources. Some of it may have been written by Aristotle or other members of the Lyceum as lecture preparation.

Scholars now agree that the following works of Aristotle have been lost: dialogues in the same style as Plato; a vast collection of natural observations; popular publications; lectures on the good and Plato's forms; as many as 158 constitutions for Greek states, of which only the one for Athens survives.

In the first century C.E., Andronicus of Rhodes organized the existing Aristotelian corpus into its present form, but the earliest transcriptions of this are from the ninth century. The first critical edition of Aristotle's works was published by the Berlin Academy in 1831. It is estimated to represent as little as a fifth of Aristotle's total output, but in amounting to about 1,500 pages of small print in typical translations of Aristotle's "collected works," it provides a substantial basis for scholarly reference today.

whom he also named his work on ethics. When Alexander, now Alexander the Great, died in 325 B.C.E., Aristotle retired to Chalcis, where he lived for the remainder of his life.

## What are some of **Aristotle's works** and what are they about?

Aristotle's *Organon* consists of six early works: *Categories, On Interpretation, Prior Analytics, Posterior Analytics, Topics,* and *Sophistical Refutations*. These, together with the *Physics* and the *Metaphysic,* address logic, language, the nature of scientific inquiry, and what philosophers have since called ontology, which is the study of things that are real or things that exist.

These works demonstrate a systematic philosophic method of analysis and provide the results of that method in general areas of human knowledge. More specific scientific accounts are found in Aristotle's *On Generation and Corruption, On the Heavens,* and *Meteorology. On the Soul* deals with the general functions of the mind, which in Aristotle's *Parva Naturalis* are applied to specific functions, such as remembering, dreaming, sleeping, and waking. Aristotle's works on biology include the *History of Animals, Parts of Animals,* and *On the Generation of Animals.* The *Nicomachean Ethics* and *Eudemian Ethics* constitute Aristotle's theory of moral virtue, whereas his political philosophy is put forth in the *Politics*. The *Rhetoric* discusses oratory and persuasion, and the *Poetics* contains his theory of tragedy as an art form.

## What was most **important** about **Aristotle's work**?

To encourage the development of certain knowledge, Aristotle produced a theory of the rules of correct thought in his development of *syllogistics,* a form of logic that dominated the field until the modern period. Regarding science, Aristotle's theory of causation was meant to show how things could come into existence and change, without reliance on Plato's idea of a more real but hidden world. Aristotle, furthermore, advocated and practiced observation and classification in all fields.

Aristotle's sense of ethics was also more down-to-earth than Plato's. He believed that happiness was an appropriate and universal goal for human beings and that it could be attained by developing and practicing virtues, which were inclinations to behave in certain ways.

Unlike Plato, Aristotle did not have an idea of a utopian form of government, but rather claimed that government arises naturally from organizations of families, clans, and villages. The purpose of government, according to Aristotle, is to support individual well-being and self-sufficiency.

While Aristotle agreed with Plato that the arts were a form of imitation, he showed that they did not necessarily falsify reality, because they could be about universal human truths, rather than mere distorted copies of actual people and events.

## What is a **syllogism**?

According to Aristotle, a classic syllogism has a major premise, a minor premise, and a conclusion. If the major and minor premises are true, then it is not possible for the conclusion to be false; the conclusion must be true. For example, "All men are mortal" is a major premise. "Socrates is a man" is a minor premise. And "Socrates is mortal" is the conclusion.

### How did Aristotle's main ideas compare to Plato's?

Aristotle rejected Plato's claim that only the forms are real and that there is another world of forms outside of the world that we perceive in ordinary life. But he agreed with Plato that knowledge must have certainty. Therefore, his main philosophical task was to describe what made objects real in this world and explain how we can have certain knowledge about them. He also developed a system of logic, or rules of thought, that would guarantee certainty if one began with premises that were certain.

## What are Aristotle's **10 categories of existing things**?

Aristotle posits 10 categories of existing things: substance, quantity, quality, relation, place, time, position, doing, having, and being affected. Each of these terms was defined by Aristotle in pretty much the same way we would define it today, the one exception being substance. For Aristotle there were primary and secondary substances. A primary substance was a whole thing, such as a man or a dog. A secondary substance was a quality of that thing, such as rationality or loyalty.

To take the rest in turn: *quantity* is the number of something, a mathematical amount or measure; *relation* is a connection or comparison between things, such as above, below, before, or after; *place* refers to where a physical thing is; *time* is both the passage of events and a specific time on a clock or a calendar; *position* refers to how something is oriented, for example, right side up or upside down; *doing* refers to action, such as playing the harp or curing the sick; *having* refers to both the possession of a thing other than the possessor (for example, your wallet), or to something that is happening to you, such as having a good time; being *affected* refers to the effect of one thing on another, for example, your being affected by heat when you put your hand in the flame of a candle.

Aristotle's main unit of existence was primary substances. A primary substance is a specific thing, such as a cow in a field, a dog, or a tree outside the Lyceum. Secondary substances are the groups to which the primary substances belong, such as bovines, canines, or plants. Primary substances have accidents—which are changing qualities that we would call attributes—that can only exist in them; for example, tallness, fatness, furriness, or greenness. Our scientific knowledge is all about secondary substances, which have no real existence of their own but are abstractions in our mind based on the common nature of members of groups of similar primary substances.

## What are the **four causes** as defined by Aristotle?

Scientific knowledge provides causal explanations of real kinds of things. Aristotle asserted that there are four causes: formal, material, efficient, and final. The formal cause of your dog is what makes the animal a dog—it is its dog essence. The material cause of the dog is the physical stuff of which it is made—its matter. (Aristotle believed that matter or physical reality is the same in all things but uniquely informed by their specific forms.)

The efficient cause of the dog is its birth and the food and water it consumes. The final cause of the dog is its ultimate purpose or function as a dog—its full development as a dog and its ability to be a loyal friend and helper to human beings in general, and because it is your dog—"yours" in particular. Form is the actuality of a substance and matter is its potential. The particular puppy you first brought home had the physical potential to become the fully excellent creature it grew into.

## What is Aristotle' notion of the "unmoved mover"?

According to Aristotle, all of nature develops, changes, comes into being, and passes out of being through the operations of the four causes. However—and here Aristotle's metaphysics and philosophy of science take on a theological tone, not unlike Plato's—causal chains cannot be infinite, so there must be a first cause, something that is not itself caused, an "unmoved mover." The unmoved mover that is the cause of everything cannot be an efficient, material, or even a formal cause, because all of those are contained in things that exist. The unmoved mover is the ultimate final cause, that to which everything is aiming. It is the greatest good and the purpose of life, and Aristotle tells us that it is "noûs"—or mind—and its essence is thought, which is always active. It thinks about itself: noûs contemplating noûs.

## What was **Aristotle's theory** of the **virtues**?

Aristotle believed that virtue, or moral goodness, is a form of practical wisdom. It is neither determined by nature, nor is it precluded by nature; it is the result of thought, action, and habit. However, not everyone can be virtuous, according to Aristotle. His necessary conditions for virtue included: high social status, wealth, good looks, being male, and being a free citizen. The specific virtues Aristotle talked about were limited to the traits admired in the ruling classes of the ancient world: pride, generosity, courage, nobility, temperance. This was partly the result of snobbery, and partly due to his sense that the practice of virtue required freedom from labor and drudgery. Still, Aristotle's ideas about how virtue is acquired and practiced can be made relevant to all adults in our own more democratic times. Moreover, we can add the virtues we care about (for example, compassion) to his limited list.

Aristotle thought that we become virtuous, first through proper training as children and second by doing the acts that correspond to the virtues in question. For example, to become courageous, it is necessary to perform courageous acts over a period of time. Virtue for human beings (as for all other things) is the excellence of what makes them human, and what makes us human is our reason, our ability to think actively. Therefore, it is important that we deliberate before acting in ways that will develop our virtues. For example, the courageous acts performed by a courageous person must be done for the right reasons.

The virtuous actions of good people will be performed because they already have the virtues in question. But every situation is unique, which is why virtuous action calls for rational deliberation beforehand. Aristotle advised that a good rule of practical reason is to aim for the middle or mean. Courage, for example, is usually somewhere between cowardice and fool-heartedness. In aiming for the mean in this way, we

37

should over-correct for our known faults. Thus, because we tend to be fond of pleasure, we should subject choices that are pleasant to a special scrutiny.

### Was anything **absolutely wrong** in Aristotle's view?

Yes. Aristotle thought that some actions were wrong in themselves and did not allow for moderation or for a mean—for example, adultery and murder.

### Did **Aristotle** think that **morality** had a **purpose** or **"final cause"**?

Yes. Aristotle thought that in human life—as in nature, generally—everything has a purpose and there cannot be an infinite regress of purposes (that is, there is an "unmoved mover") Because we are goal-directed, there must be some goal that is valuable to us in itself, and not because it will lead to some other goal. The goal that is good in and of itself is happiness. Aristotle thought that happiness is not pleasure or any other feeling, but a quality that settles over life when we are actualizing our essence by behaving virtuously for the right reasons. Our essence is our rationality.

### What did **Aristotle think** about **government and politics**?

Aristotle believed that human beings are social by nature, so the right form of government is necessary to support happy and self-sufficient citizens. He posited three main forms of government, each of which could degenerate: monarchy that could fall into tyranny; aristocracy that could fall into oligarchy (rule by a few based on wealth); and polity that could fall into democracy. Like Plato, Aristotle viewed democracy as mob rule because the great masses of people in their day were uneducated and unrefined. Aristotle thought that the best form of government was polity, a kind of democratic rule within an aristocratic class, where turns were taken for top positions and all of the privileged members had their say.

# HELLENISTIC AND ROMAN PHILOSOPHY

### How did **political events** after the **decline** of **Greece change philosophy**?

The death of Alexander the Great (356–323 B.C.E.) marked the end of the classical period in Greek philosophy. The Greek cities were unable to unify after great losses in the Peloponnesian War (431–404 B.C.E.). The next 800 years marked a period of great instability, as the political and cultural center of Western civilization shifted to Europe. As Rome came to dominate Greece, the uncontested brilliance of the Greeks faded into the past. Toward the end of this historical period, Christian thought and practice began to define almost every aspect of civilized life.

Some Pre-Socratic thought—particularly the ideas and practices of Pythagoras—lived on after the decline of Greece; Plato's work endured in new forms that were compatible with early Christianity. The Hellenistic or Greek-based forms of the new philosophies of skepticism, stoicism, Epicurianism, and cynicism spread throughout the Mediterranean world. There was little awareness of Aristotle's work at the time, although empiricism was easily accepted.

### What happened in **Athens** after both **Plato and Aristotle** were **gone**?

Athens remained the center of philosophy until the Romans sacked it in 87 B.C.E. Much of our knowledge of Hellenistic philosophical activity comes from the first century B.C.E. Roman writers Lucretius (99–55 B.C.E.) and Cicero (106–43 B.C.E.), and secondary medieval sources. Plato's Academy became the New Academy, which was devoted to critical work on the thought of other schools. This was the beginning of the skeptics. Aristotle's Lyceum, or the Peripatos, was first led by Theophrastus in 322 B.C.E., but after 287 B.C.E., it fell into decline until the middle of the first century B.C.E.

Roman statesman and writer Cicero was influenced by the philosophers Panaetius and Posidonius (iStock).

### What was **skepticism**?

Skepticism was founded by Arcesilaus, who was head of the New Academy from c. 268 to 241. His work was carried on by

39

Carneades, head of the Academy in the second century B.C.E. The skeptics held that nothing could be known, and they preached *epocé,* which is the doctrine that all judgments, or conclusions or assessments, should be suspended. These academic skeptics posed problems, or *tropes,* to show that sensory knowledge is prone to error and reasoning does not necessarily result in certainty. They concluded that because we have no absolute standards for distinguishing between truth and falsehood, the best we can hope for is probable knowledge.

## Who was **Pyrrho of Elis**?

Pyrrho (c. 360–275) started out as a painter and then became interested in Democratus' (c. 460–371 B.C.E.) atomism. He travelled with Alexander the Great to the East, where he studied with the Gymnosophists in India and the Magi in Persia. He had students but left no written work. When he would refuse to judge whether a chariot headed his way would hit him, his students often had to rescue him at the last second.

## Why was **Pyrrho important**?

His refusal to make judgments was an important school of skepticism that was developed after the Renaissance and during the Reformation and Counter-Reformation. Known as pyrrhonic skepticism, it was the general philosophical approach that many things in human life cannot be known.

## What was the **debate** between the **Phyrrhonian** and **academic skeptics**?

Pyrrhonian skepticism was founded by Aenesidemus in the early first century B.C.E. Aenesidemus claimed to be merely passing on the thoughts of Phyrro of Elis (c. 315–255 B.C.E.). Sextus Empiricus (160–210 C.E.) preserved Pyrrhonian skepticism in the second century after Aenesidemus. Pyrrhonian skeptics thought that the academic skeptics went too far in claiming that nothing could be truly known for certain. The Pyrrhonians preferred to suspend judgment on whether anything could be known. They held that suspending judgment led to *ataraxia*—peace of mind—in which there was simply no concern for what may or may not

Zeno of Citium was the founder of stoicism (Art Archive).

lie behind appearances or come after them. Phyrrhonian skeptics were opposed to dogmatism and believed that their chief philosophic opponents were the stoics.

## Who were the **stoics** and **what did they believe**?

Stoicism was founded by Zeno of Citium (334–262 B.C.E.), whose work was carried on by Cleanthes (331–322 B.C.E.), who was then succeeded by Chrusippus (c. 280–206 B.C.E.). The name "stoic' came from the Stoa Poikile, or painted colonnade, where stoics first gathered in Athens. According to these early stoics, the entire world is a morally good organism, with different phases in which events operate according to divine reason, or *logos*. The sequence of events is predetermined by fate. Each world phase ends in a big fire and is then repeated in a continuous, never-ending cycle.

Early stoic ethics held that only virtue is good, and only vice is bad. Other things, such as health or wealth, may be preferred, but they are morally indifferent. We each have a unique role in the world plan and our job is to learn what it is. Such learning creates concern for the self, which can and should be extended to close relatives and friends and, after them, all humanity. (The stoics may have been the first cosmopolitans.) Learning is based on assent to impressions, until all of a person's thoughts become related and "unassailable by reason." By counseling that we "assent to impressions," the stoics meant that we should not deny anything that is presented to us as either a fact or an opinion but simply acknowledge its effect on us. Such stoic certainty formed the "dogmatism" opposed by the skeptics.

## Who were the important **philosophers** of **middle stoicism**?

Middle stoicism matured in Rhodes, with Panaetius (c. 185–110 B.C.E.) and Posidonius (c. 125–50 B.C.E.), both of whom influenced the statesman and writer Cicero (106–43 B.C.E.). Posidonius (c. 125–50 B.C.E.) incorporated both Platonic and Aristotelian ideas into his views. The main accomplishment of Middle stoicism was to apply Greek ideas to military and political life in Roman culture. Middle stoicism was generally more focused on how those who were stoics could weather specific life problems, such as defeat in war, or imprisonment.

## What is **Roman stoicism**?

Roman stoicism was developed by Seneca the Younger (1–65 C.E.), Epictetus (c. 55–135 C.E.) and the emperor Marcus Aurelius (121–80 C.E.), who wrote *Meditations*. Many were moved by Marcus Aurelius' advice about restraining anger at his weak subjects: "Do not be turned into 'Caesar,' or dyed by the purple: for that happens." Roman stoicism was influential in the Renaissance and the modern period, and to this day it underlies codes of behavior and moral values in military communities.

The Roman emperor Marcus Aurelius was also a productive philosopher who wrote on stoicism (Art Archive).

Seneca was a playwright, statesman, and one-time tutor to Roman emperor Nero. He was also a contributor to stoic philosophy (Art Archive).

The basic stoic premise is that we are obligated to understand the nature of the things we deal with and be prepared to accept, without fuss, unwanted events that are not under our control. Epictetus is famous for saying that if your favorite clay pot breaks, you should remember that it was always fragile and not yours to begin with. And if your spouse or child dies, that is a reminder that they are mortals, something that we should always remember about the human beings we love.

## What is **Epicureanism**?

Unlike its namesake today, which connotes an enjoyment of good food and fine wine, ancient Epicureanism was an austere doctrine. It was founded by Epicurus (341–271 B.C.E.) and his colleagues Metrodorus of Lampsacus (331–277 B.C.E.), Hermarchus (dates unknown), and Polyaenus (dates unknown). Epicurus set up communities at Mytilene, Lampsacus, and on the outskirts of Athens, where his school was known as "The Garden." Epicurean practice required detachment from political life—although not opposition to it—and time spent in philosophical discussion with friends.

Epicurus wrote "letters" on physics, astronomy, and ethics, as well as maxims, and a major work, *On Nature,* little of which has survived. He was an atomist, as Democratus (c. 460–371 B.C.E.) had developed the theory, except that he thought atoms themselves contained sets of "minima" (parts of atoms that cannot be further divided). According to Epicurus, the atoms are in constant motion, with swerves and collisions that have resulted in the formation of bodies as we experience them. There is nothing godlike outside of life and society as we known them, and the gods should just be viewed as ideal models for our own behavior. Death is not to be feared, because we will

Today, we often associate Epicurus with the idea of Epicureanism, or enjoyment of food and drink. But Epicureanism actually began as an austere doctrine of serious reflection (Art Archive).

Antisthenes of Athens thought that a virtuous person could always be happier than a non-virtuous one and that the soul was more important than the body (Art Archive).

merely dissolve into our constituent atoms, which are incapable of feeling pain—or anything else.

Epicurean ethics held that pleasure is our only good; it is better even than virtue. Pain is the only evil. Pleasure should be sought in stable ways, which makes a simple life necessary. We should satisfy only our most necessary desires in the company of friends like us. The highest pleasures are "katastematic," or those related to satisfaction. The "kinetic" pleasures that result from stimulation merely increase our insecurity (they are like desires). Our ultimate goal should therefore be the absence of pain via a simple life for the body and the study of physics for the soul. This will result in *ataraxia,* or "freedom from disturbance."

## What is ancient **cynicism**?

The cynics were eccentrics who chose to be outcasts rather than kow-tow to social norms that did not make sense to them. Ancient cynicism was generally an attempt to reassert the importance of human nature as independent of society and custom. This

43

Diogenes, depicted in a painting by Flemish artist Pieter Van Mol, was an unusual philosopher given to rude and obscene public gestures that displayed his contempt for social conventions (Art Archive).

was very different from our modern definition of a cynic as someone who is skeptical and tends to believe the worst about people.

The cynics derived from Antisthenes of Athens (c. 445–360 B.C.E.), who studied with Gorgias (c. 485–380 B.C.E.) and was a good friend of Socrates (460–399 B.C.E.), even being present at his death. Antisthenes claimed to be proudest of his wealth, because, having no money, he was pleased with what he had. He thought that a virtuous person could always be happier than a non-virtuous one and that the soul was more important than the body.

Antisthenes' minimalist ideas about what was necessary to live well were carried on by Diogenes of Sinope (400–325 B.C.E.), who lived in a wine barrel, claimed that cannibalism and incest were fine practices, and was said to carry a lamp in daylight in search of an honest person. Diogenes' successor was Crates of Thebes (fl. 328 B.C.E.), who gave up his wealth to practice cynicism, but also married. He believed that asceticism was necessary for independence and claimed that lentils were better than oysters.

## How are **dogs** like **cynics**?

The English word "cynic" comes from the Greek "kyon," which means "dog." Diogenes of Synope thought people could learn much from dogs, who were not ashamed of their bodily functions, not picky eaters, and did not care where they slept. Dogs neither worry, nor care about academic philosophy, and they know immediately if someone is a friend or an enemy. What's more, dogs, unlike humans, are honest. Like a dog, Diogenes had no use for family structures, social organizations, politics, private property, or good reputation. He is said to have masturbated in the agora (market place) and replied to those who insulted him by urinating on them. He also gestured at others with his middle finger. Plato described him as "a Socrates gone mad."

Because of his contempt for convention and knowledge of philosophy, many considered Diogenes a man of wisdom. Alexander the Great once sought Diogenes out, when the philosopher was bathing in his wine barrel, which he did often because of a painful skin condition. When Alexander offered to give him anything in the world he wanted, Diogenes replied, "Please get out of my sunlight" (or words to that effect).

# WOMEN PHILOSOPHERS IN ANCIENT GREECE AND ROME

### Why aren't there any **women philosophers** from **ancient Greece and Rome** who became **well known**?

The history of Western philosophy has been dominated by men for several reasons: 1) until the twentieth century, few women were systematically educated in ways that enabled the practice of philosophy; 2) women's family and social roles did not afford them the leisure to practice philosophy; and 3) male philosophers have traditionally seen the field as restricted to men and have sometimes gone to lengths to exclude women. Nevertheless, in every philosophical period some women have been associated with philosophy as practiced by men, and others have been philosophers in their own right. It cannot be known how much of the work of women philosophers has been ignored, forgotten, or never received the attention it deserved because, until the twentieth century, little work by women philosophers was preserved or even mentioned as part of the tradition.

The ancient period in Greece and Rome was a foundation for this general, male-dominated trend. Upper-class women were sequestered in special quarters in their homes and not educated for public life. Poor women were heavily burdened by motherhood, domestic drudgery, and agricultural work. Women with some leisure might sew, spin, weave, or listen to men converse, but always in their homes, whereas most philosophical interaction occurred in public places. Overall, women in ancient times rarely had the rights accorded to men. Nevertheless, the names and philosophical work of a small number of women philosophers in antiquity have survived.

### Who were some important **women philosophers** from **antiquity**?

Although they probably are but the tip of an iceberg, Themostocles, Theano of Crotona, Diotima of Mantinea, Aspasia of Miletus, Aesara of Lucania, Phintis of Sparta,

Perictione I, Theano II, Hypatia of Alexandria, Ascepigenia of Athens, and Arete of Cyrene deserve specific mention.

## Who was **Themistocles**?

According to some accounts, Pythagoras (c. 570–495 B.C.E.), the Pre-Socratic who founded a "brotherhood" based on the religious idea that everything is made up of numbers, was taught his ethical beliefs by Themistocles (c. 524–459 B.C.E.), the Priestess of Delphi. It is known that Apollo was both the god at the Temple of Delphi and a deity worshipped by Pythagoreans. Pythagoras and his followers practiced self-examination and dietary and ritualistic purification (including their vegetarianism), based on a belief in the sameness of all life. This principle of sameness might have implied that women should be included in philosophical activities.

## Who were some **female Pythagoreans**?

Pythagoras' wife, Theano of Crotona (Italy, c. 546 B.C.E.), and their three daughters were members of Pythagoras' first group of followers. Theano was said to have discussed metaphysics and written about marriage, sex, women, and ethics. After Pythagoras died, Theano and her three sons succeeded him as leaders of the Pythagorean school. Theano II (her birth and death dates are uncertain except that she was not Theano I), a later Pythagorean, addressed moral contexualism, or the theory that what is right to do should take particular circumstances into account. She also believed that *harmonia* (harmony) is, or should be, the foundation of morality and education. Some historians believe that Perictione I (late fourth to third centuries B.C.E.), another Pythagorean, said to have written *On the Harmony of Women,* was Plato's mother.

## Who was **Aspasia of Miletus**?

Aspasia of Miletus (c. 470–c. 400 B.C.E.) was an influential member of the Sophistic movement. She was married to Pericles (495–429 B.C.E.), considered to be knowledgeable about statecraft, and was said to have taught Socrates himself rhetoric. When she was put on trial on charges of impiety, her husband secured her acquittal.

### Who was **Arete of Cyrene**?

Arete of Cyrene (c. 400–c. 340 B.C.E.), the daughter of Aristipus, a friend and student of Socrates, who was present at his death, succeeded her father as head of the Cyrenic school. She taught ethics in the Hedonistic tradition and natural philosophy, for 30 years.

### Was **Diotima of Mantinea** a **real or fictional** female philosopher?

Diotima of Mantinea, who is said to have instructed Socrates on love in Plato's *Symposium,* has been believed to be a fictional invention since the Renaissance. Before then, she was assumed to have been a real person.

### **When** did **women philosophers** first **start to become recognized** as part of philosophy?

Beginning in the early Christian era, the scholarly work and educational activities of at least some women philosophers were recognized, and some male philosophers made special efforts to interact with them intellectually.

# NEOPLATONISM THROUGH THE RENAISSANCE

**Did Plato and Aristotle influence early Christian and medieval philosophy?**

Yes, but both early Christian and medieval philosophy were influenced by interpretations of Plato and Aristotle's thought, which neither they nor today's scholars would accept as completely true to the sources. This was because Plato was given a Neoplatonic interpretation and Aristotle was interpreted through a Christian world view. Not until the Renaissance did the intellectual complexity and humanism of ancient Greek thinkers begin to fully re-emerge, however. Until Aristotle's texts were rediscovered in the ninth century, Plato was the major influence from antiquity, although many of his dialogues were lost. And until the Renaissance, all Greek or pagan philosophy took a distant second place to Christian theology and philosophy.

**Was Christianity the only religious influence on philosophy after the ancient period?**

No. Although, Christianity formed the dominant world view in Europe for over a thousand years, Jewish and Muslim thought also flourished.

## NEOPLATONISM

**What was Neoplatonism?**

Neoplatonism was an elaborate system of religious and intellectual belief that was based on ideas about "The One" as the unseen source of all existence. As a powerful but unseen foundation for everything in existence, the One was similar to Plato's forms.

## What was The One?

The One was like God, a creator of the universe and an ongoing standard for morality.

## How did **Neoplatonism** become **popular**?

Neoplatonism spread as the Roman Empire began to fall after the Emperor Marcus Aurelius (121–180), who was a stoic, died. While early Neoplatonism began under the Roman Empire, different forms of it persisted throughout the medieval period, the Renaissance, and into the seventeenth century.

## How was **Neoplatonism similar** to **Christianity**?

Just as Christianity promised a better emotional and spiritual world in times of great social and political upheaval, the Neoplatonists offered their followers an intellectual picture of a higher realm that could also console them personally. That is, Neoplatonism was closer to Christianity than to other ancient philosophies because of its emphasis on one creator and the importance placed on the feelings of its followers.

## **Who** were the **early Neoplatonists**?

Plotinus (205–270) founded Neoplatonism in the third century. He wrote most of his work between 253 and 270, and all of it was edited and published by his student Porphyry (233–309). Porphyry's writings on Plotinus were developed and revised in different schools throughout the educated world, including Alexandria, Athens, Syria, and Western Europe. Early Neoplatonism ended with the work of Boëthius (full name, Anicius Manlius Severinus Boëthius; 480–c.524) in the sixth century, who attempted to reconcile Plato and Aristotle with Christian theology.

## **Who** was **Plotinus**?

Plotinus (205–270) was born in upper Egypt. At the age of 28, he began an 11-year study of philosophy with Ammonius Saccas (n.d.). He left to fight with Emperor Gordianus III's (Marcus Antonius Gordianus Pius; also known as Gordian III; 225–244) army against Persia. After Gordianus died, or according to some accounts was murdered, Plotinus fled to Antioch, but then settled in Rome. He founded a school in Rome, became friends with Emperor Gallienus (Publius Licinius Egnatius Gallienus; c. 218–268), and began writing down his philosophy. Gallienus intended to give Plotinus land to set up a community in accordance with Plato's dialogue, the *Laws* (c. 360 B.C.E.), but others intervened, and Gallienus was soon assassinated by his own officers in the midst of a competitive military campaign. Plotinus himself died two years later, it is said, from leprosy.

Plotinus was the founder of Neoplatonism during the decline of the Roman civilization (Art Archive).

### What was the **relevance** of **Plato's *Laws*** to Plotinus and Gallienus?

In the *Laws* (c. 360 B.C.E.) Plato describes a stable system of government that is less utopian than the *Republic* (c. 380 B.C.E.) because it allows for private families and private property. Some commentators have claimed that Roman Emperor Gallienus was not interested in a Platonic form of government but that he liked Plotinus and agreed to the plan for a community as a favor to him. Plotinus, it was said, was mainly interested in setting up a retreat for himself and his followers.

### How was **Plotinus' system** of thought expressed in the *Enneads*?

Plotinus' (205–270) system of thought was arranged in the *Enneads,* which was made up of six groups of nine essays: the first three groups are about the physical world and human interaction with it; the fourth group is about the soul; the fifth is about intelligence; and the sixth is about the One. Although Plotinus thought he was a faithful student of Plato, he in fact added ideas from Aristotle, the stoics, and his own philosophical imagination.

Plotinus divided the Platonic imperceptible world of forms into three parts: the One, Intelligence, and the Soul. The One is above everything that is, because it is the highest principle of being and causation. As a principle, however, the One is everything, in everything. Because the One is a unity, it has no thought or awareness, which requires a separation between thinking and the object thought. Paradoxically, the One is both completely ignorant, lacking awareness even of itself, but also, in its own way, aware of everything that it has created.

After the One, there is Intelligence, which corresponds to Plato's specific forms, taken as a totality. Intelligence has an idea for everything that exists. Intelligence also contains number, which corresponds to souls, and it contains original matter. However, there is not an endless multiplication of ideas because, as the stoics proclaimed, every so often the entire world is destroyed.

### Where does the **soul fit** into Plotinus' system of **Platonic entities**?

All individual souls form one world soul, which comes after Intelligence. Some souls are disembodied, but those that are in bodies have additional "accretions." Humans, animals, and plants all have souls that are immortal, substantial (that is, they are substances) and incorporeal (not physical). Because they are incorruptible, individual souls may be reincarnated in different bodies.

The soul *emanates* or *effulgurates* from Intelligence, just as Intelligence emanates or effulgurates from the One. These emanations from the One and Intelligence neither detract from them nor are they willed. The same is true of the emanation of matter from the soul. Although the processes of emanation from the One, Intelligence, and the Soul are very natural, Plotinus (205–270) sometimes speaks of them as selfish descents to lower states. In emanating from Intelligence, the soul is actualizing a desire to rule and it becomes too attached to its body, which can lead to its deterioration. However, even when it is incarnated, the soul also lives in Intelligence.

### How do we know the One?

Plotinus (205–270) taught that the soul can know the One by becoming one with it, which he called "ecstasy," "surrender," "simplicity," "touching," or "flight of the alone to the alone." This re-ascension of the soul, which has been described as a union with God, in the Christian sense, was experienced many times by Plotinus. To prepare for it, Neoplatonists practiced virtues and Platonic dialectics, which included the study of mathematics.

### How did Iamblichus practice Neoplatonism?

Iamblichus of Syria (c. 245–325) was a student of Porphyry's (233–309) who set up his own school in Apamea (in what is modern Syria). Porphyry had practiced theurgy—or magic—based on vegetarianism and other physical restrictions, but he thought the effectiveness of theurgy was limited to lower levels of spiritual ascent. Iamblichus developed a more elaborate system of theurgy for every stage of salvation, which was similar to Christian sacramental theology and became an integral part of Neoplatonism from then on. Iamblichus also embellished Plotinus' system, dividing the One into two: one responsible for the creation and the other transcending it. The Roman Emperor Julian (c. 331–363) became interested in Iamblichus' system after Iamblichus incorporated many of the Greek gods into Plotinian descriptions of creation and salvation.

## What was Plotinus' association with demonology?

In his biography of Plotinus (205–270), Porphyry (233–309) wrote the following:

> An Egyptian priest came to Rome once and made acquaintance with Plotinus through a friend; the priest wanted to test his powers and suggested Plotinus to make the daimon that was born with him visible by conjuring. Plotinus gave a ready assent and conjuration took place in the Temple of Isis, because it was, as it is told, the only "pure" place the Egyptian could find in Rome. When the daimon was conjured to reveal itself, a god appeared who was not one of the daimons. And the Egyptian is said to have called out: "Blessed are you, because a god is by you as your daimon and not some low class daimon!" But there was no opportunity to ask anything from the apparition or look at it longer; because a friend who was watching and holding birds in his hands to keep the purity of the place, squeezed them to death, be it out of envy or vague fear.

> Scholars have found this passage interesting because it introduces two new elements to ideas about demons in the ancient world: first, that demons could change into benevolent gods or angels; and second, that birds could be used to protect the purity of the soul. Socrates had a "daimon" who would counsel him in times of stress or alert him to what was important. However, Plotinus' interactions with demons more resembles later ideas of magic and sorcery than simply listening to a voice, as Socrates did.

## What was the **Athenian school** of Neoplatonism?

The Athenian school was founded by Plutarch of Athens (350–433) and carried on by Syrianus (c. 370–437) whose most important student was Proclus (412–485). This school was actually the same institution that had been Plato's academy. The Athenians added new levels to Iamblichus' system in the form of gods who were interested in philosophical matters and whose thought could be understood by mortals, although they did not accept Iamblichus' notion of two Ones.

## What did **Proclus contribute** to Neoplatonism?

Proclus (412–485) wrote *Elements of Theology* and *Plato's Theology,* which had a lasting effect on subsequent philosophy, particularly that of Hegel (1770–1831) 13 centuries later. He added to the idea of emanations by adding to their downward movements, horizontal movements at different stages of their descent. That resulted

A twelfth-century illuminated manuscript depicts Philosophy visiting Boëthius. The Christian Neoplatonist wrote extensively on the Trinity and famously posed the "problem of universals" (Art Archive).

in a great multiplication of divine entities, or "henads," with which Proclus associated Greek deities. He also developed the triadic ruling principle of "remaining-proceeding-returning. That is, the deity remained what it was while its emanations proceeded downward to ordinary existence, and human understanding of this process and communion with the deity constituted returning. Aside from his spiritual work, Proclus wrote on mathematics, astronomy, physics, and literary criticism.

## Who was **Boëthius**?

Boëthius, Anicius Manlius Severinus (c. 480–c. 525) was the most famous Christian Neoplatonist in the West. He wrote extensively on the Trinity and produced many influential translations of commentaries on Aristotle, as well as works on education, science, and philosophy. His focus on logic later became a preoccupation with methods of thought among scholastic philosophers. In his commentary on Porphyry (233–309), Boëthius set up "the problem of universals," based on conflicts between the ideas of Plato and Aristotle, which was to preoccupy scholastic thinkers between 1000 and 1150.

## What is the **"problem of universals"**?

"The problem of universals," as addressed by Boëthius (480–c.525), has to do with what makes a kind of thing distinct from other things. Take, for example, the domestic dog. Dogs have the greatest genetic variety of any living species. Scientists can now identify every one of them as dogs, from Chihuahuas to Great Danes (in principle, that is—they don't actually do this), by their DNA, which has certain pre-determined resemblances to earlier lines of canines. However, well before the discovery of genes and DNA, human beings could both identify any particular animal that was a dog as a dog, even though that dog had a unique appearance and personality.

What is true of dogs in this sense is true of all natural species—all of their members seem to share "something." Plato would have said that a dog's essence is a copy of

an ideal form of dog, in which all dogs "participate." Aristotle would have said that there is an essence of "dogness," which can be known to human beings and which is shared by all dogs, but that the dog essence is in each dog and only abstracted by the mind.

Strictly speaking, for Aristotle there does not exist a dog essence apart from Rover, Jake, Lacey, Mirabelle, or any other name that designates a unique animal. The problem of universals is the question of whether Plato or Aristotle was correct. Philosophers have agonized over this question and burnt many candles, oil lamps, and computers in the process. Those who think that the essences in individual things are real have been called *realists*. Those who think that essences are abstractions or creations of the human mind have been called *nominalists*.

## Was **Boëthius guilty** or **innocent** of **plotting** against **Theodoric the Great**?

Boëthius (480–c. 525) was arrested for suspicion of treason after his correspondence with Constantinople was disclosed. He had been very critical of Theodoric during his first year as Master of Offices under Theodoric the Great (454–526), and this resulted in several enemies. They convinced Theodoric, based on his theological writings that seemed to support the Eastern Church, that Boëthius sympathized with Justinian, who ruled in the remains of the Roman Empire in the East and aspired to reunite the Empire. (The Church had split into two churches in 318 over the tenets of Arianism, which denied the trinity.)

Boëthius' executioners beat him to death after tightening a cord around his neck, which caused his eyes to pop out of his head. Theodoric later regretted this cruel

### How else has Boëthius been influential long after his death?

Boëthius (480–c. 525) is best known for his stoic-Neoplatonic text, *The Consolation of Philosophy,* which he wrote while in prison after having been accused of conspiring with Justinian to overthrow Theodoric. This text was influential throughout the Middle Ages and beyond. It was translated into Anglo-Saxon, German, and French by 1300, and it inspired the writers Dante, Boccaccio, and Chaucer, as well as many, many others.

In *The Consolation of Philosophy* Boëthius defined God as eternal and the complete and perfect sum total of never-ending life. The created universe had no beginning or end, but existed in time. Boëthius resolved the contradiction between the fact that God knows everything and the fact that man has free will by claiming that God has a simultaneous understanding of everything that happens in time, including human freedom.

death sentence, but soon after his arrest, Boëthius had said, "Had there been any hopes of liberty I should have freely indulged them. Had I known of a conspiracy against the King … you would not have known of it from me."

## How is Boëthius' *Consolation of Philosophy* both **stoic** and **Neoplatonic**?

*The Consolation of Philosophy* was written as a dialogue in which Boëthius (480–c. 525), in despair, is visited by Philosophy in the form of an uplifting and encouraging angel. Philosophy says to Boëthius:

> What is it, mortal man, that has cast you down into grief and mourning? You have seen something unwonted, it would seem, something strange to you. But if you think that Fortune has changed towards you, you are wrong. These are ever her ways: this is her very nature. She has with you preserved her own constancy by her very change. She was ever changeable at the time when she smiled upon you, when she was mocking you with the allurements of false good Fortune. You have discovered both the different faces of the blind goddess.

That Boëthius could have an angel appear to him is an occurrence with roots in Neoplatonist theurgy, or magic. And that the angel instills peace of mind in the face of turmoil and apparent misfortune evokes a decidedly stoic doctrine.

## Did **early Neoplatonism** include **women** philosophers?

Yes. Overall, Christianity emphasized the importance of the individual immortal soul, and although the Church was run by men and its dominant theologians were male, the religious lives and work of women had a recognized place in schools and convents. This change was first evident in the Neoplatonist movement.

## Who was **Hypatia of Alexandria**?

A philosopher and educator who achieved lasting renown, Hypatia of Alexandria in Egypt (c. 350–415) became famous throughout intellectual communities for her abilities in Neoplatonist philosophy and mathematics. In the Neoplatonic tradition, Hypatia used mathematics as a path toward understanding the higher world. In *Theon,* Hypatia's father comments on Ptolemy's *Almagest,* which set forth the geocentric model of the universe, and he credits her for the work of Book 3.

Although Hypatia was a pagan, the Roman Christian Egyptian government appointed her head of a school of Plotinus. Hypatia held that post for about 15 years, teaching both male and female students. She was said to have been very beautiful and was much admired personally. Synesius (c. 373–c. 414), her pupil who was to become bishop of Ptomemais, conveyed her views in essays, hymns, and letters. She was the heroine of Charles Kingsley's 1853 novel, *Hypatia; or, New Foes with an Old Face.*

Hypatia was associated with Alexandria's prefect, who was opposed by Saint Cyril of Alexandria (c. 378–444), the militant archbishop. As a result of her involvement in that dispute, Hypatia was hacked to pieces with sharp shells and her body burned by a mob of Christian monks. (The contemporary feminist philosophy journal, *Hypatia,* is named after her.)

### Did **Asclepigenia** suffer the **same fate** as **Hypatia**?

No. Asclepigenia of Athens (430–485) taught Neoplatonism in her father's school. She applied knowledge of Plato and Aristotle to Christian moral questions. Proclus (412–485) was one of her students. Asclepigenia's main interests appear to have been in mysticism, magic, and other "mysteries."

# MEDIEVAL PHILOSOPHY

### What was **medieval philosophy**?

Medieval philosophy was the historical period of thought from the fourth through the fourteenth centuries, which was dominated by religious concerns, the study of ancient Greek philosophy, and a need to reconcile rational inquiry with religious faith. It was mainly, but not completely, limited to the implications of Christian doctrine. Thus, St. Augustine (354–430) in the fourth century gave Christianity its first philosophical foundation in politics and ethics; and at the end of the era Nicolas of Oresme (1323–1382), in working out Aristotelian theories of motion that were approved by the Church, he was able to anticipate infinitesimal calculus and coordinate geometry, before Galileo's mechanical theories.

### How is **Christian philosophy** different from Christian **theology**?

The main job of medieval Christian theologians was to intellectually work out the doctrine of the Catholic Church, without questioning its basic premises or the content of the religion that was based on the New Testament. The main job of medieval Christian philosophers was to explain how accepted knowledge that did not have Christian origins was compatible with Christian theology. This distinction was not made in the early Church writings, such as those of St. Augustine.

### What was **St. Augustine's role** at the beginning of **medieval philosophy**?

St. Augustine, Aurelius Augustinus (354–430) was a pivotal figure in the transition between classical and medieval thought. Some see him as the last of the great classical thinkers, whereas others claim him as the first medieval thinker. He lived through the decline of the Roman Empire, with its political turmoil and military failures, and the

A stained glass window at the Cathedral-Basilica of St. Augustine in Florida depicts the church's namesake (iStock).

Roman state's acceptance of Christianity as the official religion. Just before Augustine died, the Vandals were burning and sacking Hippo, where he was bishop.

Augustine's most influential works are *Confessions, On the Trinity, On Genesis According to the Letter,* and *City of God.* They all reflect his own faith after conversion and provide an intellectual structure for much Christian writing that followed. Although Augustine's initial education was in rhetoric, his later studies in Neoplatonism deeply influenced his religious understanding. Still, he approached philosophy in terms of how it could serve religion, rather than as a valuable discipline in its own right. This secondary status of philosophy was widely accepted by philosophers throughout the medieval period. Augustine was one of the early Church Fathers and was canonized as a saint, by popular acclaim, as was the custom during the early centuries of the Catholic Church.

## What did **Augustine confess** in *Confessions*?

The importance of Augustine's (354–430) *Confessions* lies less in what he disclosed about himself and more in its intimate, first-person style of writing, which became a distinct genre in future religious works, as well as philosophical treatises. His *Confessions,* written when he was in his forties, relates his religious yearnings, strivings, and happiness.

Augustine's early education was in rhetoric and literature. He claims that when, at the age of 18, he read Cicero's now lost dialogue, *Hortensius,* he was inspired to devote his life to the search for wisdom. Although he converted to Christianity in 386, he made a living teaching rhetoric, and for a while his main religious interest was in Manicaeanism. (Manicaeanism denied the crucifixion of Jesus, united Christianity with Budhhism, and was preoccupied with struggles between good and evil, or light and darkness.) Augustine came into contact with Bishop Ambrose and Christian Neoplatonists in Milan and found a sufficiently sophisticated form of Christianity that appealed to him.

Augustine believed that Neoplatonism anticipated the basic Christian doctrines about God, the creation, and divine presence. When he returned to his home in North Africa, he was ordained as a priest and then became bishop of Hippo. He preached, traveled, and corresponded voluminously. In his scholarly and devotional activities, he came to believe that the Christian scriptures, particularly the Gospel account of the life of Jesus, were more important than the writings of philosophers. He concluded that more important than belief, which was an intellectual matter, was understanding, which began with faith: "Believe in order that you may understand." Understanding required a vision of God.

## What did St. Augustine mean when he said, "Please God, make me good...."?

St. Augustine (354–430) considered himself profligate in his youth, much to the distress of his mother, Monica. In his *Confessions,* which recounts some of this early history, he is famous for having written what is often repeated as: "Please God, make me good, but not just yet." However, some scholars think that a more accurate translation of the Latin is: "Oh, Master, make me chaste and celibate—but not yet!" They also think that Augustine was not so much talking about his past self as he was ironically criticizing all who lack resolve about developing their virtues and devoting themselves to God.

Augustine's sins were probably not as great as his oft-quoted remark has led many to believe. As a youth, before his conversion to Christianity, Augustine was fond of drink and women. He had an illegitimate son in 372, but was in a 15-year relationship with the child's mother, which would have been considered perfectly respectable at the time.

## How did **Augustine support** the **theology of the Church** with philosophy?

St. Augustine (354–430) tried to justify the whole of human knowledge, even though he also allowed for error. All knowledge, according to Augustine, resided within the soul as "a substance endowed with reason and fitted to rule a body." While the soul can act on the body, the body cannot act on the soul. God is always present to the soul, whether the soul is aware of his light or turns away from it. These views of Augustine established the superiority of religion to philosophy and also embedded God in the same human faculty associated with non-religious understanding to the elevation of religious understanding.

Augustine's greatest work was *The City of God,* in which he separated the temporal state (government on Earth) from the religious realm of the afterlife. The temporal state was to have a secondary role in ensuring peace, order, safety, and physical well being for its citizens. The heavenly city, by contrast, requires living according to God's rules. Although the temporal and heavenly cities may at times overlap, only God's city is eternal.

## Who are some **Dark Ages philosophers** who came **after St. Augustine**?

After St. Augustine's death in 430, the so-called "Dark Ages" (roughly 420 to 1000 C.E.) ensued. In 420 the Visigoths living inside of Rome sacked the city. In monasteries in Italy, Spain, and Britain, the Encyclopedists emerged.

## Who were the **Encyclopedists**?

They were scholars who attempted to systematically present all of human knowledge at their time. Chief among them were Boëthius (480–c. 525) of Italy, whose work went far beyond the alphabetized speculations of the other two who best represented this period: St. Isidore of Seville (560–636) and The Venerable Bede of Britain (674–735). Both Isidore and The Bede were clerics who devoted their lives to ecclesiastical service. Isidore compiled *Etymologiae* (or *Origines*), which was a systematic presentation of all available learning during his time and endured as a textbook in church schools for hundreds of years. The Venerable Bede was best known for his histories, particularly that of Britain. The next real philosophical luminary was Johannes Scotus Eriugena (c. 815–877).

St. Isidore of Seville set the ambitious goal of describing all human knowledge in an extensive encyclopedia (Art Archive).

## Who was **Johannes Scotus Eriugena**?

Johannes Scotus Eriugena (c. 810-877; also known as John Scotus Eriugena) was a Christian rationalist (literally, his name means "John the Irishman, the Irishman.") King John the Bold called him to his Palatine School to translate *The Pseudo-Dionysius*. This document was falsely attributed to St. Dionysius (d. 268), a convert of St. Paul, although it was in fact written by an unknown Neoplatonist. Eriugiena's translation was initially a success; building on its main ideas, he constructed his own system, *De Divisione Naturae*. His basic premise was that logical reasoning ought to be compatible with Christian philosophy. This meant that the teachings of the Church Fathers could be criticized, if necessary. More heretically than that, it left no room for faith in divine creation and salvation. Eriugena's treatise was condemned by Pope Honorius III (1148–1227) in 1225.

## What did **Pope Honorius III** consider **heretical** about Johannes Scotus Eriugena's treatise?

In *De Divisione Naturae* Eriugena presented a Neoplatonic view of the world and cosmos that was also pantheistic. The Catholic Church did not accept pantheism, which held that God was everywhere in the world, because He was supposed to be separate

### What was in St. Isidore's encyclopedia?

St. Isidore of Seville's (c. 560–636) encyclopedia—the *Etymologiae*—was an ambitious attempt to compile all the knowledge of its day in one source. It contained everything that was known and believed at the time, with little critical editing. For example, under "A" was an entry on the atomic theory, but there was also an entry on the mythical Antipodes, who were said to populate rocky plains in the south of Africa. Isidore related that their big toes were not on the inside of their feet, but on the outside, which afforded them greater agility in navigating their rocky terrain.

from His creation. According to Eriugena, we cannot ascribe any natural quality from our own experience to God. That view was not a problem for the pope. The problem was that he described the created world as emanating from God in different stages: God created ideas or Platonic forms, and these created perceptible objects. The perceptible objects could not create anything but instead would ultimately be one with God, which meant that God "was all in all," part of a circle that ended in himself.

## THE SCHOLASTICS

### Who were the **scholastics**?

The scholastics were the first heavyweight philosophical school of medieval times. Their eleventh-century founder was St. Anselm of Canterbury (1033–1109), who was followed by Peter Abelard (1079–1142) and Peter Lombard (1100–1160) in the twelfth century. During the same time, Jewish and Islamic philosophers reintroduced Aristotle to the West. This innovation culminated in the work of St. Thomas Aquinas (c. 1225–1274), followed by John Duns Scotus (1266–1308).

### What did **St. Anselm of Canterbury** begin?

St. Anselm (1033–1109), known as "Anselm of Canterbury," was a Benedictine monk and the second Norman archbishop of Canterbury. He is famous for his ontological proof for the existence of God in *Proslogion,* and for his model of satisfaction in the Atonement in his *Cur Deus homo*.

Anselm's ontological argument to prove God's existence amounts to this: Imagine a being that is the greatest being that can be imagined. Such a being exists in the intellect alone. If this greatest being were to exist only in the intellect, a greater one that existed in reality could be imagined. But there cannot exist in reality a greater

**61**

being than the greatest being that can be imagined. Therefore, that imagined being is the greatest being.

Now, this greatest being would be everything and have every attribute that it is better to have than not to have: living, wise, powerful, true, just, blessed, unchangeable, non-physical, eternal, beautiful, harmonious, sweet, and so forth. That is—and this is the crux of the ontological argument—because being is better than non-being, God will have being, which is to say, he will exist.

Anselm goes on to claim that God, as the greatest being that can be imagined, is simple. Everything that exists is better insofar as it more resembles the creator of all things: namely, God. All created beings, which are created by God, owe their being and well-being to God. But God is independent and has no obligations to his creations.

### Did **Anselm** face **objections** to his **ontological argument**?

Yes. Also, different forms of St. Anselm's (1033–1109) argument kept popping up in the history of philosophy after Anselm died, as did different objections to it. It remains a subject of debate in some circles to this day. Anselm had posed his argument as something that a fool, who did not believe in God, would have to agree with. His contemporary, a monk called "Gaunilon," took up the position of the fool.

Gaunilon first said that it was impossible to conceive or imagine "a being than which nothing greater can be conceived." Anselm's response was that if the words "a being than which nothing greater can be conceived" are understood, then one (the fool) has conceived of or imagined this being. And because this being is so great and existence or being is greater than non-existence or non-being, the being exists.

### What are the **roots** of **St. Anselm's ontological argument**?

First, St. Anselm's (1033–1109) argument for God's existence seems to depend on pure reason as means to truth, which goes back to the ancient Greeks. That it only depends on reason, without observation or experience, perhaps makes it closer to Plato, or the Neoplatonists, than to Aristotle. Second, the argument relies on the ancient assumption that being or having more being is "better" or more perfect than non-being or having less being.

### Has anyone succeeded in **refuting Anselm's ontological argument**?

Many philosophers believe that Immanuel Kant (1724–1804) killed Anselm's argument with his claim that existence or being is "not a predicate" or a quality that a thing can have or not have. But other philosophers continued to debate both Anselm's and others' forms of the ontological argument.

### What was **Peter Lombard's contribution** to medieval philosophy?

Peter Lombard (c. 1095–1160) was an Italian theologian who wrote the *Book of Sentences*. He was educated in Bologna, Reims, and Paris, and he taught at Notre Dame, becoming a canon there from 1144 to 1145. The *Book of Sentences* is structured around important theological questions and subjects: for example, "Is God the cause of Evil and Sin?" Peter first set out the question or issue, related what the position of the Church Fathers on it would have been, and then proposed his own answer or resolution.

### How did **Peter Lombard answer** his question of whether **God** was the **cause of evil** and sin?

God is of course good and has a good nature. Out of this good nature, God created an angel. This angel became evil after God created him and passed his evil on to man. Evil in man resulted in sin. God was therefore not the first cause of either human evil or sin. (Lombard's explanation is similar to how we would explain how a good parent has a bad child—at some point the creation or offspring is morally responsible for itself and Lombard located that point originally in an angel.)

Lombard (c. 1095–1160) wrote about this and other issues in his four-volume *Book of Sentences* (1145–1151) that soon became a standard text for theological training that was in use until the mid 1200s. Others would begin with his work and then develop their own ideas on its basis.

### What is **Peter Abelard** known for in philosophy?

Peter Abelard (1079–1149) was the French theologian who wrote *Theologia Christiana,* an attempt to use logic for explaining Christian dogmas. His expertise in logic drew students from all over Europe. He was the first scholastic to write about Aristotle's *On Interpretation,* together with Boëthius' (480–c. 525) commentary on this work.

Abelard made a distinction between the meaning of an expression—what it names—and the idea in the mind of a

Peter Abelard attempted to use logical arguments to explain Christian dogma (Art Archive).

63

## What is the romantic story involving Peter Abelard and Eloise?

The story of Peter Abelard (1079–1149) and Eloise chronicles one of the most poignant romantic relationships in the Western tradition. It was referred to in the 1999 movie about a doorway that leads into the head of the actor John Malkovich (*Being John Malkovich* in which John Cusack's character refers to Peter and Heloise in the salacious dialogue of one of his marionette shows.) Well before this movie, Cole Porter wrote: "As Abelard said to Eloise, Don't forget to drop a line to me, Please."

In real life, Eloise had written to Abelard: "The name of wife may seem more sacred or more worthy but sweeter to me will always be the word lover, or, if you will permit me, that of concubine or whore."

Abelard, at the peak of his fame and popularity, assumed the position of tutor to Eloise. They fell in love, and he is said to have seduced her. She became pregnant, and they were secretly married. Eloise's uncle discovered the whole affair. Claiming to be incensed by the secrecy of their marriage, he publicly denounced Abelard and then had him castrated. Peter himself recounted these events in his autobiographical work, *Historia Calamitatum.*

Abelard told Eloise to become a nun and he himself became a monk. They carried on a correspondence of passionate love letters. Eloise was more enamored of Abelard than he was of her. Although castration was not an unusual punishment for the kind of betrayal of trust committed by Abelard, he was humiliated by his maiming for the rest of his life, and more or less retreated into his studies. Eloise became the highly successful abbess of a convent. Peter and Eloise were eventually buried together.

speaker who uses the expression. He did not think that words signify the images in the minds of their speakers. Meanings are what true or false sentences say or signify, which lies outside the minds of their speakers. The distinctions in Abelard's innovative philosophical theory of reference remain relevant to contemporary philosophers of language.

## ISLAM'S INFLUENCE

### How and why did **Jewish** and **Islamic philosophy** become part of the **scholastic tradition**?

Arabs, Berbers, and other Muslims invaded Christian Spain in the year 711 as part of their Islamic military campaigns. These military invasions were followed by a kind of colonization, which supported lasting cultural exchange. The Muslims were inclined to tolerate Judaism as well as Christianity because it was also a monotheistic religion "of the book" (that is, like both Islam and Christianity, Judaism had its own Bible with one God). As result of the dual tolerance of Jews and Christian by Muslim rulers, the scholastic tradition, which was originally a Christian tradition, came to incorporate both Jewish and Islamic philosophy.

## How did the **Islamic religion begin**?

The Prophet Muhammad (570–632), who was born in Saudi Arabia and died in Medina, was the founder of Islam. At the age of 40, he experienced an epiphany in which the angel Gabriel appeared to him while he was meditating. Until he was 60, he experienced continuing revelations that identified him as the culmination of a tradition of prophets from Abraham in the Old Testament, or Hebrew Bible, down to Jesus of Nazareth in the New Testament. His transcription of his revelations were the basis of the Qur'an, or Koran, the bible of Islam.

Muhammad had a divine mandate to spread the new religion. Within the first 100 years of Islam, *jihad,* or holy war, reached into France, where Charles the Sledgehammer defeated the Muslims at Tours; in Spain, the Moors built luscious gardens and beautiful buildings, chief among which were the magnificent libraries in Córdoba, Granada, Seville, and Toledo. (The Muslim cultural influence is still evident in Spanish architecture to this day.)

## Was **military invasion of Europe** part of the **religious practice of Islam** during the **medieval period**?

Yes, but the Islamic religion was not opposed to Christianity. In fact, as one of three great religions "of the book," Islam had much in common with Christianity, as well as Judaism. Its doctrine included a belief in one God, the importance of prayer, the idea of a church or brotherhood for all members of the religion, and the obligation to care for the poor. What was distinctive about Islam, in comparison to Christianity, was its rejection of the idea of the Catholic Trinity, requirements of fasting and other forms of bodily purification on holy days, and the necessity for every Muslim follower to make at least one journey or pilgrimage to Mecca. The

Philosophers owe a debt of gratitude to the Muslims, because it was Islamic scholars who rediscovered the works of the ancient Greeks (iStock)

continual importance of God and homage to Old Testament prophets was shared with Judaism, although, unlike Judaism, Islam had a positive conception of Heaven.

## What was **al-Kindi**'s main **contribution** to philosophy?

Abu Yusuf al-Kindi (c. 800–850), known in Latin as Alkindus, had both a noble heritage and an important position in the caliphate (the governing body representing Islamic leaders, headed by the Caliph). He promoted the introduction of Western philosophy into the Arabic world, with a focus on Plato and Aristotle. Unlike his successors, he believed that there was a literal correspondence between the metaphysical writings of the ancient Greeks and parts of the Qu'ran. His work was closer to Neoplatonism than Aristotelianism, and the tradition he began is contrasted by scholars to that of Matta Ybn Yanus (d. 940), who founded a school of Aristotelianism in Baghdad.

## Who was **Avicenna**?

Avicenna (980–1037) was a Persian physician and commentator on Aristotle. He was born near Bukhara, which was then the capital of the Samanid dynasty (located in present-day Uzbekistan). By the age of 10, he had mastery of the Qu'ran and Arabic grammar and literature. By 16, he was highly knowledgeable about natural science, metaphysics, and theories of medicine. He also treated the sick and helped the Samanid prince Nuh Ibn Mansur (976–997). His reward for that was access to the prince's library.

Avicenna became an expert on the writings of Aristotle, wrote extensive commentaries, and also produced many treatises of his own on science, religion, and philosophy. His medical encyclopedia, *Al-Shifa* (*The Healing*) was based on Aristotle's work, and his *Al Qanun fi Tibb* (*The Canon of Medicine*), written when he was 21, became famous throughout the Middle East and Europe. As an Aristotelian interpreter, he was well known for claiming that the universality of our ideas is a product of the mind.

He was not a complete nominalist about universals, however, because he thought that there were differences and similarities among things of the same kind, which existed independently of thought. The products of thought were the formal qualities of things. This doctrine, known as *intellectus in formis agit universalitatem,* neatly corresponded with Aristotle's claim that scientific knowledge consisted in truths about forms or essences. However, although Avicenna's interpretation of Aristotle seemed to be rather staid and unoriginal, his claim that it could be reconciled with Islam was soon challenged by al-Gazali (1058–1111); and in the generation after that it was radically revised, along with al-Gazali's objections, by Averroës (c. 1126–c. 1198).

The Persian philosopher Avicenna was an erudite commentator on the philosophy of Aristotle, among other talents (Art Archive).

## Who was **al-Ghazali**?

Abu Hamid al-Ghazali (1058–1111) was a philosopher, theologian, jurist, and Sufi mystic. Born in the Middle Eastern region of Khurisan (or Khorasan), and educated in the intellectual center of Nishaur, he became head of Nizamiyah, a seminary in Baghdad, where his teachings in law and theology were renowned. He sought certainty in knowledge, and when he could not find it in his academic studies he resigned his academic post, left his family, and became a Sufi mystic. He wandered for a decade and, as the result of those experiences, returned to Nishapur to resume teaching.

Al-Ghazali came to believe that truth can be found only as the result of God's grace. In *Deliverance from Error,* his spiritual autobiography, he related his futile quest for truth and certainty through both Islamic and Western intellectual traditions and concluded that sensory information and reason were just as lacking. His alternative to rational and sensory knowledge was "a light which God Most High cast into my breast ... the key to most knowledge."

His attack on philosophical authorities as a guide to truth and certainty, particularly in the writings of Avicenna (980–1037), culminated in *The Intensions of the Philosophers*. And in *The Incoherence of the Philosophers* he offered a detailed intellectual attack on the views of Plato and Aristotle, which was again directed against Avicenna.

## What is **Sufism**?

Sufism is the mystical branch of Islam. Its classical period, or "Golden Age," was from 1000 to 1500. Sufism is believed to have branched out from Baghdad to spread through Persia, India, North Africa, and Spain. The movement supported lodges and hospices for students, Sufi adepts, and others visiting on retreat. Sufi practitioners were expected to go through different levels of spirituality. First were the "stations," requiring acts of will and actions to suppress individual egos and attachment to and desire for worldly things. This would lead to God's grace. Once God's grace was granted it could be experienced individually as love, mystical knowledge, or the loss of ego consciousness.

Sufism began as a marginal practice but was accepted by Islamic leaders in the eleventh century, mainly through al-Gazali's (1058–1111) efforts. Sufism then developed along distinct practical and intellectual directions. The practical paths required training in religious formulas and initiation into orders. It was accompanied by many fraternal and social organizations that continue in the present Islamic world.

The intellectual path developed philosophical terminology and absorbed Neoplatonic influences, culminating in Ibn Arabi's (d. 1240) system of theosophy. Within that system, God was held to be the only being. Everything else in existence was the result of his self-manifestation. The individual who could identify with all of God's self-manifestations would have the goal of becoming The Perfect Man, thus far attained only by the Prophet Muhammad. It is perhaps ironic that this intellectual path of Sufism developed when al-Gazali had embraced Sufism as part of a belief that knowledge and reasoning was not a reliable way to experience God.

## Why was **Averroës** considered **important** by other philosophers?

Averroës, known as ibn-Rushd in the Islamic world (c. 1126–c. 1198), was born in Córdoba, Spain. He brought the tradition of comparative philosophy—begun by Avicenna and rendered problematic by al-Gazali—to a new level of intellectual sophistication. His main project was to settle the debate among his contemporaries about whether Aristotle's philosophy was compatible with Islam, as Avicenna had claimed, or opposed to it as al-Galzali (1058–1111) had objected.

Averroës continued the work of Avicenna, commenting on the debate about Aristotlean philosophy and its compatibility with Islam (Art Archive).

## What was **impressive** about **Averroës' life and work**?

Averroës (c. 1126–c. 1198) was born into a prominent family of lawyers and judges and was himself trained as a lawyer in both civil and religious affairs. He traveled from Córdoba to Marrakesh in 1153 and decided that Aristotle had been correct in stating that the world was round when he was able to observe Canope, a star not visible in Spain. He served as both advisor and doctor to the sultan of Marrakesh, who encouraged a series of commentaries on Aristotle. His writings include treatises on medicine and astronomy, but he is best known for his *The Incoherence of Incoherence,* which was a reply to al-Gazali's (1058–1111) *The Incoherence of the Philosophers.* In his *Incoherence of Incoherence,* Averroës defended natural reason as a means to attain knowledge in all domains. By natural reason Averroës, and others after him, meant ordinary thought processes rather than religious intuition or revelation.

Averroës also wrote a set of commentaries on Aristotle that was influential in Western medieval scholarship. When his interpretations of Aristotle did not square with his own assumptions, he wrote detailed "supplements" of his own. For example, Aristotle's *Physics* and *On the Heavens* were composed as two separate works and based on different types of observations. Under Plato's influence, Averroës assumed that they were united.

## What were **Averroës** most noteworthy **ideas**?

Overall, Averroës' (c. 1126–c. 1198) Aristotelian views were shaped by Platonic ideas, partly because he mistakenly believed that the whole of ancient Greek thought was one unified system that had been composed cooperatively. He also believed that, according to Aristotle, all of the sciences could be studied with the same meaning of "being," whereas Aristotle had insisted that the sciences were diverse and their subject matter inherently different. Averroës viewed all of nature as one harmonious order. On the subject of immortality, this holism was related to his idea that individual souls are not distinguished from one another after death, but combine into one form.

Averroës also interpreted Aristotle as claiming that Earth was eternal, which was against Christian doctrine of the creation. In *On the Harmony between Religion and Philosophy,* Averroës tried to show that the same truth can be reached through different means: dialectic in law, philosophy for those skilled in the use of pure reason, and rhetoric for those with only a general education.

# MAIMONIDES

## What was the **importance of** Jewish philosophy **in** medieval thought?

Moses Maimonides, or Moses son of Maimon (1135–1204), who is also referred to as Rabbi Moses ben Maimon (RaMBaM), had an extensive influence on subsequent Jewish scholarship, the ideas of Thomas Aquinas (c. 1225–1274), and many scholars thereafter. Maimonides, like Averroës (c. 1126–c. 1198), was born in Córdoba, Spain, and, also like Averroës, pursued an intense interest in Aristotle. While he intended his writings to be restricted to Jewish readers, his insights about the relationship between monotheistic religious beliefs and classical philosophical insights were studied by both Catholic and Islamic thinkers, as well as Jewish philosophers and theologians.

The title page from Maimonides' *Guide of the Perplexed* in which he attempted to reconcile religion and philosophy (Art Archive).

## What were **Maimonides'** main **intellectual contributions**?

After Maimonides (1135–1204) and his family fled forced conversions in Spain, they settled in Cairo, Egypt, in 1165, where Maimonides was the physician of the vizier of Saladin (c. 1138–1193). He wrote 10 books on medicine, but it was his works on Jewish theology that represented his most important contribution to Judaism: *Book of the Commandments* treated the 613 laws from the Old Testament; *Commentary on the Mishnah* explained the practical purposes of the old rabbinical code; and *Mishneh Torah*, codified Talmudic law in 14 volumes and retains its classic status to the present. However, it was Maimonides' philosophical treatise, *Guide of the Perplexed,* that had direct influence over a broad range of Western philosophy.

## Why is Maimonides' *Guide of the Perplexed* still considered a **great philosophical text**?

Maimonides (1135–1204) addresses his *Guide* to contemporary educated men who were intellectually torn between the claims of Greek science and religion. Maimonides' intention in writing seems to be to help his readers understand philosophy, without giving up their religion. To weed out or not upset readers who lacked the mental fire power to follow his reasoning, he said that he deliberately scattered Aristotelian insights throughout the text, instead of putting those together that first occurred together. He often stated both a position and its opposite. In other words, Maimonides' first step toward guiding those already confused was to deepen their confusion. But because Maimonides deepened existing confusions so brilliantly, his *Guide of the Perplexed* has attracted lasting scholarly disputation.

## What are some **examples** of the **perplexities** Maimonides set out in his *Guide of the Perplexed*?

First, and perhaps foremost, was the question posed in *Guide of the Perplexed* of what kind of knowledge it is possible for people to have of God. According to the Doctrine of

## Why did philosophers love Maimonides?

**M**aimonides (1135–1204) provided a justification for philosophical thought in a religious context at a time when philosophers feared persecution from religious authorities. The problems Maimonides raised in reconciling Aristotelian philosophy—or the best conclusions of reason at that time—with religion brought into religion itself philosophical problems about the limits of knowledge and what ought to be concluded when reason has run out. That is, should we say that the limits of reason are the limits of human knowledge, or should we extend the limits of reason into the domain of religious faith and revelation? Strictly speaking, these are questions of how we ought to think about religion.

In the Middle Ages, which was the Great Age of Religion, philosophers were constrained to begin their philosophizing with basic assumptions that God existed and that he was good. But philosophers have always been motivated to push through to the limits of knowledge and seek certainty within those limits. By deploying Aristotle as the personification of philosophy, Maimonides was able to raise necessarily covert questions of whether reason could justify belief in the existence and teachings not only of the Judaic version of God, but also of the Christian (and perhaps Muslim) God.

We should remember that such questions, had they not been posed under the cover of the august and unquestionable authority of The Philosopher Himself—namely, Aristotle—would have resulted in loss of livelihood, excommunication (banishment or ostracism from the community of the devout and faithful) and also death itself. Philosophers were not stupid in the Great Age of Religion, not withstanding their apparent devotion to varied theological regimes and their leaders, who—it just so happened!—controlled all aspects of social, political, and economic life in Europe and the Middle East, at the same time that they upheld specific religious doctrines.

Negative Theology, which Maimonides took over from Avicenna (980–1037), nothing positive can be known about God, because God has nothing in common with any other being experienced by humans, and humans have no experience of God. All that we can know is what God is *not*. (Negative theology is the doctrine that God cannot be known by man.)

Second, there is a contradiction between the idea of God on which Judaism is founded, and the philosophical, Aristotelian idea of God. The philosophical idea is that God is intellect, whereas the religious idea is that it cannot be known what God is. Maimonides (1135–1204) sums up this problem with what he calls "very disgraceful conclusions" in the following passage.

Namely it would follow that the Deity, whom everyone who is intelligent recognizes to be perfect in every kind of perfection, could as far as all beings are concerned, produce nothing new in any of them; if he wished to lengthen a fly's wing or shorten a worm's foot, he would not be able to do so. But Aristotle would say that he would not wish it and that it is impossible to will something different from what is; that it would not add to his perfection, but would perhaps from a certain point of view be a deficiency.

Third, Maimonides rejected the Aristotelian doctrine of the eternity of the world. Although he could offer no conclusive rational justification for this rejection, neither did he affirm that this was an issue in which religion was definitively correct.

# THOMAS AQUINAS

## Who was **Thomas Aquinas** and what made him known as the greatest medieval philosopher?

St. Thomas Aquinas (1224–1274) was born in Rocaseca, Italy. He began his religious studies in a Benedictine monastery and studied liberal arts at the University of Naples. He entered the Dominican Order of Preachers when he was only 20. He studied theology in Paris, attaining his doctorate in 1256, and taught there until 1259. Aquinas then lectured on theology and philosophy at Dominican monasteries near Rome, and then returned to the University of Paris. He taught for a year in Naples in 1272. Aquinas died near his place of birth, while traveling to a church council in Lyons.

During his teaching career, which spanned from 1252 to 1273, Aquinas wrote extensively. He lucidly solved long-standing problems in the interpretation of Aristotle, made clear distinctions between Christian theology and philosophy, and demonstrated how the two were compatible on many subtle points.

## What are the **major works** of **Thomas Aquinas**?

Aquinas (1224–1274) wrote prodigiously throughout his life, and his works include commentaries on the writings of Aristotle, reports on Albertus Magnus' (1200–1280) lectures, a commentary on the *Sentences* of Peter Lombard (c. 1095–1160), and other philosophical treatises such as *On Being and Essence* and *On the Principles of Nature,* as well as *On the Unity of the Intellect against the Averroists.* He is most famous for his *Summa against the Gentiles* and *Summa on Theology.*

## What were **Thomas Aquinas'** main original **ideas**?

Although Thomas Aquinas (1224–1274) was deeply influenced by the work of the Aristotielians, as well as the stoics, Neoplatonists, and St. Augustine (354–430), his resolution of past philosophy with Christian theology is considered unique. Many of his solutions to standing problems display moderation without intellectual compromise. For instance, his position on universals (whether or not general terms name general things that exist), is even called "moderate realism." Aquinas did not believe that universals exist, but he did posit a foundation outside of the human mind for universals and truths about them. That foundation was the fact that individual things of the same kind, which are referred to by the name of that kind (e.g., specific cats that are called "cats") have real similarities and resemblances. Whether or not this solution did more than restate the problem remains an open question, but it definitely impressed many as a new way of thinking about the old problem of universals.

St. Thomas Aquinas sits between Aristotle and Plato; St. Thomas is still considered one of the most important philosophers to have ever lived (Art Archive).

## Was **Aquinas** able to solve the **conflict** between **faith and reason**?

Thomas Aquinas (1224–1274) redefined faith as a kind of knowledge, rather than as a specific feeling or attitude of mind. As such, he said that faith fell between opinion and scientific knowledge. Faith was greater than opinion because it involved strong agreement, as an act of will, and it was less than scientific knowledge because it lacked factual evidence that could compel agreement.

Aquinas thought that philosophy was reasoning based on existing knowledge or experience, leading to new knowledge, which he called "the way of discovery." He held that philosophy was also the use of reason to confirm beliefs by tracing them back to basic principles, which he called "the way of reduction." Philosophy becomes theology if the beliefs one begins with are based on faith. There are, in turn, two kinds of theology: truths in Scripture that are learned for their own sake, and metaphysics or explanations based on religious principles.

Despite his theological idea of metaphysics, Aquinas did distinguish between philosophy and theology. For instance, in *De Aeternitate Mundi,* although he held the religious belief that the universe was not eternal, he said that it might be eternal based on philosophical reasoning. In general, apart from religious revelation, Aquinas

73

## Did St. Aquinas really have a recipe for making mice?

Like many of his contemporaries, Thomas Aquinas (1224–1274) believed in the *spontaneous generation* of insects and vermin. The doctrine of spontaneous generation held that life could literally just appear without the prior presence of parent organisms. This biological mythology went back to Aristotle and is in fact strangely empirical, if you think about it. Flies, for example, do suddenly seem to appear out of rotting garbage. It took a long time—well into the seventeenth century—to discover that the maggots they spring from come from eggs laid by parent flies.

Aquinas thought that insects sprang to life in filth, owing to the Devil's influence. He thought that the development of mice, however, depended on changes in the positions of the stars. As "proof" of this origin of baby mice, Aquinas had a recipe: Take some old rags and wheat and leave them undisturbed in a drawer for a while (to give the stars enough time to exert their effects) and then take a peek. Again, there is a crude empiricism at work here. If there are mice in a dwelling, its inhabitants rarely see them breed, and rarer still do they observe female mice building nests and giving birth. If this has happened in a neglected drawer, all that may be evident when one suddenly opens it is the litter of pink babies when the last time one looked there was nothing but old rags and wheat. (If you try this at home, the wheat is probably unnecessary, although the mother mouse will doubtless appreciate it.)

believed that we get our knowledge from sense experience and our intellectual understanding of our sense experience.

## What were **Aquinas' views** on **science**?

As an Aristotelian, Thomas Aquinas (1224–1274) believed that every object has its proper place. He also held the Eudoxian astronomical view that Earth was in the center of 49 to 53 concentric spheres. However, he thought that scientific conclusions required judgment and assessment, so that all findings and reports should be considered and compared. He also believed that scientific information could be changed and revised, which is a strong tenet of modern empiricism.

## What did **Aquinas** think about the **soul**?

Although Thomas Aquinas (1224–1274) carefully and meticulously investigated what was known in general about human senses, intellect, will, and emotions, he believed that the human being is the whole of all these faculties or "powers." Simply put, the physical body is the matter or material of a human being, and its form or soul is its "substantial form." That the soul can understand general truths and exercise free will proves its non-materiality. The reality of the soul is its spirituality. Because the soul cannot be divided, it cannot be corrupted and is therefore immortal. Furthermore, because the soul cannot be divided, it cannot be the result of biological inheritance but is made directly by God, each time a person is born. This divine intervention at birth gives the biological process of human reproduction a dignity and sanctity that elevates the institution of marriage.

### Why was **Aquinas** called the **"Angelic Doctor"** by Catholics?

Thomas Aquinas (1224–1274) was called the "Angelic Doctor" because he believed there were beings with intellectual powers and abilities greater than those of humans. They existed on the highest level of the universe and were purely spiritual, although finite. They were angels.

### What did **Aquinas contribute** to **metaphysics** in the non-religious sense?

Thomas Aquinas (1224–1274) was very interested in the question, "What does it mean to be?" He sought to understand reality as a whole and tried to formulate explanations of all experience in terms of ultimate causes. About metaphysics in relation to its considerations of immaterial substances, he said, "Although this science considers these items, it does not think of each of them as its subject; its subject is simply being in general." Taken literally, this claim about metaphysics describes it as transcendent of religion, because religious entities have being and their being is the subject of the most general philosophical study. Metaphysically, Aquinas determined that every being is distinct and undivided (*unum*), it has meaning (*verum*), and there is something good about it (*bonum*).

Aquinas distinguished between what a being is and that it is. What it is, is its *essence,* and that it is, is its *esse.* We can know the essences of things without considering their existence, but it requires an act of judgment to determine *esse,* that something is.

## OTHER IMPORTANT MEDIEVAL PHILOSOPHERS

### How was **John Duns Scotus'** work **different** from **Thomas Aquinas'**?

John Duns Scotus (1266–1308) was not opposed to Aquinas (1224–1274), but he brought St. Augustine's (354–430) thought into philosophical and theological conversations that were largely dominated by interest in Aristotle. Duns Scotus also drew on Avicenna's (c. 980–1037) notion of unified being in his idea of God as Infinite Being, who had appeared to Moses as "I am who am."

John Duns Scotus helped broaden philosophical debate after Thomas Aquinas by reminding others of the work of St. Augustine and Avicenna (Art Archive).

Albertus Magnus was a theologian and philosopher who favored Catholic doctrine over the ideas of Aristotle (Art Archive).

Duns Scotus lectured at Oxford, Paris, and Cologne, where he taught that God had created each individual being with a unique nature or "haecceity." Duns Scotus thought it was the will and not the intellect that is rational, because the will can will either one thing or its opposite. The will has both an intellectual appetite for happiness and self-actualization and a desire to love things based on their inherent value. These aspects of the will incline us to love God for our own good and also because he is God. Duns Scotus introduced a new idea of "intellectual intuition," a kind of awareness that enables us to be certain of our own thoughts, and in the afterlife, be in the direct presence of God.

## Who was **Albertus Magnus**?

Albertus Magnus (1200–1280) was a German Dominican theologian who was also a dedicated scholar of philosophy. As master of theology at the University of Paris, he was a member of the commission that condemned the Jewish holy book, the *Talmud*. His philosophical contributions consisted mainly of Aristotelian commentaries; and where Aristotle disagreed with Catholic doctrine, Magnus corrected him and substituted different accounts. He relied on astrology in his view of the physical world, believing, for instance, that when the influence of Jupiter and Saturn increased the result was great fire, whereas when this influence decreased, there would be floods.

## Who was **William of Ockam**?

William of Ockam (c. 1280–c. 1349), known as the "More than Subtle Doctor," was a Franciscan monk. He studied theology at Oxford and developed a strong expertise in logic, which may have led to his foundational empirical insights. Empiricism, as a doctrine independent of theology, was not widely accepted by medieval scholastic philosophers, so neither was the principle that came to be known as Ockam's Razor: "Plurality is not to be assumed without necessity." In its modern form in science, Ockam's Razor is a rule for parsimony and simplicity in the construction of theories, and against commitment to more entities than are strictly necessary for the explanation of data or observations.

Ockam's empiricism also applied to universals, and he rejected all claims to their reality. The only real things, according to Ockam, were existent particulars. He held that universals were the names of concepts, a doctrine called *conceptualism*. He asserted that there was no willed causation in nature, which entailed that even God could not interfere in physical causal laws. Although Ockam did believe that God could intervene in human cognition.

## How well were **Ockam's ideas** first **received**?

John Lutterell, former chancellor of Oxford University, extracted over 50 heretical claims from Ockam's writings and sent them to Pope John XXII (1249–1334). Ockam was summoned to a papal commission in Avignon, where French cardinals had moved the papacy from Rome. (This relocation, which lasted from 1309 to 1377, was known as the "Babylonian Captivity" of the papacy.) Fifty-one of Ockam's offending theses were censured after two years, although no charges were brought against him. However, while he was in Avignon, Ockham conducted his own investigations of papal concessions to the Franciscans about collective poverty. He concluded that John XXII had contradicted these prior concessions in his own opposition to clerical poverty and that he was "no true pope."

When Ockam heard that Pope John XXII intended to condemn his written judgment and defense of clerical poverty, he fled to the protection of the antipapal regent in Bavaria. While he was there, the pope excommunicated him in absentia. The Black Plague was at that time rampant in Bavaria and William of Ockam is thought to have died of it.

# RENAISSANCE HUMANISM

## What **historical developments** helped to **start Renaissance humanism**?

The historical period of the Renaissance is usually considered to include the years from 1450 to 1600. This time is associated with the transition between the medieval and modern periods. From its beginnings in Italy, the Renaissance was marked by a new interest in literature, poetry, and painting in a shift of attention from the mainly religious preoccupations of life in the Middle Ages to the secular, perceptible world. The Western world changed, along with this transformation of values: the Copernican revolution radically reconfigured the place of human life in the physical cosmos; inquiries leading to the scientific revolution began; seeds for nation states were sown in political thought and action; the great age of exploration and travel by Europeans to Asia, Africa, and the Americas for adventure, science, and wealth began. All of these factors during the Renaissance changed the course of philosophy.

## What was **Marsilio Ficino's contribution** to the spirit of the Renaissance?

Marsilio Ficino (1433–1499) was ordained a priest in 1473, and from the center of cultural life in Florence he attempted to draw people to Christ through Platonism. Although he was the first to translate Plato's dialogues into Latin, he was not a purist; he also provided translations of Plotinus (205–270) and other Neoplatonists.

Ficino believed that Plato got his ideas from a legendary Egyptian magician, Hermes Trismegistus, whose work he also translated. Ficino claimed a form of wisdom that combines religion and philosophy. His own *Three Books on Life* suggested the idea of a world soul that was connected to the world's body by occult means. In human beings, a similar relationship holds insofar as the "astral body" connects body and soul. This parallel structure of the world and human beings is what makes spiritual advancement, as well as the attainment of worldly goods, possible through the practice of magic.

Marsilio Ficino was a priest who used the works of Plato to argue for Christianity (Art Archive).

Ficino's worldview and spiritual beliefs were so clearly opposed to Aristotelian Christianity—as well as probably being heretical—that their very circulation signaled important cultural changes, if not the demise of orthodoxy.

### What was **Pico Della Mirandola** known for?

Giovanni Pico Della Mirandola (1463–1494) is most famous for his "Oration on the Dignity of Man," which was the introduction to his *900 Theses,* which he wrote in order to debate publicly in Rome. A papal commission censored 13 of the theses, but after Pico attempted to justify them with his *Apology,* they were *all* condemned by Pope Innocent VIII (1432–1492).

Pico sought refuge in France, and after he was imprisoned there he went back home to Florence, where he continued his writing. He had a strong interest

Giovanni Pico Della Mirandola was persecuted by the Church for his "Oration on the Dignity of Man" (iStock).

in the same hermetic tradition introduced by Ficino, although he argued against part of it in his *Disputations against Astrology.*

While Pico's "Oration on the Dignity of Man" has been heralded as a classic example of Renaissance humanism, Pico believed that the dignity of man was located in his proper place in the cosmos. The freedom of man, which Pico is so famous for proclaiming, is thus not the freedom for human beings to create themselves or chart their own destinies, but rather the traditional Christian freedom of being able to choose between good and evil as defined by Christianity.

### What was **philosophical** about the thought of **Desiderius Erasmus**?

Desiderius Erasmus (1466–1536) was born in Holland as the illegitimate son of a priest. He became widely known and highly respected throughout England and Europe for his biblical translations and ideas about religion. He was one of the first thinkers after antiquity to admit to skepticism in religious debates. His *Moride Encomium* (*In Praise of Folly*) reintroduced the idea of a simple, pious Christianity. However, when Martin Luther (1483–1546) tried to enlist his support in the Protestant Reformation he

Desiderius Erasmus is depicted in this 1526 engraving by Albrecht Dürer (iStock).

resisted taking his side. When Luther criticized him for this, Erasmus responded with *On Free Will* in which he argued that it was impossible to know, as Luther claimed to know, that man did not have free will.

Erasmus was not himself a philosopher, but he made fun of the preoccupations of the scholastics and inaugurated their subsequent reputation as intellectually trivial. Through his influence in Europe on its educational systems, Greek, Latin, and Hebrew became more widely taught. Overall, he was a great supporter of the kind of critical spirit that many scholars believe eventually produced the Enlightenment.

### Was **Thomas More** serious about his **utopian vision**?

Although Sir Thomas More (1478–1535; later, St. More), was strongly influenced by Desiderius Erasmus' (1466–1536) mockery of scholasticism, his ideas in his most important work, *Utopia,* are quite sober and serious. The work itself became a model for modern descriptions of the ideal society. Like Erasmus, More returned to Greek philosophy and early Christianity for ideals of human life. More sought inspiration from Epicurus (341–271 B.C.E.), and, like his guide, extolled simple and natural pleasures among friends with the same tastes.

Sir Thomas More's resistance to King Henry VIII's self-serving policies eventually led to sainthood (iStock).

The principal narrator of *Utopia* is Raphael Hythlodaeus, a well-traveled philosopher who is fond of Plato, Plutarch, and Aristotle, as well as the Roman intellectuals Seneca and Cicero. The island of Utopia is a completely egalitarian, communistic society. Reflecting More's values, Utopia favors rights for women, traditional families, and a reliance on Christian virtues to support its main purpose of achieving happiness for all in their earthly lives.

### How did Sir Thomas **More** become a **martyr**?

More (1478–1535) was a lawyer by training, and beginning in 1517 he served King Henry VIII, who appointed him Lord Chancellor. In 1534 the British Parliament passed the Act of Succession, making the heirs to the English crown the children of King Henry VIII and Anne Boleyn, which resulted in Henry VIII's children from earlier marriages (including Elizabeth, who was to become Queen Elizabeth I) being declared bastards.

More refused to swear to the Act of Supremacy, which affirmed the Act of Succession, and so he was committed to the Tower of London, charged with treason, and beheaded. More had always stuck to his own principles while in high office, and his refusal has been generally interpreted as an expression of his belief that Henry VIII had overstepped his royal prerogatives, first in declaring himself Head of the Church of England, so that he could seize Church lands and marry Anne Boleyn, and then in interfering with the royal succession. More's last words were: "The King's good servant, but God's First." More was beatified by the Catholic Church in 1886 and canonized as a saint by Pope Pius XI in 1935.

### Why was **Bernardo Telesio** called **"the first of the moderns"** by Francis Bacon?

Bernardo Telesio (1509–1588) studied philosophy, physics, and mathematics at the University of Padua, receiving his doctorate at the age of 26. His subsequent pedagogical activity consisted of conversations with friends under the patronage of the Carafa family in Naples. He was also sought after by Pope Gregory XIII (1502–1585), who invited him to Rome. Telesio's major work was *On the Nature of Things According to their Principles.*

Telesio's innovation was to propose that knowledge of nature be based on sensory information about matter and the forces of heat and cold. Because of this emphasis on sensory information, Telesio is credited with laying the groundwork for more rigorous ideas about scientific investigation, which would soon follow in the work of Francis Bacon (1561–1626) and Galileo Galilei (1564–1642). However, Telesio's own theories about the workings of nature do not greatly depart from Neoplatonic perspectives.

According to Telesio, heat, represented by sky, is the source of life and the cause of biological functions. Cold is represented by Earth, and it opposes heat. Heat also emanates "spirit," which in animals and humans is located in the brain, for the purpose of anticipating and receiving sensory information. Man also has an *anima superaddita,* or mind, which is created by God and present in both spirit and body. All beings have a desire or impetus toward self-preservation, which in human beings includes a goal of everlasting life.

### Who was **St. Teresa** and what were her **main ideas**?

St. Teresa of Ávila (1515–1582) entered the Carmelite order when she was 22, and there she sought guidance in how to pray until she was 47. In 1560 she became part of the reform movement among the Spanish Carmelites. Her main works were the *Vida (Life)*, which was her spiritual autobiography, and *Way of Perfection* and *The Interior Castle.* Her main project was to help readers surrender to the divine Trinity.

Teresa held that mysticism developed in stages. In her *Life,* she says that the soul is like a garden. First, weeds need to be removed and then water must be carried from a well. The senses must be subdued to minimize distraction during this initial labor of prayer and meditation. The prayer of quiet in the second stage is like irrigation with the help of a water wheel; and in the third stage a condition of contemplation is achieved, which is analogous to having a running brook through one's garden. By this time, the senses no longer function normally and the soul wants to withdraw from the world and unite with God. In the fourth stage, this union is achieved.

In *The Interior Castle,* Teresa uses the analogy of a castle with many rooms to describe a life of contemplation. After six early stages, the soul comes into the direct presence of God.

## In what way was **St. Teresa** of Ávila a **Renaissance figure**?

St. Teresa of Ávila's (1515–1582) writings intimately recorded her spiritual development in a way that invited the reader to take the same path for him or herself. Unlike St. Augustine, whose confessional focus was ultimately on God and the religious community, St. Teresa focused on the individual heart and soul. Teresa's use of sensory imagery and her comparison of advances in mysticism to courtship and love throughout her writings, could probably not have been written during the medieval period. Neither could a distinctly female human voice have found such religious expression, before the Renaissance.

# SKEPTICISM AND NATURAL PHILOSOPHY

## How was **skepticism** related to the **scientific revolution**?

The reemergence of ancient Greek skepticism toward the end of the Renaissance was not, at first, related to the rise of scientific inquiry. Rather, Catholic and Protestant theologians used skepticism as a tool to further argue their positions during the Reformation and Counter-Reformation, and Catholics also used it to affirm mysticism and simple faith as the paths to real knowledge.

## How did **skepticism** further arguments for **faith and mysticism**?

When there were contending religions, each side would apply skepticism to the knowledge claims of the other. The Catholics used skepticism to disprove the claims about knowledge of God made by the Protestants, and the Protestants did the same thing to the Catholics. The result was that each side ended up extolling its own type of faith, rather than the knowledge claimed by the other side. (This use of skepticism to elevate faith and mysticism had its roots in Islamic philosophy, specifically in the writings of Abu Hamid al-Gazali [1058–1111]). As the two-sided religious skeptical debates wore down, the modern form of skepticism, which supports observation and the scientific method, came into wide use.

## Who were the **natural philosophers**?

"Natural philosophy" was the term used to describe what we now call science. The key players in the scientific revolution, beginning with Galileo (1564–1642) and ending with Isaac Newton (1643–1727), were called "natural philosophers" and were revered as geniuses by philosophers of their day. The lines between scientific inquiry, philosophical theories of knowledge, and philosophy of science were not clearly drawn until these "natural philosophers'" discoveries and theories helped define them.

## Who were the **philosophical rationalists**?

The philosophical rationalists believed that there was *a priori* knowledge about the world, or general truths about the world known by the mind, without experience. This was in contrast to the empiricist insistence that all of our knowledge about the world was based on experience, sensory information in particular. The seventeenth century philosophical rationalists, such as René Descartes (1596–1650), were opposed to the intellectual methods of the empiricists, but they still took science into account in their philosophies. Descartes was actively involved in scientific exploration and experimentation throughout his philosophical career. In the late-eighteenth century, David Hume's (1711–1776) empiricism posed a special problem for Immanuel Kant (1724–1804) because Hume (1711–1776) applied skepticism to basic beliefs that many had taken for granted before him, such as the existence of God and the powers of natural causes to bring about their effects. In the nineteenth century, modern reactions against empiricism took hold in the work of Georg Wilhelm Friedrich Hegel (1770–1831), Friedrich Nietzsche (1844–1900), and early existentialist philosophers, such as Søren Kierkegaard (1813–1855). These reactions shared a concern for the validity of *a priori* truths and religious knowledge.

# MICHEL DE MONTAIGNE

## Why was **Montaigne important**?

Michel Eyquem de Montaigne (1533–1592), the essayist who became mayor of his hometown of Bourdeaux, France, resurrected the ancient Greek skepticism of Sextus Empiricus (160–210 C.E.), with some reliance on Cicero. Although Montaigne lived dur-

ing the end of the Renaissance, his ideas set the stage for much thought that would follow during the scientific revolution and early modern philosophy. In the history of ideas and philosophy, he is therefore much more than a Renaissance figure.

## What is **fideism** and what does it have to do with what **Montaigne demonstrated** about **skepticism**?

Montaigne (1533–1592) demonstrated how skepticism could be a double-edged sword: it could be used to reject irrational claims, and it could be used to attack the certainty of any body of knowledge, including scientific knowledge based on the senses and the conclusions of logical reasoning. This made skepticism extremely useful for Catholic theologians attacking the claims of Protestants, and vice versa. Today, we think of skeptics as those who require careful scientific evidence for claims and judgments. Usually a skeptic is someone who will not take anything on

Michel de Montaigne showed that skepticism could be used to effectively argue for either science or religion (Art Archive).

faith. But Montaigne showed that even the best evidence, including sensory information, can be doubted, so that for him, the skeptic is someone who is better off relying on faith. What Montaigne had in mind was not only faith about knowledge that could not be proved to a certainty, but a life of faith in which all attempts at rigorous knowledge were avoided. This is known as *fideism*.

## How did **Montaigne convey** his **ideas**?

Montaigne (1533–1592) used an indirect approach to explaining his ideas, which was not surprising for someone as intellectually sophisticated about literature, philosophy, and history as he was. Montaigne translated *Natural Theology; or, The Book of Creatures,* (written from 1420 to 1430) by Raimond Sebond, a fifteenth century Spanish theologian, who had taught at the University of Toulouse, where Montaigne had studied. The University of Toulouse offered much advanced and humanistic thinking at that time in a curriculum that encouraged intellectual creativity. Montaigne's translation, *The Apology of Raimond Sebond,* was the result of Montaigne's original embellishments. His primary thesis was that sensory and intellectual knowledge are uncertain. His conclusion was that judgment should therefore be suspended concerning

85

## What were some examples of Montaigne's famous wit?

Montaigne had sayings from Sextus Empiricus (160–210 C.E.) carved into the beams of the rafters of his study. His favorite, which became his own motto and the motto of the *Essays,* was "Que sais-je?" or "What do I know?"

The following aphorisms are excerpts from his Essays.

"Wise men have more to learn of fools than fools of wise men."

"From the same sheet of paper on which a judge writes his sentence against an adulterer, he tears off a piece to scribble a love note to his colleague's wife."

"Don't discuss yourself, for you are bound to lose; if you belittle yourself, you are believed; and if you praise yourself, you are disbelieved."

"Even on the most exalted throne in the world we are only sitting on our own ass."

"Fashion is the science of appearances, and it inspires one with the desire to seem rather than to be."

"He who is not strong in memory should not meddle with lying."

"I will fight the right side to the fire, but excluding the fire if I can."

"There are some defeats more triumphant than victories."

"Age prints more wrinkles in the mind, than it does in the face, and souls are never, or very rarely seen, that in growing old do not smell sour and musty."

"Books are a languid pleasure."

"Even in the midst of compassion we feel within I know not what tart sweet titillation of malicious pleasure in seeing others suffer; children have the same feeling."

"Few men are admired by their servants."

"The greatest thing in the world is to know how to belong to oneself."

matters that go beyond experience. Along the way to that conclusion, Montaigne discussed many conflicts of opinion that were relevant to disputes current in his day.

## What are some **other notable works** by **Montaigne**?

In addition to his skeptical writings, Montaigne (1533–1592) became famous for the whole of his *Essais* (1560; literally, "Attempts"), the most substantial of which was his

*The Apology of Raimond Sebond.* The essays here were far-ranging, witty, digressive, and all about him; his tastes, opinions, and large and petty problems. He also wrote about his trip to Germany, Switzerland, and Italy in his *Journal de voyage en Italie par la Suisse et al'Allemagne en 1580 et 1581* (*Travel Journal*), undertaken after he had presented a copy of his *Essays* to the French king. Montaigne was diplomatically active in trying to quell religious antagonism and instrumental in securing Henry of Navarre's ascension to the throne as King Henry IV. He probably would have become a member of Henry's court had illness not intervened.

### What is the "problem of the criterion" as put forth by Montaigne?

Montaigne's more theoretical arguments went to the heart of theories of knowledge. All human knowledge comes from sense experience, but all humans perceive things differently and we are all vulnerable to illusions, dreams, and ordinary distortions of perception. On top of these doubts, Montaigne then introduced "the problem of the criterion." We need a criterion to determine if our experience is reliable as a basis for knowledge, but the criterion itself needs to be tested and for that a second criterion is necessary, and to test this second criterion, a third one is necessary, and on and on. All theoretical and natural philosophers after Montaigne had to come up with some sort of answer to the skeptical problems he raised: the unreliability of sensory information; the disagreement of experts; cultural differences in values and customs; individual differences in perception; the possibility of human error; and above all, the necessity for a criterion, or neutral standard to settle disagreements.

### When discussing religious belief, which did Montaigne consider to be more important: reason or faith?

In considering reason versus faith as a foundation for religious beliefs, Montaigne (1533–1592) claimed that faith, simple belief, was the best course, because all reasoning can be shown to be unsound. Philosophical views had been in conflict since the ancients, so only Pyrrhonic skepticism, with its prescribed suspension of judgment, was acceptable. There was no certainty even in the knowledge of the new sciences, since the experts disagreed and scientific knowledge was subject to change.

### Was Montaigne the only skeptical philosopher to reason in this Pyrrhonlc way?

No. Montaigne (1533–1592) derived his views from Sextus Empiricus (160–210 c.e.), who held that we could not even know whether we had knowledge in certain cases. By 1590, Sextus Empiricus' (150–210) *Hypotoses* had been published in Latin, Greek, and English. Pyrrhonic skepticism died out by the third century c.e. Desiderius Erasmus (1466–1536) was a closer predecessor to Montaigne, who defended Catholicism based

The philosopher Francisco Sánchez is portrayed in a 1979 bank note from Portugal (BigStock Photos).

on faith in *De Libro Arbitro* (1524) on the grounds that theological controversies were inconclusive. Martin Luther (1483–1546) responded to Erasmus with a dogmatic claim about his subjective certainty about God, based on his own conscience, as well as scripture.

## What was **dogmatism**?

Dogmatism, then and now, was the position that there is at least one true thing about the world that we can know with absolute certainty.

## What was some of the **Catholic response** to Martin **Luther's dogmatism**?

The Catholic response was to question whether Luther really had any knowledge at all and to emphasize the importance of Christian faith. Gentian Hervet published a 1569 edition of Sextus' *Hypotoses,* specifically as a cure for dogmatism, which would lead to serene confidence in the Church's doctrine of Jesus. Portuguese philosopher and physician Francisco Sánchez (c. 1551–1623) developed Pyrrhonic skepticism as a criticism of Aristotelianism in *Quod Nihil Scitur* (1576). (Although in his arguments for nominalism, combined with empirical observation, that led him to conclude that knowledge itself could not be obtained, Sanchez was closer to Academic than Pyrrhonic skepticism.)

## What are **academic** and **Pyrrhonic skepticism**?

In the Renaissance and early modern revival of ancient Greek ideas, academic skepticism was the position that no knowledge is possible, whereas Pyrrhonic skepticism was the position that we do not have enough evidence to know whether any knowledge is possible. The conclusion of Pyrrhonic skepticism is that all judgment on all questions about knowledge should be suspended.

## How did **Pyrrhonic skepticism** get its **name**?

It was named after Pyrrho of Elis (360–270 B.C.E.), who thought that knowledge was impossible.

## Were **Pyrrhonic skeptics anxious** about the **impossibility** of **knowledge?**

No. Pyrrhonic skeptics were reluctant to commit themselves on either opposing side of an issue and instead cultivated *ataraxia,* a mental state of peace and quiet. Pyrrhonic skepticism was supposed to be a cure for the disease of dogmatism in which positions on truths that were not evident were taken up and defended, causing distress. Third century Pyrrhonists organized this process into sets of two, five, or ten tropes, each one of which suggested how to suspend judgments about matters that went beyond appearances.

## What are the **Pyrrhonic tropes?**

They were what the skeptics took to be typical subjects of knowledge about which people disagreed.

## How did the **Pyrrhonic skeptics alleviate dogmatism?**

Their idea was that once they showed that any contentious claim could be balanced by pro and con reasons and arguments, there was no reason to believe one side or the other. This was supposed to quiet the mind and make dogmatism impossible.

## How did **Pyrrhonic skepticism** affect early modern **natural philosophy?**

If there could be no certain knowledge about the world, this left the uncertainty of "sense knowledge" as the only knowledge available about the world. Modern natural philosophy, or modern science, was based on the principle that sense knowledge is the foundation of all our knowledge about the world.

## What is **sense knowledge?**

Sense knowledge is information gathered through our senses, such as sight, touch, hearing, and so forth.

## Who were the main **defenders** of **sense knowledge** at the beginning of modern science?

Jean Bodin (1530–1596) and Pierre Le Loyer (1559–1634) offered defenses of sense knowledge between 1581 and 1605. They held that even though sense knowledge is sometimes unreliable, its errors are corrected by further sensory experience. By the 1620s two priests highly influential in both scientific and intellectual circles, Fathers Marin Mersenne (1588–1658) and Pierre Gassendi (1592–1655), used Pyrrhonic anti-Aristotelian arguments against Rosicrucianism and alchemy.

89

## What was **Rosicrucianism**?

Rosicrucianism was the practice of the secret Christian Rosicrucian Order, which was dedicated to helping mankind develop spiritually. The practices of the Rosicrucians were not published or otherwise known to the general public, but they were believed to involve ancient Neoplatonic knowledge, alchemy, and ways to cure the sick. Some believe it began after Dante degli Alighieri (c. 1265–1321) wrote *The Divine Comedy* in the early 1300s. Others locate its beginnings within a group of German Protestants in the early 1600s. Three documents circulated throughout Europe in the fifteenth century to promote what the Rosicrucians called "The Universal Reformation of Mankind": *Fama Fraternitatis Rosae Crucis, Confessio Fraternitatis,* and *Chymical Wedding of Christian Rosenkreutz anno 1459.*

Dante Alighieri is sometimes named as the inspiration for the founding of the Rosicrucians (iStock).

## Who were the **early seventeenth century "free thinkers"** after Montaigne?

The "free thinkers" after Montaigne (1533–1592) combined Pyrrhonic skepticism with anti-Aristotelianism against both religious orthodoxy and traditional authority.

The most famous free thinkers, or *libertines érudits,* were Gabriel Naude (1600–1653), Guy Patin (1601–1672), François de la Mothe le Vayer (1588–1672), Pierre Gassendi (1592–1655), and Isaac la Peyrère (1588–1672). Naude and Patin were humanists with little interest in scientific claims. But La Mothe Le Vayer took up skepticism to undermine scientific knowledge. Out of this group, only Gassendi had a lasting influence on the course of both "natural philosophy" (what we would today call science) and philosophy proper.

## What was **anti-Aristotelianism**?

Anti-Aristotelianism was a reaction against the ways in which medieval interpretations of Aristotle (384–322 B.C.E.) had for centuries been accepted unquestioningly by Catholic scholars.

## Who was **Pierre Gassendi**?

Pierre Gassendi (1592–1655) was a Catholic priest who was highly influential in justifying empirical science to religious dogmatists. He studied at Digne and Aix and became

> ## How did Pierre Gassendi's compromises about the nature and limits of knowledge help the development of science?
>
> Gassendi had shown how the development of science could take place without disturbing core religious beliefs. Like his fellow skeptics, Gassendi believed in God. Science could coexist with religion because science did not have to claim absolute truth, the way religion did.

professor of rhetoric at Digne when he was 21. After he received his doctorate in theology at Avignon and was ordained a priest, he became professor of philosophy at Aix. He also pursued astronomical research. His *Exercitationes Paradoxicae Adversus Aristoteleos* (1625) set out all that he thought was dubious and mistaken in Aristotle's writings. His principle attack on Aristotle was against the possibility of certain knowledge in science. Gassendi argued against Aristotle (384–322 B.C.E.) in his claim that certainty was neither possible nor necessary in science. At the same time, he sought to defend atomism against Church doctrine. Gassendi developed what came to be known as a mitigated or moderate skepticism that supported the conclusions of scientific inquiry.

### Why did Pierre **Gassendi** promote **mitigated skepticism**?

Pierre Gassendi (1592–1655) and his colleagues placed a high value on the new science of the time, which included the heliocentric (sun-centered solar system) theory after the Copernican revolution, the atomic theory holding that the activities of all matter were determined by its smallest particles—or atoms—and a rejection of those parts of the Aristotelian views of science that were in disagreement with these views. Gassendi's use of skepticism to attack Aristotle, and his use of moderate skepticism to support the new science, therefore made perfect sense. It helped Gassendi's cause that he was well liked and highly regarded among his colleagues in the Catholic Church, as well as by some of the more extreme skeptics of his day, and that he was careful not to go against Church doctrine. Indeed, while defending the new science on the one hand, and insisting that no scientific knowledge could be certain on the other, Gassendi was able to live and think in both the traditional Catholic world and the new scientific one.

### What was **mitigated** or **moderate skepticism** as explained by Pierre Gassendi?

Pierre Gassendi (1592–1655) argued that certainty or necessary truths could not be discovered in science. (A necessary truth is a belief or statement that it would be logically self-contradictory to deny—a necessary truth *must* be true.) Gassendi argued that all we can know is how things appear, not how they are in themselves. (In other words, we cannot know the hidden qualities of things.) We have no way to reason from what we experience to what has caused our experience, if we have not experienced that cause. Thus, if we have experienced the effect of something, but not the cause itself, we have to admit that we do not know the cause. Nevertheless, we can develop some useful bodies of information about appearances, especially if we augment that knowledge with atomism as a hypothesis.

In *Syntagma Philosophicum* Gassendi asks if there is any certain criterion to tell truth from falsehood. Clearly, some things are obvious, even to skeptics, such as "the sun is shining." It is what is concealed from us that causes difficulty: for example, whether the total number of stars is an odd or even number. Things like that can never be known. But, there are other things that are not evident that we can know by "signs." Our perception of sweat, for instance, is a sign that we have pores in our skin. There are also naturally non-evident things—such as the hidden fire that causes the smoke we see—that we know through indicative signs. While we do not know that the atomic world exists, we can infer it from indicative signs in the world we do perceive. Gassendi thought that it would be needlessly metaphysical to speculate about the property of atoms, such as claiming that they are mathematical. He also insisted that atomic explanations do not apply to the human soul, which he believed was indivisible and immortal, as held by Church doctrine.

### How did other **philosophers** and **scientists react** to Pierre **Gassendi's views**?

Jean de Silhon (1600–1667)and René Descartes (1596–1650) tried to develop positive knowledge claims that would avoid Gassendi's skepticism. Silhon argued that knowledge was possible because it existed in logic and the sciences. Descartes based his entire philosophy on an attempt to demonstrate the existence of certain scientific knowledge that would not conflict with Church doctrine. In the end, the Jesuits upheld Gassendi's view that certainty is impossible and condemned Descartes.

# THE SCIENTIFIC REVOLUTION

### **When** and **how** did the **scientific revolution begin**?

The scientific revolution began with Nicolaus Copernicus' (1473–1543) heliocentric theory and the rediscovery of ancient Greek atomism in the fifteenth and sixteenth centuries. But it was not until the end of the seventeenth century, after Isaac Newton's (1643–1727) work, that it was clear to educated people in Europe that a full-blown scientific revolution had occurred.

### What were the **main ideas** of the **scientific revolution**?

Some of the key ideas and theories that came out of the scientific revolution were that Earth revolves around the Sun, matter is composed of small particles, everything that happens can be explained mechanically or mechanistically with the help of mathematics, general principles or natural laws must be supported by observable data, and, perhaps most important, that science itself is an exciting activity that will benefit mankind.

### Who were the **key players** in the theories and practice of them in the **scientific revolution**?

Some of the key players of the scientific revolution were Nicolaus Copernicus (1473–1543), Ptolemy (90–168 C.E., who was not of this period, but highly relevant to it), Galileo Galilei (1564–1642), Johannes Kepler (1571–1630), Francis Bacon (1561–1626), Robert Boyle (1627–1691), and Isaac Newton (1643–1727).

### What were the main **philosophical aspects** of the **scientific revolution**?

From a purely philosophical perspective, given the strong influence of Neoplatonic thought in the work of almost all the natural philosophers (beginning with key Italian Renaissance thinkers, moving through Copernicus, and possibly culminating in Newton), the scientific revolution can be viewed as a sustained revolt against Aristotelianism back toward Platonism.

But it is more complicated than that. Aristotelianism was directly associated with the power of the Catholic church, which diminished as much for political and doctrinal reasons during the Reformation and Counter-Reformation as it did in philosophical circles. And, as it turned out, historically within both science and the philosophy of science, the revived influence of Neoplatonic metaphysics was relatively short-lived. By the Age of Reason, or the eighteenth-century Enlightenment, an empirically based rationality and secular reason came to form the educated world view in the West.

### What was so **revolutionary** about the **scientific revolution**?

What was revolutionary about the scientific revolution was how it emphasized objectivity and the need to look for natural causes for observable events. Many new inventions, such as telescopes, microscopes, thermometers, barometers, air pumps, and electric charge detectors, aided in this new endeavor. The principle of objectivity played out in public discovery, observation, and experimentation that could be duplicated for verification. (To be accepted, however, important experiments required credible witnesses—usually men of substantial social status.)

The goal of exact measurement and descriptions that could be quantified made mathematics a permanent part of science. But the pre-Socratics had already sought naturalistic explanations for natural events and emphasized the importance of number, so those aspects of the scientific revolution were not new. The early modern

93

## Does everyone now believe the scientific revolution was good for humanity?

Few can deny the value of an objective, factual understanding of the natural world. Modern technology that resulted from this knowledge has prolonged life, added to comfort, and made all human beings more mobile. There is also an understanding that knowledge should be open and that science is subject to revision, which goes back to the early days of the Royal Society. However, in the second half of the twentieth century, the objectivity of early modern science and its values were questioned by historians and cultural critics. Concerning the high value placed on experimentation, for example, it has been discovered that many of the experiments reported by Galileo (1564–1642) and Boyle (1627–1691) were thought experiments from which they deduced the facts, instead of having directly observed them. And Newton (1643–1727) himself did not actually base his three laws of motion on experimental data, as much as he logically deduced them from more abstract theoretical commitments.

On the cultural side, Francis Bacon's (1561–1626) perspective was based on assumptions that Earth and its creatures were all raw material for the manipulation and use of mankind. There was no sense that nature had value in its own right. In addition, some feminist critics have viewed the scientific revolution as a radical turn away from an ancient and medieval view of Earth as a living, organic whole, or mother to all who lived on it. They claim that this change in perspective privileged aggression and violence as virtues, compared to harmony and nurturance. Many crafts such as tanning, dying, and brewing, but most important, midwifery, became closed to women, as male practitioners took them over, based on "more scientific" principles, and moved them out of private households.

methods of objectivity were innovative, nevertheless. As the twentieth century historian and philosopher of science Thomas Kuhn (1922–1996) pointed out, the classical sciences of antiquity were astronomy, statics (bodies at rest or forces in equilibrium) and optics, which were all associated with mathematics and harmonics, so that advances in one led to advances in the others. In the sixteenth century, local motion (as something different from Aristotle's idea of motion as qualitative change) was added to the mathematical sciences.

In the seventeenth century, the mathematical sciences were revised by the addition of analytic geometry and calculus, new quantitative laws of motion, new theories of vision, refraction, and color, and the extension of statics to pneumatics (studies of air, fluids, and gasses). Still, Kuhn argued that Aristotle and the medievals also understood the importance of observation and experimentation. What was new was not so much the addition of new fields or striking new discoveries, but a change in perspective—new ways of looking at old things.

## What is known about **Corpernicus' life**?

Nicolaus Copernicus (1473–1543; also spelled Mikolaj Kopernick) was born in Toruñ, Prussia (in what is now Poland). He was educated in liberal arts, canon law, and medicine at the universities in Kraków, Poland, and Bologna and Padua, Italy. He received a doctorate in canon law from the University of Ferrara when he was 30. His uncle, the Bishop of Ermland, got him the post as canon of the cathedral of Frauenburg in 1497, and he also served as physician to his uncle.

Copernicus' job as canon involved diplomatic work and administration of church estates. He knew Greek and translated Byzantine poetry into Latin. He was knowledgeable about economics and developed interests in astronomy and mathematics.

He became known for his astronomical observations and calculations, and in 1514 Pope Leo X asked him to help reform the calendar. Copernicus refused because he did not think enough was known about the motions of the Sun and Moon, although he is widely reported to have contributed to calendar reform, nonetheless.

Copernicus began developing his theories in 1512 and presented a short description of his system, *Commentariolus*, to a small group of friends. His major work, *De Revolutionibus Orbium Coelestium Libri IV* (1543) was published in the same year he died. At the time of his death, he also left a treatise on monetary reform, *Monetae Cudendae Ratio,* for the Prussian provinces of Poland. First printed in 1816, but written in 1526, this work advocated a uniform coinage, preservation of the quality of the coin, and a charge to the nobility for minting the coin. Copernicus anticipated "Gresham's Law," which states that debased money drives good money out of circulation.

## How did Nicolaus **Copernicus change** the **world**?

Nicolaus Copernicus (1473–1543) changed how educated human beings viewed the world by constructing the heliocentric theory of Earth's relation to our Sun. According to the heliocentric theory, which is now considered common knowledge, Earth and the other planets revolve around the Sun. This heliocentric theory replaced the Ptolemaic geocentric theory, which held that that the Sun and other

Copernicus' heliocentric theory challenged the worldview held by the Catholic Church (iStock).

planets revolve around Earth. Copernicus became dissatisfied with the Ptolemaic system after his travels in Italy at a time when there was a lively revival of interest in ancient Pythagorian theories about the metaphysical importance of number for all aspects of nature. The Ptolemaic system was not mathematically elegant. But in Copernicus' day the Church subscribed to the Ptolemaic theory, because that was the description of the cosmos given in the Bible.

## How did **Ptolemy's view** of the **solar system** become the **accepted theory**?

Ptolemy of Alexandria (90–168 C.E.), using observations and existing written work between 127 and 151 C.E., codified the common sense of his time that the Sun and planets revolved around Earth. His work overthrew the more revolutionary writings of Aristarchus of Samos (c. 310–230 B.C.E.), who in *On the Sizes and Distances of the Sun and Moon* claimed that the Sun is much larger than Earth based on his observations of our Moon. According to Archimedes of Syracuse (287–212 B.C.E.), who combined mathematics with observations to found the science of mechanics, Aristarchus said "that the fixed stars and the Sun remain unmoved, that the Earth revolves around the Sun on the circumference of a circle, the Sun lying at the center of the orbit." Aristarchus correctly surmised that to explain the apparent immobility of the fixed stars—and assuming Earth did move—the distances between the stars would have to be huge compared to the diameter of Earth's orbit.

Aristarchus' theory was defended by Seleucus of Babylonia in the second century B.C.E., but the consensus of educated opinion was that Earth was the center of the universe, either as a floating ball that the heavens revolved around, or a stable solid, which was how it appeared to humanity. Hipparchus of Nicaea (c. 190–c. 120 B.C.E.) in Bithynia, around 130 B.C.E., put forth a theory based on the work of Eudoxus of Cnidos (c. 409–350 B.C.E.). According to Eudoxus and Hipparchus, the apparent movement of the Sun, Moon and planets was the result of their presence in crystal spheres that were concentric in relation to Earth. It was this view that Ptolemy used as a basis for his mathematical calculations.

## Was the **Ptolemaic theory** merely a matter of **religious faith**?

No, the idea that Earth was the center of the universe was not based just on religious belief. The Ptolemaic theory, constructed by Ptolemy (90–168 C.E.), did a fairly good job of describing both sensory experience and astronomical records and calculations that went back several thousand years. The movements of the heavenly bodies, which were themselves believed to be made of different and more ethereal stuff than Earth, could be more or less accurately predicted, according to this theory. It was also in accord with the existing natural philosophy that everything was made up of earth, water, fire, and air, in an ascending hierarchy. However, Ptolemy's assumption that Earth was stationary required a postulation of 80 "epicycles" to "save the appear-

## What is an epicycle?

An epicycle is a type of circular motion that is not observed but, rather, theoretically postulated. From the postulation, what could be observed became predictable, which was how it "saved the appearances," or was consistent with what was observed. In the Ptolemaic system, the 80 epicycles were necessary to account for the different speeds and directions in the observed movements of the Moon, Sun, and five known planets. They also explained differences in how far the planets appeared to be from Earth at different times. The planets themselves were believed to move in small circles, which themselves moved along "deferents," or large circles. Both the epicycles and deferents moved counter-clockwise in planes approximately parallel to the plane on which Earth was situated.

ances," which means that new complicated postulations were necessary to make the theory match observations.

### How did **Copernicus change** the **Ptolemaic system**?

The system introduced by Nicolaus Copernicus (1473–1543) was that Earth and all of the planets revolved around the sun in concentric circles. Copernicus was further able to reduce the number of postulated epicycles to 34, still saving the appearances, or not contradicting what was observed. This shifted the fundamental frame of astronomical reference from Earth to the fixed stars. As he wrote:

> First and above all lies the sphere of the fixed stars, containing itself and all things, for that reason immovable; in truth the frame of the Universe, to which the motion and position of all other stars are referred. Though some men think it to move in some way, we assign another reason why it appears to do so in our theory of the movement of the Earth. Of the moving bodies first comes Saturn, who completes his circuit in xxx years. After him, Jupiter, moving in a twelve year revolution. Then Mars, who revolves biennially. Fourth in order an annual cycle takes place, in which we have said is continued the Earth, with the lunar orbit as an epicycle. In the fifth place Venus is carried round in nine months. Then Mercury holds the sixth place, circulating in the space of 80 days.

Copernicus' conclusions were based mainly on mathematics, drawing on the perennial value of simplicity and the doctrine that nature always behaves in the most "commodious" (simple) way. To the objection that objects would fly off a moving earth, he responded that a moving sky, because it was larger, would move even faster and do more damage.

## Was **Copernicus'** new **theory purely scientific**?

No, because there was considerable mysticism in his astronomical ideas. Consider these two passages from his *De Revolutionibus Orbium Coelestium Libri IV*.

> Finally we shall place the Sun himself at the center of the Universe. All this is suggested by the systematic procession of events and the harmony of the whole Universe, if only we face the facts, as they say, "with both eyes open".

And:

> At rest, however, in the middle of everything is the Sun. For, in this most beautiful temple, who would place this lamp in another or better position than that from which it can light up the whole thing at the same time? For, the Sun is not inappropriately called by some people the lantern of the universe, its mind by others, and its ruler by still others. The Thrice Greatest labels it a visible god, and Sophocles' *Electra,* the all-seeing. Thus indeed, as though seated on a royal throne, the sun governs the family of planets revolving around it.

## Did other's share the **mystical aspects** of Nicolaus **Copernicus' system**?

In the late-sixteenth century, Giodano Bruno (1548–1600), a Dominican heretic who was burned at the stake by the Spanish Inquisition, developed mystical Copernicanism. Tommaso Campanella (1568–1639) built on Bruno's ideas for a utopia described in *City of the Sun* in which science was combined with astral magic for the good of mankind.

## Has Nicolaus **Copernicus' theory withstood** the test of **time**?

The Copernican theory that the earth and other planets revolve around the sun is still accepted as true today. Although at first Aristotelians and conservative theologians found the Copernican theory outrageous, the educated papal authorities had a deep interest in science and recognized the explanatory power of the Copernican theory. They tried to get Galileo, who was an enthusiastic supporter of the heliocentric theory, to temper his claims so that the Copernican theory would not contradict religion.

## Who was **Galileo**?

Galileo Galilei (1564–1642) was an Italian natural philosopher, physicist, and astronomer. He defended the Copernican system in *Dialogue Concerning the Two Chief World Systems,* which included a series of arguments against Aristotelian astronomy. Most strikingly, he argued that the heavens and Earth had the same kind of motion and that it was not necessary to postulate a teleological—or goal-driven—system for celestial movement. That is, it was not necessary to claim, as Aristotle had done, that the movement of the heavenly bodies was caused by what they were striving for.

## How did the **Church react** to **Galileo's theories**?

In an act that remains famous to this day, the Inquisition ordered Galileo (1564–1642) to recant his theories and placed him under house arrest during the last decade of his life. Before that time, how-

Galileo, depicted here on a 1983 Italian banknote, was another scientist who upset the Catholic Church about Earth's position in the cosmos (iStock).

ever, Cardinal Bellarmine tried for years to persuade Galileo to accept a compromise. The Church did not object to the Copernican theory so long as it was not claimed to be a description of what was true. The cardinal told a friend of Galileo's that it would be acceptable if he claimed that the Copernican theory did no more than "save the appearances"; that is, provide a hypothesis from which astronomical observations could be logically deduced without claiming that Earth actually moved. Galileo was, in the end, forced to do exactly that, although at the outset he refused to deny the truth of the Copernican theory as a true astronomical description.

## Did **Galileo** contribute more than a **defense** of **Copernicus** to science and philosophy?

Yes. Galileo (1564–1642) is credited with having founded modern mechanics by proving the laws of gravity and acceleration. He also discovered the principle of independent forces and created a theory of parabolic ballistics that accounted for the trajectory of projectiles by positing parabolic arcs for their movement. His innovations in the technology of science included an air thermoscope, a machine for raising water, and a kind of computer for geometrical and ballistic calculations. In pure science he discovered the isochronism of the pendulum (that the oscillation period of pendulums of equal length is constant) and he invented the hydrostatic balance (an accurate device for weighing things in water and in air). With the use of telescopes, he discovered the moons of Jupiter, the existence of mountains on our Moon, and Sun spots; he also described the Milky Way in greater detail. His claim that there were "blemishes" or what we would call "sun spots" on celestial bodies was in itself heretical to some Church authorities.

Philosophically, Galileo insisted on completely naturalistic causes for the observable world, but he did not object to postulating remote or unobserved causes, according to a "retroductive inference." His method of analysis involved taking effects apart and then theoretically putting them together in a new way to fit postulated causes. Insofar as this was a form of hypothetical inference, it is surprising that Galileo was unwilling to appease the Church by calling the Copernican system merely hypothetical. Galileo further angered Church officials, while supporting scientific researchers, with his claim that biblical accounts should not be taken literally by educated people.

# JOHANNES KEPLER'S INFLUENCE

### How did **Johannes Kepler** and **Tycho Brahe** help **complete** the **Copernican Revolution**?

Johannes Kepler (1571–1630) composed a mathematically precise theory of the Copernican system, and Tycho Brahe (1546–1601) furnished the measurements that constituted the factual data for the Copernican theory. Kepler's theoretical work was what completed the Copernican system. Kepler offered a religious explanation for the spacing of the planets and postulated a driving force centered in the Sun, which diminished with distance, as the cause of planetary movement.

Tycho Brahe contributed to the heliocentric model by calculating measurements that helped confirm Copernicus' theory (Art Archive).

### How did Johannes **Kepler's career** develop?

Kepler (1571–1630) studied astronomy and was prepared to become a Lutheran minister, when he was appointed a mathematician at the University of Graz. At that time, mathematics included both

ences to human life in practical ways. He believed that human beings needed to master nature and conduct experiments to discover "her" secrets—twentieth century feminists were to take Bacon to task for his assignment of a female gender to nature, compared to the maleness of scientists who were charged to conquer it.

## What were the **new logic** and **four types of idols** made famous by Francis Bacon's ***Novum Organum***?

In his *New Atlantis* (1627), Francis Bacon (1561–1626) described a social organization for scientific research. His *Novum Organum* (1620) presented a new logic of induction, which would take the place of both Aristotelian logic and a simple collection of facts. The aim was to discover real natural laws or reliable generalizations about aspects of nature

Francis Bacon believed that science could greatly improve the human condition (iStock).

Bacon's system became famous for the obstacles to acquiring such knowledge, which he described as four kinds of idols. First were idols of the tribe or natural tendencies of thought, such as a search for purposes in nature or reading human desires and needs onto natural things and events. The second were the idols of the cave or the idiosyncrasies and biases of individuals due to their education, social background, association, and the authorities they favored. The third type were idols of the marketplace or meanings of words taken for granted when the words themselves not stand for anything that existed in reality. And, finally, the idols of the the the influence of theories that had already been widely accepted.

## Once the **idols are eliminated** what did this **allow us t**

Once the mind was cleared of its idols, it would experimentation. Francis Bacon (1561–1626) tho of bodies or material objects that acted according "forms" of material objects. In seeking causes, first we which certain other things always follow. (For example, particles.) Next, we look for the cases where the effects d is absent. (No heat, no movement of particles.) When what

astronomy and astrology. In 1596 he published the *Mysterium Cosmographium,* which was the first comprehensive work on astronomy that was based on the Copernican system.

At the time, Graz was dominated by Catholics, and Kepler had to flee on religious grounds, because he was a Protestant. He went to Prague, where Tycho Brahe (1546–1601), the famous observational astronomer, had an observatory. Kepler composed a defense of Brahe's observations against Nicolaus Ursus, who had attacked them as "mere hypothesis." Kepler also claimed that, in addition to merely selecting the Ptolemaic or Copernican system, independent physical explanations are necessary. Using Tycho's observational data, Kepler then began work on the orbit of Mars. After Tycho died, Kepler was given his position as Imperial Mathematician, and also complete access to all of Tycho's data. In 1609 Kepler published *A New Astronomy Based on Causes or a Physics of the Sky*.

Kepler then had to leave Prague for the same reasons he had fled Graz. After he went to Linz, his research included music, theology, and philosophy, in addition to mathematics (which included astronomy). In his 1612 *Epitome Astronomiae Copericanae* he again emphasized the importance of causal explanation, as well as observational predictions, in studies of the movements of the planets. His 1618 *Harmonia Mundi* was the final expression of this thought. He said of this work: "It can wait a century for a reader, as God himself has waited six thousand years for a witness." Kepler was not the last great astronomer to believe he had special information about God. Isaac Newton's (1643–1727) work was to take the same high tone.

### What is **Kepler famous** for?

Based on the principle that causes needed to be sought for observed planetary motions, both regular and exceptional, Johannes Kepler (1571–1630) posited both a force between planets and the Sun and also a force to propel the planets. Isaac Newton (1643–1727) was to show that a principle of inertia could be used instead of the force to propel the planets. Kepler's most famous contribution was the discovery that the planets moved in elliptical, rather than circular orbits.

# FRANCIS BACON
# AND THE SCIENTIFIC REVOLUTION

### did **Francis Bacon contribute** to the **scientific revolution**?

acon (1561–1626) systematized the methodology of empirical science and rogram for how science could better human life. He is famous for claim-dge is power," and sought ways to further develop and apply the new sci-

greater or lesser degree, we must be able to account for the variation. Whenever possible, we should invent instruments to measure what we are investigating. (In this case, thermometers and barometers.)

## What was **Bacon's influence**?

Francis Bacon's (1561–1626) requirements for causal explanations were universally accepted as the basic principles of methodology in the new science. In the nineteenth century, the empiricist philosopher John Stuart Mill (1806–1873) restated them as the basis of scientific investigation in his time. Bacon's aspirations for an association of scientists were eventually realized in the British Royal Society. Bacon's methodological principles, combined with Kepler's theory of elliptical orbits, were built on by Isaac Newton (1643–1727) for his culminating scientific system of the fundamental structure and operating laws of the universe. And Newton's work was to hold at least until Albert Einstein's (1879–1955) theories in the early twentieth century.

## Was **Bacon's life** as direct and clear as his ideas?

No. Francis Bacon (1561–1626) lived a complex life with active political involvement in the affairs of his time, great ambition, and the appearance of deviousness. He was born in London and raised as a gentleman. His father, Nicholas, served Queen Elizabeth I as Lord Keeper of the Great Seal. Francis entered Trinity College, Cambridge, at age 12 and soon met the queen. At the age of 15, he is said to have learned that he was Queen Elizabeth's illegitimate son from her secret marriage to Robert Dudley, at which Nicholas Bacon had been a witness.

When his father died suddenly in 1579, it disturbed Francis' prospects for a substantial inheritance. This initiated a lifetime of debt. He began to study law and took a seat in Parliament in 1584 and again in 1586. He urged the execution of Mary Queen of Scots, a Catholic rival to Elizabeth's throne. Then he met Queen Elizabeth's favorite, Robert Devereux, Second Earl of Essex, who was to prove useful as his patron for a while.

Bacon applied for a succession of high offices that eluded him, although Essex helped him financially. He did get the post of Queen's Counsel in 1596, but it paid no salary. In 1586 he was briefly arrested for debt. He took an active role in investigating treason charges against his friend and patron, Essex, who was executed in 1601. At the age of 45, he married Alice Barnham, who was the 14-year-old daughter of a well-connected alderman.

After James I became king, Bacon was knighted. He served the king well and was rewarded with the office of solicitor, then attorney general, and finally lord chancellor in 1618. He again fell into debt, however. During this time he was accused and convicted of bribery. His sentence was a fine and disgrace. He continued his studies while in retirement and was honored at age 60 with a banquet held by his Rosicrucian and

## How did the British Royal Society come about?

The British Royal Society grew out of the Invisible College, and the Invisible College was inspired by Francis Bacon's *New Atlantis*.

Masonic friends. The famous poet Ben Jonson attended and said of him, "I love the man and do honor his memory above all others.

In 1626 Bacon was in London, traveling through the snow with the King's physician, when he got the idea of using snow to preserve meat. They immediately bought a fowl, had it killed, and Bacon stuffed it with snow. He came down with pneumonia and ate the bird, hoping to regain his strength from it, but died nonetheless.

## What was Francis Bacon's *New Atlantis* about?

Francis Bacon's *New Atlantis* was published in 1626 and went through 10 editions by 1670. In it was described "The House of Solomon," a research institute with laboratories for experimentation and observation in the natural sciences to include: heat, light, cold, medicine, minerals, weather, crafts, astronomy, animals, and agriculture. There would be a staff of 36 fellows and their assistants, who would set out to make discoveries. Resident scholars would read written works on past discoveries. Three "Interpreters of Nature" would assess all of this information to construct axioms and principles.

## What roles did others play in **furthering Francis Bacon's ideas**?

Samuel Hartlib (c. 1600–1662), a wealthy merchant with an interest in science, wrote *Description of the Fameous Kingdom of Macaria,* about a center of practical learning, inspired by Bacon's *New Atlantis*. Hartlib's friend, William Petty (1623–1687), the founder of modern economics, envisioned a center for teaching practical trades, which he first proposed to Robert Boyle (1627–1691). A more theoretical precedent for these plans already existed in Gresham College, which was founded by Elizabeth I's financial agent in 1598. Professors there lectured on law, physics, rhetoric, divinity, music, geometry, and astronomy to scholars, nobles, and business and professional men.

## What was the **Invisible College**?

In 1645 Robert Boyle (1627–1691) and other younger scientists met weekly over lunch to discuss current scientific news about research in England and Europe. They called themselves "The Invisible College." They discussed the Copernican theory, William Harvey's evidence for the closed circulation of blood, barometric experiments with mercury, and studies of magnetism. After England's King Charles I was beheaded, this group and their friends, who had academic posts at Oxford, organized the Philosophical Society of Oxford.

Following a lecture on astronomy at Gresham College by Christopher Wren (1632–1723) in 1660, plans were made to found a college "for providing Physio-Mathematical learning." Charles II approved their plans within a week. There were 115 original members. One third were scientists and the first president was Lord Brouncker, the leading mathematician of the day. This was The Royal Society of London for the Improvement of Natural Knowledge. It was presented with a silver mace by King Charles II at its inaugural meeting on July 15, 1662. It exists to this day, as an independent academy for scientific knowledge in the United Kingdom.

## What **ideals** for scientists did the early **Royal Society promote**?

After a rejection of Aristotelian ideals of certainty in scientific knowledge, members of the Royal Society sought what was no more than "probably true." Their ideals

Robert Boyle—a scientist best remembered for discovering the law named for him about the relationship between volume, pressure, and gases—was an inventor, theologian, and philosopher who was a member of "The Invisible College" (Art Archive).

included open-mindedness, cooperation, and good will toward colleagues. It was as important to know what one did not know as assert what one did. Here is how Thomas Sprat, in his 1667 *History of the Royal Society,* described the virtues of a virtuoso:

> The Natural Philosopher is to begin where the Moral ends. It is requiste, that he who goes about such an undertaking, should first know himself, should be well-practis'd in all the modest, humble, friendly Vertues; Should be willing to be taught, and to give way to the Judgement of others. And I dare boldly say, that a plain, industrious Man, so prepar'd, is more likely to make a good Philosopher than all the high, earnest, insulting Wits, who can neither bear partnership, nor opposition.... For certainly, such men, whose minds are so soft, so yielding, so complying, so large, are in a far better way, than the bold and haughty Assertors: they will pass by nothing, by which they may learn: they will be always ready to receive, and communicate Observations: they will not contemn the Fruits of others diligence: they will rejoice, to see mankind benefited, whether it be by themselves, or others.

## Who was **Robert Boyle**?

Robert Boyle (1627–1691) was the fourteenth child of the first Earl of Cork, who was the richest man in England. As the founder of modern chemistry, Boyle devoted his life to scientific investigation and methodology. He was well-received at the British Court, and a member of the council of the Royal Society, although he declined its presidency and the provostship of Eton because he did not want to "take oaths." When he retired to a house in Pall Mall after a stroke at age 42, he maintained his own laboratory. Boyle's goal was to replace Aristotelian mechanics with explanations using just two things: matter and motion. He was also a champion of the new atomism, or "corpuscular theory." Boyle's most famous works were *New Experiments; Physico-Mechanical Touching the Spring of the Air and Its effects, The Skeptical Chemist,* and *The Experimental History of Colors.* He also wrote a religious novel, *Seraphic Love.*

## Who were some of Robert **Boyle's scientific influences**?

Pierre Gassendi (1592–1655) and Walter Charlton (1619–1707) influenced Boyle. In 1656 Charlton brought Gassendi's ideas about atoms to England with his *Physiologia Epicuro-Gassendo-Chartonia; or, a Fabrick of Science Natural, upon the Hyopthesis of Atoms, Founded by Epicurus, Repaired by Petrus Gassendus, Augmented by Walter Charlton* (1654). Charleton revised Gassendi's view that everything, including the soul, was made up of material atoms. This view entailed that the soul was a physical thing, which was against the beliefs of most theologians and members of the clergy.

## What was Robert **Boyle's atomic theory**?

Boyle (1627–1691) claimed that the things in the world studied in physics, chemistry, biology, and inquiries into gases and fluids were all made up of atoms. He thought that because atoms could be used to explain and predict what was observable, their existence was an empirical matter and not the results of pure speculation. Unlike Gassendi, who was content to suspend judgment on whether atoms existed, Boyle claimed that atoms did exist, using the method of transdiction.

## What was Boyle's **method of transdiction**?

Boyle (1627–1691) pointed out that our senses are limited, as shown by findings from telescopes and microscopes. He thought that analogy could be used to extend sense knowledge. Atoms or corpuscles could be understood as analogous to objects we can sense. In this sense, atoms have the same principles of action as objects that can be sensed. Boyle backed up his atomic theory with reports of his own experiments, which, based on the premise that atoms exist, confirmed his predictions about gases, solids, and heat.

> ## What were some of the rather humorous experiments carried out by members of the British Royal Society?
>
> The former British comedy troop Monty Python would have had a field day with some of the early investigations conducted by the Royal Society. And King Charles II, who was very interested in experiments in general, loved to make fun of the more preposterous ones. For example, at the Philosophical Society of Oxford—hosted by founding Royal Society secretary John Wilkins (1614–1672), who had written about the "admirable contrivances of natural things" in *Mathematical Marvels*—there were, among Wilkins' own collection, transparent apiaries and a hollow statue that "spoke" through a concealed pipe.
>
> Robert Boyle (1627–1691) was considered eccentric because he doctored himself and seemed to make a hobby of collecting medical prescriptions. By the time the Royal Society had formed, alchemy had switched from being a science seeking to convert base metals into gold to one with an aim of using new medical discoveries to prolong human life. Nonetheless, in 1689 Boyle worked successfully to get Henry IV's law against "multiplying gold" repealed.
>
> When Margaret Cavendish, Duchess of Newcastle-upon-Tyne (1623–1673), was granted a visit to the Royal Society in 1667, she was shown experiments involving colors, the mixing of cold liquids, dissolving meat in oil of vitriol, weighing air, the flattening of marbles, magnetism, and "a good microscope." The Duchess wrote in her own diary that the new science was useless for solving social and spiritual problems.

## Did **Boyle's materialism** mean he was an **atheist**?

No, Boyle (1627–1691) was not an atheist. He was a very devout Protestant and wrote at length about how science and religion could be reconciled. His main publications on this subject were *The Christian Virtuoso* (1660) and *A Disquisition about the Final Causes of Natural Things* (1688). However, in his *Disquisition,* he argued that, in everyday work, a scientist should only consider the primary qualities of particles. He meant by this that a scientist, unlike everyone else, would not focus on colors, sounds, textures, and smells.

## What are **primary qualities** and **secondary qualities**?

The scientific distinction between primary and secondary qualities was to prove very important for subsequent philosophy. Primary qualities are size, shape, mass, motion, and quantity. Secondary qualities were color, texture, sound, and smell. It was believed that the primary qualities of atoms resulted in the secondary qualities that could be

107

Sir Isaac Newton was one of the greatest scientific minds of all time. (iStock).

sensed by us in objects made up of atoms. That is, the world of our perception is made up of secondary qualities, which are formed by interactions between the atoms in objects and the atoms in our sense organs. Secondary qualities are exactly those qualities of sense such as color, sound, texture, and smell that make up our everyday experience. But the "real" world was made up of atoms!

## Who was **Isaac Newton**?

Isaac Newton (1642–1727) was one of the greatest scientists and natural philosophers of the Western tradition. Alexander Pope wrote his epitaph:

> Nature and Nature's laws lay hid in sight.
>
> God said, "Let Newton be!" and all was light.

Newton made coherent, mathematically sound sense of the Copernican Theory, Kepler's and Tycho Brahe's discoveries, and Galileo's findings. He united terrestrial and celestial mechanics in a comprehensive cosmological system that supported further research for over 300 years. His scientific view of the cosmos included a place for the God of Christians, which was much appreciated in his time. Newton's equations are still useful for calculations of motion in the middle range of medium-sized objects close to the surface of Earth. (Newton's theory is not useful for sub-atomic particle research and measurements made in light years.)

## What were some of **Newton's career** accomplishments?

Newton (1642–1727) was born in Lincolnshire, England, and attended Cambridge University, graduating with a B.A. in 1665. Between 1665 and 1667, working independently while stuck at home when Cambridge was shut down due to the plague, he discovered the binomial theorem, the fundamentals of calculus, the modern principle of how light was composed, and the basics of his theory of gravity. He held the post of Lucasian Professor of Mathematics at Cambridge after 1669 and was a fellow of the Royal Society from 1671 to 1703, after which he served as its president for the rest of his life. Newton's "system of the world" or his unifying theory of mechanics and his mathematical physics was published in *Philosophiae Naturalis Principia Mathematica* (*The Mathematical Principles of Natural Philosophy*.)

## Was Isaac **Newton rewarded** for his scientific **discoveries**?

Relatively poor and without family wealth or a patron, Newton finally received the comfortable position as Warden of the Mint in 1695. He administered the complicated project of recoinage with expertise, echoing Copernicus' (1473–1543) contributions to recoinage in Poland about a 170 years earlier. (Recoinage involved calling in all of the coins in circulation and exchanging them for new ones.)

Perhaps like Copernicus, and also having the benefit of Gresham's Law (that bad coinage drives good coinage out of circulation), Newton knew that the presence of bad coins meant that people were hoarding the good ones. This was a serious economic problem at the time because England was an economy based on cash, and transactions depended on having enough physical money, or coins made of silver, in circulation. Newton's recoinage required calling in all of the silver coins that had been clipped for their metallic value (chunks literally cut out of them around the circumference) and reissuing milled coins that could not be clipped. Newton also advocated that counterfeiters be hanged!

## What were the **main elements** of **Newton's scientific system** and what did they have to do with **God**?

Newton (1642–1727) used the model of Euclidian geometry to demonstrate the mathematical axioms describing the system of the world. He held that the world consisted of material bodies, or masses made up of solid corpuscles that were either at rest or that moved according to the three laws of motion. Preceding these laws of motion was a "scholium," in which Newton stated the conditions of his entire system, which were: absolute time, absolute space, absolute place, and absolute motion.

For Newton, the universe itself was like one gigantic box that never moved. (These absolutes were to become very important in contrast to Albert Einstein's theory of relativity.) According to Newton, God played an active role in his system in several ways: he was the first cause of the whole celestial system; he keeps the stars and planets from crashing into one another; he creates absolute space and time; and he corrects for irregularities in the movements of planets and comets, which might otherwise undermine the entire harmony of the cosmos. That is, for Newton, not only did God exist outside of nature as its immaterial and transcendent soul, but God was the real and practical ruler and regulator of the physical universe. He wrote, "And thus much concerning God; to discourse of whom from the appearance of things, does certainly belong to Natural Philosophy." (This was religious science in religious times.)

## What were Newton's Laws?

**N**ewton (1642–1727) is famous for three laws of motion and the universal law of gravitation, as follows.

1. Every body continues in rest or uniform motion in a straight line unless an external force compels a change. This is the Law of Inertia.

2. A change in motion is proportional to the force impressed and occurs in the direction of the straight line in which the force is impressed. F = MA, or Force equals Mass multiplied by Acceleration.

3. To every action there is an opposite and equal reaction.

Newton's general law of gravity stated that every particle of matter in the universe attracts every other particle of matter with a force that varies directly as the product of their masses and varies inversely as the square of the distance between the particles.

### How was **Newton's system received**?

Newton's (1642–1727) laws were accepted with intellectual awe, bordering on reverence. Part of this reaction was gratitude for the comprehensive way in which he plausibly united both the atomic theory and the results of the Copernican revolution. Newton was famous for his claim of not going beyond the evidence. His motto was *Hypotheses non fingo,* or "I frame no hypotheses."

However, this was not literally true, given his scholium that assumed absolute space and time, and his postulation of force as "action at a distance." He also assumed that God existed. But Newton's stance of empiricism—he thought, for example, that with sufficiently powerful microscopes it would be possible to see atoms someday—carried the day on the issue of whether he really was an empiricist.

Newton's work was almost immediately translated into European languages and became the new view of the universe. There were also popularized versions of his ideas, and by the early eighteenth century idealized portraits of him were in wide circulation. Francesco Algarrotti published *Newton for the Ladies* in 1737, which was reprinted in many editions. (Because girls did not receive the same education as boys, it was widely believed that scientific knowledge had to be simplified and expressed in more "gentle" language for women.)

### Was **Newton** an **eccentric** personality?

According to historical anecdotes and gossip, the answer would have to be yes. There is evidence that Newton (1642–1727) was eccentric and did not interact well with others. His main quirk was his secretiveness about his work. He did not even communicate the success of his early research to others until 1669. To this day, it is not clear when he did what or which recorded intuitions correspond to what publications. After he got the position of Lucasian Professor of Mathematics at Cambridge, except for three or four weeks a year, he spent 26 years in Cambridge, lecturing on optics and elementary mathematics. That is, his life was somewhat sheltered.

Part of the reason Newton hated to publish was that he did not like the controversy that was always likely to follow. When in 1684 the Royal Society appointed a committee, led by Edmund Halley (1656–1742), to remind Newton of his commitment to publish *Principia Mathematica,* Halley had to persuade him to include the third book, which contained the application of his system. Newton at first wanted to suppress that work because he had heard that Robert Hooke (1635–1703) claimed to have had the same system before him. (Indeed, when Newton had related his discoveries about the decomposition of light, or what the components of light are, to the Royal Society in 1672, Robert Hooke and others disagreed with part of how he explained his findings. Newton refused to discuss the matter or publish his work until after Hooke died.) The *Principia* manuscript was finally delivered by a Dr. Vincent, husband of Miss Storey, at whose house Newton had lodged in his teens. Apparently she had been the sole romantic interest in his entire life.

Biographers relate that Newton had a psychological breakdown from 1692 to 1693, following unsuccessful attempts to get a prestigious and lucrative government position through the efforts of his friend Charles Halifax. Newton wrote to Samuel Pepys (1633–1703) that he was "extremely troubled at the embroilment" he was in and that he would have to withdraw from Pepys and his other friends. He then wrote to John Locke (1632–1704), apologizing for "being of the opinion that you endeavored to embroil me with women." Locke was kind and reassuring and Newton apologized further, claiming overwork and lack of sleep. Apparently, there had been no basis in fact for Newton's belief in having been "embroiled."

Newton did have an embroiled dispute over whether he or Gottfried Wilhelm Leibniz (1646–1716) had first invented the theory of "fluxions" or the differential calculus. Through his office as President of the Royal Society, Newton exerted influence over the investigation of the matter, which was finally resolved to credit him with the discovery, although it misrepresented the time sequence of correspondence on the subject between Newton and Leibniz.

Newton did no further scientific work after his position as Warden of the Mint. He referred to natural philosophy as a "litigious lady" and mentioned "another pull at the moon." He was apparently preoccupied with occult readings of biblical prophecy and alchemical theories, although the nature of these endeavors is still unclear because he often wrote in code. Some contemporary scholars now think that these occult studies were Newton's main interest and that the greatness of his scientific achievements was largely the result of "hype," after the fact. Newton's reluctance to publish or even continue his studies after he became Warden of the Mint might be less a matter of psychological instability than is often assumed.

# MEDICINE AND PHILOSOPHY

## What has **medicine** got to do with the **history of philosophy**?

The theory and practice of medicine is not usually associated with philosophers or the history of philosophy. Except for recognition of the ethical aspects of many medical decisions (for example, abortion, end-of-life issues, and cost of care), medical doctors do not seek out philosophical opinions, and philosophers do not view medicine as part of their normal range of subjects. Nevertheless, until at least the eighteenth century, medical ideas and practices concerning the human body were closely connected to philosophy in several ways.

Since ancient times, beginning with both Plato and Aristotle, philosophers used the kind of knowledge necessary for the practice of medicine as an important example of the nature of practical knowledge, in general. For instance, doctors may agree on the cause and symptoms of a disease, but deciding that a certain patient has the disease and what the appropriate course of treatment for that person should be requires making judgments that go beyond the evidence. Such judgments depend heavily on what was done in similar cases in past experience, and that says something important about the nature of practical knowledge. (Aristotle said that because of the importance of the role of experience in medicine, which was not an exact science, it would be wiser to choose an older than a younger doctor.)

In Aristotle's time there was awareness that medicine had been part of philosophy during the pre-Socratic period. Beginning in the medieval period, especially in Islamic culture, many philosophers had practical training as physicians and were employed as doctors to their patrons. That practice was also common through the Renaissance and early modern period in Europe. Another link between medicine and philosophy is that, as educated thinkers, philosophers have always had ideas about the human body and its functions, which in their scientific aspects have come from the medical views of their times. Philosophers have also maintained an interest in human emotions and thought processes, based on theories developed by psychologists and their predecessors before the science of psychology existed.

## What were **Alcmaeon's innovations** in **medicine**?

Alcmaeon (c. 500 B.C.E.) provided new answers to the question, "What is health?' He explained health as *isonomia*, or physical equilibrium. This equilibrium was a balance of opposites, which can't be restored indefinitely. Therefore, all living things die.

> ## When did medicine become separate from philosophy?
>
> **A**lthough Hippocrates of Cos II, or Hippokrates of Kos (c. 465–370 B.C.E.) is credited with being the "father of medicine," Aristotle and Theophrastus (371–c. 287 B.C.E.) wrote about Alcmaeon of Croton as the founder of medicine during the second half of the sixth century B.C.E.

Alcmaeon also investigated the functions of the different senses. Because the process of understanding was similar to the rotations of the stars, he thought that the soul, like the stars, was immortal. He speculated that sense organs relayed information to the brain through "passages." When blood moved to the large blood vessels, the result was sleep, whereas when it became redistributed the result was wakefulness. The specific nature of Alcmaeon's ideas, and his introduction to medicine of principles unique to that subject, forever changed the practice of medicine and systematic thought about the human body. As Alcmaeon's successor, Hippokrates (465–370 B.C.E.) was able to build on his thought and establish medicine as a science in its own right.

## What were **Hippocrates' accomplishments** and influence?

In founding his own school, Hippocrates (465–370 B.C.E.) formally established medicine as distinct from theurgy (natural magic) and philosophy. He himself had learned medicine from his father and grandfather. According to the Hippocratic School, illness was caused by an imbalance of four humors that were supposed to be equal in the body: black bile, yellow bile, blood, and phlegm. Every disease progressed to a crisis, from which either death or natural recovery would ensue.

Hippocratic medical practice was passive because it was believed that the body would heal itself given rest and immobilization. The therapy was always gentle, and usually only clean water, wine, or balms were used. Being able to predict the course of an illness was considered important.

In his *On the Physician,* Hippocrates stressed good grooming and a sober demeanor for doctors. It was important to keep records, not only about the patient but also about the patient's family and circumstances. Mystical causes of illness were dismissed. After Hippocrates' death, there was little advancement in the principles attributed to him, and some of his professional rules, such as taking case histories and keeping records, fell into disuse.

## How did **medicine** progress **after Hippocrates**?

Galen of Pergamum (c. 129–c. 216 C.E.) preserved Hippocratic medicine, which continued largely unchanged through the Renaissance. Galen was able to increase knowl-

An illustration from *The Great Surgery Book* (1526) by Paracelsus (Art Archive).

edge of physiology by dissecting pigs and apes, since human dissection was against Roman law. He learned how to treat trauma and wounds while working as a physician in a gladiator school. Galen performed many operations, including brain and eye surgery (the removal of cataracts), which were not attempted again for almost 2,000 years. He eventually became a physician to Marcus Aurelius (121–180 C.E.). In the ninth century, Galen's writings were translated into Arabic by Hunayn ibn Ishaq (809–873). However, the Arabs rarely practiced surgery, and among Christians, the knowledge and practice of surgery had already been abolished. Galen remained so highly regarded that when dissections during the Renaissance appeared to contradict his descriptions, they were considered anomalous. His prescription of bloodletting for almost every illness was followed as late as the nineteenth century.

## Who was **Paracelsus**?

"Paracelsus" was the pseudonym of Philippus Aureolus Theophrastus Bombast (a.k.a. Baumastus) von Hohenheim (1493–1541). His father was a medical doctor in Switzerland. Paracelsus traveled continuously after age 15 and studied medicine in Germany and Austria. He then traveled in Europe, combining surgery with his medical practice. Surgery was then considered a craft lower in status than medicine, so this was a significant risk for any physician.

In 1516 Paracelsus became a medical lecturer at the University of Basel, after he cured the famous printer Frobinius. His teachings against Avicenna (980–1037) and

## Was Paracelsus an alchemist?

Yes, Paracelsus (1493–1541) was an alchemist. But he was an adept who broke with the tradition of keeping alchemical knowledge secret and eliminated its medieval symbolism that relied on Semitic, Greek, and Roman mythology to conceal alchemists' real beliefs.

Galen (c. 129–c. 216 C.E.) were controversial, and he was forced to resume his life of travel in 1528.

Paracelsus introduced several lasting medical innovations: chemical urinalysis, a biochemical theory of digestion, wound antisepsis, the use of laudanum for pain, and the use of mercury for syphilis. His books were mainly about human nature and the place of man in the cosmos, but he also wrote important treatises on syphilis.

## What was **alchemy**?

The Latin motto of alchemy was *solve et coagula,* which means "separate and combine." Alchemy was practiced throughout the Christian, Islamic, and Jewish world until the nineteenth century and beyond. Traditionally, the central project of practicing alchemists was to discover how to turn base metals into gold. Second to this was a search for the elixir of life, which would cure all sickness and enable immortality. Medieval alchemists sought a philosopher's stone, which they believed would make both tasks possible, and they also worked on formulas for a universal solvent or aqua vitae. One form of aqua vitae has endured as a concentrated ethanol liquid: ethyl alcohol.

## How were **alchemists regarded** by their peers?

Alchemists were regarded with suspicion by traditional thinkers and theologians, but their constant experimentation with metals and plant stuff resulted in discoveries useful in tanning, dying, metallurgy, and other so-called "Baconian sciences." The figure of the Magus (or wiseman, or sorcerer, or even warlock) was associated with alchemy throughout its history.

The science of modern chemistry had its early experimental roots in alchemy, which some think is the main reason why it was not accepted as part of the scientific curriculum in higher learning until well into the nineteenth century.

The theory behind alchemy was Neoplatonic. Its main principle, "As above, so below," meant that man was a microcosm of the cosmos. In addition, time was believed to be cyclical, and the universe was seen as a being that is alive with divine spirit.

## What did **Paracelsus contribute** to **alchemy**?

Paracelsus (1493–1541) shared the Neoplatonic beliefs of most alchemists: decay is the beginning of all birth; prime matter separates out of ultimate "immaterial matter" and human creativity repeats this process; time is a cycle composed of force and growing; and above and below, or heaven and earth, are the same in form.

However, Paracelsus replaced the planetary theory of "humors" with a chemical one: salt, sweet, bitter, sour, and the fifth element—or quintessence—life. His term *Ens natural* referred to the balance of the chemical humors, and *Ens spirituale* was the balance of the mind. Unlike many of his colleagues, Paracelsus did not think that insanity was caused by demons or that nightmares represented sexual intercourse with succubi. He taught that the mind can create diseases in itself, the body, or in the minds or bodies of others via hypnosis, magic, or ill will. He thought that most diseases are curable evils but that no doctor can correct *Ens Dei,* or the will of God.

Paracelsus was accused of heresy for his Neoplatonic notion of prime matter and for asserting that illness was not evil. (Prime matter contradicted the idea that God created everything; also, saying that illness was not evil left no room for the devil.) But, after his death, his birthplace became a shrine for Roman Catholics.

## What were some **noteworthy advances** in **medicine** during the **scientific revolution**?

During the scientific revolution, William Harvey (1579–1657) correctly described and demonstrated the closed circulatory system of blood. Robert Burton (1577–1640) described (and lived out) the nature of psychological depression. With Harvey's achievement, the inside of the human body could be understood as an orderly mechanical (hydraulic) system; with Burton's achievement came the recognition of mental illness as a secular, pedestrian process. Both achievements were practical and gratifying rewards for scientific investigators, as well as their public.

## How did **William Harvey** discover the **closed circulatory system**?

William Harvey (c. 1578 or 1579–1657) was educated at Cambridge and studied at Padua, where Copernicus (1473–1543) had also studied. His father-in-law was a prominent London physician, and Harvey became a doctor at St. Bartholomew's Hospital and a fellow of the Royal College of Physicians. Ibn al-Nafis (1213–1288) and Michael Servetus (1511–1553) had described pulmonary circulation earlier, but Servetus' work was lost by the time Harvey had begun his research.

Hieronymus Fabricius, who taught Harvey at the University of Padua, had discovered valves in veins, but Harvey was not satisfied with his explanation and sought a more encompassing theory of how blood moved in the body. In his 1628 *Exercitation Anatomica de Motus Cordis et Sanguinis in Animalibus (An Anatomical Exercise on*

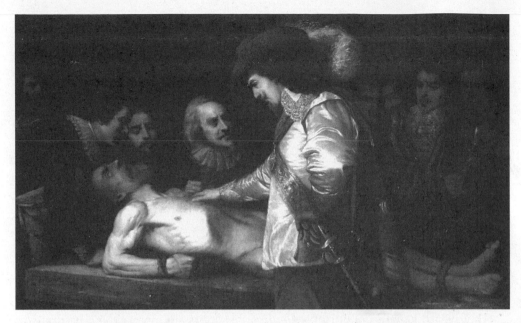

In this seventeenth-century painting, William Harvey is shown demonstrating how the blood circulates (Art Archive).

*the Motion of the Heart and Blood in Animals*) Harvey claimed that the heart pumped blood throughout the body in a closed system. Galen had believed that venous blood came from the liver and arterial blood from the heart, each of which sent blood to the different parts of the body where it was consumed.

Harvey recorded his observations during vivisections (dissections of live animals), quantifying the amount of blood that passed through the heart and counting the beats of the heart. He estimated the amount of blood pumped in a day, depending on the size of the heart. He postulated two circulatory loops—one to the lungs and the other to the vital organs—and he correctly described the role of the valves of the veins in returning blood to the heart. Harvey was personal physician to both James I and Charles I. That gave him the opportunity to vivisect deer from the royal parks for his experiments and demonstrations. He was also able to observe a pumping human heart in the hole of the chest of a viscount's son, whose wound had been covered with a metal plate. Harvey was not able to observe capillaries and could not account for the transfer of blood from arteries to veins.

## What was the **reaction** to Burton's *The Anatomy of Melancholy*?

Burton wrote *The Anatomy of Melancholy* under the pseudonym "Democritus Junior." His book was well-received. Literary historian and critic Thomas Warton (1728–1790) wrote of it: "The author's variety of learning, his quotations from rare and curious books, his pedantry sparkling with rude wit and shapeless elegance … have rendered it

117

a repertory of amusement and information." Indeed, Burton's treatise is full of satire and it constitutes a prodigious display of historical and literary knowledge.

However, the genius of Burton's *Anatomy* lies in its attempt to give a naturalistic account of the mind as both distinct from the body and yet intimately connected with it. Burton's theory of human cognition and consciousness rests on his notion of spirit, through which all of the functions and faculties of mind are physically connected with different parts of the body. While mistaken and overly literal by more modern standards, Burton's general project of investigating mind-body correspondence remains a cornerstone of empirical mind-body and mind-brain scientific research to this day.

# EARLY MODERN PHILOSOPHY

## What is **early modern philosophy**?

Early modern philosophy is mainly centered on intellectual activity in the seventeenth century, with some overlap into the early eighteenth and late sixteenth centuries. Early modern philosophy was modern in its concerns with *epistemology,* or the nature and justification of human knowledge, the fact that the scientific revolution was by then taken for granted, and a new acceptance of logical argument and fact-based reasons as necessary ingredients for the practice of philosophy.

However, what made it "early" modern was the continued importance of religious issues, the background social need for philosophers to assert a belief in God, the continued reaction against Aristotelian scholasticism, and the unstable political context prior to the existence of strong nation states.

## Who were the **main early modern philosophers**?

The customary division is between the rationalists and the empiricists. René Descartes (1596–1650), Gottfried Leibniz (1646–1716), Benedict de Spinoza (1632–1677), and Nicolas Malebranche (1638–1715) are usually listed as the epistemological rationalists, Thomas Hobbes (1588–1679) and John Locke (1632–1704) as the empiricists. However, for a more complete picture, Francisco Suárez (1548–1617) should be counted among the rationalists and Hugo Grotius (1583–1645) among the empiricists.

## What is **epistemological rationalism**?

Epistemological rationalism is the position that human beings have important ideas or principles present in their minds from birth, and that the most important truths about the world can be derived from thought, without the need for experience. These *a priori* truths are also held to be logically certain, which is to say that it would entail

119

a logical contradiction to deny them, and that they are absolutely certain, or, in current terminology, "true in all possible worlds."

# SEVENTEENTH CENTURY RATIONALISM

## FRANCISCO SUÁREZ

### Who was **Francisco Suárez**?

Francisco Suárez (also called Doctor Eximius; 1548–1617) was a Spanish Jesuit theological philosopher. He taught mainly in Spain and Italy, at Salmanca, Rome, and Coimbra. He wrote *On Law* (1612), *On the Trinity* (1606), and *On the Soul* (1612). His best known work was his 54 arguments, or treatises, known as *Metaphysical Disputations* (1597), which were believed to have influenced Descartes, Leibniz, and Grotius in the seventeenth century, and Schopenhauer in the nineteenth. Suárez treated metaphysics in the first extended systematic way in the European tradition after Aristotle, which was not an Aristotelian commentary.

### What was **Francico Suárez's** view of **metaphysics**?

Suárez defined metaphysics as the study of "being" insofar as it is real being. The idea of being was analogous to the similarities among things that existed. Suárez held that everything which exists is an individual, not capable of further division into individuals like it. Suárez' focus on the most general kinds of things that exist was echoed in Descartes' division of the world into mind and matter.

## RENÉ DESCARTES

### Who was **René Descartes**?

René Descartes (1596–1650) inaugurated modern philosophy with a pair of questions that persist to this day: How are mind and matter different? and How is the mind connected to the body? He did not set out to invent these questions, but encountered them himself while on the way toward trying to do something else. He was trying to prove to the Catholic Church that rigorous philosophy was compatible with religion and that science could be both certain and compatible with religion.

### What is the story of **Descartes' life**?

René Descartes' (1596–1650) father was a member of the minor nobility. His mother died when he was 13 months old, and after his father remarried he was raised by his

## What was René Descartes like as a person?

It is difficult to say. In contemporary terms, Descartes would probably be considered a fearful, anxious, and self-absorbed man with social disorders. He was the only seventeenth-century philosopher who never had a patron or a secure post, and he was not independently wealthy.

Descartes moved to Holland to escape the distractions of Paris, so that he could concentrate on his work. He was secretive about his personal life and moved his household about once a year during a 20-year period. Wherever he was, he conducted experiments, sometimes getting animal organs from local butchers. One account has it that when he studied vision, he literally looked through a calf's eyes.

Descartes was greatly interested in special foods and diets, possibly as a way to prolong life or even to achieve immortality. At times he was a vegetarian—it's clear this was not for moral reasons, given his belief that animals are machines—and other times he thought that the secret lay in eggs. With a servant named Helena Jans, he had an illegitimate daughter.

While Descartes' daughter, Francine, is usually described as illegitimate by biographers, her baptism was recorded in 1635 in the Reformed Church in Deventer. Francine died at the age of five from scarlet fever, and Descartes expressed great sorrow for this loss. Descartes' motto was said to have been: "A life well hidden is a life well lived." Another version has it as: "I advance masked."

maternal grandmother. At 10 he was sent to the new Jesuit college of La Flèche in Anjou, France, and there studied the classics, history, rhetoric, and Aristotelian natural philosophy. Although he considered La Flèche an excellent school, he thought that the natural philosophy he learned there was "doubtful," mainly because it was based on scholastic abstractions that had been outdated by more recent discoveries and thought.

Descartes then took a law degree at Pottiers and set off to complete his education by travel in Europe. He wrote that he had resolved "to seek no knowledge other than that which could be found either in myself or the great book of the world." He served briefly in the army and then became friends with Isaac Beeckman (1588–1637), a Dutch philosopher and scientist who inspired him to study mathematics.

Descartes' first book, *Compendium Musicae,* applied mathematics to harmony and dissonance. Descartes also began work on his discovery of analytic geometry that was published in 1637.

### How did René **Descartes'** philosophical **work begin?**

On November 10, 1619, Descartes spent many hours sequestered in a room-sized stove in a town in southern Germany. (Such very large stoves with shelves, places to sleep, and room to stand up in them were built in Germany and Russia, until the end of the nineteenth century.) Descartes had an epiphany as the result of three bizarre dreams, which set him on a course to create a new system for science and philosophy.

His inspiration was that, beginning with a few ideas known to be absolutely true, and careful methods of reasoning with them, the basic principles of all of the sciences could be logically derived from those ideas.

Descartes would go on to live briefly in Paris in 1628, before moving to Holland, where he was to remain for the rest of his life.

### What was René **Descartes' problem** with the **Inquisition?**

Descartes never had a direct problem with the Inquisition, but he was always afraid of Church authorities, and at the same time he wanted their approval. His book on cosmology and physics, which was in accord with both atomism and Copernicanism, was ready to publish, when he withdrew it after he heard of the Inquisition's condemnation of Galileo. In 1637, Descartes published his *Optics, Meteorology, and Geometry* that was prefaced with *Discourse on the Method of Rightly Conducting One's Reason and Reaching the Truth in the Sciences* (1637). Here, Descartes developed his "doctrine of clear and distinct ideas." (An idea was clear if one could be sure about what the idea was, and distinct, if it was different from other ideas.)

He next published his *Meditations on First Philosophy* (1641), partly in response to criticism he had received on the *The Discourse on Method* (1637). The *Discourse* explained Descartes' new way of deriving the first principles of the sciences from a few clear and distinct ideas. The *Meditations* was published with a set of objections and replies from his contemporaries (including Marin Mersenne (1588–1648), Thomas Hobbes [1588–1679], and Pierre Gassendi [1592–1655]), and it went to a second edition in 1642. It was a completely original work in its claims that it was possible to be certain about the nature of physical reality and the existence of God based on certainty about one's own existence.

Descartes' pre-publication discussions led to refinements in his position that related his ideas to the intellectual concerns of his peers. From these discussions, the *Meditations* became one of the most famous philosophical works. Philosophers still obsess about it in the twenty-first century!

Descartes became increasingly concerned about intellectual attacks on him by papal authorities. His friends thought that he exaggerated the personal and professional dangers of these attacks, but Descartes' own ambition was tied up with his response to them. His thinking went to the heart of the Catholic Church's use of skepticism to deny the findings of the new science that contradicted Church doctrine and scripture. It was Descartes' hope that the Jesuits would approve his ideas in the *Meditations* and even use it as a textbook.

Descartes' next publication was *Principles of Philosophy* (1644), which he believed would be a masterpiece that would gain the Church's approval.

## Who were René **Descartes'** royal **female correspondents**?

Descartes corresponded with Princess Elizabeth of Bohemia, who was very interested in applying his doctrines for clear thought. As a result of this exchange, he wrote *The Passions of the Soul* (1669), which was an account of how the mind worked and was connected to the body.

In the same year, Descartes agreed to move to Stockholm to tutor Queen Christina. Like Princess Elizabeth, she was drawn to Descartes' ideas, and wished to be well-informed and educated, in general. A small pension from the King of France had been delayed for many years, and Descartes needed the funds, as well as the honor of royal patronage. He called Sweden "the land of the bears" and was much inconvenienced by demands of the athletic young queen that he begin his lessons for her at 5:00 A.M. Descartes had always been a late riser, preferring to begin his day by reflecting in bed until noon. When he was a student at La Flèche, he had been given special permission not to rise early. Descartes' biographers believe that the change in his routine weakened him. He caught pneumonia and soon died.

## Who was **Princess Elizabeth**?

This royal friend and student of Descartes was a powerful woman with an independent mind. Elizabeth, Electress Palatine and Queen of Bohemia (1596–1662), was the oldest daughter of James VI of Scotland and Anne of Denmark, his Queen consort. Her descendants, the Hanoverians, were to occupy the British throne. In 1613 she married Frederick V, the Elector of the Palatine, an alliance designed to strengthen her father's ties to the Holy Roman Empire. Her husband was only briefly king of Bohemia, however, and after his exile, they lived in The Hague. In 1649, she entered a convent in Hertford in Westphalia, in what is now Germany, which she managed until her death.

Elizabeth's interest in philosophy had a depth that was unusual for someone with her social and familial obligations. In 1643, she wrote Descartes:

> And I admit it would be easier for me to concede matter and extension to the soul, than the capacity of moving a body and of being moved, to an immaterial being. For, if the first occurred through "information" the spirits that perform the movement would have to be intelligent, which you accord to nothing corporeal. And although in your metaphysical meditations you show the possibility of the second, it is, however, very difficult to comprehend that a

123

Descartes wrote *Passions of Soul* mainly to try to answer her questions about how the mind interacted with the body.

In that book, Descartes discusses how emotions are the mind's perceptions of disturbances in our bodies. He thought that the will was part of the soul and immaterial but that there were very delicate fluids in the pineal gland that the will could influence. The result was that parts of the body could be controlled by the mind.

soul, as you have described it, after having had the faculty and habit of reasoning well, can lose all of it on account of some vapors, and that, although it can subsist without the body and has nothing in common with it, is yet so ruled by it.

In this passage, the possibility of the materiality of the soul is deftly introduced in a way that illumines Descartes' dualism. No one, including Descartes, could satisfactorily explain how an immaterial soul could interact with a material body. One solution to this problem that Elizabeth intuited was to posit the soul as material.

## Who was **Queen Christina** and why was she important in **Descartes' life**?

René Descartes' second royal correspondent and student, Queen Christina (1626–1689) of Sweden, was a less conventional figure than his other pupil, Princess Elizabeth, although her philosophical skills and subsequent historical legacy were not as great. Christina's father raised her as a prince, and when she assumed the crown she took the title of "King Christina." During her reign she greatly expanded the number of noble titles and extravagantly spent down the treasury, most notably for "New Sweden," a colonization of America in an area near Willington, Delaware.

Christina abdicated in 1664, changing her name to Maria Christina Alexandra. She did this to convert to Catholicism, which was then illegal in Sweden. Maria Christina went first to Rome and then France. She enjoyed great attention as a former queen and was an active patroness of science and the arts. She was remembered for her shocking male dress: a short skirt, stockings, and high heels, which allowed for greater freedom of movement than the long skirts women wore at the time.

Greta Garbo portrayed Queen Christina in a 1933 film that was highly acclaimed critically but did not do well at the box office.

## What did Descartes mean by **"clear and distinct ideas"**?

Descartes thought that there was a "natural light" of reason by which one could be sure of one's thoughts. Descartes wrote in his *Principles of Philosophy (1644)*:

> I term that "clear" which is present and apparent to an attentive mind, in the same way that we see objects clearly when, being present to the regarding eye, they operate upon it with sufficient strength. But the "distinct" is that which is so precise and different from all other objects that it contains within itself nothing but what is clear."

In other words, the thinker has an intuitive or direct experience of clarity and about what he or she is clear about. Descartes was relying on our ability to recognize when we know something for sure in all its detail.

## What was the **purpose** of Descartes' *Meditations*?

In his Preface and Introduction to *Meditations on First Philosophy* (1641), Descartes said that his goal was to rationally prove the existence of God and the immortality of the soul. He claimed to be able to do that using his method of clear and distinct ideas, which would also enable him to create foundations of certainty for the sciences.

## What are some of the **major philosophical arguments** made in *Meditations*?

Descartes believed it was necessary to take the entire edifice of knowledge down to its foundations to remove existing error. His method was not to doubt everything for the sake of skepticism itself, but to doubt everything that could be doubted, so that one would be left only with what was certain. He began with the usual arguments about the errors of the senses: for instance, the observation that far away objects look smaller than they are.

He then questioned whether he could be sure that there was a world outside of his mind and noted that the insanity of that line of questioning was not unusual if one takes into account the fact that every night, during sleep, there are bizarre distortions in dreams. This raises the question of what exactly is the difference between being awake and being asleep. Descartes notes that there is nothing in the quality of either experience that guarantees which state one is in.

Descartes' project of doubt next addresses mathematical and logical thinking. Descartes said that our confidence in these processes depends on our confidence that there is a benevolent God who guarantees that what seems self-evident to us really is true, and who guarantees the accuracy of the memory of those past thought processes that are necessary to proceed to a conclusion in a chain of reasoning.

Then, Descartes advances to his most devastating level of doubt: what if there is not a benevolent, all-powerful God, but an evil demon, who instead of supporting our

Descartes' assertion that he existed led to other conclusions, such that God exists as does the external world (iStock).

true mental processes, is in fact constantly deceiving us about the workings of our own minds? So now Descartes has raised doubt to the level of doubting the existence of a good and powerful God, which he himself regards as a very disturbing and distressing predicament.

### How did Descartes **solve** his **evil demon hypothesis**?

René Descartes recounted everything that he could doubt—sensory information, the external world, his own thought processes, and the goodness of God—and noted that one thing he could not doubt was that he himself was doing the doubting. From this he concluded that he could not doubt that he existed, since someone or something must be doing the doubting. He wrote later about his famous *cogito ergo sum,* or "I think, therefore I am":

I noticed that while I was trying to think everything false, it must needs be that I, who was thinking this, was something. And observing that this truth, *I am thinking, therefore I exist* was so solid and secure that the most extravagant suppositions of the skeptics could not overthrow it, I judged that I need not scruple to accept it as the first principle of the philosophy that I was seeking.

### Was **Descartes** a **Cartesian**?

Yes, René Descartes was a Cartesian in the sense that he defended his views. But the answer is "no," too, in that he did not literally mean that the human mind and the body were two separate things. He famously wrote in Meditation II in his *Meditations on First Philosophy* (1641): "I am not in my body like a pilot in a ship." His intention was to make an abstract distinction between the mind and the body. But because he did not give a satisfactory account of their interaction, Descartes is still stuck with the mind-body dualism of "Cartesianism."

### What were Descartes' main **ideas** in *Passions of the Soul*?

René Descartes claimed that his mind or soul feels "passions," or sensations and pains, in the body. The soul is therefore connected to all parts of body, although there is one part of

## What did Descartes do once he was sure of his assertion *I am thinking, therefore I exist*?

**D**escartes asked himself what kind of thing he was and concluded that he was a *thinking thing*, that is, a mind-soul, and not the author of his own being, who must be God. God created both Descartes as an immaterial thinking thing, or soul, and the physical universe that included Descartes' body. There was a second proof for God's existence in Descartes' ontological argument: God was all powerful and all good, existence was better than nonexistence, therefore God existed.

Because God was good, he could not be a deceiver, and the earlier doubts about the existence of the external world, and the validity of logic and reason, were put to rest. The doubts about sense data could always be corrected by further sense experience. And the distinction between being awake and being asleep could be solved after one was awake and compared the two states. God had made mankind such that our perceptions of the reality of a world that existed could be trusted.

the brain, namely the pineal gland, "where it exercises its functions more particularly than elsewhere." That is, the soul directly affects the body through the pineal gland by setting animal spirits in motion, via the will. (Descartes thought that the will was infinite because it was a copy of God's will, but that human understanding is limited. Because the will often outstrips the understanding, all manner of human evils and misfortunes follow.) Consciousness, or the representation in the mind of the sensation and pains in the body, was unique to human beings, according to Descartes. He thought that animals lacked both a pineal gland and consciousness, and were therefore mere machines.

## What was the **reaction** to the *Meditations*?

Catholic theologians found René Descartes' doubt in the existence of God too convincing to be resolved by his ontological argument. Others were left with a division of the world into two radically different substances of mind and matter, a dualism very difficult to resolve. Mind could be directly introspected, but it eluded science. Matter—by which Descartes meant insensible particles that had only size, shape, quantity, and mass (primary qualities)—was the ultimate subject of science.

Descartes believed that we know less about matter than mind. The question was, "How are mind and matter connected?" Descartes' ideas of substance, his dualism, and the mind-body problem preoccupied his contemporaries and successors. Benedict de Spinoza (1632–1677) reacted with a dual-aspect theory of God and nature. Nicolas Malebranche (1638–1715) tried to answer the question of how mind and matter were connected, with his theory of *occasionalism*. Gottfried Leibniz (1646–1716) also had a

**127**

version of occasionalism in his theory of *pre-established harmony*. On the empiricist side, Thomas Hobbes (1588–1679) insisted on the nonexistence of anything non-material and John Locke (1632–1704) directly attacked Descartes' idea of substance.

Descartes thought that substance was what held matter together and what held mind together, even though substance could not be experienced directly. According to Descartes all physical things were material substance and all mental things immaterial substance.

### Why was René **Descartes' idea of substance** a **problem** for the **empiricists**?

According to Descartes, substance was known to the mind, but not through the senses. The empiricists wanted to build knowledge up from information we get through the senses.

## BENEDICT DE SPINOZA

### Who was **Benedict de Spinoza**?

Benedict (Baruch) de Spinoza (1632–1677) stands out as a loner among seventeenth century thinkers. He was excommunicated from the Jewish community in Amsterdam for his unorthodox ideas. After that, he had few contacts with other Jews, but because he was a Jew his Dutch acquaintances were not friendly to him.

In 1660, he moved from Amsterdam to Rijnsburg and then to Voorburg. In 1663, he wrote about Descartes' philosophy in *Renati Descartes Principiorum Philosophiae, Pars I et II.* His *Tractatus Theologico Politicus* was published anonymously in 1670. He was then offered the chair of philosophy at Heidelberg University, in 1673, but he turned it down because he did not want to jeopardize his peace of mind. He thought that academics were constantly arguing among themselves and engaging in petty disputes and grudges. He knew Gottfried Leibniz (1646–1716) and corresponded with the Royal Society members Henry Oldenburg and Christian Huygens.

Spinoza's *Ethics* (1677) was published after his death, as was his *Tractatus de Intellectis Emendatione* (1677). That Spinoza preferred to think on his own, with little outside influence, made his work very distinctive, but it also was part of the reason for a prolonged lack of recognition of him as a philosopher.

### What was **Spinoza's** philosophical **goal**?

Spinoza's goal was the very practical one of how a person ought to live in the world. He sought a good, or a value, that would allow independence from the unpredictable, unpleasant, and uncontrollable aspects of human life, and he concluded that the ultimate good was awareness of one's place in nature, together with an acceptance of the natural order. Natural science, politics, ethics, education, and even technology were part of what had to be understood to achieve this complete understanding. Before such understanding, Spinoza said that the human mind was like a worm in a bloodstream that thought each drop of blood was an isolated thing, instead of part of a system within an organism. His philosophical task was to describe the whole in which individual humans were parts.

Benedict de Spinoza concluded that the ultimate good was to discover one's place in nature (iStock).

## What was **Spinoza's philosophical system**?

Although Spinoza's system had very strong theological elements and he was motivated to construct it for the ethical purpose of determining how to live, he did not base morality on God, but rather on adequate human knowledge. Such knowledge would enable both an ability to control the passions and live peacefully with others. However, indirectly, this knowledge of nature amounted to knowledge of God because, according to Spinoza, God was present throughout nature.

Spinoza wrote philosophy in the form of geometrical proofs and began with axioms from which he proved his conclusions. First, he made the assumption that substance exists. Substance, he continued, has infinite attributes, but humans can perceive only two of these: extension and thought (or matter and mind).

Spinoza's metaphysics was a *monism*. Only one thing existed and that was God. God, according to Spinoza, was "a being absolutely infinite." Although God had infinite attributes, each one of which expressed His nature without limitation to itself, humans can perceive or understand only two of God's infinite attributes: thought and material bodies, or extension. Each attribute has both infinite modes and finite modes, although finite modes are infinite in number. A person, for example, is one finite mode of God, existing in God as both a mode of thought and a mode of extension.

One way of understanding Spinoza is that mind and matter are different ways of viewing the same thing that exists in God. As everything that exists, God is nature, but nature is also God. Spinoza distinguished between *natura naturans,* or God in his active role as creating, and *natural naturata,* or what we humans perceive as nature.

## How did **Spinoza consider good and evil**?

Spinoza sought to consider human actions and desires objectively, almost like mathematical questions. Virtuous actions result from understanding and are either self-preserving or altruistic, but the two are united: "Nothing is more useful to man than man." He defined good as "what we certainly know to be useful to us," and evil as "what we certainly know prevents us from being masters of some good." Because God is perfect, He has no needs from which it follows that nothing is good or evil to Him. God's blessing is not a reward for virtuous behavior, but an inevitable result of living according to reason or having "adequate knowledge." Spinoza also held that citizens of a state cannot give up their right to attain their own well being.

## How did Spinoza's system **solve Cartesianism**?

Descartes' division between mind and body depended on the existence of two separate substances: mind and material body, in addition to God. For Spinoza, there was but one substance, which was also God. That is, the human mind and the human body are the same exact thing, but are understood in different ways. We do not think of one thing as interacting causally with itself. So Cartesianism could not even get started as a problem in Spinoza's system.

## What was **Spinoza's legacy**?

Spinoza has acquired an almost saintly aura over the centuries. In 1672 he wanted to participate in a protest against the brutal mob assassination of the Dutch statesman and mathematician, Johan De Witt, and his brother, Cornelis. There was great physical risk in such participation, but the only thing that stopped Spinoza was that a friend locked him up. The nineteenth century Romantic writer Novalis called Spinoza "the God-intoxicated man." The twentieth century philosopher Bertrand Russell (1872–1970) called Spinoza "the most lovable and noble of all philosophers."

Spinoza is believed to have influenced the father of psychoanalysis, Sigmund Freud, and the scientist Albert Einstein, as well as authors such as William Wordsworth, Samuel Taylor Coleridge, Heinrich Heine, Percy Bysshe Shelley, George Eliot, George Sand, and Jorge Luis Borges. Late-twentieth century naturalists, as well as those who advocate a mind-body identity, have embraced his work. His cognitive account of the emotions as expressing beliefs has grounded branches of contemporary psychology, as well as philosophy of mind.

The contemporary playwright David Ives' *New Jerusalem: The Interrogation of Baruch de Spinoza at Talmud Torah Congregation: Amsterdam, July 27, 1656* dramatizes both the persecution of Spinoza and the concern of Jewish leaders that Spinoza's radical thought would disrupt the fragile acceptance of the Jewish community in Amsterdam. At one point in the play, the Spinoza character quips, "There is no Jewish dogma, only bickering."

After Spinoza was excommunicated from his Jewish community, he could receive neither patronage nor any other employment. He therefore made his living by grind-

## What is the Lens Crafter's Society?

**W**hile the members of the American Philosophical Association (APA) in the twentieth and early twenty-first centuries have been, for the most part, employed as academic philosophers, not everyone with a Ph.D. in philosophy is able to find work as a professor, and some of them do not have other jobs, either. The APA has tried to accommodate these unemployed philosophers at its annual meetings, and it sponsors an organization for them that is called "The Lens Crafter's Society," in honor of Spinoza, who polished lenses for a living.

ing and polishing lenses. The dust from the glass is believed to have fatally injured his lungs and been responsible for his early death.

## NICOLAS MALEBRANCHE

### Who was **Nicolas Malebranche**?

Malebranche (1637–1715) was a rationalist, like René Descartes (1596–1650), who tried to solve the problem of how the mind and body interact.

### How did Nicolas **Malebranche react** to Descartes' **mind-body problem**?

Nicolas Malebranche denied that anything, either mental or physical, could cause, or be the effect of, anything else. His reasoning was that physical bodies were inert and passive, without any force within them that could cause anything or even sustain movement. Neither can mental things cause anything, because there is no necessary connection between any human act of will and any other event. Only God has an effective will in this sense. Therefore, all causal connections in nature are in reality the actions of God. Causal chains in nature are like two clocks that are one minute apart in time. There may be an appearance of the clock that is ahead in time causing the movements of the slower clock, but this is no more than an appearance.

### Did **Malebranche** have a more **extensive philosophy** to support his **theory of causation**?

Yes, Malebranche was highly regarded as a theological metaphysician. In his major book, *The Search after Truth* (1674), he developed his theory of "vision in God." Malebranche agreed with René Descartes (1596–1650) that ideas in the mind are the basic units of perception and knowledge, but he argued that our ideas are actually in God, rather than in us. This vision in God was especially important for abstract knowledge,

131

according to Malebranche, because universals, mathematical truths, and moral under-standing were part of the vision in God. As such, they reflected God's knowledge of what was eternally true about the world He had created.

In his *Treatise on Nature and Grace* (1680), Malebranche provided an explanation of how God's goodness, omnipotence, and omniscience could allow evil in the world. He claimed that God could have created a more perfect world without the known evils of the present one. This more or mostly perfect world, however, would have been more complicated than the world God did create, and creating that world would have con-tradicted God's principle of acting in the simplest possible way, according to general laws. This simplicity and generality could also explain the unequal distribution of grace among human beings.

## Did **Malebranche** lead an **exciting life**?

If he did, it was in his inner life. To all outward appearances, Nicolas Malebranche was a scholar with the temperament of a religious recluse. He was born and died in Paris and throughout his life liked solitude.

Malebranche was sickly as a child, born with a deformed spine and prone to respi-ratory problems. He was educated at home by a tutor until the age of 16. His father, Nicolas, was a royal counselor who managed the finances of five farms. His mother was sister to the viceroy of Canada.

Malebranche entered the College de la Marche of the University of Paris, receiving an M.A. in two years, after which he studied theology at the Sorbonne in Paris for another three years. He was ordained as a priest in 1665 at Faubourg St. Jaques. His family contributed to his support by the Church, and he had no official duties beyond teaching mathematics in 1674. In 1690 the Church put his *Traité de la nature et de la grace* (1680) on the Index of books that Catholics were forbidden by the Church to read because his claim that all of our ideas are in God was controversial and because he'd been successful in spreading René Descartes' (1596–1650) mathematics. (Descartes' writings were on the Church's index of forbidden books, so Catholics were forbidden to read them and they could not be taught in Church schools.) Although his most important work, *The Search after Truth* (1674), won him wide acclaim, his stu-dents, such as Gottfried Leibniz (1646–1716), were considered of greater ability; Male-branche encouraged their research.

In 1871, Alexander Campbell Frasier, a biographer of philosophers, wrote this account of how the young philosopher George Berkeley (1685–1783) was the "occa-sional cause" of the death of Malebranche:

[Berkeley] found the ingenious Father [Malebranche] in a cell, cooking, in a small pipkin [an earthenware cooking pot that was positioned directly over a flame], a medicine for a disorder with which he was then troubled—an inflammation on the lungs. The conversation naturally turned on [George]

Berkeley's [(1685–1783)] system, of which he had received some knowledge from a translation just published. But the issue of the debate proved tragic to poor Malebranche. In the heat of the disputation, he raised his voice so high, and gave way so freely to the natural impetuosity of a man of parts and a Frenchman, that he brought on himself a violent increase of his disorder, which carried him off a few days after.

## GOTTFRIED WILHELM LEIBNIZ

### Who was Leibniz?

Gottfried Wilhelm Leibniz (1646–1715) was a German philosopher, scientist, mathematician, and historian famous for his metaphysical idealism as well as his epistemological rationalism. In addition, he made contributions to the fields of astronomy, biology (including embryology), engineering, information technology, law, logic, medicine, paleontology, philology, Sinology, social science, and topology. The calculating machine he invented could add, subtract and calculate square roots; his plans for invading Egypt are said to have been used by Napoleon. Leibniz also kept up a voluminous correspondence throughout his life.

### What is known about Leibniz's life?

Gottfried Leibniz (1646–1716) was born in Leipzig, Germany. His mother was the daughter of a professor, and his father was a professor. His father died when he was six. Leibniz studied philosophy and law at the University of Leipzig, but he was too young to be awarded a doctorate in law when he finished at age 20. He then moved to Altdorf, where he graduated and was offered a professorship that he turned down to become secretary of the Rosicrucian Society in Nuremberg. He then entered the service of Johann Philipp von Shonborn, elector of Mainz, and during this time he did not produce his own philosophy but mainly wrote histories and biographies for pay.

In 1672 Leibniz went to Paris, and after four years he entered the service of Johann Friedrich, Duke of Hanover. When Johann died, he served Ernst August (1629–1698), Duke of Hanover, and then Georg Ludwig, who became King George I of Great Britain in 1714.

You can thank Leibniz for those calculus problems you did in school (iStock).

133

## What was the dispute between Leibniz and Newton about the calculus?

Gottfried Leibniz was very sociable intellectually, and welcomed a free and cooperative exchange of ideas. Toward the end of his life, though, he was greatly distressed by the claims of Isaac Newton's (1643–1727) advocates that he had in effect plagiarized the discovery of the differential calculus from Newton. Leibniz reported that when he was in England in 1637 he was told about Newton's work on the calculus and wrote to him.

Newton replied through an intermediary, although he wrote about the binomial theory and included only the following sentence, in Latin, about the calculus ("fluxions"). The words of the sentence were presented by Newton, in code, as follows: "aaaaa cc d ae eeeeeeeeeeeee ff iiiiiii lll nnnnnnnnn oooo qqqq rr ssss tttttttttt vvvvvvvvvvvv x." It meant, "Given equation anywhatsoever, flowing quantities involving, fluxions to find, and *vice versa.*" No one has ever been able to make sense of what Newton wrote Leibniz, nor has anyone related it to the differential calculus, although the string of letters are sometimes quoted to illustrate how unreasonable Newton was. Leibniz then invented a differential calculus on his own, showed it to Newton's intermediary, and in 1684 published his method. By 1695, Newton's followers were accusing him of plagiarism.

Over the centuries, scholars have exonerated Leibniz of plagiarism. The conclusion has been that they each independently invented the calculus and that Newton did so first, although Leibniz published first.

---

He was commissioned by Ernst August to write the history of the house of Brunswick in 1685. After traveling to Munich, Vienna, and Italy, he showed, as part of his commissioned writing assignment, how Brunswick was connected with the house of Este.

Leibniz had a close correspondence with Ernst August's wife, Sophie, and her daughter, Sophie Charlotte, who became Queen of Prussia. He became president of the Berlin Society of Sciences in the same city where Sophie Charlotte lived. After her death, her family was not welcoming to him (perhaps because they had resented his relationship with her while she was alive).

Leibniz was continually involved in efforts to promote communication and cooperation in scientific research, both theoretical and practical. He also had hopes that all Christians might unite. He was honored with prestigious government posts in Vienna (1712–1714), but by the time of his death his royal patrons, and most of the intellectuals who had known him, abandoned him. They did so for several reasons: Isaac Newton was favored in Leibniz's dispute with him; Leibniz no longer had the protection of

Sophie Charlotte; and his philosophical work was not popular. Neither the Royal Society nor the Berlin Academy saw fit to honor him after he died. King George I was nearby when his funeral was held but did not deign to attend or send a representative.

Leibniz's grave remained unmarked for almost 50 years, until a descendent of Sophie Charlotte took up the cause of rehabilitating his memory. While it is not clear how damaging his dispute with Isaac Newton (1643–1727) over the discovery of the calculus was to his reputation and standing, it evidently proved more harmful to him than it did to Newton. (Newton had claimed that Leibniz plagiarized his work on the differential calculus.)

When Leibniz died, he was engaged in writing a religious work about Chinese philosophy and the *Leibniz-Clark Correspondence* in which he attacked virtually every aspect of Newton's metaphysical system.

## What were **Leibniz's views** on **embryology**?

Gottfried Leibniz believed in *preformationism,* the theory that all living things had been created at once so that their offspring unfold from completely formed seeds, or *homunculi* in the case of humans and *animunculi* for animals. Some preformationists believed that the whole of successive humanity must have been present in Adam's testicles from the time he was in the Garden of Eden, while others held that they were in Eve's ovaries. These two views were called "spermism" and "ovism," respectively.

The opposing theory to preformationism was *epigenesis,* or the idea that embryos developed in time. However, before a true knowledge of heredity or conception, together with Christian belief that mere matter could not by itself become a complex living organism, epigenesis did not seem plausible given available evidence.

Antoni van Leeuwenhoek, a highly skilled Dutch lens grinder, was able to construct microscopes that magnified items 200 times. Around 1700, after having seen bacteria, he reported viewing both male and female sperm:

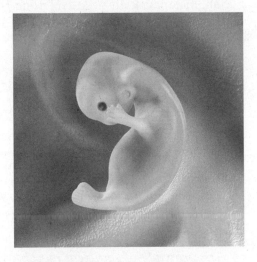

Gottfried Leibniz believed that all human beings were predetermined as homunculi from the beginning of time. In other words, each human being was completely formed before he or she was an embryo in the womb (iStock).

> I have often observed the sperm of a healthy man without waiting for it to become corrupt or fluid/watery, five or six minutes after ejaculation. I have noticed a large number of small animals, I think it must be more than a thousand, on an area no larger than a grain of sand.

135

Leeuwenhoek reported having seen tiny animals with completely formed features in pond scum and tooth plaque, as well as in the sperm of over 30 animals. He was made a member of the Royal Society, and his descriptions of miniature worlds within worlds were accepted as evidence for preformationism, as well as the original creation of everything in the universe, all at once, by God.

## What is **metaphysical idealism**?

Metaphysical idealism is the position—going back to the pre-Socratics and brought to fruition by Plato in the ancient world—that what is ultimately real is something non-material and not apparent to the senses. Insofar as God was believed to be both non-material and most real, all Christian philosophers were "idealists," but the term is usually reserved for those who posited mind or other nonmaterial substances and things as more real than matter in the natural world.

## What were some of Leibniz's **original contributions to philosophy**?

Leibniz's major works include *The Monadology* (1714), *Discourse on Metaphysics* (1686), *Theodicy* (1710), and *The Leibniz-Clarke Correspondence* (1714–1715), as well as political writings and a large body of unedited material. Leibniz had a very complex view of the universe that defied common sense, was theoretically fascinating, and preserved core Christian beliefs. His philosophical writings were highly complex and had their own terminology. He claimed that his philosophy was based on these general principles: principle of identity, principle of the best, principle of sufficient reason, metaphysically necessary principles, principles of order, principles of causation, and the principle of the natural. In addition to this, he used the idea of *monads* as the basic unit of what was real.

## How did **Leibniz define** his **principles**?

Leibniz based his philosophy on the following principles:

*The principle of identity*—This is the law of necessary truth and non-contradiction. A is A and never not-A. The opposite of a necessary truth is a contradiction.

*The principle of the best*—A contingent truth can have an opposite that is not a contradiction. God, who is perfectly wise, good, and powerful did not have to create the world. But he chose to do so and because He chose it, it is the best possible world.

*The principle of sufficient reason*—Everything that exists or occurs must have a reason that was sufficient to bring it about.

*Metaphysically necessary principles*—Leibniz had a number of these, which included: everything possible demands to exist and it will exist unless pre-

## Who was Dr. Pangloss?

The brilliant French satiric essayist François-Marie Arouet de Voltaire (1694–1778) pilloried Leibniz's philosophical optimism with the character of Dr. Pangloss in his novel *Candide*. The character Candide is the illegitimate nephew of a baron who starts out life in luxury, with Dr. Pangloss as his teacher. ("pan" is Greek for "all" and "gloss" means "tongue, speech, and words," so that Dr. Pangloss translates as "Dr. Alltalk.")

Dr. Pangloss teaches the "metaphysico-theologo-cosmolonigology" to Candide. This teaching is a caricature of Leibniz's and the poet Alexander Pope's philosophical optimism, which Voltaire found very difficult to reconcile with real human suffering, such as the devastation caused by the 1755 Lisbon earthquake and the oppression of the *ancien régime* in pre-revolutionary France.

The view of philosophical optimism held that because God is good, everything in the world must be good, as well. It is, in fact, the best world it could be, and everything in it, including what appear as evil to us, is, in the grand scheme of things, inevitable and for the best. Here's a sample of Voltaire's satire in which Dr. Pangloss expresses his belief:

> "It is demonstrable," said he, "that things cannot be otherwise than as they are; for as all things have been created for some end, they must necessarily be created for the best end. Observe, for instance, the nose is formed for spectacles, therefore we wear spectacles. The legs are visibly designed for stockings, accordingly we wear stockings. Stones were made to be hewn and to construct castles, therefore My Lord has a magnificent castle; for the greatest baron in the province ought to be the best lodged. Swine were intended to be eaten, therefore we eat pork all the year round: and they, who assert that everything is right, do not express themselves correctly; they should say that everything is best.

vented; activity is essential to substance; and states of things remain unless or until there is a reason for them to change.

*Principles of order*—These consisted of three laws of order: the law of continuity, the law that every action involves a reaction, and the law that cause and effect are equal.

*Efficient and final causation*—Efficient causes are what immediately make things happen, whereas final causes are the ends or goals of higher substances. The entire realm of efficient causation is designed to serve the realm of final causation.

*Principle of the natural*—Everything that God allows to exist and happen, he chooses from what is natural; otherwise He would constantly be performing miracles. What is natural is always in between what is essential or necessary and what is accidental.

## What was Leibniz's **monadology**?

Like René Descartes (1596–1650), Leibniz thought that the basic unit of existence was substance. But whereas Descartes posited two primary kinds of substances—mind and matter—Leibniz posited one immaterial kind of substance, which had many, many instances that he called "monads." Monads, according to Leibniz, are indivisible units of psychic or mental or spiritual force, each one of which perceived all of the other monads as an aspect of its own inner states.

Each monad had an organic body that "mirrored" what was happening in other monads, but not as a direct effect. That is, like a cell containing all of the chromosomes and genes of the animal of whose body it is a part, for Leibniz each monad contained within itself complete information about the rest of world. In addition, every monad contained its own future states, and of course, within those future states would be the monad's perception of the future states of every other monad. This world system of monads was created by God and its main feature is the *pre-established harmony* that results in human perceptions of direct inter-action and inter-relationships.

Monads form colonies and colonies of colonies with dominant monads at different levels of organization. These collections of monads constitute real physical existence. Both space and time are abstractions and not substances. Space, according to Leibniz, is the form of possible coexistences; and time is the form of possible successive existstents (things that exist).

# SEVENTEENTH CENTURY EMPIRICISM

## What was or is **natural law**?

Natural law, or the law of nature, is a set of rules for human actions, usually posited as having a divine source. As a universal moral and political code, natural law was first conceptualized by stoic philosophers, who believed that natural law was part of the fundamental structure of the universe. Some early thinkers believed that natural law applied to animals as well as humans.

Christian theorists later took up the idea of natural law as self-evident principles of human behavior that could be known only by rational beings. Thomas Aquinas (c. 1225–1274) thought that human reason could reveal God's intentions for how we ought always to conduct ourselves so as to preserve the common good, or the good of the community. Following natural law is an important part of obedience to God. The particular laws of nations and peoples might differ, but the basic principles of natural law are universal.

## What were **Grotius' influential ideas** about natural law?

Hugo Grotius (in Dutch, Huigh de Groot [1583–1645]) modified natural law from a prescription for the common good to a doctrine restraining what individuals were permitted to do in pursing their own separate goods. That is, he changed Thomas Aquinas' (c. 1225–1274) notion of natural law from a communal idea to an individualistic one. This line of thought was highly influential for the political philosophy developed by both Thomas Hobbes (1588–1679) and John Locke (1632–1704).

According to Grotius in *The Law of War and Peace* (1626), natural law could be used to settle religious disputes, as well as international ones. Grotius thought that natural law could be known by observing human nature. He concluded that humans are both sociable and combative and that every person has rights that limit what others can do. Government is the result of sacrificing some rights so that our lives will improve. Grotius thought that we would be obligated to obey natural law if God did not exist, although he also thought that God does enforce natural law.

Both Hobbes and Locke constructed theories of just and useful government, beginning from foundations of natural law. However, Hobbes emphasized the combative aspects of human nature, whereas Locke emphasized the sociable side.

## THOMAS HOBBES

### Who was **Thomas Hobbes**?

More than any other seventeenth century philosopher, Thomas Hobbes (1588–1679) directly applied the atomism and materialism of the science of his day to metaphysics. Hobbes believed that everything in existence was caused by matter and motion. He was one of René Descartes' (1596–1650) early critics and was considered an atheist by his peers. Hobbes is most famous for his description of the natural condition of mankind as "solitary, poor, nasty, brutish, and short."

### What was **Thomas Hobbes life** like?

Hobbes' father was the vicar of Westport, but he had to leave for London after his involvement in a brawl outside his church. Thomas' uncle, the alderman of Malmesbury, financed his education. Hobbes studied Greek and Latin at Oxford University from 1602 to 1608, and after graduating he took the position of tutor to Lord Cavendish's oldest son, William. (Lord Cavendish, Earl of Devonshire was to become Hobbes' main patron throughout his working career.) With William, he traveled to Europe in 1610, when

Thomas Hobbes applied the atomism and materialism of the science of his day to metaphysics (iStock).

Johannes Kepler first published his system of the elliptical shape of planetary orbits and Galileo Galilei was reporting his observations with telescopes. Hobbes met English statesman, scientist, and philosopher Francis Bacon after he returned to England and agreed with him about the need to discard Aristotelian views of science. However, Hobbes did not subscribe to Bacon's inductive method. Bacon believed that scientific knowledge could be built up from observation. Hobbes, in contrast, was to develop a system of knowledge beginning from the first principles of matter and motion from which the nature of experience could be deduced.

Hobbes then began reading the classics and translated Thucydides' history into English in 1628. By this time, Sir Cavendish had died and his widow dismissed Hobbes to cut expenses. So, Hobbes went back to Europe to work for another noble family as tutor to Sir Clinton's son. He became interested in geometry as a method for conveying a philosophical system; his interest in astronomy was piqued when he met the astronomer, priest, and philosopher Pierre Gassendi (1592–1655), as well as Galileo.

From that exchange, he conceived the idea of applying the principles of the science to the human world, specifically to politics and history. He wrote *Little Treatise* (1637), an explanation of sensation set out in a geometrical form, which was both an attack on Aristotle's theory, and his own original thought. He thought that the cause of all sensation was changes in motion of insensible particles.

In 1650, Hobbes published his *Elements of Law* in two parts: the psychological treatise *Human Nature* and *De Corpore Politico,* which defended unified government. This began a period when Hobbes' life was in danger as politics shifted, because he was suspected of atheism on account of his materialism and was disliked because of his own dislike of Catholics. Overall, his defense of a strong monarchy set Parliament against him. Meanwhile, he was briefly the mathematical tutor to Charles II, before he became king, and he published his magnum opus, *Leviathan* (1651).

Between 1645 and 1663, Hobbes became involved in several protracted and bitter controversies with other thinkers. He disputed the question of free will with John Bramwell, bishop of Derry. Two Oxford dons were angry with him: John Wallis, a professor of geometry, was scathing about Hobbes' attempts to square the circle. (This was the problem dating from antiquity of devising a method for constructing a square with an area equal to the area of any given circle.) Seth Ward, professor of astronomy, was opposed to Hobbes' entire philosophy.

## What stories did Hobbes' contemporaries tell about him?

According to the biography of Hobbes written by his contemporary John Aubrey, when Hobbes was at Oxford, he used to get up early in the morning and venture forth with lead weights, packthreads, and pairings of cheese. He would smear the threads with birdlime (an adhesive substance used to trap birds by sticking their feet to something) and bait them with the cheese. Jackdaws would spy them from far away and strike at the bait. Young Hobbes would then haul in the string and the weights would cling to the birds' wings. (Aubrey does not furnish details about what happened after that.)

After the plague of 1665 and the Great Fire of London in 1666, people sought reasons for God's wrath. Parliament passed a bill to suppress atheism, and a committee was constituted to investigate Hobbes' *Leviathan*. There was a report that Hobbes had been burned in effigy, and Hobbes was afraid that his papers would be searched, so he himself burned part of them. The king, who liked Hobbes, intervened, but from then on Hobbes was not permitted to publish his work. Neither the Roman Catholic church nor Oxford University permitted his books to be read, and they occasionally even burned them.

Hobbes played tennis until he was 75, rewrote his autobiography in Latin verse at the age of 84, and at 86 published translations of the *Iliad* and *Odyssey* in verse.

## What was **Hobbes' solution** to Descartes' **mind-body problem**?

Hobbes could not make sense of René Descartes' (1596–1650) idea of a thinking substance. He first criticized Descartes for confusing the thing that thinks with the action of thinking. And then, concerning the thing that thinks, Hobbes wrote that "a thinking thing is something corporeal. This is because it seems that the subjects of all actions are comprehensible only if they are conceived as corporeal or material." What this amounted to in the history of metaphysics was that Hobbes solved the mind-body problem by denying that there existed a non-material substance of mind, because everything that existed had to be material.

## How did **Hobbes** explain **sensation, memory, imagination, thought, and emotion**?

Hobbes described sensations as effects of movement in the body that are felt through the motions of the heart. Sense always has "some memory adhering to it," because sense organs retain the movements of external bodies acting on them. So long as the organs are moved by one object, they cannot be moved by another. Imagination is

141

Cover of illustration from Thomas Hobbes' book *Leviathan* (Art Archive).

"decaying sense," after the source of sensation is removed, and memory is similar to imagination, except that it also has a feeling of familiarity.

Hobbes believed that thought involved literal movements in the head. His idea of unguided thought led to later theories of the "association of ideas" (that one thought automatically evokes another in the mind). Guided thought is goal-directed. Hobbes thought that while humans and animals both may perform the action that is necessary to reach a goal, only humans have the distinctive trait of prudence. Prudence involves beginning with the action that one can perform and then calculating its consequences as a guide for what to do. Prudence increases with experience.

Concerning the passions, or emotions, which he called "endeavors," Hobbes postulated two types of motion in the body: vital motions, such as breathing, nutrition, and the circulation of the blood; and animal motion, such as voluntary movement. Pleasure is nothing more than motion around the heart. Appetite is an endeavor toward an object associated with pleasure, and aversion is an endeavor away from it.

## What was **Hobbes' belief** about **free will**?

In his *The Questions Concerning Liberty, Necessity and Chance* (1656) Hobbes called his position on free will "necessitarianism." He said there was nothing in the human mind to which the word "will" refers; in other words, there was no will. But there is desire, and what we call "will" is the last desire before we make up our minds to do something. The entire person can be free, however. Human freedom, according to Hobbes, consists in not being prevented from doing what one desires to do. Freedom, in his view, is thus nothing more or less than liberty.

Hobbes also believed that all actions have causes or are "necessitated." But we are responsible legally for what we do because it is just that we be punished for our decision or "will" in the matter. The purpose of such punishment is to deter others from misbehaving and preserve justice.

### What was **Hobbes' theory of government** in *Leviathan*?

Hobbes advocated a strong form of monarchy as a way of re-describing the role of the individual in his own politically volatile society. He began with the idea of a state of nature, which was a condition of life without government. Hobbes' method was to determine the uses and justification for government, from that original condition, together with an understanding of human nature.

According to Hobbes, human beings in their natural condition are each roughly equal in physical strength, because the weakest has the ability to kill the strongest. They are not sociable by nature, but rather exist in a prolonged condition in which each individual is against everyone else—a condition of war. In fact, humans only seek one another out for their own glory, greed, or to gang up and conspire against third parties. Without government and the stable organizations and institutions created and supported by government, life in a state of nature is "solitary, poor, nasty, brutish, and short."

Men do have Right Reason in nature, the first principle of which is to preserve themselves. They are also aware of the Laws of Nature, the first of which is to do whatever is possible to keep the peace. But to keep the peace, there needs to be an enforceable contract between parties, and after one side has performed there is no guarantee that the other will do his or her part. Hobbes wrote that "covenants without the sword, are but words, and of no strength to secure a man at all."

### What was **Hobbes' idea** of the **social contract**?

The social contract was Hobbes' solution to the unpleasantness of life in the state of nature. It was an agreement among citizens to give up their individual powers to harm one another and transfer all of those powers to the sovereign, or Leviathan. In return, the sovereign would keep order, which would enable all the benefits of civilized life, such as a just legal system, education, marriage, security in property, and a flourishing of the arts and sciences.

Hobbes' Leviathan, though, was to have totalitarian powers over his subjects, including the right over their lives, censorship, the right to draft them into military service, and to impose any other necessary burden of government. The only rights retained by subjects were the rights to preserve themselves and resist imprisonment or execution. Laws were literally the commands of the sovereign. Once the sovereign was made the irrevocable gift of power from the people, the only thing that could bring down the government would be its self-abdication or defeat by foreign enemies.

## JOHN LOCKE

### Why was **John Locke important**?

As a philosopher of knowledge, or epistemologist, John Locke (1632–1704) sidestepped the metaphysical problems raised by René Descartes (1596–1650) and offered a theory

John Locke's political views greatly influenced the democratization of the British government and the fundamental ideals of the U.S. Constitution (iStock).

of the mind and its capabilities that grounded modern ideas of education, psychology, and philosophy of science.

Locke's political views about democratic government and individual rights were foundational not only for the modern British parliamentary system, but also for the basic principles of the U.S. Constitution. His idea of natural law persists in practical political theories to this day.

## What happened to **Locke** during his **life** and what were some of his important **publications**?

John Locke was born in Wrington, Somerset, England. His father was an attorney and justice of the peace who fought on the Parliamentary side against Charles I. At Westminster school, which Locke began attending in 1646, he learned the classics, Hebrew, and Arabic. From Westminster, he went to Oxford University, where he disagreed with the scholastic philosophy that was taught. After he achieved his master's degree, he lectured in Latin and Greek, and in 1664 he was given the position of Censor of Moral Philosophy.

When his father died in 1661, Locke inherited enough money to be financially independent. He soon met such famed scientists as Robert Boyle, Isaac Newton, and renowned physician Thomas Sydenham, who inspired Locke to train as a medical doctor. Locke never practiced medicine but was considered knowledgeable in this area all his life.

In 1666, Locke met Lord Ashley, Earl of Shaftesbury. Shaftesbury suffered from an infected cyst on his liver, and Locke oversaw his surgery, including the insertion of a silver tube to drain the wound. The Earl's gratitude after recovery resulted in a long-term patronage. Shaftesbury supported Locke's philosophical endeavors and his nomination to the Royal Society in 1668. Conversations with colleagues Locke met through that connection resulted in the early drafts of his *An Essay Concerning Human Understanding* (1689)

Locke also served Shaftesbury in practical political ways that resulted in some of his most important contributions. He drafted a constitution for British colonial Carolina and was secretary to the Council of Trade and Plantations. Shaftesbury was tried for treason due to his leadership of the Parliamentary opposition to the Stuarts. He was acquitted, but left England for Holland. Locke also left, and while he was in Holland, his position at Oxford was taken away by the king; then James II denounced him as a traitor after the Duke of Monmouth's failed rebellion.

Locke continued to write, working on *An Essay Concerning Human Understanding* (1689) and his *First Letter Concerning Toleration* (1689). He also became involved with the plan to put the Protestants William and Mary on the English throne. Locke advised William, and after the Glorious Rebellion of 1688, he escorted Mary, Princess of Orange, on her ship back to England.

In 1689 and 1690, Locke's two major works *An Essay Concerning Human Understanding* and *Two Treatises of Civil Government* were completed. Always suffering from poor health, Locke then retired from his active involvements in politics. Still, he went on to write *Some Thoughts Concerning Education* (1693) and *The Reasonableness of Christianity,* (1695), followed by *A Vindication of the Reasonableness of Christianity* (1695). This last work sparked a controversy between Locke and Edward Stillingfleet, bishop of Worcester. Locke's denial of evidence for substance was taken by Stillingfleet to be a denial of the Anglican Church's doctrine of the Trinity, as well as a barrier to life after death through the immortality of the soul.

### How and why was **Locke's idea** of the **social contract different** from **Hobbes'**?

Locke held that the social contract was an agreement between citizens or their representatives and the government or king. Because basic amenities of human life and its fundamental social institutions were present before the social contract, government was not as essential in Locke's view, as it had been in Hobbes'. Human society existed and functioned well before government, and if government dissolved or if the governed brought it down for just reasons, society would still exist. However, if something destroyed society, that would also destroy the government.

### How did **Locke use natural law** to construct a **theory of government**?

In the *First Treatise on Government* (1689) Locke argued against English political theorist Robert Filmer, who claimed that kings, in a direct descent from Adam, had divine rights. Locke pointed out that it was impossible to trace such a direct descent with any accuracy, that human beings had female as well as male parents, and that political power was fundamentally different from patriarchal power.

In the *Second Treatise on Government* (1689), he identified natural law as God's laws for man, which included the command that man labor for his living. God had given the earth and everything on it to all mankind. Locke therefore asked how it came to be that there was private property, which was necessary to make use of the fruits of the earth. His answer was that whatever an individual mixes his labor with he

## What did John Locke mean by saying the mind was a *tabula rasa*?

Unlike the rationalists, who thought that we were born with certain ideas about the world, Locke thought that our minds are like a blank slate (*tabula rasa*) at birth. All of our ideas are the result of two different processes that happen after we are born. The first is sensory experience, and the second is our reflection on our sensory experience and on the workings of our own minds. One of his main arguments against innate ideas was that people do not all have the same ideas, but their ideas differ as their experience has differed.

comes to own. (Locke used the term "mixes labor with" for labor, in cases where we today would say "works on.")

Locke went on to claim that, in the state of nature, there were two provisos against accumulation through labor: that there be "as much and as good" left over; and that there be no waste. The first proviso assumed that natural resources would never run out. The second allowed for the store of unused items in precious objects that could be used as money, thereby allowing surplus production to be stored as wealth without the original producer being wasteful. In Locke's state of nature there was industry, cooperation, and trade. Human beings were basically peaceful, except for a few criminals. To assure justice in punishment, government was necessary, but it was merely a convenience added to a generally functional and satisfying situation.

## What was **Locke's solution** to the Cartesian **mind-body problem**?

Locke held that all of our knowledge comes to us from our ideas and that we do not have a clear idea of either material or immaterial substance. It follows from this that if substance exists, we do not know anything about it, apart from its qualities that adhere in it. For example, Locke pointed out that we can sense the hardness, color, and malleability of gold, but that we do not know what it is in gold that gives rise to these qualities.

He addressed unextended or non-material substance under the subject of personal identity, asking what it is that makes someone the same person. Locke was concerned that when a person was punished on Judgment Day, that the person being punished was the same person who had committed the crimes he or she was charged with. His answer was that in the context of divine reward or punishment "on that great day," you are the same person if you have memories of yourself in the past, so that you know it is the same "you" who committed the acts for which you are being judged.

Locke's refusal to posit a form or substance for the soul seemed to contradict the Trinitarian doctrine of three attributes or natures present in one God. Some of his critics, such as British theologian Edward Stillingfleet, accused Locke of denying the possibility of resurrection in the absence of an incorruptible, immaterial soul substance. Locke's reply to Stillingfleet was to reaffirm his belief in the immortality of the soul, as a matter of faith, rather than a fact that could be proved by reason.

Stillingfleet believed that some substantial form of a person's body was necessary for there to be a Resurrection of that person. Locke's response was to make fun of Stillingfleet by interpreting him to claim that the same body literally had to arise from the grave. Locke wrote, "And I think your lordship will not say, that the particles that were separate from the body by perspiration before the point of death were laid up in the grave."

### How were **Locke's ideas** about **substance related** to his **theory of knowledge**?

Locke confined knowledge to sensory information and the workings of the mind, and he had a moderate skepticism about claims beyond those two sources of information. Locke introduced his *Essay Concerning Human Understanding* (1689) as the result of conversations among friends which led to the question of what it was possible for them to know, given the limitations of human faculties: "It was necessary to examine our own abilities, and see what objects our understandings were or were not fitted to deal with." Locke's method was not to rely on tradition or what other philosophers had claimed, but to look to "the things themselves."

Knowledge, according to Locke, was direct awareness of some fact. The only facts we can know are those that consist of relationships among our ideas. A fact is something true about the world. Locke did not think that we had direct experience of the world. Things in the world acted on our sense organs to produce ideas. Therefore, the truths we know (facts) are about the relationships between ideas. Ideas are mental objects for Locke, some of which are representations of things in the world. In Book I of the *Essay,* Locke attacks the rationalist doctrine of innate ideas and innate knowledge. His argument is that we have innate capacities, but nothing like knowledge until there is experience—this is Locke's famous description of the mind as a *tabula rasa,* or blank slate.

In Book II, he explains our different types of ideas by tracing them to sensation and reflection on sensation. Reflection consists of combination, division, generalization, and abstraction. For Locke, our ideas are like impressions from experience. When we consider our ideas in our minds, we can combine different ideas, divide an idea into more ideas, generalize about what ideas in a group share, or abstract some property shared by a group of ideas. In Book III, Locke explains how words can mislead us about facts or "the things themselves." Book IV is a discussion of how we are obligated to conduct our minds in forming beliefs, so as not to stray too far from what we know.

### What was **original** about **Locke's thoughts** concerning **education**?

Locke originally wrote down his ideas in answer to his relative Edward Clarke, who asked how he should raise his son to grow up to be a gentleman. There was broad

The basic tenet of Cambridge Platonism was the obscure religious belief, first stated by the Giovanni Pico della Mirandola (1463–1494), that both Pythagoras and Plato based their philosophy on teachings by Moses that were expressed in the cabala and other facets of the Jewish mystical tradition. Their other beliefs affirmed God's existence, the soul's immortality, and the animation of the natural world by, or with, "spirit." They were convinced both that man had free will and that reason was of primary importance in religious matters. However, they were not empiricists, because they believed in innate ideas and innate principles of morality and religion, which were recognizable through intuition. And furthermore, it needs to be kept in mind that not all of those known as "Cambridge Neoplatonists," shared the same views.

### Who were the **Cambridge Neoplatonists**?

The founder of the group was understood to be Benjamin Whichcote (1609–1683). Whichcote called reason "the candle of the Lord." Henry More (1614–1687), Ralph Cudworth (1617–1688), and John Smith (1616–1652) were three further distinguished Cambridge Platonists. (Cudworth was the father of John Locke's lifelong friend and lady of the household in which he spent his last years, Damaris Cudworth.) Additional Cambridge Platonists of note were: Nathaniel Culverwell (1619–1651), Peter Sterry (1613–1672), George Rust (d. 1670), John Worthington (1618–1671), and Simon Patrick (1626–1707). Whichcote, More, Cudworth, and Smith were associated with Emmanuel College. Calvinism was the leading doctrine there and they all rebelled against it. Henry More was the most intellectually active member of the group.

Henry More asserted that animals, not just people, had souls (iStock).

### Who was **Henry More**?

Henry More (1614–1687) was the great-grandson of the martyred English chancellor, Sir Thomas More. Henry enrolled in Christ College, Cambridge, at the age of 17, and remained there his entire life. He became a fellow in 1641. His distinctive mission was to eradicate, or "cure," atheism and enthusiasm, which he called "two enormous distempers of the mind." He sought to convert philosophers to the Christian faith, as he understood it, and his interests included Neoplatonism, reports of witches and ghosts, science, and René Descartes' (1596–1650) philosophy.

He differed with Descartes, however, in insisting that animals have souls. He attacked Thomas Hobbes (1588–1679) and Benedict de Spinoza (1632–1677) for their presumed "atheism." He was a tutor to Cambridge Platonist Anne Conway (1630–1679) and deplored her enthusiastic conversion to Quakerism. He is said to have coined the terms "Cartesianism" and "materialist." Henry More's writings included a history of the English Jesuits, translations, and his *Life and Doctrines of our Saviour Jesus Christ* (1660).

### Who was **Anne Conway**?

Anne Conway (1630–1679) was best known in philosophy for her *The Principles of the Most Ancient and Modern Philosophy* (1690). This work was meant to overthrow both René Descartes' (1596–1650) dualism and that of Henry More (1614–1687). She posited an infinite number of ordered monads—each one of which was a "congealed spirit"—as the ultimate components of reality. She was influenced by Flemish alchemist Franciscus Mercurius van Helmont, who showed her work to Gottfried Leibniz (1646–1716). Leibniz himself acknowledged her influence, and some think he got the term "monad" from her.

### What did Anne **Conway's physical pain** have to do with **her philosophy** and **religion**?

Anne was born December 14, 1630, a week after her father, Sir Heneage Finch, who was speaker of the House of Commons, died. Having learned Latin, Greek, and Hebrew at home, she began a correspondence with Henry More (1614–1687), who had been her brother's tutor at Christ College. More held her in very high intellectual esteem, and their correspondence continued after she married Edward Conway, at the age of 20. More wrote of her that he had "scarce ever met with any Person, Man or Woman, of better Natural parts than Lady Conway."

One of her motivations for studying philosophy and possibly converting to Quakerism was her need to reconcile the existence of a good, all-powerful God with pain and suffering in the world. Anne herself was afflicted with extraordinarily severe headaches all her life. At one point, she had her jugular arteries "bled" in search of relief.

# GENDER AND EARLY MODERN WOMEN PHILOSOPHERS

### Why is **gender** an **important topic** in studies of early modern philosophy?

Social and family life, generally, and ideas about the sexes were so different in the seventeenth century compared to our own that they should not be overlooked as an

## Why were the great seventeenth century philosophers and scientists bachelors?

They were either relatively poor (Descartes, Spinoza, Locke), or prohibited from marrying because they were priests (Fathers Marin Mersenne [1588–1648] and Pierre Gassendi [1592–1655]), or it was a tradition for men of learning not to have their own families. For example, Oxford dons were not allowed to marry at that time and the seven fellows of Gresham College (founded in 1558) were all bachelors. Another reason might have been the prevailing beliefs about the nature of women. Women were not allowed to be scholars, and wives and family life was not only considered a distraction for men of learning, but sexual relations were believed to be intellectually weakening for scholars.

important background to the beginnings of modern philosophy. Interestingly, all the well-known seventeenth century philosophers—Descartes, Spinoza, Leibniz, Hobbes, and Locke—were bachelors their entire lives, as were the great majority of their colleagues in philosophy and the sciences.

### Why was the **single status** of early modern **men of science** and philosophy **important**?

Inevitably, bachelorhood would have had the negative effect of not having long-term intimate relationships or much experience with children and family life in adulthood. A bachelor's style of life would have then supported a view of the world from the perspective of a lone individual, and an assumption that the philosophical mind would always have the same gender as oneself.

### Would **marriage** have changed the **emotional lives** of seventeenth century **philosophers**?

The answer is not clear. In the seventeenth century, primogeniture, or leaving the entire inheritance of a father to his oldest son, was the norm. About one-quarter of younger sons in the middle classes did not marry because they could not afford to set up households or find brides with substantial dowries. Child mortality was between 30 and 50 percent of all live births, and after 20 years of marriage it was highly unlikely that both spouses would still be alive.

These statistics rendered family relationships more dependent on roles than on individual emotional attachments based on distinct personalities. (During the early modern period, people did not marry for what we consider to be romantic reasons.)

None of this is to say that there were not strong lifelong friendships between men and women. Philosophers such as René Descartes, John Locke, and Gottfried Leibniz had long-term female correspondents, but it is doubtful that they knew what we would call "love."

## What were the general **ideas about women** that were held by people in the **seventeenth century**?

The old Aristotelian idea that females were imperfect males was still assumed to be true in seventeenth-century Europe. The modern science of biology, which established two distinct sexes, was still in the future. Although eighteenth and nineteenth century sexual distinctions based on biology supported the idea that the capabilities of women were inherently limited and inferior to those of men, they at least focused on the distinctness of male and female identities.

The Aristotelian view has been called the "one sex theory." Many serious and well-regarded theorists of the human body solemnly insisted that the female reproductive system was no more than an inverted form of the male one. Like Aristotle, they believed that women were naturally colder and damper than men, besides being in every respect weaker. Moreover, women were considered to be the sex-desiring, aggressive gender, whereas men were often viewed as helpless and vulnerable in sexual matters.

Medical opinion concurred that blood, semen, and spinal fluid were all the same basic vital substance or fluid, albeit in different forms. Sexual intercourse was not only often viewed as a weakening form of physical dissipation, but male ejaculation was believed to draw brain tissue down the spine and out the penis—a very strong reason for a male philosopher to remain celibate. Moreover, women were viewed as the source of venereal disease, unwanted children, and burdensome financial obligations. So great was their negative sexual power held to be that they were at the same time also presumed responsible for male impotence.

## Did **women object** to this **negative view** of them in the seventeenth century?

It is difficult to see how they had much opportunity to object. Before and after Oliver Cromwell's rise to power in England, pubic entertainment and behavior were often "bawdy." By the time King William III ascended the throne in 1688, Puritanism dominated public morals, especially among the middle class. For some women, such as the successful playwright Alphra Behn, this was not good news. She wrote: "Though I the wondrous change deplore / That makes me useful and forlorn."

But even during the "wild times" of the Tory Restoration, when sexuality was freely discussed and written about, and sexual relationships and desires were acknowledged as natural and tolerated in respectable society, Behn's explicit poetry and plays had rarely gone beyond the conventional wisdom that women were the dangerous sex.     153

In her poem "The Disappointment" she relates Lysander's impotence when he is in the presence of the extremely desirable Cloris. Cloris flees, blushing with "distain and shame," and Lysander curses, "The sheppardess' charms / Whose soft betwitching influence / Had damned him to the hell of impotence."

## What was **Mary Astell's contribution** to early modern philosophy?

Mary Astell (1666–1731) used Descartes' ideas to criticize custom, insisting that tradition itself is not a sufficient justification for the subordinate position of married women. She wrote: "That the Custom of the World, has put Women, generally speaking, into a State of Subjection, is not denied, but the Right can no more be prov'd from the Fact, than the Predominancy of Vice can justify it." This willingness to criticize custom in the service of an unpopular claim was an important intellectual innovation.

Astell was interested in the use of reason as an innate capacity of women. She argued that women could find their own religious salvation, intellectually as well as morally. The target of her argument was the prevailing practice of not offering women the same education as men. In her *A Serious Proposal to the Ladies* (1694) she proposed a college for upper-class women that would prepare them for intellectual activities and religious services. Her claim was that the faults attributed to women could be corrected through education.

## How did **Mary Astell's life** affect her written work?

Astell was unmarried and spent much of her adult life in a community of women with similar backgrounds in London. She is famous for having said, "The whole World is a single Lady's family." But she never openly condemned the subordination of women in marriage because she herself believed in charitable service and the unselfish roles of women in family life. Her main objection to the nature of marriage at her time was that men chose wives mainly for material gain or temporary sexual passion; she wanted husbands and wives to have a bond of friendship.

## What was distinctive about **Elizabeth Elstob**?

Elizabeth Elstob (c. 1683–c. 1756) was the first professional scholar to compile an Anglo-Saxon grammar. In her introduction to *An English-Saxon Homily on the Birthday of St. Gregory* (1709) she argued for the usefulness of educating women on the grounds that scholarly work itself was valuable.

## What was *An Essay in Defense of the Female Sex*?

In *An Essay in Defense of the Female Sex: The "Usurpation of Man; and the Tyranny of Custom (Here in England, Especially)"* (1696) marriage was directly attacked. John Locke's (1632–1704) empiricist epistemology was put to use in a search for social causes of the inequality between the sexes. The writer did not argue that women were as good as men, claiming that they were actually better on account of their intellectual superiority, which resulted from differences in nature. The female (or male?) author announced that men had conspired to keep women subordinate to them by denying them education and imprisoning them in domestic labors. However, she (or he?) concluded that what women did domestically was more important than anything and everything accomplished by men!

# THE ENLIGHTENMENT PERIOD

### What was **Enlightenment philosophy**?

Enlightenment philosophy was written during the time associated with the Enlightenment, which occurred roughly around the eighteenth century. The Enlightenment was an historical period in which the ideas of philosophers played dominant cultural roles, in contrast to the importance of religion during the medieval period, or the importance of science and technology in the nineteenth and twentieth centuries.

### **What** was the **Enlightenment**?

The Enlightenment was known to its contemporaries and future generations as The Age of Reason. The Enlightenment went beyond intellectual activity to affect painting, literature, architecture, religion, the sciences, and, of course, politics, culminating in the American Revolution (1775–1783) and the French Revolution (1789–1799). While there were common Enlightenment intellectual themes, conditions in different nations produced distinctive types of thought. Also, there was a marked development of ideas from the first half of the 1700s to the second half, principally because of the major social and political changes preceding and accompanying the American and French Revolutions.

### What were the **common themes** of the **Enlightenment**?

The common themes were a set of values that included the following:

1. Imbuing all other values was the importance of reason and its uses to discover ideal forms of human nature and society.

2. The belief in the natural goodness of man, which was to be rediscovered by the reform of corrupt institutions.

3. An overall secularity and downplaying of traditional Christian transcendence.

4. A new aesthetic and ethics based on the goodness of nature.

5. Perhaps most important, a great faith in progress or the belief that the present is better than the past and that the future will be better than the present.

Nevertheless, none of the paramount Enlightenment thinkers simply played out these themes in direct ways. They almost all used reason or rational thought—together with a fair amount of wit—to propound and develop their ideas. The ideas themselves, though, sometimes had unforeseen consequences. That is, often the Enlightenment geniuses went too far, or were not able to fully think things through. As a result, skepticism, pessimism, and romantic madness took over when the ideas of progress and the ideals of human reason ran out.

## What was **meant by "reason"** during the Enlightenment?

Reason was considered a universal capacity of all people that was brought to fruition by logic and the knowledge of science. It required people to abandon superstition and oppressive institutions, such as absolute monarchy and doctrinaire religion.

## Is there a **sharp distinction** between **Enlightenment philosophers** and **other intellectuals**?

No, both Enlightenment philosophers and other intellectuals influenced the ideas of the time. Among philosophers, those who have endured historically as part of the present philosophical canon are limited to George Berkeley, David Hume, Thomas Reid, Jeremy Bentham, Jean-Jacques Rousseau, Immanuel Kant, and Giambattista Vico. (John Locke is also strongly associated with the Enlightenment, although he dates back to the seventeenth century). However, during their times, brilliant thought in other fields by writers and personalities such as Ethan Allen, Marquis de Condorcet, Denis Diderot, Jonathan Edwards, Benjamin Franklin, Baron d'Holbach, Thomas Jefferson, Joseph-Marie de Maistre, Charles Baron du Montesquieu, Thomas Paine, Joseph Priestly, Adam Smith, Mary Wollstonecraft, William Godwin, and Voltaire (François Marie Arouet) were part of the intellectual climate for philosophers, as well.

## Were all **eighteenth-century thinkers** in **agreement** with **Enlightenment themes**?

No. As a counter-tradition to the general rational spirit of the Enlightenment were the Romantics, such as the writers Samuel Taylor Coleridge, Johann Wolfgang von Goethe, Johann Gottfried Herder, Gotthold Ephraim Lessing, Friedrich Schiller, and William Wordsworth. There were also those, generally referred to as the "pessimists" of the

Enlightenment, who did not subscribe to the belief in progress characteristic of the age. For example, in philosophy, Giambattista Vico, Edmund Burke, and Joseph-Marie de Maistre; and in letters, William Cowper, Choderlos de Laxlos, the Marquis de Sade, and Jonathan Swift.

## GEORGE BERKELEY

### Who was **George Berkeley**?

George Berkeley (1685–1753) was the founder of modern idealism. Unlike his seventeenth century idealist predecessors, such as Nicolas Malebranche (1638–1715) or Gottfried Leibniz (1647–1716), he was

More often remembered as a German Romantic poet and playwright, Friedrich Schiller was also a philosopher; he wrote on ethics and aesthetics (Art Archive).

not a rationalist. Berkeley was completely comfortable with science and empiricism in general, and he significantly weighs in with the great triumvirate of British empiricists: John Locke (1632–1704), George Berkeley (1685–1783), and David Hume (1711–1776).

Berkeley was born in County Kilkenny in Ireland, where he went to Kilkenny College for four years, beginning at age 11. He then went to Trinity College in Dublin and was elected a fellow there in 1707, holding the position until 1724. His first book, *An Essay Towards a New Theory of Vision,* was published in 1709, followed by the *Treatise Concerning the Principles of Human Knowledge* in 1710. In 1713, he moved to London and published *Three Dialogues between Hylas and Philonas,* the first of his works to be well received. He was presented to Queen Anne by the renowned essayist and satirist Jonathan Swift (1667–1745) and became friends with the literary elite of that time.

In 1713, Berkeley traveled to Sicily as chaplain to the ambassador. His next position was as a tutor to St. George Ashe (the bishop of Derry), which involved further travel in Europe. He then wrote *De Motu* (*On Motion*) in 1721, as well as *An Essay towards Preventing the Ruin of Great Britain,* in which he argued that a recent financial crisis (the South Sea Island Bubble, which was a stock market crash that resulted from over-speculation) was the result of a decline in religion and morals. In 1723 he received a windfall inheritance from Esther Vanhomrigh, an Irish woman of Dutch descent who was a long-time correspondent and lover of Jonathan Swift, who called her "Vanessa" in his poetry. (Berkeley claimed that she was "a perfect stranger.")

In 1724 Berkeley was appointed dean of Derry, which provided him financial security, but his dream was to found a Christian college in Bermuda that would admit "Negroes" and Indians, as well as white Americans. He raised money for the project, but not enough

Dysart Castle in Thomasttown, County Kilkenny, Ireland, was the home of George Berkeley. (Art Archive).

for it to become a reality. The British Parliament awarded him 20,000 pounds, but that money never came through.

Berkeley married in 1728 and he and his wife, Anne, went to Rhode Island to set up farms to grow food for the prospective college. They remained there for three years, and then returned to live in London.

He defended Christianity in *The Minute Philosopher* in 1732, and claimed that mathematics was more mysterious than religion in *The Analyst* in 1734. That same year, he became Bishop of Cloyne, which led him to move back to Ireland, where he remained until he died in 1753, while visiting his son at Oxford University.

### What was George **Berkeley's** new **theory of vision**?

Berkeley, like René Descartes (1596–1650), sought to account for the perception of distance. Descartes had claimed in his *Dioptrics* (1647) that an innate knowledge of geometry enables even those who have never studied geometry to calculate distance by figuring out the height of a triangle formed by light rays from the visible object to each eye. Berkeley built on Irish natural philosopher William Molyneux's (1656–1698) claim that distance, as a length from the object to the eye, cannot itself be seen. Berkeley reasoned that since what is seen is a two-dimensional object, its relation to distance is contingent, dependent on sensations in the eyes and associations in the mind between what has been touched and what is seen. These associations depend on past experience.

The overall result of Berkeley's reasoning about how vision works is that visual perception is an active, learned process. He also claimed, against John Locke (1632–1704), that there are no general ideas common to both sight and touch.

### How did George **Berkeley's theory of vision** relate to the concept of **matter** and physical existence?

Berkeley is well known for his theory of vision that contributed so much to modern psychology of perception. However, in that theory he completely repudiated the primary bastion of empiricism: namely, matter. Berkeley departed from both common sense and science in elaborately insisting that matter—the entire physical world—based on our best evidence, simply did not exist in the way that the other empiri-

**Why is George Berkeley considered either an aberration or an obstacle?**

**B**erkeley is an aberration insofar as his ideas defy common sense to the point of being dismissible as simple absurdities. He is an obstacle insofar as he founded a powerful and enduring school of thought that dominated some areas of philosophy in the nineteenth century and evolved into very perplexing progressive movements in the twentieth and, it now seems, twenty-first centuries.

cists—Hobbes, Locke and Hume, and later on, John Stuart Mill and Bertrand Russell—assumed that it did. For any serious student of the history of philosophy, Berkeley is either a delightful aberration or an intractable obstacle because of this position.

### To whom is **Berkeley's idealism perplexing**?

To those who continue to cleave to the reality of the perceived existence of an external world, Berkeley's idealism can be perplexing. It is also a problematic position for many scientists, who must believe in an "objective reality" in order for their work concerning "objective facts" to make sense.

### What did George Berkeley mean when he said, **"To be is to be perceived"**?

In Berkeley's view of what exists in the world, there are only three things: minds, ideas, and God. Angels are also minds, and another way of dividing up the world is into spirits and ideas. Human beings, angels, and God are spirits. Everything else is ideas. Nothing else is known to exist. But, if only spirits and ideas exist, how can there be a world?

Berkeley thought that what we think of as an external world is just one idea added to our ideas of sense. No idea of sense can exist without being perceived by some mind. Berkeley's motto was *esse est percipi,* or, "To be is to be perceived." The idea of an external world is an isolated idea in itself, but no more than an idea. Furthermore, many of the ideas that we think we have, which support the existence of external reality, are no more than special distinct ideas combined with ideas of sense. For example, the ideas "reality" and "physical matter" are just words to which nothing like an external world corresponds. At best, they are merely additional ideas. This doctrine that reality is just another idea, in Berkeley's sense, is what made him the philosophical idealist par excellence.

### Why were **"ideas" important** to **Berkeley**?

An "idea" in this sense is a technical term, meaning some discrete thing in the mind. Berkeley's metaphysics began with the assumption that all we ever know are our ideas,

161

Occasionalism is the theory that nothing in real life ever caused anything else. God determined everything that each thing would do when he created the world. So, when one pool ball hits another and the second moves, the first pool ball does not cause the second to move because the second ball was already programmed to move that way on its own. Occasionalism holds that everything that seems to interact is like two clocks side by side with one a fraction of a second set ahead of the other. When the faster clock's handles move, it only looks like it's causing the slower clock's handles to move.

which are in our minds. (This is one reason why ideas are so important.) We tend to assume that if we have a word for something then we have an idea of it. But sometimes we fool ourselves, and our words are just empty with no ideas behind them. Therefore, we need to make sure that we actually have the ideas we think we have. Just because we are accustomed to using language in certain ways, does not mean that all words that are intelligible to us refer to ideas. If we reflect on abstract, general words, such as "man," "whiteness," "animal," or "matter," it becomes evident that there is nothing in the mind to which these words refer. All of our ideas are about particulars or combinations of particulars. We lack the capacity to create new ideas—only God can do that—although we are able to combine existing ideas in new ways and create copies of existing ideas.

### What are the **two types of ideas** according to George **Berkeley**?

Ideas, according to Berkeley, can only exist in one or another mind that is capable of perceiving them. The two types of ideas known to human beings are ideas of sense, which come into the mind from somewhere outside it, and ideas of the imagination. God, however, who creates all ideas out of nothing, does not have ideas of sense because nothing can affect Him. God has only ideas of imagination.

No idea is capable of doing anything on its own; every idea is passive. Only minds can act or do anything. All ideas must exist in minds. Without minds, there are no ideas.

### Who **influenced** George **Berkeley**?

According to Berkeley, our ideas of sense are real ideas so long as we perceive them. And in our perception of them, we are doing no more than in some way participating in what God has created. In that way, Berkeley's notion of the world is an expansion of the doctrine of occasionalism, propounded by Nicolas Malebranche (1638–1715) in the seventeenth century, and brought to an epiphany by Gottfried Leibniz (1646–1716) through his notion of "pre-established harmony." According to that doctrine and Berkeley's embellishment of it, God does all the real work, from which we, because we have been created by Him along with the rest of His creation, benefit.

Berkeley thus extended the presence of God in human cognition as something like a force constituting reality itself. Nonetheless, he endures as an empiricist due to his emphasis on sense data as a component of knowledge—never mind that for Berkeley, sense data were not signs or indications of what philosophers and the vast majority of non-philosophers call an "external world," or "reality." For Berkeley, sense data were neither real objects in themselves, nor signs of an external world, but ideas, created by God and placed in us. Period.

### What did George **Berkeley think** of **matter, extension**, and other mainstays secured by René **Descartes** and refined by John **Locke**?

According to Berkeley, matter and extension (the main property of matter that was supposed to be its occupation of space) were abstract, general ideas, which is to say that the words naming or describing them did not refer to real ideas. Since only ideas, minds, and God exist, matter and extension did not exist for Berkeley—there was nothing real corresponding to them. Berkeley applied the same criticism to our presumptive ideas of causation and the distinction between primary and secondary qualities. He looked for the ideas of sense or imagination to back them up, and found none.

In the case of causation, Berkeley was basically an occasionalist.

### How was George **Berkeley's occasionalism distinctive**?

Most occasionalists thought that the real causal connections between things took place in God's mind. Berkeley did not hold that view. According to Berkeley, we have ideas of sensory phenomena that are regularly followed by other specific ideas of sensory phenomena. But the idea of a causal link between them is an illusion.

### What did George **Berkeley** think of the **distinction between primary** and **secondary qualities**?

Seventeenth century empirical philosophers believed that secondary qualities are what we perceive—namely colors, sounds, textures, and smells. They thought that primary qualities like mass and number were the qualities of atoms that made up objects. We can't perceive primary qualities, but the seventeenth century empiricists held that it is the interaction between the primary qualities of atoms that cause our perception of secondary qualities. For example, the atoms in red paint interact with our eyes, through light, to cause the experience of red. But Berkeley denied that there was a distinction between primary and secondary qualities because it is impossible to have an idea of a primary quality such as mass, extension, size, or number without also having an idea of its color, texture, or other secondary qualities.

163

## Why did George Berkeley like tar water so much?

Some biographers claim that George Berkeley suffered the constant discomforts of constipation over his entire life, until finally, in late middle age, he found lasting relief in tar water, which is an extract of tree bark. The following appears in *A Century of Anecdotes from 1760–1860,* by John Timbs.

"Bishop Berkeley having received benefit from the use of Tar-Water, when ill of the colic, published a work *On the Virtues of Tar-Water";* and a few months before his death, a sequel, entitled *"Further Thoughts on Tar-Water";* and when accused of fancying he had discovered a nostrum in Tar-Water, he replied, that, "to speak out, he freely owns he suspects Tar-Water is a panacea."

Sir Hugh Seymour Walpole preserved the following epigram on Berkeley's remedy: "Who dare deride what pious Cloyne has done? The Church shall rise and vindicate her son; She tells us all her bishops shepherds are, and shepherds heal their rotten sheep with tar."

## What was Berkeley's answer to whether a **tree falling** in the **forest makes a sound**?

Berkeley said that objects we sense only exist insofar as we have ideas of their sensory qualities. When we do not perceive those qualities, such as the sound of a tree falling in a forest, then they do not exist as our ideas. However, this would not entitle us to conclude that such a tree makes no sound. Our ideas of sensory qualities come to us from God, who has created them. If a tree falls in the forest and God creates the sound of its crashing down, then that idea in God's mind would guarantee the occurrence of the sound, even though human beings could not perceive it. The same reasoning was applied by Berkeley to the continued existence of a room when no people are inside it. It would still exist as a series of ideas in God's mind.

## What was **Berkeley's critique** of **Newtonian science**?

Berkeley did not think that we can have an idea of absolute motion, apart from particular things that move, or of absolute space, apart from specific distances. He thought that Newton's hypothesis of force and action at a distance might be useful for mathematical calculations, but that there were no grounds to posit it as a real entity.

# DAVID HUME

## Who was **David Hume**?

David Hume (1711–1776) was the first philosopher in the Western tradition to construct a system of thought that had no intellectual reliance on God. His atheism was not merely a matter of personal belief, but was based on an application of skepticism to claims that the existence of God could be known by reason. Hume extended that skepticism to the nature of knowledge about the world, as well, and showed how limited our knowledge of both cause and effect, and the future, really is. He was the first, thoroughly modern, naturalistic philosopher.

## What are some details of David **Hume's life** and **career**?

Hume was born in Edinburgh in 1711. His father was a distant relative of the Earl of Home, and his mother's close relatives were lawyers. David was expected to study law, but he didn't like it and left Edinburgh University when he was 15 to read and think about philosophy. He subjected himself to years of intense study, and in 1734 was under a doctor's care for ailments of body and spirit. This was followed by a philosophical breakthrough, as well as work for a merchant in Bristol. He then spent three years at La Fléche, René Descartes' (1596–1650) old school. Hume anonymously published *A Treatise of Human Nature* in 1739. This work was ignored by other intellectuals, and Hume himself later described it as having fallen "stillborn from the press."

In hopes of greater recognition (Hume was consumed by what he called "love of literary fame") he composed *An Abstract of a Treatise of Human Nature,* which was anonymously published in 1740. His next major philosophical work was *Philosophical Essays concerning the Human Understanding* (1748), which was retitled *An Enquiry Concerning the Human Understanding* (1758). Then came *An Enquiry Concerning the Principles of Morals* (1751). The *Enquiry* was more explicitly anti-religious than the *Treatise*. His *Dialogues Concerning Natural Religion* was probably written during the 1750s, although published posthumously.

With his philosophical research complete, Hume applied himself to history (his *History of Great Britain* won him great fame and acclaim), economics, ethics, and political philosophy. However, he also tried, although without success,

David Hume, depicted in this 1854 engraving, sought to create a science of the mind (iStock).

165

to secure the position of chair of philosophy at the universities of Edinburgh and Glasgow. He was appointed secretary to General St. Clair for three years in 1746, which led him to Brittany and Turin; and he was in charge of the Advocates Library in Edinburgh for five years, beginning in 1752. He was then private secretary to the British ambassador in Paris and undersecretary of state.

## What was David **Hume's great ambition** in philosophy?

Hume sought to create a science of the mind, using empiricist methods in the same way that Isaac Newton (1642–1727) had created a science of the physical world.

## How did **Hume** proceed **philosophically** to create his **science of the mind**?

Hume formulated and applied, over a large range of subjects, two main principles. First, all of our knowledge is the result of either sense impressions or reflections on the workings of our own mind. Second, no matter of fact can be proved *a priori,* or before experience. As Hume put it: "All the perceptions of the human mind resolve themselves into two distinct kinds, which I shall call impressions and ideas."

He held that the sciences of the natural world and beliefs about human society are the result of empirical investigation. The truths of mathematics and logic are known without investigating the world. For this reason, they are not about the world, but about the workings of human minds. Our sensory information, which gives us immediate factual knowledge, is more compelling than our ideas. As Hume stated: "The most lively thought is still inferior to the dullest sensation."

Hume had no use for past philosophical projects that contained *a priori* speculation about the workings of this world or the next. Here is how he summed up this doctrine:

> If we take into our hand any volume; of divinity or school metaphysics, for instance; let us ask, Does it contain any abstract reasoning concerning quantity or number? No. Does it contain any experimental reasoning concerning matter of fact and existence? No. Consign it then to the flames: For it can contain nothing but sophistry and illusion.

## What was **disturbing** about David **Hume's analysis** of **causation**?

Hume attacked the scientific and common sense idea that there was a necessary connection between cause and effect. He argued that no matter how closely we observe one billiard ball striking another, there is nothing in the action of the first ball that makes the response of the second inevitable. Only through experience do we learn relationships of cause and effect. To say that an event of type A causes an event of type B is to say no more than that, in the past, events of type A have always been followed by events of type B. This is Hume's *constant conjunction theory of causation.* The mind relates causes to effects, and vice versa, based on past experience alone, which

> ## What did Hume have to say about the self?
>
> **H**ume famously denied any evidence for the existence of a self as a substance or soul. He wrote: "For my part, when I enter most intimately into what I call myself, I always stumble on some particular perception or other, of heat or cold, light or shade, love or hatred, pain or pleasure. I never can catch myself at any time without a perception, and never can observe any thing but the perception." He went on to explain that what a person calls his or her "self" is no more than a bundle or bundles of perceptions, no one of which is a direct idea of a self-thing.

produces an association of the ideas of causes and effects with each other. For example, the idea of bread is associated with the idea of nourishment.

## What was Hume's **problem of induction**?

Hume introduced an enormous problem with how we reason from past or present to the future that still plagues philosophers of science and epistemologists today. He pointed out that no matter how comprehensive our past experience, it is never a logical contradiction to deny that the same thing which happened in the past will happen in the future. Take the idea that the Sun will rise tomorrow. Although we have always known it to rise every day, it is not a contradiction to say it won't rise tomorrow. If one objects that past experience gives us regularities between events like those that occur today and the Sun rising thereafter, Hume's response would be that we do not know that those regularities will occur in the future. To take another example, oxygen, friction, and combustible material have always resulted in fire, but maybe in the future that very combination will not be followed by fire.

Hume's problem of induction goes beyond saying that we never know enough to predict the future. His claim is that even when we do know enough to predict the future, where that knowledge has been proven in past experience, we do not know that the patterns of our experience in the future will resemble the patterns of the past. Of course, he did not disregard probability or prudence. His attack was on the notion that we can be certain about the future.

## What is the big **problem** with Hume's **reduction** of **the self** to **perceptions**?

Overall, Hume saw the mind as a kind of theater stage, across which ideas pass, with each idea a separate "existence" of sense or logical relation. He did not address the implied question of whom the audience is that has access to this theater. What he was looking for and failed to find was an object of reflection that could in a unitary, distinct way, justify the term "self." He was not looking for the "reflecter," or the "I" in search of its "self." He simply assumed that this reflecter was not the self he was looking for when one enters "most intimately into what I call myself." Another way of putting this is that Hume's analysis of the self cannot account for that process of analysis (of reflecting on one's own ideas). Hume did not take into account the fact that he was reflecting, and that the thing he was that was reflecting is what is meant by the word "self."

## What was new in **Hume's views** on **religion**?

In his *Dialogues Concerning Natural Religion* (c. 1750s), Hume argued against both a priori and empirical proofs for the existence of God. This was an attack on rational grounds for religious belief. His argument against a priori arguments or the ontological argument used by René Descartes (1596–1650) was to claim that nothing that exists can exist necessarily. That is, it is not a logical contradiction to assert the non-existence of anything, including God.

His empirical arguments were mainly directed against the cosmological argument and the argument from design. Against the cosmological argument that held the world must have had a maker, Hume claimed that we do not have enough knowledge about the origins of worlds to justify a hypothesis about how this one came about. The "argument from design" held that just as things such as houses and watches must have builders, the world, insofar as it works well within itself, must have a designer. Hume's response was that we have no grounds to reason from what is true of any one thing within the world to the entire world itself. If Hume's arguments hold, then the only grounds left for religious belief are those of pure faith.

## What was **unusual** about **Hume's theory** of the **emotions**?

Although Hume exalted reason over faith when it came to knowledge, when it came to human psychology he believed that we are primarily motivated by our emotions or "passions" and that reason is always in the service of these emotions. That is, unlike Benedict de Spinoza (1632–1677), he did not have a cognitive theory of the emotions, according to which what we feel is the result of what we believe. Hume wrote: "Reason is, and ought only to be, the slave of the passions."

### Did **Hume believe** that we have **free will**?

Yes, Hume believed in free will, but in a strange way. He argued that our freedom is based on the fact that we are determined by our existing character. If there were no causal link between our motives and our actions, then there would be no moral basis for praise and blame. That is, we do not praise or blame others for what they do accidentally or as "flukes." For Hume, freedom therefore consists in the liberty to do what we want, or a lack of constraint. Our spontaneity is not the same as indifference, or the lack of a cause for doing one thing or the other. He wrote: "By liberty, then, we can mean a power of acting or not acting, according to the determinations of the will.... Now this hypothetical liberty is universally allowed to belong to every one who is not a prisoner and in chains."

### How was **Hume** a man of **contradictions**?

Hume is famous for having written, "Be a philosopher, but amidst all your philosophy, be still a man." Hume described himself as "a man of mild dispositions, of command of temper, of an open, social, and cheerful humour, capable of attachment, but little susceptible of enmity, and of great moderation in all my passions." During his last painful illness with cancer, when his friend Adam Smith (1723–1790) visited him, he was calm and had no regrets about his atheism, nor did he desire to make a religious conversion in case there was an afterlife. He did in fact have a lifelong reputation of being pleasant and highly reasonable. He was known as the "the Good David," in England and "le bon Davide" in France.

But, concerning his moderation, Hume very much enjoyed fine food and drink and weighted over 300 pounds. And as for his mildness, his "friendship" with Jean-Jacques Rousseau (1712–1778) suggests otherwise. When Rousseau was given refuge in England, partly due to Hume's efforts, in 1766, Hume soon came to regret it. Although le bon Davide had enjoyed great fame in the salons of Paris, Rousseau was a world celebrity of greater wattage. Rousseau was also financially pressed and very sensitive to public opinion. He wore exotic costumes and was made fun of in staid English society. Hume did nothing to temper this reaction. Rousseau soon became distrustful of Hume's friendship and accused him of perfidy. Instead of letting the matter rest, Hume published their correspondence, going against the advice of his close friends, who were prepared to make allowances for Rousseau, because they knew how personally troubled he was. This publication, together with Hume's denial that he had himself "leaked" the letters, destroyed his friendship with Rousseau and incurred skepticism about his own good will, good sense, and underlying motives.

# JEAN-JACQUES ROUSSEAU

## Who was Rousseau?

Jean-Jacques Rousseau (1712–1778) was an original political philosopher who may have contributed more than any other single person to the motivations for the French Revolution. He was, in addition, a highly creative novelist capable of gathering a reading public into a community that lived vicariously through his characters, some locking themselves up for days to sentimentally enjoy his latest novel. For these reasons, Rousseau may have been the first modern celebrity-philosopher.

## What was Rousseau's life like?

Rousseau's life seemed to spin out of control from time to time, although he found a degree of stability, intellectually, in his writing. He was born in Geneva, Switzerland, in 1712 and always considered himself a citizen of that canton (city-state). His mother died nine days after his birth. His father, an unsuccessful watchmaker, and his aunt raised him. His father was an emotional man, often reading sentimental novels and Plutarch.

As a boy, he was subjected to abuse outside the family. In his *Confessions*, Rousseau described the erotic effect of corporal punishment from a pastor's sister. Later, a notary and an engraver, to whom he was apprenticed, abused him. Rousseau left Geneva at the age of 16, and soon met Françoise-Louise de Warens, a Catholic noblewoman who became his lover and motivated him to convert to Catholicism.

In 1742, he went to Paris to present a new system of musical notation to the Académie des Sciences, but his system was rejected. He then became secretary to the French ambassador in Venice, Italy, in 1743, but left within a year after quarrelling with him. Back in Paris, he began a lifelong relationship with a seamstress named Thérèse Levasseur. He met Denis Diderot (1713–1784) and began contributing articles on music to his encyclopedia. He then submitted an essay for a competition at the Academy of Dijon in answer to the question of whether the arts and sciences had benefited mankind. Rousseau's resounding negative answer was *Discourse on the Arts and Sciences* (1750). It won and made him famous. His opera *Le Devin du Village* was much appreciated by King Louis XV, but Rousseau did not get a pension from him because he immediately supported Italian over French music.

Rousseau then returned to Geneva and converted back to Calvinism. He wrote *The Discourse on Inequality* in 1755, which caused an alienation from Diderot and other patrons, because it claimed that most human inequalities were the result of society, not nature; Rousseau believed man was born good. But he secured the support of the very rich Duke de Luxembourg. His romantic novel *Julie; ou la nouvelle Héloise* was a big success and was followed by *Of the Social Contract* (1762; also known as *Principles of*

*Political Right*), and *Émile; or, On Education* (1762). All of these writings were critical of established religion and therefore banned in both France and the canton or city-state of Geneva. Rousseau fled arrest in 1762 (brought on by the uproar about his political ideas), and after some disorganized travels, finally, in 1765, prevailed on the hospitality of the very English David Hume (1711–1776). The latter situation did not work out, however.

Rousseau reentered France in 1770 under the assumed name "Renou," and went to Paris. He had begun work on the *Confessions,* in England, but the completed edition was not published until after his death. He wrote *Considerations on the Government of Poland* after an invitation to make recommendations for a constitution for the Polish-Lithuanian Commonwealth. This was followed by his *Dialouges: Rousseau* (1776, published in 1782), *Confessions of Jean-Jacques*

Jean-Jacques Rousseau argued for the natural goodness of mankind (iStock).

*Rousseau* (1782), and *Reveries of the Solitary Walker* (1782). He then wrote an analysis of Gluck's opera *Alceste,* before dying suddenly in 1778.

## What were **Rousseau's** most influential **ideas**?

Rousseau proclaimed and argued for the natural goodness of man. It was society and custom that created human vice and evils in the world, he felt. For example, in the natural state, primitive man had a form of wholesome self-love, or "amour de soi," which in society became "amour proper," or pride and vanity about how he was regarded by others. In the natural condition, "Man is born free," but in society, the institution of private property, which Rousseau considered a form of theft, as well as other corrupt institutions, resulted in man being "everywhere in chains." Rousseau posited a natural sympathy in human relations, which had been corrupted by greed, and a simple piety, which was distorted by organized religion.

This vision of the goodness of man was set forth in *Discourse on the Arts and Sciences* (1750) and in his novels. In *Of the Social Contract, Principles of Political Right* (1762), Rousseau addressed the same questions treated by Thomas Hobbes (1588–1679) and John Locke (1632–1704) of how, given original freedom, a good government can be imagined to come about, and what such a government would be like.

## Was Rousseau a hypocrite?

**B**ased on his assumption that children were naturally good and that the purpose of education was to nurture this goodness, Jean-Jacques Rousseau (1712–1778) became the leading educational theorist of his age. His *Émile; or, On Education.* is a loving account of the development of a young boy under the guidance of Rousseau. The boy is raised in the countryside, where there are less corrupting influences and his mind is not taxed until he is 12. This is a progressive education set up to draw out the nature of the child: "Nature wants children to be children before being men.... Childhood has its own ways of seeing, thinking, and feeling." Émile then learns a skill (carpentry), and at 16 he is introduced to Sophie, who has been selected as his mate. Sophie has been educated to be "governed," whereas Émile is taught the principles of self-government.

Rousseau himself is said to have had five children by Thérèse Levasseur, and each one was brought to an orphanage at birth. Those individuals who already hated Rousseau, such as Voltaire (1694–1778), pointed out that most children in orphanages at that time perished. Rousseau's only defense was that he did not think he would have been a good father.

When a friend of Rousseau's noted that the course of education described in *Émile* was not practical, Rousseau wrote back: "You say quite correctly that it is impossible to produce an Émile. But I cannot believe that you take the book that carries this name for a true treatise on education. It is rather a philosophical work on this principle advanced by the author in other writings that man is naturally good."

If Rousseau did not take himself seriously as an educational theorist, then his own behavior as a parent would not have meant that he was a hypocrite on that score. The question, however, remains whether this behavior qualifies him as "naturally good," so the question of hypocrisy does not go away that easily.

Rousseau postulated that individual rights are given up to the community in the founding contract. In return, the individual becomes a citizen whose rights are protected. But this is an active model of citizenship because the individual is required to agree to the general will at the same time that he or she acts in self-interest.

### Did **Rousseau** support a **free society**?

Not exactly. Like Thomas Hobbes (1588–1679), he held that structure and government authority are necessary to safeguard individual freedoms. Once they have entered into the social contract, citizens retain sovereignty, but the general will, or what is good for the community, is enacted by legislators into laws. This general will, or communal good, may at times be opposed to what is simply good for the majority. Rousseau's proposal for the ideal society was thus focused on the end or goal of that society. He thought that direct democracy was usually the best means for achieving that end in small societies, but in larger societies representative democracy, or even monarchy, would be more appropriate. Rousseau also advocated some form of state religion that would be binding on all citizens and require their participation for the sake of social coherence and stability.

# THOMAS REID AND JEREMY BENTHAM

### Why was **Thomas Reid important**?

Thomas Reid (1710–1796) was the founder of Scottish Common Sense Philosophy, which was prominent in English thought during the first half of the nineteenth century, and was revived by G.E. Moore (1873–1958) in his attack on idealism in the twentieth century. Reid's basic contribution was a criticism of the doctrine of ideas in philosophy, which in his own time was famously deployed by David Hume (1711–1776), although it had strong predecessors in John Locke (1632–1704) and George Berkeley (1685–1783).

Reid believed that it is impossible that what we know are sensations or ideas in the mind because this can't account for the immediacy of our experience of objects present to the senses, motion, or our experience of our own selves. Reid thought that we directly know real objects in the world, just like we assume in common sense. For example, when you look at a computer screen as you type, you do not perceive the idea of the screen, but rather the screen itself. His common sense was to insist on the location of the knower directly in the world, with no mediation in the mind by ideas, sensations, or impressions.

### Did Thomas **Reid** have his **own ideas**, in addition to saying why the empiricists were wrong?

Yes, and Reid was highly influential for a while, although he is often overlooked as an Enlightenment philosopher. He lectured at King's College, Aberdeen, and held the chair of moral philosophy at Glasgow. His main publications were *An Inquiry into the Human Mind on the Principles of Common Sense* (1764), *Essays on the Intellectual Powers of Man* (1785), and *Essays on the Active Powers of Man* (1788).

After rejecting the empiricist representative theory of knowledge, Reid developed an intuitionist theory of knowledge in terms of mental faculties: Reid thought that we have innate powers of conception and conviction. There are first principles that we can identify by their early appearance, universality, and irresistibility. We could not deny an irresistible principle. For instance, sensations are operations of the mind that, together with impressions made on our sense organs, cause our conceptions of primary and secondary qualities. A sensation of smell thus suggests that there is a quality in the object causing the sensation. In analyzing vision, Reid reasoned that the data are received on the round surface of the eye, but processed within it. He concluded that visual space must have a non-Euclidian geometry of curved space (he was about a century ahead of his time in postulating non-Euclidian geometry).

In addition to faculties of perception and memory, Reid posited a moral faculty resulting in conceptions of justice or injustice that may differ, depending on different people's conceptions of the same action. He also posited active powers, leading to action, according to principles of action. When Reid spoke of "powers" in this way, he seemed to mean capabilities in the mind. The principles of action were animal principles (such as appetites and physical desires) and rational principles that include understanding and will.

### What did **Thomas Reid** believe about **free will**?

Reid believed that we are able to will something because we have a conception of the action and we will to do that thing. Concerning freedom, Reid thought it was not sufficient, as David Hume (1711–1776) had claimed, that we act according to our will, but that we must also have the power to choose what to will. This is because willing is instrumental to the goal of an action, and without the power over means there is no power over the end. Your free actions are those caused by you and you know that you are their cause because your conviction of your freedom arises from your faculties, as a first principle.

### Who was **Jeremy Bentham**?

Jeremy Bentham (1748–1832) was the founder of the moral system of utilitarianism, which is considered to be one of the three major systems of ethics in Western philosophy, along with Aristotelian virtue ethics and Kantian deontology, or duty ethics.

### What were **Bentham's life** and **career** like?

Bentham was born in Houndsditch, London, and began studies at Queen's College, Oxford, when he was just 12 years old. After his graduation, he entered Lincoln's Inn to become a lawyer and was called to the bar in 1767. He never practiced law, though, instead dedicating himself to reforming the entire system of civil and criminal law. Existing legal theory seemed incoherent, he felt, and the penal system was cruel and very expensive to administrate. Bentham's legal writings began with work on legal reform that was not published until 1811, and his *Comment on Blackstone's Commentaries* was not published until 1928. Bentham wrote voluminously, but there was a certain disorganization in his methods of completing any one thing. He published part of his Blackstone criticism as *A Fragment on Government* (1776) and *Introduction to the Principles of Morals and Legislation* (1789).

Bentham attempted to gain Catherine the Great of Russia's support for his Constitutional Code. He was made a citizen of France after the Revolution, in 1792, and his ideas also reached the United States. But he was most influential politically in England, where he was leader of the philosophical radicals and an inspiration to the Benthamites. Both of these groups thought that Bentham's pleasure principle or principle of utility could be used to change the world for the better. James Mill, father of John Stuart Mill (1806–1873), the great nineteenth century English utilitarian, was a close friend of his. Bentham also founded the journal *Westminster Review,* as well as University College.

### What was Bentham's **Principle of Utility**?

Jeremy Bentham intended it to guide legislators for the sake of reforming the legal system. He thought that legislators were too influenced by "the principle of sympathy and antipathy," which he called "ipse-dixitism." They punished what they did not like, even if, as in the case of sexual transgressions, no one was harmed, and they failed to punish sources of great suffering. Bentham wanted legal obligations to be based on the goal of increasing happiness and lessening pain and suffering. This was his principle of utility. With this principle, no other value was necessary, and legal fictions could be abolished. Concerning rights, Bentham believed that they were "nonsense upon stilts."

### What is **hedonic calculus**?

According to Jeremy Bentham, courses of action should be chosen based on their consequences in terms of the pleasure and pain experienced by all involved. Everyone counts for one, and no one counts for more than one. All pleasures are on the same level, and in Bentham's famous words, "all quantity of pleasure being equal, pushpin is as good as poetry." (Pushpin was a bowling-type game of the time.) The value of justice reduces to its greater utility over injustice. Punishment, for example, is only just or unjust in terms of its consequences as a deterrent to future crime. Bentham's hedonic calculus consisted of literally quantifying pleasures and pains according to these factors: how near or far, how long-lasting, how intense, how likely to cause pleasure or pain of the same kind, and how many are affected.

### What was Betham's main proposal for **prison reform**?

In his *Panopticon Letters* Jeremy Bentham proposed a new type of prison building so that every prisoner would be under continual observation. He drew elaborate blueprints for this kind of building, which would regulate every aspect of the lives of prisoners. It was intended as a humane but highly effective method for controlling the minds of prisoners.

# IMMANUEL KANT

### Was Immanuel Kant an **important figure** of the **Enlightenment**?

Yes, Immanuel Kant (1724–1804) was more intellectually influential in the nineteenth century and beyond than any other Enlightenment philosopher because he constructed a system of reason from which empiricism and the sciences could be derived. Kant thereby, theoretically, ended any residual tensions between rationalism and empiricism because his rationalism allowed for empiricism. In that sense, he was the epitome of the Age of Reason. Of course, for those who ignored Kant, the business of philosophy remained empiricism, idealism, or rationalism, as usual.

### What is known about Immanuel **Kant's life**?

Immanuel Kant was born in Königsberg in East Prussia. His father was a saddler, and his grandfather was a Scottish immigrant. After attending the local high school, he was taught by the philosopher Marin Knutzen at the University of Königsberg. He worked as a tutor and returned to take a master's degree, after which he was employed as a Privatdozent (Private docent, or P.D.) to teach physics, mathematics, anthropology, geography, and some philosophy. (In his courses on anthropology and geology, he taught the prevailing view of European racial supremacy over Asians and Africans.) He was poor until 1770, when he secured the position of chair of logic and metaphysics at Königsberg.

Other European intellectuals, such as Jean-Jacques Rousseau (1712–1778), whom Kant greatly admired, constantly moved and traveled to secure their fame and livings, with amorous and political adventure, as a kind of byproduct of their intellectual careers. But that was not for Kant. He never left the area of East Prussia, and remained a bachelor in Königsberg (now Kaliningrad) all his life. When the Prussian king asked him not to publish further about religion in 1794, he duly complied. Kant's health was fragile, but he took care of himself, living until he was 80. He relied on travelers and published works for information about the outside world and was content to dine with friends and fulfill his professorial duties, including a term as rector of the university.

Immanuel Kant constructed a system of reason from which empiricism and the sciences could be derived (iStock).

Kant's early works were about natural science, the most notable being his *General History of Nature and Theory of the Heavens* (1755). His magnum opus was *The Critique of Pure Reason,* but when it finally appeared in 1781 few could understand it. He tried to make his ideas more accessible in his *Prolegomena to Every Future Metaphysics* (1783). This was followed by his 1790 *Critique of Practical Reason* and the *Critique of Judgment*. In 1793 and 1797, he published *Religion within the Bounds of Mere Reason* and the *Metaphysic of Morals*. Kant was by then famous, but younger thinkers undertook to explain his system better than he had. He was working on his response to them in his *Opus Postumum* when he died.

## Why are Immanuel Kant's **epistemology** and **metaphysics transcendental**?

To this day, philosophers dispute whether Kant was providing a theory of how the mind in fact works or instead a critical theory of how we ought to view knowledge. In either case, Kant's epistemology and metaphysics are both transcendental. His epistemology is transcendental in that he reasons *a priori* from what is known to what must be the case in order to account for what is known. And his metaphysics is transcendental in that what ultimately exists exceeds and eludes both our direct knowledge and full understanding, even though we are justified in postulating it according to certain principles of reason.

## What was Immanuel Kant's **Copernican Revolution**?

Just as Copernicus changed the center of our universe from Earth to Sun, Kant relocated the basic principles and categories of reality, as studied by science, from the external world to the mind. Like John Locke (1632–1704), he began with an examination of the powers of the mind and an aim to reject metaphysical claims that could not be rationally justified. He posited a human rational necessity to understand real experience in space and time and a practical need to live with other rational beings, seeking the principles that could fulfill those requirements.

In 1770 Kant argued in *On the Form and Principles of the Sensible and Intelligible World* that our knowledge of space and time is only about appearances, but that we are still justified in making limited claims about what lies behind those appearances. This was the foundation for what became known as critical philosophy. Kant's revolutionary claim was that we have *a priori* knowledge of both space and time because they are the forms of our perception: space is the organization of experience in the outer world, while time is the organization of experience in the inner world. (This was followed by the two editions of his *Critique of Pure Reason,* with his *Prolegomena to any Future Metaphysics* published in between to respond to criticism.)

## What was Immanuel Kant's notion of **synthetic *a priori* knowledge**?

Knowledge is "synthetic" or "ampliative," according to Kant, if it is about objects that can be experienced in the world. It is *a priori* if it can be known without experience. Kant's motivating metaphysical question was, "How is it possible to know certain principles about the world, without prior experience?"

Kant's solution was to apply a "transcendental deduction" to such principles and show that without them experience would not be possible. For example, concerning causation, he argued that consciousness itself requires orderly experience based on necessary connections in reality. This was Kant's answer to David Hume's (1711–1776) reduction of causation to constant conjunction. He rejected Hume's skepticism that constant conjunction is all that there is by claiming that the world could only make sense to us if we assumed that that there were real causal connections in it. In his *Prolegomena to Every Future Metaphysics* (1783), Kant famously said that Hume had awakened him from his "dogmatic slumbers."

## What was Immanuel **Kant's moral system**?

Kant's moral starting point is the distinction between things that are instrumentally or hypothetically good because they have good consequences, and things that are good in and of themselves. The only thing that is good in itself is a good will or benevolence, without which every other gift of fortune can be just cause for resentment. Morality is for rational beings, and rational beings require principles of action. In the community of rational beings, or the Kingdom of Ends, actions are good if they are autonomous, which is to say freely chosen.

According to Kant, a rational being is autonomous or self-ruling. The rules that a rational being uses to regulate himself are absolute—what Kant called "categorical." Such rules are imperatives and are followed for their own sake. Hypothetical rules, by contrast, are followed in order to make something else happen. For example, "Do not harm innocent people" would be a categorical rule and "Eat your vegetables" would be a hypothetical rule.

## What was Immanuel **Kant's categorical imperative**?

Kant is usually interpreted to have two formulations. First, "Act so that the maxim of your action, or the generalization describing it, can be willed by you to be a general rule, to be followed by all rational agents." In other words, only do those things that you as a benevolent, rational being can will that everyone do.

The test of a categorical imperative is what happens if everyone follows it. Something that has good consequences in a particular case might not have good consequences in all cases. For example, if the maxim is "Obey traffic rules," and you come to a red light with no other cars in attendance, you may not drive through it, even though the consequences in this particular case would be benign. Or, to use an example of Kant's, if the maxim is not to lie, and a madman is looking for a friend of yours whose whereabouts you know, you may not lie in this case, because overall you can't benevolently will that everyone be permitted to lie whenever the consequences are good for them. To take another example of Kant's, you may not take your own life, no matter how miserable you are, because you categorically can't will suicide as a good action.

## Was Immanuel Kant a recluse?

**Y**es. He lived a very precise and orderly life, and his neighbors claimed to be able to set their clocks by his daily walks. During the 1770s, he retreated into what biographers call his "silent decade." He set himself the task of figuring out how perception and intellect are connected. Never a *bon vivant,* he withdrew from even minimal social contact. But he was very forthright about what was going on in his life and did not make the usual social excuses. When a former student tried to coax him out, he responded in this manner:

> Any change makes me apprehensive, even if it offers the greatest promise of improving my condition, and I am persuaded by this natural instinct of mine that I must take heed if I wish that the threads which the Fates spin so thin and weak in my case to be spun to any length. My great thanks, to my well-wishers and friends, who think so kindly of me as to undertake my welfare, but at the same time a most humble request to protect me in my current condition from any disturbance.

### Is Immanuel Kant's **categorical imperative** different from the **Golden Rule**?

Yes, it is. According to the Golden Rule, we should act as we would have others act toward us. If our tastes are perverted or we do not care for our own welfare, the Golden Rule could permit acts of depravity and violence, but such acts could never be willed categorically. Moreover, Kant's system is strongly based on individual good will toward the community of all other rational individuals. There is a debt to Jean-Jacques Rousseau's (1712–1778) idea of the "common good" here; indeed, Kant greatly respected Rousseau's moral philosophy.

### What was Immanuel Kant's **second formulation** of the **categorical imperative**?

According to Kant, all rational beings are intrinsically valuable, and in the Kingdom of Ends, no one is a means to the end of anyone else. In the world of affairs what we do and who we are have prices, but in the Kingdom of Ends there are no prices, only dignities. The second formulation of the categorical imperative is that one must always act to treat humanity (either as another person or oneself) as an end and never as a means. In other words, don't use people!

### What was Immanuel **Kant's theory** of the **self**?

Kant distinguished between the empirical ego and the transcendental ego. The empirical ego is what we normally think of as the self and are able to experience. The transcendental ego is the necessary origin of those fundamental structures of thought and intuition that are necessary for experience. The transcendental ego is known only as an object of thought, and not as an object of direct experience.

### What was Immanuel **Kant's proof** of **God's existence**?

Kant rejected the ontological argument on the ground that existence is not a quality or characteristic of things. According to Kant, we cannot say that the sweater is red, wool, and it exists. He rejected the first cause argument as partly relying on the ontological argument; and he rejected the argument from design on the grounds that, at best, it proves only an architect or designer of the universe, and not a creator. Kant himself thought there was a moral proof for God's existence because the moral agent knows that he cannot achieve his goals on his own without God. The resulting belief in God becomes a matter of individual, personal conviction—not "It is morally certain that there is a God," but "I am morally certain that there is a God."

# MARY WOLLSTONECRAFT
# AND WILLIAM GODWIN

### Which of the **other Enlightenment thinkers** were most directly **relevant** to philosophy?

Among the other Enlightenment thinkers of note in the area of philosophy is Mary Wollstonecraft (1759–1797), the mother of *Frankenstein* novelist Mary Wollstonecraft Shelley. She contributed the foundations for feminist thought. Her husband was anarchist and political philosopher William Godwin (1756–1836), known for his determinist utilitarianism. The French *philosophes,* particularly the encyclopedists, contributed radical ideas about society and government. Voltaire (François-Marie Arouet; 1694–1778) brought key philosophical ideas to a wider audience. Enlightenment thought in general had a powerful effect on the American colonies and the establishing principles of the United States of America.

### Who was **Mary Wollstonecraft**?

Mary Wollstonecraft (1759–1797) is considered the founder of modern feminism in the West. She wrote at the time of the French Revolution and contributed to democratic ideas, generally, in *Vindication of the Rights of Men,* as well as to arguments for the equality of women in *Vindication of the Rights of Women.* She also wrote novels, an autobiographical travel essay, and shorter works on education.

## What were **Wollstonecraft's** main **political ideas**?

In *Vindication of the Rights of Men* (1790) she argued against Irish statesman and political theorist Edmund Burke's (1729–1797) conservative attack on the ideals of the French Revolution (liberty, equality, fraternity). Her claim that Burke's endorsement of custom and tradition implied that slavery was acceptable made her famous overnight. *Vindication of the Rights of Women* (1792), in which Wollstonecraft sounded a clarion call for the recognition of women as human beings, was innovative in its progressive thought.

## What did **Wollstonecraft** claim on **behalf of women**?

Mary Astell (1666–1731) and Elizabeth Elstob (1683–1756) preceded Wollstonecraft in arguing for women's recognition as thinking persons. Astell claimed that women were entitled to be educated. Her reason for this was that women had the same God-given capacity to reason as men. Her justification for educating women was that this could help them be better wives and mothers. Wollstonecraft shared Astell's views and defended them more systematically. She also claimed that the current treatment of privileged women as "spaniels" and "toys" was demeaning to them. She took Jean-Jacques Rousseau (1712–1778) to task for claiming in his hugely popular novel *Émile* (1762) that women should be educated to provide soothing pleasure to men. She wrote openly about female sexuality and the emotional vulnerability of women to "rakes," arguing that women were educated to be impulsive, emotional, and gullible.

## What were **Wollstonecraft's theoretical innovations**?

Mary Wollstonecraft developed the arguments of the seventeenth century anonymous writer who said in *An Essay in Defense of the Female Sex: The "Usurpation of Man; and the Tyranny of Custom (Here in England, Especially)"* that women had the traits they did because of the roles society assigned them. However, Wollstonecraft stopped short of condemning men for this or claiming that women were superior or equal to men in character or strength.

Wollstonecraft's general contribution to political and social theory was twofold. First, in the case of women, she offered a detailed analysis of how their customary upbringing and assigned roles in society caused them to develop those traits that were considered "natural" to the female sex: emotionality, submissiveness, impulsiveness, vanity. Second, she pursued the assumption that reason could be used to improve human happiness. In both of her major works, she assumed that it was the obligation of rational people of both sexes to endorse social progress and human equality. Wollstonecraft's progressiveness was focused on the life conditions of those who were disadvantaged and oppressed, which was not the case with leading male political philosophers in the seventeenth century, or even during the Enlightenment. In that sense, she was a revolutionary thinker.

## Was Wollstonecraft opposed to marriage?

No. Mary Wollstonecraft believed that marriage should be reformed so that husbands and wives would be true friends. She did not think that the whole of women's virtue lay in their sexual chastity, but that they should have opportunities to develop their character, just as men did. Turning around the seventeenth-century belief that women were the sexually dangerous and aggressive sex, she wrote that the biggest danger to women's chastity was the failure of men to consider chastity a serious virtue of their own.

## How did the facts of **Wollstonecraft's life obscure** her **work**?

Mary Wollstonecraft's life was tumultuous in a way that was shocking to her peers and many later thinkers. Her husband, the philosopher William Godwin (1756–1836), wrote *The Memoirs of the Author of A Vindication of the Rights of Woman* a year after Mary had died in childbirth at the age of 37. Godwin, the founder of modern anarchism, was vilified by the poet Robert Southey for "the want of all feeling in stripping his dead wife naked," and in a satire called *The Unsex'd Females, A Poem* (1798) published by Richard Polwhele.

Mary Wollstonecraft was born in Spitalfields, London, and her father squandered their money and took over her own small inheritance. He drank excessively and beat Mary's mother. Her sisters, Everina and Eliza, were also to have unhappy marriages. In her teens, Mary became friends with Jane Arden, whose family had intellectual interests, and Fanny Blood, with whom she later started a school in Newington Green, which was known as a "dissenting community."

Blood married, became ill, and died. The school fell apart, and Wollstonecraft worked as a governess, leaving after a year when she decided to support herself by writing. This was a very daring ambition for a woman at the time, and Wollstonecraft called herself "the first of a new genus." In London, she was assisted by the publisher Joseph Johnson; she became part of a circle that included Thomas Paine and William Godwin, and supported herself by translating French and German texts after learning those languages. She had an affair with the married artist Henry Fuseli, who rejected her when his wife refused a platonic ménage à trois.

She then wrote *Vindication of the Rights of Men* (1790), followed by *Vindication of the Rights of Women* (1792), and traveled to France a month before Louis XVI was guillotined. There she fell in love with the adventurer Gilbert Imlay, with whom she had her daughter, Fanny. Imlay rejected Mary, and when she returned to England she twice tried to commit suicide. Eventually, she became romantically attached to Godwin and they married so that their child would be legitimate, though they lived in separate houses. Their daughter, Mary, became Mary Shelley, the author of *Frankenstein*. Fanny committed suicide at the age of 22.

### Who was **William Godwin**?

Mary Wollstonecraft's husband, William Godwin (1756–1836), was well known as a novelist and political radical. In his *Enquiry Concerning Political Justice* (1793) he advocated utilitarianism and anarchism. He believed that the institution of government has an artificially corrupting effect on individuals because it creates prejudices. He proposed that instead of large nation-states humans should live in small communities without government so that they can get to know each other as unique individuals. Only then will it be possible for human beings to feel sympathetic regard for their neighbors.

Godwin thought that, because there is no free will, there is no point in punishment. Virtue, according to Godwin, was based on sympathy, and sympathy motivates us to bring about the greatest happiness for the greatest number of human beings. Godwin had no use for other values beyond this happiness principle. He also thought that rights were unnecessary because sympathy could do the work of protecting everyone.

# THE *PHILOSOPHES*

### Who were the *philosophes*?

The term "*philosophe*" can and has been applied to virtually all intellectuals who advocated change in the world order during the decades leading up to the American and French revolutions. In that sense, David Hume, Jeremy Bentham, and Benjamin Franklin were all *philosophes*. However, to tell a manageable history of philosophy it is useful to narrow the term down to the French encyclopedists and Adam Smith, Edward Gibbon, Gotthold Lessing, and Cesare Beccaria.

### What was the **goal** of the **encyclopedists**?

The goal of the encyclopedists was to gather together, in a collection of contemporary volumes, everything known at the time in all fields. Their main contributors were Denis Diderot (1713–1784), Jean le Rond d'Alembert (1717–1783), Baron Paul-Henri-Dietrich d'Holbach (1723–1789), and Charles-Louis de Secondat, Baron de La Brède et de Montesquieu (1689–1755), as well as Jean-Jacques Rousseau (1712–1778) and Voltaire (1694–1778). Their work was humanistic and scientifically inclined. However, its anti-clerical themes resulted in royal censorship in 1750, although the project endured until 1777. There were 140 contributors and almost 150 additional writers and engravers to the project. The 32 volumes produced had more than 70,000 entries, with 11 volumes of plates and 21 of printed text.

## What was individually **noteworthy** about **Diderot, d'Alembert, Holbach,** and **Montesquieu**?

- Denis Diderot (1713–1784) was the general editor of the *Encyclopedia*. His *The Skeptics Walk* (1747) was a robust attack on Christianity. His claim that the universe was wholly material and evolving, as asserted in *Letter on the Blind* (1749), resulted in a brief imprisonment. Diderot's comedies were considered second-rate, but his literary analyses created the new genre of literary criticism.

- Jean le Rond d'Alembert (1717–1783) was the chief philosopher in the encylopedists' project. In his *Discours préliminaire* he divided a philosophy of man into pneumatology (or the human soul), logic, and ethics. He held that the substance of the universe cannot be known, and in *Essay on the Elements of Philosophy* (1759) defined the field as a comparison of phenomena (that is, appearances).

Denis Diderot is credited with creating the field of literary criticism (Art Archive).

- Baron Paul-Henri-Dietrich d'Holbach (1723–1789) was a major contributor to the encyclopedia. He was a solicitor at the Paris Parlement and hosted philosophical dinners. He systematized Diderot's naturalism and published anonymous, irreligious treatises applying philosophy against the Catholic Church. He argued that everything in existence was based on matter and motion in a completely determined universe. Holbach thought that Christian virtues were unnatural, that piety was fanaticism, and that church officials were immoral. He was also a utilitarian.

- Baron de La Brède et de Montesquieu (Charles-Louis de Secondat; 1689–1755) was the chief political encyclopedist. His most famous work is *The Spirit of the Laws* (1740–1748) in which he argued that governments can be divided into republics, monarchies, or despotisms, which are respectively motivated by political virtue, honor, and fear. Types of government depend on the character, history, and geography of a people. A constitutional government with a separation of executive, legislative, and judicial powers is the only form that can protect liberty. This idea influenced the framers of the U.S. Constitution.

## Why was **Adam Smith's work** important?

Adam Smith defined the economic system of capitalism and founded the science of modern economics (iStock).

Adam Smith (1723–1790) defined the economic system of capitalism and at the same time founded the science of modern economics in his *An Inquiry into the Nature and Causes of the Wealth of Nations* (1776). He sought to answer the question of how nations grow richer, assuming that human life would improve as nations prospered. He analyzed the importance of the ongoing division of labor in the industrialization process, and argued for free competition based on the profit motive. This would be a system of economic liberty or "laissez faire" ("Let them do it"). He argued that selfishness in acquiring wealth would result in better conditions for all, through the "invisible hand" of the market place.

## What did **Edward Gibbon** contribute?

Edward Gibbon (1737–1794) wrote *The Decline and Fall of the Roman Empire,* which was published between 1776 and 1788. This tome is still read today. Gibbon argued that Rome fell because of invasions by barbarians and the corruption of Christianity that rendered the citizens of Rome "servile and pusillanimous."

## Who was **Gotthold Lessing**?

Gotthold Lessing (1729–1781) represented the *philosophes* in Germany, which was a difficult task, owing to the conservatism and strict censorship there. In *Nathan the Wise* (1779) he argued for the toleration of Jews and for human equality across religions. In *On the Education of the Human Race* (1780) he claimed that all religions are part of a progression of humanity to the point when it will turn away from religion and toward pure reason.

## What **reforms** did **Cesare Beccaria** advocate?

Cesare Beccaria (1738–1794) wrote *On Crimes and Punishments* (1764), which was influential against the idea that punishment serves retribution. He reasoned that the purpose of imprisonment was the protection of society and the reform of criminals. Beccaria's book is believed to have been influential in the abolition of torture and maiming as routine criminal punishments by the mid-nineteenth century.

## Who was **Voltaire**?

"Voltaire" was the pen name of François-Marie Arouet (1694–1778), a playwright, poet, essayist, and widely read popularizer of Sir Isaac Newton. His *Philosophical Letters* (1734) and *Philosophical Dictionary* (1764) both express his brilliant wit and underlying sense of social justice. He made great fun of Gottfried Leibniz (1646–1716) as Dr. Pangloss in the satire *Candide,* but although he thought that this was not the best of all possible worlds, as Pangloss did, he believed improvement was possible on specific issues.

Voltaire's empiricism was similar to that of John Locke (1632–1704) in that he was a moderate skeptic who also thought that human knowledge is generally adequate for the lives most people lead. In other words, we know what we need to know. He argued for toleration and objected to the narrowness of church Christianity. By the same token, he did not go as far as Jean-Jacques Rousseau (1712–1778) in extolling simplicity over civilization. He replied to Rousseau after he gave him a copy of *The Social Contract*: "I have received your new book against the human race, and thank you for it. Never was such a cleverness used in the design of making us all stupid. One longs, in reading your book, to walk on all fours. But as I have lost that habit for more than sixty years, I feel unhappily the impossibility of resuming it."

## What was interesting about **Voltaire's life**?

Voltaire (1694–1778) led a very dramatic life. After his classical education at a Jesuit school, he chose literature over law, and his subsequent satires resulted in his banishment from Paris as well as exile to Holland. He spent almost a year imprisoned in the Bastille. All of this happened by the time he was 24.

Voltaire was believed to be the best playwright in France for half a century. A disagreement with a chevalier resulted in another sojourn in the Bastille, after which he went to England and learned the language, philosophy, and politics of that country. In 1734 he had to flee Paris again, and for the next 15 years he studied physics, metaphysics, and history with the highly intelligent Marquise Du Châtelet, in Lorraine. During this time he was also at court, protected by Madame de Pompadour, who was the mistress of King Louis XV.

Voltaire became historiographer of France and a member of the French Academy in 1746. In 1750 he was appointed philosopher-poet to Frederick the Great of Prussia, but they had disagreements after three years; Voltaire then bought a château in Geneva, Switzerland, and then an estate in France. In France he defended Jean Calas, a Protestant who in 1762 was tortured on the rack and executed. Voltaire was by then very rich and he devoted himself to causes against the oppression of the Church. When he returned to Paris at age 83, he was highly acclaimed, but died soon afterwards. He was first buried outside Paris, but then his remains were moved to the Pantheon, only to be again disinterred during the Restoration. (Voltaire's body was never completely reassembled after that.)

## What were **Voltaire's main contributions** to philosophy?

A witty playwright, poet, and essayist, Voltaire was a widely read French popularizer of Isaac Newton and John Locke (iStock).

In his *Letters Concerning the English Nation* (1734), published as part of his *Philosophical Letters,* Voltaire introduced a French audience to the ideas of John Locke (1632–1704) and Isaac Newton (1643–1727). At the same time, he offered political criticism of the ancient regime, which was to motivate the French Revolution. Against Blaise Pascal (1623–1662), who in the previous century had counseled quietism and claimed that suffering on Earth was excellent preparation for heaven, Voltaire argued for the betterment of human life in the here and now.

Voltaire's "Letter on Mr. Locke" in his *Philosophical Dictionary* took up a possibility raised by Locke of matter being able to think. However, later in life, he retreated to a skeptical position on such materialism after it was taken up by the *philosophes* in defense of atheism.

## What were **Voltaire's religious views**?

Voltaire rejected the wager of the brilliant seventeenth century mathematician Blaise Pascal (1623–1662). The following passage from Pascal's *Pensées* constitutes the famous wager:

> "God is, or He is not." But to which side shall we incline?

> Reason can decide nothing here. There is an infinite chaos which separated us. A game is being played at the extremity of this infinite distance where heads or tails will turn up…. Which will you choose then?

> Let us see. Since you must choose, let us see which interests you least. You have two things to lose, the true and the good; and two things to stake, your reason and your will, your knowledge and your happiness; and your nature has two things to shun, error and misery. Your reason is no more shocked in choosing one rather than the other, since you must of necessity choose…. But your happiness?

> Let us weigh the gain and the loss in wagering that God is…. If you gain, you gain all; if you lose, you lose nothing. Wager, then, without hesitation that He is.

In other words, if we don't know whether God exists, we have two choices. We can base our life on the premise that he is. In that case, if he exists, we will go to heaven. But suppose he doesn't exist?

Founding Fathers of the United States such as Benjamin Franklin (left) and Thomas Jefferson were energized by the Age of Enlightenment and the flourishing ideals of liberty and democracy (iStock).

It's still better to bet that he is, because if he isn't, we lose nothing. Whereas, if we bet that he isn't and he isn't, we are merely confirmed in our misery, but if he turns out to exist, we go to hell when we die. Voltaire would have none of this.

Voltaire believed that the design evident in nature was proof of God's existence, as First Cause, Prime Mover, and Supreme Intelligence. However, he thought that God was indifferent to human concerns, and tried to resolve the problem of evil: How can a benevolent and omnipotent God permit evil to exist?

Votaire was very distressed by the Lisbon earthquake and tidal wave that struck on All Saints Day in 1755, killing thousands. In his "Poème sur le désastre de Lisbonne" (1755) he rejected both Leibnizian optimism and the doctrine of original sin. He concluded that all humans can do is accept such evil and continue to worship. In *Zadig and Other Writings* his sense of religious awe was further stressed; he maintained an attitude of tolerance for the rest of his life, with ongoing interests in the teachings of Confucius and the Quakers. In his final years, Voltaire overtly attacked the Catholic Church for its intolerance. He proclaimed, "Those who can make you believe absurdities, can make you commit atrocities."

## Who was **Jonathan Edwards**?

Jonathan Edwards (1703–1758) was the third president of Princeton University, although he died a year after he was elected. He was educated at Yale, preached in New

## How did the Enlightenment affect the United States?

Amerca did not develop its own philosophical tradition until the late nineteenth and early twentieth centuries. In the period before the American Revolution and the founding of the new republic, the excitement of liberty from oppressive government, the dignity of the individual, and rights to private property were all highly motivating ideas.

These optimistic ideas were inspirational in the writings of Thomas Paine, Benjamin Franklin, Thomas Jefferson, and others. The American separation of church from state, as an article of individual liberty—against oppressive government religion, and for free thought and speech—came directly from Enlightenment ideas, as did the division of the powers of government and the distrust of government.

It should be noted, however, that libertinism and outright atheism were to remain European phenomena for a very long time. Under the inspiration of Jonathan Edwards (1703–1758), American Protestant religious philosophy flourished in the late eighteenth century in a New England Born-Again movement known as "the Great Awakening."

York City, and became a leader of the Great Awakening in 1729 in Massachusetts. His theology was a Puritan form of Calvinism.

Edward's interest in philosophy included Nicolas Malebranche (1638–1715), the Cambridge Platonists, and John Locke (1632–1704). He was himself an idealist, similar to George Berkeley (1685–1783), who held that human minds are made up of thoughts and sensations, God being the only true substance.

## What was **original** in **Jonathan Edwards' view of God**?

Jonathan Edwards developed the idea that God loves and is delighted by Himself and creates us and other creatures as part of this joy in Himself. Edwards taught that God's love is disinterested and that he is supremely beautiful, infusing the entire world with "His Loveliness." By comparison, the beauty seen by mortals is "secondary," an imperfect copy of what God sees.

## Was Jonathan **Edwards merciful** toward sinners?

Not in the least. Jonathan Edwards thought that many humans were depraved and that a real Hell awaited them. There is a tone of delight in these facts in his 1741 sermon, "Sinners in the Hands of an Angry God." Edwards not only believed that sinners would be punished, but that God himself had no pity for their agony. He wrote:

If you cry to God to pity you, he will be so far from pitying you in your doleful case, or showing you the least regard or favour, that instead of that, he will only tread you under foot. And though he will know that you cannot bear the weight of omnipotence treading upon you, yet he will not regard that, but he will crush you under his feet without mercy; he will crush out your blood, and make it fly, and it shall be sprinkled on his garments, so as to stain all his raiment. He will not only hate you, but he will have you in the utmost contempt: no place shall be thought fit for you, but under his feet to be trodden down as the mire of the streets.

And, insofar as the virtuous strive to emulate God, Edwards felt it is fitting that they enjoy the suffering of such sinners in Hell. In 1758, in his "Why Saints in Glory Will Rejoice to See the Torments of the Damned," Edwards wrote:

When they shall see how miserable others of their fellow-creatures are, who were naturally in the same circumstances with themselves; when they shall see the smoke of their torment, and the raging of the flames of their burning, and hear their dolorous shrieks and cries, and consider that they in the meantime are in the most blissful state, and shall surely be in it to all eternity; how will they rejoice!

# COUNTER-ENLIGHTENMENT FIGURES

### Which **Counter-Enlightenment figures** had **lasting effects** on philosophy?

Giovanni Battista (Giambattista) Vico, or Vigo (1668–1744), has in recent years been rediscovered, or discovered, as an important philosopher. Edmund Burke (1729–1797) was the most explicit conservative of modern times, although Joseph-Marie de Maistre (1753–1821) held similar views. Also, Jonathan Swift (1667–1745) deserves mention as a mordant critic of the establishment in general, and the Marquis de Sade (1740–1814) represents a kind of extreme marginality in his depravity, which marginality was later taken up by nineteenth and twentieth century progressives—he also remains genuinely outrageous!

### How was **Giambattista Vico** a **unique philosopher** of his time?

Giambattista Vico (or Giovanni Battista Vico; 1668–1744) was an Italian philosopher and jurist who is credited with having founded the philosophy of history, as well as the modern understanding of history. He provided painstaking analyses of ideas in the past and accounts of how they developed over time, due both to varied circumstances and events, as well as the content of the ideas themselves. In that sense, Vico invented intellectual history.

### Did **Vico interact** with other **Enlightenment thinkers** over his lifetime?

No. Giambattista Vico's circumstances did not afford him the leisure of an intellectual vocation. Outside of Italy, only the German intellectuals, such as Johann Georg Hamann and Johann Gottfried von Herder, knew of his work. Italy was not united during his lifetime. Naples endured constant upheavals as Spain, Austria, and France took it over. Additional political stress resulted from the strength of the Jesuits within the city.

Vico's father was a bookseller in Naples. After fracturing his skull as a child, Vico could not attend school for three years, so he read on his own. When he did enroll in university, he proved to be an undisciplined student. He concentrated on logic and medieval scholasticism before settling on law. But, after assisting his own father in a lawsuit in his teens, he never practiced law again. For 10 years after 1685, Vico worked as a tutor, reading on his own in philosophy, history, ethics, jurisprudence, and poetry. He did not like mathematics, nor was he particularly interested in science.

By the time Vico became professor of rhetoric at the University of Naples in 1695, it was a Cartesian center dedicated to the study of René Descartes' philosophy. And Vico was opposed to many aspects of Cartesianism, especially his rationalism. From 1699–1708, Vico delivered the beginning lecture for the University every year. Of the essays that developed from those lectures, "On the Study Methods of Our Time" (1709), was well received for its advocacy of liberal education. This was quickly followed by his 1709 lecture, "On the Most Ancient Knowledge of the Italians." In 1722 his three volume *Universal Law* was complete, and in 1725 both his autobiography and *The New Science,* which was to be revised in 1730 and 1744, were released. Vico failed to be promoted to chair of civil law and had to write poems and vanity pieces for hire to make a living. He grew bitter and his lifelong melancholy worsened. His death in 1744 followed an agonizing illness.

### How was **Vico**'s thought **opposed** to the **Enlightenment**?

Vico's main thesis was: "the order of ideas follows the order of things." The Enlightenment thesis, by contrast, was: "the order of things follows the order of ideas." That is, Vico thought that ideas are the result of physical reality, whereas Enlightenment optimists held that reality can be directed by reason. Also, Vico believed in a cyclical progression of human events, whereas an overarching faith of the Enlightenment was in the existence of progress, which meant real change.

### Why did **Vico oppose Cartesianism**?

Vico concluded that René Descartes (1596–1650) had been too enamored of mathematics and natural philosophy (science) to the neglect or dismissal of art, law, and history as valid fields of knowledge. Vico also did not think that Descartes was right in

## What was unusual about Vico's autobiography?

Vico told the story of his life, *Life of Giambattista Vico Written by Himself* (1725–1728), in the third person, and he analyzed both the effect of his circumstances on his temperament and how his ideas developed before he began writing. His autobiography is thus his intellectual history. Here is how it begins:

Signor Giambattista Vico, he was born in Naples in the year 1670 of upright parents, who left behind them a very good reputation. The father was of cheerful humor, the mother of a quite melancholy temper; and both came together in the fair disposition of this little son of theirs. As a boy he was very lively and restless; but at the age of seven he fell headfirst from high on a ladder to the floor, and remained a good five hours motionless and senseless, fracturing the right side of the cranium without breaking the skin, hence from the fracture arose a shapeless tumor, and from the many deep lancings of it the child lost a great deal of blood; such that the surgeon, having observed the broken cranium and considering the long state of unconsciousness, made the prediction that he would either die of it or he would survive stolid. However, neither of the two parts of this judgment, by the grace of God, came true; but as a result of this illness and recovery he grew up, from then on, with a melancholy and acrid nature which necessarily belongs to ingenious and profound men, who through ingenuity flash like lightning in acuity, through reflection take no pleasure in witticism and falsity.

seeking the same kind of certain knowledge in science that mathematics yielded. In his first book, *On the Ancient Italian Knowledge,* (1710) Vico argued that Descartes was wrong in holding awareness of his own existence as a first philosophical principle, and in trying to prove God's existence through reason alone.

Vico's own view was that the mind does not make itself and for that reason cannot know how it has knowledge of itself. Concerning mathematical and even scientific certainty, Vico did not think we can arrive at it through clear and distinct ideas, as Descartes claimed. He claimed that mathematical knowledge is certainly true because the human mind has created the very standard for mathematical truth, or because we have made mathematics. However, God has made the physical universe, and only He can have certain knowledge about that. Vico did concede that when we do make things in nature, or through scientific experiment, we can gain knowledge from the confirmation of our hypotheses.

## What was **Vico's new view** of **history** as knowledge?

Unlike the Cartesians, who dismissed history as a hodgepodge of fiction and unconnected facts, Vico thought that the historian can achieve more certainty than the scientist because he is studying the story of a world made by humans.

He disagreed with Hugo Grotius (1583–1645), Thomas Hobbes (1588–1679), and others, who began with the idea of a state of nature or some other way of positing a static, unchanging human nature. He was wary of what we would call "anachronism," or assuming that words had the same meanings in the past as they do now, or that people have always thought the same way. Vico believed that historical events change human ideas. Vico asserted that every theory "must start from the point where the matter of which it treats first began to take shape." According to Vico, the way the historian can discover the minds and feelings of those in past times is to decode their language, myths, and customs. For example, he believed that what are considered metaphors, myths, and fables at one time may have been the literal truth to people in the past.

## What was Vico's **cyclical idea** of history?

Vico believed that there are cultural patterns that dominate in different societies. Thus, law, religion, politics, art, and manners all tend to match up at any given time and place. For example, he drew connections between Athenian law and its pre-Socratic and Socratic philosophies. In his cyclical account of history, or what he called *corsi e ricorsi,* societies organically develop and then age and rot. He posited a bestial condition, a time of the gods, and a time of heroes, which also leads to oligarchies, or rule by the richest. This is followed by an age of men, characterized by class conflict, until the society decays. Vico applied this theory to the history of Rome, beginning with the mythical founders Romulus and Remus and ending with its overthrow by external barbarians.

## From what did Vico believe the **cycles of history originated**?

Vico thought that God ordained the cycles of history in his "divine providence," an idea that Vico held to be compatible with the fact that human beings might have other aims or goals than what actually does transpire. This idea is believed to have been influential in Friedrich Hegel's (1770–1831) notion of "the cunning of reason." The general idea is that history always turns out to be something different from what people intended.

## What were **Edmund Burke's political background** and **beliefs**?

Edmund Burke (1729–1797) was a member of the British House of Commons from 1765 to 1794. In his early career, which was more literary than philosophical, he propounded a romantic view of art. As a statesman, he resisted political and social change based on ideals and abstract ideas, although he supported political change that would reestablish proven rights or customs. For example, while he was opposed to the French Revolution for its ideals of "liberty, equality, fraternity," he was in favor of the Irish movement for independence and the American Revolution.

## What are some key facts about Edmund Burke's life?

Edmund Burke was born in Ireland in 1729. He attended Trinity College in Dublin, and then moved to London, hoping to read law, but he was never "called to the bar." Instead, he wrote *A Vindication of Natural Society* and *Philosophical Inquiry into Our Ideas on the Sublime and the Beautiful,* both published in 1756

British politician Edmund Burke was philosophically a pessimist, believing that equality among all people was an unachievable goal (Art Archive).

by the bookseller Robert Dodley, who also commissioned him to write an *Abridgement of the History of England,* which he never completed. His *Vindication* was deliberately written in the style of the Tory statesman Lord Bollingbroke, who in overblown ways praised a pure state of nature compared to civilization. Although Burke argued for the opposite, his imitation of Bollingbroke was so convincing that many readers thought Bollingbroke had written it.

Burke's theory of art was opposed to the classicist value of clarity. He thought that great art is mysterious and evocative and that the sublime inspires fear. He wrote: "It is our ignorance of things that causes all our admiration and chiefly excites our passions."

## What were **Burke's main ideas** in **political theory**?

Edmund Burke was a Christian pessimist who believed that there was real evil in the world and that inequality was inevitable. According to Burke, the best prospect for human society was to cling to traditions and customs that had proved their stability over generations. He thought that the French Revolution showed how great harm resulted from attempts to change society. Such attempts at change, motivated by abstract ideals, led to "false hopes and vain expectations in those destined to travel in the obscure walk of laborious life." In his 1790 *Reflections on the Revolution in France,* he called talk of fraternity "cant and gibberish."

## How were Joseph-Marie **de Maistre's ideas similar** to Edmund **Burke's**?

Joseph-Marie de Maistre (1753–1821) was a Roman Catholic political theorist who sought to restore traditional society according to Thomism (the teachings of Thomas

195

Joseph-Marie de Maistre believed that the Catholic Church would eventually triumph over the objective, scientific ideas of the Enlightenment (Art Archive).

Jonathan Swift, known for his satires such as *Gulliver's Travels,* did not believe that humans were particularly rational creatures (iStock).

Aquinas [c. 1225–1274]). He viewed the French Revolution as "satanic," in his 1796 *Considerations on France.* However, de Maistre went beyond Burke in his belief that the Catholic Church would triumph over Enlightenment philosophy. In his 1810 *Essay on the Generating Principle of Political Constitutions,* he described a fundamental human and God-ordained desire for order and discipline.

### How **important** was Joseph-Marie **de Maistre**?

In his *Freedom and Its Betrayal,* philosopher and historian Isaiah Berlin (1909–1997) listed de Maistre as a major opponent to liberty in the Enlightenment. In the nineteenth century, French literary critic Émile Faguet (1847–1916) described de Maistre as "a fierce absolutist, a furious theocrat, an intransigent legitimist, apostle of a monstrous trinity composed of Pope, King and Hangman, always and everywhere the champion of the hardest, narrowest and most inflexible dogmatism, a dark figure out of the Middle Ages, part learned doctor, part inquisitor, part executioner."

### How was Jonathan **Swift opposed** to **Enlightenment values**?

Jonathan Swift (1667–1745) is considered to have been at heart a sincere Christian who did not believe in the rationality of human nature, but rather thought that whenever order is established, it then begins to disintegrate. In 1709, in *A Project for the Advancement of Reason and the Reformation of Manners,* he implored Queen Anne to begin a moral crusade against contemporary vice. However, the great irony about Swift was that his characteristic path to moral reform was through satire and sarcasm.

## Did Jonathan Swift go mad?

Some thought he did, based on the scatological and prurient interests that his later writings expressed. For instance, in his 1732 poem "The Lady's Dressing Room," after morbidly describing a long list of disgusting physical effluvia from a woman's process of cleaning, grooming, dressing, and applying makeup, he wrote at the end: "Disgusted Strephon stole away / Repeating in his amorous Fits, / Oh! Celia, Celia, Celia shits!

At the same time, Swift also wrote another strange poem, "A Beautiful Young Nymph Going to Bed," which is about a woman who repulsively removes all the parts of herself, including prostheses, that made her seem attractive. Swift apparently had an obsession about the falseness of women. Although he was a priest in the Anglican Church, he had a 17-year love affair with Esther Vanhomrigh, a former tutee, whom he rejected for the younger Esther Johnson, known in his writings as "Stella." Esther Vanhomrigh, or "Vanessa" to Swift, was the friend who left money to George Berkeley (1685–1783). She died soon after Swift finally rejected her. Esther Johnson also died young.

In 1742, Swift was pronounced of unsound mind and memory, incapable of looking after himself or his affairs. When Swift died in 1745, he left his estate to found an insane asylum, but he was apparently not insane from psychological causes. Rather, he had labyrinthine vertigo, known as "Ménière's Disease," a physiological ailment that was not well understood in his day. His final words were, "I am a fool." Swift's Latin epitaph reads in English: "When savage indignation can no longer torture the heart, proceed, traveler, and, if you can, imitate the strenuous avenger of noble liberty."

He "sent up" the established respectability of his age through forays into fiction, as well as the rhetoric of a pamphleteer. Thus, when it became clear that he would not get support for the plight of the poor in Ireland, he and his friends founded the Scribelous Club for the sake of engaging in activity against the "dunces."

Swift is most famous for his 1726 satire, *Gulliver's Travels*. His 1729 "A Modest Proposal for Preventing the Children of Poor People from Being a Burthen to Their Parents or Country, and for Making Them Beneficial to the Public" was a shocking criticism of the treatment of the Irish poor in which he suggested that their babies be substituted for the traditional goose that graced the tables of absentee English landlords.

## Who was the **Marquis de Sade**?

Dinatien Alphonse François de Sade (1740–1814) was a French nobleman and revolutionary best known for his shocking pornographic works *Justine (The Misfortunes of*

The ruins of the Marquis de Sade's castle. The marquis was known for his prurient pursuits, but his ideas on human sexuality influenced the fields of psychology and philosophy (iStock).

*Virtue), Juliette (Vice Richly Rewarded), 120 Days of Sodom (The School of Licentiousness), Incest,* and *The Crimes of Love*. In an age that was not strongly focused on vice and sin, he managed to spend over 30 years of his life incarcerated—in an insane asylum, as well as in prison—mostly on account of his writing. The term "sadism" is based on his name.

## What are some details of the Marquis de Sade's life?

De Sade was born in the palace of Condé. His father was a count, his mother a lady-in-waiting to the princess. He attended a Jesuit college and was captain of a cavalry regiment in the Seven Years' War, after which he married the elder sister of the woman he loved, fathering two sons and one daughter. In 1766 he had a theater constructed at his castle in Lacoste (in the 1990s, fashion designer Pierre Cardin acquired the ruins of de Sade's castle as a site for theater productions). He was a libertine, said to have sexually abused young people of both sexes, both servants and prostitutes. He was accused of kidnapping and abusing a woman named Rose Keller in 1768; after she escaped, he was also accused of blasphemy, which was a more serious offense at the time than the sexual crimes.

When prostitutes in Paris complained of de Sade's abuse, he was exiled to his castle. Then he had an affair with his sister-in-law, for which his mother-in-law secured an arrest warrant from the king. A series of arrests and escapes in which his wife was his accomplice ensued. He was confined to an insane asylum at Charenton after being imprisoned in the Bastille. In the asylum, the Abbé allowed him to produce plays. When he was released in 1790, his wife divorced him.

## What was the **intellectual merit** of **de Sade's endeavors**?

De Sade was elected to the National Convention in 1790 and wrote political pamphlets calling for a direct vote. Simone de Beauvoir (1908–1986) and other twentieth century existentialists interpreted a radical doctrine of freedom in his writings. His emphasis on the importance of sexuality in human life is said to have anticipated Sigmund Freud. Others have seen seeds of nihilism in his work. The twentieth century psychoanalyst Jacques Lacan claimed that de Sade's ethics were a counterpart to Immanuel Kant's (1724–1804) categorical imperative. The twentieth century feminist Andrea

Dworkin (1946–2005) analyzed de Sade to illustrate the inherently violent misogynistic nature of all heterosexual pornography.

## Is there **interest** in the Marquis **de Sade today**?

Yes. The Marquis de Sade has endured as a glamorous and enigmatic film subject. The 1969 film *De Sade* was shot in Germany, and speculation about who its director really was continues to the present time. In 1996, the Marquis was revisited in *Dark Prince,* which was not a blockbuster. The most recent reprise is the 2000 movie *Quills,* starring Geoffrey Rush as the Marquis, Kate Winslet as Madeleine (a teenager with whom de Sade has an affair), Joaquin Phoenix as the Abbé du Coulmier, and Michael Caine as Dr. Royer-Collard.

The setting of *Quills* is an insane asylum in Napoleonic France, where the Marquis has been confined because of his licentious, depraved ideas that he graphically expresses in writing. Even while incarcerated, he has been getting his manuscripts out to be published. Napoleon himself is disturbed by this travesty and sends Dr. Royer-Collard, a mental health "specialist" to deal with the Marquis and "cure" him. Dr. Royer-Collard is a hypocrite who abuses his young wife. The film turns on the conflict between the Abbé and de Sade. The Abbé slowly goes mad, and the Marquis experiences remorse for the effect of his ideas on another.

Overall, *Quills* is an aesthetically sophisticated film that dramatizes the continuously mordant wit of the Marquis de Sade, which coexisted with what would otherwise be unadorned pornography. In defying the optimism of the Age of Reason, he used its reigning weapon.

# NINETEENTH CENTURY PHILOSOPHY

## What characterizes **nineteenth century philosophy** as a **foundation** for **current philosophical thought**?

Philosophy became fully modern in the nineteenth century in the sense that nineteenth century philosophical schools of thought and methods of analysis are still practiced by professional philosophers today. Modern philosophy is characterized by empiricism on the one side and a reaction against empiricism on the other. It consists of a series of inquiries that continue to be used as classic foundations for contemporary thinkers, who build upon it still. Its primary founders flourished in the nineteenth and early twentieth centuries, and they set the stage with problems that gave rise to existentialism and phenomenology, or continental philosophy; American philosophy, or pragmatism; Anglo-American analytic philosophy, including what is now known as "philosophy of science"; and the new philosophies of post-structuralism, post-modernism, feminism, and race and post-colonialism.

The hallmark of modern philosophy has been a constantly renewed awareness of other fields as philosophically interesting, such as social criticism, political science, physical science, psychology, mathematics, logic, and literature, and new understandings of the human subject as both a generator and subject matter of philosophical thought.

## NINETEENTH CENTURY EMPIRICISM

### What **happened** that **affected empiricism** in the nineteenth century?

Empiricism became systematized as an overall philosophical methodology with applications for science, ethics, and political science. This was largely the work of two men who did not agree with each other, William Whewell (1794–1866) and John Stuart Mill

(1806–1873), and a third, Auguste Comte (1798–1857), who founded the new school of thought called positivism.

Comte was also important in founding sociology, but can be considered here as an empiricist for his methodology. Whewell was primarily focused on science and its popularization. Mill was able to bring a coherent explanation of empirical science into philosophy because his empiricism was more easily accepted by empiricist philosophers than was Whewell's. Mill also extended empiricism to ethics, political philosophy, and rights for women. Comte was the most extreme empiricist to date, and in the twentieth century positivism was revisited as a method for doing philosophy in general.

## WILLIAM WHEWELL

### Who was **William Whewell**?

William Whewell (1794–1866) was a polymath who contributed work to mechanics, mineralogy, geology, astronomy, political economy, theology, education, law, architecture, ethics, the philosophy of science, and what he named "tideology." He was a founder and president of the British Association for the Advancement of Science, and a fellow of the Royal Society. Whewell invented the term "scientist" analogously with "artist." He was the most influential figure in British education in the nineteenth century.

### What were the main facts about **Whewell's life**?

William Whewell was born in Lancaster in 1794. His father was a master carpenter, and his mother wrote poetry. He studied at Heversham Grammar School and attended Trinity College, Cambridge, on a scholarship. He was elected to the Royal Society in 1820, when he was just 26. After being ordained as an Anglican priest—a requirement for the post—he was chair of mineralogy at Trinity College from 1828 to 1832. He became professor of moral philosophy in 1838.

Whewell married Cordelia Marshall and became master of Trinity College and vice chancellor of Cambridge in two separate terms. When Cordelia died, he married Lady Affleck, who was the sister of a friend. Lady Affleck died, and then Whewell himself passed away after he was injured in a riding accident. His work was largely neglected until the mid-twentieth century; the revival of interest in his empirical and theoretical achievements has been substantial ever since.

### What was William Whewell's **fundamental antithesis** of **knowledge**?

Whewell claimed that "in every act of knowledge … there are two opposite elements, which we may call Ideas and Perceptions." Whewell was influenced by Immanuel Kant (1724–1804) and shared Kant's belief that scientific information is not a pure collection of objective facts in the world, but that a prior system of ideas is required to arrive

> ### How did William Whewell describe the method of science?
>
> In his 1837 book, *History of the Inductive Sciences,* Whewell described scientific methodology as a three-part process, beginning with a "prelude" of isolated facts, progressing toward laws or generalizations, and culminating in "colligation" by scientists during an "inductive epoch" in which a theory is created. The last stage is a "sequel" in which the theory is refined and applied to new facts.

at scientific knowledge. However, he did not go as far as Kant in locating the possibility for scientific knowledge wholly within the mind. That is, unlike Kant, Whewell thought that the world as it is known to human beings exists independently of human minds. Neither did Whewell go as far as the empiricists, who emphasized induction and observation, in what he called the "sensationalistic school."

## What did William **Whewell** mean by the **sensationalistic school**?

Whewell meant to belittle the view of empiricists who held that all knowledge was the result of sensory experience, or what Whewell thought was "mere" sensation.

## What were William **Whewell's main ideas**?

Whewell posited certain "Fundamental Ideas," such as Space, Time, Cause, and Resemblance, which enabled "unconscious inference" so that we could structure and relate our sensations in ways that resulted in our perceptions of objects. He thought that each science has a distinct Particular Fundamental Idea that makes sense of its subject matter: For instance, the idea of Space for geometry, Cause for mechanics, and Substance for chemistry. The fundamental idea of a science can be further modified to fit the requirements of that science, such as the idea of force as a modification of the idea of Cause in mechanics.

## In what ways did William **Whewell disagree** with **Immanuel Kant**?

Whewell disagreed with Kant (1724–1804) in not limiting the number of Fundamental Ideas, and claiming that we can have objective knowledge of the world as it exists in itself, independently of our Fundamental Ideas. Kant, on the other hand, held that we cannot know things as they are in themselves, but only things as our categories enable us to understand them. Whewell posited God as the creator of our Fundamental Ideas. Because God had created them, these ideas matched reality.

## What was William **Whewell's theory of induction**?

In his *Philosophy of the Inductive Sciences, Founded upon Their History* (1840; revised, 1847; expanded, 1858), Whewell focused on "Discoverers' Induction" as used to construct phenomenal laws or generalizations, and causal laws, or explanations. This is where he described "colligation" as a "renovation" of Francis Bacon's (1561–1626) principles.

In colligation, the mind "superinduces" upon facts some conception that can be used to generalize. For example, Whewell described astronomer Johannes Kepler as having colligated the points of the Martian orbit. Whewell argued that discovery occurs not as the result of new facts, but in applying the right conception to existing facts. Thus, according to Whewell, Kepler applied his ellipse conception to the facts of Mars' orbit that were already collected by the Danish astronomer Tycho Brahe.

Whewell believed that choosing the right conception to colligate facts cannot be done by simple observation or guesswork, but requires a "special process in the mind" in which "we infer more than we see." Once theories are created, theories can be extended to what cannot be observed, such as light waves, orbit shapes, and gravity. In other words, Whewell thought that we always approach experience with something in mind that helps us interpret experience and go beyond it.

### How did William Whewell think **consilience, coherence,** and **predictions** should be applied to **test theories**?

Scientific theories must withstand the tests of consilience, coherence, and prediction. "Consilience" refers to new kinds of cases confirming the theory. A theory's coherence is its ability to explain new kinds of facts. The theory's "coherence" ought to increase over time. Predictions should turn out to be accurate. Once they have withstood such tests, theories and basic scientific principles become necessary—it is a contradiction to deny them, given an understanding of their meaning.

# JOHN STUART MILL

### Why was **John Stuart Mill important**?

John Stuart Mill (1806–1873) is to this day studied most for his work on ethics, which codified utilitarianism, one of the three major philosophical moral systems, along with virtue ethics and deontology. However, he had important political influence, too, as a British progressive, and also codified the empirical philosophy of science. His contributions to both democratic progress and the philosophy of science were so influential that they are often taken for granted politically and in definitions of science, without a perceived need to trace their authorship.

### What were some of **John Stuart Mill's achievements**?

Mill's father's interests and connections set the direction for his son, although Mill ultimately chose his own path based on life experience and the influence of his wife. Mill's father, James, was a philosopher and economist, as well as an official in the East India Company. J.S. Mill also worked in that company until he retired when the British government took over the company's administration in India in 1857. Mill edited the *Westminster Review* in the 1830s and was a member of Parliament between 1865 and 1868. Overall, Mill was dedicated to getting the educated public of Great Britain to accept scientific solutions to political, social, and economic problems, although he also placed great value on humanistic concerns as informed by the arts and life itself.

### What are some of John Stuart **Mill's influential publications**?

In his *System of Logic* (1843), Mill added to formal logic a system of evidentiary proof to show how conclusions about matters of fact were justified. He also updated Francis Bacon's (1561–1626) analysis of causation, and built on David Hume's (1711–1776) theory that causes are not logically connected to their effects, and that causal relationships are no more than constant conjunctions of types of events.

In *Principles of Political Economy* (1848) Mill identified a gap between what was measured in economics and

John Stuart Mill was a Member of Parliament, political theorist, economist, and philosopher who was a utilitarianian (Art Archive).

205

human values, such as the preservation of the environment and limited population. He argued that the ideal economy would be made up of worker-owned cooperatives.

Mill's *On Liberty* (1859) was his most contested work because it was an attack on the leveling effects of social opinion. Mill thought that democratic societies imposed conventions on their members that did not allow for much individual experimentation in life styles. His more conservative contemporaries objected to the freedoms of opinion he championed, as well as his idea that if what others consider a vice does not harm them, they have no right to interfere with an individual who practices it. His *Utilitarianism* (1861) argued for the greatest good for the greatest number of people, in which the greatest good is defined as happiness.

His *On the Subjection of Women* (1869) has endured as a classic feminist work. His last major work, *Three Essays on Religion* (1874), was a rational perspective on religion, but was neither agnostic nor atheistic. Mill reasoned that there probably was a God, but that the amount of human suffering in the world made it unlikely that God was very benevolent toward human beings.

### What did John Stuart **Mill think** about Jeremy Bentham's **"pleasure principle"**?

Jeremy Bentham (1748–1832) had introduced the idea that the only thing good in itself was pleasure. By the time Mill wrote his ethics, this was widely known as Bentham's Pleasure Principle. Mill recognized the value of pleasure, but was more interested in happiness.

### How did John Stuart **Mill** define the difference between **higher** and **lower pleasures**?

Mill did not think that a simple quantitative calculus could be used to make moral decisions. He argued that there were "lower pleasures" that were mainly connected with immediate physical gratification and delight, and "higher pleasures" that involved delayed gratification or prior diligence. The higher pleasures, such as those found in the cultivation and enjoyment of art, literature, poetry, and friendship, were better than the lower pleasures. Mill's proof that they were better was the testimony of those who had experienced both the lower and higher pleasures.

### Was John Stuart **Mill** a **socialist** or a **capitalist**?

In applying the principles of utility to government and social institutions, Mill recognized the productive consequences of free markets. But he thought that public ownership of production might benefit a greater number by eliminating the extremes of

## Did John Stuart Mill have much chance to indulge in the pleasure principle as he grew up?

The pleasure principle was certainly not applied to Mill's young life in the same sense as Jeremy Bentham's (1748–1832) formulation, although it possibly was in Mill's more nuanced version of utilitarianism, which distinguished between higher and lower pleasures. Mill's father, James, with help from his friend Bentham, educated the young Mill at home. Young John knew Greek at three, Latin at five, logic by 12, and economics by 16. He was also deeply schooled in a social mission to increase the good for the greatest number through progressive political programs. Mill had a nervous breakdown at 20. Biographers believe that his highly structured and rigorous childhood education was the cause of an emotional imbalance. The humanities had been neglected in his education, and his social interactions with peers were limited by the demands of his studies.

Mill then began a course of study in literature to develop his more humanistic sensibilities. He read romantic poetry and Johann Wolfgang von Goethe, and he began to rethink Bentham's simple hedonic calculus. The result was Mill's famous distinction between higher and lower pleasures and a scathing assessment of Bentham's character as oblivious and uncultured: "Bentham," an essay first published in the *London and Westminster Review* in 1838, and revised in 1859 for his own *Dissertations and Discussion,* Volume 1.

poverty. He believed in democratic government, provided that citizens were well-informed and it was not a simple majority rule based on emotions.

## Why did John Stuart Mill **distrust majority rule**?

Mill argued in *On Liberty* (1859) that the whole of society could be swayed by the mere opinions and passions of a majority. For this reason, free speech was essential. Even if those who seek to suppress free speech are correct, if they are not willing to present their arguments afresh they might come to hold their correct conclusions as mere superstitions. Mill thus believed in freedom of opinion for its utility in promoting a generally rational pubic epistemology or shared theory of what constitutes knowledge.

He thought it was important that people have standards based on what is known as opposed to mere opinion. If there is free speech and public disagreement, then the parties that prevail have to give reasons for their views, according to Mill. In other words, Mill thought that free speech would encourage good arguments, and that good arguments would result in an informed public. Knowledge, according to Mill, required both reasoning and a justification of beliefs.

## What was John Stuart **Mill's formulation** of **utilitarianism**?

Mill showed how the principle of utility can be used to account for individual action and collective values. As a consequence of individuals seeking their own happiness, the good of society as a personal goal might be a result. Social values such as justice, in Mill's account, do not benefit society as mere abstractions, but only if individuals seek them out in their own lives.

## What was John Stuart **Mill's** final **assessment** of **religious belief**?

Mill concluded that, given the evils of this world, it is impossible that there is a God who is both all powerful and loves humankind. He did think, though, that it was likely that there exists a less than omnipotent but nonetheless benevolent deity. Overall, Mill believed that human beings can control their happiness on Earth through improvements in education and social institutions. Still, he saw the utility of religion for some who modeled their own morality based on Jesus Christ's teachings.

## What are John Stuart Mill's progressive ideas in *The Subjection of Women*?

Mill begins *The Subjection of Women* (1869) by saying that it is more difficult to argue against a position that is held on irrational grounds than one based on reasoning. (René Descartes [1596–1650] made a similar claim at the beginning of his *Meditations*.) Those who hold irrational views will not be persuaded to change them by rational argument but will just look for a more "profound" basis of their opinion, even to the point of claiming it is the result of instinct.

This set the stage for Mill's claim that the condition of women at the time he wrote was the result of a long historical tradition of "might makes right," combined with the power enjoyed by all men "simply by being born male." He compared this condition to slavery on a number of counts: women were completely dependent on men for their livelihood, being deprived of education and means for productive employment; women did not have control over their own bodies or children in marriage; women lacked civil rights, such as the right to vote or own property; and women were subject to violence and rape within marriage, without legal recourse.

Mill also claimed that women were trained to display the traits of mind and character (or lack thereof) that would make them desirable subordinates to men: stupidity, preoccupation with appearance, and adoration of and submission to men. Men assumed that all women wanted to be wives and mothers, which made their exclusion of them from education and the professions ironic, to say the least. But although marriage appeared to be a contractual relationship, women did not have any real freedom to withhold their consent because they could not earn a living on their own.

Against existing arguments that women were not the equals of men, Mill claimed that insofar as women had been so suppressed by their circumstances in marriage and lack of education, men knew very little about what their true capabilities were. He claimed that "the highest masculine and the highest feminine characters" were clearly equal.

## What were John Stuart **Mill's views** on **marriage**?

Mill concluded that human virtue flourishes best in friendships between equals, and that was his ideal for marriage, "by a real enrichment of the two natures, each acquiring the tastes and capacities of the other." As a utilitarian, Mill justified this ideal of friendship between equals for marriage by claiming that it would allow half of the human population to make contributions to civilized life, which had not yet been made. He also believed that women had already demonstrated distinctive moral strengths and altruistic impulses, so that their participation in civic life and the professions would advance civilized values in general.

## How were John Stuart **Mill's views** on **women influential**?

Mill expressed these views at a time when it was fashionable for educated men to sentimentalize the traditional role of women. Such sentimentalization, for example, can be seen in social thinker and critic John Ruskin's *Sesame and Lillies,* or English writer and critic Coventry Patmore's poem "The Angel in the House." Many religious authorities and political leaders were outraged and shocked by Mill's opinions on this matter. On the other hand, the suffragist movement had already begun in both England and the United States, and the support of a famous philosopher and public figure was perceived to be a great help in the cause.

Nonetheless, it wasn't until about 50 years after *The Subjection of Women* (1869) was published that women got the vote in both countries. Although the rights Mill advocated for women are now largely taken for granted, some feminists believe that Mill's failure to address the issue of the division of labor within the family rendered his arguments for the liberation of women incomplete, as did his basic assumption that, even once liberated, the vast majority of women would still choose to be wives and mothers. And although Mill stressed the personal development of women, he did so more within the context of their traditional roles than in terms of their autonomy as human beings.

## What was John Stuart **Mill's view** of **logic** and **scientific methodology**?

Foremost, Mill argued that deductive logic does not depend on intuition for its proof, but rather on internal consistency. The foundational assumptions or axioms of all sciences are based on experience. Even the shared scientific axiom that nature is uniform or law-like is proved through simple enumeration of confirming examples, that is, through induction. More specific causal explanations do no more than summarize necessary and sufficient conditions: A necessary condition is always present when the effect occurs; the effect is always present when a sufficient condition is present. For example,

## Who was Harriet Taylor?

**H**arriet Taylor (1807–1858) was John Stuart Mill's wife. He met her when he was 25, while still recovering from his nervous breakdown. She had been married since the age of 18 to John Taylor, with whom she had three sons. Mill and Harriet Taylor had what they described as a platonic relationship, until the death of her husband after 20 years of marriage. At one point, the Taylors separated, with Harriet taking her daughter to live with her, while John raised their sons.

Some feminist writers believe that Harriet was actually the author of Mill's *The Subjection of Women,* (1869) as well as other writings, such as *On Liberty* (1859), for which Mill gave her great credit. Taylor's contemporary detractors referred to her as "that stupid woman," and said she only appeared to have been Mill's collaborator because she was adept at repeating what he had already said or written. Taylor published very little in her own name. She was a founding member of the Kensington Society, which circulated the first petition for the rights of women, and she contributed articles to the Unitarian journal, *Monthly Repository*. Mill was without question extremely devoted to her, and after her death he wrote:

> Were I but capable of interpreting to the world one half the great thoughts and noble feelings which are buried in her grave, I should be the medium of a greater benefit to it, than is ever likely to arise from anything that I can write, unprompted and unassisted by her all but unrivalled wisdom.

a bullet to the brain is sufficient to cause death in most cases, but it is not necessary because people die from other causes. Or, oxygen is necessary to cause fire, but it is not sufficient because fire requires friction and combustible material, as well as oxygen.

Mill also thought that the basic principles of arithmetic and geometry could be proved by induction. He agreed with Isidore Marie Auguste François Xavier Comte (1798–1857) about a unified view of the social sciences, whereby the laws for more general sciences could be derived from what is known about more specific sciences. For example, observations of individual human behavior could result in a science of psychology, and observations of individual psychology could result in a science of society or sociology. It should be noted that much subsequent theoretical work in mathematics and social science did not find Mill's ideas useful.

# AUGUSTE COMTE

## Who was **Auguste Comte**?

Isidore Marie Auguste François Xavier Comte (1798–1857) was famous and influential in his day as a sociologist, and even coined the word *"sociologie."* He was the first Western sociologist. Comte has also endured as the founder of positivism.

Comte taught mathematics for a while at l'École Polytechnique in Paris, where he himself was educated. Although mental illness—to the extent of psychotic episodes that required hospitalization—interfered with his work, his condition stabilized enough for him to complete his major work during a marriage that ended in divorce. After the woman he loved in a subsequent platonic relationship died, he formulated his mission to create a new "religion of humanity." Comte published *Cours de philosophie positive (Course in Positive Philosophy)* in six volumes from 1830 to 1832.

## What was Auguste **Comte's positivism**?

Comte advocated the use of mathematics for making decisions in ways that still influence statistics and business models today. He believed that our knowledge all comes from observation and asserted that it was impossible to know anything about physical objects that could not be observed. The goal of science was prediction, said Comte, and explanation has the same structure as prediction. He meant by this that a theory that generates predictions about what will happen can also explain what has happened. For example, suppose our theory is that friction, oxygen, and combustible material will cause fire. From this we can predict that striking a match will result in a flame, and we can also explain why striking the match causes the flame. Comte also thought that imagination should always be kept in check by observation.

Auguste Comte is credited with coining the term "sociology" (Art Archive).

## What were Auguste **Comte's sociological ideas**?

Comte believed that in all the sciences, there are three historical phases: theological, metaphysical, and scientific or positive.

The theological phase contains religious restrictions and belief in the supernatural. The metaphysical phase involves the justification of political rights above authority. In the scientific phase, solutions to social problems can be found. By combining these laws of phases, Comte developed an "Encyclopedic Law," according to which all of the sciences could be ordered into a hierarchy in which sociology was the greatest and included all of the others. Comte wrote: "If it is true that every theory must be based upon observed facts, it is equally true that facts can not be observed without the guidance of some theories." He thus posited an interconnection between facts and theories, which holds to this day.

### Did Auguste **Comte** believe in **altruism**?

Yes. In fact, Comte coined the word "altruism," meaning an obligation to help and serve others, even at cost or harm to one's own self-interests.

# INTUITIONISM

### **What** was nineteenth century **intuitionism**?

To some extent all philosophical systems have a place for intuition: direct knowledge that is non-inferential or cannot be proved by prior argument and for which there is no way to resolve doubts. Mill thought that William Whewell's (1794–1866) philosophy of science was "intuitive," although it was in places quite inferential. However, Whewell did have an explicitly intuitionist moral theory. Other noteworthy nineteenth century intuitionists were William Hamilton, F.H. Bradley, Henry Sidgwick, James Martineau, and, toward the end of the century and into the next, Henri Bergson.

### What was William **Whewell's intuitionist moral philosophy**?

Whewell (1794–1866) claimed that conscience enables direct perception of moral goodness and badness. However, he did not describe conscience as a separate moral faculty but as "reason exercised on moral subjects." Moral rules are primary principles of reason, discoverable by reason itself. He took them to be self-evident necessary truths.

### What was **Scottish Common Sense Philosophy**?

It was the realist view of human knowledge put forth by Thomas Reid (1710–1796) that what we know are real objects in the world and not our ideas, as claimed by David Hume (1711–1776).

### Who was **William Hamilton**?

William Hamilton (1788–1856) was a professor at Scotland's University of Edinburgh. He is famous for his "philosophy of the conditioned" in Scottish Common Sense Phi-

believe that morality is an intrinsic value, which, depending on their social status, they "self-realize" in their actions. Good selves could be actualized only if bad selves were suppressed. Therefore, the good self requires the bad self and morality can never be completely actualized unless oneself "dies" through surrender to Christianity.

## Was F.H. **Bradley** also an **idealist**?

It's not clear whether Bradley was an idealist, though he did believe that our direct experience of particular existence is what we can call reality. In his second major work, *The Principles of Logic* (1883), Bradley attempted to construct the metaphysical system that would explain his ethics. Thought is embodied in judgments, which must be true or false. Ideas are the contents of judgments and they represent reality. Ideas also represent kinds of things, each member of which is a particular individual (in the sense of an object). For example, you can have the idea of your particular pet dog, Rover, and that idea represents just Rover; but you also have the idea of dogs that represents all dogs.

However, all judgments are hypotheticals claiming that certain universal connections exist in reality. For example, if one makes the judgment that dogs are good companions for humans, one is claiming that dogs—in a general sense that applies to all dogs—are good companions in a general sense that applies to all human beings. But such a judgment is hypothetical because you might have a dog that is not a good companion for you.

Reality is the sum total of everything that there is in the world and as such, reality is what Bradley called a "concrete whole." One encounters reality by the experiences that one has. That is, judgments are abstract, whereas reality is particular. For this reason, thought can never fully represent reality. Another way of putting this is that the real world cannot be completely described and classified by us.

Finally, in his *Appearance and Reality* (1893), Bradley further explained that reality, as experience, is all blended in harmony. Bradley thought that relations such as "bigger," "smaller," "before," and "after" are appearances, not reality. Relations are abstracted by thought from direct experience of reality. This direct experience taken altogether is "the Absolute," and, in a surprising turn, Bradley concluded that the Absolute, or the totality of our experience, is the real reality (as opposed to something that our experience could be "experience of"). In other words, Bradley held both that our experiences are experiences of reality and that all of our experiences added up constitute reality.

## Who was **Henry Sidgwick**?

Henry Sidgwick (1838–1900) was not so much an intuitionist as the first modern moral theorist who used a combination of common sense and shared intuitions to assess the competing moral theories of his day. As a professor at Cambridge University, he was active in founding Newnham, the first college for women. His wife, Eleanor Mildred Balfour, whose brother, Arthur, was later Prime Minister of England, became Prin-

> ## How did John Stuart Mill criticize William Whewell's view of moral intuitionism?
>
> **M**ill's criticism of Whewell's moral intuitionism was that it implied that morality could not progress because necessary truths are always true. Mill further claimed that Whewell's necessary moral truths would preserve the status quo, and he charged Whewell with conservatively supporting slavery, marriage without women's consent, and cruelty to animals. What Mill missed, however, was that, as with Fundamental Ideas in science, Whewell held that we may not know all of the relevant rules of morality. Thus, discovering these rules allowed for moral progress.

losophy. He agreed with Immanuel Kant (1724–1804) that we cannot know things in themselves, but also with Thomas Reid (1710–1796) about naturalism. Reid's idea that we know things in the world directly and Kant's idea that we do not know things in themselves are contradictory. Hamilton believed that they could be mysteriously combined through intuition.

John Stuart Mill (1806–1873), in *An Examination of Sir William Hamilton's Philosophy* (1865), vigorously attacked Hamilton's notion that scientific principles are intuitively valid, rather than valid on account of their ability to provide causal explanations, as Mill thought.

## What was William Hamilton's **philosophy of the conditioned**?

Hamilton called "the conditioned" something that has been described or classified, and "the unconditioned" things that are without descriptions or classifications. His philosophy was an attempt to create a balance between the conditioned and the unconditioned. Hamilton wrote that "all that is conceivable in thought lies between two extremes, which, as contradictory of each other, can not both be true, but of which, as mutually contradictory, one must be true.... The law of the mind, that the conceivable is in every relation bounded by the inconceivable, I call the law of the conditioned." Hamilton held the theological belief that the Infinite is "incognizable and inconceivable."

## Who was **F.H. Bradley**?

Francis Herbert (F.H.) Bradley (1846–1924) was a main architect of nineteenth century British idealism, but he was also highly influential as an intuitionist. His principal work was *Ethical Studies* (1876) in which he sought to explain how morality can be part of individual consciousness and social institutions. He argued that individuals

> ## What was F.H. Bradley like as a person?
>
> **B**radley was made a fellow at Merton College, Oxford, in 1870. This was a life-time position with no teaching duties, which only marriage could terminate. Bradley never married, and he lived on campus until he died. A kidney inflammation in 1871 left him careful of his health, and although he participated in the governance of the college, he avoided other social occasions. For instance, he turned down an opportunity to be a founder of the British Academy.
>
> Bradley detested cats and shot them on the college grounds, during the night. R.G. Collingwood, his neighbor for 16 years, later wrote: "Although I lived within a few hundred yards of him … I never to my knowledge set eyes on him."

cipal of Newnham in 1892. The Sidgwicks collaborated on many reform and intellectual projects, including investigations into parapsychology. Sidgwick's principal works are *The Methods of Ethics* (1874) and *Outlines of the History of Ethics* (1886).

## What was the **Sidgwick's interest** in the **paranormal**?

Henry Sidgwick helped found the Society for Psychical Research in 1892, and his wife, Eleanor, was an active participant. The Sidgwicks believed that the work of society could help confirm religious claims, such as life after death. They believed that an afterlife was necessary as a motivation for morality in this life. However, their investigations were inconclusive, even though Eleanor believed that Henry communicated with her after his death in 1900.

## What is **moral theory**?

Moral theory is the intellectual assessment and comparison of different moral or ethical systems. For instance, if we compare consequentialism and deontology, then we are working within moral theory. To some extent, anyone who argues for their own moral system does some amount of moral theory. For example, Jeremy Bentham (1748–1832) in his dismissal of human rights as "nonsense upon stilts," wanted to replace discourse about rights with calculations about pleasure, and Immanuel Kant (1724–1804) in distinguishing between hypothetical and categorical judgments and elevating the latter, were both engaged in moral theory.

## What did Henry **Sidgwick contribute** to **moral theory**?

First, Sidgwick is considered to have offered the clearest exposition of the classic utilitarianism of Jeremy Bentham (1748–1832) and John Stuart Mill (1806–1873) to such an extent that he is often counted as a utilitarian himself. But second, it is his comparative assessment of egoism, utilitarianism, and intuitionism that remains most instructive. ("Egoism" is the moral system according to which we should always act in our own self-interest.)

Sidgwick examined both common sense moral principles and the main claims of all three systems and concluded that none is self-evident or certain according to intuition. He thought that utilitarianism could be useful when we do not know what to do and seek guidance, but that the basic principles of utilitarianism depend on intuition for their acceptance. But egoism also seems self-evident, and it often conflicts with utilitarianism. Sidgwick admitted that he could not resolve this contradiction.

### Who was **James Martineau**?

James Martineau (1805–1900) was an English religious intuitionist. His main works were *Types of Ethical Theory* (1885) and *A Study of Religion* (1888). His distinct contribution was to develop a specifically religious interpretation of Immanuel Kant's (1724–1804) metaphysics.

Henri Bergson is most famous for arguing that objective measurable time is not the same as real time (Library of Congress).

### How did James **Martineau** make Immanuel **Kant's metaphysics religious**?

Martineau relied on intuition to claim that the phenomenal world mirrors a noumenal world (the world of things we cannot experience) in which real objects are causally related. He held that this reality is the result of God's will. In ethics he claimed that we choose our motives first and then our actions. Intuition tells us which ones are the higher motives and that the highest one is reverence. (He meant that the desire to revere motivates our best actions.)

### Who was **Henri Bergson**?

Henri Bergson (1859–1941) was professor at the Collège de France and winner of the 1927 Nobel Prize for Literature. He is most famous for his *Time and Free Will* (1889) in which he argued that objective

## What did Henri Bergson have to say about laughter and the human sense of humor?

**B**ergson wrote a 1900 analysis of laughter, which shows he was pretty interested in the concept of humor. He thought that the comical is a part of life that cannot be fully understood by reason alone. Laughter requires a state of indifference, according to Bergson, "for laughter has no greater foe than emotion." He went on to say that "the comic demands something like a momentary anesthesia of the heart.... [I]t's appeal is to intelligence pure and simple."

To be comical, something must be rigid, like a facial grimace or a mechanical walk. Our perception of this rigidity is broken up by our laughter. Ordinary language bears Bergson out on this because we talk about being "cracked up," or "broken up" when something is funny. Anything that switches our attention from the soul or moral realm to the body can be comical, said Bergson: for example, a speaker sneezing at a dramatic moment in his presentation. Bergson saw the overall purpose of comedy as a reassertion of life in an age of machines.

measurable time, which can be divided into equal segments, is not the same as real time, which we experience directly. In *Matter and Memory* (1896) he offered a mind–body theory consistent with his later work on evolution in which he argued that a creative urge, rather than Darwinian natural selection, is what causes evolution. In *An Introduction to Metaphysics* (1903) he provided further support for his theory of time. In *Creative Evolution* (1907) he claimed that a life force is necessary to explain evolution, and in *Two Sources of Morality and Religion* (1935) he claimed that there are two kinds of society: one free and allowing for reform and creativity, the other stagnant, conservative, and repressive.

## How did Henri **Bergson relate real time** to **free will**?

Real time, according to Bergson, cannot be imagined as points on a line in space, like scientific clock time. Real time is intuited directly and within us; it is the ground of spontaneous free acts. Our free will is our spontaneous free acts, which are unpredictable. Intuition and analysis parallel this distinction. Intuition apprehends duration directly and examines it, whereas analysis breaks duration up into unchanging concepts.

# PHILOSOPHY OF MATHEMATICS AND LOGIC

## Why did **philosophers** become **interested** in **mathematics, geometry,** and **logic**, during the nineteenth century?

Philosophers have always been interested in these subjects, but in the nineteenth century there were even more innovations in science and technology than before. Changes in the world had an invigorating effect on higher learning, and philosophers took an interest in new research in the sciences and mathematics. Logic had been a philosophical subject since Aristotle, so new forms of logic were of interest to many philosophers who were not logicians.

## What **advances** were made during the **nineteenth century** concerning the **philosophy of mathematics and logic**?

During the nineteenth century, a logical theory of probability was propounded, non-Euclidian geometry was discovered, the objectivity and necessary truth of scientific first principles were questioned, a new system of logical notation was devised, and the possibility that mathematics could be reduced to logic was introduced.

## Who was **Pierre-Simon Laplace**?

Pierre-Simon Laplace (1749–1827) was a mathematician and astronomer who explicated what was to be the classic theory of probability. He taught in Paris at different schools, such as the École Militaire (military school).

## What is Pierre-Simon **Laplace's theory of probability**?

The fact that we do not know certain things gives rise to the idea of probabilities. Because we view the world as determined in assuming that every event has a cause, the probability of an event depends on a combination of what we do know and what we do not know. Laplace's theory of

Mathematican and astronomer Pierre-Simon Laplace was famous for his theory of probability (Art Archive).

218

## Who was Pierre-Simon Laplace's most famous student?

The man who would later become the most famous French dictator in history, Napoleon Bonaparte, was one of Laplace's students. Laplace's definitive *Analytic Theory of Probabilities* (1812) was, in fact, dedicated to Napoleon.

probability was that if there is no reason to believe that one of a number of events, n, will occur, then the probability of each happening is 1/n. For example, the probability that any day of the week chosen at random will be either a Tuesday or a Thursday is 2/7.

## What is **non-Euclidian geometry**?

Euclidian geometry depends on a number of axioms, most important of which concerns the property of parallel lines. Non-Euclidian geometry changed Euclidian axioms. It was to have application in physics, particularly Albert Einstein's theory of relativity, when it enabled a concept of "the fourth dimension."

Carl Friedrich Gauss (1777–1855) was the first to figure out the principles of non-Euclidian geometry, although because he did not publish his ideas, the credit was given to Janos Bolyai (1802–1860) and Nikolai Lobachevsky (1792–1856), who were working independently. They rejected the Euclidian assumption that could not be proved in which only one line passes through a point in a plane that is parallel to a separate coplanar line. In their new system, a line can have more than one parallel and the sum of the angles of a triangle may be less than 180 degrees.

By the middle of the nineteenth century, Bernhard Riemann (1826–1866) developed a geometry in which straight lines always meet, thereby having no parallels, and in addition allowing for the sum of the angles of a triangle to be greater than 180 degrees. (In Euclidian geometry, parallel lines never meet and the sum of the angles of a triangle is always 180 degrees.) Reimann also went on to distinguish between the unboundedness of space as part of its extent, and the infinite measure over which distance could be taken that is related to the curvature of the same space. Riemann returned to Gauss' now-published work and explained the new ideas of distance first introduced by Loybachevski and Bolyai in terms of trigonometry. The bottom line was that "arc length" could be understood as the shortest distance between two points on a surface, without reference to the geometric properties or applicable geometry of that in which the surface itself was imbedded.

In 1868, Eugenio Beltrami (1835–1899) demonstrated a model of a Bolyai-type two-dimensional space, inside a planar circle. This proved that the consistency of non-Euclidian geometry depended on the consistency of Euclidian geometry, thus reassuring skeptics that non-Euclidian geometry was valid.

219

## How did **non-Euclidian geometry affect** other fields?

The relationship between space and geometry changed forever in people's minds, thanks to non-Euclidian geometry. The question arose of whether space itself was curved. This made the whole of geometry seem hypothetical and led some to question the possibility of *a priori* knowledge. That is, if space is not necessarily Euclidian and there are other unknown geometries of space, then what does it mean to say that we have "*a priori* knowledge of space?" Also, the idea of the curvature of space was conducive to Albert Einstein's theory of relativity, thus influencing physics and our concept of the universe.

## What are **Venn diagrams**?

British philosopher and logician John Venn (1834–1923) invented the system of logic diagrams named after him, which consisted of the overlapping circles. They can be used to test and demonstrate the validity of inferences. Venn diagrams illustrate collections of sets and their relationships to each other, which are useful in logic theory.

## Who was **Jules Henri Poincaré**?

Jules Henri Poincaré (1854–1912) was a mathematician, physicist, and philosopher of science. He responded to the discovery of non-Euclidian geometry by suggesting a modification of Immanuel Kant's (1724–1804) claim that we have synthetic *a priori* knowledge of the world (that is, certainly true knowledge that applies to reality, which is not based on experience).

His proposal was what became known as "conventionalism," namely that physicists will retain Euclidian geometry because it has the simplest geometrical conventions and is therefore appropriate for them. This proposal was short-lived in mathematics, because Albert Einstein was to show in his General Theory of Relativity that the curvature of space obeyed the principles of non-Euclidian geometry. However, the broader principle of conventionalism, namely that truth in science depends on agreement about specified rules, was to be revived as an idea of scientific truth in the twentieth century.

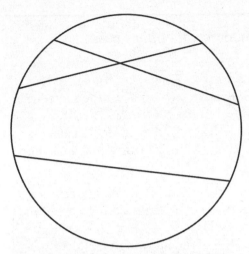

Beltrami's model of n–dimensional hyperbolic geometry in which points are represented by the points in the interior of the n–dimensional unit ball (or unit disk, in two dimensions, in this schematic) and lines are represented by the chords or straight line segments with endpoints on the boundary sphere (here, it is the circumference of the two–dimensional disk.)

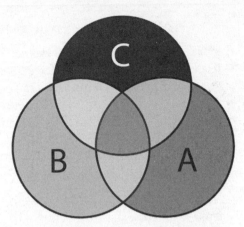

A Venn diagram of sets A, B, and C. Where one or more sets overlap, it means that they have members in common. It can be seen by the overlapping in this diagram that some things are A, B, and C, some things are A and B, some things are B and C, and some things are A and C.

## Who was **Gottlob Frege**?

Gottlob Frege (1848–1925) was a professor of mathematics at the University of Jena, who thought that Immanuel Kant (1724–1804) was mistaken in claiming that mathematical truth is synthetic—that is, about reality. (Kant had claimed that mathematical truths were synthetic *a priori,* which is to say both true of the world and known independently of experience of the world.) His task was to show how the concepts of mathematics could be defined in terms of logic alone, so that the theorems of mathematics would then appear as logical truths. If mathematics could be reduced to logic in this way, it would be shown that mathematics was merely true by definition, meaning that it had no empirical content, so that it could not be about the world. Mathematics would thereby be *a priori*, but not also synthetic, as Kant had insisted.

## What was Gottlob **Frege's** main **innovation** in the philosophy of **logic**?

Frege treated predicates as functions and subjects as arguments. Thus "Socrates is mortal" becomes "function 'mortal' is applied to argument 'Socrates.'" In his *Conceptual Notation* (1879), Frege also introduced a simple way to treat words and terms such as "all" and "there is" as logical quantifiers. Logical quantification is a notational system that connects a variable with what is being talked about. For example, in the sentence "Every person alive today will die some day," "person alive today" is being talked about and "every" is the quantifier. This treatment of Frege's still stands today.

221

## What was Gottlob Frege's landmark insight about meaning?

Frege's theory of language was set forth in three essays: "Function and Concept," "On Concept and Object," and "Sense and Reference." He noted that some identity statements are true and informative. For example, the sentence "Venus is Venus," does not tell me anything, but the sentence, "The Morning Star is the Evening Star," is informative, although it means the same as "Venus is Venus," because Venus is in fact both the Morning Star and the Evening Star.

How can this be? Frege's explanation was that there is a difference between "sense" and "reference." Reference is the actual planet Venus, in this case. But sense is *how* the planet is referred to by the term "Morning Star" (i.e., a bright object in the eastern sky before sunrise). Thus, "The Morning Star" does not stand for Venus itself, but for the sense of how Venus is presented. This is why the two sentences that appear to be equivalent really are different. It explains why it is not informative to say that Venus is Venus or that The Morning Star is the Morning Star, but it is informative to say that Venus is the Morning Star.

## How did Gottlob **Frege** attempt to **reduce mathematics** to **logic**?

In his *Foundations of Arithmetic* (1884), Frege argued that logic, or the laws of thought, are not descriptive of how we think and that words do not have meaning in isolation but only within context. Then in his two-volume *Basic Laws of Arithmetic* (1893 and 1903), Frege began his project in earnest by showing that every predicate determines a class that can be described logically. For example, red is a predicate and red determines a class of red things.

## Did Gottlob **Frege succeed** in **reducing mathematics** to **logic**?

Alas, no. When the second volume to Frege's *Basic Laws of Arithmetic* (1893) had been sent to the printer, he received a letter from British philosopher, historian, and mathematician Bertrand Russell (1872–1970) in which Russell introduced his famous paradox: "Is the class of all classes that are not members of itself a member of itself or not?" The question is coherent but it entails a contradiction, so it has no answer.

Frege had to admit that he had no foundation for his reasoning: "A scientist can hardly encounter anything more undesirable than to have the foundation collapse just as the work is finished. I was put in this position by a letter from Mr. Bertrand Russell when the work was almost through the press." The great irony in this is that Russell embarked on his own project to reduce mathematics to logic—and failed!

# GERMAN IDEALISM

## What is **German idealism**?

It was the philosophical perspective developed in the nineteenth century that reality is not physical but psychic, or mental. Its main author was Georg Wilhelm Friedrich Hegel (1770–1831). There were also British and American versions of Hegelian thought.

## How were **nineteenth century German idealists different** from **Plato** or George **Berkeley**?

Before the nineteenth century, idealism tended to be a train of thought in individual writers who posited the existence of unseen entities and claimed greater reality for them than the things in the world that could be sensed. Except for Plotinus (205–270) and other Neo-Platonists, idealism before the nineteenth century was limited to positing entities or structures that existed in a separate realm, independently of perceived reality, as humans perceive reality.

The nineteenth century idealists, in contrast, posited ideal entities and structures and also described their functions in ways that directly influenced the perceived world and events within it. A medical analogy is that before the nineteenth century, idealists were like philosophical "anatomists," whereas in the nineteenth century, idealists also worked as philosophical "physiologists." This last is especially true of Friedrich Hegel (1770–1831), although he could not have constructed his system without Immanuel Kant's (1724–1804) work before him, and the directions in which Johann Gottlieb Fichte (1762–1814) and Friedrich Schelling (1775–1854) tried to take Kant's work.

## JOHANN GOTTLIEB FICHTE

### Who was **Johann Gottlieb Fichte**?

Johann Gottlieb Fichte (1762–1814) is regarded as an intellectual bridge between Immanuel Kant (1724–1804) and Friedrich Hegel (1770–1831), as well as the founder of the nineteenth century school of German idealism.

### What are some highlights of Johann Gottlieb Fichte's career?

As a student at Leipzig University, Fichte studied Benedict de Spinoza's (1632–1677) philosophy. After he discovered Immanuel Kant (1724–1804), he wrote *An Attempt at a Critique of All Revelation,* (1792) in which he tried to show that morality was the major part of religion. This was inspired by Kant's view that an understanding of morality requires an understanding of religion.

223

Soon after Fichte met Immanuel Kant (1724–1804) in Königsberg, his first book, *Attempt at a Critique of All Revelation* (1792), appeared. It drew connections between religious revelation and Kant's philosophy. Fichte had not shown it to Kant before publication, and Fichte's name did not appear as the work's author, so the book was assumed to be by Kant. Kant generously cleared up this misunderstanding, giving high praise to Fichte, who immediately became famous. The accolades were hyperbolic. One reader wrote: "The most shocking and astonishing news … nobody but Kant could have written this book. This amazing news of a third sun (the other two being Kant and René Descartes [1596–1650]) in the philosophical heavens has set me into such confusion."

## What are some important facts about Johann Gottlieb **Fichte's career**?

Fichte was appointed professor of philosophy at the University of Jena in 1794, where he extended his Kantian idea of duty to criticize the drunkenness, lewdness, and brawling of the students. In 1795 he became an editor of the *Philosophiches Journal,* and in the preface to an article he was going to publish that had been written by a friend of his, he wrote that God was the moral order of the universe. There were complaints that this was an atheistic view, and so the governments of Saxony and other German states suppressed the *Philosophiches Journal* and demanded that Fichte be kicked out of Jena.

Fichte defended himself in writing and then threatened to resign his university position. The Jena University authorities interpreted his threat as an offer, which they immediately accepted, so he lost his position there. Much later, in 1810, he became the first professor of philosophy at the University of Berlin.

Fichte's independent philosophy was first stated in *Foundation of the Science of Knowledge* (1794) and popularized in *The Vocation of Man* (1800). In 1796 he wrote *Foundations of Natural Right,* which was his treatment of natural law. In 1808 he gave a series of "Speeches to the German Nation" in French-occupied Berlin (published as "Addresses to the German Nation" in 1922). In those talks, Fichte supported resistance against French dictator Napoleon Bonaparte, arguing for the common good.

## What were the main **original ideas** that were important to Johann Gottlieb **Fichte's philosophy**?

Fichte was opposed to what he called dogmatism, or the idea that there was an external world that was independent of human beings and what they valued. He thought that atheism, materialism, and determinism were the results of such beliefs in objective reality, and this was to the detriment of morality. Even Immanuel Kant's (1724–1804) system had a dogmatic strain in his positing of things-in-themselves, which could not be known. Fichte's solution to these problems of dogmatism was idealism: mind creates everything.

### How was Johann Gottlieb **Fichte's idealism** connected to **freedom**?

Fichte thought that our spontaneity is something we can become aware of through reflection on ourselves as active beings, who think, as well as do things in the world. This entails that the ultimate reality is a "transcendental ego," a locus of pure activity. Following Kant, Fichte meant that behind the self of which a person is aware while thinking, there is an unperceived self. Fichte believed that maturity was required to realize this freedom of the self. Those who were immature would cling to dogmatism.

### What was Johann Gottlieb **Fichte's political philosophy**?

In his *Foundations of Natural Right* (1796), he supported individualism, but his views changed over time. His "Speeches to the German Nation" (1808) advocated concern for the common good and condemned selfish acts. He argued that egoism was untenable, morally, but that the German people could rise to a higher level because of the innate excellence of their character and language.

## FRIEDRICH SCHELLING

### Who was **Friedrich Schelling**?

The literary and artistic Romantics of his era deeply influenced the philosophy of Arthur Friedrich Wilhelm Joseph Schelling (1776–1854). He studied at Tübinger Stift (the seminary of the Protestant Church in Württemberg) and graduated from the philosophy faculty there in 1792. He then attended lectures at the University of Leipzig while working as a tutor to aristocratic youth. At the age of 23 he received an unprecedented offer to teach philosophy at the University of Jena. He subsequently held chairs at the universities at Würzberg, Erlangen, Munich, and finally Berlin, where he was expected to oppose the Hegelians. His primary motivation in philosophy appears to have been aesthetic, and he became known for his "nature philosophy," as developed in his *System of Transcendental Idealism* (1800).

### What was Friedrich **Schelling's** major **thesis**?

Schelling believed that the entirety of Nature, physical as well as mental, was Mind on the way toward consciousness. But consciousness, or the human self, is the creator of nature. Life cannot be explained in mechanistic or inert terms.

Schelling resurrected a type of alchemical thought whereby "magnetism," which is the general form of particular existence, either becomes evident in light or maleness, or else becomes evident in heavy inertia, or femaleness. In ordinary language (although there was nothing ordinary about this belief) the alchemists believed that things that exist are all made up of a magnetic something that can manifest itself in either light-weight and airy (or male) beings, or else in heavy and dense (or female) beings.

He believed that existent reality became separated from the Absolute in a spontaneous act of freedom, which created time itself, along with the world as we know it. That is, there occurred in the Absolute a spontaneous burst of freedom that resulted in the separation of what we perceive as reality from the Absolute. Another consequence was the appearance of time. This is to say that the Absolute exists outside of time.

Schelling had a following among Romantics in the sciences, as well as in the arts because Romantics in the nineteenth century, as today, loved quasi-mystical explanations of the world. Lorenz Oken (1774–1851), for example, postulated that all of life in Schelling's sense in which nature is unconscious mind, originated in "primeval slime." The connection between Oken's idea and Schelling's thought is not at all clear, except to indicate how one wild set of ideas is capable of inspiring others.

### How were Friedrich **Schelling's views** of **culture aesthetic?**

Schelling believed that history is a drama that will be resolved when the Absolute discloses itself. God is an artist, the universe his artwork. The main value of religion lies not in its morality, but in its beauty.

## FRIEDRICH HEGEL

### Who was **Friedrich Hegel?**

For sheer intellectual fire-power, Georg Wilhelm Friedrich Hegel (1770–1831) was probably the most brilliant thinker of the nineteenth century. He was a philosopher who could think about the entire world with an Aristotelian comprehensiveness, if not an Aristotelian lucidity. He is best known for his idealist positing of an Absolute, a kind of non-religious, Neo-Platonic, post-Enlightenment "One," which was observed only through its workings in the ordinary reality experienced by mere mortals, but deduced (divined?) through the logic of Hegel himself.

### What are some highlights of Friedrich **Hegel's career?**

Hegel was the eldest of three children. His father was a minor government official in the Duchy of Wittenberg; his mother died when he was 11. He attended the theological seminary or "Stift," which was a subsidiary of the University of Tübingen. His roommates were the great German Romantic poet Johann Christian Friedrich Hölder-

## What is the story behind Friedrich Schelling's scandalous romantic affair with August Wilhelm von Schlegel's wife?

When he was teaching in Jena, Schelling was close friends with German poet August Wilhelm von Schlegel, who was highly esteemed by other German Romantics, and with Karoline, who would later be the poet's wife. There was discussion of marriage between Schelling and the Schlegels' daughter, Auguste. But Auguste died from dysentery in 1800, after Schelling had supervised her treatment. At first, Schelling was blamed, but later biographers exonerated him because her death was probably medically inevitable at that time.

Schelling and Karoline then recognized their love for each other, and August moved out, leaving Jena for Berlin. Later, Johann Wolfgang von Goethe, another famous literary figure, helped secure a divorce, and Schelling and Karoline married, after they had left Jena to avoid the predictable scandal.

lin and the philosopher Friedrich Schelling (1775–1854), who would be his colleague and intellectual opponent. (They disputed the importance of Reason, with Hegel proudly affirming it and Schelling expressing a lack of enthusiasm for it.) When he graduated, Hegel first worked as a tutor for a Bern family, and then he moved to Frankfurt. His father's death provided him with sufficient income to concentrate on his own scholarly work in hopes of getting a university position. His early interests were in reconciling fluid notions of reason with non-institutionalized Christianity.

In 1805, Schelling assisted Hegel in moving to Jena, where he lectured for several years and became a professor at the University of Jena. By this time, as expressed in his early essays, Hegel was having doubts about the freedom promised by the Enlightenment. He loved the thought and ways of life of ancient Greece and believed that Enlightenment rights would result in new forms of repression. One motivation for this concern might have been his experience of the French Revolution. On a deeper philosophical level, he thought that what was most noble in human beings required society and government for its development. This view conflicted with the individual rights doctrine, which assumed that government was the enemy of natural human rights.

At Jena, he co-edited the *Critical Journal of Philosophy* with Schelling, which was dedicated to exploring the consequences of Immanuel Kant's (1724–1804) transcendental idealism, in light of Johann Gottlieb Fichte (1762–1814) and Schelling's own work. Hegel left Jena when the University closed after Napoleon Bonaparte's victory in October 1806. He then edited a pro-Napoleon newspaper in Bavaria, and became headmaster of a Nuremberg high school in 1808.

Friedrich Hegel was a philosopher who could think about the entire world with an Aristotelian comprehensiveness (AP).

In 1807 Hegel's important *Phenomenology of Spirit* was published, and then his *Science of Logic* (1812) resulted in a professorship at Heidelberg. In 1818 he assumed his last post, which was as a professor at Berlin, lecturing widely on philosophy of history, history of philosophy, aesthetics, and philosophy of religion, much of which was unpublished until it was posthumously compiled from his notes and those of students. Hegel's *Foundations of the Philosophy of Right: Natural Right and Political Science in Outline* was published in 1821.

## What were Friedrich **Hegel's** main ideas?

Hegel's system is difficult to describe because all of its parts are inter-related, and so to describe one aspect of it is to evoke all of the others; it is not clear exactly where an interpreter might begin. Hegel's order of exposition in the progression of his work is not a good guide because the structure of his system has to be presupposed in order to make sense of the progression. In other words, Hegel had his whole system in mind as he wrote about different parts of it. This said, there are several important elements that can be identified as Hegel's premises:

- Man has a history, but nature does not.
- All men do not have the same categories of fact.
- Human thought develops.
- Philosophy should give a rational account of religion.
- Social stability is possible after the French revolution.
- Individual autonomy is possible in a unified society.
- The nature of things is a system and a system of knowledge must reflect that.

## What was Friedrich **Hegel's system**?

Knowledge, according to Hegel, begins with logic, the subject of which is pure being, although logic is always "mediated" in history, so that we do not see or experience logic in its pure form, but have to infer it from relations among events. Past philosophy represents different forms of consciousness that have progressed toward absolute knowledge or philosophical science. The progression of consciousness occurs because different forms of consciousness are contradictory and their inner dialectic resolves the contradictions via the emergence of new forms. This dialectic is not a dialogue between consciousnesses, but the inner development of what consciousness is conscious of. Hegel is able to chronicle this development of consciousness toward absolute knowledge, because it is presumed to be attained through his philosophical work.

## What happens after **absolute knowledge** is **attained**?

Friedrich Hegel's science is aimed at uniting Immanuel Kant's (1724–1804) system of transcendental categories to Aristotle's (384–322 B.C.E.) logic about the real world. Hegel divides his thought process into treatments of being, essence, and concept, which are each divided into three parts, and so on. The contradictions in each category of nature require resolution leading to the categories that succeed it.

According to Hegel, nature itself has developed in a logical way, leading to ever greater abstractions in the form of our knowledge of nature. Hegel did not make clear distinctions between things in themselves in an ordinary, realist sense, and our knowledge of those things. For Hegel, then, the progression toward more complexity in nature corresponds with a progression in human knowledge.

## Is **Hegel's system** purely **abstract**?

Very abstract thinking is necessary to understand Hegel's system, but the system itself is presented by him as a literal account of reality. Categories are at the outset literally embedded in physical nature, which expresses them. Space expresses a lower category of being, whereas living organisms embody and express the higher categories of concept, purpose, and life. Thus, the development of the system of thought is evident in the development of the real world, except that thought, or the Absolute, is the ultimately real actualizing and defining principle of everything that exists.

## Where does the **human mind fit** into **Hegel's idealism**?

Human *Geist,* or mind, or spirit, is made up of the same categories that form reality, according to Friedrich Hegel. These categories, as ideas, develop in the individual life and in humanity as a whole over time. There are three stages of spirit, with the second higher than the first, and the third higher than the second. The first stage is subjective spirit, which is individual psychology. The second stage of Geist is objective spirit, or the traditions, rules, and institutions of society. The third stage of Geist is Absolute Spirit, evident in the arts, religion, and philosophy. As spirit understands itself, it becomes free and aware of itself, or self-conscious. Spirit preserves, destroys, and raises up what is not spirit.

## Was Hegel a political radical or a romantic?

**F**riedrich Hegel was not a radical in his mature writings in which he praised the status quo. But in his youth, perhaps he was. At 18 he began studies at the Stift Theological Seminary in Tübingen, but he was bored by the course of study and sermons, preferring to read Aristotle, Spinoza, Voltaire, and Rousseau. Nevertheless, he was a good student, earning a Ph.D. by 20 and a theological certificate three years later. His peers called him "old man" when he accompanied them in hiking, beer drinking, and carousing. They were all excited by the French Revolution, and in 1792 Hegel was called the "most enthusiastic speaker of freedom and equality" in a student club that was devoted to the study of Plato, Kant, and F.H. Jacobi.

Hegel's roommates were the poet Christian Friedrich Hölderlin and the philosopher Friedrich Schelling (1775–1854). From Hölderlin he learned to love the ancient Greeks even more. They all protested against the political and ecclesiastical stasis of Tübingen. On July 14, 1792, Hegel, Hölderlin, and Schelling were said to have planted a liberty tree on a meadow near the Tübingen Seminary, although not all biographers think this in fact happened.

Hegel was hardly a Romantic philosopher, but there was some romantic drama in his life. As he was finishing *The Phenomenology of Spirit* (1807), Christina Burkhard informed him that she was pregnant with their child. Ludwig, his illegitimate son, was born in February 1807. He completed the manuscript on the same day Napoleon Bonaparte captured Jena: October 18, 1807. In 1811, at the age of 41, he married Marie von Tucher, who was 20. Marie's aristocratic family was not enthusiastic about the match, though, and a government official friend had to intervene to negotiate it. During their courtship, Hegel wrote her a romantic poem (which most describe as hackneyed); he referred to his hope of marrying her as an ascension into "eternal bliss."

## What did Friedrich **Hegel think** was the **highest form** of **spirit**?

The modern state of Hegel's own time is considered by him to be the epitome of Absolute spirit. This state is a unity that molds its members and also allows them individual freedom.

## Who were the "**Right**" and "**Left**" **Hegelians**?

Active interest in Friedrich Hegel's ideas died out soon after his death in 1843, but his influence has nonetheless continued in much twentieth-century thought. His ideas were immediately interpreted by the "Right Hegelians," who believed that the Prussian state represented the final union of philosophy and Christianity, and the "Left Hegelians," including Ludwig Andreas von Feuerbach (1804–1872) and Karl Marx (1818–1883), who interpreted a politically revolutionary future for the dialectic propounded by Hegel.

## ARTHUR SCHOPENHAUER

### Who was **Arthur Schopenhauer**?

Arthur Schopenhauer (1788–1860) was influenced by the other German idealists, whom he despised as optimistic fools. Unlike Friedrich Hegel (1770–1831) and both the Right or the Left Hegelians, his view of the Idea that formed and worked the world was pessimistic.

### What are some highlights of Arthur **Schopenhauer's life**?

Educated in Germany, Schopenhauer traveled throughout his childhood to France, Holland, Switzerland, Austria, and England. After his father's death, which biographers attribute to suicide, his mother, Johanna Troisner, moved to Weimar and became a celebrated novelist. She introduced Arthur to Johann Wolfgang von Goethe, August Wilhelm Schlegel, and the Brothers Grimm.

Schopenhauer studied medicine at the University of Götttingen and philosophy at Berlin, getting his doctorate at the University of Jena. After that, he lived in Frankfurt. His doctoral dissertation, *On the Fourfold Root of the Principle of Sufficient Reason* (1813), formed the basis of his philosophy, which appeared systematically in his most important work, *The World as Will and Representation* (1818).

### What were Arthur **Schopenhauer's** main **ideas**?

Schopenhauer offered an original interpretation of Immanuel Kant's (1724–1804) metaphysics based on additional inspiration. He wrote: "I owe what is best in my own development to the impression made by Kant's works, the sacred writings of the Hindus, and Plato." In his dissertation, he argued that Kant's phenomenal world, or the world of our experience, which Schopenhauer called "the world of representation," obeys the "principle of sufficient reason," which he stated this way: "every possible object … stands in a necessary relation to other objects, on the one hand as determined, on the other as determining." That is, everything is both a cause and an effect and these relations are necessary, which is to say that they cannot be denied without logical contradiction.

Kant's noumenal world, or the "things in themselves," of which we can know nothing except that they exist, became knowable, according to Schopenhauer, through our inner reality, which is our will. Again following Kant, because mathemat-

Arthur Schopenhauer was known for having a more pessimistic view of the world than German idealists like Friedrich Hegel (iStock).

ics or numbers are projections of the mind that enable us to experience phenomena, Schopenhauer felt that the noumenal world has no number—it is "one." This claim would have no consequences in experience if it were true, since it is an effort to describe what underlies experience.

## How did Arthur **Schopenhauer** think we could best **become aware** of **noumenal will**?

Through aesthetic experience, especially of nature and music, we can become aware of the noumenal world. Schopenhauer's theory of nature appreciation is a modification of Immanuel Kant's (1724–1804) notion of the sublime. Schopenhauer thought that there is tranquility in the experience of the beautiful, but that the experience of the sublime, such as in watching a storm, requires an active participation. Thus, the observer tears himself away from his own will in contemplating the sublime object "by a free exaltation." Music is a pure expression of the absolute noumenal will. In listening to music, which expresses the universal will, we directly become universal subjects, bypassing our own individual wills.

## What did Arthur **Schopenhauer** mean by his **acronym WELT**?

Schopenhauer thought the omnipresence of will was an endless cause of suffering; he even created an acronym to express this with the word *Welt,* or "world." The letters in WELT stood for Weh (woe), Elend (misery), Leid (suffering), and Tod (death). Schopenhauer thought that the only way out of this was to give up will by affirming the Noble Truths of Buddhism: life is suffering; desire causes suffering; eliminating desire eliminates suffering; desire can be eliminated only through a saintly life, which requires chastity, humbling of the body, and extreme poverty.

## What was Arthur **Schopenhauer's moral system**?

Schopenhauer believed that we should harm no one and help others as much as we can. Only on the level of appearance, when we are in direct contact with our own individual wills, is this difficult. In the noumenal realm, there is only one will and we are all part of it, so to harm another person is, in effect, to harm ourselves.

## What was Schopenhauer like as a person?

Schopenhauer was willful, misanthropic, and misogynistic—in short, not much of a "people person." While at the University of Berlin, he called Johann Fichte (1762–1814) a "charlatan." And he later wrote:

> Fichte, Schelling and Hegel are in my opinion not philosophers, for they lack the first requirement of a philosopher, namely a seriousness and honesty of enquiry. They are merely sophists who wanted to appear to be, rather than to be, something. They sought not truth but their own interest and advancement in the world.

So much for men, in Schopenhauer's opinion. In his twenties, Schopenhauer experienced unrequited love for the mistress of the Duke of Weimar. He and his mother, a successful novelist, quarreled over his treatment of her guests and he never saw her again after age 26. Women, in general, he said:

> ...are directly fitted for acting as the nurses and teachers of our early childhood by the fact that they are themselves childish, frivolous and short-sighted; in a word, they are big children all their life long ... an undersized, narrow-shouldered, broad-hipped and short legged race.... [T]hey have no proper knowledge of anything; and they have no genius.

Schopenhauer was also said to have abused at least one female servant. In his old age, he lived alone, except for a poodle.

### What was Arthur **Schopenhauer's influence**?

Schopenhauer's philosophical ideas influenced Friedrich Nietzsche (1844–1900), and his idea of an unconscious will was formative for Sigmund Freud's (1856–1939) ideas of psychology. Schopenhauer had profound effects in literature and was the first significant Western philosopher to incorporate Eastern thought in his system.

# BERNARD BOSANQUET

### Who was **Bernard Bosanquet**?

Bernard Bosanquet (1848–1923) was an English Hegelian who taught at University College (from 1870 to 1881) and at St. Andrews (from 1903 to 1908), Oxford. His name was inherited from French Huguenot forebears. He left Oxford when an inheritance enabled him to pursue social activist causes in London. His major works appear as the published editions of the Gifford Lectures that he gave in 1911 and 1912: *The*

Yes, Bosanquet actively served for years, during the 1880s and 1890s and the first two decades of the twentieth century, within a number of charitable and educational organizations such as the London Ethical Society, Charity Organization Society, and the London School of Ethics and Social Philosophy. His *Philosophical Theory of the State* (1923) and *Psychology of the Moral Self* (1897) were based on public lectures he gave to adult education groups.

In 1895 he married Helen Dendy, who was a social activist and reformer. She served on the Royal Commission on the Poor Laws from 1905 to 1909. Both Bosanquets believed that the best way to secure social reform was through education that developed individual character. This viewpoint often brought them into conflict with leading socialists of the time.

*Principle of Individuality and Value* (1912) and *The Value and Destiny of the Individual* (1913). Bosanquet explained the existence of the Absolute with his own system of logical doctrines; he advocated for community values as opposed to individualism, and he was the leading British philosopher of aesthetics in his day and beyond.

## What was Bernard **Bosanquet's idealist doctrine**?

Bosanquet acknowledged a tremendous debt to Friedrich Hegel's (1770–1831) notion of the Absolute and was modest about his own contributions to Hegelian philosophy, although they were a significant departure. According to Bosanquet, contradictions occur in experiences when there are opposing views of the same fact. Truth is attained by eliminating such contradictions by incorporating them into a larger picture. The totality of human experience contains all of such truths and that is "The Absolute." It can be seen from this that Bosanquet had an empiricist interpretation of Hegel—a view that itself was a contradiction!

Bosanquet also held that the Absolute contains all conflicting desires and satisfies all of them. The value of anything lies in its ability to satisfy desires, so the Absolute is the standard of all values. We can best realize all of our desires by surrendering our particular forms of them to the Absolute. This surrender is religious consciousness.

## What were Bernard **Bosanquet's** main **ideas** concerning **social philosophy**?

Humans, said Bosanquet, can only achieve their individual goals within communities. Both individually and collectively, we all wish for those things that produce harmony where once there were conflicting desires. On a community level, this is the general will. Being ruled by the general will results in liberty. The general will is the foundation of the modern state that has as its aim the actualization of what is best for all of its citizens.

## What was Bernard **Bosanquet's aesthetic theory**?

Bosanquet, in his *A History of Aesthetic* (1892), provided an historical development of beauty. In the ancient world, beauty was imitation, whereas in Hegel's objective idealist philosophy, beauty is reality itself. Following Immanuel Kant (1724–1804), he held that we experience objects as beautiful because they present the structures and organizing qualities of reason in perceptible forms.

# MATERIALISM, MARXISM, AND ANARCHISTS

## What is the **origin** of **materialism, Marxism,** and **anarchism** in the modern era?

Intellectually, they were all reactions against Hegelianism. In society, as political movements, they represented a natural historical progression from the French Revolution, and a reaction against the industrial revolution in Europe, as well as against feudalism in Russia.

## What is **materialism**?

In a general philosophical sense, materialism is the doctrine that only physical, material things are real. In a political Marxist sense, materialism is the doctrine that economic conditions and transactions determine the course of history.

## What is **Marxism**?

Marxism is the doctrine attributed to Karl Marx (1818–1883) that human society is divided into social classes and that the material or economic struggles among classes are the most important events on the big stage of history.

Karl Marx viewed human history in terms of a continuing struggle between economic classes (iStock).

## What is **anarchism**?

Anarchism is the political doctrine that human happiness and well being are best served without powerful political structures. Anarchists seek the decentralization of power, into small units, controlled by the people.

## LUDWIG ANDREAS VON FEUERBACH

### Who was **Ludwig Andreas von Feuerbach**?

Ludwig Andreas von Feuerbach (1804–1872) criticized German Idealism as a form of theology, or a rationalization of religion. His project was to invert Friedrich Hegel's (1770–1831) relationship between the individual and the Absolute. Whereas for Hegel, the individual was an effect or expression of the Absolute, for Feuerbach the Absolute was an effect or expression of the individual. Feuerbach's main works were: *Toward a Critique of Hegel's Philosophy* (1839), *The Essence of Christianity* (1841), *Principles of the Philosophy of the Future* (1843), and *The Essence of Religion* (1846). He collaborated with Karl Marx (1818–1883) and was active in the late 1840s revolutionary period, but then retired from public life and died poor.

### What kind of a **materialist** was Ludwig **Feuerbach**?

Feuerbach was an historical materialist. He sought to bring out the implicit Hegelian assumption that "truth, reality, and sensibility are identical." But Feuerbach thought that by locating reason and consciousness in the Absolute, Friedrich Hegel (1770–1831) had alienated man's essence from him. He asserted that "only a sensible being is a real, true being," and that thought is the product of this human being, and not the other way around. God or the Absolute is no more than the appearance of ourselves to ourselves. The work of philosophy was to begin with man, in his situation. Man was neither mere matter nor consciousness alone.

### How were Ludwig **Feuerbach's ideas received**?

After his early publication of work critical of Christianity, Feuerbach was dismissed from a teaching position at Erlangen University, where he had gotten his doctorate in philosophy; after that, he could not secure further academic employment. His ensuing criticism of Friedrich Hegel (1770–1831) did not help his situation.

### What **influence** did Ludwig **Feuerbach** have on others?

Feuerbach directly influenced Karl Marx (1818–1883) and many others. His philosophical starting point of the existing individual predated existentialism. His ideas of

## What did Ludwig Feuerbach conclude man was?

In his *Principles of the Philosophy of the Future* (1843) Feuerbach wrote the rallying cry for many vegetarians: *Der Mensch ist, was er isst,* or "Man is what he eats." However, his full thought on this was not merely dietary. The preceding sentences, written in 1850, read:

> The doctrine of foods is of great ethical and political significance. Food becomes blood, blood becomes heart and brain, thoughts and mind-stuff. Human fare is the foundation of human culture and thought. Would you improve a nation? Give it, instead of declamations against sin, better food.

> Feuerbach struggled with how "human fare" became human thought. His solution was to convert "the essence of religion into the essence of *man*," but Marx criticized him for his location of abstractions in the individual, preferring to understand the individual as a collection or intersection of social and economic relations.

how religion should be studied made possible sociologies, histories, and other non-religious studies of religion.

# MARXISM

## Who was **Karl Marx**?

Karl Marx (1818–1883) was the German revolutionary and philosopher of modern society and economics who is most often credited with having founded communism and socialism as political movements and systems of thought. He is also credited with the impetus behind the modern labor union movement. Marx's early works are considered utopian and were not published in his lifetime. His *magnum opus* is *Das Kapital* (*Capital,* released in 1867, 1885, and 1894), although the *The Communist Manifesto* (1848) that he wrote with Friedrich Engels (1820–1895) is less hypothetical and more accessible to the reader.

At the time Marx and Engels wrote, the following did not exist for workers in industrialized nations: minimum wage laws, health care insurance, pension plans, workplace safety regulations, laws against child labor, or specified hours for shifts or work weeks. Neither was there widespread and compulsory public education for the children of workers. While some of these goods do not universally exist at this time in industrialized nations and may not exist at all in parts of Asia, Africa, and South America, they are now generally taken for granted as fundamental human entitlements.

## Who was **Friedrich Engels**?

Friedrich Engels (1820–1895) founded Marxism with Karl Marx (1818–1883). In addition to *The Communist Manifesto* (1848), they collaborated on *The Holy Family* (1844) and *The German Ideology* (1845). Engels' *The Condition of the Working Class in England* (1844) described the suffering in the lives of workers at that time. Engels also published *Socialism: Utopian and Scientific* (1880) and *Anti-Düring* (1878). In *The Dialectics of Nature* (1883) Engels related historical materialism to natural science and claimed that there were universal laws of nature and thought.

Along with Karl Marx, Friedrich Engels established the ideals of communism (Art Archive).

Engels' greatest contribution was a presentation of Marx's ideas in more accessible and popular formats and terms. Engels' father was a textile manufacturer, and the young Engels worked at his mill in Manchester, eventually owning it. Engels helped Marx financially throughout his life and also supported his children after Marx died. He edited Marx's *Das Kapital* after Marx's death.

## In a nutshell, what did Karl **Marx** and Friedrich **Engels** write in **their philosophy**?

Human beings must work to live. History, noted Marx and Engels, is a Hegelian dialectical process in which different divisions of labor have developed, resulting in the nineteenth century in a bourgeois owning class that controls the government and an exploited *proletariat,* or working class, that furnishes the labor for capitalists. Capitalism is an economic system in which owners seek profits through ever-expanding production and markets. Their profit is the result of subtracting the costs of material and equipment, or capital, plus wages paid to workers, from the money they take in.

Within the producing system, labor, or the work of the working class, results in a "surplus value," because workers are exploited by employers. The worker is paid just enough to go home and eat, sleep, and engage in familial acts of reproduction, which altogether "reproduce" his labor so that he can continue to function as a worker. That is, every aspect of the worker's life is "squeezed" by their employers so that they can maximize their profits. The result is that workers, especially those who made up the vast pool of labor in nineteenth century industrial society, were poor.

## Did Karl Marx live in poverty himself?

**Y**es. After he was kicked out of Brussels and Paris for his revolutionary writing, Marx and his family found refuge in London. In 1850 they were ejected from their two-room flat in Chelsea for failing to pay the rent. They found cheaper accommodation in Soho, where they stayed for six years. In order to help Marx with an income, Friedrich Engels returned to work for his father in Germany. The two kept in constant contact, and over the next 20 years they wrote to each other about every other day. During this time, Marx sought to understand capitalism by reading back issues of *The Economist,* as well as journal articles, in the Reading Room of the British Museum.

The Marxes' fifth child, Franziska, was born at their Soho flat, but she only lived for a year. Eleanor was born in 1855, but later that year Edgar became the Marxes' third child to die. The family owned very little, and some days Marx could not leave the house because Jenny had to pawn his trousers to buy food. But on some Sundays, they all went to Hampstead Heath for picnics.

After Marx began earning money from his articles for the *New York Daily Tribune,* and Jenny's mother left her a small inheritance, they were able to move to Kentish Town. In 1856, Jenny had a baby that was still-born, and after that she caught smallpox. Although she survived this illness, it left her deaf and badly scarred. Marx also grew ill, and he wrote to Engels that "such a lousy life is not worth living." But when he had an outbreak of boils in 1863, he was consoled that it was "a truly proletarian disease."

Both the working class and the owning class have their own ideologies, which unreconstructed are the ideology of the owning class. That is, the owning class sees the world in a way that justifies their position: for example, in believing that all who have great wealth have earned it by hard work. The politically dominant class in a society is the class that economically controls the main means of production. In general, the ideology of any social class is the result of where that class is located in terms of the dominant means of production in its society.

Workers and others need to realize that workers are human beings who become alienated from their own labor when it is merely treated as a commodity on which their employers make a profit. The short-term solution to this situation is for workers to unite and demand better pay and working conditions. The long-term solution is a historical process through which capitalism will destroy itself through its own internal contradictions. The erstwhile workers will then become socialist owners who are able to pursue self-fulfilling activities, instead of merely laboring to survive from one day to the next.

# ANARCHISM

## What is **anarchism**?

Anarchism is a theory and political movement that is based on ideals of freedom and equality. All forms of domination, authority, and subordination are considered unjust and backed up by force. The state and all of its supporting institutions, as well as the institutions supported by the state, are deemed unacceptable. Society should be reorganized into small, self-governing communities in which members cooperate toward the same ends and produce their livelihood together. English journalist and political philosopher William Godwin (1756–1836) initiated modern anarchism in the eighteenth century, and in the nineteenth, Pierre-Joseph Proudhon (1809–1865), Mikhail Alexandrovich Bakunin (1814–1876), and Pyotr Alexeyevich Kropotkin (1842–1921) were leading figures.

## Who was **Pierre-Joseph Proudhon**?

Pierre-Joseph Proudhon (1809–1865) was the French social theorist who coined the word "anarchism." In his *What Is Property?* (1840) he famously proclaimed that "property is theft."

## What was **new** about Pierre-Joseph **Proudhon's thought**?

Jean-Jacques Rousseau (1712–1778), in talking about property in land had made a similar assertion to Proudhon's about property being theft, but Proudhon's innovation was to argue that owners deprive workers of most of the results of their labor. Because workers had a right to the results of all of their labor, as well as that labor itself, the amount of private property concentrated in individual or small group hands should be limited. This would require reform in the economic system to establish banks that would grant interest-free loans to poor people. The state would dissolve and there instead would be associations of collectives on a worldwide basis.

A 1948 French cartoon lampoons Pierre-Joseph Proudhoun's ideas about the poor. Proudhon asks a servant why he left the door open, and the servant responds that since there is no such thing as property, why does it matter? (Art Archive).

## What was Pierre-Joseph **Proudhon's** lasting **influence**?

Although his thought, along with that of other nineteenth century anarchists, was

> ## Did Mikhail Bakunin get along with Karl Marx?
>
> **B**akunin and Marx were bitter enemies. Marx campaigned to expel Bakunin from the International Working Men's Association. The tempestuous relationship between Marx and Bakunin is a well known part of the history of Western socialism. As a co-member of the International Working Men's Association, Marx referred to Bakunin as "a man devoid of all theoretical knowledge." Bakunin said that Marx was "from head to foot an authoritarian.... [T]he instinct of liberty is lacking in him." Although Marx said that Bakunin was "in his element as an intriguer," it was Marx who in 1848 published an untrue rumor, begun by the Russian ambassador, that Bakunin was a Russian agent responsible for the arrest of Poles.

neglected after World War I, some of Proudhon's social ideas remain influential in contemporary economic organization. Examples of this include the representation in management of workers in large industries, as well as cooperative housing units and food growing and buying projects.

### Why was Pierre-Joseph **Proudhon against women's rights**?

In his *Pornocractie* (1875) Proudhon argued that if women were allowed to vote and secured other legal equalities with men, the institution of marriage would decline over time, because women would not need men to support them financially. Proudhon thought that this single state of men and women would result in widespread prostitution.

### Was Pierre-Joseph **Proudhon** a **friend** of Karl **Marx**?

Very briefly. Marx (1818–1883) wrote to him after *What is Property?* (1840) was published and they became friends in Paris, where Marx was then living in exile. But Marx responded to Proudhon's subsequent *The Philosophy of Poverty* (1847) with *The Poverty of Philosophy* (1880). The ensuing dispute divided the anarchists from the Marxists in the International Working Men's Association. Proudhon also had a dispute with Mikhail Bakunin's (1814–1876) followers, who objected to his idea of worker's cooperatives and peasant ownership of land and factories after a peaceful revolution.

### Who was **Mikhail Bakunin**?

Mikhail Bakunin (1814–1876) was a Russian anarchist and revolutionary who was active in Europe from 1840 to 1849, and 1861 to 1871. During the years between these periods, he was imprisoned in both Europe and Russia, and for a time was exiled to

Peter Kropotkin was a Russian prince whose views on communism were mitigated by science and the ideas of evolutionary theory (Art Archive).

Siberia. His views are held to be contradictory because he believed both that the "instinct for freedom" in the masses would lead to revolution and that revolution would need to be the result of a plan by educated elite.

In his first period, Bakunin criticized liberal projects to reconcile the demands of workers with the establishment, and he was particularly excoriating about both the Church and the state. In his second period, he attacked scientism, or the dominance of technical approaches to public policy, calling for a "revolt of life against science." Overall, Bakunin and his followers were opposed to the development of Marxism.

## Who was **Peter Kropotkin**?

Peter Kropotkin (1842–1921) was perhaps the mildest of all the Marxists and anarchists. He mainly sought to provide a scientific foundation for anarchist-communism by drawing on his own work in geology and his knowledge of Charles Darwin. He was a Russian prince, claimed to be descended from Rurik, who was said to have founded Russia. (Some say Rurik was not an actual historical person, and even if he were it would be hard to prove who his descendants were.)

Kropotkin also wrote the entry for anarchism in the famous eleventh edition of the *Encyclopedia Britannica* that was published in 1911. This edition was mainly composed by the experts in leadings fields of nineteenth century knowledge and is still highly regarded. (All volumes of this edition are now available free online.)

## **How** did Peter **Kropotkin** come to form his **life philosophy**?

Kropotkin's father was a general, and Kropotkin was educated in the Corps of Pages, becoming an attendant to Tsar Alexander II. He received a commission in the Mounted Cossacks of the Amur and went to Siberia, where he investigated the penal system. What he saw turned him against the repressive form of government in place.

In his twenties, Kropotkin led expeditions into unchartered areas of Siberia, which resulted in discoveries about glaciation, the deserts of eastern Asia, and mountain structure.

He read Pierre-Joseph Proudhon's (1809–1865) writings, which led him to resign his commission in protest of an execution of Polish prisoners, who had attempted to

## What was Peter Kropotkin's doctrine of anarchist-communism?

Kropotkin's proposals proceeded from the needs of consumers. He envisioned a free-distribution warehouse, instead of the collectivist production cooperatives proposed by Pierre-Joseph Proudhon (1809–1865). The main cohesive forces were to be based on social ties, rather than production goals. In his *La Conquête du pain* (*The Conquest of Bread*), Kropotkin attempted to work out the details of his system, which was based on ideas previously developed in Thomas More's 1516 work, *Utopia*, and directly made known to Kropotkin by François Dumartheray, who had worked with Kropotkin in setting up the journal *Le Révolté*.

escape. After exploring the eskers of Finland, he was offered the position of secretary of the Russian Geological Society in 1872, but instead went to Switzerland to meet exiled radicals.

Kropotkin decided he was an anarchist after moving interactions with Bakunin's followers among the watchmakers of Jura. (The watchmakers were conscientious craftsmen who were not part of the wider industrial revolution, and their cooperation in a close-knit community inspired Kropotkin.) When he returned to Russia, he joined the underground, and in 1874 was imprisoned in the Peter and Paul Fortress. He escaped to Europe, where he founded the journal *Le Révolté* in 1879 and participated in the London International Anarchist Congress in 1881. In Lyons, France, in 1882, he was sentenced to five years imprisonment for being a member of the International Workingmen's Association, but public outcry led to an early release. After that, he went to England and remained there, returning to Russia after the Russian Revolution of 1917.

When Kropotkin lived in England, he worked mainly as a scholar. Leading scientific journals and publishers printed his work. His most important publications were *Memoirs of a Revolutionist* (1899), *Mutual Aid: A Factor in Evolution* (1902), and *Modern Science and Anarchism* (1912). His last work, *Ethics,* was published in 1924 after he died in Russia. Kropotkin's final years were disappointing to him because the aftermath of the Russian Revolution defied his anarchist ideals. He denounced the Bolshevik reign of terror after the October Revolution.

## What was Peter Kropokin's view of Darwinism in society?

Kropotkin did not think that competition was a good survival strategy, whether in the animal or human worlds. In his *Mutual Aid: A Factor of Evolution* (1902) he wrote the following:

In the animal world we have seen that the vast majority of species live in societies, and that they find in association the best arms for the struggle for life:

243

understood, of course, in its wide Darwinian sense—not as a struggle for the sheer means of existence, but as a struggle against all natural conditions unfavourable to the species. The animal species, in which individual struggle has been reduced to its narrowest limits, and the practice of mutual aid has attained the greatest development, are invariably the most numerous, the most prosperous, and the most open to further progress. The mutual protection which is obtained in this case, the possibility of attaining old age and of accumulating experience, the higher intellectual development, and the further growth of sociable habits, secure the maintenance of the species, its extension, and its further progressive evolution. The unsociable species, on the contrary, are doomed to decay.

However, Kropotkin did hold that revolution is part of human evolution and that anarchism was a return to a condition that had been distorted by modern repressive institutions. Because human beings are naturally social, government is unnecessary.

# PSYCHOLOGY AND SOCIAL THEORY

## What was **philosophically significant** about **nineteenth-century psychology** and **social theory**?

In the nineteenth century, the foundations were laid for psychology and sociology to develop as distinct fields separate from philosophy. The reasons for their separation are differences in subject matter as well as methodology. Concerning the latter, Wilhelm Dilthey (1833–1911) put the case of his age best in claiming that human sciences such as history, psychology, philology, and philosophy were characterized by a need to understand, whereas the physical sciences sought causes.

However, in the twentieth century, quantitative methodology and experiments in search of causes were to characterize important parts of both psychology and sociology. Quantification and causal explanation were also to characterize economics, which did not become distinctly independent from political philosophy, sociology, and philosophy until the twentieth century. But in the nineteenth century, the establishment of psychology and sociology as separate from epistemology, ethics, and political philosophy, as well as revolutionary critique, was a major achievement.

## FRANZ BRENTANO

### Who was **Franz Brentano**?

Franz Brentano (1837–1917) taught in Würzburg and at the University of Vienna, influencing Austrian philosopher Alexius Meinong (1853–1920); Edmund Husserl

## What was Franz Brentano's psychological theory of right and wrong?

Brentano thought that judgments can be correct or incorrect and that the same held for loving and hating. If a thing is good, then it is impossible to love it incorrectly. Correctness in loving and hating is objective, as is incorrectness. Brentano was an intuitionist concerning such correctness. He thought that we could be immediately and directly aware of the "fit" between the emotion and the object.

(1859–1938), the founder of phenomenology, and Sigmund Freud (1856–1939), the father of psychoanalysis. He was ordained as a Roman Catholic priest in 1864, but renounced his vows after engaging in a dispute about papal infallibility. He resigned his professorship at the University of Vienna, so that he could marry, and was not able to regain that position. Later years left him blind, but he continued to write in virtually every subfield of philosophy until he died. Brentano's principal writings are *Psychology from an Empirical Point of View* (1874) and *Our Knowledge of the Origin of Right and Wrong* (1889).

## What was Franz **Brentano's** main **contribution** to **empirical psychology**?

Brentano's lasting importance lies in his emphasis on the *intentionality* of conscious states and attitudes. He pointed out that thoughts, beliefs, hopes, desires, and the like—which Bertrand Russell (1872–1970) was to term "propositional attitudes"—are directed toward some object. For instance, if you are thinking about an apple then your *intentional object* is the apple you are thinking about; if you want a new car, it is the car you *intend* as an object of that desire.

Because physical states are not intentional in this way, intentionality is a basis on which what is mental can be distinguished from what is physical. Brentano identified three different kinds of intending: ideas, judgments, and the phenomena of love and hate. The last, also known as emotions and volitions, are directly related to morality.

Although an earlier version of Brentano's doctrine—called "immanent intentionality"—suggested that the object intended was in some way literally in the mind, he later explained that although there is always a mental object for consciousness the object need not literally exist. The point is that one can think of a thing that does not exist. Objects of thought that do exist have "strict relations" with other objects that exist, whereas those that do not exist lack them.

# Alexius Meinong

## Who was **Alexius Meinong**?

Alexius Meinong (1853–1920) was born in Lemberg, Austria, and studied philosophy with Franz Brentano (1837–1917), who set him the task of reading David Hume (1711–1776). This resulted in two early books on Hume, the first on abstraction and the second on relation, which appeared as *Hume-Studien* in 1877 and 1882, respectively. Like Brentano, Meinong is considered an analytical phenomenologist. Unlike those phenomenologists in the so-called continental tradition, he applied the rigors of logic to introspection. He established the Institute of Psychology in Graz, Austria, where he was a professor. Meinong is best known for his theory of objects and values, and his principle publication is *On Assumptions* (1902).

## What was Alexius **Meinong's psychological theory**?

Meinong divided mental experience into act, content, and object. He worked on the basis of Brentano's theory of intentionality, whereby all mental states intend objects. The mental act, or "act element," is the way that the subject is directed toward the object, whereas the specific content, or "content element," is its focus in that case. For example, it is a different act to think of an apple versus to desire an apple. Thinking of an apple and thinking of a car is a difference in content, and going from one to the other is a change in focus.

Meinong's object theory bypassed traditional ontology because as intended objects (in the sense of Franz Brentano [1837–1917]), it was not necessary that all objects exist. In fact, Meinong stressed a bias toward existence in the history of metaphysics, which he called a "prejudice in favor of the actual." Each object has a *sosein,* or character, which is given through its "nuclear features." Because objects truly possess their characters, even statements about nonexistent objects can be true, because how objects are is independent of their existence. For example, a pink unicorn is genuinely pink, even though unicorns do not exist.

## Was Alexius **Meinong** serious about **nonexistent objects**?

Yes, and it cost his reputation dearly, because Bertrand Russell (1872–1970) was to make great fun of him for it in his famous article "On Denoting" (1905). Still, other twentieth-century philosophers, such as Terence Parsons (1939–) and Roderick Chisholm (1916–1999) were to defend the consistency of Meinong's ontology and the usefulness of being able to talk about non-existent objects. Meinong believed that non-existent objects include the merely possible, as well as the impossible. He thought that existence was just a property of objects, like smell or shape, so that, for example, fictional characters lack that property, while Meinong himself had it.

## What was Alexius **Meinong's theory of value**?

Our emotions and desires have a cognitive ability to discern value. This does not mean that our emotions and desires can "think" but that they tell us something about the world, often faster than our minds. Objects—those things intended by us—present themselves with value features. For instance, the smell of the apple directs me to eat it—it has the value of being good to eat. Or a sunset presents itself as beautiful, a property that does not reduce to facts about the refraction of light or the amount of pollution in the air. There are also value universals, such as the good, the beautiful, the agreeable, the desirable, and different kinds of the obligatory (the general category of our duties). Meinong distinguished between "dignitatives" that are associated with ideas of the good, and "disideratives" associated with ideas of duty.

# SIGMUND FREUD

## How are **psychology** and **philosophy related**?

Up until the nineteenth century, no clear distinction was made between philosophy of mind and psychology. The science of psychology did not yet exist in its own right until the early twentieth century. Early historical figures in the science of psychology, such as Sigmund Freud (1856–1939), are of interest to philosophers because their theories of the human mind changed ideas about human nature in ways that philosophers had to take into account.

## Who was **Sigmund Freud**?

Sigmund Freud (1856–1939) was the founder of psychoanalytic theory and clinical practice. He developed the idea that early childhood experience has a lifelong influence in shaping personality and character. The importance of childhood education was emphasized as early as Plato (c. 428–c. 348 B.C.E.), but Freud was the first to stress childhood emotional experience. Freud was also responsible for the popular acceptance of the idea that self-understanding does not occur immediately and automatically, but requires a special kind of reflection. The ancient Greeks are famous for the maxim, "Know Thyself," but Freud's distinct contribution was that there are different layers of the self to be known.

Sigmund Freud was the father of psychoanalysis and clinical practice (Art Archive).

247

Freud's principle works are *The Interpretation of Dreams* (1900), *Three Essays on the Theory of Sexuality* (1905), and *Civilization and Its Discontents* (1930). Also of particular interest in his application of his theories to healthy people in ordinary life is *Psychopathology of Everyday Life* (1901).

## What are some details of Sigmund **Freud's life** that led him to his work?

Freud was born in Freiberg, Germany, but raised in Vienna, Austria. He studied medicine at the University of Vienna, specializing in neurology. In 1886, Freud married Martha Bernays. They had six children, and the youngest, Anna, herself became a noted psychoanalyst. Freud's youngest son, Ernst, was the father of Lucien Freud, the celebrated twentieth century portrait painter. Biographers of Freud assess his family life as happy and stable, providing much needed support for the controversy that swirled around his startling and original psychological theories.

Freud's mentors J.M. Charcot and Josef Breuer investigated hysteria, and Freud became interested in the psychological aspects of this disorder because hysterical patients have physical symptoms without underlying disease. Freud and Charcot published their clinical findings of how talk can change patients' ideas, as a treatment for hysteria, in their *Studies in Hysteria* (1895). As Freud developed a sexual interpretation of the causes of hysteria, Breuer distanced himself from him.

## What was Sigmund **Freud's interpretation** of **hysteria**?

At first, Freud, along with his mentor Josef Breuer, advanced the hypothesis that people suffering from hysterics have buried memories of trauma. Treatment consisted in recovering those memories and a cathartic discharge of the affect or emotion associated with them at the outset. Freud thought that the source of the repression was sexual molestation by male relatives. He revised this "seduction theory" when he realized that if the sole cause of hysteria was repressed memories, there was no reason why it should not resolve itself by being discharged in hysterical symptoms. Taking a page from Franz Brentano, and perhaps Alexius Meinong (1853–1920), as well, he theorized that it could be fantasy revealing itself in the form of repressed desires that was the key. This led to Freud's oedipal theory.

## What was Sigmund **Freud's oedipal theory**?

The oedipal theory, or Freud's idea of the Oedipus complex, was based on Freud's *instinct theory* that there are enduring sexual desires in the human psyche, as well as opposition to their expression. Sexuality and its opposition take the form of *libido* versus *ego,* or self-preservation in early and middle life, and the form of *Eros,* or desiring life, versus *Thanatos,* or a wish to die, toward the end. (It's interesting that Freud thought the wish to die was a human expression of a longing in all life to return to an inorganic state.)

Freud named the child's attraction for its mother after the fictional character Oedipus, who is the tragic figure from the Sophocles play who accidentally falls in love with his mother (Art Archive).

The Oedipus complex results from a situation in which the child desires the mother as a result of prolonged human dependency on one caregiver. Male children fear that their fathers will punish them through castration. Female children transfer their original oedipal yearnings for their mothers to their fathers in an "Electra complex," which is also accompanied by "penis envy." This all occurs unconsciously in terms of active and passive principles that later come to be expressed and identified as male and female, respectively.

Because the primary process of the psyche tends toward a cathartic discharge of repressed energy, the *pleasure principle* is Freud's main explanatory tool. He applied this principle to the way in which the emergence of unconscious material can account for humor and also everyday failures in function and memory. In psychoanalysis, both dreams and free association could be used to access unconscious conflicts and particularly oedipal fantasies.

### Did Sigmund Freud analyze himself?

Yes, he did, and several examples show that he aimed for complete disclosure. On his own Oedipus complex, he wrote a friend:

> I have found, in my own case too, [the phenomenon of] being in love with my mother and jealous of my father, and I now consider it a universal event in early childhood, even if not so early as in children who have been made hysterical.

249

He was also just as willing to analyze literary characters and authorship; thus, he famously wrote about Shakespeare's Hamlet:

> Fleetingly the thought passed through my head that the same thing might be at the bottom of Hamlet as well. I am not thinking of Shakespeare's conscious intention, but believe, rather, that a real event stimulated the poet to his representation, in that his unconscious understood the unconscious of his hero.

Freud also collected his own memory lapses, slips of the tongue, and dreams for analysis. In the 1936 article "A Disturbance of Memory on the Acropolis," he explained why he felt doubtful and uneasy when he visited the Acropolis in Greece in 1904:

> It must be that a sense of guilt was attached to the satisfaction in having gone such a long way: there was something about it that was wrong, that from earliest times had been forbidden. It was something to do with a child's criticism of his father, with the undervaluation which took the place of the overvaluation of earlier childhood. It seems as though the essence of success was to have got further than one's father, and as though to excel one's father was still something forbidden.

Freud's father had been too poor to make such a trip, and not educated enough to have been interested in the Acropolis.

## HERBERT SPENCER

### Who was **Herbert Spencer**?

Herbert Spencer (1820–1903) was a philosopher and social reformer who was assistant editor-in-chief of *The Economist*. He also wrote for the *Westminster Review,* while George Eliot was its editor. Spencer was an atheist, without any training in the humanities, and he believed that only science could yield useful knowledge. In his ethics, he combined Jeremy Bentham's (1748–1832) version of utilitarianism with John Stuart Mill's (1806–1873) view that happiness is the true end. Spencer thought that pleasure and pain were evidence of happiness or unhappiness.

Spencer is best known for his evolutionary views that predated Charles Darwin's publication of *On the Origin of the Species by Means of Natural Selection* (1859). Spencer's main publications were works he published in his major project

Herbert Spencer was an atheist who believed science was the only way to uncover true knowledge (Art Archive).

## What was Herbert Spencer like as a person?

Spencer was a sickly child and received home schooling from his father and his uncle, a strict dissenting Protestant clergyman. Once, at a social event, someone asked the uncle why his nephew wasn't dancing. "No Spencer ever dances." he answered.

Mary Ann Evans, the novelist better known by her pen name, George Eliot, had a warm friendship with Spencer. Although he did not enjoy public places and entertainment, he took her to restaurants and the opera. Biographers believe that Eliot would have married Spencer, if he'd asked her, but he never did. She said that "the life of this philosopher, like that of the great [Immanuel] Kant, offers little material for the narrator."

After *First Principles of a New System of Philosophy* (1880) was published, Spencer developed an illness that led to insomnia and self-medication with opium. He became very reclusive and would sometimes wear ear plugs so that he did not have to listen to what others said. Although he advocated for public causes such as the metric system, and against the Boer War, he spent his last years with very little human interaction.

*System of Synthetic Philosophy,* beginning in the 1850s, and 1884's *The Man versus the State.*

## What were Herbert **Spencer's** ideas about **evolution**?

Spencer believed that change occurs according to the Law of Evolution, which dictates a progression from simplicity to homogeneity to uniformity to more complexity to heterogeneity to variety. At any stage, all of the parts that are changing are also part of one whole. Spencer cited as evidence examples from the physical, biological, psychological, and social sciences. Society itself evolves from primitive homogenous forms to complex advanced ones, he pointed out, whereby component parts have different functions.

Because Spencer thought that change follows its own internal rules, he believed that social progress cannot be the result of external actions, such as social welfare or the regulation of trade. In education, he believed that children should be taught skills that would best enable them to compete with others. Spencer's views were taken up by Social Darwinists, who advocated the principles of the "survival of the fittest" for society, against social reform generally, and in favor of capitalistic competition, specifically.

251

# SOCIOLOGY AND PHILOSOPHY

## How is **sociology related** to **philosophy**?

Social and political philosophers discuss society and criticize culture. Sociology is the science that can give them factual information about what they are discussing.

## Who was **Emil Durkheim**?

Emil Durkheim (1858–1917) taught at the universities in Bordeaux and Paris and is credited with having founded the academic field of sociology in France. His goal was to develop sociology as a positive science with its own subject matter. His major contribution in this regard was an insistence that society could not be reduced to the nature and behavior of the human individuals that constituted it. His principle works were *The Division of Labor in Society* (1893), *The Rules of Sociological Method* (1895), *Suicide* (1897), and *The Elementary Forms of Religious Life* (1912).

## What were Emil **Durkheim's** main **ideas**?

Durkheim thought that the "horde," or non-organized group, was the simplest kind of society, and he analyzed existing tribal societies as having developed simple methods of social organization from their recent horde past. Social complexity was an evolutionary process, and in the societies of his day, Durkheim addressed the problems attending their complexity, such as individualism and dissolution of older forms of solidarity. Because modern societies were based on divisions of labor, the best way to solve these problems was through professional and trade organizations. Durkheim believed that religion could be understood as a reverence for those social norms and traditions that shaped human life.

## What did Emil **Durkheim contribute** to the **study** of **suicide**?

First of all, Durkheim defined suicide as follows: "[T]he term suicide is applied to all cases of death resulting directly or indirectly from a positive or negative act of the victim himself, which he knows will produce this result." Second, he systematically catalogued suicide rates in modern society and analyzed his data into four main types: egoistic, altruistic, anomic, and fatalistic. Egoistic suicide resulted from insufficient social ties, altruistic from too much involvement in social relationships. Anomic suicide was the result of acute or chronic crises typical of conditions in contemporary life, especially economic deprivation. Fatalistic suicide occurred only in exceptional conditions of difficult life circumstances, such as slavery.

## Who was **Georg Simmel**?

Georg Simmel (1858–1918) was a philosopher and early sociologist. He was born in Berlin and lived most of his life there. Simmel wrote about a wide range of subjects, including ethics, philosophy of history, education, religion, art, and money. His writing style was digressive rather than tightly analytic, as was expected in German philosophy at that time.

Overall, as a *Lebensphilosphe,* or philosopher of life, Simmel saw life as more than itself—in other words, more than the human biological organism and its processes—because it was productive, particularly in cultural creativity. Perhaps Simmel's most distinctive work was his *Philosophy of Money* (1900), a subject that few philosophers have directly addressed, then or since. He also wrote about fashion.

## What were Georg **Simmel's thoughts** on **fashion** and **money**?

Simmel distinguished between individuals' personal selves and social selves, the latter being necessary for functioning in complex societies. Both fashion and money had symbolic uses in this sense. Simmel believed that fashion was limited to life in cities, because, as he wrote, "it intensifies a multiplicity of social relations, increases the rate of social mobility and permits individuals from lower strata to become conscious of the styles and fashions of upper classes."

His view of money was similar in that he felt it can operate as an impersonal form of exchange, as well as having value. Through money, subordination and domination can be expressed, while at the same time money permits more freedom within society. Simmel was also aware of the disadvantages of the use of money in its ability create special hardships and crises in social identity.

## Who was **Marie-Luise Enckendorf**?

"She" was the pseudonym of Gertrud Kinel, Georg Simmel's wife, under which she published her own philosophical writings. The Simmels maintained a salon for intellectuals but otherwise enjoyed a conservative, bourgeois family life. They had one son.

## Who was **Max Weber**?

Max Weber (1864–1920) held chairs at the universities at Freiburg, Heidelberg, and Munich, although what biographers refer to as a "nervous ailment" curtailed

Max Weber interestingly combined ideas of economics with religion (Art Archive).

his career as an academic. His main project was to understand the dominant features of modern life in its Western development. His most famous work was *The Protestant Ethic and the Spirit of Capitalism* (1904).

## How did Max **Weber** connect **Protestantism** to **capitalism**?

Weber observed that capitalism required investment, which itself required an excess of money over what was needed for existence. He believed that such saving was a form of asceticism encouraged in Protestant churches that valorized work and devalued enjoyment of the results of work. Weber noted that other religions dominated in societies that were not capitalistic.

Weber called the mental process that made capitalism possible "rationalization," and he analyzed its presence in efficient, rule-based Western government, as well as economics. He thought that liberal political systems could be an advantage to nations—Germany, in particular—in their international struggles. But he also believed that the accompanying scientific world-view, which downplayed custom, led to a "disenchantment of the world."

Weber thought that a possible course of correction to the rationalization of bureaucracies was mass democracy, which would result in charismatic leaders.

# CONTINENTAL PHILOSOPHY

## What is **continental philosophy**?

Existentialism, phenomenology, critical theory, and structuralism all represent what is now called "continental philosophy." Existentialism is a philosophical perspective on the world, which begins from the standpoint of one individual in ways that apply to all individuals. Phenomenology is a more abstract and systematic development of the processes of individual knowing and understanding. (Existentialists have tended to be more literary than phenomenologists.) Critical theory is a twentieth-century development of the theoretical methodology of Marxism. Structuralism is an application of a number of continental traditions to social criticism, resulting in analyses of social structures.

One thing they all have in common is that their original foundational ideas came from European thinkers. But more than geography is at stake with this name. Continental philosophy is often contrasted with Anglo-American analytic philosophy, which has dominated in twentieth-century philosophy departments in American colleges and universities, since philosophy became a profession in higher education during the 1930s. It should be noted that what is true of American academic philosophy departments has not been true of English, French, and German departments in the United States, which over the twentieth century welcomed continental philosophy into their curricula. Moreover, continental philosophy is not alone in its stepchild status among American professional philosophers, because the same thing happened to American philosophy, also known as pragmatism, after the 1950s.

# EXISTENTIALISM

### What is **existentialism**?

Existentialism is a kind of philosophy that begins from the concrete reality of the human individual's existence in the world. What is shared by all humans in their day to day life becomes a foundation for knowledge and the nature of reality. Existentialism is focused on human experience from the first person, some "me" or "I."

### How are **existentialism** and **phenomenology historically related**?

Existentialism and phenomenology both begin with the facts of human reality, from the standpoint of the first person. As distinctive traditions of thought, both have roots in the nineteenth century, existentialism going back to Fyodor Dostoyevsky (1821–1881), Søren Kierkegaard (1813–1855), and Friedrich Nietsche (1844–1900), and phenomenology originating with Franz Brentano (1837–1917). Strictly speaking, existentialism is older than phenomenology, although some twentieth-century existentialists have sought to base their work on that of more contemporary phenomenologists, rather than their nineteenth-century existentialist predecessors.

## SØREN KIERKEGAARD

### Who was **Søren Kierkegaard**?

Søren Aaybe Kierkegaard (1813–1855) was a Danish Christian existentialist who extolled religious faith as an individual and emotional "leap" from all that was reasonable and rational. He wrote from his heart and the emotional circumstances of his own life.

Danish Christian existentialist Søren Kierkegaard based his philosophy on his religious faith (Art Archive).

### What were the **emotional conditions** in Søren **Kierkegaard's life**?

Kierkegaard's father, Michael, was a very gloomy man who had married a former maid as a second wife. He felt himself under a cloud of God's wrath and expected punishment through his children predeceasing him—five of them did. The sins of Kierkegaard's father apparently consisted of his having impregnated his wife before they were married and in

256

cursing God during severe weather as a 10-year-old shepherd. He later became well off as a wool merchant.

Kierkegaard was sickly as a boy, but he could reduce larger boys to tears with his sarcasm and mockery. At the University of Copenhagen, he did not find Hegelianism congenial because it did not address "a truth, which is true *for me,* to find *the idea for which I can live and die."* The religion of Lutheranism did not speak to him, either, and for a while he indulged in expensive food and drink and wore fashionable clothes because he believed that immediate pleasure was the most important thing. But his father's despair haunted him and became his own.

Kierkegaard was intending to become a pastor when he became engaged to Rigene Olsen in 1841. He had met her when she was 14, three years earlier, and they were deeply in love. But Kierkegaard broke off the engagement, and she subsequently married her tutor, Frederick Schlegel (who became governor of the Danish West Indies). An original life's path was taking shape for Kierkegaard, and when he decided not to marry he also decided not to become a Lutheran pastor.

Kierkegaard believed that philosophy was neither about system-building nor analysis, but rather the expression of individual existence. He had no respect for professors because he did not think there was any way they could comprehend his subjectivity.

Kierkegaard's most important works were all written in the 1840s: *Either/Or: A Fragment of Life* (1843), *Fear and Trembling* (1843), *The Concept of Dread* (1844), *Philosophical Fragments* (1844), *Concluding Unscientific Postscript* (1846), and *The Sickness unto Death* (1849). His autobiographical writings and journals shed considerable light on his personal thoughts and feelings. Nonetheless, it was not his intention to disclose everything. He wrote:

> After my death no one will find among my papers a single explanation as to what really filled my life (that is my consolation); no one will find the words which explain everything and which often made what the world would call a trifle into an event of tremendous importance to me, and what I look upon as something insignificant when I take away the secret gloss which explains it all.

When Kierkegaard was near death he refused a pastor's sacrament, remarking: "Pastors are royal officials; royal officials have nothing to do with Christianity." His epitaph read, as he had requested: "That individual."

## What did Søren **Kierkegaard** deem his main **vocation** in life?

Kierkegaard felt his main vocation was "to reintroduce Christianity into Christendom." For him, Christianity was a way of existing. He thought that only humans existed, because they have "internal reality," in contrast to God, who has "external reality." Faith for him was an inward leap in answer to one burning question about God.

## What was Søren **Kierkegaard's burning question**?

For Kierkegaard, the most important question was whether there was a God, and thereby an afterlife. He did not think that question could be answered by any marshalling of the appropriate facts or through an intellectual process of any kind. It was a rational question, but there was no answer to it. The only acceptable answer was an actual leap of faith within and by the individual. Furthermore, insofar as the facts of the world rendered the possibility of God and an afterlife absurd, this absurdity itself is a test of faith. The more absurd something seems to be, the greater the faith necessary to believe it. Kierkegaard thought that great faith was the key to being a Christian. To this end, he deployed the biblical story of Abraham and Isaac. God commands Abraham to take Isaac up a mountain and then sacrifice him. This act is pathological in ordinary terms, but in religious terms, for Kierkegaard, it is the quintessential example of a leap of faith.

## What were Søren **Kierkegaard's "stages of life's way"**?

Kierkegaard claimed that faith required choices in self-development through three "stages on life's way." Each stage is a different viewpoint on life. First, there is the aesthetic life, lived in the moment, dedicated to the satisfaction of desire, and, in its refined form, to the appreciation of the arts. Lacking in this life is commitment. Commitment is found in the second stage in the ethical life, which seeks a unified self over time. The third stage is the religious life.

## Was Kierkegaard "cursed"?

**K**ierkegaard had a self-fulfilling way of being cursed. There was not only the matter of Regine Olson—after he broke off his engagement, he spent the rest of his life tormented by her loss. There was also the "Corsair Affair" of 1845 to 1846, when, after an unfavorable review, he wrote the following in "Dialectical Result of a Literary Police Action":

> With a paper like *The Corsair,* which hitherto has been read by many and all kinds of people and essentially has enjoyed the recognition of being ignored, despised, and never answered, the only thing to be done in writing in order to express the literary, moral order of things— reflected in the inversion that this paper with meager competence and extreme effort has sought to bring about—was for someone immortalized and praised in this paper to make application to be abused by the same paper.... May I ask to be abused—the personal injury of being immortalized by *The Corsair* is just too much.

> And abused he was, in a campaign so bitingly satiric and mocking of all his personal weaknesses and defects—he was short and frail, and had been born with a hump on his back—that he described himself as apprehensive of everyone with whom he came into contact, "even the butcher boy." This was not self-indulgent paranoia because Kierkegaard experienced the modern phenomenon of a celebrity degraded by the gutter press everywhere he walked in Copenhagen. It was a catastrophe for him because walking and talking to people in all stations of life had been his principal diversion.

## Was there only **one kind** of **religious life** for Søren **Kierkegaard**?

No, Kierkegaard distinguished between two. In the first, the individual relates to God, using his idea of God to deal with guilt. In the second, there is a "teleological suspension of the ethical," as in the story of Abraham and Isaac. The implication of this transcendence of the ethical is that real religion is higher and more important than what is accepted as goodness in society.

## FYODOR DOSTOYEVSKY

## Why have **existentialist philosophers** claimed **Dostoyevsky** as one of their own?

The great Russian novelist Fyodor Mikhailovich Dostoyevsky (1821–1881) is considered an inspiration to the modern philosophical tradition of existentialism because of the depth of his appreciation for the difficulty of the human condition and the universal problems he and his fictional characters agonized over. Friedrich Nietsche (1844–1900) said that Dostoyevsky was "the only psychologist from whom I have something to learn." He praised Dostoyevsky's *Notes from the Underground* (1864) for having "cried truth from the blood."

Indeed, in *Notes from the Underground* Dostoyevsky introduces a self-deprecating narrator, who became an iconic anti-hero for subsequent existentialist writers. The narrator's first words are, "I am a sick man," and his ensuing reflections, rantings, and ruminations make it clear that the sickness at issue is primarily a malaise of the soul. Not the least of this sickness is a disgust with reason.

Although Dostoyevsky is well known for valorizing simplicity in religious faith, he did not arrive at that viewpoint easily, either in works of fiction such as *Crime and Punishment* (1866), or in his own life. In his masterpiece, *The Brothers Karamazov* (1881), Ivan is an atheist, while his brother, Alyosha, is studying to become a monk. In the famous "Grand Inquisitor" dialogue within this novel, Ivan presses Alyosha on his faith, going to the heart of the matter in asking how a good God can permit the suffering of innocent children. Ivan recounts the story of a peasant's child whom the lord allows his dogs to tear apart, because the child threw a stone at one of them. The character of Alyosha is said to be modeled on Dostoyevsky's close friend, the Russian philosopher Vladimir Sergeyevich Solovyov (1853–1900), who longed to reunite the Roman Catholic and Russian Orthodox churches.

Russian Fyodor Dostoyevsky expressed his belief in the extreme difficulty of the human condition through such novels as *The Brothers Karamazov* and *Crime and Punishment* (iStock).

## What aspects of **Dostoevsky's life influenced** his deep **interest** in **human difficulty**?

Dostoyevsky's father was a violent and abusive alcoholic. He was also the doctor of the Mariinsky Hospital for the Poor in Moscow. Dostoyevsky himself suffered from epilepsy from the age of nine. As a child, he used to disobey his parents and explore Mariinsky Hospital, absorbed by the misery of the patients and the stories about their lives that they told him. His first book, *Poor Folk* (1846), brought out the individual humanity of the poor, who were otherwise be ignored and dismissed by the educated reading public of the time.

In 1849 Dostoyevsky was arrested for his participation in the liberal group of intellectuals called the Petrashevsky Circle. He was sentenced to death, although Czar Nicholas II did not really intend for the execution to be carried out. Nevertheless, the experience of standing for hours in the freezing cold in anticipation of a firing squad was believed to have scared Dostoyevsky for life. He was then exiled to Siberia for four years of hard labor. He wrote of this period: "In summer, intolerable closeness; in winter, unendurable cold. All the floors were rotten. Filth on the floors an inch thick; one could slip and fall.... We were packed like herrings in a barrel.... Fleas, lice, and black beetles by the bushel."

When Dostoyevsky's brother and wife died in the same year, he fell into a deep depression and became a gambler. During that period he wrote *Crime and Punishment* (1866), in a frenzied haste, because he was out of money. His life evened out after 1867, when he married his 20-year-old stenographer to whom he had dictated *The Gambler* (1867). While this book is about an elderly woman who gambles self-destructively, some think that Dostoyevsky was describing his own compulsion.

Dostoyevsky lived at the Russian resort Staraya for years before his death from emphysema and an epileptic seizure that brought on a lung hemorrhage. Forty thousand people went to his funeral.

# FRIEDRICH NIETZSCHE

## Who was **Friedrich Nietzsche**?

Friedrich Nietzsche (1844–1900) was a brilliant philosophical iconoclast whose devastatingly direct critical writing style might in itself have qualified him as an existentialist. More substantively, though, was how he developed critiques of bourgeois culture, Christianity, empirical reason, and altruistic morality from the standpoint of a protesting individual who was grander, smarter, more creative, and in odd ways for a much later readership, "hipper" than those who championed accepted values of the time. While Dostoyevsky and others had criticized modernity in the hope of a return to more conservative religious values, Nietzsche looked ahead to coming generations, who would use science as an art to transcend the dreariness of Western history.

## How did Friedrich **Nietzsche's life** presage **his philosophy**?

The great irony is that in life Nietzsche was very unlike his heroes, either those of the aristocratic past that he so admired, or of the new age of knowledge and courage that he heralded. His life began in a somewhat sheltered way in Prussia. His father, a Lutheran minister and the son of a Lutheran minister, died when he was four of what the doctors called "softening of the brain." His mother, Franziska, was only 18 when Friedrich was born; she was the daughter of a Lutheran minister. Contrary to Nietzsche's belief that his forebears were Polish noblemen, many of them were butchers.

When Nietzsche was six, his younger brother died, and he, his mother, and his sister moved to Naumburg. Nietzsche grew up in a household consisting of his mother and sister, his paternal grandmother, and two unmarried aunts. Biographers have remarked that this all-female environment was detrimental to his psychological health as an adult. They have referred to this environment in trying to make sense of the hostility Nietzsche displayed toward women in some of his writings, such as this from *Thus Spoke Zarathustra* (1883–1885): "When thou goest to woman, take thy whip."

At boarding school, Nietzsche suffered from migraines. He was inspired by the poetry of Johann Hölderlin, who had gone insane, so this was not considered a "healthy" subject by Nietzsche's teachers.

Friedrich Nietzsche was more forward thinking than many of his contemporaries, rejecting many of the values of his time (BigStock Photos).

Nietzsche studied theology and classical philology at the University of Bonn, but only philology at the University of Leipzig. He served briefly in the army from 1867 to 1868, and was discharged after a chest injury, which was incurred when he landed on the pommel of his saddle while mounting. When he was only 24, his teachers considered him so promising that he was appointed associate professor of classical philology at Basel. Nietzsche moved to Basel, became a Swiss subject, and, in 1869, a full professor.

In 1870 he received leave to serve as a medical orderly in the Franco-Prussian War, returning to Basel with both dysentery and diphtheria. He received his doctorate in 1873 and resigned from his academic position in 1879 for health reasons. After that, he continued to write and to travel for nine years.

## What are some of Friedrich **Nietzsche's important works**?

Nietzsche's principal works consist of 10 books, which are universally held to be a major achievement. His most famous works include *The Birth of Tragedy* (1872), *The Gay Science* (1882), *Thus Spoke Zarathustra* (released in four parts from 1883 to 1885), *Beyond Good and Evil* (1886), *On the Genealogy of Morals* (1887), and *The Anti-Christ* (1888). Not to be forgotten is *Ecce Homo,* or *Behold the Man* (1888),

## What was the nature of Nietzsche's disability?

**M**uch controversy swirls around this question. There is evidence that he was treated for syphilis at Leipzig, while being kept ignorant of the diagnosis. He is believed to have had tertiary syphilis when he died. It is not clear when Nietzsche might have caught this disease, since he lived an ascetic life, but it was perhaps the result of visiting a brothel only once or twice while he was a student.

Nietzsche's health was poor throughout his life. His eyesight was weak and he had gastro-intestinal pains that he treated himself by walking and by taking a plethora of pills. In January 1889, Nietzsche broke down in a street in Turin, his arms around a horse that had been beaten. Over the next few days, he wrote demented letters to his friends, claiming to have been "crucified by German doctors in a very drawn-out manner," and ordering the Emperor of Germany to report to Rome so that he could be shot. His friends brought him back from Italy, and his mother put him in a clinic in Jena. The treatment was unsuccessful, though, and his mother brought him home.

In 1893, his sister, Elisabeth, returned from Paraguay, where her husband had committed suicide. She took charge of the editing and publication of Nietzsche's manuscripts and isolated him from his friends. When their mother died in 1897, Elisabeth brought Nietzsche to Weimar, where she allowed people to see him. Nietzsche was not communicative, but she had him dressed up anyway, so that she could display him. He was by then very famous.

which he dedicated to Voltaire and in which Nietzsche included his own endearing essay about his own works, "Why I Write Such Good Books" (1888).

## What did Friedrich Nietzsche mean by **"the birth of tragedy?"**

Nietzsche was influenced by Arthur Schopenhauer (1788–1860), who thought that the real world underlying everyday reality was composed of Will, best perceived by us in music. According to Nietzsche, tragedy as an art form was an invention of the ancient Greeks, before Socrates, in order to cope with the chaotic and sorrowful nature of their lives, and indeed of life itself. The tragic play was a rational and beautiful dramatic structure, created by Apollo, the god of reason, which allowed the audience to participate in the underlying, frenzied reality of disorder. This underlying disorder and merging of everything into an anguished but expressive drunken whole was what Nietzsche called the "Dionysian" element in Greek life. Thus, the Apollonian element of reason allowed the Dionysian element of disorder to emerge in the dramatic form of the tragedy, for the vicarious participation of the audience, who was represented by the chorus in the tragic play. In *The Birth of Tragedy* (1872), which was his doctoral dissertation, Nietzsche quoted the great tragic playwright, Sophocles:

> There is an ancient story that King Midas hunted in the forest a long time for the wise Silenus, the companion of Dionysus, without capturing him. When Silenus at last fell into his hands, the king asked what was the best and most desirable of all things for man. Fixed and immovable, the demigod said not a word, 'til at last, urged by the king, he gave a shrill laugh and broke out into these words: "Oh, wretched ephemeral race, children of chance and misery, why do you compel me to tell you what it would be most expedient for you not to hear? What is best of all is utterly beyond your reach: not to be born, not to *be,* to be *nothing*. But the second best for you is—to die soon."

## What was Friedrich Nietzsche's idea of a **"gay science?"**

In a series of aphorisms, Nietzsche advocates philosophy as a celebration of life, in contrast to the stultified and stultifying practices of the German intellectuals, whom he had criticized as philistines throughout his writings during the 1870s. He caps his scientific ideals with the cosmological and possibly Neoplatonistic doctrine of life as a cycle, which he calls the "eternal recurrence." Everyone's life recurs an endless number of times, and the test of a life worth living is that every moment one can will the infinite return of that moment in some future life, and do so with joy.

Nietzsche applauded "the ideal of the most high-spirited, alive, and world-affirming human being who has not only come to terms and learned to get along with whatever was and is, but who wants to have *what was and is* repeated into all eternity." And although he thought that we eternally recur, built into what happens again and again is continuous choice, in a chance spectacle of endless opportunity. (In form, this perspective is a re-enactment by Nietzsche of the birth of tragedy, with the forces of high spirit and reason affirming the worst that has, can, and will happen.)

## What did **Zarathustra say** in Friedrich Nietzsche's ***Thus Spoke Zarathustra***?

In *Thus Spoke Zarathustra* (1883–1885) Nietzsche presents the thoughts of his eponymous hero, who is named after the prophet who founded the Persian religion of Zoroastrianism. Zarathustra's goal, presented in a series of aphorisms, is to prepare for the coming of the *Übermensch,* or Overman, who will fill the vacuum left by the death of the Christian God and the absence of real human heroes. Human life will be created as artists create their works.

## What are the **qualities/characteristics** of Friedrich **Nietzsche's Overman**?

Nietzsche posited the Overman as a new type of human being who would create values in an age when Christianity was no longer a living religion. Unlike the ideal Christian, the Overman would not be meek or ashamed of his strength. He would love life on earth completely, with no need to believe in heaven.

## What were Friedrich **Nietzsche's views** on **religion**?

In *Beyond Good and Evil* (1886), *The Genealogy of Morals* (1887), and *The Anti-Christ* (1888), Nietzsche described Christianity as a sickly ethics of weak people's resentment of the strong. He thought that before Christianity "blond beasts" had become masters of their subjects through daring acts of ferocity. That ancient ruling class was naturally cruel to those not as strong. These fierce rulers saw their weak subjects as "base," while their own traits of pride, courage, reverence for tradition, and loyalty to one another constituted their virtues. The old aristocratic system of values was in time destroyed through the machinations of a

The prophet Zoroaster (or Zarathustra), who founded the ancient Persian religion, inspired Nietsche's idea of the "Overman" (Art Archive).

priestly class, which denied itself by turning its cruelty inward, and encouraged the oppressed masses to identify what hurt them as morally bad—evil.

Christianity was thus a slave morality in Nietzsche's opinion, its uselessness for living fully evident in the worship of a slain God and a rejection of earthly vitality for hopes of joy in heaven. He thought that Christianity was a powerless religion for powerless people, a slave religion with a slave morality for slaves. But he cautioned the strong:

> One has to test oneself to see that one is destined for independence and command—and do it at the right time. One should not dodge one's tests, though they may be the most dangerous game one can play and are tests that are taken in the end before no witness or judge but ourselves.

## What did Friedrich **Nietzsche mean** by **power**?

In his *Will to Power* (compiled posthumously in 1901) Nietzsche is more concerned with the power and strength of the individual than in the individual's control over others. Nietzsche believed that the world was in constant flux and that the only way living things could enjoy being alive was not by knowledge of ideal or unchanging

Some people have, indeed, interpreted Nietzsche in this way because he does celebrate the strong overcoming the weak. When the Nazis came to power in Germany, Nietzsche's sister tried to benefit by presenting her brother's works to them as an appropriate philosophy for the Third Reich. This tarnished Nietzsche's reputation until Walter Kaufmann, in his own translations and edited editions of Nietzsche's works in the 1960s, reinterpreted him as a philosopher of individual freedom. Most current philosophers who like Nietzsche believe that he meant every individual has the freedom to become strong and detach himself from the "herd."

entities, but by constantly increasing their own power. The will to live was for him identical to the will to power because existence is a continual struggle. The "transmogrification" of values by the Overman would represent a future stage of this will to power in the form of new, successful life.

# Jean–Paul Sartre

## Who was **Jean-Paul Sartre**?

Jean-Paul Charles Aymard Sartre (1905–1980) was the icon of twentieth century existentialism. Popular versions of his ideas gave existentialism its dark glamour of atheistic, nihilistic, cigarette-smoking, absinth-drinking, café-frequenting, French intellectuals, arguing about ideas, and practicing "free love." Sartre himself smoked a pipe, was short, stocky, near-sighted, and wall-eyed. He was well known by his contemporaries for his work in the French resistance against the Nazis, and later on, for his Marxism and opposition to the Vietnam conflict. Sartre refused to accept the Nobel Prize for Literature in 1964 on the grounds of his political objections to the bourgeois militaristic culture that made such a prize possible.

Sartre's main existentialist works consisted of numerous plays and essays; the novel *Nausea* (1938); and the philosophical works *The Imagination* (1936), *The Transcendence of the Ego* (1937), and *Being and Nothingness* (1943). His Marxism was developed in the uncompleted, three-volume work *The Critique of Dialectical Reason* (1958–1959).

## What was Jean-Paul **Sartre's** version of **existentialism**?

Sartre was an atheist, so he began with the premise that man is alone in the world and there is no higher power. There is no fixed human nature because man is the inventor of the very idea of nature: "man makes himself." This ability to make oneself is accompanied by a responsibility for what one makes and it leads to considerable anguish because one must choose what to be on one's own. The living human being is always in a situation of varying degrees of difficulty from which there is no escape.

Others are also present in one's life, of course, and they have the same kind of freedoms you do, which renders cooperative and lastingly loving human relationships extremely difficult. One can never fully see the other as he or she is to himself or herself. Because others are in the same situation, the net effect is that "hell is other people." Sartre's view of intimate relationships was bleak because the person desired always eludes being the object desired. The desired person can never fully become an object because he or she has their own freedom.

Jean-Paul Sartre was the icon of twentieth century existentialism (Art Archive).

To accept one's freedom and one's situation, or "facticity," are both necessary in order to be in "good faith." The person who lives in bad faith either denies his own freedom and responsibility or denies the reality of his situation. Everything is chosen, even emotions that carry one to extremes, or insanity. Even the most difficult situation, which one has not chosen, does not negate one's freedom. It is the individual who gives the situation the meaning it has for him or her as a difficult situation. With a gun to one's head, for instance, one still has the choice of whether or not to live.

## What was Jean-Paul **Sartre's basis** for his **idea of freedom**?

Sartre argued that freedom was inherent in the very structure of human consciousness. To be conscious is to be free. Consciousness has no prior cause but is a spontaneous upsurge. Consciousness is nothing in itself, because it is always aware of something other than itself. Consciousness is freedom. Thus, consciousness is not a thing in itself. Sartre called consciousness the "for-itself," or *pour-soi,* and everything else is the "in-itself," or *en-soi.* At first glance, his division of the human cosmos into for-itself and in-itself resembles René Descartes' (1596–1650) doctrine of mental and physical substance, but Sartre went beyond Descartes' idea of the "mental substance."

For Sartre, as his hero in *Nausea* (1938) discovers in the course of a research project, even a person's past meritorious acts or traits of character have the status of *en-soi.* It is a form of bad faith, for example, to pretend that one is determined to fulfill his or her duty because that is how he or she was raised, or that one's laziness makes

## Was Jean-Paul Sartre Jewish?

This question is deeply imbedded in the disputes among Sartre's closest followers that followed his death. Their disputes were not so much matters of philosophy as they were a competition for who would inherit Sarte's legacy and be able to speak for him after his death. According to Bénny Levy, a former Maoist who had been Sartre's secretary for several years and transcribed 40 hours of taped conversations in *Hope Now: The 1980 Interviews* (1996), Sartre expressed hope for the coming of the Messiah.

disciplined work impossible. People are responsible for allowing their own background, weaknesses, or strengths to be motives for action in the immediate present.

## What kind of a **Marxist** was Jean-Paul **Sartre**?

In his introduction to the *Critique of Dialectical Reason* (1960) Sartre first claimed that his own existentialist philosophy was merely an addendum to Marxism as an historical process. But when he went on to explain what he meant, he said that the success of Marxist liberation for the oppressed would be necessary for the freedom he had described to be accessible to everyone. In other words, he saw the goal of Marxism as the realization of the very freedom he had described.

In one sense, this contradicted his description of freedom as a universal human condition. But in another sense, Sartre believed that the oppressed have the power, based on their individual freedom, to unite and cooperate for collective liberation. So, although he embraced Marxism, he did not embrace its premise of determinism that the individual's consciousness is the result of the political and economic factors forming his or her social class.

## Who was **Simone de Beauvoir**?

Simone de Beauvoir (1908–1986) is now most famous as the philosopher who began the "Second Wave" of feminism in the West. She began writing when she was eight years old and was a novelist and political writer who helped Jean-Paul Sartre (1905–1980), her main lifelong companion, found *Le Monde*. De Beauvoir's major works include the novels *She Came to Stay* (1943), *The Blood of Others* (1945), and *The Mandarins* (1954), and her philosophical texts *The Ethics of Ambiguity* (1947), *The Second Sex* (1949), and *Old Age* (1970). She also wrote evocative autobiographical works, such as *Memoirs of a Dutiful Daughter* (1958). De Beauvoir ruthlessly described Sartre's great decline toward the end of his life in *Adieu: A Farewell to Sartre* (1981).

Beauvoir also quarreled fiercely with Arlette Elkaim, the young Jewish Algerian student who had contacted Sartre when she was 18. Sartre enjoyed discussing his philosophy with Elkaim, and he preferred to write in her apartment, instead of following his lifetime habit of writing in cafés. Then he adopted her and bought her a house in the south of France, which became their summer vacation home.

Beauvoir had an adopted daughter of her own, Sylvie Le Bon de Beauvoir, with whom she had had an erotic relationship, although Sylvie later described it as "platonic." Sylvie wrote *Tête-à-Tête* (2005) about de Beauvoir and Sartre.

In 2005, Sylvie and Sartre's daughter were not on speaking terms. Each in her sixties, they continued to bitterly contest their respective rights to Sartre and de Beauvoir's literary properties. Since Sartre and de Beauvoir are inextricably linked through letters in which they discussed each other, the complexity of the dispute between their literary heiresses can only be imagined. By 2005, Sylvie was a retired philosophy teacher and Arlette was described as "extremely reclusive." Geographically, these women had lived close to each other in the same Parisian *arrondisement,* for some years.

Beauvoir had a high tolerance for alcohol all her life (she liked its "taste") but drank more heavily in her later years. She was also hooked on amphetamines. When she died in 1986, she was buried in Sartre's grave, thereby sealing their link for posterity.

### What did **Simone de Beauvoir** mean by an **ethics of ambiguity**?

Beauvoir expressed a disappointment with politics after World War II, and she addressed the importance of mass action and relations between political party leaders and their followers and colleagues. She applied Jean-Paul Sartre's (1905–1980) existential philosophy to politics, criticizing "the spirit of seriousness" that characterized those who did not take responsibility for their political actions as free individuals. Although Sartre had never written on ethics, she thought that ethical positions and decisions would arise from compelling passions and circumstances. The best interpretation of Beauvoir's *The Ethics of Ambiguity* (1947) is not that ethics is itself ambiguous but that ethics is somewhat arbitrary from an existentialist perspective.

Simone de Beauvoir is credited with beginning the Second Wave of feminism (AP).

## How was Simone de **Beauvoir influential** as a **feminist**?

Writing at a time when women did not have a recognized voice in public life—they had only received the right to vote in 1944 in France—or opportunities to pursue professions, Beauvoir offered a comprehensive account and analysis of the position of women in Western society with a focus on their life stages. For women, unlike men, "biology is destiny," she said. She was not particularly sympathetic to the subordinate condition of women, generally, because she thought that they too easily accepted their secondary passive roles in comparison to the leading, active roles allowed and expected of men.

Beauvoir did not clearly indicate ways in which women could realize their human freedoms and transcend their object-like status, or *immanence,* as human beings who were not only objectified by men, but who seemed too content to objectify themselves. However, she began a trend in social and political activism, as well as intellectual life, which recognized and addressed the ways in which women were "the second sex."

## OTHER EXISTENTIALISTS

### What did the **religious** and **humanist existentialists contribute**?

The religious existentialists reconciled Sartrean ideas of freedom with the Judaic-Christian tradition. The humanist existentialists brought the more abstract aspects of existentialism into literature or developed them in different directions philosophically.

### What were the **ideas** of the main **religious existentialists**?

Martin Buber (1878–1965) connected existentialism to Judaism by emphasizing that whereas Christians have direct individual relationships to God, the Jewish relationship to God is mediated by membership in a community. As a professor at the Hebrew University in Jerusalem, after he left Vienna in 1938, Buber tried to reconcile Jews and Arabs.

Buber criticized the subject–object form of knowledge as a mode in both human and religious relationships. In its place, he advocated an "I–Thou" relationship that recognized the subjectivity of the other. His main work is *I and Thou* (1923).

Karl Jaspers (1883–1969) thought that philosophy should help human beings with their projects of self-discovery toward a goal of *Existenz,* or authentic selfhood, based on an understanding of one's own life. Although not a traditional theologian, Jaspers nevertheless addressed individual spiritual yearnings. His main works are *Philosophy* (1932), *On the Origin and Goal of History* (1949), and *Way to Wisdom* (1950).

Gabriel Marcel (1889–1973) was both a philosopher and a playwright who addressed human existence in terms of community and personal relationships. He emphasized "we are," instead of "I am," drawing on both Søren Kierkegaard

(1813–1855) and Buber. He also approached philosophy as a Bergsonian intuitionist by relying on his immediate insights for his views, rather than arriving at them through argument. His main works include *Mystery of Being* (1951) and *Man against Mass Society* (1955). His William James Lectures at Harvard University (1961, 1962) were published as *The Existential Background of Human Dignity*.

Simone Weil (1909–1943) was born into a Jewish Parisian family but converted first to leftist syndicalism, which was a Marxist political movement with the goal of putting labor unions in control of both industry and government. Her subsequent religious thought was a combination of Neo-Platonism, Christianity, and Jewish mysticism. She was an activist on behalf of the democratically elected government during the Spanish Civil War, and for the French resistance during World War II. She criticized the way in which Marxism had become a religion to some and objected to the dehumanizing effects of capitalism. Her solution was meaningful work as a fundamental human need. Her main writings, published posthumously, are *Gravity and Grace* (1947) and *Oppression and Liberty* (1955).

## What were the **ideas** of some of the **humanist existentialists**?

Hans Jonas (1903–1993) was influenced by phenomenology as well as existentialism, but some of his most original work has been directly relevant to environmental concerns and thought about the nature of life. In *The Imperative of Responsibility* (1979) he argues for ethical responsibility for the planet to fight the incursions of technology. In *The Phenomenon of Life* (1966) he argues against standard biological approaches that objectify living things and seek to explain their behavior via mere chemistry or mechanistic hereditary forces. Jonas' positive thesis is that all life forms, even single cells, have some form of awareness and they strive from their own physicality and perspective on the world. (Awareness on a cellular level does not imply the presence of the *cogito*—a mind—it is sufficient if the living entity "behaves" in a way that enhances its life, or attempts to do so.)

Emmanuel Levinas (1905–1995) was a French Jewish philosopher who was originally from Lithuania. Levinas criticized the philosophical tradition in which things other than an individual mind are represented to that mind in ideas or some other "mental content." He thought that the paradigm for understanding consciousness was the face-to-face interactions between human beings. Such interactions are both particular and indescribable, as well as of inestimable importance. Levinas' main works are *Totality and Infinity* (1964), *Otherwise than Being or beyond Essence* (1974), *Difference and Transcendence* (1999), and *Between Us* (1998).

Albert Camus (1913–1960), like Søren Kierkegaard (1813–1855), had a "burning question." In his case, it was, "Why should a human being not commit suicide?" The question arose for him from his apprehension of the human condition as absurd, together with the absence of God and a forever frustrated search for meaning. Camus

271

Albert Camus, the brilliant author of novels like *The Rebel,* struggled to understand the meaning of human life in a godless world (Art Archive).

was a friend of Jean-Paul Sartre (1905–1980), but they became alienated from each other as a result of Camus' critique of communist tyranny in his essay im favor of revolutionary struggle, *The Rebel* (1951). His novel *The Plague* (1947) dramatized the ever-presence of death in human life. In his nonfiction essay *The Myth of Sisyphus* (1942) Camus claims that meaning can be found by affirming the absurd and then rebelling against it, as in "imagine Sisyphus happy." Sisyphus' punishment by Zeus consists of eternally rolling a large boulder up a mountain, only to begin again after he has reached the top and the boulder has rolled down again. His crimes were first to put Death in chains and then escape death himself. Camus was awarded the Nobel Prize for Literature in 1957; his own death in a car crash raised the question of his suicide.

Paul Ricoeur (1913–2005) wrote on a variety of subjects, including existentialism, phenomenology, ethics, psychology, and theory of language. All of his work was distinguished by a deep engagement with key figures in the history of philosophy. His *Freedom and Nature* (1950) was received as a rejection of Sartre's theory of freedom. Ricoeur argued that willing always has an involuntary component, which works as a kind of built-in resistance. What is voluntary consists of motive, decision, and consent, each of which has its own involuntary "moment." The involuntary moments include birth, death, character already developed, the body, and the unconscious. (First, it's not clear that Sartre equated freedom with acts of will, because freedom is present in all consciousness. Second, Sartre would have said that what we accept or recognize as involuntary requires a free choice of bestowing that particular meaning.)

# PHENOMENOLOGY

## EDMUND HUSSERL

### Who was **Edmund Husserl**?

Edmund Husserl (1859–1938) is recognized as the founder of phenomenology as a systematic method of philosophy. He also created an important and new perspective on logic and mathematics, which distinguished them from empirically discovered psychological "rules of thought." Husserl's major works are *Logical Investigations* (1900), *The Idea of Phenomenology* (1907), and *Ideas Pertaining to a Pure Phenomenology and to a Phenomenological Investigation* (1913).

## What are some key facts about Edmund **Husserl's life** and **career**?

Husserl was born in Prossnitz, Moravia, which became part of Czechoslovakia after World War I and is now in the Czech Republic. His family was Jewish. Husserl studied mathematics in Leipzig and Berlin, and then got his Ph.D. in Vienna in 1883, writing *Contributions to the Calculus of Variations* that year. For the next two years, he studied psychology and philosophy with Franz Brentano (1837–1917) and then went to the University of Halle for his habilitation (preparation for university teaching) under a student of Brentano. He wrote *On the Concept of Number*, which he revised four years later, in 1891, as *Philosophy of Arithmetic*.

In 1886 Husserl converted to Christianity, taking the name "Edmund Gustav Albrecht Husserl." The next year, he married Malvine Steinschneider, who was to prove a valuable source of information about his work and intentions to academic colleagues. They had a daughter and two sons. In 1901, the Husserls moved to the University of Göttingen. He was promoted to "ordenlichen" professor in 1906, and the next year he traveled to Italy to see Brentano.

Husserl was at this time in correspondence with Wilhelm Dilthey and leading mathematicians, as well as philosophers, about their work and his. German psychologist and philosopher Karl Jaspers (1883–1969) visited him in 1913, the same year *Ideen* was published. While visiting his son Wolfgang, who was injured in World War I, Husserl experienced nicotine poisoning.

In 1916 Husserl was appointed to a professorship in Freiburg. Wolfgang was killed in action that year. For the next two years, Edith Stein was his assistant, as was philosopher Martin Heidegger (1889–1976), for whom he obtained a lectureship and helped get an assistant professorship in 1919. The next year, his son Gerhard was wounded, although he recovered. Over the following decade, Husserl and Heidegger were in contact, exchanging ideas and manuscripts.

Because of his Jewish birth, in 1933 the German government barred Husserl from using the library at Freiburg University, or any other German academic institution, although after an immediate public outcry, he was reinstated a week later by a decree. Husserl resigned from the Deutsche Akademie several months after that. His leaving was not only a matter of what had happened at Freiburg but of the growing danger to all Jews in Germany at that time. He was then appointed to the School of Philosophy at the University of Southern California, but declined because his assistant, Eugen Fink, was not permitted to accompany him. Husserl was not allowed to participate in the Paris Congress of Philosophers in 1937. At his cremation the next year, Eugen

Fink eulogized him. Fink had been Husserl's dedicated and collaborative research assistant for 10 years. In his own work, Fink was to eventually turn from Husserl's philosophical perspective to that of Heidegger.

Husserl had only published six books during his lifetime, but he had a huge collection of papers and manuscripts. Fearing that the Nazis would destroy them, the Belgian philosopher Herman Leo Van Breda (1911–1974) took them out of Germany, where they became part of the Husserl Archives in Louvain after World War II.

## Who was **Edith Stein**?

Edith Stein (1891–1942) was canonized by Pope John Paul II in 1998 as Saint Theresa Benedicta of the Cross. She was born into an observant Jewish family in the central European region of Silesia, which was then part of the German Empire. In 1932 she denounced the Nazi regime to Pope Pius XI. She converted to Roman Catholicism in 1922 and was received into the Discalced Carmelite Order in 1934. In a retaliatory move against Jewish converts in the Netherlands, where the Carmelites had sent Stein for safety, she and her sister Rosa were transported to the Auschwitz concentration camp. They died there in the gas chamber in 1942.

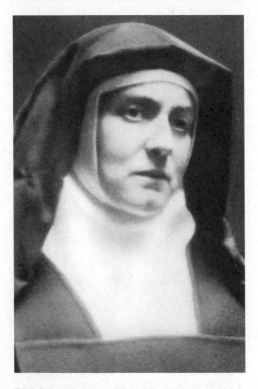

Edith Stein, a student of Edmund Husserl, was canonized after performing a miracle to save a child who overdosed on acetaminophen (AP).

Stein was a student of Edmund Husserl (1859–1938), first at Göttingen University and then at Freiburg, where she became his assistant. Her doctorate was "On the Problem of Empathy." She became a faculty member at Freiberg University after working with Martin Heidegger in preparing Husserl's manuscripts for publication. As a Jewish woman, she was barred from further postgraduate studies at Freiberg and other German universities. She finally gave up her assistantship to Husserl and began to teach in Catholic girls' schools, learning about Thomas Aquinas (c. 1225–1274) and Catholic philosophy in general. She did become a lecturer at the Institute for Pedagogy at Münster, but had to give it up due to anti-Semitic laws in 1933, the same year that her former colleague, Martin Heidegger (1889–1976), was made rector of Freiburg University.

The miracle Edith Stein is supposed to have performed—that of curing a child

## How did Edmund Husserl separate mathematics and logic from psychology?

First, Husserl distinguished between numbers that are the result of counting actual objects before us and numbers as symbols. Clearly, most of mathematics deals with numbers as symbols. Husserl claimed that symbolic numbers, as well as propositions and universals, cannot be reduced to mental states, as *psychologism* claimed. As intentional objects of consciousness, in Franz Brentano's (1837–1917) sense of intentionality, these logical and mathematical entities are objective.

who had overdosed on acetaminophen in response to a prayer from relatives—is disputed by some Jewish groups who claim it is not clear whether she is a genuine martyr. Her legacy includes numerous writings, some of which were translated into English in the 1980s and 1990s: *Life in a Jewish Family: Her Unfinished Autobiographical Account* (1986), *On the Problem of Empathy* (1989), *Essays on Women* (1996), and *The Hidden Life,* (1993). Stein also wrote *Knowledge and Faith, Finite and Eternal Being: An Attempt to an Ascent to the Meaning of Being, Philosophy of Psychology and the Humanities, Self-Portrait in Letters,* which have not yet been translated into English or published.

## What was Edmund **Husserl's doctrine of intentionality**?

Husserl thought that the same objectivity of intentional objects that mathematical symbols have holds for all sorts of other objects, as well, including objects of perception and "categorical objects," such as causal connections, states of affairs, and relations. When we describe an object we have an intellectual intuition of it, or our intention is "fulfilled," although in terms of what we do not know our intention of the object may be "empty."

At first, Husserl thought that what was given to us in consciousness was not the Kantian "thing in itself," but he later claimed that in a "manifold of appearances," the thing-in-itself can be given to consciousness, which is to say, known. This view was criticized as idealism because all "objects" for Husserl were objects of consciousness. Husserl later qualified his position by stating that the thing-in-itself given to consciousness, was only given to consciousness as a complete object of consciousness, not as its own total reality.

Basically, Husserl was claiming that everything we know, even if what we know is true, is nonetheless something like an idea in the mind (e.g., My cat is now sitting on my computer as I write this. That's a fact. But as something that I am consciously aware of, it is also something in my mind.)

## What was Edmund **Husserl's phenomenological method**?

Husserl thought the task of the philosopher was to perform an empirical "reduction" of intentional objects of consciousness by describing what is in the mind without making a commitment to the reality of the mental content. That is, Husserl thought that we should describe what appears to be so to us without making a commitment that it is so (e.g., My cat is sitting on my computer, but Husserl would prefer that I stick to my impressions or the "representations" in my mind of the cat sitting on the computer.)

This is a special perspective, distinctive from the natural attitudes of ordinary people and scientists who address actual things that exist in the world. For Husserl, there is no philosophical distinction between a content of consciousness that is a dream or a fantasy and one that corresponds to something happening in reality. There were, however, different types of reduction for Husserl, most notably *epoche* in which the truth and reality of the objects of consciousness are "bracketed." This bracketing of truth or reality was exactly the same thing as not making a commitment to the truth or reality. Husserl would have wanted me to describe the cat on my computer and my perception of it, but to stop short of claiming that the cat really is sitting on my comuter.

Also influential was Husserl's *eidetic* reduction that had as its subjects acts of consciousness itself, and *eidetic intuition* that pertained to the essences of objects of consciousness.

Thus, analysis of perception, which is something that consciousness does, would be an example of eidetic reduction, whereas analysis of what is being perceived would be an example of eidetic intuition. This distinction was to prove very influential in Jean-Paul Sartre's philosophy, where he distinguished between consciousness as awareness and what we are conscious or aware of.

## How did Edmund **Husserl distinguish** between two **types** of the **self**?

First, Husserl explained that there is the "psychological ego" or the "self" that owns or makes the intentional acts of consciousness. The psychological ego exists in the world, because one can be aware of it as a self. But there is also the *transcendental ego* for which there is a world and which is concerned about truth—the transcendental ego intends the world. The transcendental ego makes it possible for the psychological ego to exist and it determines how it will function.

## MARTIN HEIDEGGER

## Who was **Martin Heidegger**?

Martin Heidegger (1889–1976) was the phenomenological "ontologist" who first united existentialism with phenomenology, but later revealed that his true concern was ontology. He is considered one of the titans of Western philosophy and had more direct enduring influence over twentieth century continental philosophy than any other thinker.

Heidegger wrote extensively on the history of philosophy, developing his own phenomenological analyses. His main books include his doctoral dissertation *The Doctrine of Judgement in Psychologism* (1914), his habilitation (in Europe, Ph.D.s write two dissertations, one to get a degree as a scholar and the second to qualify them to teach on a university level) *The Doctrine of Categories and Signification in Duns Scotus* (1914), his most famous *Being and Time* (1927), and then *Introduction to Metaphysics* (1953), *What Is Called Thinking* (1954), *What Is Philosophy?* (1956), *On the Way to Language* (1959), *Nietzsche* I and II (1961), and *Phenomenology and Theology* (1970). Transcripts of Heidegger's lec-

Martin Heidegger was a phenomenological ontologist who united existentialism with phenomenology (AP).

tures were partly published in 1975 (the complete works would constitute over 100 volumes). Heidegger is also known for articles on art and poetry, as well as his essay *The Question Concerning Technology*.

## What did Martin **Heidegger** mean by **"ontology?"**

The term "ontology" refers to the study of being in a general sense that is relevant to all thinkers and theorists. Empiricists, for example, have ontologies in that there are some entities that they believe exist. According to Heidegger, ontology, as the first and last subject of philosophy, is the study of Being, with a capital "B." Being is existence itself, including everything that exists, but in particular human consciousness for which Being is first and foremost the condition of its own being.

For readers who find this confusing, excellent relaxation can be found in Günter Grass' 1963 novel, *Dog Years,* which contains a parody of Heidegger's terminology in the literal description of a canine's wanderings during the Nazi era. For the more scholarly inclined, there is Theodor Adorno's *The Jargon of Authenticity* (1973).

## How does Martin **Heidegger embarrass** the **Heideggerians**?

Heidegger's political beliefs and behavior when the Nazis came to power have generated much controversy, based on the following documented facts.

277

Heidegger paid dues as a member of the NSDAP, or Nazi Party, from 1933 to 1945. In his inaugural address in May 1933 as rector of Freiburg University, three months after Hitler came to power, he called for the students and faculty to serve the new regime, referring to "the march our people has begun into its future history" and to "the power to preserve, in the deepest way, the strengths which are rooted in soil and blood." In June 1933, he told the Heidelberg Student Association that the university "must be integrated into the *Volksgemeinshaft* (people's community) and be joined together with the state." In August 1933, he established the rule that the rector would no longer be elected by the faculty but appointed by the Nazi minister of education, a position to which he was himself appointed in October 1933. In November 1933, he applied the Nazi laws on racial cleansing to the students at Freiberg, awarding financial aid to Aryan students, but not to Jews or Marxists.

Heidegger also secretly denounced to the Nazi government a number of Jewish or politically suspect professors at Freiburg, such as Hermann Staudinger, who won the Nobel prize in chemistry in 1953, and Eduard Baumgarten, the pragmatist philosopher who was teaching at Göttingen. Max Müller, the Catholic intellectual, was fired by Heidegger as student leader and prevented from getting a lectureship. Edmund Husserl (1859–1938), Heidegger's former teacher, was denied use of the University Library at Freiburg because he was a Jew even though he had converted to Lutheranism. (Heidegger and Husserl's intellectual relationship is examined in the film *The Ister*, directed by David Barrison and Daniel Ross in 2004.)

Although Heidegger resigned as rector in 1934, the next year he referred to the "inner truth and greatness of National Socialism." At least until 1960, Heidegger maintained a friendly acquaintance with Eugen Fisher, the head of the Institute of Racial Hygiene in Berlin that employed the infamous Dr. Joseph Mengele as a researcher. Heidegger never repudiated Nazism after World War II. In his lecture on technology in 1949, he referred to the mechanism of agriculture, saying: "Agriculture is now a motorized food-industry—in essence, the same as the manufacturing of corpses in the gas chambers and the extermination camps, the same as the blockade and starvation of the countryside, the same as the production of the hydrogen bombs."

Many were offended by this comparison by Heidegger of murdered Jews to agricultural products. In a last interview before his death, Heidegger described the main task of thought as achieving a satisfactory relationship to technology. He said that National Socialism had that goal but that "those people were far too limited in their thinking to acquire an explicit relationship to what is really happening today and has been underway for three centuries." In other words, his greatest disappointment with the Nazis was their failure in addressing the problem of technology!

## What are some important facts about Martin **Heidegger's life**?

Heidegger was born in 1889 in the Black Forest in Messkirch, Germany, an area to which he maintained close ties throughout his life. He attended gymnasium (high school) in Freiberg, beginning in 1906, where he read Franz Brentano's (1837–1917) *On the Manifold Meaning of Being According to Aristotle* (1862). He intended to become a Jesuit priest, but he was rejected, so he prepared for the Catholic priesthood at Ludwig University in Freiberg. He read the works of Edmund Husserl (1859–1938) there and, at the urging of his teachers, changed from theology to philosophy and mathematics.

After marrying Elfride Petri in March 1917, he joined the German army, advancing rapidly to corporal, although he was discharged for reasons of health. As Husserl's assistant and a colleague of Karl Jaspers (1883–1969), Heidegger was successful in philosophy, becoming an associate professor at the University of Marburg, where he wrote *Being and Time* (1927) in a matter of months to secure that post. After this work, he experienced the well-known *Kehre,* or turn in thought, which led to his *An Introduction to Metaphysics* (1953).

Among his students were future philosopher Herbert Marcuse (1898–1979) and political theorist and philosopher Hannah Arendt (1906–1975), who became his lover before she had to leave Germany. (As a Jewish intellectual, it became evident that she was in danger after being questioned by the Gestapo [the German secret police].) During this time, Heidegger was influenced by Lao Tzu's work on meditation, which led to his own understanding of Being through language.

Heidegger became rector of the University of Freiburg in 1933 and was a member of the National Socialist Party. In 1945, the French Military government removed his professorship, although he was able to gain emeritus status, provided he did not teach again. He had a nervous breakdown in 1946 but wrote his "Letter on Humanism" to make it clear that, regarding his study of Being, his work was not as humanistic as Jean-Paul Sartre (1905–1980) and other existentialists had mistakenly assumed. In 1950 his professorship was restored, and in 1951 he was allowed to be professor emeritus. To recap, he was first given emeritus or retired status without having been reinstated as a professor. Then he was reinstated as a professor and was given a normal emeritus status after that. He continued his work until he died in 1976.

## What is **Dasein**?

"Dasein" is Martin Heidegger's term for a human being. Its literal meaning is "being there." Heidegger intended by this term to convey that human beings are not simple, self-contained biological beings but that they are always concerned with things beyond their physical selves, with things in the world, other people, and the future.

## Why do some people consider Martin **Heidegger** to be an **existentialist**?

In *Being and Time* (1927) Heidegger analyzed the human being or "Dasein," which in German means "being-there." Heidegger's insight was that Dasein cannot be understood as a biological thing because its main objects of concern, which is a fundamental structure of what it is, are always somewhere other than where Dasein itself is. Although Dasein in its being is concerned for its own being (understood in the ordinary sense as "life"), its own being is caught up "in-the-world." Furthermore, Dasein fails to understand its own being authentically, because in its ordinary existence it accepts the interpretation of its being that has already been constructed by "the they," or the mass mind. The they is particularly mistaken about the nature of death.

## What is **"the they"**?

Martin Heidegger's term "the they" was meant to refer to ordinary people who go about their everyday lives with no philosophical awareness of their existence.

## What were Martin **Heidegger's views** on **death**?

Heidegger thought that the individual's death had to be wrested away from "the they," who made of death something impersonal that was ordinary, but which somehow didn't happen to anyone in particular. Heidegger claimed that death is "in each case my own" and that authentic existence requires an attitude of "anticipatory resoluteness" toward one's own death. It is nothing less than conscience, "the call of care," which draws a person to attend to his or her own death.

The problem is that Dasein cannot be completed until Dasein is no more. But when Dasein is no more, Dasein will no longer "be" as a concrete individual, and furthermore, its own death is a nothing. Heidegger took this to mean that we are constantly being called to a nullity in a paradoxical need to authentically be that which we most fully are. This nullity in the essence of Dasein, which in Heidegger's terminology is "always out-standing," so long as Dasein is, creates a primordial anxiety in Dasein. Heidegger meant that the fact that our death is always in the future is what makes us always anxious. But of course, if our death were in the present, we would no longer exist. So we mortals have to put up with the fact that we will die as something that we are always aware of while we are alive.

## What was Martin **Heidegger's theory of space**?

Dasein creates space by assigning proximity or distance to objects in the world with which it is concerned. And the space that results from existence in this way does not necessarily line up with abstract dimensions and distances. The eyeglasses on a person's nose, for example, are farther away to the wearer than the picture hanging on the wall that he or she looks through the glasses to see.

Objects in space acquire a characteristic of being "ready-to-hand"—they are things that we use and manipulate. The ready-to-hand, although literally in space, has its real meaning through human action over time. For example, if you pick up a hammer, you intend to do something with it in the next few minutes, and you are doing that to achieve a goal after that, such as hanging a picture on the wall.

## What was Martin **Heidegger's theory of time**?

As with space, time, explained Heidegger, is a creation of Dasein based on its concern for things beyond its immediate self. Dasein in the mode of *temporality* even creates abstract or clock time because it is a goal-oriented being. Something that is "not-yet" becomes located in the future. On the basis of the "having-been," which is the past, the immediacy of the present emerges from Dasein's concern about something in the future. As a structure of human existence, temporality thus temporalizes itself. This is Heidegger's terminology, and what he seems to mean is that when you think about the future, you think about how the present will be a memory to you then. People do this when they deliberately take photographs to "create memories."

## Why did Martin **Heidegger claim** that **existentialism** was **not** a type of **humanism**?

In going back to Presocratic thought, Heidegger concluded that the original concern of man, or Dasein (in a cultural line that linked contemporary Germans to ancient Greeks), was Being. Heidegger believed that the Presocratics had only started to formulate the primary questions concerning Being, when the Socratics introduced a subject-object kind of metaphysics that already foreclosed one kind of answer to the original question of Being. Heidegger makes it clear to the reader that he does not know what this original question concerning Being was. Indeed, he devoted his philosophical work to trying to reconstruct the question, thereby inviting readers to ponder the same problem he did, with no conclusive answer. In this sense, Heidegger provides an exercise in meditation to those of his readers who take the time to understand him.

Heidegger wrote much about what that question might be, relying on a phenomenological intuition that "language is the house of Being." He did not mean by this the language of "the they," or even the discourse of French existentialists, such as Jean-Paul Sartre (1905–1980), with its insufficiently general concerns. Until the question of

Being could be formulated, the kind of humanism that existentialism could be could
not even be properly imagined, according to Heidegger.

## What was Martin **Heidegger's question** concerning **technology**?

Heidegger's question was the same question that hangs over us at this time: will technology destroy the world as we know it? But Heidegger's understanding of technology
was unlike environmentalist thought that distinguished the artificial from what is
natural. As part of what it means to say that "the world worlds," Heidegger believed
that technology was a process arising from Being, insofar as human beings are the
custodians of Being in their own being, albeit without a full understanding of what is
involved in their relationship to Being.

Technology, according to Heidegger, was an "enframing" force and process that
emerges from Dasein's relationship to being: all beings are marshalled and regiment-
ed to present themselves as uniform types of objects; human activities and the beau-
ties of nature are also enframed and presented back to Dasein as items for use or consumption. In Heidegger's terms, a particularly plaintive example of such processing is
the redirection and artificialization of the River Rhine as a tourist attraction.

As part of his analysis of the historical force of technology that has arisen from a
distinctively human understanding of Being, Heidegger insists that technology is not
an effect of science, but the reverse. Science and scientific research are no more than
the results of more general technological forces.

# MAURICE MERLEAU-PONTY

## Who was **Maurice Merleau-Ponty**?

Maurice Merleau-Ponty (1908–1961) was an anti-empiricist who sought to reconstruct the world based on a phenomenology of human perception. He was influenced
by Edmund Husserl (1859–1938), was friends with Jean-Paul Sartre (1905–1980) for a
while, and continues to be of great interest to phenomenological philosophers of

## What was ironic about Maurice Merleau-Ponty's last lecture?

Merleau-Ponty died suddenly of a stroke while preparing to give a lecture on René Descartes (1596–1650). He repeatedly returned to Descartes' split between the mind and the body in composing his own philosophy. He did not accept the Cartesean split, but sought to address the mind and body as a united whole. Merleau-Ponty thought that a person's own body, *le corps propre*, should be, in its personal, individual, lived reality, a scientific subject. It is one's own body that makes consciousness corporeal. He wrote: "Insofar as I have hands, feet, a body, I sustain around me intentions which are not dependent on my decisions and which affect my surroundings in a way that I do not choose."

Clearly, Merleau-Ponty's stroke proves this point because it was not something he chose, but definitely something that conclusively affected not only his surroundings but the possibility of his even having those surroundings. What's ironic is that he made his point by having a stroke, which is very different from making a philosophical argument.

mind. His principal works are *The Phenomenology of Perception* (1945), numerous essays, and his unfinished *The Visible and the Invisible*.

## What are some facts about Maurice **Merleau-Ponty's life** and **career**?

Merleau-Ponty's father was killed in World War I. He completed his philosophical studies at the École Normale Superieure in 1930 and then taught in high schools throughout France. He wrote two dissertations for his doctorate and was given the chair of child psychology at the Sorbonne in 1949; next, he was made chair of philosophy at the College de France in 1952. With Jean-Paul Sartre (1905–1980) he founded the journal *Les Temps Moderne*. But he resigned from the publication as editor, partly in objection to Sartre's subject-object dichotomy. Merleau-Ponty wrote about their dispute in *Adventures of the Dialectic* (1955). Overall, Merleau-Ponty opposed dualisms and he also criticized self-versus-world ideas. He thought that the self was as much a body as a mind and that our bodies are always in the world.

## What did Maurice **Merleau-Ponty** mean by a "**phenomenology of perception**"?

Merleau-Ponty opposed the abstract natures of both empiricism, which generalized, and idealism, which denied the direct experience and existence of physical reality. He proclaimed that "the perceiving mind is an incarnate mind," meaning that it was "in" the body in the sense of being co-incident with the body. Perception is a physical process involving eyes, ears, the nose, the hands, rather than only the mind. His focus was thus on the human body as a perceiving, living part of world, a position theretofore much neglected in philosophical inquiry.

According to Merleau-Ponty, perception is neither abstract nor scientific. Rather, all perception is lived; it is the experience of human beings in the world. Consciousness is, to use a later term, "embodied" and always engaged in perceiving the world. What is "phenomenological" about human experience is that what is perceived cannot be separated from how it is perceived or from how it is described. In conversation with Ferdinand de Saussure (1857–1913), Merleau-Ponty composed *The Prose of the World* (1969), claiming that meaning is not determined by history but by the subject's actual experience in the world. Language is itself continually changing as a result of this experience. In *The Visible and the Invisible* Merleau-Ponty had intended to show how communication and thought can go beyond perception, but he died before completing that project.

# CRITICAL THEORY AND STRUCTURALISM

## What is the **difference** between **critical theory** and **structuralism**?

There is no clear distinction of practice that practitioners of both schools of thought would accept. Many structuralists denied being structuralists and some critical theorists were unaware of the term "critical theory." But from the standpoint of a reader, it may help to keep in mind that both structuralism and critical theory provide analyses of society that need not be accepted by the members of society being analyzed. The term "critical theory" is associated with the Frankfurt School, which developed the twentieth century version of scholarly Marxism. The term "structuralism" refers to a study of mental structures in society. Critical theory seeks to provide analyses that further progressive and egalitarian social goal, structuralism also uses critical theory. Although the members and followers of the Frankfurt School were not narrowly political, their Marxist legacy tended to point them in certain political directions. While structuralists might have shared certain goals with Marxian critical theorists, their subjects were other social institutions besides government. They also took up Freudian psychology and were instrumental in laying the foundations for a new focus on language and symbols as an important philosophical subject. In some quarters, given the successors or intellectual heirs of structuralism, language and the "symbolic order" became the only intellectual subject. That is, the structuralists paved the way for intellectual postmodernism, which is also known as "post-structuralism."

## CRITICAL THEORISTS

## What was the **Frankfurt School**?

The Frankfurt School was the intellectual activity associated with the Institute for Social Research in Frankfurt am Main, Germany. The Institute was made possible by a

The president of Italy visits Antonio Gramsci museum. Gramsci (whose photo is seen in the background on the right) came up with the idea that a society's dominant class defines the ideology of all classes within that society (AP).

gift from Felix Weil (1898–1975) in 1923, following the First Marxist Week, which was very well-received by intellectuals. The Institute was, in addition, funded by Frankfurt University and, during the Nazi period (1933–1944), Max Horkmeier (1895–1973) and Theodore Adorno (1903–1969) secured the support of Columbia University to set up its exiled version as The International Institute of Social Research in New York City.

The Institute in Frankfurt was reinstated after World War II ended in 1945. Walter Benjamin (1892–1940), Herbert Marcuse (1898–1979) and Erich Fromm (1900–1980), were also among its first generation of members. Jürgen Habermas (1923–) remains its most famous contemporary member. Hannah Arendt (1906–1975) had political interests that implied she had more in common with the Frankfurt School than any other movement, despite striking out on her own as an American philosopher after leaving Germany. Although not part of the Frankfurt School because he was imprisoned by the Italian fascist government in 1926, the Marxist theorist Antonio Gramsci (1891–1937) deserves mention in this context.

## Who was **Antonio Gramsci**?

While Antonio Gramsci (1891–1937) was in prison he worked out his version of Marxism, which was mainly a revolt against Karl Marx's (1818–1883) historical determinism. Gramsci's *Prison Notebooks* (compiled after his death, beginning in 1971) was edited for publication by Palmiro Togliatti, who succeeded him as leader of the Italian

285

communists. According to Togliatti, education and persuasion were the paths to reform toward a classless society, rather than Bolshevism or direct political revolution.

Gramsci's most influential idea has been what Togliatti called Gramsci's "theory of hegemony," whereby the dominant class in society creates not only its own ideology, but also that of the classes dominated by it—all classes share the ideology of the dominant class. Hence, education and persuasion are important to change the social mass mind, so that political change can evolve. In this sense, it could be said that Gramsci was not only a member in spirit of the Frankfurt School, he was also a structuralist.

## Who were **Max Horkheimer** and **Theodore Adorno**?

Max Horkheimer (1893–1973) and Theodore Adorno (1903–1969) were founding members of the Frankfurt School and they were its leaders in exile. Horkheimer was a cultural critic and social philosopher; Adorno was a cultural critic and musicologist. Horkheimer's ideal was a general understanding of the place of human beings in society. He thought, contrary to orthodox Marxists who often viewed society from the standpoint of the proletariat, that no social class at that time escaped distortions in its social world view. Adorno thought that Austrian composer Arnold Shönberg's atonal music supported human autonomy or freedom, and he strongly condemned jazz as a form of "music for the masses," in contrast.

In a way, given their shared view that Marxism should not be culturally centered on the proletariat, it is not surprising that Horkheimer and Adorno collaborated, producing *Dialectic of Enlightenment* (1974). They argued that the progress sought in the Enlightenment could not be achieved and that instead the result would be either mass capitalistic vulgarity in a consumer economy, or totalitarian brutality.

## Who was **Walter Benjamin**?

Walter Benjamin (1892–1940) is highly regarded for the ways in which he combined Jewish religious insights with Marxism. He died from taking morphine pills in Pourtbou on the French-Spanish border, while traveling with a group of intellectuals escaping from the Nazis. Different theories have been advanced about his death: that he committed suicide to avoid torture by the Gestapo for himself and his colleagues, or that Stalinists killed him. Benjamin was Hannah Arendt's (1906–1975) first husband's cousin. Before he died he gave Arendt the manuscript to his *The Concept of History* (1939), which she gave to Theodore Adorno (1903–1969), who had it published in the United States.

In his major work *The Work of Art in the Age of Mechanical Reproduction* (1936), he combined Jewish mysticism with Marxism. Benjamin thought that logic was limited as a philosophical tool because in modern times the philosophical is best accessed through literature and music. He was studied mainly for his theories in musicology, until his work was recognized to be highly relevant for postmodernism in the late-twentieth century.

## Who was **Hannah Arendt**?

Hannah Arendt (1906–1975) was a German-American social and political philosopher, who taught at The New School after World War II. She attended the University of Marburg, where she began the affair with Martin Heidegger (1889–1976) that was to become a lifelong relationship. They broke up and came together repeatedly. Arendt wrote her dissertation on Saint Augustine with Karl Jaspers (1883–1969) at Heidelberg University. She was married to the philosopher Günther Anders (1902–1992) in 1929, but they divorced in 1937. She was not allowed to continue her habilitation because she was a Jew; after beginning an investigation on anti-Semitism, she was questioned by the Gestapo. She then went to France, and worked with Walter Benjamin (1892–1940) in helping Jewish refugees. Her own imprisonment at Camp Gurs ended with her escape.

In 1940 Arendt married Heinrich Blücher (1899–1970), a poet, philosopher, and former Communist. With Blücher and her mother, she escaped to the United States from Vichy, France on phony visas (with the assistance of Hiram Bingham IV, an American diplomat). After World War II, Arendt testified for Heidegger in a de-Nazification hearing, and she wrote an admiring essay about his work in a philosophical celebration of his eightieth birthday.

Arendt was director of research for the Commission of European Jewish Cultural Reconstruction, which led to frequent returns to Germany after 1944. In the United States she taught at the University of California at Berkeley, Princeton University, Northwestern University, and The New School. She was not particularly progressive in the American social context, supporting racial segregation at the beginning of the Civil Rights movement, and refusing to be identified as a feminist during the period of "women's liberation." Her main works are *The Origins of Totalitarianism* (1951), *The Human Condition* (1958), *On Revolution* (1963), *On Violence* (1970), *Eichmann in Jerusalem* (1963), and *The Life of the Mind* (1978).

## What was Hannah **Arendt's political philosophy**?

Overall, Arendt was a strong critic of totalitarianism and an advocate of individual freedom, offering distinctive insights. She believed that both fascism and communism arose under illusions of inevitability based on the lack of real political community in modern life. She did not consider

German-American social and political philosopher Hannah Arendt was an ardent critic of all forms of totalitarianism (AP).

287

herself an existentialist because she thought "we are" is a more important starting point for philosophy than "I am." Her positive model of society was active citizen participation in ways that leave social and private interests out of civic identities.

Arendt's analysis of the trial of the Nazi Adolf Eichmann, in which she introduced the concept of the "banality of evil," was very controversial for her criticism of how Eichmann's trial was conducted in Israel, and how Jewish leaders had behaved under German dictator Adolf Hitler. Arendt's last work was an examination of practical judgment in political contexts in which she used the figure of Socrates (460–399 B.C.E.) to posit inner dialogues. Conscience, she said, had the role of supporting friendship with one's self.

## Who was **Herbert Marcuse**?

Herbert Marcuse (1898–1979) generally inspired left wing thought in the United States after he was exiled from Germany in 1933. He was, for example, African American political activist Angela Davis' dissertation adviser, and Abbie Hoffman, one of the radical founders of the "New Left," studied with him as well.

Marcuse's primary theme was that philosophy is necessary to combat political oppression. He drew on Friedrich Nietzsche (1844–1900) and Sigmund Freud (1856–1939) to criticize Marxism for its underlying Enlightenment faith in reason. He thought that Western democracies, as well as communist regimes, used scientific methods to deprive people of freedom through mass education and the trivialization of culture into entertainment. His major theme was the ways in which political repression was mirrored in psycho-sexual repression. His main works include *Reason and Revolution* (1941), *Eros and Civilization* (1955), *One-Dimensional Man* (1964), and *Critique of Pure Tolerance* (1969).

African American social critic and political activist Angela Davis has remained relevant since the 1970s by continuing to write on race and gender issues (AP).

## Who is **Angela Davis**?

Angela Davis (1944–) is a world-famous African American social critic and political activist. In 1970, she was acting assistant professor in the philosophy department at the University of California, Los Angeles, and a member of the Communist Party USA. She was also once associated with the Black Panther Party. Davis was criminally indicted for helping Black Panther member George Jackson to escape from a courtroom in Marin County, California, in 1970. The guns Jackson used were registered in Angela Davis' name. She was for a while on the FBI's most wanted list after she fled arrest. In the end, Davis was acquitted of criminal charges and was rehired at the university. Davis claimed that she never completed her dissertation because it was "lost" in papers confiscated by the FBI. She has since developed a distinguished career in critical writings about race and gender as well as the "prison industrial complex" in contemporary American culture.

Davis' principal works include *If They Come in the Morning: Voices of Resistance* (1971), *Frame Up: The Opening Defense Statement Made* (1972), *Angela Davis: An Autobiography* (1974), *Women, Race and Class* (1981), *Violence against Women and the Ongoing Challenge to Racism* (1985), *Women, Culture and Politics* (1989), *Blues Legacies and Black Feminism: Gertrude "Ma" Rainey, Bessie Smith, and Billie Holiday* (1999), *Are Prisons Obsolete?* (2003), and *Abolition Democracy: Beyond Prisons, Torture, and Empire* (2005).

## Who was **Erich Fromm**?

Erich Fromm (1900–1980) established his reputation in political psychology with *Escape from Freedom* (1941), which was a condemnation of authoritarian societies. His *Art of Loving* was an international best seller in 1956. His distinction between different types of love in that work was a revelation to some Western readers. Fromm drew on the Talmud to extol individuality and criticize totalitarianism. Many of his readers were inspired by his combination of Marxism with psychoanalysis in a way that respected individuality.

# STRUCTURALISTS

## Who was **Ferdinand de Saussure**?

Ferdinand de Saussure (1857–1913) was a Swiss structuralist whose lectures were published by students after his death as *Course in General Linguistics* (1916). A manuscript of his that was found in his house in 1996 emerged as *Writings in General Linguistics* (2002). Saussure's most influential idea was that language can be understood as a formal system, apart from its actual production and understanding. As a formal system, the elements of language get their meanings from other elements, apart from references to anything outside of language. This insight of the self-contained nature of language and other symbolic systems proved to be a foundation for what across many disciplines, philosophy included, developed as "the linguistic turn."

## What is the **linguistic turn**?

During the last half of the twentieth century, at different times in different humanistic disciplines, scholars turned from talking about people and events in the world to talking about language, symbols, and how people and events were represented in popular culture, as well as academic disciplines. Language became the new main subject across disciplines.

## Who was **Jacques Lacan**?

Jacques Lacan (1901–1981) was a psychoanalyst who was barred from the International Psychoanalytic Association for his ideas, which nonetheless were very influential. His main works are *Ecrits* (*Writings;* 1966), *The Language of the Self* (1978), and his published seminars.

Lacan applied a Saussurian notion of the linguistic order to Freudian psychology. He thought that metaphor and metonymy (substitution of an attribute of a thing for a thing itself) were the main unconscious mechanisms and that psychotherapy literally works as a form of speech that corrects speech by reinserting into discourse what has been obscured from it by neurosis. Lacan is famous for his claim that the ego consists merely of identifications made imaginatively. He meant that human beings imagine themselves as having certain characteristics at an early age and that is how the self develops. Speech creates social connection, but language is a formal system in which words derive meanings from other words only.

## Who was **Claude Lévi-Strauss**?

Claude Lévi-Strauss (1908–) is a French social anthropologist, who is best known for *The Elementary Structures of Kinship* (1949) and *The Savage Mind* (1962). He applied Saussurian ideas of the system of language to social structures, analyzing human relations and systems of exchange, particularly in kinship relations.

Claude Lévi-Strauss applied theories of language systems to the ways people relate to each other (AP).

## Who was **Louis Althusser**?

Louis Althusser (1918–1990) was a philosopher who was also a member of the French Communist Party. He is known for *For Marx* (1965), *Reading Capital* (1968) and especially *Lenin and Philosophy and Other Essays* (1978). His main project was to derive from Karl Marx's (1818–1883) writings a scientific system. He viewed science as governed by systems of concepts, or "problematics," that set questions, evidence, and importance. Althusser argued that structures which express ideologies are self-perpetuating and not subject to changing historical forces, as Marx had claimed. Althusser killed his wife in 1980 and was committed to a psychiatric facility, thereby ending his academic career.

## Who was **Michel Foucault**?

Michel Foucault (1926–1984) was an acclaimed French philosopher who also had French licenses in psychology and psychopathology. His father and both grandfathers were medical doctors, and the ways in which he analyzed European culture, through an archeology of concepts, probably owes as much to medical diagnostic methodology as it does to continental intellectual criticism.

His principle works are his published dissertation, *Madness and Unreason: A History of Madness in the Classical Age* (1961), *The Birth of the Clinic* (1963), *The Order of Things* (1966), *The Archaeology of Knowledge* (1969), *Discipline and Punish: The Origin of the Prison* (1975) and the multi-volume *History of Sexuality* (1974). *The Order of Things* was a best seller in France, leading to his world-wide fame. In that book, Foucault argued that sciences do not simply pop up as sources of truth on their own, but require prior ideas of human nature and truth in order to be supported and accepted as sciences.

## What was Michel **Foucault's method** for forming his **cultural criticism**?

Foucault studied institutions and ideas by understanding their histories. In the course of that anthropological "archeology," he often pinpointed the emergence of new forms of human discourse and personal identity. In the case of sexuality, for example, Foucault argued that new forms of power create new forms of sexuality, as do new practices of observation and medical diagnosis.

One of Foucault's most enduring contributions was to demonstrate how many human traits and practices that are believed to be natural are in fact the effects of social and political institutions that exert unexamined power on individuals. At the same time, the individuals are complicit in remaking themselves to conform to institutional expectations. A primary example would be ideas of gender such as athletic ability in women. Before the second half of the twentieth century, women were believed to be unable to participate or excel in sports due to "natural" limitations.

Foucault is famous for having claimed to invert Plato (c. 428–c. 348 B.C.E.), who had said that the soul is imprisoned in the body, meaning that our natural physical needs and desires oppress our higher spiritual selves. Foucault thought that "the soul is the prison of the body," meaning that our ideas shape our physical existence.

## How did Michel **Foucault's philosophy develop**?

Foucault went back to René Descartes (1596–1650) to show that the designation of insanity was the product of an age that valued reason in a certain form. He thought that medical practice in general required a certain kind of seeing before specific pathologies could be detected. In *The Order of Things* (1966), he argued that part of the development of economics, science, and linguistics in the eighteenth and nineteenth centuries entailed the invention of the idea of "man" as a universal subject. (Man, the universal subject, was supposed to be always the same and always rational.)

In *The Archaeology of Knowledge* (1969), Foucault showed how the sciences themselves are constituted by "discourses," or background ways of forming and transmitting knowledge. Without prior standards that make scientific knowledge acceptable as knowledge, scientific discoveries would have no importance. For example, if we hear that scientists have discovered a gene that predisposes people to a certain kind of cancer, we accept this as true, because we accept the authority of science. *Discipline and Punish: The Origin of the Prison* (1975) marks the beginning of Foucault's investigation of power. He argued that institutions such as the prison, the army, the factory, and the school wield power through specific techniques in which oppression can co-exist with representative democratic political structures.

## Was Michel **Foucault** an **existentialist**?

Foucault's philosophy was mainly social criticism rather than the theory of self-creation associated with existentialism. However, in his own life, he became notorious for unconventional and spontaneous behavior in ways that the public has associated with existentialism. During the last years of his life, Foucault was active in the world in ways that some found shocking, both politically and personally. In a late interview he said, "Well, do you think I have worked all these years to say the same thing and not be changed?"

Foucault first visited the United States in 1970 to lecture at the University at Buffalo, State University of New York, later visiting the University of California, Berkeley. He took LSD at Zabriskie Point in Death Valley National Park, and referred to the experience as life changing in positive ways. In the late 1950s, he went to Iran, and after the revolution he supported the new reactionary government. His essays about

Iran, published in the Italian newspaper *Corriere della Sera*, provoked controversy when they were translated into French and English in 1994 and 2005, respectively.

Foucault was in a committed 25-year relationship with Daniel Defert, a former student. He described it as having lived in "a state of passion," adding that "at some moments this passion has taken the form of love." Much has been said and written about Foucault's exploration of homosexual bars and sex clubs in the Castro district of San Francisco. Foucault died of an AIDS-related infection, although this was not admitted at first, when his death was announced in *Le Monde*. Before he died, Foucault destroyed massive amounts of his unpublished writings and directed that other manuscripts be destroyed also.

# AMERICAN PHILOSOPHY

### What is **American philosophy**?

The term "American philosophy" most often refers to the school of pragmatism, which began in the late-nineteenth century. Pragmatism is internationally recognized to be a distinct form of philosophy, not only created by philosophers from the United States, but also reflective of American culture. There were, of course, intellectuals in the United States before the pragmatists, and some of their work was highly original, linked to distinct cultures: seventeenth, eighteenth, and nineteenth century political theorists, abolitionists, suffragists, evolutionists, Native American thinkers, American Hegelians, and New England transcendentalists.

Many American philosophers after the pragmatists have worked within analytic, empirical, continental, and postmodern traditions, as well as later forms of pragmatism. American philosophy, broadly understood as an intellectual aspect of culture, would include all of these fields. However, American philosophy, as systematic philosophy, traditionally understood, narrows the subject down.

## EARLY AMERICAN PHILOSOPHICAL STRAINS

### Which **early American philosophical strains** were most **influential**?

The thought of several Native American orators, the St. Louis Hegelians, the transcendentalists of New England, and writers on evolution all influenced pragmatist philosophy, either directly or by their emphasis of what were to become enduring American themes to be taken up by pragmatists and others.

## What was the **Native American philosophical tradition**?

There are as many Native American philosophies as there are distinct nations and tribes. Over most of its history, their philosophies were transmitted orally from one generation to the next. As American indigenous cultures and tribes were destroyed by war and the loss of ancestral lands, these transmissions were largely lost. Some transmissions were recorded by early anthropologists in condescending ways that distorted them. There are contemporary attempts to reconstitute Native American traditional oral knowledge, as critiques of Western philosophy, religion, technology, and economics. Such critiques now form the content of Native American or Indigenous American Studies, as well as the late-twentieth century philosophical subfield of Native American Philosophy.

For Native American tribes it has been a struggle to preserve their rich artistic and spiritual values. Native American philosophy has become a subject of interest at universities in recent years (iStock).

However, the speeches of eighteenth and nineteenth century Native American leaders who sought to resist removal to reservations and preserve the lives, cultures, and lands of their peoples endure as unreconstituted early American philosophy. Noteworthy in this regard is Teedyuscung, who, when he spoke at treaty councils in Pennsylvania, began: "I desire all that I have said … may be taken down aright." Teedyuscung, Tenskwatawa, and Sagoewatha spoke like Americans.

## Who was **Tenskwatawa**?

The Prophet, Tenskwatawa (also known as Tenskatawa, Tensquatawa, or by his original name, Lalawethika; 1775–1834) was the brother of the Shawnee leader Tecumseh. Tenskwatawa was a powerful orator who preached a return to Native American traditions as a form of resistance against destruction and oppression suffered. In a speech to Governor William Henry Harrison in 1810, he expressed what was later to become a broadly American form of self-creation, combined with biting wit:

> It is true I am a Shawnee. My forefathers were warriors. Their son is a warrior. From them I take only my existence; from my tribe I take nothing. I am the

maker of my own fortune; and oh! that I could make of my own fortune; and oh! that I could make that of my red people, and of my country, as great as the conceptions of my mind, when I think of the Spirit that rules the universe. I would not then come to Governor Harrison to ask him to tear the treaty and to obliterate the landmark; but I would say to him: "Sir, you have liberty to return to your own country."

## Who was **Sagoewatha**?

Sagoewatha, or Chief Red Jacket (1757–1839), gave many speeches on the problems posed by diverse populations with different appearances and religions sharing the same country. In this sense, he anticipated twentieth century American concerns about racial difference and immigration.

## What was the **most striking Native American contribution** to American philosophy?

There is growing recognition of the influence of Native American thought on eighteenth and nineteenth century Euro-American ideas, as well as later on in history. Contemporary pragmatist scholars have traced contemporary concerns with community well-being in a pluralistic society to early Native American attempts to negotiate with Euro-Americans. Others have identified deeper mainstream American cultural debts to indigenous peoples.

Robert Pirsig, the author of *Zen and the Art of Motorcycle Maintenance* (1974), in his second book, *Lila* (1991), draws a fascinating and neglected comparison between what was to become the distinctly direct and plain American style of speech (if not always writing) and speeches in English made by Native American Great Plains leaders. Pirsig quotes Ten Bears, speaking in 1867 to other Native Americans and representatives from Washington:

I was born on the prairie, where the wind blew free, and there was nothing to break the light of the sun. I was born where there were no enclosures, and where everything drew a free breath. I want to die there and not within walls.… I lived like my father before me, and like them I lived happily.

While pragmatists such as John Dewey (1859–1952) were often prolix, their writing was nevertheless direct and innocent of the high style of European abstraction and unnecessary embellishment. Their ideas were not unnecessarily complicated. The same can be said of much New England transcendentalist writing, although maybe not of the St. Louis Hegelians, of the more idealist pragmatists such as Charles Sanders Peirce (1839–1914) and Josiah Royce (1855–1916), or the process philosophers Alfred North Whitehead (1861–1947) and his follower Charles Hartshorne (1897–2000).

# ST. LOUIS HEGELIANS

## Who were the **St. Louis Hegelians**?

They were a group of philosophers and teachers who founded The Saint Louis Philosophical Society in 1866 and began to publish *The Journal of Speculative Philosophy* in 1867. The founding members were Henry C. Brokmeyer (1826–1906), William T. Harris (1835–1909), and Denton Jacques Snider (1841–1925). Brokmeyer was a Prussian immigrant who had come to the United States in 1844, attended Brown University, plied several trades, and lived in a hut (like Henry David Thoreau [1817–1862]). Harris was a Yale dropout who came to St. Louis to teach Pittman shorthand. Brokmeyer and Harris undertook the project of translating Hegel's *Science of Logic* (1812) into English. Snider, who had graduated from Oberlin College, came to St. Louis in 1865 to teach at Christian Brothers College.

## How did the **St. Louis Hegelians apply** their **philosophy**?

The St. Louis Hegelians tried to apply their philosophy directly to current events. They were very proud of St. Louis, in contrast to Chicago. Due to an error in the 1870 census, the St. Louis Hegelians, along with other residents of the city, were thrilled by the statistic that the population of St. Louis was greater than that of Chicago. On October 8, 1871, the day of the great Chicago fire (believed to have been started by a kick to a lamp from Mrs. O'Leary's cow, although overall conditions were extremely dry and inflammable), Snider asked Brokmeyer what he thought of this disaster. Brokmeyer's reply (note: Snider spelled Brokmeyer's name as "Brockmeyer"), according to Snider, was:

> Chicago was the completely negative city of our West and indeed of our time, and now she has carried out her principle of negation to its final universal consequence; she has simply negated herself. The positive result of that negative is bound to arrive, but not over there in the same place again, but here, here in our St. Louis.

But Alas, the 1880 census put the population of St. Louis below that of Chicago. The Saint Louis Philosophical Society hired a mathematician from Washington University to check the census figures. He told them that the 1870 census had been in error and that the population of St. Louis really was 350,000 compared to 503,000 in Chicago!

## Did the **Eastern philosophers interact** much with the **St. Louis Hegelians**?

Although they were not academic philosophers, the St. Louis philosophers were in conversation with the Eastern transcendental thinkers, such as those of the Concord School of Philosophy, which had been organized by William Harris (1835–1909) and transcendentalist Amos Bronson Alcott (1799–1888). The Concord School held conferences during the summer from 1879 to 1887, and when Alcott first visited Harris in St. Louis, he was abused by Henry C. Brokmeyer (1826–1906) in what the Hegelian observers called "the first bout between East and West." The result was celebrated as a victory for the West. Another famed Eastern philosopher, Ralph Waldo Emerson (1803–1882), also visited the St. Louis Philosophical Society.

### What were the shared **goals** of the **St. Louis Hegelians**?

Although Friedrich Hegel (1770–1831) was chosen as the guide for the group by Henry C. Brokmeyer (1826–1906), their interests were not so much in theoretical abstractions as in understanding their own life and times, particularly the U.S. Civil War. According to Denton Jacques Snider (1841–1925), their goals were "to philosophize ... practical life," to be able to give a rational account of their vocations, and achieve self-realization. They also wanted to contribute to the future greatness of society. Philosophy for them was closer to a religious practice than an academic one.

### What **happened** to the **founders** of the **St. Louis Philosophical Society**?

They went on to distinctive careers. Henry C. Brokmeyer (1826–1906) set up a law office and was elected to the Missouri Senate. He composed the Missouri constitution in 1875, became lieutenant governor, and was acting governor from 1876 to 1877. Then he moved farther west, lived with the Creek Indians, and attempted to get his translation of Friedrich Hegel's (1770–1831) *Science of Logic* (1812) published, which he never did. He ended up whittling wood and making toothpicks, which he brought to St. Louis to sell.

William Harris (1835–1909) became a journalist and lecturer, head of the Concord school, and Missouri's first commissioner of education. Denton Jacques Snider (1841–1925) wrote more than 60 books, including the intellectual history of the St. Louis Hegelians. He taught from kindergarten to college level at the Communal University of Chicago, and set forth his "Sniderian psychology" in 10 volumes. Snider's most famous work is *The St. Louis Movement in Philosophy, Literature, Education, Psychology* (1920).

Thomas Davidson (1840–1900), who was another early member of the St. Louis Society, founded the Breadwinner's College in New York City and a summer school in Glenmore, New York, where he later lived.

### How did Denton Jacques **Snider interpret** Friedrich **Hegel**?

Denton Jacques Snider (1841–1925) thought that Friedrich Hegel (1770–1831), in the *Lectures on the History of Philosophy* (Berlin, 1820 and published as the *Philosophy of History* in 1858), was not able to achieve a full system of thought, but that his "principle of evolution" held the greatest promise for future philosophy. He read Hegel's *Phenomenology of Mind* (1910, first published as *Philosophy of Spirit* in 1817) as a guide for how the individual can achieve total self-understanding through the analysis of his experience as a mirror of the history of his times.

So the St. Louis Hegelians tried to analyze their own times as an expression of the Absolute. There was thus a comparison between Hegel's vision of the Absolute in Napoleon Bonaparte and Snider's understanding of the U.S. Civil War and the end of the Great St. Louis illusion (which was shattered by the civic realization that Chicago had outpaced them in population). Snider's insight that Hegel's *Phenomenology of Mind* "is a book written in a Romantic style, which destroys Romanticism," has been considered subtle and sophisticated by his commentators. He meant by this that Hegel had a grand project but ran out of optimism about human history and the Absolute itself.

## New England Transcendentalists

### **Who** were the **New England Transcendentalists**?

They are considered to be the American counterparts to European Romantics, who valued emotion as much or more than reason and stressed the importance of individual and private yearnings. The distinctively American form of Romanticism, as seen in the novels of Herman Melville (1819–1891), the prose of Ralph Waldo Emerson (1803–1882), the poetry of Walt Whitman (1819–1892), and the essays of Henry David Thoreau (1817–1862), emphasized the condition of the solitary and courageous private person in nature. As well, there were distinctly philosophical transcendentalists, such as Amos Bronson Alcott (1799–1888).

### Who was **Amos Bronson Alcott**?

Amos Bronson Alcott (1799–1888) was the father of writer Louisa May Alcott. He founded a school and a utopian community called "Fruitlands." As a transcendentalist, he combined Platonism, German mysticism, and American Romanticism. He largely followed the teachings of the leading Unitarian minister, William Ellery Channing, who preached a gentle form of religious belief and practice, against Calvinism. Alcott's publications include *New Connecticut, Tablets* (1868), *Concord Days* (1872), and *Sonnets and Canzonets* (1882). Most of his other work is still unpublished, except for his vague "Orphic Sayings" that appeared in *The Dial,* and which is representative of transcendental thought.

## What was Henry David **Thoreau's philosophical contribution**?

Henry David Thoreau (1817–1862) was a naturalist, writer, school teacher, and pencil maker (he invented the pencil with an eraser on its end). He was born in Concord, Massachusetts, attended Harvard, and then returned to Concord. He was not a political reformer but is famous for his civil disobedience in not paying the poll tax (he felt it supported slavery and the Mexican-American War, both of which he found objectionable) and for helping runaway slaves escape.

Thoreau is best known for the two years he spent in a hut he built on Walden Pond, an experience he describes in *Walden* (1854). His lifestyle there and protest against materially driven lives of "quiet desperation," set an aesthetic ideal for many American intellectuals in generations to come. Thoreau's love of nature and ideals of simplicity were in themselves a form of revolt against industrial life and have been reclaimed in intellectual revolts against post-industrial life.

However, Thoreau's striking intellectual contribution is not the ideal of "roughing it" in nature, because his time at Walden Pond, punctuated as it was by frequent visits from his literary friends, as well as his own habit of walking back into town, was hardly a withdrawal from society. Indeed, the hardships he endured scarcely compared with the hardships of pioneers and homesteaders farther west, who lived in rural poverty out of necessity rather than choice.

By contrast, Thoreau set a different example for a different American group of strivers. He combined a naturalistic aesthetic of simplicity with cultural criticism and intellectual creativity. This "life of the mind in the woods" stands in stark social class and regional contrast to the genuinely hard-scrabble background of several of the early twentieth century pragmatists, as well as with their efforts

A stamp depicting naturalist philosopher Henry David Thoreau (iStock).

## What happened to Henry David Thoreau's hut?

A replica of Thoreau's hut can now be visited. It is adjacent to Walden Pond near Concord, Massachusetts. Visitors can also walk around that three-mile circumference, across which Thoreau wrote that he liked to have "big conversations" with his guests. But none of this is the real thing.

After Thoreau left his hut to stay at Ralph Waldo Emerson's (1803–1882) house, it was moved around Brooks Clark Farm as a structure for storing corn. It was finally placed in the northwest pasture of the farm to memorialize Thoreau and left there until 1867, although the windows were gone by then. In 1868, the roof was taken off to cover a pig yard, and in 1885 the floor and some other wood from the hut were used to make a shed off the barn. The remainder of the hut was then taken apart to replace planks in the barn. Others say that these boards were used to remodel the farm house.

to build a broad community and support democratic social interactions through writing and public speaking. But both Thoreau's privileged love of nature and the pragmatists' more common touch represent a cultural sea change from much of the thought discussed in the salons, drawing rooms, and formal church-like architectural settings of Europe.

## Who was **Ralph Waldo Emerson**?

Ralph Waldo Emerson (1803–1882) was the leading nineteenth century American transcendentalist. His essays and activism not only established him as an intellectual for his time, but also provided a model for subsequent American intellectuals, particularly the pragmatists.

Emerson's main writings, which are still read today—most are free on-line—include *Nature* (1836), his first book, which contains the essays "Nature," "Commodity," "Beauty," "Language," "Discipline," "Idealism," "Spirit," "Prospects," "The American Scholar," "Divinity School Address," "Literary Ethics," "The Method of Nature," "Man the Reformer," "Introductory Lecture on the Times," "The Conservative," "The Transcendentalist," and "The Young American"; there is also *Essays: First Series* (1841), containing "History," "Self-Reliance," "Compensation," "Spiritual Laws," "Love," "Friendship," "Prudence," "Heroism," "The Over-Soul," "Circles," "Intellect" and "Art"; and *Essays: Second Series* (1844), which includes "The Poet," "Experience," "Character," "Manners," "Gifts," "Nature," "Politics," "Nominalist and Realist," and "New England Reformers." Other books include *Poems* (1847); *Miscellanies; Embracing Nature, Addresses, and Lectures* (1849); *Representative Men* (1850), including essays on Plato and Johann Wolfgang von Goethe; *English Traits* (1856), which is about his travels; *The Conduct of Life* (1860); the poetry collection *May-Day and Other Pieces* (1867); and *Society and Solitude* (1870). Emerson's last series of essays were lectures given at Harvard University in 1871 and posthumously published as *Natural History of Intellect* (1904). There is also the *Correspondence of Thomas Carlyle and R.W. Emerson* (1883).

### How did Ralph Waldo **Emerson define transcendentalism**?

He considered transcendentalism a kind of philosophical idealism that held that the ultimate reality was spiritual and not material. He thought that experience was limited in telling us what things are in themselves or what to value. Emerson also referred to a Kantian notion of "ideas or imperative forms," which made experience possible, and he ascribed to Immanuel Kant (1724–1804) the label "Transcendental Forms," for these realities of the mind and spirit.

### What kind of **life** did **Ralph Waldo Emerson lead**?

Ralph Waldo Emerson (1803–1882) lost his father when he was just eight years old, and was sent to Boston Latin School the next year. He attended Harvard College at 14,

where he waited on tables at the commons and tutored to pay for his education. After graduation, he helped his brother in a school for young ladies, which his mother ran in her home. In 1829 Emerson graduated from Harvard Divinity School as a Unitarian minister. But he resigned from that vocation in 1832 because of a disagreement with church administrators. He had married Ellen Louisa Tucker in 1829, but she died of tuberculosis two years later at the age of 20. He mourned her deeply, but had also described himself as "strangely attracted" to a young man while at Harvard, and was later believed to become infatuated with other young men, including author Nathaniel Hawthorne.

During travels in Europe after his wife died, Emerson met authors William Wordsworth, Samuel Taylor Coleridge, and Thomas Carlyle (he would correspond with Carlyle [1795–1881] until his death in 1881), and philosopher John

Ralph Waldo Emerson was the leading American transcendentalist of the nineteenth century (Art Archive).

Stuart Mill (1806–1873). In 1835 Emerson bought a house in Concord, Massachusetts, and married Lydia Jackson, with whom he had four children. He was reasonably well off financially (partly due to a lawsuit securing his inheritance from his first wife) and he used part of the money to help Amos Bronson Alcott (1799–1888), his neighbor. Many considered Emerson the greatest orator of his day.

### What did Ralph Waldo **Emerson mean** by the **"over-soul"**?

Emerson's idea of the soul came to him from reading the *Bhagavad Gita* and commentaries on it. Nonetheless, his ideas bear a striking similarity to European Neoplatonic thought. Emerson wrote:

> The Supreme Critic on the errors of the past and the present, and the only prophet of that which must be, is that great nature in which we rest, as the earth lies in the soft arms of the atmosphere; that Unity, that Over-soul, within which every man's particular being is contained and made one with all other; that common heart, of which all sincere conversation is the worship, to which all right action is submission; that overpowering reality which confutes our tricks and talents, and constrains every one to pass for what he is, and to speak from his character, and not from his tongue, and which evermore tends to pass into our thought and hand, and become wisdom, and virtue, and power, and beauty. We live in succession, in division, in parts, in particles. Meantime within man is the soul of the whole; the wise silence; the universal beauty, to which every part and particle is equally related; the eternal ONE.

### What were Ralph Waldo **Emerson's requirements** for a **scholar**?

Emerson thought that much could be learned from ordinary experience and that spirituality was not separate from what was familiar or "common." He did not have a high opinion of American academic philosophers, dismissing their thought as "derivative," but he did posit necessary conditions for a scholar. These are: closeness to and experience with nature, knowledge of the past, and action as the clearest expression of thought. Emerson wrote that thinking is a "partial act," but living is a "total act."

### Was Ralph Waldo **Emerson** an **abolitionist**?

Yes, but it took him a while to develop his position. From childhood, he thought that slavery was evil, but he relied on persuasion rather than outright opposition to it until 1837. At that time he was shocked by the murder of Elijah P. Lovejoy, an abolitionist publisher in Illinois. By 1844 he said of the abolitionists: "[W]e are indebted mainly to this movement, and to the continuers of it, for the popular discussion of every point of practical ethics." After that, he was considered a strong voice for abolition; the

## What was Ralph Waldo Emerson's infamous "Divinity School Address"?

In 1838 Emerson was invited to give the graduation address at Harvard Divinity School. He said that while Jesus was a great man, he was not God. This enraged the Protestant community, who termed him an atheist and corrupter of young minds. He was not asked back to Harvard for 30 years. However, by the late-nineteenth century, the doctrine that Jesus was not God was routinely accepted by Unitarians. (Unitarians to this day reject the idea of the Trinity, which entails that Jesus was God, although they recognize him as an extraordinary human being, perhaps even supernatural.)

*Atlantic* magazine—which also published essays by the African American intellectual Frederick Douglass—printed these words by Emerson, referring to the slave-owning and free American states, in 1862:

> We have attempted to hold together two states of civilization: a higher state, where labor and the tenure of land and the right of suffrage are democratical; and a lower state, in which the old military tenure of prisoners or slaves, and of power and land in a few hands, makes an oligarchy.... But the rude and early state of society does not work well with the later, nay, works badly, and has poisoned politics, public morals, and social intercourse in the Republic, now for many years.

## Who was **Margaret Fuller**?

Margaret Fuller (1810–1850) organized weekly Saturday conversations with women in Boston to supplement their education and discuss their condition in society. She co-founded *The Dial* with Ralph Waldo Emerson (1803–1882) in 1840, which was the official Transcendentalist publication for four years. Fuller left the magazine in 1842 to write for the *New York Tribune*.

Fuller interviewed intellectuals for the *Tribune* in England and Italy in 1846, including George Sand, Thomas Carlyle, and the Italian revolutionary Giovanni Ossoli, with whom she fell in love. The couple had a child and married. The entire family drowned in a sea accident while returning to the United States, when their ship hit a sandbar one hundred yards away from Fire Island.

Fuller's main work is *Woman in the Nineteenth Century* (1845) in which she argued for women's independence and equality between the sexes. Her great-nephew was the twentieth-century architect of geodesic domes, Buckminster Fuller.

## What was *The Dial*?

The name for this publication was suggested by Amos Bronson Alcott (1799–1888) and Ralph Waldo Emerson (1803–1882). The simile was explained in the first issue this way:

> And so with diligent hands and good intent we set down our *Dial* on the earth. We wish it may resemble that instrument in its celebrated happiness, that of measuring no hours but those of sunshine. Let it be one cheerful rational voice amidst the din of mourners and polemics. Or to abide by our chosen image, let it be such a Dial, not as the dead face of a clock, hardly even such as the Gnomon in a garden, but rather such a Dial as is the Garden itself, in whose leaves and flowers the suddenly awakened sleeper is instantly apprised not what part of dead time, but what state of life and growth is now arrived and arriving.

*The Dial* became dormant in 1844, but was revived for a year in 1860. In 1880 it reappeared as a political magazine, and in 1920 as a literary modernist magazine, publishing essays, poetry, and art reviews until 1929.

## Who was **Frederick Douglass**?

Many contemporary scholars of race consider Frederick Douglass (born Frederick Augustus Washington Bailey; 1818–1895) to be the first liberatory African American intellectual. In 1873, he was the vice-presidential candidate when Victoria Woodhull was the first woman to run for U.S. president.

The famous abolitionist, suffragist, orator, and statesman Frederick Douglass is considered by many to have been the first liberatory African American intellectual (Art Archive).

Douglass began life as a slave, but was taught to read at the age of 12 by his owner's sister-in-law. He taught other slaves to read, and after a series of failed escapes he finally gained his freedom and became active in the Massachusetts anti-slavery movement. At 23 he began his distinguished and inspiring career of public speaking. He was present at the Seneca Falls convention, where the American suffragist movement originated in 1848.

Douglass toured Ireland and England in the mid 1840s, and his supporters raised money to legally purchase his freedom in 1856. Back in the United States, Douglass published newspapers, the most famous of which was *The North Star,* which had as the motto "Right is of no Sex—Truth is of no Color—God is the Father of us all, and we are all brethren."

In the 1850s, Douglass spoke for school desegregation in New York. During the U.S. Civil War, he promoted the rights of blacks to fight for the Union. When the Emancipation Proclamation was issued in 1862, he said: "We were waiting and listening as for a bolt from the sky … we were watching … by the dim light of the stars for the dawn of a new day … we were longing for the answer to the agonizing prayers of centuries."

In 1884, after his first wife had died, Douglass married Helen Pitts, a white suffragist from New York. Pitts had worked on *Alpha,* the nineteenth-century radical women's publication, while living in Washington, D.C.

Douglass' main writings are *A Narrative of the Life of Frederick Douglass, an American Slave* (1845), *The Heroic Slave: Autographs for Freedom* (1853), *My Bondage and My Freedom* (1855), and *Life and Times of Frederick Douglass* (1881; revised, 1892); he edited *The North Star* from 1847 to 1851, after which it became the *Frederick Douglass' Paper.*

## SOCIAL DARWINISM

### What was **evolutionary thought** like in **America** during the **nineteenth century**?

Within educated communities, Charles Darwin's theory of evolution was broadly accepted as an accurate history of living beings. Since Deism, or the idea that God was suffused throughout nature, was a widespread perspective at the time, there was not an obvious conflict between religious accounts of creation and evolution. Discussion more commonly centered on whether social forms of evolution were ruthlessly competitive or cooperative. As in nineteenth century European thought, there were two perspectives: life in society, as in nature, was "red in tooth and claw" and a matter of "survival of the fittest"; or, life in society, as in nature, evolved through cooperation. It is not surprising that the transcendentalists favored the cooperative view.

### What was **Social Darwinism**?

Social Darwinism was an application of the Darwinian idea of the "the survival of the fittest" to inequalities and opportunities in contemporary nineteenth century society. It was an age in which the enterprising could amass large fortunes in a short period of time, although they had to compete with other capitalists. And those who labored, often in unhealthy and exhausting conditions for barely enough pay to support themselves, also competed among themselves for available jobs.

Social Darwinists wrote popular books, sometimes consisting of what today would be considered racist or class-based eugenics, and their claims made a strong impres-

Charles Darwin's ideas on evolution were adapted to Social Darwinism (Art Archive).

sion on general readers. They shared a belief that competition was valuable in itself and that those who failed in life's contests failed a deeper test of evolutionary survival. Instead of social reform, their ideals were to encourage the traits that enabled success at competition by means of selective human breeding, as well as moral approval of the winners.

## Who were the main Social Darwinists?

William Graham Sumner (1840–1910), professor at Yale, was the American version of the English evolutionist Herbert Spencer (1820–1903). Sumner was a strong advocate of unrestricted capitalism. He was famous for his essay "The Man of Virtue," which promoted self-interest as a primary duty for individuals. The industrialist Andrew Carnegie (1835–1919) built on these ideas in his "The Gospel of Wealth," which further enshrined the "law of competition" as a natural principle of progress.

## Did nineteenth-century American philosophers directly take up evolution?

Yes. Both John Fiske (1842–1901) and Chauncey Wright (1830–1875) believed in the evolution of consciousness and human morality. Fiske was best known as an historian for his two volume *The American Revolution* (1891). Wright was an empiricist philosopher of science who opposed transcendentalism and was to be influential in subsequent pragmatist thought, although he himself published very little. Lester Ward (1841–1912) was a sociologist best known for *Dynamic Sociology* (1883), but his main ideas in favor of intervention in social evolutionary processes proved to be relevant for future social and political philosophy.

## Was nineteenth century evolutionary thought connected to ideas of progress?

Not directly, because evolution was an external force, whereas progress depended on individual human effort. But the two notions were frequently associated, as in the ideas of American industrialist Andrew Carnegie. In general, notions of progress formed both ideals and practical motivations. Society as a whole was believed to be progressing, and individuals were motivated to advance in life by becoming materially prosperous. The prosperity of society was largely believed to be a matter of technology. The nineteenth century was the first full-fledged "machine age," and it saw the inventions and wide use of the cotton gin, locomotive, telegraph, and electric lights, to name just a few.

## Was Social Darwinism a beneficial set of beliefs?

**M**ost progressives thought not. First, Social Darwinism tended to accept, if not applaud, the suffering of the poor, as though it reflected their personal weakness rather than the structure of society. And second, Social Darwinism "evolved" into a reactionary type of white supremacy.

Toward the end of the nineteenth century and the beginning of the twentieth, Social Darwinism and its associated eugenics merged with white American racialist beliefs that would later be considered racist or discriminatory. For example, in 1916 amateur anthropologist and lawyer Madison Grant published *The Passing of the Great Race; or, The Racial Basis of European History.* Grant propounded a theory of "Nordic Superiority" and argued for a public eugenic program to save the Nordics from being overrun by non-white racial groups. Grant's book sold 1,600,000 copies by 1937. It was widely influential in individual beliefs and public policy that restricted immigration from Asia and discriminated harshly against African Americans.

## Did **all nineteenth-century thinkers** believe in **progress**?

Thomas Edison (1847–1931) certainly did. In 1876, when he set up his laboratory in Menlo Park, New Jersey, he committed himself to "a minor invention every ten days and a big thing every six months or so." (Edison did get about 40 patents a year and over 1,000 before he died.)

Not everyone was so enthusiastic about new machines, though. Thomas Carlyle (1795–1881), for example, wrote in 1829 in "Signs of the Times," an essay that was published in the *Edinburgh Review*. (the signs being "The Age of Machinery") that "the shadow we have wantonly evoked stands terrible before us and will not depart at our bidding." Henry David Thoreau (1817–1862) wrote in *Walden* (1854): "We do not ride upon the railroad; it rides upon us."

Still, many did share Edison's optimism, and it was the popular national view. Timothy Walker, a lawyer from Ohio, wrote in the *North American*

The idea of progress through technological innovation was certainly the faith held by such prominent thinkers as inventor Thomas Edison (AP).

*Review* in 1831 that machines free ordinary people from burdensome labor and promote democracy.

# PRAGMATISM AND PROCESS PHILOSOPHY

## What is **pragmatism**?

Pragmatism is a distinctively American philosophy that originated in community discussion groups and came to define the philosophy department at Harvard University during the late nineteenth century. While not as scientific in perspective as some philosophy in Europe during the same time, it represented an effort to think in a practical way.

## CHARLES SANDERS PEIRCE

### Who was **Charles Sanders Peirce**?

Charles Sanders Peirce (1839–1914) is recognized as the founder and originator of pragmatism, although his intellectual expertise extended to logic, mathematics, economics, social science, the physical sciences, and geodesic work. Peirce's published writings date from 1857 until his death and constitute 12,000 printed pages. There are, in addition, 80,000 pages of his unpublished hand-written work. His principal works, published posthumously, are edited volumes, such as *The New Elements of Mathematics* (four volumes, 1976), *The Essential Peirce* (two volumes, 1992 and 1998), and *Writings of Charles S. Peirce: A Chronological Edition* (five volumes, 1882–1993).

### What are some key facts about Charles **Peirce's career** and **life**?

Charles Sanders Peirce (1839–1914) was born in Cambridge, Massachusetts. His father, Benjamin, was professor of mathematics at Harvard University and a founder of the U.S. Coast and Geodetic Survey and the Smithsonian Institution. (Benjamin Peirce is also said to have built the Harvard department of mathematics.) At the age of 12, young Charles discovered logic, and at 16, he began his independent study of philosophy. In 1859 he graduated from Harvard, unsure of "what I would do in life." His primary interest was in logic, for which there were no career opportunities. He practiced geodesy for several years and returned to Harvard to study natural history and philosophy in 1861. He got a Ph.D. in chemistry in 1863, graduating *summa cum laude*.

Peirce continued his studies of logic on his own and has been considered to be one of the greatest logicians of all times. Although he disagreed with Immanuel Kant's (1724–1804) insistence that space was Euclidean and later moved to Friedrich Hegel's

## Why were all of Charles Peirce's works published posthumously?

**P**eirce neither published nor prepared for publication the greater part of his work. When he died, his widow, Juliette, sold his papers to the Harvard University Philosophy Department (for $6,000). Josiah Royce (1855–1916) was supposed to supervise their organization, but he died two years later; many of the papers were subsequently lost, misplaced, allowed to become disorganized, or simply taken. The late mathematics historian Carolyn Eisele, while conducting some research, chanced upon a trunk of Peirce's writings in the mid 1950s in a corner of the basement of Widener Library.

The first edition of *Peirce's Collected Papers* was put together by Charles Hartshorne, Paul Weiss, and Arthur Burks during the 1930s. Critics have deemed this collection arbitrary and not truly representative of Peirce's thought because it makes Peirce seem unnecessarily obscure and does not clarify the progression of his ideas. *A Chronological Edition* (1989) of Pierce's work, edited by the Peirce Edition Project of the Indiana University at Indianapolis, has produced more coherent results, covering the period from 1857–1886. Two other well-regarded efforts are *Peirce's Cambridge Conferences Lectures of 1898* (1992) and *Peirce's Harvard Lectures on Pragmatism of 1903* (1997).

(1770–1831) objective idealism, Kant remained a dominating influence over his philosophical ideas. Peirce's philosophy was a distinct form of pragmatism, which he called "Pragmaticism."

## What was Charles **Peirce's philosophical system**?

Peirce's philosophical views had idealist underpinnings. He had four systems. In his first system (1859–1861), he agreed with Immanuel Kant (1724–1804) that things-in-themselves could not be known either in science or philosophy. Science is concerned with phenomena, or what appears in experience. But there is an objective world underlying phenomena, or what is known. There are three kinds of things: 1) matter; 2) mind; and 3) God, or "It," "Thou," and "I," which Peirce called "Firstness," "Secondness" and "Thirdness," respectively. Peirce thought that ideas in God's mind are as material as objects in our experience. However, he encountered logical problems with this system and was not quite satisfied with the relation between the Kantian categories and the things in themselves.

In his second system of thought (1866–1970), Peirce used Hegelian methodology and assumptions to conclude that what was most real was a dynamic system. He thought that the world of experience or phenomena, which he called "the phaneron," is entirely made up of signs which are qualities, relations, things, events—everything—and that these signs are all meaningful. The meaning of each sign is part of a system that also contains the object and the "interpretant." The object is what the sign is a sign of. The interpretant is the feature or activity of mind that experiences the sign. And, the interpretant is also a sign—because everything is a sign—so it also has an object and a second interpretant.

This structure of sign—object—interpretant, interpretant-as-sign → object → new interpretant goes on infinitely. But the reality of the object consists of a limiting form that is approached as cognitions approach infinity. That is, if an object is real, our process of inquiry and experience can go on almost forever. Reality for Peirce was a "convergence of inquiry," and since what we know is always general or a universal, the object is made up of universals. This makes reality mental, hence Peirce's philosophical idealism.

However, Peirce ran into difficulties with the logic of these relations, and after discovering an original (and still not widely understood, except by logicians) logic of relations, he constructed his third system (1870–1884), which more closely resembled what is now considered pragmatism and is based on the operating principles that most now associate with Peirce, although he called his system "pragmaticism" to distinguish it from the ideas of other pragmatists, who were less concerned with science.

### What was Charles **Peirce's pragmaticism**?

Peirce's starting point in his pragmaticism was his activity and self-identification as a scientist. Peirce thought that philosophy was philosophy of science and that logic was the logic of science. As a pragmaticist, Peirce is best known for two articles: "The Fixation of Belief" and "How to Make Our Ideas Clear," published in *Popular Science Monthly* (under different titles) in 1877 and 1878, respectively. In these works, he defended science as the best way to overcome doubt and presented the pragmaticist idea of clear concepts. He claimed that concepts, or the meanings of scientific terms, must have "cash value." The "cash value" of a concept is the difference it makes in experience to have the concept, compared with not having it. The entire meaning of a clear concept lay in its consequences. The consequences—meaning—of a scientific concept were possible observations under conditions that could be specified. That is, the concept had to generate predictions and it doesn't matter if the predictions were accurate or not, just so long as it could predict something that would happen.

### What was Charles **Peirce's fourth system**?

Peirce's fourth system (1885–1914) introduced evolution to his second system. The whole system of sign-object-interpretant, with its infinite implications, is an evolving system. The system has evolved over time and continues to evolve, as does our knowledge of it, and every sign within it. Peirce worked out many details of this process, in logic and in what others considered "pragmatism." He ended up with an extreme form

## Why wasn't Charles Peirce ever a professor of philosophy?

Pierce did have a job as lecturer in logic at Johns Hopkins University, in Baltimore, from 1879 to 1891. But in 1883 he divorced Harriet Melusina Fay, to whom he had been married since 1862, and married Juliette Froissy. Froissy was thought to be a gypsy, and Peirce was said to have lived with her before their marriage. A scandal ensued, and Peirce left his academic position. Peirce's only subsequent employment was for the U.S. Coast and Geodetic Survey, which ended in 1901 due to congressional curtailment of funding. Peirce then did odd jobs and was employed as a consultant in chemical engineering. Sometimes, William James (1842–1910) and other friends assisted him financially.

of idealism that posited the entire universe as a living, feeling organism, with habits that are mirrored in our general laws of nature (descriptions of regularities).

# WILLIAM JAMES

## Who was **William James**?

William James (1842–1910) built on Charles Peirce's (1839–1914) pragmaticist ideas to create a more humanistic form of pragmatism. James was also the founder of modern psychology as a science independent of subjective introspection. His principal works include *The Principles of Psychology* (1890), *The Will to Believe and Other Essays in Popular Philosophy* (1897), *The Varieties of Religious Experience* (1901–1902), and *Pragmatism* (1907).

## What are some interesting facts about William **James' life**?

James was the oldest of five children. His brother Henry was the famous novelist, and his sister Alice became well known for her posthumous diaries. James' father, Henry James Sr., was both wealthy and eccentric. The James children were educated in the United States, England, and Europe, and William grew up with a cosmopolitan perspective. James was at first interested in studying art, but then turned to science. In youth he suffered from eye, back, stomach, and skin problems and was diagnosed as "neurasthenic." He experienced depression and, at times, prolonged suicidal thoughts. While some of his ailments might be considered "psychosomatic" today, he did eventually die of heart failure.

James began medical studies at Harvard in 1864 and took time off to travel on expeditions to the Amazon and to Germany for cures of various physical complaints. He was awarded his M.D. in 1869. It was his only academic degree, although he never practiced medicine. He married Alice Gibbens in 1878 and spent the remainder of his life teaching at Harvard, in both psychology and, after the early 1880s, philosophy. James' students included such luminaries as President Theodore Roosevelt, author and philosopher George Santayana, civil rights activist W.E.B. Du Bois, philosopher Ralph Barton Perry, author Gertrude Stein, philosopher and legal scholar Morris Raphael Cohen, Alain Locke (sometimes called the "Father of the Harlem Renaissance"), logician and pragmatist C.I. Lewis, and psychologist and philosopher Mary Calkins.

### What was Williams **James'** main **contribution** to **psychology**?

James developed the same theory that was independently developed by Carl Georg Lange (1834–1900), the Danish physician and psychologist. It became known as the James–Lange theory of the emotions. The theory is that emotions are our experience of changes in our bodies. Benedict de Spinoza (1632–1677) had held that emotions are the effects of our beliefs, while René Descartes (1596–1650), in *Passions of the Soul* (1649), had expressed an earlier version of the James-Lange theory.

Our common sense assumption is that emotions are reactions to events in the world that are mediated by our understanding. By contrast, the James–Lange theory held that our bodies react directly to the world and our awareness of this physical reaction constitutes our emotions. In "What Is an Emotion?," his famous 1884 article published in *Mind,* James wrote:

> Our natural way of thinking about … emotions is that the mental perception of some fact excites the mental affection called emotion, and that this latter state of mind gives rise to the bodily expression. My thesis on the contrary is that the bodily changes follow directly the perception of the exciting fact, and that our feeling of the same changes as they occur is the emotion.

### How did William **James** come to **develop pragmatism**?

During the 1870s, James participated in a discussion group that became known as "the Metaphysical Club." Its members included Charles Sanders Peirce (1839–1914), U.S. Supreme Court Justice Oliver Wendell Holmes (1841–1935), and mathematician and philosopher Chauncey Wright (1830–1875). While the group was meeting, there was some concern on the part of civic leaders in New England that religion, particularly Protestantism, was suffering as a result of the popularity of Darwinism and intense interest in the sciences. At the time James began to teach philosophy, Harvard administrators had an interest in the potential of philosophy to support religion. When James began his career, the disciplinary boundaries between psychology and philosophy were fluid. Largely as the result of his work, the two fields were distinct by the end of his career. (To this day, William James Hall houses the Harvard Department of Psychology.)

Intellectually, James' pragmatism grew out of the limitations of psychology to provide answers to the moral questions that interested him: How can religion be justified intellectually? Is there free will? What is the nature of truth?

## What were William James' main pragmatic interests?

James attributed his pragmatic maxim to Charles Sanders Peirce (1839–1914): "To attain perfect clearness in our thoughts of an object ... we need only consider what conceivable effects of a practical kind the object may involve—what sensations we are to expect from it, and what reactions we must prepare." James applied pragmatism to epistemology, ethics, religious theory, and free will.

## What was William James' pragmatic epistemology?

He accepted that statements are true-or-false claims about what exists, but within our experience the world is "really malleable" so that truth is also imposed on reality. Truth, as "agreement with reality," varies, depending on the nature of what may be true. For example, in ordinary experience, beliefs are true if we are not painfully surprised when we act on them. Scientific truth emerges in ways that make entire systems coherent.

## What was William James' pragmatic ethics?

James thought that values require beings with emotions and wants. Judgments of value are objective when care for one another results in a standard for a community. This results in a shared or common world. Moral choices determine our character. Besides decisions connected to physical pleasure and pain, there are higher ideals that should direct our future experience, and, if necessary, be modified by that experience. Moral progress results when more inclusive ideals are substituted for less inclusive ones. Nevertheless, all ideals are only "provisional."

## What were William James' theories concerning religion and free will?

James thought that whether or not to believe in God, or to believe that we have free will and that there are objective values, cannot be decided neutrally by an appeal to facts. The facts in such matters are inconclusive, and a neutral intellectual position does not address the importance to us of whether or not God exists, or if we have free will, or whether there are objective values. Because our beliefs in such matters will make a difference in our lives and those of others, we must "will to believe" that God exists, that we have free will, and that there are objective values. In the case of free will, to motivate ourselves toward actions that are unpleasant, we should think about their positive consequences. James' offered an example of this: when one is reluctant to arise from bed on a cold morning, if one thinks about what one will do that day the necessary physical motion becomes almost automatic.

### How did William **James express** his own **will to believe?**

In the 1880s, James wanted to apply scientific methodology to mind-reading and "spiritualism." He could not find collaborators in the Harvard academic community, but in England at that time both Alfred Russell Wallace, who had discovered the theory of evolution at the same time as Charles Darwin, and the moral philosopher Henry Sidgwick (1838–1900) and his wife, Nora, were already interested in subjects of this sort. James became part of a group of intellectuals who went to séances and carefully investigated reports of supernatural events. They also counted reports of "apparitions" that occurred on the same day the person, whose apparition appeared, had died.

This so-called "Census of Hallucinations" resulted in a statistically significant correlation between day of death and appearance of that person's ghost. However, James thought that the sample of 17,000 would have yielded more reliable results if it were 50,000 and included American as well as British apparitions. James was also very skeptical of the table rapping and spirit-directed writing that were routine at séances, and he wanted to exclude mediums from the ranks of reputable spiritual researchers.

## JOSIAH ROYCE

### Who was **Josiah Royce?**

Josiah Royce (1855–1916) is known as an "absolute pragmatist." He sought to combine German and British absolute idealism with American pragmatism.

Royce was born in Grass Valley, California, which, at the time following the gold rush, was a mining town. His family moved to San Francisco when he was 11 and he graduated from the University of California in 1875; he then received a Ph.D. from Johns Hopkins University in 1878. Royce also studied at universities in Leipzig and Göttingen, after which he taught English at the University of California for four years.

In 1882, he was invited to join Harvard's philosophy department, where he eventually became a professor and led a highly acclaimed and distinguished career. Royce's major publications are *The World and the Individual* (1899), *Sources of Religious Insight* (1912), *The Problem of Christianity* (1913), *War and Insurance* (1914), *The Hope of the Great Community* (1916), and *Lectures on Modern Idealism* (1919). Also available is *Royce's Logical Essays: Collected Logical Essays of Josiah Royce* (1951).

## What were some of Josiah **Royce's metaphysical ideas**?

Royce's metaphysical system was intended to solve the problems posed by a religious worldview. He believed that what exists is a totality of everything that is known, so that the nature of Being can be understood by understanding how it comes to be known. Although knowledge starts with data from the senses, to arrive at the idea of a public object, as well as a past and future, transcendence is necessary. Transcendental judgment is not isolated, but part of a system of judgments. Such a system can account for error as a failure to define an object. An idea is a purpose that seeks an object, but the object in turn clarifies the original idea. The infinite is real, because the Absolute, which is One, represents itself along with everything else that mirrors it.

## What were Josiah **Royce's ethical** and **religious views**?

The primary virtue according to Royce was "loyalty to loyalty." While some people are loyal to bad causes, only good causes could support the loyalty to themselves that constituted loyalty to loyalty. In Royce's interpretation of Christianity, the Church, sin, and atonement were united by God as Spirit. Royce's idea of the role of God as Spirit, in community, was perceived as addressing a neglected aspect of the doctrine of the Trinity. (Christian religious history, in emphasizing God and Jesus, had often minimized the Holy Spirit.) Although it should be noted that his emphasis on community is similar to Martin Buber's (1878–1965) description of how Judaism differs from Christianity.

# JOHN DEWEY

## Who was **John Dewey**?

John Dewey (1859–1952) was the most famous philosopher in the United States during the early twentieth century. He was a public intellectual during the decades when ordinary people, as well as intellectuals, filled halls to hear intellectually stimulating and edifying speeches. His interactive, pragmatic approach to ordinary life, education, and art appreciation has shaped American experience in fundamental ways that do not always refer to him by name.

Although, or because, Dewey was shy, he wrote 37 books and more than 700 articles. His main publications include *Psychology* (1887), *Human Nature and Conduct*

(1922), *Experience and Nature* (1925), *The Public and Its Problems* (1927), *The Quest for Certainty* (1929), *Philosophy and Civilization* (1932), *A Common Faith* (1934), *Art as Experience* (1934), *Liberalism and Social Action* (1935), *Logic: The Theory of Inquiry* (1938), *Freedom and Culture* (1939), and *Problems of Men* (1946).

## What are some key facts about John **Dewey's life** and **career**?

Dewey was born in 1859 in Burlington, Vermont, where his father was a grocer. He attended the University of Vermont and then taught classics, science, and algebra at a high school in Oil City, Pennsylvania, and then in Burlington, Vermont. Unsure of his future direction, but encouraged by former teachers, he applied to the new graduate program in philosophy at Johns Hopkins University but was turned down for a fellowship twice. Dewey finally borrowed $500 from an aunt to attend. He thereby became part of the first generation able to obtain Ph.D.s in philosophy in the United States. Dewey's teachers at Johns Hopkins were philosophers George Sylvester Morris (1840–1889) and Charles Sanders Peirce (1839–1914), and psychologist G. Stanley Hall (1844–1924).

At first, Dewey was very interested in Hegelian ideas of organism, that the living being interacts with its environment, and that society is an organic whole that can be

viewed as an organism. After writing a dissertation on Immanuel Kant (1724–1804), he taught at the University of Michigan from 1884 to 1894. At this time he became interested in public education and progressive politics, as well as psychology. In 1894 Dewey became chair of the department of philosophy, psychology, and education at the University of Chicago. At Chicago, working with colleagues, he began to develop activist social theories. This resulted in the 1903 *Studies in Logical Theory,* which was dedicated to William James (1842–1910).

Dewey had a national reputation when he left Chicago for Columbia University. The *Journal of Philosophy,* published by the Columbia Philosophy Department, became an outlet for his ideas and a forum for discussion of them over the decades. Dewey lectured in Tokyo, Peking, and Nanking, and studied education in Turkey, Mexico, and Russia.

John Dewey was the most famous philosopher in the United States during the early twentieth century (AP).

In retirement, Dewey chaired the 1937 Mexican commission investigating charges against Russian revolutionary Leon Trotsky, which produced a report, *Not Guilty*. He also defended Bertrand Russell in 1941, when Russell was denied a teaching opportunity at City College, New York, because of his political ideas.

## What were John **Dewey's** main **philosophical ideas**?

Dewey brought ordinary life into philosophy. His main concept was experience, first for a cognitive Hegelian subject, and later as a more inclusive emotional and active dimension of human life. Dewey argued, against philosophical idealists and indeed most other philosophers of his day, that most of what is important in our experience is not reflective. Unlike the Hegelians, he also insisted that there was not a unified whole of all experience, but many interlocking versions or kinds of experience. Experience, for Dewey, was thus *pluralistic*. But the experience of the concrete human individual, or the real person, was the primary form of experience for Dewey.

Dewey sought to articulate the anthropological and biological nature of lived human experience. He saw this as a new form of empiricism. Against criticism that he was neglecting what was objective in writing and speaking as though experience was everything, Dewey developed a metaphysical account of experience.

## What was John **Dewey's metaphysics**?

Dewey held that nature has different "transactions," or kinds of action, that have mutual causes and effects between or among their components. Dewey's transactions are thus interactions. There are three evolutionary levels, or "plateaus," of transactions: physiochemical, psychophysical, and human experience. Physiochemical reactions are simply what can be studied by physics and chemistry; psychophysical transactions are connections between mind and body; human experience is exactly how things seem to human beings as they go about their lives.

## What was John **Dewey's theory** of art?

First, Dewey thought that inquiry is an art, and he rejected what he called the "spectator theory of knowledge," whereby knowing is believed to be passive contemplation. According to Dewey, ordinary human life itself is a form of art because it is permeated with aesthetic qualities in human experience. For Dewey, all experience, or anything that can be called "an experience," has an aesthetic quality that can be directly appreciated. An experience has an immediacy that is directly felt or *had* and which unites its constituents into the same whole. Dewey meant by this that we are not aware of the physical or chemical aspects of our experience but of holistic actions and qualities. For example, the runner does not experience her sprained ankle in the same way that the sports doctor examining her does. She has a united qualitative experience of strain and pain, whereas the sports doctor understands her condition in terms of which exact tissues have been damaged.

## Did John Dewey hold views on education for children?

**Y**es, and some have considered this unusual in a philosopher. He was married twice and had six children himself and adopted three. Although Dewey did not want to be known as an "educator," because it would detract from his philosophical reputation, his contribution to education was at least as lasting as his philosophical innovations.

When Dewey began to consider education, school children were expected to sit quietly and absorb information passively. While Dewey did not believe in a completely child-centered method of instruction, he emphasized the activity of learning, with an understanding that children are already curious and energetic participants in common, ordinary life outside the classroom.

Dewey thought that children should be taught skills to solve problems, including moral problems. When he became chair of the department of philosophy, psychology, and education at the University of Chicago, he founded The Laboratory School. It was based on his theory of education, the motto of which was "Learn by Doing!"

However, he acknowledged practical advice from Ella Flagg Young, the first woman president of the National Education Association, who was able to translate his ideas into actual practices and exercises in the classroom. He was also in contact with Jane Addams, who had cofounded the educational mission at Hull House. Dewey spent considerable time there himself, talking to working people about their problems and aspirations. His 1899 *The School and Society* was a best seller. Dewey's subsequent works on education were *The Child and the Curriculum* (1902), *How We Think* (1910), and *Democracy and Education* (1916).

Dewey called the aesthetic qualities of experience "tertiary qualities." Because experience is a kind of transaction, the aesthetic quality of an experience can change and become more meaningful toward a "consummation." A consummation is the reconstruction of an experience by intelligence: for example, solving a problem. What is not aesthetic according to Dewey is what is slack or overly rigid. There is nothing in either scientific inquiry or practical action that precludes the presence of aesthetic qualities.

## JANE ADDAMS

### Who was **Jane Addams**?

Jane Addams (1860–1935) was the first woman public intellectual in the United States. She was a close colleague of both John Dewey (1859–1952) and George Herbert Mead

(1863–1931). In 1931 Addams was awarded the Nobel Peace Prize for her progressive public activities in beginning the settlement house movement. The settlement
movement involved locating places for
assisting members of impoverished
immigrant communities, directly in their
neighborhoods. Addams began the services of Hull House with art appreciation
classes and quickly developed a program
of education for youth, child care,
instruction in domestic skills, and adult
education. She was only "recovered" as a
philosopher and feminist in the late-
twentieth century. Her main works
include *Democracy and Social Ethics*
(1902), *Newer Ideals of Peace* (1906),
*Twenty Years at Hull House* (1910) and
*Second Twenty Years at Hull House* (1930), *The Long Road of Woman's Memory*
(1916), and *Peace and Bread in Time of War* (1922).

Famous for founding Hull House in Chicago, Jane Addams
won a Nobel Peace Prize for her work helping the
impoverished (Art Archive).

## What are some highlights of Jane **Addams' life** that led her to found **Hull House**?

Addams' father was a mill owner and politician in Cedarville, Illinois. Her mother died
when she was two, while giving birth to her ninth child. Addams attended Rockford
Seminary (a women's college), failed in medical school, and became depressed for a
decade, during which she traveled throughout Europe. Along the way she visited Lon-
don's Toynbee Hall, which was a young men's community that helped poor Jewish and
Irish immigrants in East London by working within these people's neighborhoods.
Addams resolved to duplicate this plan, and in 1889 she founded Hull House in the
Near West Side community of Chicago. Hull House was run and operated by women.
Addams had long-term relationships with her cofounder and college friend, Ellen
Gates Starr, and, later on, with her colleague Mary Rozet Smith.

Addams' work at Hull House, and other settlement houses based on it, made her
well known; she became a very popular public speaker. She was involved in the
founding of other progressive organizations, such as the National Association for the
Advancement of Colored People, the American Civil Liberties Union, and the
Women's International League for Peace and Freedom. Former President Theodore
Roosevelt asked her to second his nomination for the presidency by the "Bull Moose"
Progressive Party in 1912. (Roosevelt had served three years as U.S. president after
1901, and a full term after 1904.) The Progressive Party strongly supported women's
rights and suffrage.

However, Addams became a target for intense public criticism when she expressed both pacifist and feminist views before World War I. Toward the end of her life, she dedicated herself to world peace and African American civil rights.

## How did **Hull House** fulfill **pragmatist ideals** of knowledge?

Addams saw Hull House as an epistemological (theory of knowledge) project, as much as a charitable program. She wrote: "The ideal and developed settlement would attempt to test the value of human knowledge by action, and realization, quite as the complete and ideal university would concern itself with the discovery of knowledge in all branches."

# GEORGE HERBERT MEAD

## Who was **George Herbert Mead**?

George Herbert Mead (1863–1931) was a philosopher, social theorist, and reformer whom John Dewey (1859–1952) described as "a seminal mind of the first order." (Dewey brought him to the University of Chicago when he accepted his position there.) Mead had been raised in a New England Puritan community, but in his mature thought he became an empiricist.

Mead's most important contribution to both pragmatic theories of education and sociology was his idea of "symbolic interaction." He offered an explanation of the development of the human mind and self, through the development of language and role playing. Although something of a behaviorist in his insistence on the social nature of individual mental development, Mead also believed that there were different developmental stages of adjustment to the external environment. Mead worked with Dewey in the Chicago Laboratory School and was a friend of Jane Addams (1860–1935) and a close observer of her work at Hull House.

## Who was **George Santayana**?

George Santayana (born Jorge Agustín Nicolás Ruíz de Santayana y Borrás; 1863–1952) was a philosopher, poet, art critic, and author of the international best selling novel *The Last Puritan* (1935; new edition, 1936). His father was Spanish and he was born in Madrid, but his Scottish mother brought him to the United States when he was nine and enrolled him in the Boston Latin School. In 1889 he received a Ph.D. in philosophy from Harvard, with Josiah Royce (1855–1916) as his advisor. In 1892 he accepted an instructorship at Harvard and later became professor of philosophy, teaching there for 20 years. Santayana's students included authors Conrad Aiken, T.S. Eliot, Robert Frost, Wallace Stevens, and Walter Lippman, as well as U.S. Supreme Court Justice Felix Frankfurter.

### What did George Herbert Mead contribute to philosophy?

**M**ead was a philosopher of "emergence," in his studies of Darwinian evolution. He proposed that new forms of life change the nature of the past, because after a new form exists, what preceded and led to it needs to be reinterpreted. Mead did not publish while he lived, although his works were prepared by his students to appear posthumously as *Mind, Self, and Society* (1934).

Santayana retired from Harvard in 1912 and spent the remainder of his life writing and traveling in Europe. His main publications are *The Sense of Beauty* (1896), *Interpretations of Poetry and Religion* (1900), *The Life of Reason* (five volumes, 1905–1906), *Skepticism and Animal Faith* (1923), *The Realms of Being* (four volumes, 1927–1940), *Persons and Places* (1944), *The Middle Span* (1945), and *My Host the World* (1953). In addition to numerous other books and essays, Santayana's published correspondence to over 350 respondents runs to eight volumes.

## What was George **Santayana's contribution** to **pragmaticism**?

Other than the fact that Josiah Royce (1855–1916) was his teacher and C.I. Lewis (1883–1964) argued against his intuitive theory of knowledge, it is not always clear how Santayana was a pragmatist. The philosophical convention places him within that group, mostly due to time and place and the pragmatist philosophers he interacted with while living in the United States. Still, Santayana's ideas about aesthetics, reason, philosophy itself, and human nature share a common spirit with William James (1842–1910) and John Dewey (1859–1952).

Santayana's theory of aesthetics was that beauty is the experience of pleasure in the form of an object, rather than the effects on the sense organs of the person experiencing the artwork. He claimed that all preference is basically irrational and that values are based on pleasure. His take on reason emphasized human creativity in science, religion, society, and ordinary life, as well as more obviously in art. Overall, he identified human beings as animals, inhabiting a physical world, oriented toward food, and fearful of danger. Santayana thought that nature was a kind of backdrop within which we have our experience. In *The Life of Reason* (1905–1906), he described nature as "drawn like a sponge, heavy and dripping from the waters of sentience." The "nature of nature" is thus conditioned by our experience of it. These views characterize his early work.

After he left Harvard, Santayana wrote about metaphysics and ontology, emphasizing objective reality as opposed to human experience. But Santayana himself did not acknowledge this change in his subject matter, and in his later writing he claimed to be providing a more comprehensive and rigorous foundation for his earlier theories of art and experience.

## What was George **Santayana's ontology**?

He rejected the kind of philosophical skepticism about physical reality that had led to idealism. But he thought one positive effect of that skepticism was to show that "essence" is what is ultimately real. However, people can't experience pure essences. Our "animal faith" posits a world beyond our immediate experience. That world is made up of essence and matter, and also truth and spirit. Matter is constantly changing, but it has a continuity, which renders it a "substance." Truth is about matter and what exists, whereas spirit is pure transcendental consciousness. Spirit intuits. Santayana described intuition as "the direct and obvious possession of the apparent without commitments of any sort about its truth, significance, or material existence."

# RALPH BARTON PERRY

## Who was **Ralph Barton Perry**?

Ralph Barton Perry (1876–1957) is best known for his theory of value and his realist views. But he received a 1936 Pulitzer Prize for his biography of his mentor and colleague, *The Thought and Character of William James* (1935).

Perry received his Ph.D. from Harvard in 1899 and taught there from 1902 to 1946. His main publications include a 1925 revision of Alfred Weber's *History of Philosophy*, *The New Realism* (1912), *General Theory of Value* (1926), *Puritanism and Democracy* (1944), *The Realms of Value* (1954), and *The Humanity of Man* (1956).

## What was Ralph Barton **Perry's theory of value**?

Perry wrote that value worked like a target: any object becomes valuable or acquires value when interest is taken in it. The moral good is the promotion of "harmonious happiness," which is achieved when all interests are harmonized and fulfilled.

## What was Ralph Barton **Perry's realism**?

Perry wrote *The New Realism: Cooperative Studies in Philosophy* (1912) with five others: Edwin B. Holt, Walter T. Marvin, William Pepperell Montague, Walter Boughton Pitkin, and Edward Gleason Spaulding. They were in revolt against both idealism and dualism, holding that what we perceive and remember are what they appear to be, as we are conscious of them. Their conclusions were similar to those of G.E. Moore's (1873–1958) common sense attack on idealism.

# C.I. LEWIS

## Who was **C.I. Lewis**?

C.I. Lewis (1883–1964) was the most Kantian of all the pragmatists, although he did not become a pragmatist until he read Charles Sanders Peirce's (1839–1914) papers, when he was given an office in the library room where they were stored at Harvard.

Lewis was born in Stoneharn, Massachusetts. His father was a shoe maker who became barred from employment due to union activism. Lewis attended Harvard as an undergraduate and returned to get his Ph.D. there after teaching in Colorado. He then went through the tenure process at the University of California and became well known for his work in symbolic logic. But he gave up his position as associate professor there to be an assistant professor in the Harvard department of philosophy in 1920, where he remained until 1953, serving twice as chair.

Lewis was the most famous philosopher of his generation during the 1940s, but he had become obscure by the 1960s, largely due to the success of his student W.V.O. Quine (1908–2000). Quine's success was largely based on the widespread acceptance of his refutation of the analytic/synthetic distinction, which was the cornerstone of Lewis' entire philosophical edifice. Lewis' main works are *A Survey of Symbolic Logic* (1918); *Symbolic Logic* (1932), which was written with C.H. Lanford; *Mind and the World Order* (1929); *An Analysis of Knowledge and Valuation* (1946); and *The Ground and Nature of the Right* (1965).

## What was the **analytic/synthetic distinction** and why did C.I. Lewis need it?

"Analytic" truths are true by definition and tell us nothing about the world. "Synthetic" truths are about the world, but they can turn out to be false. Along with this distinction is the *a priori/a posteriori* distinction: *a priori* knowledge is known without, or before, experience, whereas *a posteriori* knowledge can only be known after, or as a result of, experience.

Empiricist philosophers traditionally hold that there are no *a priori* synthetic truths, and they have tended to assume that what is analytic is also *a priori,* and what is synthetic is *a posteriori.*

Lewis' main philosophical tool, in accounting for both ordinary experience and scientific knowledge, was to distinguish between the *a priori* and what he called "the given." Quite simply, he thought that our knowledge and experience was the result of the interplay between the *a priori* and the given. There is something "brute" in our experience that we have no control over, but we make sense of it by projecting *a priori* principles and categories onto it.

## What was C.I. **Lewis' form** of **pragmatism**?

Lewis believed that all knowledge about the world, even simple perceptual truths, is hypothetical, taking the form of "If I do X, then Y will result." For example, to say that the wall is hard, means that I will have a certain sensation if I bang my head against it, just as the claim that the peach is ripe means that if I bite into it, I will experience certain expected flavors.

In ethics, Lewis believed that value judgments are appraisals of the consequences of action. Aesthetic valuation, however, involves an apprehension of an objective qualitative mode of experience. Lewis, like John Dewey (1859–1952), believed that values are in the world, as objective qualities, and not the result of human preferences or judgments. According to Lewis, every experience has both a value dimension, according to where it is on a scale from good to bad, and an aesthetic dimension from pleasing to unpleasant, or of high to low aesthetic quality. In both ethics and aesthetics, some things can be seen to be intrinsically good, upon reflection. And in ethics, the aim and purpose of action is often what is intrinsically good.

## Who was **Alain Locke**?

Alain LeRoy Locke (1885–1954) was the first African American Rhodes scholar. He wrote a dissertation in philosophy at Harvard University in 1918, but was told that he would not be hired to teach philosophy, except at a black institution. Locke's dissertation was *The Problem of Classification in the Theory of Value*. Ralph Barton Perry (1876–1957) was his adviser.

In 1921 Locke returned to Howard University, where he had previously taught English, to chair the philosophy department; he held that position until 1953. Locke has been primarily remembered for his work in the creation and support of the Harlem Renaissance, and for his writings on black art and music. However, he also developed his studies in pragmatism and applied them to issues of racism and racial identity in complex ways that were only first recovered in the late-twentieth century. Locke's principle pragmatic philosophical work was *When Peoples Meet: A Study in Race and Culture Contacts* (1942). Locke's other philosophical writings have since been edited and re-interpreted by Leonard Harris (1948–) and others.

Although Americans are taught that their country is a wonderful "melting pot" of races, race relations and cultural pluralism prove to be complex issues. Alain Locke was well known for studying their dynamics (iStock).

### How did Alain **Locke apply pragmatism** to issues of **race** and **culture**?

Locke was interested in values and valuation, cultural pluralism, and race relations. He argued that each cultural group has a distinct identity, which should not conflict with the citizenship of its members in a wider whole. Thus, African Americans could have the cultural identity(ies) supported by the Harlem Renaissance and remain Americans. This model of identity was the intellectual foundation of Locke's efforts in promoting black culture. But some now view it as an applied pragmatic strategy.

Locke believed that black identity was largely the result of economic and political forces and not biology. However, his pragmatic strategy was not to argue this belief directly, but to promote an understanding of race as culture—within a broader society that emphasized false biological notions of race—toward the goal of eventual "racial" equality.

## PROCESS PHILOSOPHY

### What is **process philosophy**?

Process philosophy was an early twentieth century system of thought that was strongly influenced by Albert Einstein's theory of relativity and other scientific ideas, such as the wave theory of light and sub-atomic physics. The fundamental metaphysical premise of process philosophy is that the basic unit of existence is not a stable thing, such as an atom, but events, or change over time. The two most prominent process philosophers were Alfred North Whitehead (1861–1947) and Charles Hartshorne (1897–2000).

### Who was **Alfred North Whitehead**?

Alfred North Whitehead (1861–1947) was famous in analytic philosophy for his collaboration with his student Bertrand Russell (1872–1970) on *Principia Mathematica* (three volumes; 1910, 1912, 1913). *Principia* took almost 10 years to complete and was highly regarded as an impressive but ultimately unsuccessful attempt to reduce mathematics to logic. Whitehead was also the American originator of process philosophy, a version of philosophy of science and metaphysics that is similar to pragmatism in its emphasis on change and the dynamic nature of experience.

### What are the highlights of Alfred North **Whitehead's career**?

Whitehead spent the first 25 years of his teaching career at Trinity College, Cambridge. Whitehead and Bertrand Russell (1872–1970) distanced themselves from each other after Russell became a pacifist during World War I and Whitehead's son was killed in that war. Whitehead taught at the University of London and began publishing works on philosophy of science, such as *Principles of Natural Knowledge* (1919), *The Concept of Nature* (1920), and *The Principle of Relativity* (1922). His most important work as a process philosopher was *Process and Reality* (1927–1928), which was published after he moved to the United States to accept a position at Harvard.

### What was Alfred North **Whitehead's process philosophy**?

Whitehead believed that it is impossible to have an idea of simple spatial or temporal location. He claimed that in our immediate experience nothing possesses "this character of simple location." Instead, Whitehead held that simple location requires a process of "constructive abstraction" that is made up of considerations of existing volumes extended over one another, such as a nest of baskets, Russian dolls, or pots of different sizes. Every location has an aspect of itself in every other location and thereby mirrors the entire world. (It's unlikely that Whitehead meant literally "mirrors," so much as he wanted to emphasize that things are not completely self-contained or isolated from other things.)

Moreover, what we imagine to be objects are actually constructed events and processes. Process, not substance, is the basic unit of the world. The work of philosophy is to explain the relations or connections between scientific and logical descriptions of reality and our everyday experience (of nested volumes). To believe that science directly describes experience is to commit the "fallacy of misplaced concreteness."

> ## How did Charles Hartshorne's system of the universe work?
>
> All human sensations, according to Hartshorne, are feelings, and nature itself is the totality of all interactions of sentient, creative beings, which exist for all time in God's memory. The entire universe is literally God's body. The most important values—which can be sensed and are immortal as events of sensation—concern beauty. Beauty can be theoretically understood as a mean between order and disorder and/or simplicity and complexity.

## What did Alfred North **Whitehead** think the **world was composed of** in reality?

According to Whitehead, the most primitive real unit is an *actual occasion,* which is not any thing or substance that persists in time, but a process, a process of becoming. This process of becoming is related to every other process of becoming, or as Whitehead's commentators have explained, the basic unit of reality is a Leibnizian monad that has windows on every conceivable "surface." The entire world is organic and "nature is a structure of evolving processes." Reality is process. Moreover, Whitehead believed that his ontology, unlike the scientific ontology of inert objects, allowed for the existence of an evolving God.

## Who was **Charles Hartshorne**?

Charles Hartshorne (1897–2000) wrote over 20 books dedicated to developing the theological side of Whitehead's philosophy. Hartshorne posited a dynamic form of evolution that included human events, time, history, and God. God is "di-polar." He has an abstract pole and a concrete one. Hartshorne thought that the necessity of God's existence could be proved in his version of St. Anselm of Canterbury's ontological argument. Hartshorne believed that Anselm was mistaken in attempting to prove the existence of God from thought, but that what can be proved is the necessity of God's existence.

Hartshorne's major works are *Beyond Humanism: Essays in the New Philosophy of Nature* (1968), *The Logic of Perfection and Other Essays in Neoclassical Metaphysics* (1962; revised, 1973), *Anselm's Discovery* (1965), *A Natural Theology for Our Time* (1967; revised, 1992), *The Philosophy and Psychology of Sensation* (1968), *Creative Synthesis and Philosophic Method* (1970), *Reality as Social Process* (1971), *Omnipotence and Other Theological Mistakes* (1984), and *Born to Sing: An Interpretation and World Survey of Bird Song* (1992).

# ANALYTIC PHILOSOPHY

### What is **analytic philosophy**?

Analysis is a mental process that breaks down ideas, beliefs, arguments or trains of thought, and systems of thought into their simpler components. Insofar as philosophy is about "mental products" in its own field and others, all philosophy is analytic. However, in American philosophy departments, and internationally, the term "analytic philosophy" has come to designate twentieth century mainstream philosophical thinking, as opposed to continental philosophy, pragmatism, and subjects that now fall under "new philosophy" because they are recent additions to the field.

### What is **distinctive** about the practice of **analytic philosophy**?

Analytic philosophy is as much a method as a set of traditional subjects. The method is a combination of empiricism and conceptual analysis, with as little speculation as possible.

## EARLY TWENTIETH CENTURY ANALYTIC PHILOSOPHY

### What were the **important themes** in early twentieth century **analytic philosophy**?

Analytic philosophy before World War II began with a rejection of British idealism via G.E. Moore's (1873–1958) well-received common sense philosophy and a new rigor in theories of meaning, introduced by the empiricist Bertrand Russell (1872–1970). The doctrine of logical atomism, as developed by Russell and Ludwig Wittgenstein (1889–1951), flourished for a while.

331

Logical atomism was dependent on truth-functional logic for its explication. In other words, analytic philosophers generally turned to logic as the science par excellence that set the standard for philosophy.

# G.E. MOORE

## Who was **G.E. Moore**?

George Edward Moore (1873–1958) successfully revived epistemological and metaphysical realism and supported a common sense philosophical method. He spent most of his career at Cambridge University, becoming a professor there in 1925. As an undergraduate, Moore was a member of the Cambridge Apostles, a select intellectual group of Cambridge University undergraduates. He was editor of the top analytic journal, *Mind* (1921–1947). Moore's main books are *Philosophical Studies* (1922), *Principia Ethica* (1903), and *Some Main Problems of Philosophy* (1953).

## What was G.E. **Moore's common sense** philosophy?

Moore made a distinction between what philosophers claim and what ordinary people believe. He wrote:

> I do not think that the world or the sciences would ever have suggested to me any philosophical problems. What has suggested philosophical problems to me is things which other philosophers have said about the world or the sciences.

> His own philosophical approach was to analyze concepts or the meanings of words by determining the difference between any one concept "before the mind" or under consideration as an object of thought, and other concepts. In his writing, Moore demonstrated a methodical and thorough style of analysis. It was this calm, painstaking clarity that established his philosophical stature in the twentieth century.

## How Did G.E. **Moore** develop his **common sense philosophy**?

Moore's first major article was "The Refutation of Idealism," which was published in *Mind* in 1903. In it he argued that no idealist or skeptical argument was as convincing as common sense beliefs that the world is real, and that, therefore, idealism and skepticism can just be dismissed. Moore became famous for "proving" the existence of the external world with his legendary "two hands argument" (derived from his 1939 "Proof of an External World" argument against skepticism concerning the existence of the external world.)

Moore said that by raising his right hand and saying, "Here is a hand," and then raising his left and saying, "And here is another," the skeptical position was disproved. This was not as "off hand" a dismissal as it seems. Moore's premise was that he knew

## Who or what were the Cambridge Apostles?

This was the undergraduate club at Cambridge University to which G.E. Moore, and some of the male writers who held him in high esteem, belonged. The Cambridge Apostles, or "Cambridge Conversazione Society," was founded in 1820 by George Tomlinson, who was later bishop of Gibraltar. There were originally 12 members; hence the name. They met on Saturday nights for discussion after one member presented a paper and they ate "whales," which were sardines on toast. The Apostles have always been a quasi-secret society with an annual dinner and a meeting in London every so often. Women could not be considered for membership until 1970.

When the "Cambridge spy ring" was disclosed in 1951, four of its members were former Apostles, and two, who were employed in high government offices, had given the KGB sensitive information. (The Cambridge spy ring consisted of five British young men who attended Cambridge University and were recruited to spy for the Soviet Union during the 1930s. They infiltrated the highest levels of British government and betrayed top secrets to the Soviet Union.)

he had two hands, from which it followed that the external world existed, from which it followed that there was no ground for the skeptic's doubt about its existence.

## How was G.E. **Moore** a **realist**?

Moore was at times a *naïve realist* and at other times a *representative realist*. All realists believe that there is a real, external world. Naïve realists hold that we directly perceive objects in this world. Representative realists think that what we perceive are the effects of those objects on our organs of sense, or, in other words, that what we perceive are not objects but *sense data* caused by real objects.

# TRUTH–FUNCTIONAL LOGIC AND LOGICAL ATOMISM

## What is **truth-functional logic**?

Truth-functional logic preserves logical truth by substituting terms according to the rules of logic. The truth or falsity of a statement can be calculated according to the truth of its parts. For example, if A or not-A (the law of non-contradiction) is a rule, then if A is true, not-A must be false; if A is false, then not-A must be true. Compound sentences are true or false depending only on whether their components are true or false. For example, the sentence "It is raining and cold" is true if "It is raining" is true and "It is cold" is true.

Truth functional logic is typically applied according to tables that indicate the truth values of sentences that contain clauses linked by the connectives "if," "and," "not," "if-then," and "if and only if." The truth or falsity of the whole sentence depends on the truth or falsity of its components, according to the rules of logic that apply to each of the connectives.

## What was **logical atomism**?

The main claim of logical atomists was that the world is made up of logical facts. These logical facts are like atoms because they can't be divided into smaller facts. Single logical facts can be combined by truth-functional logic into molecular facts.

To apply the theory of logical atomism to more complex statements, such as the claims of science, the method of logical construction was posited. In logical construction, any "S' represents a logical construction of "Ps" if statements about S can be reduced to atomic statements about Ps. For example, a salad is a logical construction of its ingredients, and perceptions of ordinary objects are logical constructions of sense data. Bertrand Russell (1872–1970) and Ludwig Wittgenstein (1889–1951) were the main proponents of this perspective.

## What was the **influence** of **logical atomism**?

As a philosophical doctrine, logical atomism was surpassed by logical positivism. However, its main rhetorical force did demolish what Bertrand Russell (1872–1970) termed "logical holism," or the notion that the world is a whole, no part of which can be known independently of all others. Logical holism was the epistemological doctrine associated with absolute idealism.

## BERTRAND RUSSELL

## Who was **Bertrand Russell**?

Arthur William Bertrand Third Earl Russell (1872–1970), who was known to his friends as "Bertie," is hailed as the founder of analytic philosophy, along with G.E. Moore (1873–1958) and Ludwig Wittgenstein(1889–1951). He studied and lectured at Cambridge University, losing his position there between 1916 and 1944 because of his pacifist views and activism. He won the Nobel Prize in 1950. His writings on philosophical, political, scientific, and social reform topics are all in beautifully executed prose, which he was said to have been able to compose from the first draft.

Russell is now best known for his failed attempt with Alfred North Whitehead (1861–1947) to reduce mathematics to logic, his theory of descriptions, his theory of types, and his ruling doctrine that the work of philosophy is to analyze propositions (the meanings of sentences) and that the only propositions worthy of such analysis must have "constituents" with which we are acquainted (have direct knowledge of).

Russell was one of the most productive philosophical authors of all time. He published hundreds of articles and essays and scores of books. Among the most noteworthy are "On Denoting," *Mind* (Vol. 14, 1905); *Philosophical Essays* (1910); *The Problems of Philosophy* (1912); *Principia Mathematica,* with Alfred North Whitehead, three volumes (1910–1913); *Why I am Not a Christian* (1927); *A History of Western Philosophy and Its Connection with Political and Social Circumstances from the Earliest Times to the Present Day* (1946); and *The Autobiography of Bertrand Russell* (1967–1969).

His pacifist activities won Bertrand Russell a Nobel Prize, while as a philosopher he was the most productive author of his day, publishing scores of books (AP).

## What was Bertrand **Russell's theory of knowledge**?

Russell distinguished between two kinds of knowledge. Knowledge by acquaintance was direct knowledge of "sense data," mental states, thoughts, and feeling. More indirect "knowledge by description" was ultimately based on knowledge by acquaintance. For example, I have knowledge by acquaintance of this page as I am typing it into my computer, but knowledge by description of Burma, where I have never been.

## What was Bertrand **Russell's** theory of **definite descriptions**?

Russell gave an account of how it is possible to talk meaningfully about things that do not exist. According to his theory of definite descriptions, what a proposition of the form "X is Q" means is: "There is exactly one thing that is X and that one thing is Q," or, "At least one thing is X and no more than one thing is X and whatever is X is Q."

Russell's theory makes it possible to distinguish between the contradiction of "X is Q" and "X is not-Q." To use Russell's example: (A) "The King of France is bald" has as its contradictory, (A') "There is no King of France, or there is more than one King of France, or there is one King of France who is not bald." But, (B) "The King of France is not-bald" means, according to Russell's theory, (B') "There is one King of France, no more and no less, and he is not bald." And, A' and B' do not have the same meaning.

## What is Bertrand **Russell's theory of types**?

Russell began with a puzzle inspired by the German philosopher Gottlob Frege's (1848–1925) attempt to reduce mathematics to logic: Is the class of all classes that are not members of themselves, or C, itself a member of itself? This question seems valid, but Russell showed that it leads to contradictions: If C is a member of itself then it should not be in D, which is the class of classes that are not members of themselves, but if C is a member of itself, it will be in D. But if C is not a member of itself, then it should be in D, and C is a member of itself. Russell's answer was that there is a hierarchy of types of things that restricts what can be said about them. So we can say that Russell is an analytic philosopher, but not that a group of people are an analytic philosopher.

## What did Bertrand **Russell** think about his **use of logic**?

Russell believed that logic could be used to solve both philosophical problems and everyday ones, if propositions were translated into the correct logical form. To accomplish this, he held the ideal of a "logically correct" language. For a while he thought that his student Ludwig Wittgenstein (1889–1951) was on the right path toward supplying that. But Wittgenstein only alluded to such a language in his early work and abandoned the project later on.

# LUDWIG WITTGENSTEIN

## Who was **Ludwig Wittgenstein**?

Ludwig Wittgenstein (1889–1951) had two distinct philosophical periods. First, was his ambitious development of logical atomism that was influenced by his teacher Bertrand Russell (1872–1970), resulting in his writing *Tractatus Logico-Philosophicus* (1921). Second was Wittgenstein's original, "ordinary language" theory of philosophy. This was an original insight about ordinary language. Wittgenstein was unquestionably a genius.

## What are some facts about Ludwig **Wittgenstein's life**?

Quite a lot is known about Wittgenstein's life, although not everything is completely understood. Some stories seem to be in the realm of legends. Wittgenstein was born in 1889 in Vienna, Austria, to a famous and wealthy family of Jewish ancestry. His paternal grandparents were Jews who converted to Protestantism, and his mother was Catholic, although her father was of Jewish descent. Ludwig was the youngest of eight children, who were all exposed to high culture (composer Johannes Brahms was a friend of the family).

Although Ludwig was baptized as a Catholic, when he "confessed his sins" to friends later in life, among his admitted transgressions was the fact that he allowed others to assume he was not Jewish. Ludwig had four brothers, three of whom committed suicide. When his father died in 1913, Ludwig inherited a vast fortune, which he gave away. In 1938, after Germany annexed Austria, he was able to protect his sisters from being sent to concentration camps by giving the German government millions of dollars in gold.

Wittgenstein's education included studying mechanical engineering in Berlin; in 1908 he moved to England to study aeronautics, which included experimenting with kites. This led to mathematics and then to philosophy, insofar as it was a current pursuit to seek the foundations of mathematics in logic. A visit with the mathematician Gottlob Frege (1848–1925) led Wittgenstein to meet Bertrand Russell (1872–1970) at Cambridge University, where he studied logic with both G.E. Moore (1873–1958) and Russell. But his studies were interrupted by World War I, during which he volunteered for the Austrian army and distinguished himself for bravery.

Russell assisted Wittgenstein in publishing *Tractatus Logico-Philosophicus* (1922). Wittgenstein then taught elementary school in a rural area of Austria and also designed and built a modernist house in Vienna for his sister Gretl.

Returning to Cambridge in 1929, he taught philosophy, becoming a professor at Trinity College 10 years later. He was a hospital porter during World War II and resigned his professorship in 1947, moving to Ireland to write. Just before dying, he said, "Tell them I've had a wonderful life." Ray Monk's biography *Wittgenstein: The Duty of Genius* (1991) is considered definitive as both an intellectual and personal account of Wittgenstein's life.

## What did Ludwig **Wittgenstein** accomplish in his *Tractatus Logico-Philosophicus*?

Although the work is considered one of the greatest achievements in philosophy, it's really not clear. Wittgenstein's stated intention was to address the problems of philosophy that had preoccupied Gottlob Frege (1848–1925) and Bertrand Russell (1872–

> **What are some examples of**
> **Wittgenstein's propositions in his *Tractatus*?**
>
> - The world is all that is the case.
> - A proposition is a picture of reality.
> - Propositions *show* the logical form of reality. They display it.
> - What *can* be shown, *cannot* be said.
> - The general form of a proposition is: This is how things stand.
> - All the propositions of logic say the same thing, to wit nothing.
> - *The limits of my language* mean the limits of my world.

1970)—Arthur Schopenhauer (1788–1860) was another influence on the work—although he said at the end of this work: "My propositions serve as elucidations in the following way: anyone who understands *me* eventually recognizes *them* as nonsensical." At the beginning of the book, Wittgenstein claims that his main purpose is ethical.

*The Tractatus Logico-Philosophicus* consists of seven sets of numbered propositions or statements, which are believed to be about the connection between language and the world. It seems to present an account of the essence of language as expressive of thought. Thought, according to Wittgenstein, is limited to what is factual so that the propositions of language are representations of the world. The propositions of logic, on the other hand, convey no factual information—logic consists of *tautologies*. Logic is very useful, but all of its conclusions are true by definition.

Wittgenstein believed that a meaningful sentence must have a precise structure that is made up of simple (in Russell's language, "atomic") sentences or simple names. Atomic sentences are pictures of states of affairs. Working backwards from this "picture theory of meaning" it would follow that, given the ideal logical language, the world itself has a logical structure.

Wittgenstein was to later abandon this view in favor of philosophical activity that consisted of descriptive analysis of ordinary language. But before he did that, the *Tractatus* had enormous influence on the new twentieth century school of thought known as logical positivism.

## OTHER LOGICIANS

### Who was **Kurt Gödel**?

Kurt Gödel (1906–1978) is famous for his theorem about mathematical systems, which appeared in a 1931 article titled "On Formally Undecidable Propositions in

*Principia Mathematica* and Related Systems," originally published in German in the 1931 volume of the journal *Monatshefte für Mathematik* (*Monthly Journal of Mathematics*). According to Gödel's Theorem, every formal (mathematical or logical) system is incomplete because there can always be a sentence expressing a truth that can't be proved in the system. To prove his theorem, Gödel invented a method for correlating formulas in logic with positive integers.

### Who was **Alfred Tarski**?

Alfred Tarski (1902–1983) was a logician. Born in Poland, he taught at the University of California at Berkeley from 1942 to 1958. He is famous for his theory of truth that appeared in "The Concept of Truth in Formalized Languages" (1933), which appeared in the Polish journal *Prace Towarzystwa Naukowego Warszawskiego, Wydzial III Nauk Matematyczno-Fizycznych,* and was translated into English in *Logic, Semantics, Metamathematics, Papers from 1923 to 1938* (1983). According to Tarski, any theory of truth should imply the truth of "T-sentences" in natural languages. For example, "'Snow is white' in English is true if and only if snow is white" is a T-sentence. It is important to notice that Tarski's theory of truth does not specify what constitutes truth but is rather about how true sentences can be defined.

# LOGICAL POSITIVISM

### What is **logical positivism**?

A new generation of thinkers who were influenced by Bertrand Russell (1872–1970) and Ludwig Wittgenstein (1889–1951) created a twentieth century version of Auguste Comte's (1798–1857) nineteenth century intellectual endorsement of science. The term "logical positivism" was coined in 1930 by two supporters: E. Kaila and A. Petzäll, philosophers who were part of the early movement that logical positivism came to represent. The twentieth century positivists Moritz Schlick (1882–1936), Rudolf Carnap (1891–1970), Otto Neurath (1882–1945), and in England, A.J. Ayer (1910–1989) were members of what became known as the "Vienna Circle."

## THE VIENNA CIRCLE

### Was the **Vienna Circle** an actual organization?

Yes, it was a discussion group of scientists and philosophers in Vienna, who held meetings from 1922 to 1938. Its members were highly influential in setting the subject matter of future analytic philosophy, ethics, political philosophy, philosophy of science, philosophy of language (excluding ordinary language philosophy), and philosophy of mind.

The manifesto of the Circle was *Wissenschaftliche Weltauffassung: Der Wiener Kreis* (*The Scientific Conception of the World: The Vienna Circle*) was published in 1929 and translated by Otto Neurath (1882–1945) in his *Empiricism and Sociology* (1973). The manifesto proclaims that the scientific world-conception of the Vienna Circle is distinguished "essentially by two features. First it is empiricist and positivist: there is knowledge only from experience. Second, the scientific world-conception is marked by the application of a certain method, namely logical analysis." Logical analysis is a way of using symbolic logic to determine whether sentences or their components refer to experience. Many logical positivists were also phenomenalists.

## What is **phenomenalism**?

Not to be confused with phenomenology, phenomenalism is the empiricist doctrine that sense data, or the sensory organ's impression of perception, could be used to explain the meaning of sentences about perceptual objects. Some believed that perceptual objects themselves, such as a computer, a desk, or a car, could be reduced to sense data. This last ontological version of phenomenalism would involve a general commitment to philosophical idealism or the doctrine that the only things that are real are mental phenomena.

## What is **verificationism**?

Verificationism is a theory of meaning. The meaning of a statement is its empirical methods of verification that ultimately yield sensory information. For contemporary verificationists such as Michael Dummett (1925–) this meant that the truth of sentences must be related to the ways in which they are or can be verified.

## What was tragic about Schlick's death?

After the Nazis came to power in Germany and Austria, many members of the Vienna Circle fled to the United States and England. Schlick remained. Although not Jewish, he was distressed by what was then happening in Germany. While walking up some steps at the University of Vienna to teach a class on June 22, 1936, Johann Nelböck, a former student, confronted Schlick with a pistol and shot him. Schlick died of a chest wound. Nelböck was convicted but soon pardoned, after which he became a member of the Nazi Party. Although Schlick was not Jewish, logical positivism was condemned as "Jewish thought" by the Nazis.

## Who was **Moritz Schlick**?

Moritz Schlick (1882–1936) is famous for claiming that philosophy was dependent on science, intellectually. He was a philosopher who studied with the physicist Max Planck before arriving in Vienna, Austria, in 1922. His presence was the inspiration for the mathematician Hans Hahn to inaugurate the discussion group of the Vienna Circle, which, in addition to Hahn and Schlick, at first contained Otto Neurath (1882–1945) and the physicist Philip Frank. Rudolf Carnap (1891–1970) joined them in 1926.

Schlick was professor of the philosophy of inductive sciences at the University of Vienna, while he led the Vienna Circle. He believed that empirical knowledge was not about the content of experience, which could not be communicated, but about the form of experience. He maintained that all genuine philosophical problems and questions were either mathematical or logical, or could be solved by scientific investigation.

Schlick believed that this implied that philosophy had no subject matter of its own that was distinct from the sciences. However, unlike other logical positivists, he thought that ethics were practical and that moral goodness was simply whatever is approved by society; moral obligation could be studied as what is generally required by society. His main works include *General Theory of Knowledge* (second edition, 1925) and *Problems of Ethics* (translated, 1939).

## Who was **Rudolf Carnap**?

Rudolf Carnap (1891–1970) is famous for his work on scientific verification. He received his Ph.D. from the University of Jena. He was a member of the Vienna Circle until he left Germany in 1935 to teach at the University of Chicago and the University of California at Los Angeles. In his early work he focused on the logical structure of language and what it implied about the world. In the 1940s, Carnap worked on logic and introduced the idea of a "state description," which is the linguistic form of a possible world, or the most complete description of the world that can be given in any language.

Unlike earlier logical positivists, Carnap addressed the problem of inconclusive evidence for actual scientific verification and the meaning of scientific terms. He argued for the use of probability in determining "degrees of confirmation" in place of absolute verification. Carnap's principle works include *The Logical Structure of the World* (1928; English translation, 1967), *Philosophy and Logical Syntax* (1935), *Introduction to Semantics* (1942), *Formalization of Logic* (1943), *Meaning and Necessity: A Study in Semantics and Modal Logic* (1947), and *Logical Foundations of Probability* (1950).

## Who was **Otto Neurath**?

Otto Neurath (1882–1945) was a polymath who had begun by studying mathematics in Vienna, earning a doctorate in the subject in Berlin. During World War I he was assigned to the planning ministry by the Austrian government because he had earlier written about barter economies. The Marxist governments of Bavaria and Saxony hired him to implement their post-war socialist economies; he was charged with treason when the German government took over, although he was soon released. In graphic design, he contributed to the Viennese Social and Economic Museum with his invention of "Isotype," a system of symbols for iconographically presenting quantitative information to the public.

As a logical positivist, Neurath was the main architect of the manifesto of the Vienna Circle. Along with Rudolf Carnap (1891–1970), Bertrand Russell (1872–1970), John Dewey (1859–1952), and others, he advocated the Unity of Science project, which was to result in the *International Encyclopedia of Unified Science* that would unify language and method and interdisciplinary dialogue across the sciences. It was never published.

Neurath's ambition was to render the social sciences as predictive as the physical sciences. His main works include *Through War Economy to Economy in Kind* (1919), *Personal Life and Class Struggle* (1928), *Empirical Sociology* (1931), and *Neurath–Carnap Correspondence* (1943–1945), as well as numerous articles in edited collections, as well as work on *The International Encyclopedia of Unified Science*.

Neurath was married three times and his last wife, Marie, carried on his Isotype work after his death.

## What was Otto **Neurath's main** philosophical **contribution**?

First, Neurath thought that the only connection between language and reality was metaphorical, and he believed that, at best, language and world "coincide" only because reality is all previously verified sentences. This required a "coherence theory of truth" for each individual sentence: a sentence is true if it *coheres* with already verified sentences. Only the entire language system can be verified. Neurath famously wrote:

We are like sailors who on the open sea must reconstruct their ship but are never able to start afresh from the bottom. Where a beam is taken away a new one must at once be put there, and for this the rest of the ship is used as support. In this way, by using the old beams and driftwood the ship can be shaped entirely anew, but only by gradual reconstruction.

Second, Neurath did not think that phenomenalism could provide a valid foundation for scientific language because sense data are subjective. His alternative was to propose that mathematical physics be used for objective descriptions, a doctrine known as *physicalism*. Furthermore, language itself could be described in the language of mathematical physics because it is material, constituted by sounds and graphic symbols.

## Who was **A.J. Ayer**?

Sir Alfred Jules ("Freddie") Ayer (1910–1989) was the British logical positivist who became famous for his *Language, Truth and Logic* (1936), which was followed by *The Problem of Knowledge* (1956). Ayer's main contribution was to relate logical positivism to traditional philosophy, which in no uncertain terms resulted in a devastating attack on metaphysics, ethics, and religion. The attack was on the meaning of terms used in these fields and resulted in the claim that they were meaningless.

Ayer was the Grote Professor of the Philosophy of Mind and Logic at the University College London from 1946 until 1959, and after that the Wykeham Professor of Logic at the University of Oxford. From 1951 to 1952 he was president of the prestigious Aristotelian Society. In 1973 he became a Knight in the Legion of Honor.

Ayer's publications include *Philosophical Essays* (1954), *The Concept of a Person and Other Essays* (1956), *The Origins of Pragmatism* (1958), *Metaphysics and Common Sense* (1969), *Russell and Moore: The Analytical Heritage* (1971), *Probability and Evidence* (1972), *Bertrand Russell* (1972), *The Central Questions of Philosophy* (1973), *Hume* (1980), *Philosophy in the Twentieth Century* (1982), *Freedom and Morality and Other Essays* (1984), *Ludwig Wittgenstein* (1986), *Part of My Life* (1977), and *More of My Life* (1984), as well as numerous articles on related topics.

## What are some **other interesting facts** about A.J. **Ayer's life** and career?

Ayer was a prominent subject of academic gossip for his "womanizing" (he was married four times) and for his engagement in fashionable popular culture. There was an overall glamour to his life. Ayer's mother's family founded the French Citroën car company, and his father worked for the wealthy Rothchild family of bankers. He attended Eton, won a scholarship to Oxford, and served in the SOE (Special Operations Executive) during World War II. Before the war, while on a visit to New York, Ayer made a record with actress Lauren Bacall. He supported the Tottenham Hotspur Football Club and was known to its fans as "The Prof."

## How did A.J. Ayer defeat Mike Tyson?

This is an oft-told story that those who knew Ayer said sounded exactly like him. When, at the age of 77, Ayer was a visiting professor at Bard College in 1987, he went to a party hosted by fashion designer Fernando Sanchez. Ayer noticed that the professional heavyweight boxer Mike Tyson was annoying model Naomi Campbell. Ayer told Tyson to back off, and Tyson responded, "Do you know who the f*** I am? I'm the heavyweight champion of the world!" Ayer shot back, "And I am the former Wykeham Professor of Logic. We are both pre-eminent in our field. I suggest that we talk about this like rational men." Ayer and Tyson did have a conversation, and Naomi Campbell, who was not yet famous, took advantage of this diversion to elude them both.

Ayer was also a secular humanist. He was honorary associate of the Rationalist Press Association after 1947, and a successor to evolutionary biologist and humanist Julian Huxley when he became president of the British Humanist Association. In 1965, Ayer was named the first president of the Agnostics' Adoption Society. He edited the anthology *The Humanist Outlook* in 1965.

At the peak of his career, Ayer served as a sort of in-house atheist for the British Broadcasting Corporation. He debated the Jesuit philosopher Frederick Copleston (1907–1994) on the subject of religion. Copleston was the author of the nine-volume *History of Philosophy* (1946–1975), so the two were matched in erudition.

Ayer (apparently briefly) revised his life-long atheism after a near-death experience in 1989—brought on by choking on a piece of smoked salmon. Toward the end of his life, though, he said, "What I should have said is that my experiences have weakened, not my belief that there is no life after death, but my inflexible attitude towards that belief."

## What was A.J. **Ayer's version** of **logical positivism**?

In *Language, Truth and Logic* (1936), published when he was just 26, Ayer forcefully and with great panache presented the main tenets of logical positivism as a doctrine broadly relevant to philosophy. He asserted the empiricist doctrine that all of our knowledge of the world comes from sensory experience. The truth or falsity of statements was dependent on whether they could be verified in terms of that experience. Only statements that could be true or false were meaningful. It followed from these bold claims that metaphysical, religious, and ethical statements, if they were not true by definition, could assert nothing meaningful about reality. Statements about the self, the external world, and the minds of others had to be confirmed by sensory experience, if they were to be meaningful. Concerning the existence of God, for example,

Ayer maintained that the question itself was not meaningful because no possible experience could determine its truth or falsity. Ayer's ethical theory was emotivist, that is, ethical judgments were held to be expressions of emotions.

### How was A.J. **Ayer** a **phenomenalist**?

According to Ayer, meaningful factual statements can be reduced to claims about sense data. While he seemed at times to temper this view, over his career he stuck to sense data as the foundation of empirical knowledge. In a famous exchange with the ordinary language philosopher J.L. Austin (1911–1960), Ayer defended his theory of sense data. Ayer's position was that sense data are not directly intuited until they have led to a perception of the ordinary world, with all of its normally perceptible objects, such as tables and chairs. Austin, who was a colleague of Ayer's at Cambridge, held that Ayer's theory of sense data could not be a form of foundationism because it presupposed common sense reality. That is, Austin's claim against Ayer was that, contrary to how Ayer seemed to present his case, perceptual knowledge was not built up of sense data. Ayer defended his view by claiming that in the process of verification sense data were necessary to confirm perceptions.

# ORDINARY LANGUAGE PHILOSOPHY

### What is **ordinary language philosophy**?

First, ordinary language philosophy should be distinguished from philosophy of language, which is a subfield of analytic philosophy. Ordinary language philosophy is an historical episode in analytic philosophy whose practitioners, inspired by Ludwig Wittgenstein (1889–1951), believed that all of the major problems of philosophy were either pseudo-problems that could be dispelled with reference to ordinary language, or genuine problems that could be solved by investigating how certain words were used. It should be stressed, however, that although ordinary language philosophers focused on how words were used, they were not interested in simply describing common usage. Rather, they were interested in the meanings of words or the concepts named by words; ordinary usage was investigated in order to determine meaning.

Indeed, Wittgenstein himself was aware that language, taken superficially, could be "bewitching." Furthermore, this determination of meaning seems to have been a reflective, rather than an empirical process. The ordinary language philosophers conducted no surveys; neither did they attempt to determine actual usage by consulting with sociologists or linguists. (This is important, because in the early twenty-first century experimental philosophy proceeds by just such empiricism.)

In addition to Wittgenstein, prominent practitioners in the heyday of ordinary language philosophy included the American advocates O.K. Bouwsma (1898–1978)    345 and Norman Malcolm (1911–1990), and the British discussants John Wisdom, (1904–1993), J.L. Austin (1911–1960), and H.P. Grice (1913–1988).

## What was Ludwig **Wittgenstein's major insight** concerning **ordinary language** and **philosophy**?

Wittgenstein's (1889–1951) work in ordinary language philosophy was published posthumously; his lecture notes and notebooks came out as *Philosophical Investigations* (1953) and *The Blue and Brown Books* (1948). Wittgenstein's interest in ordinary language represented a shift from his earlier interest in an ideal representational or "picture theory" of language to the ways in which human beings actively use language to go about the business of life.

Words and their meanings might seem like simple concepts on the surface, but Ludwig Wittgenstein maintained that language usage is not easily defined at all. (iStock).

Wittgenstein believed that the multiple uses of language cannot be codified and that key words cannot be neatly defined, but rather that we are engaged in overlapping series of "language games." Language games are like other games that are loosely related through "family resemblance," even though it is impossible to provide a definition of a "game" that will cover all of them. Wittgenstein used the simile of family resemblance because if one looks at the members of a large family, while they do not look exactly alike, there may be features that some share. For example, siblings and cousins might have the same hair color, or they might share certain similar facial structures inherited from their parents.

What Wittengstein meant in calling language a game was that how we use language is a self-contained system of practices with many implicit rules. Sometimes we cannot even say what the rules are, so Wittgenstein thought it was better not to concentrate on describing the rules, but to pay attention to actual language usage instead.

## What is the **method** behind **ordinary language philosophy**?

The correct philosophical approach in ordinary language philosophy is not to construct abstract systems of meanings but to "look and see" how words actually function in real life. Such investigation is a kind of philosophical therapy against an occupational tendency to create abstractions and strictly imposed generalizations. Philosophers should turn to language so as to "let the fly out of the bottle."

This was Wittgenstein's metaphor and philosophers still use it when they want to describe solving a problem by changing the framework in which the problem is posed. For example, in "letting the fly out of the bottle," one doesn't try to influence the fly directly, but instead changes the angle at which the bottle is held.

## What was Ludwig **Wittgenstein's private language argument**?

In applying his method to introspection or the reports of people's feelings, intentions, and beliefs, Wittgenstein constructed his well known and controversial "private language argument." He reasoned that because words derive their meaning from public criteria that influence correct usage, there can't be a wholly private language used to report only the private states of one person. He did not mean to claim that we do not have inner experiences, accessible only to those whose experience them, but rather that there are natural expressions of such experiences (pain, for example) that enable us to know the minds of others.

## Who was **O.K. Bouwsma**?

Oets Kolk (O.K.) Bouwsma (1898–1978) was famous for his humorous manner of teaching Ludwig Wittgenstein's (1889–1951) ordinary language philosophy over a 50-year teaching career, most memorably at the University of Texas at Austin. He would classically expose the absurdity of philosophical claims with elaborately silly examples of the kind of world that would be necessary for them to be true or plausible. René Descartes' (1596–1650) dreaming and evil demon sources of doubt were among Bouwsma's favorites. In a course on prophecy, he lauded Wittgenstein as follows:

> What is a prophet like? Wittgenstein is the nearest to a prophet I have ever known. He is a man who is like a tower, who stands high and unattached, leaning on no one. He has his own feet. He fears no man. "Nothing can hurt me!" But other men fear him. And why? Not at all because he can strike them or take their money or their good names. They fear his judgment…. [T]he acquaintance with Wittgenstein has given me some inkling as to what the power of the prophet was among his people. "Thus saith the Lord" is the token of that being high above all fear and all blandishment, fearless and feared, just and conscience. Thus saith the Lord!

Bouwsma's papers are collected in *Philosophical Essays* (1965), *Toward a New Sensibility,* (1982), *Without Proof or Evidence* (1984), and *Wittgenstein Conversations* (1949–1951). The Humanities Research center in Austin, Texas, has archived Bouwsma's notebooks and class notes.

## Who was **Norman Malcolm**?

Norman Malcolm (1911–1990) was an American interpreter of Ludwig Wittgenstein (1889–1951), perhaps even his leading U.S. advocate. He had met both Wittgenstein and G. E. Moore (1873–1958) during studies at Cambridge University, and described his association with Wittgenstein in *Ludwig Wittgenstein: A Memoir* (1958). O.K. Bouwsma (1898–1978) was also an early influence.

Malcolm discussed Wittgenstein's private language argument in *Wittgenstein's Philosophical Investigations* (1954) and argued that dreams are not genuine experiences in *Dreaming* (1958). In *Memory and Mind* (1976) Malcolm analyzed philosophical and psychological ideas of memory, concluding that there was no scientific foundation for "memory traces." (By "memory trace," it was not clear what earlier thinkers had meant. Anyone can imagine different meanings for such a term, but none of them has objective, observable qualities.) He rather thought that the idea of memory traces was an example of how thought can be falsely "tempted."

## What is the **other minds problem** in philosophy?

To the philosophically innocent, this question sounds ridiculous: "Do other people have minds?" The ordinary answer is something like, "Of course they do!" However, the philosophical problem is the theoretical one of explaining how we know that other people have minds in accord with other philosophical commitments. Thus, an intuitionist might say that we know or feel the mind of another directly. A logical positivist would have to base our knowledge of other minds on what we perceive of the physical behavior of others and justified inferences that we can make based on those perceptions. This approach generates the interesting question of whether it would matter to us if someone close to us turned out to be a robot. Insofar as language usage does not cover interactions with robots that are sophisticated enough to perfectly mimic human behavior, it's difficult to see how an ordinary language approach could solve this problem.

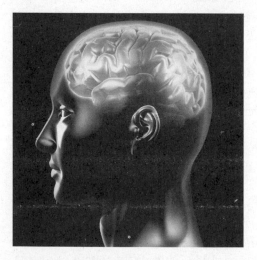

You may think it's obvious that other people have minds just as you do, but for philosophers this notion is not so easily proven (iStock).

## Who was **John Wisdom**?

Arthur John Terrence Dibben Wisdom (1904–1993) was educated at Cambridge University and became a professor there in 1952. His early work was on Jeremy Bentham (1748–1832) and logical atomism, but under Ludwig Wittgenstein's

(1889–1951) influence he began a project of examining different approaches toward philosophical problems. Wisdom's publications in that area include *Other Minds* (1952), *Philosophy and Psychoanalysis* (1953), and *Paradox and Discovery* (1964).

Wisdom discursively reflected on why philosophers say and write "very strange things," and refuted skepticism about the existence of other minds. Wisdom brought the discussion of the "other minds problem" into twentieth century analytic contexts by ruling out the possibility of direct knowledge of other minds and at the same time showing why the claim that our knowledge is restricted to momentary sensations does not hold up. Overall, he argued that philosophers have always relied on the use of language and that there are historical precedents in philosophy for deciding when language gets the main subjects of philosophy right, as well as wrong.

Wisdom thought that the main subjects of philosophy were categories of being in reality and kinds of statements in language. He held that relevant distinctions within these subjects were implicit in language. He is also the author of *Philosophical Papers* (1962).

## Who was **J.L. Austin**?

John Langshaw (J.L.) Austin (1911–1960) was educated in the classics at Oxford and served in military intelligence during World War II. He was appointed White's Professor of Moral Philosophy at Oxford University in 1952, and he also visited at Harvard University and the University of California at Berkeley. Austin did not think that all philosophical problems were the results of confusions about language, but he referred to ordinary speech for important distinctions. In *Sense and Sensibilia* (edited from his lecture notes in 1962), Austin attacked the sense-data theory on the grounds that we do not perceive sense data, but real objects.

Austin is best remembered for his performative theory of certain types of language. For example, saying "I promise," or "I do" in a wedding ceremony, constitutes the actions of promising and marrying someone. While everybody knows such things in common sense, previous theories of language had not attended to this performative function. He further elaborated his theory of speech with the following distinctions among what he called "forces" in speech: *locutionary forces* are associated with meaning, *illocutionary* with intention, and *perlocutionary* with the consequences of saying certain things.

## Who was **H.P. Grice**?

H. Paul Grice (1913–1988) is most famous for his doctrine of *conversational implicature* that he introduced in 1968. This doctrine was developed as a logical thesis about the "if-then" conditional, but its applications to understanding linguistic usage go beyond its original technical purpose. Grice demonstrated that the meanings of words used in sentences, and the sentences themselves, are highly dependent on the context

349

of utterance, as well as certain rules of cooperation in speech. These rules include: be informative, do not be more informative than required, do not state what you know is false, do not state what you have no evidence for, be relevant, do not be obscure, do not be ambiguous, do not use more words than you must, and observe order.

When speakers break one or more of these rules, the result is that what speakers say is not always equivalent to the literal meaning of their words. For example, if a speaker is asked how a play was and responds that the furniture used in the set was very nice, this irrelevance will imply a negative judgment of the play.

Grice developed his speech theory with considerable complexity, and it is of interest to logicians and analysts of language. Grice was thus was able to demonstrate the existence of a lot of linguistic structure—with possibilities for neatly implied alternative meanings in contexts of conversation. This was a huge setback to the confidence of ordinary language analysts that meandering investigations of overlapping linguistic practices could yield stable meanings for certain words. Grice showed that meaning depends on context. But on the other hand, Grice's work emphasizes the complexity of ordinary language as life practices, similar to self contained games, like baseball, but unlike baseball, capable of adding meaning to the most important events in our existence. Grice's writings have been collected and published as *Philosophical Grounds of Rationality* (1986), *Studies in the Ways of Words* (1989), and *Aspects of Reason* (2001).

# ANALYTIC ETHICS

## What is **analytic ethics**?

Analytic ethics is the application of both or either logical positivism and ordinary language analysis to ethics.

## What is the **difference** between **ethics** and **morals**?

Philosophers tend to use the terms interchangeably. In ordinary usage, however, "morals" refers to private behavior, whereas "ethics" refers to public, professional, or civic behavior. Thus, while judgments about a person's morals can be about sexual behavior and drinking habits, judgments about ethics often concern the obligations of people in positions of responsibility, for example, "medical ethics."

## What is the **difference** between a **moral system** and a **moral theory**?

A moral system specifies principles according to which people should act, such as deontological or duty ethics, utilitarianism, or virtue ethics. A moral theory is an account of basic moral terms such as "good" or "evil" and the nature of moral judgments and arguments. Moral theorists may also compare different moral systems.

We all have times when we feel conflict within ourselves. In ordinary life, ethics has to do with how we make good versus bad judgments regarding public behavior, whereas morals deals with this conflict on a personal level (iStock).

## What is **moral conventionalism**?

Ethical or moral conventionalism is the view that what makes something good or an action right is a general cultural belief. Ethical conventionalism has descriptive and prescriptive forms. Prescriptive conventionalism says that we ought to follow conventions; descriptive conventionalism says that we do follow conventions.

## What is **ethical (or moral) relativism**?

There are two kinds: descriptive moral relativism is the view that different cultures have different moral beliefs; prescriptive or normative moral relativism is the view that the whole of what's right is what people in a given society think is right. The result of this view is that moral disagreement can't be rationally debated.

## How do **philosophers deal** with **ethical relativism**?

Philosophers intensely dislike prescriptive ethical relativism. It makes the analysis of moral terms and the construction of moral systems pointless because there is no way to justify them. Different positions have been taken about descriptive moral relativism. Some philosophers deny it, claiming that once we understand moral systems that seem to be different from our own, we can derive universal moral principles from all moral systems that apply to all human beings. Others have argued that even

351

though there are different viewpoints about what is morally right, some of those viewpoints are simply wrong, and then their job is to show how they are wrong.

## What was G.E. **Moore's naturalistic fallacy**?

Moore (1873–1958) contended that goodness cannot be analyzed in terms of any other property. In his *Principia Ethica* (1903) he wrote:

> It may be true that all things which are good are also something else, just as it is true that all things which are yellow produce a certain kind of vibration in the light. And it is a fact, that Ethics aims at discovering what are those other properties belonging to all things which are good. But far too many philosophers have thought that when they named those other properties they were actually defining good.

Moore thought that we know what is good directly, just as we know the color yellow when we see it. Thus, "We can only point to an action or a thing and say 'That is good.' We cannot describe to a blind man exactly what yellow is. We can only show a sighted man a piece of yellow paper or a yellow scrap of cloth and say 'That is yellow.'" The same is true of what is good. Whenever what is good is defined in terms of some "natural" property, such as "resulting in the good for the greatest number," the naturalistic fallacy has been committed because it is always possible to ask of something that has the natural property, "Yes, but is it good?"

Moore's notion of the non-reducible nature of goodness became for a while a concept and standard for other ethicists to both refute and match in rigor.

## What was the **emotivist theory** of ethics?

According to the logical positivists, statements had meaning only if it could be said what would verify or falsify them, in terms of descriptions of sensory experience. Because both moral and aesthetic statements could not meet this test, they were considered not to have empirical meaning but to be expressive of how the person uttering them felt. So, to say, "This is right," would be equal to saying, "I like this."

The novelist and feminist essayist Virginia Woolf was part of the Bloomsbury group (AP).

## What was the Bloomsbury group?

The Bloomsbury group was a loose group of friends, the men of which were Cambridge graduates. They met in the evenings for drink and talk at the house of author Virginia Woolf's sister, Vanessa Bell. (The house was in the Bloomsbury district of London, and hence this name.) Its initial members, before 1910, were: the novelists E.M. Forster, Mary MacCarthy, and Virginia Woolf; economist John Maynard Keynes; the novelist, biographer, and critic Lytton Strachey; and the painters Duncan Grant, Vanessa Bell, and Roger Fry. All were close or intimate friends long before they individually became famous.

G.E. Moore (1873–1958) served as an intellectual ideal and mentor to the group. He was particularly revered by the others for his *Principia Ethica* (1903), and the model of clarity he provided for all intellectual work. Above all, the Bloomsbury members were inspired by Moore's idea that art and friendship have intrinsic value—they're good in themselves and serve no "higher purpose."

A.J. Ayer (1910–1989) put forth this view in *Language, Truth and Logic* (1936). A more comprehensive account was given by Charles L. Stevenson (1908–1979) in *Ethics and Language* (1944). Stevenson argued that moral judgments do not have cognitive meaning, but rather emotive meaning. He meant that moral judgments are not factual in nature, but are rather emotional reactions to facts, which are sometimes meant to influence others. If the facts or other circumstances changed, so could the moral judgment.

## What is **ethical subjectivism**?

Ethical subjectivism is either the same as ethical emotivism, or the view that ethical judgments express our shared emotions, or else it refers to an individual's private moral views as the meaning of morality, so that in principle there could be as many moral systems as there are individuals.

## How were **virtue ethics rediscovered** in **analytic philosophy**?

Aristotelian virtue ethics, mainly as expressed in Aristotle's (384–322 B.C.E.) *Nicomachean Ethics*, were revisited in analytic philosophy to create rationalist moral systems. According to Aristotle, we develop our individual virtues through a rational process of deliberating and then choosing what to do in action. The revival of Aristotelian ethics was sometimes pursued in opposition to other prominent moral systems and moral theories. Philippa Foot (1920–) and Alasdair MacIntyre (1929–) are noteworthy twentieth century virtue ethicists.

## What was **Philippa Foot's contribution** to **virtue ethics**?

Phillippa Ruth Foot (1920–), who is the granddaughter of U.S. President Grover Cleveland, opposes subjectivism or emotivism in ethics and insists on a connection between morality and rationality. She has tried to undermine a fact/value divide in claiming that moral judgments are determined by facts about our lives and nature. In this sense, she is a "moral naturalist." Moral naturalism is the view that what is morally good is not some distinct and special quality but ordinary things and actions that have been rationally chosen as best in a particular set of circumstances.

Overall, Foot has consistently supported virtues as conducive to self-interest. Her main publications are *Virtues and Vices and Other Essays in Moral Philosophy* (1978), *Natural Goodness* (2001), and *Moral Dilemmas: And Other Topics in Moral Philosophy* (2002).

## What is **ethical naturalism**?

Ethical naturalism holds that goodness is a natural property and that morality can be understood without intuitions, conscience, or religion.

## What was **Alasdair MacIntyre's contribution** to **virtue ethics**?

Alasdair MacIntyre (1929–) has approached ethics with a rejection of both Marxism and late-twentieth century consumer capitalism. In his return to Thomistic Aristotelianism, or Aristotelianism influenced by the altruistic and religious values of Christianity, he considers the nature of moral argument about competing systems and has reclaimed Edith Stein (1891–1942) as a phenomenologist.

MacIntyre views virtues as moral qualities needed to fulfill human potential. He has focused on the combination of practice, virtue, and tradition: practice is communal action; virtue is the individual dispositions and habits that are necessary to participate in practice; tradition is the history of a community as an object of reflection. MacIntyre thus thinks that virtues develop and are practiced in communities and that moral communities must be understood in terms of their history.

MacIntyre's view is not intended to be conservative in a social or political sense, but is instead developed as an understanding of Aristotelian virtues that would not have been possible without the fact of all the history that has ensued since Aristotle wrote. MacIntyre's main works on this subject include *After Virtue* (1981), *Whose Justice, Whose Rationality?* (1988), and *Three Rival Versions of Moral Inquiry* (1990).

## Who was **Ayn Rand**?

Ayn Rand (1905–1982) was a Russian-born American novelist who reacted strongly against communist and socialist political ideals, as well as Christian virtues of altruism. She is most famous for extolling "the virtue of selfishness" in both her novels and her philosophy of objectivism. Her most popular novels are *We the Living* (1936), *The Fountainhead* (1943), and *Atlas Shrugged* (1957).

### What was Ayn **Rand's virtue of selfishness**?

Rand believed that the highest human good was individual happiness, which is achieved through rationality. Every individual has an elevated duty to further his or her own self-interest, and others do not have a right to demand that one sacrifice oneself or one's interests simply because they are weaker or in need. In this sense, Rand was an "ethical egoist."

In novels like *Atlas Shrugged* author Ayn Rand put forth her ideas that people should selfishly pursue their own happiness (AP).

### What is **ethical egoism**?

Ethical egoism is the moral system that everyone ought to pursue his or her own self-interest above all other goals. As with ethical relativism, it has both a descriptive and prescriptive form. Descriptive ethical egoism holds that everyone always pursues their own self-interest; prescriptive ethical egoism holds that everyone should always pursue his or her own self-interest. Insofar as she thought that communism and socialism were evil and widespread, Ayn Rand (1905–1982) was not a descriptive ethical egoist, although she was clearly a prescriptive ethical egoist.

### What was Ayn **Rand's** philosophy of **objectivism**?

Most professional philosophers refer to Rand's (1905–1982) objectivism as a "so-called philosophy." Rand claimed to have taught herself the history of Western philosophy in a matter of months, which left her a passionate follower of Aristotle (384–322 B.C.E.). She believed that Aristotle's law of identity, or "A is A," is a metaphysical principle on which can be based the existence of an objective world that is knowable through reason. Rand remains popular on many contemporary college campuses, although more for her novels and doctrine of selfishness than for her metaphysics. (Most professional philosophers before and after Rand have held "A Is A" to be a tautology, telling us nothing about the world, be it objective or otherwise.)

### What is **consequentialism**?

Consequentialism is the twentieth century version of nineteenth century utilitarianism. The utilitarian moral system held that we should act so that the greatest pleasure or happiness for the greatest number results, with everyone counting for one and no one counting for more than one. G.E. Moore's (1873–1958) ideal utilitarianism specified that the goods we should seek as the result of our actions are aesthetic experiences and relations of friendship.

Consequentialism is a more general form of utilitarianism that holds that we should act so as to bring about the best consequences, or act to maximize the results. Contemporary consequentialists often speak of "preference-satisfaction" as the ultimate consequence that has intrinsic value. (Preference satisfaction is getting what one wants.) There is also discussion about the distribution of consequences, whether it is better that all involved get equal shares or whether it is sufficient if the total good or average good is increased.

*Act consequentialism* specifies that we should do the action that has the best consequences, and *rule consequentialism* specifies that we should do the action that is an instance of the rule that has the best consequences.

All of these issues and others have been discussed in J.J.C. Smart (1920–) and Bernard Williams' (1929–2003) *Utilitarianism: For and Against* (1973) and Samuel Scheffler's (1951–) *The Rejection of Consequentialism* (1994). There have also been attempts to relate consequentialism to ordinary language philosophy, most notably by R. Hare (1919–2002).

## Who was **R. Hare**?

Richard Mervyn Hare (1919–2002) was a professor of moral philosophy at Oxford University, and he later taught at the University of Florida. In his *The Language of Morals* (1992) he argued for the prescriptive nature of moral judgments and their "universalizability," or ability to be generalized.

In *Freedom and Reason* (1963) and *Moral Thinking, Its Levels, Method, and Point* (1981), Hare held that ethical concepts are used according to logical rules that support the truth of utilitarianism. The utilitarianism propounded by Hare was "two-tier," providing for both act utilitarianism and rule utilitarianism. Act utilitarianism requires that we do singular actions that will result in the best consequences, whereas rule utilitarianism requires that we follow rules that will result in the best consequences.

## Have some philosophers **criticized consequentialism**?

Elizabeth Anscombe (1910–2001) in a 1958 article, "Modern Moral Philosophy," coined the term "consequentialism" when she criticized twentieth century versions of utilitarianism that did not distinguish between intended and unintended consequences. Anscombe argued that only intended consequences have moral value.

Anscombe is also famous for her defense of Thomas Aquinas' (c. 1225–1274) doctrine of double effect (DDE). According to DDE, an action is morally permissible if it

## What is applied ethics?

**A**pplied ethics is the study of existing ethical principles in practical fields of human endeavor, such as medicine, engineering, business, law, and environmentalism. Applied ethics also extends to new moral rules for new situations, such as the rights of airline passengers and disaster victims, moral issues involved in human cloning, and consumer protection. In this sense, applied ethics is practical ethics—it is a study of ethics of practice.

In addition, applied ethics can be more critical as it applies theoretical moral systems and moral theories to practices and fields outside of philosophy. Existing rules and behavior in a given field may be theoretically justified or criticized by philosophical ethicists. In some cases, new moral directions may emerge. Environmental ethics is a good example of the theoretical dimension of applied ethics.

has known bad consequences but it is not the intention or goal of the person performing the action to bring about those consequences. In Jesuit moral reasoning about performing craniotomies (operations to crush a baby's skull so that the baby can be extracted to save its mother's life), DDE has been used. If it is not the obstetrician's goal to kill the baby but merely to extract it, craniotomies are deemed permissible.

Anscombe provided this example: say she meets her mortal enemy on a cliff. If her enemy falls off because she accidentally falls against him, she is blameless, even though the unintended effect of the enemy's death is welcome to her (after the fact).

Others have criticized the ways in which consequentialism seems to ignore issues of justice in cases where an unjust act or even a human sacrifice might serve to maximize benefits for others.

## How have **consequentialists responded** to **criticism**?

Some consequentialists, such as philosophy professor and author Kai Neilsen (1926–), have simply bitten the bullet and asserted that whatever saves the most lives is good. Neilson is famous for his 1972 article in *Ethics,* "In Defense of Utilitarianism," which provides the example of a fat man wedged in a cave; the waters are rising and his companions are trapped behind him. Nielsen asserts that if the fat man were humanely dispatched by an exploding stick of dynamite (conveniently on the scene) there is no violation of morality.

Consequentialists have responded to the criticism of being unjust by claiming that rule consequentialism can allow for justice because a just rule will result in better consequences, and in the long run unjust behavior will fail to improve people's lives. For example, in an immediate situation a doctor might sacrifice a healthy patient so that six others who need organ transplants may live. But the rule followed in the sacrifice of the healthy patient would undermine confidence in doctors, and in the long term more harm than good would result from killing the healthy patient.

Others have pointed out the obvious problem of calculating consequences in the future. Another strong objection to consequentialism, voiced by Bernard Williams (1919–2003), is that the focus on results with everyone counting the same undermines the integrity of an agent by ignoring the importance of personal projects to that agent. In a famous example, Williams imagines that a traveler is asked to kill one Indian to save nine more from being shot. He argues that the consequentialist approach violates the importance to the traveler of his own moral identity as someone who does not kill others.

# ANALYTIC POLITICAL PHILOSOPHY

### What is **distinctive** about **analytical political philosophy**?

Twentieth century analytic political philosophers have for the most part supported liberal and egalitarian values, and they have done so in formal writing that is in itself apolitical.

### Who was **Isaiah Berlin**?

Isaiah Berlin (1909–1997) was renowned for his work on ideals of liberty in democratic societies. He was born in Latvia and educated at Oxford. He was president of Wolfson College, Oxford, from 1966 to 1975. He is famous for his distinction between "positive" and "negative liberty" and his criticism of Marxist ideas of history. Berlin was a brilliant and elegant speaker and delivered lectures on the British Broadcasting Corporation, often without notes. Berlin's major works include *Historical Inevitability, Two Concepts of Liberty* (1959), *Four Essays on Liberty* (1969), *Russian Thinkers* (1978), *Against the Current: Essays in the History of Ideas* (1979), *Personal Impressions* (1980), *The Crooked Timber of Humanity: Chapters in the History of Ideas* (1990), and *The Sense of Reality: Studies in Ideas and Their History* (1996).

### What were Isaiah **Berlin's two concepts** of **liberty**?

Berlin developed the distinction in his 1958 inaugural address as Chichele Professor of Social and Political Theory at Oxford University. Negative liberty is the absence of constraints or interference with individual action, as in a person being free to vote, write a book, or study ballroom dancing. Positive liberty is the human capacity for self-development and determination of one's destiny. For example, some people live in countries without negative liberties, which in turn hampers their positive liberty.

Others with positive liberties may not be able to fully exercise them due to economic or social limitations.

Berlin argued that, largely due to the Romantic and German idealist tradition, political theorists had been preoccupied with positive liberties as effects of particular forms of government. He believed that the idea of positive liberty was co-opted by both German national socialism and communism. In the case of communism, the goal of liberty became identical to the goal of state control in the name of "collective rationality." For the Nazis, it was the destiny of Germany and its "master race" that became an overriding value affecting individual lives.

Isaiah Berlin was famous for his work on ideals of liberty in democratic societies (AP).

Berlin was an advocate of negative liberty in the tradition of John Stuart Mill (1806–1873), which emphasized the importance of minimal government constraint. In other words, he did not think government was a viable source of values or projects for individual life plans because when government did assume that function it was likely to become totalitarian and repressive.

### How did Isaiah **Berlin oppose Marxist historicism**?

Berlin did not think that impersonal or absolute forces could determine history, apart from the free will of "exceptional individuals." He wrote in "Does Political Theory Still Exist?":

> It is seldom … that there is only one model that determines our thought; men (or cultures) obsessed at their models are rare, and while they may be more coherent at their strongest, they tend to collapse more violently when, in the end, their concepts are blown up by reality.

By the same token, Berlin was not enthusiastic about harmony or agreement in political life. He believed that well-intentioned individuals could hold opposing values, resulting in inevitable moral conflict: "These collisions of values are of the essence of what they are and what we are."

### Who was **Karl Popper**?

Sir Karl Raimund Popper (1902–1994) is well known for his insistence that it be necessary to be able to say what would make scientific claims false. He was born in Austria and grew up near Ludwig Wittgenstein (1889–1951) in Vienna, Austria, but not under wealthy circumstances. He had to leave Germany in the late 1930s, and after teaching in New Zealand he was a professor at the London School of Economics. Popper is as famous for his philosophy of science as for his political thought, which he developed in *The Open Society and Its Enemies* (1945, fifth revised edition, 1965).

## What was Karl **Popper's notion** of the **open society**?

Beginning with a criticism of Plato (c. 428–c. 348 B.C.E.) and Karl Marx (1818–1883), Popper argued that Plato's philosopher-kings represented an unattainable ideal of human wisdom and that Marx was mistaken in believing that human history has a moral dimension. Popper reasoned that rulers are always fallible human beings. Furthermore, Popper rejected "historicism," or the view that history is determined by group actions, and "holism," or the view that only groups are causal agents in society. He did not think that the social sciences had evidence for either the existence of impersonal forces in history or the view that anything other than individuals could make things happen.

Popper did not think it was possible for rulers to predict the consequences of their actions and policies. His grounds for this were the philosophical impossibility of anyone being able to predict the future. In an open society, policies should therefore be undertaken as hypotheses that are open to being proved false. Because rulers were capable of fooling themselves and others about the success of their policies, it should be left up to the people to evaluate whether a program was successful. And if it were assessed unsuccessful, then another program should be instigated, subject to the same corrections. Popper believed that if societies were not "open" in this way, then totalitarianism and repression of individual liberties would ensue.

## Who was **John Rawls**?

John Rawls (1921–2002) was educated at Princeton University and taught at Princeton, the Massachusetts Institute of Technology, Cornell University, and Harvard University. He is credited with almost single-handedly reviving Anglo-American political philosophy in his *A Theory of Justice* (1971). Relying on both Kantian morality and the basic principles of consent by those governed from social contract theory, Rawls outlined a model for a just society. His additional publications include *Political Liberalism* (1993), *The Law of Peoples* (1999), *Collected Papers* (2000), and *Essays in the History of Philosophy* (2001).

## What was John **Rawls' theory** of **justice**?

Rawls (1921–2002) began by positing justice as the cardinal virtue of society. All societies value the concept of justice in a primary sense, although they have different

## Did John Rawls believe in complete equality?

**N**o, Rawls (1921–2002) was not an advocate of total "distributive justice" or the ideal that all members of society should receive equal amounts of everything. But he applied the standard of fairness to inequalities through his "difference principle:" inequalities must "be of the greatest benefit to the least-advantaged members of society."

"conceptions of justice." Rawls' conception of justice was that it can be understood as fairness. On that model he proposed that a society would be just if its fundamental institutions were just, which would entail equal access to official positions. As a way of determining how fundamental institutions could be just, Rawls proposed a thought experiment that posited an "original position."

In the original position, the framers of just institutions would do their work behind a "veil of ignorance." This veil of ignorance would prevent them from knowing their own positions or interests in the society whose institutions they were framing. Rawls wrote:

> No one knows his place in society, his class position or social status, nor does anyone know his fortune in the distribution of natural assets and abilities, his intelligence, strength, and the like. I shall even assume that the parties do not know their conceptions of the good or their special psychological propensities. The principles of justice are chosen behind a veil of ignorance.

Rawls' thought experiment guarantees a hypothetical condition of disinterestedness on the part of original framers. This posits them as Kantian rational agents, who because they are autonomous or self-ruling, can and should make choices about what is most important in their lives. That they do not know their personal interests but nonetheless frame institutions that will affect everyone's personal interests is fair in the same way as having one child cut a piece of cake and the second child choose the piece she wants. The premise that individuals with interests in society consent to the basic institutions echoes the necessity for the consent of those governed in social contract theory.

Social contract theory is also based on the premise that government must justify itself as beneficial to those governed. Rawls' original position promises a test of even greater benefits than allowed by original social contract theorists, such as John Locke (1632–1704), who assumed that only property owners would be represented in government. Rawls' model permits us to ask whether anyone in society who could be represented behind the veil of ignorance would choose a given state of state of affairs. If not, then that state of affairs is not just or fair.

361

## Who was **Robert Nozick**?

Robert Nozick (1938–2002) is considered important for his idea of minimal government. He was educated at Columbia, Princeton, and Oxford universities and became a philosophy professor at Pellegrino University and Harvard. His most influential work was *Anarchy, State, and Utopia* (1974), which was written in response to John Rawls' (1921–2002) *A Theory of Justice* (1971). Additional books by Nozick include *Socratic Puzzles* (1997), *The Nature of Rationality* (1993), and *The Examined Life* (1989).

## What was Robert **Nozick's response** to John **Rawls**?

First, Nozick (1938–2002) held that rights were inviolable. Second, he argued that a minimal state could develop without violating rights, but that a Rawlsian state could not because of the difference principle. Nozick argued that any state based on the principle of helping the disadvantaged required the violation of property rights where property had been acquired through free exchange.

## What was Robert **Nozick's** own **political theory**?

Nozick (1938–2002) held that any form of distribution is just if those involved are entitled to what they own. Entitlements concern acquisition and transfer of property, as well as the rectification of prior wrongs and errors.

He favored a minimal state that served a policing function and defended strong private property rights for its citizens. Although when analyzing John Locke's (1632–1704) idea that private property is based on mixing labor with something, he posed this question:

> Why does mixing one's labor with something make one the owner of it.... If I own a can of tomato juice and spill it in the sea ... do I thereby own the sea, or have I foolishly dissipated my tomato juice?

Nozick resolved this puzzle by moving from a metaphysical ground to a utilitarian one, the same way Locke did. We are entitled to what we mix our labor with because the added labor increases the value of the original material.

### What does the Locke-Nozick solution leave out?

It doesn't account for how we can come to own both the parts of something we have mixed our labor with and the parts we haven't. How is it possible that in owning property—which first became a commodity because someone improved it—one comes to own the mineral rights to that property? Also, how do we decide when something is too big to mix our labor with, so that we cannot, as in Nozick's ocean example, come to own all of it?

# Who was **Leo Strauss**?

Leo Strauss (1899–1973) is important for his work relating philosophical texts to politics in real life. He was a German-born American philosopher who left a position at the Academy of Jewish Research in Berlin, Germany, to study in Paris, France, on a Rockefeller Fellowship in 1932. Because, as a Jew, it was unsafe for him to return to Germany when the Nazis came to power, he taught at Cambridge University and in New York, until he became professor of political science at the University of Chicago in 1949, remaining there until 1969.

Strauss taught classical political philosophy. His work became inspirational to American neoconservatives after his death. His students and purported followers in real-world politics during the administration of President George W. Bush included Deputy Secretary of Defense Paul Wolfowitz, and Abram Shulsky, who headed the Pentagon's Office of Special Plans. The political writer William Kristol was also a student, but so were the liberal social critic Susan Sontag and the apolitical literary critic Alan Bloom.

Strauss' principle publications include *The Political Philosophy of Hobbes* (1935; reprinted, 1952), *Persecution and the Art of Writing* (1952), *Natural Right and History* (1953), *Thoughts on Machiavelli* (1958), *The City and Man* (1964), *Political Philosophy: Six Essays by Leo Strauss* (1975), and *Socrates and Aristophanes* (1980).

# What were Leo **Strauss'** main **politically relevant** ideas?

Strauss (1899–1973) was mainly a classical political theorist. He believed that an important connection between real-life politics and philosophy began with Socrates' (460–399 B.C.E.) trial and conviction. He argued that, since Socrates, philosophers had hidden their meanings to escape political persecution. Strauss developed a theory of reading as a way for independent thinkers to uncover the true intentions behind necessarily obscure texts.

Strauss did not believe that the social science distinction between facts and values was fundamental. This distinction held that statements about what should be the case cannot be logically deduced from statements about what is the case. He held that politics could not be studied without prior values. Strauss thought that human excellence and political virtue had been neglected as a result of the importance placed on individual freedom in modern liberalism. Because liberalism as a doctrine led to relativism, it could be subject to two kinds of nihilism: a "brutal" nihilism, as in Nazi Germany or communist Russia, which erased existing foundations of society to enshrine new ideals; or a "gentle" nihilism that led to "permissive egalitarianism," as in American culture.

Strauss apparently endorsed "noble lies" as a political means for correcting contemporary abuses, according to new political philosophy based on the esoteric readings of classical texts. (A "noble lie" is a lie told to people who will benefit from believing it.) However, he himself had no clear solutions to tensions between reason and religion, or modern versus ancient political philosophy.

363

# EPISTEMOLOGY AND METAPHYSICS
# AFTER LOGICAL POSITIVISM

## What was new in **metaphysics** and **epistemology after logical positivism**?

Metaphysics and epistemology made a new empirical start that was thoroughly informed by science. P.F. Strawson (1919–2006) defended a common sense metaphysics, and, like Wilfred Sellars (1912–1989), he developed the idea of a common perspective that was opposed to science. Strawson did much to reclaim for philosophy a common sense approach to the world, which the logical positivists would have thought was meaningless, because it was not about science. Nelson Goodman (1906–1998) resurrected the perennial problem of induction—reasoning that begins with experience and builds toward knowledge. W.V.O. Quine (1908–2000) uniquely redirected the course of twentieth century philosophy by combining pragmatist insights with a rigorous philosophical method. Also, perhaps partly as a result of Quine's work, Hilary Putnam (1926–) reinterpreted pragmatist epistemology by applying its insights to questions of truth in the sciences.

## Who was **P.F. Strawson**?

Sir Peter Frederick (P.F.) Strawson (1919–2006) was educated at Oxford University, where he became a professor in 1968. He disagreed with Bertrand Russell's (1872–1970) theory of definite descriptions because the statement "The king of France is bald" presupposes the truth of "There exists a king of France." This created problems because if there is no king of France then "The king of France is bald," is neither true nor false, or it is not a statement.

Although Strawson was strongly influenced by ordinary language philosophy, he was less interested in linguistic usage than in implied conceptual systems and categories of existence in ordinary reality. In *The Bounds of Sense* (1966) he argues for a "manifest image," or common (shared) way of understanding the world.

## Who was **Wilfred Sellars**?

Wilfred Sellars' (1912–1989) goal of combining analytic philosophy with logical positivism, resulted in his founding the journal *Philosophical Studies*. Educated at Michigan and Harvard universities, he spent his professional life after 1963 at the University of Pittsburgh. His work centered on the problems of reconciling the scientific world view with our ordinary conception of ourselves as having minds and intentions in a world with meanings, sounds, and colors. Sellars developed his resolution in a union of empiricism and philosophy of mind, which introduced the philosophy of "functionalism." His main books include *Science, Perception and Reality* (1963), *Philosophical Perspectives* (1967), and *Essays in Philosophy and Its History* (1974).

## Who was **Nelson Goodman**?

Nelson Goodman (1906–1998) criticized the idea that similarity existed in the world independently of our linguistic inclinations. Goodman was educated at Harvard, was an art dealer in Boston from 1929 to 1941, and became a Harvard professor in 1968. In his *The Structure of Appearance* (1951) he developed Rudolf Carnap's (1891–1970) insights about the logical structure of the world. Later, he came to the conclusion that there are many different world structures, depending on the perspectives of observers. In *Fact, Fiction and Forecast* (1954) Goodman extended his argument that structure in nature depends on our interests with his famous "grue" example.

## What is **grue**?

Nelson Goodman (1906–1998) supposed that all emeralds before time T, which is the present, are green. But if this is true, then "G" is also true: "Emeralds before time T are green or emeralds after time T are blue." The reason it is true that emeralds after time T are either green or blue is that the time after time T is the future and we do not know what the future will hold for emeralds—or for anything else.

G defines the predicate "grue" (a term Goodman made up) as a quality of emeralds: All of the emeralds that qualify as "grue" could be blue after time T. Nevertheless, Goodman maintained that we would prefer to call them "blue" after time T. He believed this showed that confirmation cannot be a purely logical or syntactic process, but that it reflects our linguistic preferences, which go beyond what we actually know.

## W.V.O. QUINE

## Who was **W.V.O. Quine**?

W.V.O. (Willard Van Orman) Quine (1908–2000) represents the apogee of twentieth century scientific philosophy; in many ways he combined the best of logical positivism, pragmatism, and scientific empiricism. He was born in Akron, Ohio, and studied at Oberlin College and then Harvard. He earned his Ph.D. in 1932 and then became a Harvard Fellow. This allowed four years for research and travel before beginning his 50-year Harvard teaching career in 1936.

Scientific philosopher W.V.O. Quine believed: "To be is to be the value of a variable." (AP)

His influence is considered monumental, and he has been highly regarded, even revered, as a person. Quine's main books are *Word and Object* (1964), *The Ways of Paradox, and Other Essays* (1976), *Ontological Relativity* (1977), *From a Logical Point of View: Nine Logico-Philosophical Essays* (1980), *From Stimulus to Science* (1998), *Theories and Things* (1986), *Pursuit of Truth* (1992), and *Quiddities: An Intermittently Philosophical Dictionary* (1989).

## What were W.V.O. **Quine's** most **influential ideas**?

Quine did not think that the "analytic-synthetic distinction" could be defended, because he did not think that "analytic" could be defined in a non-circular way. He had a holistic view of knowledge, likening the whole of all of our theories to a "web." He believed that assertions of existence were relative to specific theories, and he thought that philosophical epistemology should be "naturalized." By this he meant that philosophical epistemology should be consistent with standards for scientific truth.

## What was W.V.O. **Quine's attack** on the **analytic-synthetic distinction**?

In "Two Dogmas of Empiricism," published in the journal *The Philosophical Review* (1951), Quine began with the accepted view that analytic statements are true based only on the meaning of the words they contain. There is nothing in the world that can affect the truth of an analytic statement. Synthetic statements are factual claims about the world. Quine then showed how it is impossible to define analyticity without a prior notion of sameness of meaning that itself presupposes analyticity. What this means is that unless you already know what "analytic" means you will not understand any definition of it, or that "analytic" cannot be defined without circularity.

If we do not know what analyticity is, there is a strong implication that for all practical purposes all of our beliefs are in some sense synthetic and subject to revision based on experience. The second dogma of empiricism that Quine attacked in the same article was the prevailing view that statements in a theory all face reality one by one. Quine claimed that all of the statements face reality together. Here, Quine meant that a whole theory or account of the world gets confirmed at once, rather than parts of the theory being confirmed separately.

## Did W.V.O. Quine practice what he preached about philosophical relevance?

No, and many have been grateful for this. As a philosopher, Quine has been criticized for his "ivory tower" view of the field and his claim that philosophers are not particularly qualified for "helping to get society on an even keel." However, in real life, Quine was very involved in resisting Nazism. After he visited Germany as a Harvard fellow in the 1930s and met the logical positivists of the Vienna Circle, he reacted against the Nazis' incursions into philosophy (one of which was an avowedly racist mathematical journal, *Deutsche Mathematik*) by volunteering for the U.S. Navy. After he returned to teaching at Harvard, he organized symposia and talks for members of the Vienna Circle from 1938 to 1941, particularly for Rudolf Carnap (1891–1970), although Carnap was later hired by the University of Chicago. Quine also helped Alfred Tarski (1902–1983) gain employment at City College in New York.

## What was W.V.O. Quine's view of existence?

He is famous for claiming: "To be is to be the value of a variable." He meant by this that we should be committed to the existence of only those entities that need to be posited in order to understand and apply scientific theories. He wrote:

> For my part I do, *qua lay* [amateur] physicist, believe in physical objects and not in Homer's gods; and I consider it a scientific error to believe otherwise. But in point of epistemological footing, the physical objects and the gods differ only in degree and not in kind. Both sorts of entities enter our conceptions only as cultural posits.

## How did W.V.O. Quine naturalize epistemology?

He did not think that knowledge could have a foundation apart from science, and that instead of philosophical epistemology there should be a scientific explanation of how we construct our web of knowledge and why and how that web is successful.

Quine had a flexible view of knowledge and thought that theoretical terms did not have definite or fixed meanings, that translation was "indeterminate," and that it was unclear how words referred to objects.

## What was W.V.O. Quine's holistic view of knowledge?

Quine's holistic view was his positive account of knowledge after he attacked the second dogma of experience, that single statements or parts of a theory can be confirmed

367

independently of each other. Quine thought that all of our scientific and lay theories were interconnected with the most general and abstract truths—for example, the truths of arithmetic—in the center of a web. Toward the periphery of this web were more specific generalizations and factual claims that were easier to give up in the face of an experience that contradicted them. It is this aspect of Quine's thought that places him in the tradition of pragmatism.

# HILARY PUTMAN

## Who was **Hilary Putnam**?

Hilary Putnam's (1926–) extraordinarily productive career has encompassed metaphysics, epistemology, philosophy of mathematics, philosophy of mind, and philosophy of language. He began to flourish in the philosophical generation after W.V.O. Quine (1908–2000), becoming a professor at Harvard in 1965. He collaborated with Quine on the ontology of mathematical entities and agreed with him about the analytic-synthetic distinction. In collaboration with his wife, Ruth Anna Jacobs, he helped revive late-twentieth century interest in the work of John Dewey (1859–1952). Putnam has also revived interest in William James' (1842–1910) work.

Putnam's major publications include *Mathematics, Matter and Method, Philosophical Papers,* vol. 1. (1975), 2nd ed. (1985); *Mind, Language and Reality, Philosophical Papers,* vol. 2 (1975); *Meaning and the Moral Sciences* (1978); *Reason, Truth, and History* (1981); *Realism and Reason, Philosophical Papers,* vol. 3 (1983); *The Many Faces of Realism* (1987); *Representation and Reality* (1988); *Renewing Philosophy* (1992); and *Pragmatism: An Open Question* (1995).

## How did Hilary **Putnam agree** with W.V.O. **Quine** on the **analytic-synthetic distinction**?

In 1957 Putnam published the article "The Analytic and the Synthetic," in the anthology *Minnesota Studies in the Philosophy of Science,* edited by H. Feigl and G. Maxwell

(1962), in which he showed how the history of the definitions of kinetic energy made it impossible to divide statements about kinetic energy into "analytic" and "empirical," or synthetic ones.

## What was Hilary **Putnam's neo-pragmatism**?

In the 1970s he began to regret the lack of historical knowledge in analytic philosophy. He applied Ludwig Wittgenstein's (1889–1951) notion of ordinary language to advocate for pluralism within philosophy. He lost confidence in the ability of philosophers to describe the world better than ordinary language users. Given his increased interest in the social sciences, particularly economics, he rejected the fact/value dichotomy. Putnam argued that scientists were not as "objective" or free of value concerns as they presented themselves to be, and that value judgments can be objective.

# PHILOSOPHY OF SCIENCE

## What happened in **analytic philosophy** of **science** over the course of the **twentieth century**?

The twentieth century was an extraordinary period of conceptual upheaval in how science was regarded. There was a rejection of hard-core logical positivism, beginning with Hans Reichenbach (1891–1953). Just as metaphysics and epistemology drew closer to the actual sciences, philosophy of science itself began to look more humanistic as traditional inductive confidence in objective facts was first dislodged by Karl Popper (1902–1994). Thomas S. Kuhn (1922–1996) then inverted the relationship between facts and theories with his notion of a paradigm and scientific revolutions.

Over the same time period, any lingering hopes in "vitalism" or some non-objective life force were put to rest by James D. Watson and Francis Crick's discovery of the double helix structure of DNA. However, the mapping of the human genome at the turn of the twenty-first century did provoke more nuanced views on biological determinism, opening the possibility of a new philosophy of science of biology.

## Who was **Hans Reichenbach**?

Hans Reichenbach (1891–1953) was the leader of "logical empiricism." He was born in Hamburg and studied mathematics, physics, logic, and philosophy. He became a professor of philosophy of science at the University of Berlin and was a close associate of Albert Einstein. He founded *Erkenntnis* with Rudolf Carnap (1891–1970), which was the premier journal of scientific philosophy in the 1930s.

As with thousands of other Jews at the time, Reichenbach had to leave Germany in 1933. He first went to Istanbul before settling down at the University of California at Los Angeles. His main works include *Experience and Prediction* (1938), *The Theory of Probability* (1939–1949), and the posthumous *The Direction of Time* (1956).

## What was **Reichenbach's** theory of **logical empiricism**?

Reichenbach disagreed with the logical atomists and logical positivists, who felt that objects of scientific study could be described as if they were made up of sense data. His own realist view became known as *physicalism*. He argued on pragmatic grounds for a probabilistic interpretation of induction, so that induction could be expressed in terms of probabilities of future events based on the occurrence of these events in the past.

Reichenbach also developed a triple-valued logic in which statements could be true, false, or indeterminate, for quantum theory. He added the option of "indeterminate" to "true" and "false." Quantum theory specifies that some events could not be determined even though their causes were known, so it was important to add indeterminacy to a system of formal logical notation. Although much of his work is highly technical, his *The Rise of Scientific Philosophy* (1951) is a clear and somewhat generalist account of his perspective.

## How did **ideas about life change** when it came to the **philosophy of science**?

Many notions of a mysterious "vitalism," or "life force," at the heart of the reproduction of living beings were exchanged for materialist (physical) accounts after James Watson and Francis Crick discovered the double helix in 1953. Watson and Crick's discovery of the structure of DNA took the mystery out of the idea of life because it could account for the reproduction of genetic material in purely chemical terms. The double helix was a three-dimensional model of the twisted-ladder structure of deoxyribonucleic acid (DNA), which showed how sequences of acids and bases would replicate themselves through chemical reactions. Watson and Crick's discovery paved the way for gene-based studies in heredity, culminating in the "mapping" of the human genome (totality of genes) by the early twenty-first century.

## Has **science removed** all of the **mystery of life**?

Not exactly. The radical materialist idea that organisms are "computations" of their genes and environmental conditions has had critics, most notably Richard Lewontin (1929–) in his *Biology as Ideology: The Doctrine of DNA* (1991) and *The Triple Helix: Gene, Organism, and Environment* (2000). Lewonton's main contribution has been to point out that seemingly random factors in the development of organisms, which cannot be predicted before the fact, are the third element in biological replication.

## Who was **Ernest Nagel**?

Born in Czechoslovakia, Ernest Nagel (1901–1985) lived in the United States after 1910 and was a member of the Columbia University philosophy department for over

40 years. His *The Structure of Science* (1961) is probably the last important logical positivist account of scientific investigation. Nagel extended the principles of the "covering law model," whereby explanation is based on a generalization that has been inductively built up, for the social sciences. He argued that although historical events are unique and non-recurring, historical explanation implies that such events would happen again, given the same conditions and proven generalizations.

## What was **Karl Popper's contribution** to **philosophy of science**?

In his *The Logic of Scientific Discovery* (1935; English translation, 1959), Popper (1902–1994) attacked the logical positivist assumption that scientific hypotheses could be derived from experience and confirmed by it inductively. Popper claimed that hypotheses can never be completely confirmed because we can't know what the future will hold with certainty, or even with high probability. It requires an unspecifiably high number of positive instances to confirm a hypothesis and only one negative case to falsify or discredit it. Popper's theory of falsification was very well received by working scientists.

## What was Karl **Popper's theory of falsification**?

Popper (1902–1994) did not think it mattered how hypotheses were inspired or arrived at, so induction was not necessary for their formation. In fact, he thought that the more bold and imaginative a hypothesis, the more scientific it was because it would be possible to specify what would falsify it. He argued that science progresses through a process of falsification, or, if hypotheses withstand crucial tests, then "corroboration," but never confirmation. Hypotheses or theories that cannot be falsified, such as religious, Marxist, or Freudian claims, according to Popper, could never qualify as scientific claims.

## How did **falsification work** according to Karl **Popper**?

Popper (1902–1994) postulated a *hypothetico-deductive method*. From the hypothesis—together with descriptions of initial conditions—certain future events, or known past events could be logically deduced. If the hypothetico-deductive method were applied to the past, it worked as a form of explanation. If it was applied to the future, it was the form of prediction. Prediction and explanation thus had the same logical structure.

Karl Popper claimed that hypotheses can never be completely confirmed because we can't know what the future will hold with certainty (AP).

**W**itnesses disagree, but the most neutral account is that there was a meeting of the Moral Sciences Club in Room H3 at Kings College, Cambridge, on October 25, 1946. Bertrand Russell (1872–1970) presided, and Karl Popper (1902–1994) came to give a critical paper on Ludwig Wittgenstein's (1889–1951) language game theory of truth and how to do philosophy. For one thing, Popper thought that there were moral rules.

At some point, Wittgenstein picked up a poker from the fireplace. He either did this to make a point or out of anger; stories differ. When Wittgenstein asked Popper what the example of a moral rule was, Popper is said to have replied, "Not to threaten visiting lecturers with pokers." Bertrand Russell, who was by then alienated from Wittgenstein, may or may not have interceded and told them to calm down.

A very entertaining book has been written about this episode and the lives and times of Popper and Wittgenstein by British Broadcasting Corporation journalists David Edmonds and John Eidinow: *Wittgenstein's Poker* (2001).

Popper's notion of falsification required that one falsifying instance either lead to the rejection of the original hypothesis, or more likely, to a reexamination of initial conditions. For example, if the hypothesis is that water freezes at 32 degrees Fahrenheit and a body of water does not freeze at that temperature, the rule or hypothesis that water freezes at that temperature is unlikely to be discarded. Rather, the thermometer may need to be checked, as well as the chemical composition of the liquid presumed to be water.

## Who was **Thomas Kuhn**?

Thomas S. Kuhn (1922–1996) became world famous for his idea that scientific progress requires new ways of looking at the world. He was educated at Harvard and taught at the University of California at Berkeley, Princeton University, and the Massachusetts Institute of Technology. He began as a physicist and then studied the history and philosophy of science. While teaching a course on physics to humanities students, he realized that Aristotle's (384–322 B.C.E.) physics were not as wrong as commonly assumed, but rather made sense in their own intellectual context.

His first book, *The Copernican Revolution* (1957), explained the intellectual transition from Aristotelian geocentricism to the heliocentric theory. But it was Kuhn's second book, *The Structure of Scientific Revolutions* (1962) that reverberated throughout

intellectual communities, because he showed how science proceeds by quantum leaps when new theories overthrow old theories. After Kuhn became very famous and attended a conference on his work, where everyone used his term "paradigm" almost as loosely as they do today, he is reported to have told someone, "I am not a Kuhnian."

## What was Thomas **Kuhn's paradigm theory**?

Although Kuhn himself noted that he used the word "paradigm" in at least 23 different ways in the first edition of *The Structure of Scientific Revolutions* (1962), the core meaning is that a paradigm defines and prescribes how research is conducted in a science, and it also presents a picture of the world as studied by that science.

During normal science, all practitioners are expected to work within the reigning paradigm of their field and extend accepted theories to new circumstances. There is widespread agreement on one coherent world view in a mature science. In immature sciences, competing schools of thought have followers who defend the paradigm of the viewpoint they subscribe to. Paradigms are not absolutely true for all time and can be literally overthrown by the adoption of new paradigms.

## What is a **scientific revolution** according to Thomas **Kuhn**?

A scientific revolution, said Kuhn (1922–1996), is preceded by a time of crisis in which the leading paradigm is no longer able to guide investigation and produce new discoveries in the field. A competing paradigm arises that is able to both explain the data accounted for in the old paradigm and explain new data.

Eventually, the new paradigm wins, because its adherents get control of the field in question. Along with their victory comes the authority to rewrite the textbooks so that the entire history of the science can be viewed as leading up to the new paradigm. Most of the practitioners of the old paradigm do not change their minds, but literally leave the field, either through retirement or death. The new paradigm then establishes a new era of normal science that persists until the next revolution.

## Who was **Imre Lakatos**?

Imre Lakatos' (1922–1974) main contribution to the philosophy of science was to reconcile the work of Karl Popper (1902–1994) and Thomas Kuhn (1922–1996). He was born Imre Avrum Lipschitz to a Jewish family in Debrecen, Hungary. His mother and grandmother were killed at the Auschwitz concentration camp. Lakatos (which would be written "Lakotos Imre" in Hungarian) studied mathematics, physics, and philosophy at the University of Debrecen, changing his name to Imre Molnár to save himself from the Nazis.

He was a communist during World War II and took the name "Lakatos" as a tribute to the Hungarian general and prime minister Géza Lakatos. He studied at Moscow

State University, but then was imprisoned for "revisionism" from 1950 to 1953 for ideas that reinterpreted Marxist doctrine in a way that Marxist authorities considered to be undermining to their official views. He then fled Hungary after the 1956 Soviet invasion. Lakatos earned his doctorate at Cambridge University in 1961 and lectured at the London School of Economics.

Lakatos' major works include *Proofs and Refutations* (1976), which is based on his doctoral dissertation, *The Methodology of Scientific Research Programs: Philosophical Papers Volume 1,* and *Mathematics, Science and Epistemology: Philosophical Papers Volume 2* (1978).

## What needed to be **reconciled** between Carl **Popper** and Thomas **Kuhn**?

Karl Popper (1902–1994) claimed that scientists ought to change their theories when they were falsified and that the hallmark of a scientific theory was its ability to be falsified. Thomas Kuhn (1922–1996) believed that, in fact, many accepted scientific theories had plenty of known, falsifying data. The problem was that Kuhn's account did not allow for progress in science, according to Popper's criterion of falsification, and that Popper's theory seemed to be unrealistic.

## How did Imre **Lakatos' research** program **reconcile Popper** and **Kuhn**'s work?

Lakatos (1922–1974) described a scientific method to both allow for progress and explain how science had developed. Instead of talking about theories, he introduced the notion of a "research program," which consisted of both theories and accepted research practices in a given field. Every research program has a core, or "protective belt," of claims that could not be falsified.

*Degenerating research programs* have growing protective belts and fail to predict new facts or create new projects for discovery; they survive by adding *ad hoc* hypotheses. *Progressive research programs* are able to support new projects of discovery that

do not produce vast amounts of falsifying data requiring revision of the core; they do not significantly rely on *ad hoc* hypotheses.

The way that Lakatos reconciled the discrepancy between Popper and Kuhn's account of science was to shift ground from the static relationship between facts and theories to the dynamic nature of scientific practice. Popper's view was that scientific truth changes when theories are falsified, whereas Kuhn thought that theories were not falsified so much as overthrown. Lakatos made scientific practice, rather than beliefs about the truth of theories, his subject.

## Who was **Paul Feyerabend**?

Paul Feyerabend (1924–1994), who was a friend and colleague of Imre Lakatos (1922–1974), is famous for his anarchist view of science. He was born in Vienna, Austria, and served in the German army during World War II, sustaining a bullet to the spine. After the war, he studied at the London School of Economics, with Karl Popper (1902–1994) as his advisor. During this time he began a dialogue with Lakatos, taking a stand against Lakatos' rationalist scientific project. But publication of this joint work was curtailed by Lakatos' death. Feyerabend had a lifelong interest in theater and opera and taught at the University of California at Berkeley after 1958.

Feyerabend's main writings include *Against Method: Outline of an Anarchistic Theory of Knowledge* (1975), *Science in a Free Society* (1978), *Realism, Rationalism and Scientific Method: Philosophical Papers, Volume 1* (1981), *Problems of Empiricism: Philosophical Papers, Volume 2* (1981), and the recklessly titled *Farewell to Reason* (1987). His autobiography is *Killing Time: The Autobiography of Paul Feyerabend* (1995).

## What was Paul **Feyerabend's view of science**?

He did not think it was possible to construct a philosophy of science that set out invariable rules for scientific progress. Instead, he argued that the most important scientific revolutions proceeded in violation of standing accepted methodological rules. He believed, for example, that the "consistency criterion," which posits that new theories not contradict older ones, is not a rational rule but an aesthetic one, insofar as old theories have been falsified.

Feyerabend also argued against Karl Popper's (1902–1994) idea of falsification on the grounds that interesting theories are not constructed in accordance with all relevant facts. One example of this was how the Renaissance astronomer Galileo Galilei (1564–1642) and his followers disregarded some of their telescopic observations during the construction of their optical theory. Feyerabend claimed that Lakatos' notion of a research program was a form of his own anarchism in disguise; he dedicated *Against Method: Outline of an Anarchistic Theory of Knowledge* (1975) to Lakatos as his "fellow-anarchist."

375

# PHILOSOPHY OF MIND AND PHILOSOPHY OF LANGUAGE

## What is the **connection** between **philosophy of mind** and **philosophy of language** in analytic philosophy?

Their development has been intertwined since the end of the behaviorist explanation of language learning. The new field of cognitive science, which arose from Noam Chomsky's (1929–) philosophical treatment of linguistics that disproved behaviorism, shows how philosophy of language is connected to philosophy of mind. When Chomsky proved that language learning required innate linguistic capacities, the whole tabula rasa or blank slate theory of mind came tumbling down.

## What is **behaviorism**?

Propounded by psychologists Ivan Pavlov (1859–1936) and John Broadus (J.B.) Watson (1878–1958) and streamlined by Burhus Frederick (B.F.) Skinner (1904–1990), behaviorism was the thesis that introspection had no use for a science of mind. Behavior is modified by its consequences in ways that can be described without any recourse to the

Psychologist Ivan Pavlov helped show that people's behaviors can be modified over time (Art Archive).

mind in terms of intentions, beliefs, or prior knowledge. Human psychology was no more than behavior that could observed in the laboratory, without considering that behavior from the point of view of the subject who was "behaving." Learning is *conditioning,* a series of automatic responses to repetitive rewards and punishment. Watson propounded the theory of behaviorism in his book *Behaviorism* (1925).

Noam Chomsky's (1929–) review of Skinner's 1959 classic tome *Verbal Behavior* is taken to have demolished Skinner's behaviorist theory of language learning, and behaviorism more generally. This is important to philosophy in two ways. First it restores the importance of how things seem or are experienced by a human subject. Second, it allows for speculation and analysis of how what is going on in the subject's mind is organized and processed in the brain.

# Noam Chomsky

## Who is **Noam Chomsky**?

Avram Noam Chomsky (1928–) is an American philosopher of linguistics and one of the most widely influential critics of contemporary politics over the twentieth century and beyond. Now a professor emeritus of linguistics at the Massachusetts Institute of Technology, Chomsky is recognized as an important founder of cognitive science in linguistics, psychology, and philosophy of mind, as well as computer science.

His major publications that are relevant to philosophy of language and mind include: *Syntactic Structures* (1957), *Cartesian Linguistics* (1966), *Current Issues in Linguistic Theory* (1964), *Aspects of the Theory of Syntax* (1965), *The Sound Pattern of English* (with Morris Hall; 1968), *Language and Mind* (1968), *Studies on Semantics in Generative Grammar* (1972), *The Logical Structure of Linguistic Theory* (1975), *Reflections on Language* (1975), *Essays on Form and Interpretation* (1977), *Rules and Representations* (1980), *Language and the Study of Mind* (1982), *Modular Approaches to the Study of the Mind* (1984), *Knowledge of Language: Its Nature, Origin, and Use* (1986), (*Barriers Linguistic Inquiry Monograph Thirteen*) (1986), *Language and Thought* (1993), *The Minimalist Program* (1998), *On Language* (1998), and *New Horizons in the Study of Language and Mind* (2000).

## What was Noam **Chomsky**'s argument **against behaviorism**?

Chomsky (1928–) objected on the grounds that the speed with which a child learns a language and demonstrates an ability to form correct new sentences, even without hearing grammatically correct speech, implies that this language ability has not been learned. Behaviorism was fundamentally a theory that all human knowledge and behavior, including language use, was learned.

## What is Noam **Chomsky's** own **theory** of **language**?

While Chomsky has developed different versions of his theories over the years, often abandoning his own followers of previous versions, most commentators agree that overall themes and trends in his thought amount to the claim that linguistic ability or language in a general syntactic or grammatical sense is "hard wired" into the human brain as a physical structure enabling a linguistic "faculty."

Chomsky has posited a "Universal Grammar" that limits the group of possible human languages. In philosophical terms, this is a rationalist, rather than an empiricist, approach to language. Thus, in *Cartesian Linguistics* (1966), Chomsky clearly stated, in affinity with René Descartes (1596–1650), that human language is innate and that human beings universally share this capacity. It should be noted, however, that Chomsky is a materialist concerning mental activity, whereas Descartes believed that the mind was a non-material substance.

Noam Chomsky is a brilliant linguist who developed a Universal Grammar that limited possible languages and showed that the human mind can be studied like a natural phenomenon (AP).

## Why has Noam **Chomsky's theory** of **language** been so **influential**?

Chomsky's principle of a Universal Grammar is compatible with materialism. It entails that the mind can be scientifically studied like a natural phenomenon. Moreover, the output of speakers can be used as data from which to infer deeper linguistic structures than those evident in spoken language. Insofar as language is an important, if not primary, mental activity, the idea of innate physical structures determining language production has implications for understanding other mental functions. Chomsky's work in linguistics has had a strong influence on the philosopher of mind Jerry Fodor (1935–), for example.

## Why is **materialism** important regarding the **analytic philosophy of mind**?

Whether the mind is equated with the physical brain or held to be closely connected to it, analytic philosophers of mind have been united in a materialist view since Gilbert Ryle (1900–1976) wrote *The Concept of Mind* (1949).

## Who was **Gilbert Ryle** and what was his **thesis**?

Gilbert Ryle (1900–1976) was the Oxford philosophy professor who edited the journal *Mind* after G.E. Moore (1873–1958). He is famous for having conclusively taken philosophers to task for talking about the mind as though it were "the ghost in the machine." He attacked the lingering Cartesian idea of the mind as a non-physical entity related to the body in ways that could not be explained. Instead, he said statements that were about the mind should be viewed as meaningful only if they could be explained in terms of actual behavior or behavioral tendencies.

## JERRY FODOR

### Who is **Jerry Fodor**?

Jerry Alan Fodor (1935–), a philosopher of cognitive science at Rutgers University, is perhaps best known for his "modular theory of mind" and his concept of the "language of thought." Fodor's books include: *Psychological Explanation* (1968), *The Language of Thought* (1975), *Representations: Essays on the Foundations of Cognitive Science* (1979), *The Modularity of Mind: An Essay on Faculty Psychology* (1983), *Psychosemantics: The Problem of Meaning in the Philosophy of Mind* (1987), *A Theory of Content and Other Essays* (1990) *The Elm and the Expert, Mentalese and Its Semantics* (1994), *Concepts: Where Cognitive Science Went Wrong* (1998), *In Critical Condition* (1998), *The Mind Doesn't Work that Way: The Scope and Limits of Computational Psychology* (2000), and *Hume Variations* (2003). Fodor also writes about opera for the *London Review of Books*. His writing style is uniquely witty and peppered with joyful mockery, as well as homespun analogies and references.

## What is Jerry **Fodor's modular theory** of **mind**?

First of all, Fodor said the mind is largely innate and mental development is not formed by experience, but rather set off by experience. Cognition can be described in the same way as the operations of computers, in terms of representations. The mind is modular in that many of its computational processes are independent of others. They may "send" their results to other computational processes without having their own processes "observed" by the other processes.

## What are the **modules of the mind**, according to Jerry Fodor?

In his *The Modularity of Mind* (1983) Fodor posits "transducers" (senses that connect us with the outside world), "input systems," and "central systems." Input and central systems are distinguished by the fact that input systems are modular and central systems are not. Modules each have one kind of cognitive material (for example, the visual module), and their information is encapsulated so that they can work very quickly, although they are inaccessible to conscious introspection. One module can be destroyed without impairing the others, as in cases of "aphasia."

Besides the different sensory systems, language is a module. It should be noted that Fodor does not hesitate to compare his theory with the system of phrenology propounded by Franz Joseph Gall (1758–1828), which is usually taken to be an example of early pseudo-science. The non-modular central systems correspond to thinking and believing and have access to other contents of the mind. Unlike language, the non-modular central system is not localized.

## What is Fodor's **language of thought hypothesis**?

The language of thought and thinking, as a mental language, is a system of symbols in the brain. Its content are "propositional attitudes" such as: thinks that, desires that, intends that, believes that, hopes that, and so forth. Each attitude has a distinct computational relation to a representation. Computation is information processing based on syntax. As Fodor puts it, there is "no computation without representation."

379

Thus, having a belief is being in a computational relation to a representation, as is having a desire. Every primitive concept in thought has a neural symbol in the brain. The end result of this in behavior is that the representation that is a belief causes an individual to behave as if it were true, whereas the representation that is a desire causes the individual to behave to make it true.

## What was **Wilfred Sellars'** idea of **functionalism**?

Wilfred Sellars (1912–1989) introduced the concept in his 1956 paper, "Empiricism and Philosophy of Mind." According to Sellars, there can be no mental foundations of knowledge such as sense data, and he also rejected the pragmatists' "myth of the given." (By "the given," the pragmatists referred to that part of experience that is not influenced by the perceiver or thinker.) Functionalism, as developed by Sellars, as well as Hilary Putnam (1926–) in his early writings, is the thesis that mental states can be defined by three things: what causes them, their effects on other mental states, and their effects on behavior. That is, mental states can be understood in terms of their functions, which operate like the software of a computer.

## What are **problems** with **functionalism** as a theory of mind?

Functionalism may result in attributing minds to complex systems that we otherwise would not consider to have minds. It might result in denying the presence of minds that operate according to different causal principles than our own. Indeed, Hilary Putnam (1926–) himself later rejected functionalism on the grounds that beliefs could not be computational states because their content was determined by external facts, and beliefs were also part of a whole system of knowledge. At the same time as Paul Kripke (1940–) and Keith Donnellan (1931–), he developed a new causal or direct theory of meaning, which was published in *The Meaning of "Meaning"* (1975).

## What is the **causal theory of meaning?**

This theory was first developed by Paul Kripke (1940–), Keith Donnellan (1931–), and Hilary Putnam (1926–) in the 1970s. There used to be a distinction between denotative and connotative, or "intensional" (with an "s," which is different from intention with a "t"), meaning. Denotative meaning was the thing or types of things in the world to which a word referred. Connotative or intensional meaning was the conditions of application of a word or the definition of the word in other words.

According to the causal theory of meaning, also known as "the causal theory of reference," there is a causal history that makes proper names the names of the individuals they are (something like a "baptism.") Natural kind terms, such as water and gold, work in much the same way. To take an example, the term "water" designates the natural $H_2O$; if a substance were called water that was not $H_2O$ it would not be water. Putnam famously said of meanings in this regard that they "just ain't in the head." Articles by Kripke, Donnellan, and Putnam on this subject appear in *Naming, Necessity and Natural Kinds* (1977), edited by Stephen P. Schwartz.

## How did **Thomas Nagel object** to **functionalism**?

Thomas Nagel (1937–), who is not related to Ernest Nagel (1901–1985), became famous for his 1974 article in *The Philosophical Review,* "What Is It Like to Be a Bat?" Nagel's point in that article was that the subjectivity of bats eludes us because of the nature of our objective methods of measuring consciousness. He makes the same point in another way with an example of a person tasting chocolate while a brain surgeon observes the part of his brain that is activated. No amount of such observation will allow the observer to taste the chocolate—not even if he licks the part of the brain in question!

Thomas Nagel criticized reductionist views of the human mind with his famous article "What Is It Like to Be a Bat?" (AP).

381

## What is the story about Nagel and the spider?

While Nagel was working in William James Hall at Harvard University one summer, he noticed a spider that lived in the men's urinal. Every time the urinal flushed, the poor arachnid would make a mad dash for its life so as not to drown. Nagel was concerned about what would happen to it when classes were in session and the urinal was flushed with greater frequency.

After long and careful deliberation, Nagel decided to liberate the spider. He carefully removed it from the urinal with a paper towel and placed it in a corner of the room. At first the spider did not move, and Nagel assumed it was getting its bearings. He left town over a holiday weekend, and when he returned the poor spider had still not moved. It was quite dry and quite dead.

Nagel recounts this episode in *The View from Nowhere* (1986). His implication seems to be that even the greatest compassion and best intentions may miss their objective, due to a lack of understanding of the circumstances of another.

---

Nagel's main motivations for holding out for the irreducibility of subjective experience are both moral and epistemological. He has shown that the whole of scientific investigation proceeds to increasing points of objectivity toward an ideal "view from nowhere," whereas concrete experience is always someone's view from somewhere. Books by Nagel include: *The Possibility of Altruism* (1970), *Mortal Questions* (1979), and *The View from Nowhere* (1986). Nagel's short introduction to philosophy, *What Does It All Mean?* (1987), is very accessible.

## What is **eliminative materialism**?

Eliminative materialism is the doctrine, first proposed by Paul Feyerabend (1974–1994) in the early 1960s, that science will eventually make it possible to eliminate all customary talk that presupposes non-material minds in favor of references to brain states only. The Canadian-born American philosopher Paul Churchland (1942–) and his wife, Patricia Churchland (1943–), have developed this view into a distinct branch of philosophy of mind. The Churchlands have held that our ordinary common sense theory of mind—consisting of intentions, desires, and motives—is mere "folk psychology," which, like other "folk beliefs," ought to be put aside in intellectual and scientific endeavors. Churchland wrote:

> Eliminative materialism is the thesis that our commonsense conception of psychological phenomena constitutes a radically false theory, a theory so fundamentally defective that both the principles and the ontology of that theory will eventually be displaced, rather than smoothly reduced, by completed neuroscience.

Principal publications by Paul Churchland include *Scientific Realism and the Plasticity of Mind* (1979), "Eliminative Materialism and the Propositional Attitudes" (published in the *Journal of Philosophy* in 1981), and *The Engine of Reason, the Seat of the Soul* (1996); both Paul and Patricia penned *On the Contrary* (1998).

## How do the Churchlands account for perceptions of meaning?

Meaning is fixed by networks of association. Ultimately, meaning will be replaced by connectionist networks with activation along "preferred vectors." Sameness of meaning is no more than a sameness of patterns. In the library of the future, there will be "plugs" for directly activating relevant brain states and patterns, bypassing the need to transmit meanings via language as we now know it.

## Who was Alan Mathison Turing?

Alan Mathison Turing (1912–1954) was a British cryptologist and mathematician who is credited with founding modern computer science. His Turing Machine, which was an extensive thought experiment, formalized the concepts of algorithms and computation. The Turing Machine consists of a possibly infinite paper tape with a stream of binary symbols that is continually scanned by a "read-write" device moving left or right and erasing or writing symbols on the tape, according to a program.

Turing showed that any such machine could be programmed to simulate any other one, meaning that it was a "universal machine." This universal machine could implement every known mathematical method. He extended this model to machines that cannot be simulated by a universal Turing machine, called Oracle machines. Turing proposed that intellectual activity can be understood as networks of universal and non-universal machines that can learn, through "training," to become something like universal machines.

After the invention of actual electronic computers, Turing suggested that theories of "artificial intelligence" could be tested. If there were a computer that could perform the same calculations as a human being—to the point where a human being could not tell whether the results were produced by the computer or by another human being—then there could theoretically exist artificial intelligence. Turing's 1950 article in *Mind*, "Can Machines Think?," continues to be

Alan Turing was a British cryptologist and mathematician who is credited with founding modern computer science (Art Archive).

383

## What was John Searle's "Chinese Room Argument"?

In his *The Rediscovery of the Mind* (1992), Searle supposed that a person who understands no Chinese is locked in a room with Chinese symbols and an algorithm or computer program that can be used to automatically answer questions in Chinese. The answers are good enough to be indistinguishable from answers by a Chinese speaker. Searle insists that what is missing from this picture, which is the overall computational theory of the mind in contemporary philosophy, is understanding—the person in the room does not understand Chinese!

Adherents to a computational theory of mind, in response to Searle's position, would probably claim that unless we go back to a mysterious "ghost in the machine," the behavior of the person locked in the room is exactly what is meant by "understanding Chinese."

As to who is right in this argument, no one knows for sure. As Jerry Fodor (1935–) noted, "we," meaning philosophers of mind, do not yet have an adequate theory of mind. If you think you do, then try explaining exactly how your desire to raise your right arm results in that arm going up.

highly influential in philosophy of mind discussions, in part as a result of John Searle's (1932–) treatment of it.

## How did John **Searle disagree** with Alan Mathison **Turing**?

The American philosopher John Searle (1932–), a professor at the University of California at Berkeley since 1959, has described his own work as an attempt to reconcile the world of science with the human self-conception of mindful animals with free will. In his *Intentionality: An Essay on the Philosophy of Mind* (1983), Searle argued that mental states are both caused by and realized in neurobiological brain processes. He called this view "biological naturalism."

In his Chinese room argument, he attempted to refute a broad Turing-inspired Strong Artificial Intelligence view that mind could be duplicated by the right computational device. Additional works by Searle, which advocate the non-reductionality of consciousness, while also acknowledging contemporary science, are: *Expression and Meaning: Studies in the Theory of Speech Acts* (1979), *The Rediscovery of the Mind* (1992), *The Mystery of Consciousness* (1997), and *Mind: A Brief Introduction* (2004).

# NEW PHILOSOPHY

## How can there be **"new" philosophy**?

Western philosophy began during the seventh century B.C.E., so it's a good question how there can be anything new in the field. Toward the end of the twentieth century, philosophy began a revitalization by adding fields and reconfiguring old problems. Some of the subjects added had originated in philosophy, developed as other disciplines, and then returned to philosophy so that philosophers could sort out the "real" intellectual issues. Feminism, environmentalism, and to some extent studies of race all fall under this category, as does cognitive science and new philosophies of psychology and biology.

Post-structuralism, or deconstructionism, which is also known as "postmodern philosophy," always was considered philosophy in Europe, but it has only recently been recognized as such at philosophy departments in American universities. So-called "other philosophies" from Latin America, Asia, and Africa have also begun to achieve recognition in the United States. There has been a revival of pragmatism, too.

Brand new on the horizon is "experimental philosophy." There is, in addition, a new philosophy of biology, philosophy of film and television, philosophy of technology, and philosophy for children, not to mention the new "mysterianism."

## Which of these **new philosophies** are **fads** and which **will last**?

The history of philosophy teaches that the focus of a generation or two can slip into obscurity as new methods and subjects catch attention. So it is impossible to predict which philosophers and books will be read 100, 50, or even 20 years from now. In one way or another, the ideas and writers considered in this chapter signal the end of philosophy via its dissolution into literature, cultural criticism, or empirical science.

But philosophy has endured for over 2,000 years, so news of its death may be premature at this point. It also remains to be seen whether these new strains of thought will themselves become entrenched in ways that are distinctly philosophical according to the old tradition, or whether the old tradition will just sail on grandly, oblivious of current distractions.

## What are the **major themes** in **new philosophy**?

Several factors stand out: a perceived need for philosophy to be relevant to current social concerns, the value of democracy, cultural pluralism, the importance of including women and non-whites who did not fully contribute to a history dominated by white males, and, above all, a strong revolt against ideas of objectivity, truth, and the perceived arrogance and hubris of previous philosophers. There is also a desire to make the subject of philosophy interesting to new students in a multimedia, electronic age.

# POSTMODERN PHILOSOPHY

## What world **facts** inform **postmodernism**?

The term "postmodern" came from the field of architecture. Meaning "after modern," it is a phrase that connotes, sometimes ironically, borrowing from the past in irreverent ways. Postmodern philosophy arose after major historical changes: the different scientific world views represented by Albert Einstein's theories of relativity and sub-atomic physics; the enormous destructive power of twentieth century warfare; the liberation of former colonies, as well as women and nonwhites in Europe and the United States; the economic, political, and social conditions of "post-colonialism"; and a breakdown in traditional social institutions such as the nuclear family, changes in women's roles, global capitalism, new economic inequalities, and environmental crises.

## What are the distinctive **methods** of **postmodern philosophy**?

Building on the work of structuralists, particularly Ferdinand de Saussure (1857–1913) and Jacques Lacan (1901–1981), most postmodern philosophers take social systems of language and symbols as their primary subject matter. More than that, they view the entire human world as existence within and through language. Their methods of analysis are variably hermeneutic, critical, and genealogical.

More specifically, deconstructionism proceeds by identifying *aporia,* or contradictions in Western thought that rested on theological principles insofar as they were ultimately inaccessible to consciousness. Typically, modern aporia required binary pairs, such as "right and wrong," or "being and non-being," each member of which was falsely defined in opposition to the other.

## JACQUES DERRIDA AND DECONSTRUCTIONISM

### Who was **Jacques Derrida**?

The Algerian-born French intellectual theorist, Jacques Derrida (1930–2004), is widely considered to be the founder of deconstructionism, which he presented in his introduction to a 1962 translation of Edmund Husserl's (1859–1938) *The Origin of Geometry*. In a later interview, Derrida said of this work, using his distinctive terminology that has made so many Anglo-American philosophers dismissive of deconstruction:

> In this essay the problematic of writing was already in place as such, bound to the irreducible structure of "deferral" in its relationships to consciousness, presence, science, history and the history of science, the disappearance or delay of the origin, etc. ... this essay can be read as the other side (recto or verso, as you wish) of *Speech and Phenomena*.

Using Husserl's standard that for something to be known it must be known by human consciousness, Derrida developed a critique of the "metaphysics of presence," the tradition that imagined knowledge as a thing known to God or the Absolute Consciousness. He called the whole history of Western philosophy "a search for a transcendental being that serves as the origin or guarantor of meaning."

His principle books include *"Speech and Phenomena" and Other Essays on Husserl's Theory of Signs* (1973), *Of Grammatology* (1976), *Writing and Difference* (1978), *Spurs: Nietzsche's Styles* (1979), *The Archeology of the Frivolous: Reading Condillac* (1980), *Margins of Philosophy* (1982), *The Post Card: From Socrates to Freud and Beyond* (1987), *Edmund Husserl's Origin of Geometry: An Introduction*

(1962, 1989), *Of Spirit: Heidegger and the Question* (1989), and *The Gift of Death* (1995). Derrida is most famous for *Of Grammatology* (1972).

## What is **deconstructionism**?

Deconstructionism is a method for interpreting "texts" (the term for written works used by deconstructionists) that is based on the premise that the meaning of texts depends as much on the writer's background historical conditions and those of the reader, as it does on what is in the text itself.

## How did **Derrida explain deconstructionism** in his *Of Grammatology*?

Derrida's *Of Grammatology* (1972) is about the instability of texts, due to the fact that all writing depends on the meanings readers bring to it, which may change, so that it cannot be claimed that a given piece of writing has a specific and stable meaning. All signs depend on other signs for their meanings, so there is never an ultimate meaning—meaning is always "deferred."

Jacques Derrida (1930–2004) speaks of "arche-writing" in this regard, which refers to gaps in the meaning of what is sacrosanct. All writing is split between its intention and how a reader understands it, and there is a gap between the writer and the reader.

Derrida's description of the reality of writing is meant to be an accurate account of the nature of intellectual life. The imagined presence of a being before whom the intentions and meaning of the philosopher is grasped, is the illusion under which philosophers and others have labored for so long.

Derrida thought that there was an ambiguity in the spoken word, which made the written word necessary, and he introduced the term "differance" to write about this difference. If one says "differance" and "difference" aloud there is no audible difference between them. The relevant difference can only be expressed in writing, although we have already seen how meanings are inconclusive in writing.

It is this insight about the dynamic nature of meaning—against Ferdinand

Jacques Derrida was the founder of deconstructionism (AP).

## How has Jacques Derrida's poststructuralism been received?

**D**errida's contemporary Michel Foucault (1926–1984), who many have regarded as a structuralist, accused him of practicing a terrorism of obscurantism. Foucault meant that those who could not understand Derrida (that is, most of his philosophical contemporaries) were attacked by Derrida as idiots. American philosophers such as Noam Chomsky (1929–), John Searle (1932–), and Richard Rorty (1931–2007) have mocked and dismissed Derrida. Searle referred to "the deliberate obscurantism of the prose, the wildly exaggerated claims, and the constant striving to give the appearance of profundity by making claims that seem paradoxical, but under analysis often turn out to be silly or trivial."

Chomsky thought that Derrida's work was typical of the local eccentric tradition of Parisian intellectuals. Without it being an explicit issue for them, Chomsky and Searle assume that meaning itself is stable and their theoretical work proceeds on that basis. However, Rorty, who has claimed that it might be impossible to understand Derrida's metaphysics, has a view similar to Derrida's about the false pretensions to truth that philosophers entertain.

de Saussure's (1857–1913) structuralist view that there is a system of meaning constituted by speech, for which the written word is somewhat secondary, if not unnecessary—that earned Derrida the label "poststructuralist," beginning in 1968. Derrida criticized the structuralist tradition as "moving from center to center in futility."

# RICHARD RORTY

## Who was **Richard Rorty**?

Richard McKay Rorty (1931–2007) was probably the most widely read contemporary American philosopher who is not considered to be doing philosophy by analytic and empirical philosophers. He taught at Wellesley, Princeton, the University of Virginia, and Stanford. Rorty began as an analytic philosopher, arguing in favor of eliminative materialism, but with *Philosophy and the Mirror of Nature* (1979) he began in the late 1970s to criticize analytic philosophy from a pragmatic perspective that drew on Continental thought.

As a neo-pragmatist, Rorty believed that most philosophical problems are illusions caused by language, that truth is a somewhat arbitrary and relative ideal, and that philosophy is just a literary genre. His main writings include *Philosophy and the Mirror of Nature, Consequences of Pragmatism* (1982), *Philosophy in History* (1985), *Contingency, Irony, and Solidarity* (1989), *Objectivity, Relativism and Truth: Philo-*

*sophical Papers I* (1991), *Essays on Heidegger and Others: Philosophical Papers II* (1991), *Achieving Our Country: Leftist Thought in Twentieth Century America* (1998), *Truth and Progress: Philosophical Papers III* (1998), *Philosophy and Social Hope*, (2000), *Against Bosses, Against Oligarchies: A Conversation with Richard Rorty* (2002), *The Future of Religion* with Gianni Vattimo (2005), and *Philosophy as Cultural Politics: Philosophical Papers IV* (2007).

Richard Rorty believed that most philosophical problems are illusions caused by language and that truth is an arbitrary ideal (AP).

## What was Richard **Rorty's view** of **truth**?

Rorty (1931–2007) criticized the idea that all we know are ideas that represent the world, or "representationalism"; he also challenged the special intellectual role of philosophers. He thought that "true" is just an honorific term used within linguistic and knowledge communities to mean "justified to the hilt." Rorty called this epistemological position "liberal ironism" because it rested on ideals of human freedom. He thought that commitment alone is adequate justification for belief. This view led Rorty into relativism.

## What was Richard **Rorty's concept** of **philosophy**?

Rorty (1931–2007) viewed philosophy as an ongoing free conversation or exchange of ideas that might be pursued passionately but nonetheless could not arrive at a kind of truth that did not exist. Philosophy was an opportunity to creatively reinvent oneself. Although he continually expressed liberal views, he did not think a rational view of universal human rights was possible to construct but that empathy and related sentiments could be cultivated by reading literature and through the right early education.

## JÜRGEN HABERMAS

### Who is **Jürgen Habermas**?

Jürgen Habermas (1929–) is a German philosopher and social theorist who combines the critical theory of the Frankfurt School with American pragmatism. With this combination he is postmodern in his emphasis on public speech and dialogue as a political way of life. His engagements with contemporary thinkers—from Jacques Derrida (1930–

## How did Richard Rorty illustrate relativism to his audience?

Rorty (1931–2007) practiced a highly sophisticated relativism that allowed him to present a position that his audience would agree with, and at the same time show how that position could be plausibly contested by those who held a very different position that was unacceptable to him and his audience. Concerning fundamentalist religious beliefs, for example, he taught views opposed to them with apparent strong commitment, and at the same time tried to show how his perspective was deeply offensive and even counter-productive in changing the minds of those who held those beliefs.

2004) to John Rawls (1921–2002) to Pope Benedict XVI (when he was Cardinal Ratzinger)—exemplify his theory. However, it should be noted that unlike most avowed postmodern philosophers, Habermas defends Enlightenment democratic values.

Habermas' major works include *The Structural Transformation of the Public Sphere* (1962), *Theory and Practice* (1963), *On the Logic of the Social Sciences* (1967), *Knowledge and Human Interest* (1967), *Toward a Rational Society* (1967), *Technology and Science as Ideology* (1968), *The Theory of Communicative Action* (1981), *On the Pragmatics of Communication* (1992), *The Postnational Constellation* (1998), *Old Europe, New Europe, Core Europe* (2005), *The Divided West* (2006), and with Joseph Ratzinger *The Dialectics of Secularization* (2007).

## What are Jürgen **Habermas' main ideas**?

Habermas' (1929–) quest has been to find a normative or prescriptive basis for social criticism. As a graduate student, he identified the importance of the public sphere of political discourse in the eighteenth century, which did not endure. In his early work, he rejected positivism, Marxism, and the psychoanalytic tradition for their failures to provide a normative foundation. His own goals were liberatory, and he thought that modernity could best be criticized from communicative rationality, or progressive discourse, as opposed to merely instrumental or goal-oriented rationality.

Habermas has held that formal "pragmatics" is necessary to clarify the implicit rules that determine who participates in official and institutional discourse. In criticizing these rules, Habermas' conclusion is that such discourse is biased toward bureaucracy and technology or mastery of nature, which is not limited to capitalism. The correction lies in an ongoing dialectic or public discussion, with the ideal of obtaining the agreement of all interested groups. This pluralistic dialectic is itself an ideal speech situation. Habermas' ideal speech situation is understood by many to be a revival of Enlightenment rationality.

German philosopher and social theorist Jürgen Habermas is a postmodernist who has defended Enlightenment democratic values (AP).

## Is Jürgen **Habermas' work** wholly **theoretical**?

No. First, he holds that the ability to see the worthiness of other people's goals is a condition for participation in a discourse community. And second, the subject under discussion should determine what will count as convincing argument. He has expressed optimism that his notion of discourse is compatible with likely global peace among nation states.

Habermas has struggled with the idea of self-determination as an individuating criterion for states, and tried to determine the kinds of negotiations necessary for mutual cooperation within Europe. He has also claimed that dialogues between religious thinkers and secularists can be mutually beneficial even though some of the core beliefs of each group cannot be fully translated into the worldviews of the other.

Generally speaking, Habermas' views on rationality, cosmopolitanism, and democratically negotiated universal human goals represent a re-casting of modern ideals. Other post-modernists, such as Jean Baudrillard (1929–), Gilles Deleuze (1925–1995), and Pierre-Félix Guattari (1930–1992), regard such ideals with greater skepticism and suspicion.

## MORE FRENCH POSTMODERN PHILOSOPHERS

### Who was **Jean Baudrillard**?

Jean Baudrillard (1929–) is a social theorist who writes about the absence of the kind of educated public discourse described by Jürgen Habermas (1929–) in pessimistic but elegant and evocative prose. He is, like Richard Rorty (1931–2007), a very readable postmodernist, but less sanguine.

Baudrillard's thought on terrorism in *In the Shadow of the Silent Majority* (1982) and *The Spirit of Terrorism: And Requiem for the Twin Towers* (2002) identifies it as a media-manipulating appropriation of public attention in a culture where only the spectacle is taken seriously. This is not a frivolous view insofar as it is based on a thorough-going analysis of contemporary life as in large part virtual, made up of *simulacra* of previous forms of human existence.

An example of this would be the way that newly constructed "old towns" are simulacra of historical places, and American pizza is a simulacrum of Italian food. This is apparently not just a question of things lacking authenticity, according to Baudrillard, but of a mass preference for virtuality instead of reality. Thus in *The Gulf War Did Not Take Place* (1991) he describes how experiences of the first Gulf War, even and especially for the troops, were mediated by its representation on television, radio, and other media forms, according to externally determined scripts that only captured bits and pieces of the actual experience.

## Who was **Jean-François Lyotard**?

Jean-François Lyotard (1924–1998) was educated at the Sorbonne and attended Jacques Lacan's (1901–1981) psychoanalytic seminars. His *The Postmodern Condition: A Report on Knowledge* (1979), which was commissioned by the Québec government, won him worldwide fame, and he taught and lectured widely throughout the United States.

Lyotard sought to articulate the principles of postmodernism as both an intellectual attitude and a condition of contemporary life.

## What was Jean-François **Lyotard's view** of **postmodernism**?

Lyotard defined postmodernism as "incredulity toward metanarratives," or a skepticism that is not satisfied by legitimate orthodoxy. An example of the sort of narrative Lyotard had in mind was the Enlightenment account of the triumph of rationality and the liberation of the "rational subject." Lyotard proposed that "little narratives" about unique events be constructed instead. In his *The Différend* (1983) Lyotard considers disagreement between or among participants who cannot agree on the rules. As a result, the dispute cannot be resolved, so the best result that can occur is for all sides to be recognized.

## Who were **Gilles Deleuze** and **Pierre-Félix Guattari**?

Gilles Deleuze (1925–1995) and Pierre-Félix Guattari (1930–1992) were collaborators best known for *Anti-Oedipus: Capitalism and Schizophrenia* (1972), *A Thousand Plateaus* (1980), and *What Is Philosophy?* (1991). Their last book, *Chaosmose* (1992), summed up their previous questioning about subjectivity: "How to produce it, collect it, enrich it, reinvent it permanently in order to make it compatible with 'mutant Universes of value?'"

Engaged with both the history of philosophy and contemporary culture, as well as political activism, they thought that the task of the theorist was to invent connections, since there was no preformed relation between theories and reality. Thus, certain structures were better understood as having "rhizomes" that traveled horizontally and popped up in surprising ways, rather than "roots," which could be uncovered straight down. Rhizomes were something like social trends that are decentralized, such as

Gilles Deleuze collaborated with Pierre-Félix Guattari to write several philosophy books that often used recondite terminology (AP)

individuals creating their own news outlets through blogging, rather than people all relying on the same few sources for information. Progressive trends could be identified as "micropolitics," "schizoanalysis," and "becoming-woman."

## What was Gilles **Deleuze like** as a **person**?

He did not like to furnish autobiographical information, claiming: "Academics' lives are seldom interesting." His fingernails were extremely long, but when it was suggested that this was a sign of eccentricity, he replied, "I haven't got the normal protective whorls, so that touching anything, especially fabric, causes such irritation that I need long nails to protect them." In the same interview he said that the fact that he did not travel did not mean an absence of "inner journeys."

## How did **Alan Sokal attack postmodernism**?

New York University physicist Alan Sokal wrote a spoof of postmodern scholarship titled "Transgressing the Boundaries: Towards a Transformative Hermeneutics of Quantum Gravity," which was published by the postmodern journal *Social Texts* in its 1996 spring/summer "Science Wars" issue. When his article came out, Sokal simultaneously confessed his hoax in the academic gossip journal *Lingua Franca*. He referred to his *Social Text* article as "a pastiche of left-wing cant, fawning references, grandiose quotations, and outright nonsense," which was "structured around the silliest quotations I could find about mathematics and physics" that recent postmodernist academics had written. Why did Sokal do this? He explained it this way:

> I'm an unabashed Old Leftist who never quite understood how deconstruction was supposed to help the working class. And I'm a stodgy old scientist who believes, naively, that there exists an external world, that there exist objective truths about that world, and that my job is to discover some of them.

In other words, besides thinking that, and showing how, postmodern thought was of poor intellectual and scholarly quality, Sokal did not believe it served a worthy political purpose. Sokal, along with Jean Bricmont, a physicist professor and philosopher of science, further developed the critique implied by Sokal's article in their book *Fashionable Nonsense* (1997).

## What do Deleuze and Guatarri mean by their bizarre terminology?

Gilles Deleuze (1925–1995) and Pierre-Félix Guatarri (1930–1992) took pride in using new terms that they did not define, but which they thought readers would understand. "Mutant universes of value" seems to refer to new systems of value that are unconventional and popular. Examples in our time would be interests in vampires in entertainment, the growing importance of electronic communication, and the change in household pets from mere pets to members of the families with whom they live.

The importance of townhall meetings in the United States would be an example of "micropolitics." "Schizoanalysis," which suggests contradictory meanings, was used to refer to Deleuze and Guatarri's project of getting rid of the idea of the Freudian idea of the unconscious as a way of explaining human behavior. "Becoming-woman" refers to the fact that contemporary women are actively involved in defining their own social roles.

The question left by Sokal's work is this: "Does such political condemnation of an entire field of thought respect hard-won principles of academic freedom? And if standards of political worthiness are being applied to postmodernism, is that application fair, given over two and half centuries of philosophy that has been largely irrelevant to its immediate political contexts?

While it's true that much postmodern work was sparked by widespread student protests in France in 1968, so has much politically ineffective, if not irrelevant, work in the history of philosophy been inspired by instant political events. Moreover, political criticism of postmodernism requires some understanding of its intellectual, poststructuralist context, which Sokal seems to lack. Finally, the issue of political relevance is separate from the question of whether a body of work is nonsense.

# OTHER AMERICAN PHILOSOPHIES

## What are the **other American philosophies**?

The term here refers to philosophies that represent groups in the Americas that have been politically subordinate to the groups historically represented by the U.S. government. These philosophies themselves have long histories in their cultures of origin, but their concerns have recently become part of Anglo-American mainstream academic philosophy. As a result, new philosophical subfields emerged toward the end of the twentieth century: African American, Native American, and Latin American philosophy. Each of these traditions has developed as a form of cultural criticism, and insofar as its analyses of oppression would not immediately be recognized as such by perpetrators, each is a distinctive critical theory.

## What makes the concerns of these **historically disadvantaged groups** part of **philosophy**?

When philosophers take up these concerns, as many have in recent decades, they become part of the official curriculum of philosophy in higher education. In addition, the issues raised require the methods of both analytic and continental philosophy to resolve. Some of these issues are ethical and others are directly related to political philosophy and public policy, both of which are now part of the canon of contemporary philosophy.

# AFRICAN AMERICAN PHILOSOPHY

## What is **African American philosophy**?

African American philosophy has had at least three periods: in the nineteenth century period it is usually associated with abolitionism, most notably in the writings of Frederick Douglass (c. 1818–1895); in the early twentieth century, it is distinguished by the work of Alain Locke (1885–1954) and W.E.B. Dubois. Not until the 1970s did African American philosophy begin to function as a subfield within academic philosophy, and that was the beginning of its third period, which continues until the present day.

Aside from recognizing historically overlooked thinkers and ideas, African American philosophy has focused on identity, racism and its remedies, questions of reparations for black chattel slavery before the U.S. Civil War, and the question of whether there is a scientific foundation for the division of human beings into biological races.

Among the many luminaries of African American philosophy was W.E.B. Dubois, a civil rights activist, historian, sociologist, and Pan-Africanist who dedicated his life to solving the problem of racism (Library of Congress).

A skeletal list of core classic readings in African American philosophy would include: Alexander Crummell's (1819–1898) *Destiny and Race: Selected Writings, 1840–1898* (2000), Frederick Douglass' *A Narrative of the Life of Frederick Douglass, an American Slave* (1845), W.E.B. DuBois' (1868–1963) *The Souls of Black Folk* and *Dusk of Dawn* (1945), Alain Locke's (1886–1954) *The New Negro* (1925), Booker T. Washington's (1886–1915) *Up from Slavery: An Autobiography* (1901), and Martin Luther King's (1929–

> ## Which important books helped create late-twentieth-century African American philosophy?
>
> **A**n abbreviated core bibliography would include the following books: Kwame Anthony Appiah and Amy Gutmann, *Color Conscious: The Political Morality of Race* (1996); Bernard Boxill, *Blacks and Social Justice* (1992); Angela Davis, *Women, Race, and Class* (1983); Lewis R. Gordon, *Bad Faith and Antiblack Racism* (1996); Jacquelyn Grant, *White Women's Christ and Black Women's Jesus* (1989); Leonard Harris, ed., *Philosophy Born of Struggle: Anthology of Afro-American Philosophy from 1917* (1983); Bill E. Lawson, ed., *The Underclass Question* (1992); Tommy L. Lott, ed., *Subjugation and Bondage* (1998); Howard McGary, *Race and Social Justice* (1998); Charles W. Mills, *The Racial Contract* (1997); Michele M. Moody-Adams, *Morality, Culture and Philosophy: Fieldwork in Familiar Places* (1997); Greg Moses, *Revolution of Conscience: Martin Luther King, Jr., and the Philosophy of Nonviolence* (1997); Albert Mosley, *Affirmative Action: Social Justice or Unfair Preference?* (1996); Lucius Outlaw, *On Race and Philosophy* (1996); Rodney C. Roberts, ed. *Injustice and Rectification* (2002); Laurence Thomas, *Vessels of Evil: American Slavery and the Holocaust* (1993); Cornel West, *Prophesy Deliverance! An Afro-American Revolutionary Christianity* (1982); George Yancy, editor, *African-American Philosophers, 17 Conversations* (1998); and Naomi Zack, *Thinking about Race* (2006).

1968) *A Testament of Hope: The Essential Writings and Speeches of Martin Luther King, Jr.* (1986).

## What were the main **themes** and claims in **classic African American literature**?

Until the Emancipation Proclamation (1862), the main issue was the abolition of black slavery. From the end of the Civil War until the Civil Rights movement of the late 1950s that resulted in legislation against discrimination in 1964, the issue was discrimination against blacks and their social and legal exclusion from opportunities in employment, education on all levels, housing, adequate medical care, and fairness in the criminal justice system. At the same time, support for and construction of positive identities for African Americans was a central concern.

## What are the **philosophical issues** about **racial identity**?

They come down to the question of whether African Americans should envision themselves and their communities as race-specific or generically American. Traditionally, strong racial or ethnic identities have developed among members of oppressed groups, sometimes based on the very things that are used against them by racists. On the other hand, strong racial identities among disadvantaged groups may prevent young people from aspiring to and achieving success in a dominant white society. Beyond these pragmatic concerns is a current consensus that all social and psychological racial identities are socially constructed, rather than biologically determined.

### What have been the **major themes** and issues in **African American philosophy**?

Analyses of racism, questions about racial identity, and questions about the reality of race are all important issues in African American philosophy.

### What is the **philosophical issue** regarding **biological race**?

In ordinary reality, it seems obvious that most people belong to one or another of a few major races due to biological differences. Actually, human biological sciences have failed to identify any physical essences that distinguish a race; and there are no stable physical traits that all members of any race share. For example, some black people have lighter skin hues than some white people, and overall there is greater variation of so-called racial traits within races than between races. When the human genome was mapped at the turn of the twenty-first century, geneticists reporting on the research emphasized that they had found no genes for race.

Of course, the physical traits that count as racial are genetically inherited, but there is no difference in principle between those traits and others. Both globally and historically, criteria for racial membership have varied. In colonial times, a person was considered white if most of their great grandparents were white. By 1900, the "one-drop" rule was in effect throughout the land: a person was considered black if there were any black ancestors, no matter how far back they were. The one-drop rule erased positive racial identities for Americans with both black and white ancestry—they were, and to a large degree still are, considered black, rather than multiracial, mixed race, or biracial.

The lack of a biological foundation for black or white racial identity has led some writers to suggest either that racial categories be eliminated or that racial identities be recognized as purely social. On that social basis, there is no rational reason why people with both black and white ancestry should not be recognized as mixed race, instead of automatically assigned to the black category. Others have tried to reconstruct less rigorous "biological" bases for race, and still others have argued that, within the African American tradition, race has always been understood to involve something more than biology.

# NATIVE AMERICAN PHILOSOPHY

## What is **Native American philosophy**?

Native American tribes and nations have held well-developed world views, religions, epistemologies, metaphysics, and social and political views long before Europeans invaded and appropriated their lands. Much of this knowledge was transmitted orally and subject to loss and fragmentation, following what many indigenous people call the Native American Holocaust.

The development of Native American philosophy as a subfield in academic philosophy requires not just reconstruction of past knowledge but some acceptance of the methods of Western philosophy. The problem is that these methods are highly problematic for most indigenous thinkers. Furthermore, after centuries of distorted descriptions of their cultures by anthropologists and government officials, most Native American philosophers have a strong preference for speaking in their own voices, rather than agreeing to let others present their perspectives.

There are not very many Native Americans in U.S. university philosophy departments at this time—perhaps fewer than 50. Nevertheless, since the 1980s a "canon" of Native American philosophy has developed, which includes the following sources: *The Sacred Hoop* by Paula Gunn Allen (1986); *How It Is: The Native American Philosophy of V. F. Cordova by Linda Hogan,* by Kathleen Dean Moore, Kurt Peters, and Ted Jojoba (2007); *Cultural Sites of Critical Insight: Philosophy, Aesthetics, and African American and Native American Women's Writings,* by Angela L. Cotton and Christa Davis (2007); *American Indian Thought: Philosophical Essays,* by Anne Waters (2003); and *Defending Mother Earth: Native American Perspectives on Environmental Justice,* by Jace Weaver (1996).

## What are some of the **current issues** in **Native American philosophy**?

The concerns address politics, ecology, religion, and feminism. The Native American claims are both straightforward and difficult to solve. Political activist and former ethnic studies professor at the University of Colorado at Boulder, Ward Churchill, has argued that progressive movements within mainstream American society do not address Native American ideals because those progressive movements are dedicated to getting more of the prizes of technology and capitalism. Traditional Native Americans, by contrast, seek to withdraw from the dominant system and into self-sufficient traditional communities.

To some extent, the current political issues of Native Americans concern ecology and environmentalism. On the one hand, Native Americans may refuse to be used as symbols of ecological virtue, even though ideals of self-sufficiency on tribal lands do rely on sustainable ecological practices. It is a significant irony that some Native

American communities have been able to use profits from their casinos to purchase those ancestral lands that the U.S. promised them in unfulfilled treaties.

Viola Cordova (1937–2002), a university professor and the first Native American to earn a doctorate in philosophy (she was also part Hispanic), argued that the history of Western philosophy has an overwhelming Christian bias and influence in ways that are incomprehensible to thinkers in Native cultures. Anne Waters, another Native American philosopher, as well as an attorney who teaches at California State University at Bakersfield, has challenged the myth of European discovery of the "Americas," referring to oral traditions claiming that Native Americans have always inhabited the Americas.

Native American women writers such as Paula Gunn Allen have traced matriarchal patterns in indigenous political history, which were dislodged by European settlers who refused to negotiate with female leaders. This suggests very different feminist concerns among Native American women compared to Western feminists, recovering political power instead of attaining it.

## LATIN AMERICAN PHILOSOPHY

### What is **Latin American philosophy**?

Latin American philosophy is either or both the thought of philosophers who reside in Latin American countries or the newer work of Latino-Latina/Hispanic-American philosophers. Like African American and Native American philosophy, it is a subfield to the academic discipline that formed after 1930, although it was not duly recognized until after 1980.

Contemporary considerations of philosophy in Latin America, written by philosophers who also reflect on the Latino-Latina/Hispanic-American experience include the following books: Linda Alcoff and Eduardo Mendieta, *Thinking from the Underside of History: Enrique Dusell's Philosophy of Liberation* (2000); Jorge J.E. Gracia, Mireya Camurati, editors, *Philosophy and Literature in Latin America* (1989); Jorge J.E. Gracia and Elizabeth Millan-Zaibert, editors, *Latin American Philosophy for the 21st Century: The Human Condition, Values, and the Search for Identity* (1989); Eduardo Mendieta, *Global Fragments: Critical Theory, Latin America and Globalizations* (2007); Susana Nuccetelli, *Latin American Thought: Philosophical Problems and Arguments* (2002); and Ofelia Schutte, *Cultural Identity and Social Liberation in Latin American Thought* (1993).

### What are the **issues** addressed by **Latino-Latina/Hispanic-American philosophy**?

Identity, immigration, the experience of multinational persons, and the nature of cultural difference are considered. As well, there are unique feminist issues for Latina-

Americans and questions centered on the difference between race (as false biology) and ethnicity (as culture).

## What have been the **major trends** in **Latin American philosophy**?

Many commentators identify four periods in the 500 year history of philosophy in Latin America: colonial, independentist, positivist, and contemporary. Overall, Latin American philosophers have been actively involved in political and social events in their countries; they have not, until very recently, incorporated indigenous world views into their intellectual perspectives.

The colonial period (1550–1750) was characterized by interest in medieval scholastic philosophy, such as the work of Thomas Aquinas (c. 1225–1274) and Francisco Suárez (1548–1617). During this time, Mexico and Peru were important in intellectual life and the influence of Spain dominated. The Royal and Pontifical University of Mexico, founded in 1553, was where Alonso de la Vera Cruz (1504–1584), Tomás de Mercado (1530–1575), and Antonio Rubio (1548–1615) flourished. Antonio Rubio's *Mexican Logic* (1605) was a celebrated textbook on Aristotelian logic throughout Europe. Bartolomé de Las Casas' (1474–1566) *In Defense of the Indians* is still widely read.

During the independentist philosophical period (1750–1850) intellectual interest was focused on political issues, although European rationalism, empiricism, and ethics were also taken up. The positivist period (1850–1910) embraced European positivism and had local social and political applications. It was assumed by many, after independence, that positivist philosophy, backed up by social science, would usher in "Order and Progress." Juan Bautista Alberdi (1812–1884), in his *Idea* (1842), sought to modify European positivism to the specific circumstances of Latin America.

# OTHER CONTINENTAL TRADITIONS

## What other **continental traditions** are **new** to Western philosophy?

Recent decades have seen renewed interest in African, Japanese, Chinese, and Indian philosophies among Euro-American philosophers. Some of this work has been called comparative philosophy because it seeks to relate themes that are well-established and well-developed philosophies in their continents of origin to traditional interests in Western philosophy. Japanese, Chinese, and Indian philosophies admit to the comparative treatment because they have long, well-established textual traditions. However, African philosophy is a less clear case, not because it fails to treat issues that in the Western tradition would without doubt be considered "philosophical," but because much of it has endured through oral traditions. Still, a broad recognition of African culture and its historical civilizations, after the 1960s, led to the Euro-American perspective of Afro-centrism among some members of the "African Diaspora."

## What are **Afro-centrism** and the **African Diaspora**?

In the United States, Afro-centrism begins with the premise that American slaves and, through inter-generational cultural inheritance—if not a now-untenable biological essentialism—their descendants, came from Africa. At the time when the original slave populations were kidnapped from Africa, Africa had fully developed religions, cultures, cities, and civilizations dating before ancient Western philosophy. The involuntary implantations of Africans, as slaves, in the Americas and Europe resulted in a forced scattering, or diaspora, from those African origins.

The reclamation of their African heritage on the part of African Americans results in a different perspective than the dominant white view that African slaves were forced immigrants without original cultures comparable to the cultures of those who enslaved them. Afro-centrism is thus a foundation for a new African-American pride, in both origins and contemporary identity, through cultural inheritance, for all groups and their members who are part of the African diaspora.

A new legitimate foundation of culture, complete with its own art, architecture, poetry, styles of clothing, food, and everyday habits, is therefore claimed. It needs to be emphasized that this is in contrast to the culture of slave cabins, slave field labor, or slave service in the homes of masters, complete with a loss of original names, on through the oppressively degrading conditions of segregation, disproportionate incarceration, ghetto living conditions, the destruction of traditional black nuclear families and neighborhoods, and a general sense of being both the cause and object of America's unique "race problem."

Afro-centrism is thereby a perspective of encouragement and racial uplift. Sources on Afro-centrism include Martin Bernal's *Black Athena: The Afroasiatic Roots of Classical Civilization* (three volumes, 1987–2006), Lewis R. Gordon's *Her Majesty's Other Children: Sketches of Racism from a Neocolonial Age* (1997), and Molefi Asante's *The Afrocentric Idea* (1987).

## Is there or has there been an **African philosophy**?

There is a millennially long tradition of oral African philosophy, as well as many active twentieth century African philosophers. Once this thought is presented in established Western philosophical terms, however, it does not so much support Afro-centrism as a perspective of racial uplift as it evinces a philosophy by asking questions about its own philosophical enterprise. That is, a great deal of contemporary African philosophy is itself concerned with the question of whether it is philosophy and what that means in an African, although not Afro-centrist, context.

The context is not Afro-centrist because Africans who remained in Africa and were not brought to Europe or the Americas had no need for the distinctive uplift of Afro-

> ## What does Afro-centrism have to do with philosophy?
>
> **A**frican philosophy is of interest to philosophers as a theoretical system of thought. Also, some philosophers have accepted the challenge raised by Afro-centrism that Western philosophy has excluded the intellectual perspectives of Africans.

centrism. Instead, the focus on Africa from an African perspective turns on the question of what the multiplicity of countries and cultures in Africa, each with distinct languages and traditions, have in common so that they can view themselves as African. They share a colonized past and poverty in the present world; they have been designated by biological race, though this is an illusion.

Contemporary philosophical sources for African philosophy include Kwame Anthony Appiah, *In My Father's House: Africa in the Philosophy of Culture* (1992); Kwame Gyeke, *Tradition and Modernity* (1997); Emmanuel Eze, editor, *Postcolonial African Philosophy* (1970); Paulin J. Hountondji, *African Philosophy: Myth and Reality* (1983); John Mbiti, *African Religions and Philosophy* (1970); Albert Mosley, editor, *African Philosophy: Selected Readings* (1995); H. Odera Oruka, editor, *Sage Philosophy* (1990); Tsenay Serequeberhan, editor, *African Philosophy: The Essential Readings* (1991); Kwasi Wiredu, editor, *A Companion to African Philosophy* (2004); and Richard Wright, editor, *African Philosophy: An Introduction* (1984).

## BUDDHISM AND CONFUCIANISM

### How have **Japanese, Chinese**, and **Indian philosophy** recently **entered Anglo-American philosophy**?

Asian philosophy came to the West as Buddhism from Japanese, Chinese and Indian philosophy, and Neo-Confucianism from Chinese philosophy. Given the common thread of Buddhism throughout Asia, many might be tempted to designate all philosophy from Japan, China, and India as "Asian philosophy" or "Eastern philosophy," but there are other systems of thought and religion just as diverse as Buddhist traditions.

Also, the different Buddhist traditions derive from cultures that have very distinctive histories, as well as very different current political and economic situations and ties to the West. That their theological dimensions are not Christian, Jewish, or Muslim, is probably all that the philosophies of these areas—broadly understood to be more than Buddhism and Confucianism—have in common.

Although Euro-American intellectuals in other fields have well-developed scholarly traditions based on Eastern texts, it should be noted that philosophers, as a profession, are relative latecomers to Eastern philosophy. For instance: the British biochemist Joseph Needham (1900–1995) wrote extensively on technology and science in the history of China; the nineteenth century German novelist Herman Hesse introduced an international readership to Indian thought and Buddhism in his 1922 novel, *Siddhartha*; and philosophy's own Gottfried Leibniz (1646–1716) was fascinated by Chinese thought. The question is what do philosophers put on their curricula from Eastern thought in new ways that emphasize a commonality of philosophical interests? Again, the answer is Buddhism, on account of its resonance with Western metaphysics and epistemology, and Confucianism for what it teaches about virtue ethics.

## What is **Buddhism**?

Buddhism was founded in India by Siddhartha Gautama. The majority of Indian scholars place his lifespan as c. 563–c. 483 B.C.E. Indian Buddhism divided into Theravada, or Hinayana or "Lesser Vehicle," and Mahayana, or "Greater Vehicle." Indian Buddhism was no longer a vibrant religion in India after the thirteenth century, but it had by then spread geographically. Theravada Buddhism is practiced in Thailand, Laos, Cambodia, and Sri Lanka. Mahayana Buddhism is practiced in China, Japan, Nepal, and the United States. Tibetan Buddhism, in addition to including the Greater and Lesser Vehicles, has a form known as Vairayana. All of the three vehicles are practiced in Himalayan parts of Mongolia, Northeastern China, and Russia.

Zen Buddhism is practiced in Japan as a kind of meditation called "zazen" that repudiates texts (even though there is a written tradition) and focuses on unmediated direct experience. Zen originated in India and emerged in China in the seventh century C.E., from which it spread to Vietnam, Korea, and Japan. Zen includes Yogācāra, which is a form of philosophical idealism that uses yoga exercises to achieve disbelief in the existence of physical objects.

Buddhism is often associated with China, Japan, and Nepal, but it actually began in India, where it was started by Siddhartha Gautama, the Buddha (iStock).

## What is the **school of thought** of **Buddhism**?

The general structure of Buddhism as a school of thought is based on a religious belief in reincarnation, which is known as "the wheel of life." The spiritual ideal is for the individual to stop being reincarnated by adopting behavior with the correct karma, or consequences. The wheel of life is propelled by the flame of desire. The main obstacle to Enlightenment is thereby identified as desire: desire for

people, money, power, fame, objects, and anything else. By following the Eightfold Path, a practitioner will snuff out his or her "flame" of desire and no longer need to return to this earth.

There are three precepts or self-evident truths: that all life is unhappy or unsatisfying, that all life is impermanent, and that there is no eternal or even permanent self or soul. From these precepts, the Eightfold Path manifests itself: right speech, right action, right livelihood, right effort, right mindfulness, right concentration, right views, and right intentions.

## What have **Western philosophers recognized** in **Buddhism**?

Buddhist thought rejects ideas of substance or substances as entities that endure through time and change. Speculation about the eternity of the world, its infinity, or the connections between the soul or mind and the body are not considered worthwhile. In the Theravada schools of thought, perceptual experience is believed to justify mind-independent entities, but we do not experience them directly. Some commentators hold that there are independent entities, otherwise our inference from experience that they exist could not be justified. Furthermore, we do not control what we perceive, which suggests that things exist outside of our perception. Others distinguish between reliable and unreliable sensory experience. Some Buddhists believe that both minds and bodies are collections of transitory perceptions.

According to the Madyhamika School, there can't be individual objects because everything is dependent on everything else. However, enlightenment can result in an awareness of an underlying reality behind or beyond this flux. The Yogācarā branch of this school holds that because there are no minds, there is no one to see the truth and no way to discover it. Given the lack of substances (which would include minds), all that exist are mental states. Our lack of control over perception or the apparent objectivity of things is merely the effect of our own memories.

It should be evident at this point that Buddhism has grappled with the same kinds of questions about what really exists as those that have held the attention of Western philosophers throughout history. One difference is that, with the exception of ancient stoicism and epicurianism, and perhaps contemporary Buddhism, Western philosophers do not have life practices directly linked to their intellectual beliefs. Useful sources for philosophical comparison include Masao Abe and Steven Hein, *Zen and Comparative Studies* (1997); Dan Lusthaus, *Buddhist Phenomenology: A Philosophical Investigation of Yogacara Buddhism* (1997); and Anil Kumar Sarkar, *Buddhism and Whitehead's Process Philosophy* (1991).

## What is **Confucianism**?

Confucius (551–479 B.C.E.) was born in Shantung, China, where he advanced from poverty to an influential administrative post. He was a member of the *Ju* (the literal

meaning of "ju" is weaklings), a social group of ritualists and teachers. Confucius and his colleagues and followers became members of the *Ju-chia,* the School of the Ju. They sought to develop and restore traditional ideals of concern for all living things and reverence toward other human beings by determining and following proper rules of conduct.

In 496 Confucius left his position to talk to rulers about the Ju-chia's doctrines. During a time when warlords were chaotically vying for control of the declining Chou dynasty, he sought to import moral principles and the traditional virtues into government. Confucius' thoughts were put together by his pupils in the *Lun Yü,* or *Analects.*

## What is the **Tao**?

The Tao, or "way," advocated by Confucius involves appropriately performing one's roles in the family and society according to *jen,* or loving respect for others. All are presumed to be equal in acting according to jen, and if all act in this manner, the whole of society and the world will be improved.

## What was **Confucius' influence**?

Confucius was the most highly regarded teacher, moralist, and poet in Chinese history. Mencius (372–289 B.C.E.), the most prominent Confucian philosopher after Confucius himself, held that all human beings are born with moral inclinations. Mencius' teachings have persisted as the dominant form of Confucianism to the present time. Hsun Tzu (c. 312–230 B.C.E.) taught Confucianism as a way of following formal hierarchical social structures to achieve personal happiness.

A statue of Confucius at the Confucious Temple in Suzhou, China (iStock).

For additional information on the teachings and history of Confucianism refer to: Xinzhong Yao and Hsin-chung Yao, *An Introduction to Confusianism* (2000), and Chung-Ying Cheng, *New Dimensions of Confucian and Neo-Confucian Philosophy* (1991).

## How is **Confucianism relevant** to contemporary Western philosophy?

Confucianism is conservative and does not appear to be based on individual autonomy or self-rule; its highest moral principle seems to be social conformity: to this extent it is not easily imported into Western moral, political, and social philosophy.

However, a number of contemporary moral philosophers have found some appeal in the Confucian egalitarian ideal of respect for all beings. Confucianism has also been received as an alternative virtue ethics theory, as well as for its utilitarian/consequentialist notion that correct behavior will maximize happiness.

Such comparative ideas, as well as contemporary interpretations and applications of Confucianism, can be found in the following sources: Bo Mou, *Comparative Approaches to Chinese Philosophy* (2003), Li-Hsiang Lisa Rosenlee, *Confucianism and Women: A Philosophical Interpretation* (2006); Philip J. Ivanhoe, *Ethics in the Confucian Tradition: The Thought of Mengzi and Wang Yangming* (2002); Bryan W. van Norden, *Confucius and the Analects: New Essays* (2002); and Kwong-loi Shun and David B. Wong, *Confucian Ethics: A Comparative Study of Self, Autonomy, and Community* (2004).

# FEMINIST PHILOSOPHY

## What is **feminism** and **feminist philosophy**?

Feminism involves both thought and practice aimed at improving the well-being of women. On the side of practice it is often thought of as the "women's movement." Intellectually, feminism is a critical theory because it contains analysis of social conditions and prescriptions for improving them toward its end. Also on the intellectual side, feminism is now a multidisciplinary academic field with participation from all of the humanities, contemporary cultural criticism, the social sciences, and women's studies.

Feminist philosophy is the philosophical dimension of intellectual feminism. Many feminist philosophers understand their intellectual history and the history of the women's movement in terms of three "waves."

## What are the **three waves of feminism** according to feminist philosophers?

The first wave began on the eve of the French Revolution with Mary Wollstonecraft's (1759–1797) writings and continued until women in both Great Britain and the United States were granted the right to vote in 1918 and 1920, respectively.

After women gained suffrage in the United States, the women's movement seemed to go into a dormant period, perhaps because until the end of World War II progressive thought was concentrated on socialism and communism. However in the middle of the twentieth century, the publication of two books began what many view as the second wave: the French existentialist philosopher Simone de Beavoir's (1908–1986) *The Second Sex* (1952) and Betty Friedan's *The Feminine Mystique* (1963).

Betty Freidan (1921–2006) was an American writer and left-wing political journalist and activist. In 1957, at the 15-year reunion of Smith College (an institution for

Prominent feminist Betty Friedan wrote about the disatisfaction many American women were feeling about their lives in the mid-twentieth century (AP).

women), she interviewed her classmates, who had graduated in 1942. Many had achieved the approved social ambition of a husband, home, and children, but they were dissatisfied with their lives and in some instances agonizingly unfulfilled. Friedan argued, in ways that resonated throughout American society and Europe, that women as human beings needed education and meaningful work, mental stimulation, and fully adult responsibilities.

By the 1970s, further development of Friedan's ideas found expression in the third wave. The women's liberation movement was associated with the following achievements: Title VII of the Civil Rights Act of 1964 prohibited discrimination in employment on the grounds of gender, as well as race; the U.S. Supreme Court decision of *Roe v. Wade* in 1973 legitimized the right to abortion based on bodily privacy. These legal innovations combined with "the pill" (birth control medication), provided a new degree of sexual freedom, huge increases in women's employment outside the home, and access to higher education. Women entered the professions in unprecedented numbers and "the rest is history" in the sense that it is now taken for granted by American society that women should have opportunities equal to men's.

## What were the **goals** of activist **second wave feminists**?

Equality with men in employment, an end to violence against women, full equality of women in public life, including access to the highest offices of government, and top executive positions in all social institutions were all goals of the second wave. Full acceptance of lesbians and nontraditional families remain ongoing political ideals, as do universal health care and child care for working mothers in the United States. The problem of the "second shift," or the fact that working women still do disproportionate amounts of domestic work and child care in their homes, is another overhanging problem. (See in *The Second Shift* [1990] by Arlie Russell Hochschild and Anne Machung.)

## What is **philosophical** about **feminist philosophy**?

Unlike women's studies, which is focused on the factual and historical aspects of women's lives, feminist philosophy rethinks much of social philosophy and ethics from the perspective of women and the interests of women. Some feminist philosophers have created new philosophical subject matter, whereas others have revisited traditional philosophical approaches that were created by male philosophers. For example, political philosophers have often assumed that the basic political unit is a male head of household, thereby neglecting both female workers and the kind of unpaid work performed by women in traditional families. Feminist philosophers seek revisions and expansions of such assumptions so as to include women.

## What have been the main **themes** in **philosophical feminism**?

Philosophical feminists have thus far been very open to theoretical work from other disciplines. They have concentrated on theorizing the oppression of women in the history of philosophy, as well as contemporary culture. The result in the United States alone has been a vast body of work with many facets.

Although feminism is hardly part of mainstream philosophy in academia, most philosophy departments now have women members. Examples of influential feminist scholarship include feminist reclamation, feminist epistemology, feminist political theory, and gender theory. An excellent overview of these subjects is Alison M. Jagger and Marion Young's *A Companion to Feminist Philosophy* (2000).

## What is **feminist reclamation**?

In philosophy, as well as other fields, feminist reclamation has been the rediscovery of women thinkers, who have been neglected in traditional intellectual history, especially before the 1980s. Some of these women are considered philosophers only if philosophy is broadly construed. But others worked comprehensively on issues central to their field, influenced their peers, and have only recently been fully recognized for their achievements. A strong example of this category is Ruth Barcan Marcus.

## Who is **Ruth Barcan Marcus**?

Ruth Barcan Marcus (1921–) was educated at Yale, received a Guggenheim fellowship in 1952, and was a founding chair of the philosophy department at the University of Illinois at Chicago. After working as a professor at Northwestern University, she was Halleck Professor of Philosophy at Yale University from 1973 to 1991. She worked in the formal subjects of quantification theory and modal logic, sometimes in disagreement with W.V.O. Quine (1908–2000).

One of her most striking achievements was an early formulation of the new causal theory of reference, made famous by Hilary Putnam (1926–) and Saul Kripke (1940–). The causal theory of reference held that words for things have a history from the first time someone used a specific word to stand for a specific object or idea. For example, we call apples "apples" because that word was the first at some time, in some specific place, to be used to name the fruit. As proponents of the causal theory of reference put it, apples were baptized "apples."

Marcus' ground-breaking journal articles are collected in *Modalities: Philosophical Essays* (1993). She received the American Philosophical Association Quinn Prize for service to the profession in 2007.

## How did **feminist epistemology** develop?

Nancy Chodorow (1944–) showed in *The Reproduction of Mothering* (1978) how social roles within the nuclear family are "reproduced" socially by girls identifying with their mothers and boys becoming unlike their mothers. Recognition of the social construction of female gender resulted in broad rejection of biological determinism of women's traditional roles. This cleared the way for feminists to seek social causes for the disadvantageous status of women.

Carol Gilligan's (1936–) *In a Different Voice* (1982) criticized Lawrence Kohlberg's account of moral development because it left out the relational nature of girls' moral perceptions, in contrast to the more abstract and individualistic nature of boys' moral development. The idea that women had relational identities led to an ethics of care, most notably based on Stanford University psychologist Nell Noddings' *Caring* (1982), which was foundational for the work of Sandra Lee Bartke in *Femininity and Domination* (1990) and Eva Kittay's *Love's Labor: Essays on Women, Equality and Dependence* (1999).

Genevieve Lloyd's *The Man of Reason: "Male" and "Female" in Western Philosophy* (1984) sparked a view that philosophy itself had been identified with distinctively masculine capabilities of reason to the intellectual as well as literal exclusion of women. These perspectives led to the articulation of feminist epistemology, stressing connected, rather than individual knowers (or people who learn and come to know things), and the role of emotion and action in knowledge. The collection of papers in Linda Alcoff (1955–) and Elizabeth Potter's (1947–) edited work *Feminist Epistemologies* (1993) relates some of this ground-breaking work to traditional epistemology. An additional development of feminist epistemology is feminist philosophy of science.

## What is **feminist philosophy of science**?

Feminist philosophy of science consists of analyses of scientific methodology and standards for truth. Its focus has been on the ways that the idea of objectivity have excluded knowledge of importance to women.

## Who are some key **feminist philosophers of science**?

Sandra Harding (1935–) addresses questions of whether women have privileged ways of knowing, in Third World, as well as Euro-American societies, whether the exclusion of women from science can be corrected within science, and whether scientific knowledge is itself misogynistic. Harding's groundbreaking work includes *The Science Question in Feminism* (1986) and *Whose Science? Whose Knowledge?* (1991). Janet

## Are all philosophical feminists women?

**B**y no means. A number of male philosophers have endeavored to both learn and support feminism and include feminist subjects in their own more traditional work. These men have published such books as *Rethinking Masculinity: Philosophical Explorations in Light of Feminism* (1992), edited by Larry May and Robert Strikwerda; *Men Doing Feminism* (1998), edited by Tom Digby; and Michael A. Slote's *The Ethics of Care and Empathy* (2007).

There were women's separatist social movements in the 1970s, but this has never been a viable option in academia. The radical feminist philosopher of religion Mary Daly (1936–), who taught at Boston College for 33 years, was forced to retire in 1999 for barring men from some of her classes. Daly was always on thin ice at this Jesuit institution, especially after the publication of her first book, *The Church and the Second Sex* (1968). Daly's work is about how men have appropriated the roles and power of women in religion, particularly in Catholic ritual.

Philosophical feminism has evinced strong support for lesbian feminism on the grounds that lesbians have been oppressed in society and that lesbians may recognize the personhood of women more easily than men. Nevertheless, freedom of sexual preference entails that heterosexuality remains a respected preference, just as freedom of choice in abortion has not led feminists to invalidate, on moral or political grounds, pregnancy and childbirth. On motherhood, for example, Sara Ruddick's *Maternal Thinking: Toward a Politics of Peace* (1990) shows how childcare develops distinctive ways of thinking, although childbirth and rearing is not limited to heterosexual women. Much of French feminist writing assumes strong male-female sexual differences.

Kourany (1943–) edited *The Gender of Science* (2002) and *Scientific Knowledge* (1987, 1998), which relate some of the feminist critique of traditional science to standing issues in mainstream philosophy of science.

## What has been important in **second wave feminist political philosophy**?

The concept of patriarchy, or rule by "fathers," throughout human history sparked much social and textual analysis, which was brought to theoretical completion by Carole Pateman in *The Sexual Contract* (1988). Pateman argued that when modern social contract theory was constructed by Thomas Hobbes (1588–1679) and John Locke (1632–1704), women were left out of the political equation and relegated to private life.

Iris Young (1949–2006), a professor of philosophy at the University of Chicago, addressed the connection between female social roles and political structures in *Jus-*

411

*tice and the Politics of Difference* (1990) and *Inclusion and Democracy* (2000). Young also addressed women's disempowered bodily comportment in her 1980 essay "Throwing Like a Girl" (included in a book by the same name in 1990). In addition, feminist philosophers have welcomed and discussed the work of University of Michigan Law School professor Catherine MacKinnon.

## What is **Catherine MacKinnon's contribution** to second wave feminist political philosophy?

In the 1970s Catherine MacKinnon (1946–) began to argue that sexual harassment is a form of sexual discrimination, outlawed by the 1964 Civil Rights Act. MacKinnon and Andrea Dworkin also developed legal theory to outlaw pornography. The U.S. Supreme Court ruled against sexual harassment in 1986, largely based on MacKinnon's work; and the Supreme Court of Canada has partly accepted her arguments against pornography.

MacKinnon's books include: *In Harm's Way: The Pornography Civil Rights Hearings* (edited and introduced with Andrea Dworkin; 1997), *Toward a Feminist Theory of the State* (1989), *Pornography and Civil Rights: A New Day for Women's Equality* (with Andrea Dworkin; 1988), *Organizing Against Pornography* (1988), *Feminism Unmodified: Discourses on Life and Law* (1987), and *Sexual Harassment of Working Women: A Case of Sex Discrimination* (with Thomas I. Emerson; 1979).

## What is Catherine **MacKinnon's argument** against **pornography**?

According to MacKinnon, pornography not only exploits and objectifies those women who are its subjects, but it also expresses and supports the overall oppression of women in society. The subordinate status of women in pornography, as well as the violence against women depicted in so many of its forms, is part of an unjust sex-gender system.

## How have **second wave feminists** addressed **gender**?

They have criticized the social norm of "compulsive heterosexuality," on the grounds that the human sex-gender system is a system of power that benefits men at the expense of women. Some of this work has consisted of the "deconstruction" of gender as natural and a valorization of love between women. Judith Butler, the Professor of Rhetoric and Comparative Literature at the University of California at Berkeley, has challenged "heteronormativity" in *Antigone's Claim: Kinship Between Life and Death* (2000) and *Gender Trouble: Feminism and the Subversion of Identity* (1999). Butler is famous for her deconstruction of gender into performances of gender. Sara Lucia Hoagland, in *Lesbian Ethics: Toward a New Value* (1988), and Marilyn Frye in *The Politics of Reality: Essays in Feminist Theory* (1983), developed foundational views of this perspective.

## What is **French feminism**?

French feminism is a school of thought named by feminists outside France to refer to work mainly proffered by Luce Irigaray (1932–), Hélène Cixous (1937–), and Julia Kristeva (1941–). But none of these three is originally from France, and from time to time each has denied being a feminist. What Irigary, Cixous, and Kristeva all share is that their work is based on considerations of philosophical and psychoanalytic texts. They all assume that to improve the situation of women, fundamental psychological structures need to be revised. That is, they are working within the tradition of structuralism.

By comparison, there is another group of French feminists whose work is more sociological and activist than theoretical. Known as French materialist feminists, they address the situation of women by attempting to change society through political activism and work in the social sciences. Key figures are: Simon de Beauvoir (1908–1986), Christine Delphy (1941–), Monique Wittig (1935–2003), and Colette Guillaumin (1934–). Some of their theoretical work, which has been especially influential in the Communist Revolutionary League, describes the ways in which the free labor of women in the family supports capitalism.

## Who is **Julia Kristeva**?

Since arriving in France in 1966 from Bulgaria, Julia Kristeva (1941–) has achieved international recognition for her writings about women in the psychoanalytic tradition. Her work is considered multi-disciplinary, encompassing art criticism, philosophy, and cultural critique. Kristeva's primary theoretical contribution has been a distinction between the symbolic aspects of language and what she calls the semiotic, a psychic level of meaning based on a child's relationship to its mother. Primary human desires are attached to the semiotic, which is based on the biological rhythms of the maternal body, although the semiotic eludes symbolic translation.

## What is Julia **Kristeva's idea** of the **abject** and the **nature of women**?

Kristeva has emphasized the rejection of mothers by both male and female children due to male-dominated cultural patterns that render the mother herself abject, which is to say, totally other, disgusting, and monstrous. Kristeva thinks that the solution to this problem requires a rediscovery and healing of narcissism in women's psyches and an acceptance of adult love between women. However, Kristeva rejects the label "woman" as a universal term, and has refused to define women. She apparently believes that every woman is fundamentally different in how she is a woman or what being a woman means. As she wrote:

> It is there, in the analysis of her difficult relation to her mother and to her own difference from everybody else, men and women, that a woman encounters the enigma of the "feminine." I favour an understanding of femininity that would have as many "feminines" as there are women.

413

Kristeva's main theoretical writings are: *About Chinese Women* (1977), *Desire in Language: A Semiotic Approach to Literature and Art* (1980), *Powers of Horror: An Essay on Abjection* (1982), *Revolution in Poetic Language* (1984), and *New Maladies of the Soul* (1995).

## Who is **Luce Irigaray**?

Luce Irigaray (1932–) was born in Belgium and attended Jacques Lacan's psychoanalytic seminars in the 1960s. She is famous for having written, "Sexual difference is probably the issue in our time which could be our 'salvation' if we thought it through," and "One must assume the feminine role deliberately. Which means already to convert a form of subordination into an affirmation, and thus to thwart it." Irigaray's main writings include *An Ethics of Sexual Difference* (1982) and *Je, Tu, Nous: Toward a Culture of Difference* (1990).

## For what is Luce **Iragary most famous**?

The publication of Irigaray's (1932–) doctoral thesis, *Speculum of the Other Woman* (1974), led to her expulsion from further study at Lacan's Freudian School at Vincennes. (In Europe a Ph.D. is not sufficient for university teaching, as it is in the United States, and a second dissertation or habilitation is required.) Irigary's dissertation consisted of her theoretical analyses of a lecture by Sigmund Freud (1856–1939) on femininity and long quotations from the works of male philosophers, from Plato (c. 428–c. 348 B.C.E.) to Hegel (1770–1831). It was evident in the work that by a "speculum" she was referring to the concave mirrored medical instrument inserted into a woman's body.

## Was Luce Irigaray's *Speculum of the Other Woman* socially **relevant**?

Yes, and it has also had a tremendous influence on students and scholars of French feminist philosophy. In the context of the women's health movement in the United States during the 1970s, it expressed part of the spirit of the gynecological aspect of women's liberation. Women began to rebel about the fact that there were so few women doctors and that male doctors treated their reproductive and child birth issues in repressive ways. Women began to talk more openly about their feelings of shame about their own bodies.

Members of some women's collectives began giving themselves and their friends gynecological examinations, and others, without prior medical training, taught themselves how to administer abortions. At the same time, the practices of natural childbirth (childbirth without medication) and nursing, which until then had been the only resort for many poor women, were advocated for privileged women, for the health of both mothers and babies. These examples of women taking responsibility for their health were motivated both by an ideology of rebellion against patriarchy and the goal of improving women's health.

Since the 1970s, feminist advocates have pointed out that clinical medicine has traditionally been based on the male body. Some diseases have different symptoms in men and women—for example, heart disease. At this time, female doctors are commonplace, particularly in the practice of gynecology, and there is greater attention, overall, to women's health problems.

Historical information on the 1970s women's health movement can be found at CWLU Herstory Project: The Online History of the Chicago Women's Liberation Union is at http://www.cwluherstory.com.

## Who is **Hélène Cixous**?

Hélène Cixous (1937–) is best known to philosophers for her *The Laugh of the Medusa* and *Sorties* (both 1975). These works constitute an anti-essentialist exhortation for women to reclaim their bodily experience in a new form of feminine writing, *écriture féminine*. Cixous has been interpreted to advocate bisexuality and multiplicities of sexuality in ways believed to have prefigured queer theory.

## Why are **LBGT studies** and **queer theory** part of **philosophy** now?

They have become part of philosophy along with an overall interest in expanding cultural studies to include attention to issues previously neglected. This change has been part of the humanities, generally, and philosophers have focused on conceptual issues related to these fields.

Queer theory emerged in the 1990s, along with LGBT (Lesbian Gay Bisexual Transsexual) studies, as a positive affirmation of sexual difference that does not fit into any of its predecessor categories, including lesbianism. Good overviews on the subject may be found in Naomi Schor's *Feminism Meets Queer Theory* (1997), and helpful works on transsexuality are Susan Stryker's *Transgender History* (2008), and Laurie Shrage's *You've Changed* (2009).

## Why has there been a **third wave in feminism**?

According to its critics, the second wave was presumed to speak for all women while it merely propounded the interests of a small group of white, privileged American intellectual women. Two books crystallized this complaint: bell hooks' (she spelled her name in all lowercase letters) *Ain't I a Woman?: Black Women and Feminism* (1981) brought attention to oppression due to race suffered by women of color. Elizabeth V. Spelman pointed out the problems of a universalizing trend within feminism that left out differences among women in *Inessential Woman: Problems of Exclusion in Feminist Thought* (1988).

White feminist complaints about "glass ceilings," or invisible barriers to top positions in business, on the one hand and the stultifying aspects of home-making on the other, did not resonate with all other women. Poor women and women of color had worked outside their own homes, in factories and fields, or the homes of other women, for centuries; the "second shift" was not new to them. Because of this, a third wave was needed to address *all* women's needs.

### How did **race** become **important** in **feminist philosophy**?

The complexity of feminist issues of race were underscored by University of California at Los Angeles law professor Kimberle Crewshaw's groundbreaking paper, "Demarginalizing the Intersection of Race and Sex: A Black Feminist Critique of Antidiscrimination Doctrine, Feminist Theory and Antiracist Politics" (*University of Chicago Legal Forum* 139–67, 1989). Kimberle's work introduced the problems of intersectionality, whereby oppressions due to race and gender can't simply be added because they result in distinctive new identities that form a situation of new forms of discrimination.

Kimberle argued that black women are not protected by either discrimination laws for women or by discrimination laws for blacks—white women take precedence over them in the first instance and black men in the second. That is, anti-discrimination laws are satisfied in the letter of the law by protecting groups of women in which white women dominate, and groups of blacks in which men dominate. The result is that black women are not legally protected as black women.

### What is the **problem** caused by **intersectionality**?

The result of all the intersectionalities has been a widely accepted equation that race + class = gender, resulting in a multiplicity of women's genders that prevents the possibility of women working together or even identifying in the same way. And the result of that is an unspecified number of feminisms. Once different women's genders are recognized, it can be very difficult for them to reunite as women. For example in their essay "Have We Got a Theory for You!" (1998), María C. Lugones and Elisabeth V. Spelman use a dialogue to show how some differences in Angla and Latina cultural experience simply cannot be translated into each other's framework of understanding.

### Can the **problem** of **intersectionality** be solved?

Many theorists believe it can if there is a shared understanding of what women have in common. One possibility, developed by Naomi Zack in *Inclusive Feminism: A Third*

## What further problems of inclusion did second wave feminists face?

The problem of not having addressed racism was compounded by neglect of social class inequalities in the second wave. Furthermore, while the goals of Western feminists appeared to be androgynous equality with men, women in the Third World were constructing feminisms based on their traditional roles as wives and mothers in times of political upheaval. Some of these projects are discussed in *Decentering the Center: Philosophy for a Multicultural, Postcolonial and Feminist World* (2000), edited by Uma Narayan and Sandra Harding, and Haleh Afshared's *Women and Politics in the Third World* (1996). The way in which poor American women have been left out of the abortion debates is treated by Laurie Shrage in *Abortion and Social Responsibility: Depolarizing the Debate* (2003).

*Wave Theory of Women's Commonality* (2005), is that all women share a relation to an historical category that has been oppressed: the group of mothers, or birth females, or men's heterosexual choices. A second, developed by Cressida J. Heyes in *Line Drawings: Defining Women Through Feminist Practice,* is that women share Wittgensteinian "family resemblances."

## Why is the **unity** or commonality of **women important**?

Although the entire world knows which human beings are "women" and not "men," if feminists cannot agree on this matter then it is not clear how feminism can advocate for the well-being of women. Third World, poor, and racially marginalized women need the support of First World women, who in turn might learn from the practical forms of organizations developed in less advantaged countries and cultures. Without a perceived commonality among women, there is no basis on which common political ends, such as health care, education, child care for working mothers, and preservation and care of the natural environment, can be collectively pursued by feminists.

# ENVIRONMENTAL PHILOSOPHY

## What is **environmentalism**?

Environmentalism is the study of the relationship between living organisms (including human beings) and natural environments, usually with the aim of preserving natural environments and renewable resources. Environmentalism is now a multifaceted, multi-disciplinary field, extending widely into both theory and practice.

Environmental philosophy has drawn on many traditions and subfields within philosophy, including: ethics, social philosophy, continental philosophy, aesthetics, and feminism. Each of these areas refers basic questions about our relation to the environment to fundamental philosophical viewpoints.

## What, besides ethics, is **philosophical about environmentalism**?

As mortal beings, we are all dependent on our environments, and a good part of human spirituality is centered on gratitude for how the earth supports human life, as well as the beauty of natural living and nonliving things. Overall, environmentalism has encouraged a reverence for the goods of life and a good life that flows from what is not artificial or man-made and mass-produced.

There are, of course, direct practical human concerns when it comes to environmentalism, as well as quality-of-life issues related to diminishing resources. For example, not all of the multi-disciplinary experts who have studied global warming agree on its dangers or on how much of it is due to human fossil-fuel consumption. Some believe that Earth has had similar changes in temperature before human industrialization. Recent and emerging studies assign high percentages of global warming to the

Philosophical environmentalists, analyze humanity's relationship to nature (BigStock Photos).

flatulence of domestic animals raised for food (which could be considered an indirect human activity). Sorting out an issue as complex as global warming would require extensive philosophy of science!

## What general **philosophical problems** does **environmentalism pose**?

In more traditional philosophical terms, there are ontological and metaphysical issues involved in what counts as a "unit" in environmentalism. (It is important to define the unit because that defines the subject matter theoretically and makes it possible to keep track of what should be preserved, in practical terms.) Is it one animal, a group, an entire ecological niche, a region, a country?

In broad human terms, the problems related to our natural environment are likely to be central in twenty-first century life—everywhere. The dependence of humans on the natural planet and the dependence of the natural health of parts of the planet on human activity will probably become an even more absorbing, distressing, and contentious subject than it already is.

Since of all the new subjects in philosophy, environmentalism is probably the most popular, it should be noted that the following books are all good sources of additional information: William F. Baxter, *People or Penguins: The Case for Maximum Pollution* (1974); Ted Benton, *Natural Relations: Ecology, Animal Rights & Social Justice* (1993); Jay Bernstein, *Adorno: Disenchantment and Ethics* (2001); J.B. Callicott, *In Defense of the Land Ethic: Essays in Environmental Philosophy* (1989); B. Devall and G. Sessions, *Deep Ecology: Living as if Nature Mattered* (1985); Robert Heilbroner, "What Has Posterity Ever Done for Me?," in *New York Times Magazine* (January 19, 1975); Thomas E. Hill, "Ideals of Human Virture and Preserving the Natural Environment," in *Ethics,* Volume 5 (1983); D. Jamieson, editor, *A Companion to Environmental Philosophy* (2001); Aldo Leopold, *A Sand County Almanac* (1949); A. Naess, *Ecology, Community, Lifestyle* (reprint, 1989); R. Nash, *The Rights of Nature: A History of Environmental Ethics* (1989); V. Plumwood, *Environmental Culture* (2002); and Peter Singer, *Animal Liberation: A New Ethics for our Treatment of Animals, (1975, 1977, 1983).*

## How did **environmental philosophy** get **started**?

Popular environmentalism began in the 1960s and 1970s when marine biologist Rachel Carson (1907–1964) traced the movement of toxic pesticides (specifically, DDT) through the food chain in her classic book, *Silent Spring* (1962). Intellectually, this led to a rediscovery of ecologist and forester Aldo Leopold's (1887–1948) land ethic, *A Sand County Almanac* (1949), and the thought of John Muir (1838–1914), founder of the Sierra Club.

Leopold had written: "That land is a community is the basic concept of ecology, but that land is to be loved and respected is an extension of ethics." This moral tone set the basic philosophical orientation toward environmentalism as a moral/ethical matter. The Norwegian philosopher Arne Naess (1912–) was inspired by his encounter with the Himalayan Sherpas' reverence for their great mountains when his guides would not take him to sacred places. Naess developed an important distinction between deep ecology and shallow ecology.

## What is the **distinction** between **deep** and **shallow ecology**?

According to Arne Naess (1912–), shallow ecology is concern of affluent Westerners for their own clean air and water, abundant resources, and beautiful scenery. Deep ecology, by contrast, is based on biospheric egalitarianism, or the inherent value to all natural beings of their own existence, shared equally by them all.

Naess envisioned the world as a "total-field" or "biospherical net" in which individual organisms are related to the whole of their environments. As individuals, human beings, for example, are mere "knots" in the net and ought to forgo some of their preoccupation with their own individual existence and selfish interests.

## What has been Arne **Naess' philosophical influence**?

Naess' (1912–) broadest influence has probably been from his overall sense that there are spiritual, if not religious, values in our proper connection with natural environments. People should respect and care for such environments as an elevated activity. Many contemporary environmentalists, theoretical and practical, share Naess' intuition that human beings benefit from contact with nature and animals in deeply nourishing ways that cannot be duplicated by commercial forms of entertainment, or even human interaction. Acknowledgment of such benefits has led virtue ethicists such as Thomas E. Hill Jr. (1951–) to claim that how we treat non-human beings both reveals our own character and partly constitutes it.

In contemporary environmental debates, another way of stating the deep–shallow ecological distinction is via instrumental and intrinsic values. A being has intrinsic value if it is good in and of itself, whereas its value is instrumental if its good is what it is good for. This theoretical point is important ethically in thought going back to Immanuel Kant (1724– 1804), which distinguishes between categorical or absolute imperatives and hypothetical or instrumental ones. But whereas Kant thought that the only thing with intrinsic value is the good will of a rational creature (a human being), some environmentalists have extended intrinsic value to all living beings.

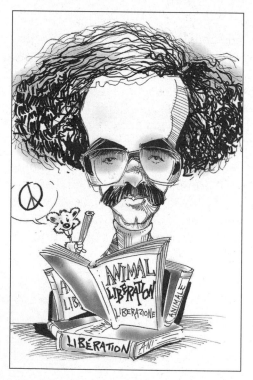

A caricature of Peter Singer, who has been criticized for saying that healthy adult animals are more valuable than severely impaired human infants (BigStock Photos).

420

## What **question** does **deep ecology pose** for philosophers?

The question that arises is this: "How can we justify the intrinsic value of non-human beings?" Jeremy Bentham (1748–1832) famously wrote that this question turns not on whether "they" can think or reason, but on whether they can suffer. A contemporary utilitarian, the Australian philosopher Peter Singer (1946–), developed this idea of worth in his now world-famous book *Animal Liberation* (1973).

## What are some of Peter **Singer's views**?

Singer (1946–) has at times argued that the lives of healthy, adult animals are of greater value than those of severely impaired human infants. Such views have met with great controversy. When Singer was hired by Princeton University in 1999, there were dramatic public demonstrations by and for disabled people, and the university administration hired armed guards to protect him.

Singer, proceeding on utilitarian grounds, does not believe that animals have rights, but rather that their well-being is intrinsically good and their pain and destruction intrinsically bad. Singer is not a deep ecologist, because he does not attribute intrinsic value to the well-being of mountains, rivers, or plants, or whatever is not sentient. Singer has claimed that the privileging of human life and well-being over that of animals is speciesism, which, in principle, is no different from racism and sexism.

## **Who** has **claimed** that **animals** have **rights**?

Tom Regan (1938–) has based a deontological doctrine of the wrongness of killing innocents, including animals, on the premise that they have intrinsic or inherent worth. It follows from this that humans have an obligation not to harm animals, or at least some of them, for recreation, food, or experimentation. Paul W. Taylor (1923–) has extended Regan's view in claiming that every living thing, from a germ to an elephant, has a "teleological-center-of-life" that is worthy of moral respect.

## What do **critics** of the **deep ecological** and animal value views **claim**?

William F. Baxter, a law professor who passed away in 1998, argued in *People or Penguins: The Case for Maximum Pollution* (1974) that the cost of a pollution-free society would be harmful to humans. He assumed that humanism requires that humans are what matter above all else. Baxter expressed a general critical view of environmentalism held by human beings who do not believe that animals have intrinsic worth or rights equal to those of humans.

## What **religious issues** are involved in **environmental thought**, pro and con?

Some of the critical perspective derives from a Christian view imbedded in Western political philosophy that God gave the earth and everything on it to humankind to rule over for our use; only humans have the spark of divinity that justifies intrinsic value. Nonetheless, many religious groups have proclaimed an obligation of benevolent stewardship over parts of the earth. But, insofar as part of this stewardship is for the sake of future generations, a perplexing question arises: How can we have obligations to those who do not exist? Robert Heilbroner (1919–2005) has examined this issue in "What Has Posterity Ever Done for Me?," a widely quoted and reprinted 1975 essay that first appeared in *New York Magazine*.

## How is **environmental ethics** a **secular matter**?

In secular terms, animals and other natural entities do not have legal standing in human courts, unless there is human advocacy for them. Endangered species and anti-cruelty laws are instances of such advocacy. Other critics of environmentalism and animal rights point out that 99.9 percent of all species that have ever existed are now extinct and that human predation on nature is just as natural as animal predation.

## How is **environmentalism related** to **feminism**?

Feminists have addressed the exploitation of natural environments as part of overall cultural misogyny insofar as the earth is at least metaphorically female. Also, some of the exploitation of animals is centered on female animals. Chris Cuomo explores this last thesis and characterizes living beings in an interesting way as having "dynamic charm" in *Feminism and Ecological Communities* (2002).

## How is **environmentalism** related to **racial and international studies**?

Theorists of racial discrimination such as Laura Westra and Bill E. Lawson have identified "environmental racisms." Minorities, who live in poor neighborhoods, are more vulnerable to having toxic dump sites in their immediate environments, for example. Some indigenous philosophers have criticized the whole Western technological project. By contrast, international scholars have criticized Western environmentalists for assuming that development in poor countries for the improvement of human life is less important than the preservation of nature.

# OTHER TRENDS IN NEW PHILOSOPHY

## What is the **philosophy of biology**?

Strictly speaking, philosophy of biology is not new because it has been part of philosophy since Aristotle (384–322 B.C.E.). However, recent thought about how living systems are different from the inert subject matter of physics and chemistry have resulted in new philosophies of biology as a distinct theoretical/philosophical subject. Moreover, social controversies, such as popular debates about creationism and evolution, and beliefs in individual self-determination versus genetic determinism, have injected new vitality into older issues in philosophy of biology.

## What are some of the main **themes** in **philosophy of biology**?

Philosophers of biology are interested in how biological explanations differ in form from explanations in the other sciences regarding whether the behavior of living things can be predicted, and in how environment, genetics, and processes of development interact to result in organisms. They are also interested in evolutionary theory.

Useful texts in philosophy of biology include: Alexander Rosenberg, *Structure of Biological Science* (1985); Elliot Sober, *The Nature of Selection* (1984); and Michael Ruse, *Philosophy of Biology* (1973). Most contemporary philosophers of biology rely on Ernst Mayr's *The Growth of Biological Thought: Diversity, Evolution and Inheritance* (1982) and *Towards a New Philosophy of Biology: Observations of an Evolutionist* (1988). Additional thought by biologists have also resulted in new perspectives on biology that include work by: Patrick Bateson, Richard Dawkins, Jared Diamond, Stephen Jay Gould, Richard Lewontin, John Maynard Smith, and Edward O. Wilson. Also, evolutionary biology has inspired new philosophical systems of thought—for example, by Daniel Dennett.

## Who is **Daniel C. Dennett**?

Daniel C. Dennett (1942–) is an American philosopher of mind and science. He is professor of philosophy at Tufts University and co-director of the Center for Cognitive Studies there. He has been influential in combining cognitive science and evolutionary theory in philosophy of biology, most notably in these works: *Darwin's Dangerous Idea: Evolution and the Meanings of Life* (1996), *Kinds of Minds: Towards an Understanding of Consciousness* (1997), *Brainchildren: Essays on Designing Minds (Representation and Mind)* (1998), *Freedom Evolves* (2003), *Sweet Dreams: Philosophical Obstacles to a Science of Consciousness* (2005), and *Breaking the Spell: Religion as a Natural Phenomenon* (2006). Dennett is also a supporter of the Brights Movement.

## What is Daniel C. **Dennett's philosophy of biology**?

Dennett (1942–) engages evolutionary theory by asking the question, "Skyhooks or cranes?" Skyhooks are unexplained leaps from one stage of development to the next, whereas cranes are ways of understanding a later stage based on the design of an earlier one. Dennett has argued that consciousness, the contents of consciousness, and even the products of consciousness, such as Shakespeare's plays, can be naturalistically understood in the same way that physical evolution is understandable. Neural systems create "multiple drafts" of the same thing so that the brain itself is "a sort of dung heap in which the larvae of other people's ideas renew themselves." Dennett is also a proponent of the doctrine of "memes," whereby certain patterns of behavior are products of evolution that are physically inherited. His extreme materialism has attracted many critics, as well as supporters.

## What is a **meme**?

In *The Selfish Gene* (1976) British evolutionary biologist, professor, and author Richard Dawkins coined the term as being on a par with "gene." A meme—for instance, a tune, recipe, moral system, or style of dress—gets passed on from one generation to the next via cultural interaction. Although memes are not usually held to be physically inherited the way that genes are, social biologists believe them to be subject to natural selection and mutation.

## What is **experimental philosophy**?

It is a very new philosophical approach that aims to use empirical information to back up the "ordinary intuitions" to which philosophers refer. People are given philosophical problems or solutions to them and asked if they agree with the philosopher's answer. Experimental philosophy has been applied to philosophy of language, philosophy of action, and "intuitions" that free will is not compatible with determinism.

## What are some **results** of **experimental philosophy**?

Thus far, Bertrand Russell's (1872–1970) theory of descriptions has "failed" at least one intuitive test. Respondents are inclined to blame people for what they do unintentionally, which, according to philosophers, they should not. Free will is also held to be compatible with determinism, which philosophers have assumed not to be the case.

## What are the **pitfalls** and **promises** of **experimental philosophy**?

In its degenerate forms, experimental philosophy could resemble philosophy by opinion poll, but that is not its goal or method. Rather, the view is that before relying on ordinary intuitions, philosophers should check what non-philosophers

Richard Dawkins, an evolutionary biologist, coined the term "meme" (AP).

actually believe. That is, if philosophical theories depend on a certain view of intuitions, then philosophers should begin with the empirically accurate view: they should make sure that when they say the public thinks X, that the public does think X. The promise of philosophy is that experimental philosophy has the potential to make social and political philosophy more scientific.

This does not deprive philosophers of the freedom to construct theories that explain why ordinary intuitions are incorrect, insofar as they are complex judgments and not mere expressions of taste. Recent work in experimental philosophy includes: Joshua Knobe and Shaun Nichols, *Experimental Philosophy* (2008); Joshua Knobe, "Intentional Action in Folk Psychology: An Experimental Investigation," in *Philosophical Psychology,* 16, (2003); and K. Anthony Appiah, *Experiments in Ethics* (2008). Critical responses to experimental philosophy include: Ernest Sosa, "Experimental Philosophy and Philosophical Intuition," in *Philosophical Studies,* 132 (2006); Kirk Ludwig, "The Epistemology of Thought Experiments: First vs. Third Person Approaches," in *Midwest Studies in Philosophy,* 31 (2007); and Antti Kauppinen, "The Rise and Fall of Experimental Philosophy," in *Philosophical Explorations,* 10 (2007).

## What is **philosophy of technology**?

Ideas of technology go back to Plato (c. 428–c. 348 B.C.E.) and Aristotle (384–322 B.C.E.), who spoke of *techne,* or knowledge of art and craft, which included arithmetic

What is our relationship to technology? How does it affect our lives and our perception of our world? These are questions the philosophy of technology may address (BigStock Photos).

and medicine. Such knowledge understands itself, according to universals and causes. It can be taught and is distinct from *physis,* or nature.

Contemporary philosophy of technology is a multi-disciplinary field dedicated to studying the cultural effects and causes of technology, both historically and in its emergent forms. The American Philosophical Association publishes a newsletter on *Philosophy and Computers,* and there are academic journals such as *Ends and Means, NetFuture—Technology and Human Responsibility,* and *Techné: Research in Philosophy and Technology.*

### What are the main **themes** and **influences** in **philosophy of technology**?

Most of the writing is on the progressive/environmentalist/feminist/postmodern side of contemporary philosophy. While not anti-technology *per se,* there is a deep suspicion of technology as a force in its own right that stems from Martin Heidegger's (1889–1976) *The Question Concerning Technology*. By contrast, more optimistic views of technology stem from the writings of John Dewey (1859–1952).

Key issues are: whether technology can be controlled independently of radical economic and political changes; whether technology can correct its own excesses; and the roles played by technology in the history of science. Contemporary books of interest include: Michael Adas, *Machines as the Measure of Men: Science, Technology, and*

## What is philosophy for children?

Philosophy for children is an attempt both to introduce critical thinking and the subject of philosophy to high school students and to explore and develop natural interest in philosophical questions among younger children. In Europe, high school age students have traditionally had at least some philosophy on their curricula; the question in the United States is not whether teenagers are capable of learning philosophy, but how to introduce it and find teachers qualified to do so, as well as funding.

While psychologist Jean Piaget set the paradigm that children are not able to "think about thinking" or engage in philosophy before about age 12, philosopher Gareth Matthews (1929–) argues in *Philosophy and the Young Child* (1980) that there was evidence of philosophical thought and speech in Piaget's own young subjects. Before then, Matthew Lipman (1922–) had introduced philosophy to middle school children in Montclair, New Jersey, with his 96-page philosophical novel for children, *Harry Stottlemeier's Discovery* (1974). (A philosophical novel for children is a story that raises philosophical issues in language that a child can understand.)

Both Mathews and Lipman have stressed the active nature of children's philosophical interests. By contrast, Norwegian author Jostein Gaarder's best-selling young adult novel *Sophie's World: A Novel about the History of Philosophy* (1994) leads the reader through a series of studies about philosophy. Thus, philosophy for teenagers may be more didactic than the philosophy already taught to children.

Contemporary journals devoted to teaching children philosophy include *Analytic Teaching, The Community of Inquiry Journal, Critical & Creative Thinking, The Australasian Journal of Philosophy for Children, Questions: Philosophy for Young People,* and *Thinking: The Journal of Philosophy for Children.*

*Ideologies of Western Dominance* (1990); Eric Higgs' anthology *Technology and the Good Life* (2000); and Hans Achterhuis, *American Philosophy of Technology* (2001).

## What is **philosophy of film**?

Film criticism, both scholarly and popular, has a history as long as visual media. But philosophy of film, as a contemporary subfield in aesthetics, or philosophy of art, dates from the 1970s. As in other fields, the philosophy of film is similar to the theory of film undertaken by specialists in film or film studies.

There are philosophers who, like film theorists and critics, specifically study film as a self-contained medium, philosophical cultural critics who use film as "evidence" of broad beliefs in contemporary culture, and philosophers who turn to film for examples in ethics, aesthetics, political philosophy, feminism, and many other philosophical interests and subfields.

As well, some films directly raise philosophical questions, such as the questions about what is real in *The Matrix* (1999) and its sequels, and the nature of memory and identity raised by *Momento* (2000) and the children's film *The NeverEnding Story* (1984). There are, moreover, films that are directly about philosophy and philosophers such as *The Ister* (2004), which is about Martin Heidegger (1889–1976).

Contemporary sources on philosophy and film include: Richard Allen and Murray Smith, editors, *Film Theory and Philosophy* (1997); Gregory Currie, *Image and Mind: Film, Philosophy, and Cognitive Science* (1995); and Cynthia A. Freeland and Thomas E. Wartenberg, *Philosophy and Film* (1995). The online journal *Film-Philosophy: A Philosophical Review of Film Studies and World Cinema* is an ongoing source of contemporary work and additional sources.

## What is **mysterianism**?

Mysterianism is the view that it is impossible for us to explain consciousness. This perspective, sometimes held by philosophers, is now called "the new mysterianism" and is based on the writings of Colin McGinn (1950–), such as *The Problem of Consciousness* (1991), *The Mysterious Flame* (1999), and *Consciousness and Its Objects* (2004).

The name "new mysterians" was bestowed by Owen Flanagan (1949–) in his *Science of the Mind* (1991), and it was based on the rock group Question Mark and the Mysterians. Past philosophers such as Gottfried Leibniz (1646–1716) similarly believed that the emergence of consciousness could not be fully understood by conscious beings.

What is striking about the new mysterianism, though, is that it cropped up after almost a century of rigorous philosophical attempts to provide theories of consciousness and cognition. It is different from claiming, as Jerry Fodor (1935–) does, that we do not now know how the mind is connected to the body because it claims that we can't ever know that, or even what the mind itself is. Some aspects of this thought are reminiscent of skepticism in the ancient world and in the sixteenth century.

# Glossary

*Note: words and terms that appear here have broad philosophical use and meaning. More specific references to the text, as well as individual philosophers are listed in the index.*

**abolitionism** Nineteenth century arguments and action to abolish chattel slavery in the United States and Great Britain.

**absolute** Hegel's idea of a non-material something developing over history and determining the progression of events, forms of society, and types of knowledge, while at the same time being expressed in them.

**accidents** Non-essential qualities or characteristics of a thing, which can change while the thing remains what it essentially is (see *essence*).

**aesthetics** Philosophical study of what constitutes beauty and of the creation and appreciation of artworks.

**affirmative action** A policy of affirming minority racial identities or those of women by giving them opportunities in employment and education on the basis of race or gender instead of, or in addition to, the opportunities they would get given their other skills, largely illegal at present if based solely on race, without considering other skills and aptitudes.

**a fortiori** Reasoning from a premise stronger than the one needed to come to a conclusion at hand.

**African American philosophy** Moral, social, and political philosophy based on the American experience, identities, and concerns of African Americans.

**African philosophy** Broadly understood as the oral and written traditions and knowledge of varied cultures in Africa; as a distinct philosophy, occupied with both philosophical problems of its own identity, questions about the possibility of one African philosophy, and engagement with questions in traditional Western philosophy.

**alchemy** Medieval and Renaissance proto-chemical practice with goals of turning base metals into gold and concocting the elixir of life (*aqua vitae*).

**altruism** Doctrine that we do or should help others, even to the extent of sacrificing our own interests.

**American Philosophical Association (APA)** Contemporary professional organization of American philosophy.

**American philosophy** Philosophy that originated in and is mainly practiced in the USA, refers mainly but not exclusively to pragmatism.

**analogy** A comparison based on functions or structures (e.g., swimming in water is analogous to walking on land).

**analysis** Intellectual process of breaking complex ideas down into simpler components; examination of whether an argument is logically valid.

**analytic philosophy** A form of philosophy that analyzes concepts, proceeds with respect for science and does not rely on metaphysical speculation.

**analytic truth** A statement that is true wholly because of the meaning of its terms (e.g., "All bachelors are unmarried men.")

**anarchism** Political theory that society can be improved with the elimination of central government and be replaced by local cooperative organizations formed by workers; action toward achieving anarchist goals.

***a posteriori*** "After experience." *A posteriori* truths require experience or observation to be formulated.

***a priori*** "Before experience. *A priori* truths do not require experience or observation to be formulated.

**artificial intelligence (AI)** Idea of higher cognition in machines, proposed by mid-twentieth century cognitive philosophers to both solve the mind–body problem and create models for how the human mind works.

**artificial language** Formal language constructed for a precise purpose—such as in logic, computer science, mathematics—or the use of formal language by analytic philosophies.

**atomism** Metaphysical principle that all physical objects and things are made up of particles that cannot be further divided; scientific principle that some part of reality or language has small parts that are foundational for larger parts or objects and that it is the task of thinkers to discover what those atoms are in a particular domain.

**argument** A train of thought or sequence of sentences that is meant to prove or be persuasive. Proof requires logical validity; persuasion can be achieved with a probable conclusion or appeal to common sense or intuition.

**assumption** A statement believed to be true before proceeding on to another subject.

**atheism** Theological or non-religious position that there is no deity or supernatural entity; belief that God does not exist.

**autonomy** Self-rule or control by the individual over important aspects of his or her life.

**axiology** Study of values.

**bad faith** Self-deception; in existentialism bad faith consists of denying the nature of consciousness, evading responsibility, or denying the reality of one's situation.

**begging the question** Fallacy in reasoning whereby one assumes beforehand what remains to be proved.

**behaviorism** Early twentieth century psychological theory of human learning, attributed to J.B. Watson and B.F. Skinner, that is based on stimulus and response model of conditioning, with strong rejection of introspection as source of information for all human mentation or psychological theories.

**Buddhism** Way of thought and life founded in India by Siddhartha Gautama during the sixth century B.C.E. and later practiced all over the world.

**canon** A set of traditional writings that the student is expected to master in a field.

**Cartesian** Pertaining to or derived from the thought of René Descartes, usually in reference to claims that the mind is separate from the body, or that the mind and body are two radically different things or substances.

**categorical imperative** Absolute moral obligation formulated by Kant in two ways: Act so that you can will the maxim of your action to be a general law for rational beings; never treat another, or yourself, as a means, but always as an end (with intrinsic worth).

**catharsis** Release of pity and fear caused by viewing tragedy in Aristotle's sense.

**causal theory of meaning** Also known as reference theory of meaning; view that meaning is not mental but in the objects named by words and that words come to name objects based on an original "baptism" linking the word to the object.

**causation** The reality and study of how events are connected so that one event or one type of event results in another event or another type of event.

**chance** An occurrence of two events or type of occurrence, with no known causal connections. Chance may be an appearance only, due to lack of information about relevant courses, or chance may be viewed as an effect of the randomness of some events that cannot be determined.

**character** Human disposition to act in certain ways, which may be good or bad.

**choice** A situation in which it is possible to do one or more of several things, or an exercise of autonomy.

**circular argument** An argument where the conclusion is the same as its premises.

*cogito* Latin, literally meaning "I think"; name for René Descartes's conclusion that he exists, in the argument: "I think, therefore I am."

**cognition** Mental processes that impart or transmit knowledge, often presumed to be unemotional or not determined by emotion.

**cognitive science** Study of human and primate mental processes, including the processing of perceptual information, and learning.

**common sense** What most people believe and are considered correct or justified in believing; received opinion.

431

**common sense philosophy** Approach to philosophical problems that relies on common sense or ordinary opinions, attributed to Thomas Reid, G.E. Moore and others.

**concept** An idea, or more accurately, the meaning of a word.

**conceptual analysis** Philosophical analysis of the meaning of terms.

**confirmation** Proof of truth.

**Confucianism** Moral and social theory begun in sixth century B.C.E. China, which is based on the individual virtues and wider social benefits of specific familial and social roles.

**conscience** Moral intuition that a person has certain obligations, or that some kinds of behavior are morally wrong.

**consciousness** Awareness, the human mind in operation, or the human subject as self-aware.

**consequentialism** Moral system in which an action is right if it has good consequences, or better consequences than another action.

**constructed** Not natural, a human trait or activity is constructed or socially constructed if it is the result of custom or social rules and practices.

**contingent** Uncertain to happen or something that could be or could have been otherwise.

**contradiction** A statement that both asserts and denies the same thing. The law of non-contradiction in logic states that either A or not-A must be true, not both, and not neither.

**contrary** Two things or statements are logical contraries if they cannot both be true, but can both be false.

**conversational implicature** Theory of spoken language developed by H.P. Grice, according to which accepted rules of communication, together with a speech context, determine meaning, and the meaning is understood to change when the rules are violated.

**Copernican revolution** Named after Nicolaus Copernicus, change in world view from geocentric to heliocentric theory.

**corroboration** Scientific standard of confirmation that is less than full proof; the statement that is corroborated could turn out to be false in the future.

**cosmological argument** Argument for the proof of God as the creator of the universe, on the grounds that something must have created the universe; because all events and things have causes, then so must the universe as a whole.

**cosmopolitanism** Idea throughout intellectual history that one should be a "citizen of the world," opposed to localism and chauvinism.

**counter-factual** Hypothetical about the past; e.g., if Aristotle's texts had been lost forever, Western philosophy would have been more platonic.

**covering law model** Standard for scientific explanation whereby specific events are explained by showing how they are instances of generalizations; e.g., The pond is frozen because it's below 32 degrees Fahrenheit and water freezes at 32 degrees.

**critical theory** A system of thought that makes assertions about social reality in critical ways. The assertions are often negative evaluations in contrast to a desired ideal and those who they are made about need not agree with them for critical theorists to accept them. May also mean Marxist analysis produced by twentieth century scholars.

**critique** Verb or noun referring to criticism that originates from a well-formed intellectual perspective.

**cynicism** Ancient doctrine of withdrawal from society and return to what is simple and natural, which may be obnoxious to those who are refined.

**deconstruction** Postmodern philosophical perspective that regards meanings as unstable and analyzes classic writings in ways that go beyond authors' stated intentions.

**deduction** Method of logical reasoning that is determined by the laws of logic alone.

**deep ecology** Position that non-human and non-sentient natural beings have intrinsic value that humans should respect.

**deliberate** Quality of an action where the agent is aware of what he or she is doing.

**demonology** Form of practical magic involving calling up, using, and interacting with demons or daimons.

**deontology** Moral system based on obligations or duties.

**determinism** Doctrine that all events, including human actions, have causes and that the future can in principle be predicted.

**dialectical** A progressive process involving what are believed to be opposites, in either conversation or reality, which aims toward truth in conversation and creates change in reality; a philosophical method that posits an initial set of terms or principles and shows how they interact and result in new terms and principles.

**dialogue** In philosophy, a conversation about a topic in which different views are argued back and forth so that more of the truth is uncovered than would be if one person spoke or if the discussants stated their views separately and independently.

**dichotomy** A compelling difference in meaning between two things, so that they are of an "either-or" nature.

**dignity** Intrinsic worth that deserves respect. According to Immanuel Kant, rational agents have a dignity that cannot be bought or sold (priced).

**disposition** Tendency to behave in a certain way, without there being an inherent substance causing the behavior. For example, according to Aristotle, virtues are dispositions to behave, fully evident in past and present behavior, and not inert or fixed qualities of mind or soul.

**doctrine of double effects (DDE)** Principle that a person is morally responsible only for what she intends, even if an unintended consequence of an action, of which she was aware, is something desired.

**duality** Separation or split between two things, so that they are radically different, for example, the Cartesian duality between mind and body.

**Eastern philosophy** Philosophical study of religions and thought systems from Asian cultures and nations such as, for example, India, China, and Japan.

**egoism** Principle that humans act out of self interest, egoism can be a description of human behavior or a prescription for it.

**eliminative materialism** View in analytic philosophy of mind that references to subject states and attitudes (wanting, willing, intending, feeling, etc.) should be eliminated from scientific and empirical philosophical discourse.

**emotivism** Theory of ethics and aesthetics, according to which moral and aesthetic judgments are only the expression of emotions and desires.

**empiricism** Philosophical position that all knowledge of the world is and should be based on perceptual experience, either directly or indirectly.

**Enlightenment** A large part and theme of eighteenth century philosophy according to which mankind will progress based on reason, universal human rights, and the fundamental dignity and goodness of humankind.

**environmental philosophy** Moral and social philosophy based on environmental concerns.

**epicurianism** Philosophy attributed to Epicurus, which includes atomism, and living well by pursuing only enduring, quiet pleasures.

**epigenisis** Early modern idea that living things develop over time, opposed to preformationism.

**epistemology** Theory of knowledge, what counts as knowledge, and how beliefs are justified so as to qualify as knowledge.

**essence** Aristotelian idea of that in a thing which makes it what it is and which is also present in all other things of the same category.

**ethics** Philosophical study of what is right and wrong, good and bad, in matters that primarily concern human harm or well-being.

**etymology** Study of the history and development of words and concepts.

**events** Occurrences in time, usually distinguished from things or substances.

**evidence** Grounds for believing something is true, usually used in empirical context.

**existentialism** Philosophical doctrine that truth for humankind begins in concrete human existence instead of from abstractions, and that humans have no pre-constructed nature or essence but must create their characters and lives through actions that they choose to do, and values and meanings that they actively bestow.

**experience** Everything or anything that happens to or is encountered by a subject; in empirical philosophy, perceptual or sensory occurrences; in pragmatism, the whole of all events, without a subject-object distinction.

**experimental philosophy** Early twenty-first century philosophical method of checking the intuitions philosophers have about widespread beliefs by empirically investigating those beliefs.

**external reality** Everything except consciousness or the human mental subject, including the subject's physical body.

**faith** Type of belief or attitude that does not require empirical evidence or logical reasoning.

**fallacy** Mistake in logic or informal argument.

**falsifiability** Standard for the scientific nature of theories and hypotheses, according to Karl Popper; so that if how a theory would be falsified cannot be specified, then it is not scientific.

**falsification** Process whereby an empirical belief is proved false by a prediction that fails to happen or an event that contradicts an hypothesis.

**fatalism** Non-philosophical form of determinism that does not posit causal chains but specific inevitable events.

**feminism** Intellectual theory and practical programs that have the aim of furthering the well-being of women.

**forms, platonic** Timeless, ideal entities that enable the appearance of entities in this world and set standards for their excellence.

**freedom** Ability of the human subject to choose and determine his or her life, usually discussed in the context of "free will." Freedom is not the same as "liberty," which often refers to the absence of external constraints.

**functionalism** Analytic philosophical theory of mind that defines mental processes in terms of computations that are related to brain states.

**gender** In the modern period, the social roles and psychology assigned to biological males and females, believed to be based on their biology; in the early modern period, the social roles of male and female were believed to determine their male or female biological sex in some cases; in postmodern feminism, a generally sexed category of women determined by race and social class.

**God, gods** Transcendent immortal beings with or without high moral qualities, who are more powerful than mortals and are capable of affecting human life as well as creating its material conditions.

**hedonism** Doctrine that the aim of life is pleasure, that people always or should pursue their own pleasure; hedonism is often opposed to altruism, although some accounts of pleasure address pleasures of friendship and helping others.

**hermeneutic** Philosophical method in which texts and also reality are interpreted, usually on the basis of their relation to human consciousness.

**historicism** Theory of society and human nature, attributed to Karl Marx, holding that impersonal historical forces determine individual situations and life destinies, as well as social and historical events.

**holism** Doctrine that the components in an area of study are inter-connected in ways that form one coherent whole.

**hypothetical** Not certain or declarative; a classic hypothetical has the form "If _____, then _____."

**idea** Something before the mind intellectually, which may or may not represent something outside of the mind.

**idealism** Philosophical doctrine that what is ultimately real is mental, rather than physical, sometimes leading to a denial of the existence of an external world.

**identity** The nature of a thing whereby it is what it is; in contemporary social philosophy, the social nature, understood as constructed, of different types of human beings in terms of race, ethnicity, or gender.

**identity of indiscernibles** Gottfried Leibniz's principle that if two things are exactly the same then they are the same thing, from which it follows that two things cannot be exactly the same.

**ideology** Set of beliefs about how things ought to be or interpretations of events based on ideas of how they ought to be; ideologies are not easily falsified.

**incommensurable** Two theories or systems of thought are incommensurable if their key terms cannot be translated into one another.

**individualism** Doctrines that value the separate individual, distinct from relationships with others.

**induction** Process of reasoning that proceeds from experience to build up knowledge.

**infinite** Immeasurably and unthinkably great in magnitude; magnitude without limit.

**innate ideas** Ideas or structures present in the mind from birth, which may be literally present in fully developed form, or emerge as the child develops.

**intentionality** The aspect of consciousness that is about something other than itself, such as wanting, thinking, willing, desiring, etc.

**intuitionism** Doctrine that some things, qualities, or truths, are known directly, with no need for empirical evidence or logical proof.

**ipse-dixitism** Jeremy Bentham's term for moral systems based on sympathy and antipathy.

**irony** In postmodern philosophy, a mode or attitude in speech and writing that does not view itself as ultimately true or certain, and which may be playful, humorous, self-doubting, or tentative.

**James-Lange theory of emotion** View that emotions are experiences of the person's bodily processes, first developed by René Descartes, named after William James and C.G. Lange, who proposed it independently in the late-nineteenth century.

**justice** As fairness, justice is treating those who are equal in some respect, the same way, or treating equals equally; distributive justice pertains to how the goods of life are divided among members of a community, nation, or the world.

**knowledge** The goal of intellectual activity; in classic epistemology, knowledge is defined as true belief that has been arrived at in justified ways; i.e., I do not know something if I believe it and it is true, but I do not know why I believe it or how I have come to believe it. Neither do I know it, if it is true and I think it's true because I dreamt it or I heard a voice in my head.

**Latin American philosophy** The intellectual tradition of philosophical work in Latin America, dating from 1550 and composed of colonial, independentist, positivist, and contemporary periods. Some contemporary Latin American philosophy overlaps with Latino-a/Hispanic American philosophy.

**Latino-a/Hispanic American philosophy** Contemporary emerging philosophy about questions arising from the experience of Latin American groups in the United States, together with reflection on the history of Latin American philosophy and dialogue with both Latin American and North American philosophers, especially on questions of ethnic and racial identities.

**laws of nature** Regularity, so that events of one type are always followed by another; causal regularity; in religious philosophy, God's laws for human behavior.

**liberty** The absence of external constraints on important aspects of human autonomy or self-rule; e.g., freedom of speech and religion are liberties.

**lifeworld** The artificial, natural, and social world inhabited by human beings in their daily lives; term attributed to Jürgen Habermas, referring to human existence; term coined by Edmund Husserl to mean "what appears to consciousness."

**logic** Formal systems of rules of inference.

**logical atomism** View that an ideal philosophical language can be constructed in which basic terms will represent fundamental units of reality, usually attributed to Bertrand Russell and Ludwig Wittgenstein (in his early work).

**logical positivism** Philosophical doctrine that the physical sciences should set the concerns and subject matter of philosophers; epistemological doctrine that a statement is meaningful if it can be said what in perceptual experience would have some bearing on its truth, or ideally, verify or falsify it.

**manifest image** Idea of a world view, attributed to W. Sellars, in which philosophy matches the findings of the relevant sciences.

**Marxism** Intellectual doctrines that derive from the work of Karl Marx and Friedrich Engels, who focused on the material conditions and needs of human existence and created an ideology with the goal of distributive justice; in practical politics Marxism is associated with socialist ideals.

**materialism** Doctrine that what is ultimately real is physical.

**matter** Physical stuff or things, the material world.

437

**meaning** The concept (connotation), or thing(s) in the world (denotation), that a word or term symbolizes.

**mechanism** Explanation of reality in terms of causes and effects that do not make reference to anything distinctive about living things, but refer only to the movements of inert objects in space.

**metaphysics** In philosophy, abstract explanations of ordinary things, events, and experience, that refer to entities or processes that are not directly accessible to human perception, but are believed to be foundational for what is perceived.

**mind** What is not matter, pertaining to the conscious human subject, a synonym for soul; the complex of perceptions, ideas, thoughts, emotions, memory, feeling, and self-reflection, considered as a whole.

**modernity** Period of time from about 1800 to 1950 and its corresponding intellectual products; philosophical thought associated with the modern historical period.

**monad** Self-contained, individual unit of awareness or perception, which is the basic unit of substance; in modern philosophy a monad is a single oneness deriving from Gottfried Leibniz's philosophical system.

**monism** Doctrine that there is only one thing in the whole of existence, or that all things are part of the one thing.

**moral conventionalism** View that what is right is what social conventions hold to be right.

**moral philosophy** In the modern period, all philosophical subjects that pertain to ethics, politics, values, and society.

**morals** In ordinary life, personal behavior that can be judged right or wrong.

**moral system** A theory of the moral rules according to which human beings ought to behave, such as virtue ethics, deontology, or consequentialism.

**moral theory** Abstract branch of philosophical ethics that analyzes meanings of core terms, such as "good" and "right," and which may compare different moral systems.

**mysterianism** Doctrine that we cannot know the ultimate causes or reality of our most important concerns; new mysterianism is the doctrine that we will never know the nature of consciousness or how the mind is related to the body.

**mysticism** System of belief that posits knowledge without logical reasoning processes or sensory experience.

**mythology** In Western intellectual history, term used to refer to accounts, usually poetic or literary, of the nature and actions of ancient deities; broadly used to refer to narratives within a culture pertaining to beliefs that have no scientific foundation.

**Native American philosophy** Broadly construed, the religion and worldviews of indigenous peoples in the Americas, largely transmitted via oral traditions; in philosophy, a new subfield that seeks to present Native American thought and work from Native American perspectives to critique Western philosophy.

**naturalism** Analytic and pragmatic philosophical methodology that seeks explanations and solutions to philosophical problems in ways that are compatible with or derived from scientific explanations.

**naturalistic fallacy** G.E. Moore's doctrine that goodness is a non-natural quality so that if one defines it in terms of desired consequences or pleasure, or any other natural property, it can always be asked of something fitting the definition, "Is it good?"

**natural kind** A type of thing that is naturally formed to be what it is and where all members of the kind share certain characteristics.

**natural language** Human languages developed over time, such as English, Italian, French, German, Chinese, and so forth.

**natural philosophy** Term for early modern physics, astronomy, and proto-chemistry.

**natural religion** Belief in a deity based on combination of reason and experience, rather than revelation.

**nature** The non-human world, or the human idea of the non-human world.

**necessary causal condition** An event or thing that is always present if an effect is present (the effect need not be present if it is present; e.g., oxygen is a necessary condition for fire).

**necessity** Type of connection that is logical in that it cannot be denied without contradiction, or connection between real events such that effects are inevitable given their causes.

**Neoplatonism** Doctrine from the ancient world, influential throughout philosophical history thereafter, that there exists a transcendental reality in which events determine what happens in this world.

**nominalism** Doctrine that all natural kinds are arbitrarily designated as such by human intellectual concerns and activity and that there are no universals in reality, but only in language; in its modern form, credited to John Locke though Boëthius first formulated it, that essences are in the mind and made up by the mind.

**non-Euclidian geometry** Coherent geometries with principles other than those laid down by Euclid, allowing, e.g., that parallel lines meet and angles in triangles add up to less than 180 degrees; geometric revolution in the nineteenth century that paved the way for Albert Einstein's theory of general relativity.

**noumena** Things in themselves that are not directly perceived or describable by us, contrasted by Immanuel Kant with phenomena, which we can perceive.

**numerology** Ancient doctrine, attributed to Pythagoras and his followers, that numbers are real entities, present throughout reality, in ways that determine the non-numerical properties of things.

**objective** Independent of the mind, as in "objective reality"; in human discourse, a lack of bias; in science, the presumption that the same experiments will yield the same data to different observers.

439

**objectivism** Philosophical system developed by Ayn Rand based on the existence of an external objective world and belief that that the Aristotelian law of identity, *A is A,* yields a metaphysical truth about that world.

**observation** Perceptual process, with or without the use of manmade instruments (e.g., thermometers, cameras), for recording what happens.

**occasionalism** Causal doctrine attributed to Nicolas Malebranche and others that because we cannot perceive causal connections, there are none in reality, although they do exist in the mind of God.

**One, the** In Neoplatonism, ultimate ontological, ruling, moral and unified basis of existence that is itself separate from existence and/or may be expressed in it.

**ontological argument** Proof for the existence of God, used by René Descartes and others, that proceeds from God's qualities, as we think them, to his necessary existence.

**ontology** The science and study of what exists, pursued as a distinct inquiry, or of what is believed to exist, in a specific domain of inquiry, pursued as a distinct inquiry. Martin Heidegger treated ontology in the first sense, W.V.O. Quine in the second.

**ordinary language philosophy** View developed by Ludwig Wittgenstein in his later writings that ordinary language assigns varieties of meanings through usage in different contexts, and that the analysis of ordinary language can yield solutions to many traditional philosophical problems.

**other minds, problem of** The problem of how we know that other people have minds, since we cannot directly experience the mind of another as that person experiences it.

**paradigm** According to Thomas Kuhn, a paradigm is an agreed upon set of beliefs in a mature science that determines the ontology of the field, its experimental methods, and appropriate objects of study. Used more loosely after Kuhn, a paradigm is any dominant worldview, in any area of human activity.

**particulars** Concrete, variable instances of something.

**patriarchy** Feminist notion of "rule by the fathers" as a social principle that has historically been oppressive to women.

**phenomena** The appearances of things or things as they show themselves; evidence; in Heideggerian philosophy, that which shows itself to man.

**phenomenalism** Logical atomist or logical positivist view that material objects are made up of sense data.

**phenomenology** Philosophical methodology, attributed to Edmund Husserl, in which the structures, processes, and intentional objects of consciousness are observed and analyzed.

*philosophes* Term for French intellectuals whose work preceded and influenced the French Revolution, usually including Diderot, Montesquieu, Rousseau, Voltaire, and others.

**philosophy of biology** New twentieth century subfield in philosophy of science that addresses the distinct nature of living things and the scientific questions and methodologies that characterize biology.

**philosophy of science** Study of the principles used for scientific discovery and theory construction, as well as progress in science. Philosophy of science may and has been both descriptive and prescriptive.

**phrenology** The now-held-to-be-pseudo-scientific views of F.J. Gall that a person's psychological traits were evident by the bumps and other configurations on the surface of the skull.

*phronesis* Practical wisdom; in ancient Greece, both good judgment in ordinary affairs and knowledge of the ultimate goods and ends of life.

**Platonism** Systems of thought or ideas deriving from Plato, according to which there are transcendent entities that support the existence of, and are the ideals or essences of, every kind of thing in the world that humans experience.

**pleasure principle** Utilitarian principle that pleasure is the greatest value, and moral goodness consists in increasing pleasure for the greatest number of sentient beings.

**pluralism** Pluralistic views of thought accept different belief systems and methodologies for arriving at truth; pluralism in political theory advocates a multiplicity of perspectives and groups with different agendas and interests, democratically coexisting in society; pluralism in ontology holds that there is more than one type of thing in a given domain.

**positivism** View developed by Auguste Comte that social sciences should use mathematics, explanation has the same logical structure as prediction, and social science findings can be used to solve major problems of governing and society.

**possible** Not logically contradictory to imagine; what is possible in events need not be probable or likely.

**post-modernism** Also known as post-structuralism or deconstructionism, the continental school of thought after Jacques Lacan, principally attributed to Jacques Derrida, in which meanings are considered dependent on other symbols in an unstable system.

**pragmatism** American philosophy, known for an analysis of experience and social relevance; a method that analyzes experience as an interactive process between the conscious subject and the world.

**pre-formationism** Pre-modern biological theory that sperm and eggs contain miniature versions of fully developed humans or animals.

**Presocratics** Literally, those philosophers who lived before Socrates; Greek philosophers from the seventh to fifth century B.C.E., who are viewed as the originators/founders of both Western science and Western philosophy.

**prime mover** Aristotle's idea of the ultimate cause of the universe, posited because without it causal chains would be infinite; interpreted theologically as an argument for God's existence.

**probability** Likelihood of an event happening; standard for prediction that is considered reliable, although it falls short of certainty; theory of how probability is assigned, the logic of likelihood.

**process philosophy** Usually attributed to A.N. Whitehead, an ontological perspective that reality and everything in it is made up of events, instead of stable entities; method of analysis whereby what were believed to be things, turn out to be events or happenings over time.

**proof** A process involving the manipulation of symbols, which is required to proceed in a certain way in mathematics or logic, for the conclusion to be justified; whenever the conclusion of an argument cannot be false if its premises are true.

**proper name** The name of an individual that is not usually believed to have any meaning beyond its reference to that individual; e.g., "Naomi Zack" and "Ed D'Angelo" are proper names.

**proposition** The meaning of a sentence.

**qualities** In ancient philosophy, qualities were considered "accidents" of substances. In early modern philosophy, a distinction was made between primary and secondary qualities. Primary qualities were mass, size, velocity, number of atoms, etc., whereas secondary qualities were color, odor, sound, etc.; the primary qualities were believed to cause the secondary qualities of perceptions as the result of the effects of the atoms in perceptible objects on sense organs.

**quietism** Withdrawal from the world based on intellectual reasons, such as in ancient skepticism, the impossibility of knowledge.

**race(s)** Group or groups of human beings believed to be different biologically and culturally; the biological difference now believed not to have scientific support; the cultural difference accepted as a fact of social reality.

**rationalism** Doctrine opposed to empiricism, according to which knowledge about the world can be present or developed by means of reason, without prior experience.

**rationality** Good sense, following the rules of logic and accepting available evidence in forming beliefs and making decisions about action.

**realism** Naïve realism is the philosophical version of the ordinary belief in the existence of an external physical world, which common sense philosophers think requires no special proof; in medieval philosophy, the belief that universals exist apart from particular objects that are similar, or exist in those objects.

**reductionism** Doctrine that some things are "nothing but" other more fundamental or perceptible things, as in reducing material objects to atoms or sense data; methodological principle of explanation, whereby one statement or theory is reduced to another if it can be logically derived from it; e.g., the reduction of statements about chemical interactions in chemistry to statements about atoms in physics.

**reference** Process by which a symbol or sign points to or designates an object; for example, a road sign ("Tulsa City next exit") refers to a town along the road.

**relativism** Descriptive moral doctrine that different circumstances, agents, and cultures have different and often conflicting rules of behavior or value; prescriptive moral doctrine that there are no universal rules of behavior or human values.

**research program** Concept of scientific progress and change, developed by Imre Lakatos, encompassing both research activity and scientific theory; progressive research programs need few *ad hoc* hypotheses, while degenerative ones need increasing numbers of *ad hoc* hypotheses to provide explanations of data.

**rhetoric** The art or skill of speaking or writing to persuade or impress listeners or readers.

**rights** Legal conditions necessary to preserve a prior condition of human worth and dignity, as in universal rights, property rights, rights to free speech, and rights to own property.

**scholasticism** Tradition of commentary on ancient sources in relation to then-contemporary philosophical problems, or in relation to Christian theology, practiced during the medieval period.

**science** Precise, rigorous, and formal system of thought and study of the world, including human beings, which in Aristotelian and Cartesian thought was believed to yield certain knowledge, but by the modern period was accepted as most probable knowledge. Since the nineteenth century the sciences have been divided into the physical sciences (e.g., physics, astrology, mathematics, chemistry, geology, biology) and the social sciences (e.g., psychology, sociology, anthropology, history), with more theoretical agreement and precision about data attributed to the physical sciences.

**scientific revolution** The beginning of modern empirical science, in practice and theory, during the sixteenth and seventeenth centuries, following the Copernican revolution and epitomized by Isaac Newton; term used by Thomas Kuhn to refer to radical change in perspective within a scientific field.

**semantics** Meanings or theory of meaning.

**sense data** Sensory impressions of different senses (e.g., greenness, hardness, coldness) directly experienced in the present; believed by logical positivists to be the foundation of empirical knowledge.

**sex** Traditionally, the biological difference between males and females; sexual activity; in early modern and postmodern feminism, male or female sex was believed to be the result of male or female gender that was determined by social roles and hierarchies.

**sexism** Term used during early Second Wave (1960–1980) feminism to refer to contempt, bias, aversion, or other devaluation of women based solely on their sex.

**skepticism** Doubt about otherwise plausible claims, as in skepticism about the existence of the external world or other minds. Before the modern period, skepticism was often used to show that knowledge was impossible so that other men-

443

tal attitudes, such as quietude or faith, could be pursued. Academic skepticism was the view that no knowledge is possible, pyrrhonic skepticism the view that we cannot know whether any knowledge is possible.

**social contract theory** Foundational theory for modern democratic government, attributed to Hobbes, Locke, Rousseau, and others, according to which legitimate government requires the original explicit or implied consent of those governed. The contract may be between subjects and rulers or among subjects to designate rulers.

**Social Darwinism** Late-nineteenth century application of principles of Darwinian evolution to human society, stressing competition and "survival of the fittest," often used or misused to support social inequality and advocate eugenics programs.

**social philosophy** Analysis of problems and meanings in culture and society; theories for public policy.

**solipsism** Doctrine that I cannot know anything except my own mind and its contents; doctrine that I cannot know that anything exists beyond myself and my mind.

**sophism** Form of rhetoric in ancient Greece whereby either side of an argument could be taken up; also associated with cultural relativism and cosmopolitanism during that time.

**soul** Immaterial part of the self, considered paramount for morality and identity, and which may or not be believed to survive death.

**soundness** A sound argument is in accordance with the rules of logic, so it is valid, and its premises are also true, so that its conclusion is true.

**space** According to Isaac Newton, space is an objective reality; according to Immanuel Kant it is a condition for human experience.

**speciesism** Animal rights activists and theorists' designation of the view that human beings are of greater value than other life forms. Some believe specieism to be as unjust as racism or sexism.

**state of nature** An historical or hypothetical human condition, without or before civil government, usually posited to justify the need for a particular type of government, in social contract theory.

**stoicism** Beginning in ancient Greece, doctrine of accepting or withdrawing from what the individual cannot control; associated with universal humanism and cosmopolitanism.

**structuralism** Philosophical and social theory that takes psychic or social structures as its subject matter.

**subjectivism** Belief or implication that knowledge is completely dependent on the wants, needs, experience, or distortions of each individual.

**substance** According to Aristotle and medieval philosophers, a living thing or other being that can exist independently; ultimate substratum of reality, as in René Descartes's material and immaterial substances; category of thought according to Immanuel Kant. The idea of substance as underlying substratum was rejected by empirical philosophers beginning with John Locke.

**sufficient cause** Something that if present always has a certain effect, although it need not be present whenever the effect is.

**sufficient reason** The principle of sufficient reason states that all things that exist must have causes that necessitate them.

**sufism** Mystical branch of Islam.

**symbolic order** The arrangement of language and other symbols in a culture that mediate all human psychic activities and is a source of meaning generally. One subject of structuralism.

**synthetic truth** A statement that is true of the world.

**teleological** Determined by a future end, goal, or purpose.

**theism** Belief in transcendental or non-natural beings or god(s).

**theology** A rational system of thought that has a particular religion as its subject; for example, Christian theology, or Jewish theology.

**theoretical terms** Symbols for unobserved, or even unobservable entities that are posited in scientific theories in order to explain what can be observed.

**theory** A linguistic system that can be used to explain experience, although everything asserted in the theory may not have a foundation in experience.

**time** Aristotle defined time as a measurement of events. Since then, distinctions have been made between objective time as measured by clocks, time as a condition of perceptual experience (Immanuel Kant), and time as subjective experience (Henri Bergson), and time as constructed by the human apprehension of past, present, and future (Martin Heidegger). Bertrand Russell said that it was a contingent matter that we remember the past instead of the future.

**token-type distinction** The type is the general kind, the token an instance of it, as in dogs and my dog, "Maggy."

**tragedy** A dramatic genre that dates before the time of Aristotle in which the hero is a good man who makes an error, from which his doom ensues. Tragedy has universal themes and a plot that is determined by events within the play. It moves the audience to great pity and fear that, according to Aristotle, provokes a process of *catharsis*.

**transcendental argument** Philosophical method attributed to Immanuel Kant of determining what must be true for human beings to be able to have the kind of experience they do; this process of "transcendental deduction" is rigorous in that it does not posit more than is necessary to account for experience.

**transcendentalism** Positing entities that exist separately from experience; New England transcendentalism was a nineteenth century philosophical and literary movement that combined romantic ideas of the individual in natural environments with philosophical ideas from both Plato and Immanuel Kant.

**truth** In modern analytic philosophy, a quality of statements or propositions. A statement is true according to the correspondence theory of truth if it accurately represents reality; in the coherence theory, true statements are compatible or consistent with other accepted knowledge.

**universal grammar** Innate grammar present in all human beings, enabling them to learn a finite number of natural languages, as posited in different formulations by Noam Chomsky.

**universals** General terms like "cat" and "dog." From ancient Greek through early modern philosophy there was a debate about whether universals themselves were real or only particulars were real, or universals were real insofar as they existed "in" particulars.

**utilitarianism** Moral system attributed to Jeremy Bentham and John Stuart Mill holding that an action is good if it promotes the greatest happiness for the greatest number, whereby everyone counts as one unit and no one counts for more than one.

**utopia** Theory or imaginary depiction of an ideal human society which does not exist; the term was coined by Thomas More whose novel of the same name depicted an ideal society that existed nowhere, derived from the Greek words *ou*, meaning "not," and *topos*, meaning "place." More's novel makes frequent mention of Plato's *Republic*, perhaps the first example of a utopian society in the history of philosophy.

**validity** Characteristic of an argument that proceeds according to rules of logic.

**value** Something worth having, striving for, or retaining, which has intrinsic, usually non-monetary worth, or imparts such worth to other things.

**verificationism** Logical positivist doctrine that the meaning of a sentence is how it would be verified or falsified in perceptual experience and that only sentences that can be verified or falsified by perception are meaningful.

**vice** Trait of character considered immoral or unethical, or a disposition to behave in such ways.

**virtue** Trait of character considered excellent or morally good, or a disposition to behave in such ways.

**vitalism** Scientifically outdated view of a life force accounting for what is distinct about living things and their abilities to reproduce themselves, which was largely put to rest by James Watson and Francis Crick's discovery of the model of DNA.

# Select Bibliography

More extensive lists of primary sources are given in the text of the chapters. The sources below are for the key figures and subjects. The most up-to-date, in-print editions have been selected. Many recent compilations do not have the same titles as the original works, although they contain the original works.

Many of the classic sources and other important philosophical texts are available free online at Project Gutenberg: http://www.gutenberg.org/wiki/Main_Page. Wikipedia, the Stanford Encyclopedia of Philosophy, and other free sources listed in online searches have entries for many of the philosophers and schools of thought covered in this book, but all secondary sources should be checked against primary sources by scholarly students.

Websites for environmental philosophy include: The International Association for Environmental Philosophy, http://www.environmentalphilosophy.org/; Erratic Impact—The Philosophy of Nature, http://www.erraticimpact.com/~ecologic/; The Center for Environmental Philosophy, http://www.cep.unt.edu/centerfo.html; and The International Society for Environmental Ethics, http://www.cep.unt.edu/ISEE.html.

## THE BASICS

### One-Volume Histories of Philosophy

Durant, Will. *The Story of Philosophy: From Plato to Voltaire and the French Enlightenment* (read by Grover Gardner) 9 CDs. Audio Partner Publishing Company, 2004.

Popkin, Richard H. *The Columbia History of Philosophy*. New York: Columbia University Press, 1999.

Russell, Bertrand. *History of Western Philosophy*. New York: Simon & Schuster, 1967, Routledge Classics, 2004.

*For a continental history of philosophy, from the ancient Greeks through Heidegger, see:*

Schürmann, Reiner. *Broken Hegemonies.* tr. by Reginald Lilly. Bloomington, IN: Indiana University Press, 2003.

*For a general account of some philosophers' lives, see:*

Sharfstein, B.A. *The Philosophers: Their Lives and the Nature of Their Thought,* New York: Oxford University Press, 1980.

## ANCIENT PHILOSOPHY

### Greek Pre-Socratics

Burnet, John. *Early Greek Philosophy*. Meridian Books, New York, 1957.

Colli, Giorgio. *The Greek Wisdom* (*La Sapienza greca*). 3 vols. Milan 1977–1980.

Curd, Patricia, ed. *A Presocratics Reader*. Indianpolis, IN: Hackett, 1996.

Kirk, G.S., J.E. Raven, and M. Schofield. *The Presocratic Philosophers,* 2nd ed. Cambridge University Press, 1983.

### The Sophists

Guthrie, W.K.C. Vol. 3 of *History of Greek Philosophy,* Cambridge: Cambridge University Press, 1969.

Jarratt, Susan C. *Rereading the Sophists: Classical Rhetoric Refigured,* Carbondale & Edwardsville: Southern Illinois University Press, 1991.

### Plato

Cooper, John M., and D.H. Dutchinson, eds. *Plato, Complete Works.* Indianapolis, IN: Hackett Publishing Co., 1997.

Grube, B.M.A. *Plato's Thought.* Indianapolis, IN: Hackett Publishing Co., 1980.

### Aristotle

Aristotle. *Selections* (from all major works). Indianapolis, IN: Hackett Publishing Co., 1995.

Aristotle. *Nicomachean Ethics.* Terrence Irwin, tr. Indianapolis, IN: Hackett Publishing Co., 2000.

Robinson, Timothy A. *Aristotle in Outline.* Indianapolis, IN: Hackett Publishing Co., 1995.

### Hellenistic and Roman Philosophy

Epicurus. *The Epicurus Reader.* Indianapolis, IN: Hackett Publishing Co., 1994.

Fanthan, Elaine, et. al. *Women in the Classic World.* New York: Oxford University Press, 1994.

Inwood, Brad, and Lloyd P. Gerson, eds. *Hellenistic Philosophy: Introductory Readings.* Indianapolis, IN: Hackett Publishing Co., 1999.

Inwood, Brad, and Lloyd P. Gerson, eds. *The Stoic Reader.* Indianapolis, IN: Hackett Publishing Co., 2008.

### Women Philosophers in Ancient Greece and Rome

Elaine Fanthan, et. al. *Women in the Classic World,* New York: Oxford University Press, 1994.

Ward, Julie K., ed. *Feminism and Ancient Philosophy.* New York: Routledge, 1996.


## NEOPLATONISM THROUGH THE RENAISSANCE

### Neoplatonism

Gerson, L.P., ed. *Cambridge Companion to Plotinus.* Cambridge, UK: Cambridge University Press, 1996.

Gerson, L.P., and John Dillon, eds. *Neoplatonic Philosophy: Introductory Readings.* Indianapolis: Hackett Publishing Co., 2004.

### Medieval Philosophy

Clark, Marty T. *An Aquinas Reader: Selections from the Writings of Thomas Aquinas.* New York: Fordham University Press, 2000.

Debus, Allen G. *Man and Nature in the Renaissance.* Cambridge, UK: Cambridge University Press, 1978.

Gracia, J.G., and T.B. Noone. *A Companion to Philosophy in the Middle Ages.* London, 2003.

Hyman, J., and J.J. Walsh. *Philosophy in the Middle Ages,* Indianapolis, IN: Hackett, 1973.

Kretzmann, N., and E. Stump. *The Cambridge Companion to Augustine.* New York: Cambridge University Press, 2000.

Luscombe, David. *Medieval Thought,* New York: Hill & Wang, 1980.

Schoedinger, Andrew B., ed. *Readings in Medieval Philosophy.* New York: Oxford University Press, 1996.

### Renaissance Humanism

Copenhaver, Brian P. *Renaissance Philosophy: A History of Western Philosophy, no. 3.* New York: Oxford University Press, 1992.

Doughert, M.V., ed. *Pico della Mirandola, New Essay.* New York: 2007.

Fallico, Herman, and Arturo B. Fallico. *Renaissance Philosophy, vols. I and II, The Italian Philosophers and Transalpine Thinkers.* New York: Modern Library, 1969.

Hankins, James. *Cambridge Companion to Renaissance Philosophy.* New York: Cambridge University Press, 2007.

Keith, Thomas, ed. *Renaissance Thinkers.* New York: Oxford University Press, 1992.

# SKEPTICISM AND NATURAL PHILOSOPHY

## Skepticism

Bradford, R.G., ed. *Sextus Empiricus: Outline of Pyrrhonism*. Cambridge, MA: Harvard University Press, 1967.

Kurtz, Paul. *The New Skepticism: Inquiry and Reliable Knowledge*. Buffalo, NY: Prometheus Books, 1992.

Moser, P., ed. *The Oxford Handbook of Epistemology*. Cambridge, MA: Harvard University Press, 2002.

Popkin, Richard H. *History of Skepticism from Savonarola to Bayle*. New York: Oxford University Press, 2003.

Popkin, Richard, and Avrum Stroll Popkin. *Skeptical Philosophy for Everyone*. Buffalo, NY: Prometheus, 2001.

## The Scientific Revolution

Bacon, Francis. *Works and Letters and Life*. Spedding, James, et al., eds. 4 volumes, London, 1857–1874 (standard edition available in facimile), also available in a facsimile reprint, Stuttgart: Bad Cansstatt, 1989.

Butterfield, Herbert. *The Origins of Modern Science, 1300–1800*. New Haven, CT: Yale University Press, 2004.

Galileo Galilei, *Two New Sciences*. tr. Stillman Drake. Madison: University of Wisconsin Press, 1974.

Gaukroger, Stephen. *Francis Bacon and the Transformation of Early-Modern Philosophy*. Cambridge, UK: Cambridge University Press, 2001.

Grant, Edward. *The Foundations of Modern Science in the Middle Ages: Their Religious, Institutional, and Intellectual Contexts,* Cambridge, UK: Cambridge University Press, 1996.

Kuhn, Thomas S. *The Copernican Revolution: Planetary Astronomy in the Development of Western Thought*. Cambridge: Harvard Univeersity Press, 1957.

Lindberg, D.C. *The Beginnings of Western Science: The European Scientific Tradition in Philosophical, Religious, and Institutional Context, 600 B.C. to A.D. 1450*. Chicago: University of Chicago Press, 1992.

Merchant, Carolyn. *The Death of Nature: Women, Ecology and the Scientific Revolution*. New York: HarperCollins, 1980.

Shapin, Steven. *The Scientific Revolution*. Chicago: University of Chicago Press, 1996.

Spratt, Thomas. *The History of the Royal Society of London* (facimile of 17th century edition). Whitefish Mountain, MT: Kessinger Publishing, 2003.

Westfall, Richard S. *The Construction of Modern Science*. New York: John Wiley & Sons, 1971.

Zack, Naomi. *Bachelors of Science: Seventeenth Century Identity, Then and Now*. Philadelphia: Temple University Press, 1997.

## Medicine and Philosophy

Burton, Robert. *The Anatomy of Melancholy*. William H. Gass, ed. New York: New York Review of Books, 2001.

Gregory, Andrew. *Harvey's Heart: The Discovery of Blood Circulation*. Cambridge, UK: Icon Books, 2001.

Nutton, Vivia. *Ancient Medicine: Sciences of Antiquity*. New York: Routledge, 2004.

Ragner, Louis N. *A History of Medicine*. Boca Raton, FL: Taylor & Francis, 2005.

# EARLY MODERN PHILOSOPHY

*For a collection of standard readings, see:*
Popkin, Richard H. *Philosophy of the Sixteenth and Seventeenth Century*, New York: Simon & Schuster, 1966.

## Seventeenth Century Rationalism

Descartes, René. *The Philosophical Writings of Descartes*. John Cottingham, Robert Stoothoff, and Dugald Murdoch, eds., 3 vols. Cambridge, UK: Cambridge University Press, 1985.

Leibniz, Gottfried Wilhelm. *Philosophical Essays*. Roger Ariew and Daniel Garber, tr. Indianapolis, IN: Hackett, 1989.

Spinoza, Baruch. *Complete Works*. Michael J. Morgan, ed. Indianapolis, IN: Hackett, 2002.

## Seventeenth Century Empiricism

Alan, Graham, John Rogers, Jean-Michel Vienne, and Yves Charles Zarka, eds. *The Cambridge Platonists in Philosophical Context*. Dortrecht: Kluwer Academic Publishers, 1997.

Hobbes, Thomas. *Leviathan, with Selected Variants from the Latin Edition of 1668*. Edwin Curley, ed. Indianapolis, IN: Hackett, 1994.

Jones, Tod E. *The Cambridge Platonists*. Lanham, MD: Rowman & Littlefield, 2005.

Locke, John. *Essay Concerning Human Understanding*. Kenneth P. Winkler, ed. Indianapolis, IN: Hackett, 1996.

Locke, John. *The Political Writings*. David Wooton, ed. Indianapolis, IN: Hackett, 2003.

## Gender and Early Modern Women Philosophers

Atherton, Margaret. *Women Philosophers of the Early Modern Period*. Indianapolis, IN: Hackett, 1994.

Newcastle, Margaret Cavendish. *Observations on Experimental Philosophy*. Eileen O'Neil, ed. Cambridge, UK: Cambridge University Press, 2001.

Wiesner, Merry E. *Women and Gender in Early Modern History*. Cambridge, UK: Cambridge University Press, 2000.

## THE ENLIGHTENMENT PERIOD

*A classic intellectual history of the period is:*

Cassirer, Ernst. *The Philosophy of the Enlightenment*. Princeton, NJ: Princeton University Press, 1968.

*A reader for the Enlightenment is:*

Gilmour, Peter, ed. *Philosophers of the Enlightenment*. Barnes & Noble Books, 1990.

### Enlightenment Philosophers

Bentham, Jeremy. *An Introduction to the Principles of Morals and Legislation*. James Henderson Burns, Herbert Lionel Adolphus Hart, and F. Rosen, eds. New York: Oxford University Press, 1996.

Berkeley, George. *Philosophical Works Including the Works on Vision*. Michael Ayers, ed. Rutland, VT: C.E. Tuttle, 1993.

Hume, David. *Moral Philosophy*. Geoffrey Sayre-McCord, ed. Indianapolis, IN: Hackett, 2006.

Kant, Immanuel. *Metaphysical Foundations of Natural Science*. Michael Friedman, ed. Cambridge, UK: Cambridge University Press, 2004.

Kant, Immanuel. *The Moral Law: Groundwork of the Metaphysics of Morals*. H.L. Paton, ed. New York: Routledge, 2005.

Reid, Thomas. *An Inquiry into the Human Mind on the Principles of Common Sense*. Derek R. Brookes, ed. Edinburgh, UK: University of Edinburgh Press, 1997.

Rousseau, Jean-Jacques. *The Basic Political Writings*. Donald A. Cress, tr., Peter Gay, ed. Indianapolis, IN: Hackett, 1987.

### Other Enlightenment Writers

Voltaire, *The Portable Voltaire*. Ben Ray Redman, ed. New York: Penguin Books, 1977.

Wollstonecraft, Mary. *A Vindication of the Rights of Women*. Miriam Brody, ed. New York: Penguin, 1992.

### Counter-Enlightenment Figures

Edmund Burke, Edmund. *Reflections on the Revolution in France: A Critical Edition*. J.C.D. Clark, ed. Palo Alto, CA: Stanford University Press, 2001.

Edwards, Jonathan. *The Sermons of Jonathan Edwards*. Wilson H. Kimnach, Kenneth P. Minkema, and Douglas A. Sweeney, eds. New Haven, CT: Yale University Press, 1999.

Sade, Marquis de. *The Complete Marquis de Sade*. Paul J. Gillette, and John S. Yankowski, eds. Los Angeles, CA: Holloway House Publishing Company, 2006.

Swift, Jonathan. *A Modest Proposal and Other Satirical Works*. North Chemsford, MA: Courier Dover Publications, 1996.

Vico, Giambattista. *On the Most Ancient Wisdom of the Italians*. L.M. Palmer, ed. Ithaca, NY: Cornell University Press, 1988.

# NINETEENTH CENTURY PHILOSOPHY

## Nineteenth Century Empiricism

Comte, Auguste. *The Positive Philosophy.* Sunrise, FL: AMS Publisher, 1974.

Fish, Menachem. *William Whewell, Philosopher of Science.* Oxford, UK: Clarendon Press, 1991.

Mill, Harriet Hardy Taylor. *Enfranchisement of Women.* London, UK: Virago, 1988.

Mill, John Stuart. *On Liberty and the Subjection of Women.* New York: Penguin, 2007.

Mill, John Stuart. *Utilitarianism.* Rutland, VT: Tuttle, 1993.

Scarre, Geoffrey. *Logic and Reality in the Philosophy of John Stuart Mill.* New York: Springer, 1988.

## Intuitionism

Bergson, Henri. *Time and Free Will: An Essay on the Immediate Data of Consciousness.* North Chemsford, MA: Courier Dover, 2001.

Bradley, Francis H. *Appearance and Reality: A Metaphysical Essay.* Boston, MA: Adamant Media, 2002.

Sidgwick, Henry. *The Methods of Ethics.* foreword by John Rawls. Indianapolis, IN: Hackett, 1981.

## Philosophy of Mathematics and Logic

Dummett, Michael. *Frege: Philosophy of Language.* Cambridge, MA: Harvard University Press, 1981.

Gillespie, Charles Coulston, Robert Fox, and Ivor Grattan-Guinness. *Pierre-Simone Laplace, 1749–1827: A Life in Exact Science,* Princeton, NJ: Princeton University Press, 2000.

Greenberg, Marvin Jay. *Euclidian and Non-Euclidian Geometries: Development and History.* New York: W.H. Freeman, 1993.

Poincaré, Henri. Forward by Bertrand Russell. *Science and Method.* North Chemsford: Dover Courier, 2003.

Shapiro, Stuart, ed. *The Oxford Handbook of Philosophy of Logic and Mathematics.* New York: Oxford University Press, 2005.

Venn, John. *Symbolic Logic.* Providence, RI: American Mathematical Society, 2007.

## German Idealism

Beiser, Frederick C. *Hegel.* New York: Routledge, 2005.

Bosanquet, Bernard. *Logic or the Morphology of Knowledge.* Germantown, NY: Kraus Reprint Co., 1968.

Bourcher, David. *The British Idealists.* New York: Cambridge University Press, 1997.

Bowie, Andrew. *Schelling and Modern European Philosophy: An Introduction.* New York: Routledge, 1993.

Fichte, Johann Gottleib. *The Science of Knowledge.* New York: Cambridge University Press, 1982.

### Materialism, Marxism, and Anarchists

Engels, Friedrich. *The Condition of the Working Class in England.* New York: Penguin Classics, 1987.

Kropotkin, Peter. *Mutual Aid: A Factor of Evolution.* London: Freedom Press, 1987.

Marx, Karl. *Selected Writings.* Lawrence H. Simon, ed. Indianapolis, IN: Hackett, 1994.

Wartofsky, Marx W. *Feuerbach.* New York: Cambridge University Press, 1977.

Woodcock, George. *Anarchism: A History of Libertarian Ideas and Movements.* Peterborough, Ontario: Broadview, 2004.

### Psychology and Social Theory

Brentano, Franz Clemens. *Psychology from an Empirical Standpoint.* Atlantic Highlands, NJ: Humanities Press, 1973.

Chisholm, Robert M. *Brentano and Meinong Studies.* New York: Rodopi Press, 1982.

Dilthey, Wilhelm. *Descriptive Psychology and Historical Understanding.* The Hague, Netherlands: Nijhoff, 1977.

Durkheim, Emile. *Suicide: A Study in Sociology.* New York: Free Press,(Simon and Schuster) 1979.

Freud, Sigmund. *The Psychopathology of Everyday Life.* New York: A.A. Brill, 2005.

Freud, Sigmund. *The Interpretation of Dreams.* Nu Vision Publications (www. nuvision.com), 2007.

Simmel, Georg. *The Philosophy of Money,* New York: Routledge, 1978.

Weber, Max. *The Protestant Ethic and the Spirit of Capitalism.* North Chelmsford, MA: Dover Courier, 2003.

## CONTINENTAL PHILOSOPHY

### Existentialism

*Useful general overviews are:*

Barnes, Hazel. *An Existentialist Ethics.* New York: Knopf 1967.

Arendt, Hannah, *The Human Condition.* Chicago: University of Chicago Press (1958).

Barrett, William. *Irrational Man: A Study in Existential Philosophy.* Garden City: Doubleday, 1962.

Kaufmann, Walter. *Existentialism from Dostoevsky to Sartre.* Cleveland: Meridian Books, 1968.

McBride, William, ed. *The Development and Meaning of Twentieth Century Existentialism.* New York: Garland Publishers, 1997.

Warnock, Mary. *Existentialist Ethics.* London: Macmillan & Co., 1967.

*Primary existentialist texts are:*

Beauvoir, Simone de. *The Second Sex*. H.M. Parshley, tr. New York: Vintage Books, 1989.

Buber, Martin. *Between Man and Man*. Ronald Gregor Smith, tr. New York: Macmillan, 1978.

Buber, Martin. *I and Thou*. Walter Kaufmann, tr. New York: Scribner, 1970.

Camus, Albert. *The Myth of Sisyphus and Other Essays*. Justin O'Brien, tr., New York: Knopf, 1955.

Camus, Albert. *The Stranger*. Matthew Ward, tr. New York: Knopf, 1988.

Dostoevsky, Fyodor. *The Brothers Karamazov: The Constance Garnett Translation Revised by Ralph E. Matlaw*. New York: Norton, 1976.

Jaspers, Karl. *Reason and Existenz*. William Earle, tr. New York: Noonday Press, 1968.

Kierkegaard, Søren. *The Essential Kierkegaard*. Howard V. Hong and Edna H. Hong, eds. Princeton: Princeton University Press, 2000.

Kierkegaard, Søren. *Concluding Unscientific Postscript*. David Swenson and Walter Lowrie, trs. Princeton: Princeton University Press, 1971.

Kierkegaard, Søren. *Fear and Trembling*. Howard V. Hong and Edna H. Hong, trs. Princeton: Princeton University Press, 1983.

Marcel, Gabriel. *The Philosophy of Existentialism*. New York: Citadel Press, 1968.

Marcel, Gabriel. *Being and Having*. Katherine Farrer, tr., London: Westminster, 1949.

Nietzsche, Friedrich. *On the Genealogy of Morals*. Walter Kaufmann, tr., New York: Vintage Books, 1969.

Nietzsche, Friedrich. *The Gay Science*. Walter Kaufmann, tr. New York: Vintage Books, 1974.

Nietzsche, Friedrich. *Thus Spoke Zarathustra,* in *The Portable Nietzsche*. Walter Kaufmann, tr. New York: Viking Press, 1975.

Sartre, Jean-Paul. *Nausea*. Lloyd Alexander, tr. New York: New Directions, 1965.

Sartre, John Paul. *Being and Nothingness*. Hazel Barnes, tr. New York: Washington Square Press, 1992.

Sartre, Jean-Paul. *Search for a Method*. Hazel Barnes, tr. New York: Vintage Books, 1968.

Tillich, Paul. *The Courage to Be*. New Haven, CT: Yale University Press, 2000.

Wahl, Jean. *A Short History of Existentialism*. Forrest Williams and Stanley Maron, trs. New York: Philosophical Library, 1949.

## Phenomenology

Arendt, Hannah, "Heidegger at Eighty," in *Heidegger and Modern Philosophy*, Michael Murray, ed., New Haven, CT: Yale University Press, 1978.

Heidegger, M., *Being and Time*. John Macquarrie and Edward Robinson, trs. New York: Harper & Row, 1962.

Husserl, Edmund. *Logical Investigations.* Dermot Moran, J.N. Findlay, and Michael Dummet, eds. New York: Routledge, 2001.

Lacan, Jacques. *Psychology.* Sean Horner, ed. New York: Routledge, 2005.

Merleau-Ponty, M. *Adventures of the Dialectic.* Joseph Bien, tr. Evanston, IL: Northwestern University Press, 1973.

Saussure, Ferdinand. *Course in General Linguistics.* New York: McGraw Hill, 1966.

### Critical Theory and Structuralism

Poster, M. *Existential Marxism in Postwar France: From Sartre to Althusser.* Princeton: Princeton University Press, 1975.

Ricoeur, P. *Freud and Philosophy: An Essay on Interpretation.* Denis Savage, tr. New Haven: Yale University Press, 1970.

Ricoeur, P. *Oneself as Another.* Kathleen Blamey, tr. Chicago: University of Chicago Press, 1995.

Wigershaus, Paul. *The Frankfurt School: Its History, Theories, and Political Significance.* Boston: MIT Press, 1995.

## AMERICAN PHILOSOPHY

*For a general overview of American Philosophy, see:*

Kuklick, Bruce. *A History of Philosophy in America 1720–2000.* New York: Oxford University Press, 2001.

### Early American Philosophical Strains

Emerson, Ralph Waldo. *The Essential Writings of Ralph Waldo Emerson,* Brooks Atkinson, and Mary Oliver, eds. New York: Modern Library Classics, 2000.

Gill, Jerry H. *Native American World Views: An Introduction,* Amherst NY: Humanities Books, 2002.

Pirsig, Robert. *Lila.* New York: Bantam, 1992.

Snider, Denton J. *St. Louis Movement in Philosophy, Literature, Education, Psychology—with Chapters of Autobiography.* Sterling, VA: Thoemmes Press, 2001

Thoreau, Henry David. *The Portable Thoreau.* Carl Bode, ed. New York: Penguin Classics, 1964.

### Pragmatism and Process Philosophy

Dewey, John. *Dewey and His Critics, Essays from The Journal of Philosophy.* Sidney Morgenbesser, ed. Indianapolis, IN: Hackett, 1977.

James, William. *Pragmatism.* Bruce Kuklick, ed. Indianapolis, IN: Hackett, 1981.

Lewis, Clarence Irving. *Mind and the World Order: Outline of a Theory of Knowledge.* Mineola, NY: Dover Books on Western Philosophy, 1991.

Peirce, Charles S. *The Essential Peirce: Selected Philosophical Writings, 1893–1913.* Peirce Edition Project, Nathan Houser, and Jonathan R. Eller, eds. Bloomington, IN: Indiana University Press, 1998.

Royce, Josiah. *The Philosophy of Josiah Royce.* John K. Roth, ed. Indianapolis, IN: Hackett, 1982.

Santayana, George. *Persons and Places.* William G. Holzberger, Herman J. Saatkamp, Jr., and Richard C. Lyon, eds. Cambridge, MA: MIT Press, 1988.

White, Alfred North. *Process and Reality.* New York: The Free Press, 1978.

## ANALYTIC PHILOSOPHY

### Early Twentieth Century Analytic Philosophy

Feferman, Anita Burdman, and Solomon Feferman. *Alfred Tarski: Life and Logic.* Cambridge, UK: Cambridge Concise Histories, 2008.

Levy, Paul. *Moore: G.E. Moore and the Cambridge Apostles.* New York: Oxford Paperbacks, 1981.

Moore, G.E. *Philosophical Studies.* Cambridge, UK: Cambridge University Press, 2007.

Russell, Bertrand. *The Basic Writings of Bertrand Russell.* New York: Routledge, 2002.

Smith, Peter. *An Introduction to Gödel's Theorems (Cambridge Introductions to Philosophy).* Cambridge, UK: Cambridge University Press, 2007.

Wittgenstein, Ludwig. *Tractatus Logico Philosophicus.* New York: Routledge Classics, 2001.

### Logical Positivism

Ayer, A.J. *Language Truth and Logic.* New York: Penguin Modern Classics, 2001.

Carnap, Rudolf. *The Logical Structure of the World and Pseudoproblems in Philosophy.* Peru, IL: Open Court Classics, 2003.

Schlick, Moritz. *General Theory of Knowledge.* New York: Library of Exact Philosophy, 1985.

Stadler, Friedrich. *The Vienna Circle: Studies in the Origin, Development, and Influence of Logical Empiricism.* New York: Sprnger-Verlag Wien, 2001.

### Ordinary Language Analysis

Anscombe, G.E.M. *Human Life, Action and Ethics: Essays by G.E.M. Anscombe* (St. Andrews Studies in Philosophy & Public Affairs). Exeter, UK: Imprint Academic, 2006.

Austin, J.L. *How to Do Things with Words,* Cambridge, MA: Harvard University Press, 1975.

Bouwsma, O.K. *Philosophical Essays.* Kansas City, KS: Landmark Edition, 1982.

Malcolm, Norman. *Ludwig Wittgenstein: A Memoir.* New York: Oxford University Press, 2001.

Wittgenstein, Ludwig. *Philosophical Investigations: The German Text, with a Revised English Translation, 50th Anniversary Commemorative Edition*. London: Blackwell, 2003.

## Analytic Ethics

Foot, Philippa. *Natural Goodness*. New York: Oxford University Press, 2002.

MacIntyre, Alastair. *After Virtue: A Study in Moral Theory*. Notre Dame, IN: University of Notre Dame Press, 2007.

Moore, G.E. *Principia Ethica* (Principles of Ethics). Mineola, NY: Philosophical Classics, Dover, 2004.

Smith, Tara. *Ayn Rand's Normative Ethics: The Virtuous Egoist*. New York: Cambridge University Press, 2007.

Smart, J.J.C., and Bernard Williams. *Utilitarianism: For and Against*. New York: Cambridge University Press, 1973.

Scheffler, Israel. *The Rejection of Consequentialism*. New York: Oxford University Press, 1995.

Stevenson, Charles L. *Facts and Values: Studies in Ethical Analysis*. New Haven, CT: Yale University Press, 1963.

## Analytic Political Philosophy

Berlin, Isaiah. *The Proper Study of Mankind: An Anthology of Essays*. New York: Farrar, Straus, Giroux, 2000.

Nozick, Robert. *Anarchy, State and Utopia*. London: Blackwell, 2003.

Popper, Karl. *The Open Society and its Enemies*. New York: Routledge Classics, 2002.

Rawls, John. *A Theory of Justice*. Cambridge, MA: Harvard University Press, 1971.

Strauss, Leo. *Liberalism Ancient and Modern*. New York: Harper Collins, 1995.

## Epistemology and Metaphysics after Logical Positivism

Goodman, Nelson. *Fact, Fiction and Forecast*. Cambridge, MA: Harvard University Press, 2006.

Putnam, Hilary. *Pragmatism: An Open Question*. London: Blackwell, 2000.

Quine, W.V.O. *From a Logical Point of View: Nine Logico-Philosophical Essays*. Cambridge, MA: Harvard University Press, 2006.

Sellars, Wilfred. *Science, Perception and Reality*. Atascadero, CA: Ridgeview Publishing 1963.

Strawson, P.F. *The Bounds of Sense: An Essay on Kant's Critique of Pure Reason*. New York: Routledge, 1990.

## Philosophy of Science

Feyerabend, Paul. *Against Method: Outline of an Anarchistic Theory of Knowledge*. Brooklyn, NY: Verso, 1993.

Kuhn, Thomas. *The Structure of Scientific Revolutions.* Chicago: University of Chicago Press, 1990.

Lakatos, Imre. *Proofs and Refutations: The Logic of Mathematical Discovery.* New York: Cambridge University Press, 1976.

Lewontin, Richard. *The Triple Helix: Gene, Organism, and Environment.* Cambridge, MA: Harvard University Press, 2000.

Nagel, Ernest. *The Structure of Science.* Indianapolis, IN: Hackett, 1979.

Popper, Karl. *The Logic of Scientific Discovery.* New York: Routledge, 2002.

Reichenbach, Hans. *Experience and Prediction.* Notre Dame, IN: University of Notre Dame Press, 2006.

## Philosophy of Mind and Philosophy of Language

Chomsky, Noam. *Reflections on Language.* New York: Pantheon, 1975.

Churchland, Paul. *Scientific Realism and the Plasticity of Mind.* New York: Cambridge University Press, 1979.

Dreyfus, H. *What Computers Can't Do: The Limits of Artificial Intelligence.* New York: Harper Colophon, 1979.

Fodor, Jerry Alan. *The Mind Doesn't Work That Way: The Scope and Limits of Computational Psychology.* Boston, MA: MIT Press, 2000.

Nagel, Thomas. *The View from Nowhere.* New York: Oxford University Press, 1986.

Ryle, Gilbert. *The Concept of Mind.* Chicago: University of Chicago Press, 2000.

Schwartz, Stephen P., ed. *Naming, Necessity and Natural Kinds.* Ithaca, NY: Cornell University Press, 1977.

Skinner, B.F. *Verbal Behavior.* New York: Prentice Hall, 1957.

Turing, Alan Mathison. *The Essential Turing.* New York: Oxford University Press, 2004.

Watson, J.B. *Behaviorism.* New Brunswick, NJ: Transaction Publishers, 1997.

# NEW PHILOSOPHY

## Postmodern Philosophy

Baudrillard, Jean. *Simulacra and Simulation.* Shiela Faria Glaser, ed. Ann Arbor: University of Michigan Press, 1994.

Deleuze, Gilles, Felix Guattari and Brian Massumi. *A Thousand Plateaus: Capitalism and Schizophrenia.* Minneapolis, MN: University of Minnesota Press, 1987.

Derrida, Jacques. *Philosophy Guidebook to Derrida on Deconstruction.* Barry Stocker, ed. New York: Routledge, 2006.

Findlayson, James Gordon. *Habermas: A Very Short Introduction.* New York: Oxford University Press, 2005.

Lyotard, Jean Francois. *The Postmodern Condition: A Report on Knowledge.* Frederic Jameson, ed. Minneapolis, MN: University of Minnesota Press, 1984.

Rorty, Richard. *Contingency, Irony, and Solidarity.* New York: Cambridge University Press, 1989.

## Other American Philosophies

### African American Philosophy—Classic

Crummell, Alexander. *Destiny and Race: Selected Writings, 1840–1898.* Wilson Jeremiah Moses, ed. Amherst, MA: University of Massachusetts Press, 1992.

Douglass, Frederick. *A Narrative of the Life of Frederick Douglass, an American Slave.* New York: Penguin Classics, 1982.

DuBois, W.E.B. *The Souls of Black Folk.* New York: Signet Classic, 1995.

King, Jr., Martin Luther. *A Testament of Hope: The Essential Writings and Speeches of Martin Luther King, Jr.* New York: Macmillan, 2002.

Locke, Alain. *The New Negro.* Oxford, UK: Johnson Reprint Corp., 1998.

Washington, Booker T. *Up from Slavery: An Autobiography.* Harwich, MA: Reed Books, 2006.

### African American Philosophy—Contemporary

Allen, Anita. *Uneasy Access: Privacy for Women in a Free Society.* Lanham, MD: Rowman & Littlefield, 1988.

Appiah, Kwame Anthony and Amy Gutmann. *Color Conscious: The Political Morality of Race.* Princeton, NJ: Princeton University Press,1996.

Boxill, Bernard. *Blacks and Social Justice.* Lanham, MD: Rowman & Littlefield, 1992.

Davis, Angela. *Women, Race, and Class.* New York: Random House, 1983.

Gordon, Lewis R. *Bad Faith and Antiblack Racism.* Atlantic Highlands, NJ: Humanities Press, 1995.

Grant, Jacquelyn Jacquelyn. *White Women's Christ and Black Women's Jesus.* Atlanta, GA: Scholars Press, 1989.

Harris, Leonard, ed. *Philosophy Born of Struggle: Anthology of Afro-American Philosophy from 1917.* Dubuque, IA: Kendall/Hunt Publishing Co., 1983.

Lawson, Bill E., ed. *The Underclass Question.* Philadelphia, PA: Temple University Press, 1992.

Lott, Tommy L. ed. *Subjugation and Bondage.* Lanham, MD: Rowman & Littlefield, 1998.

McGary, Howard. *Race and Social Justice.* London: Blackwell, 1998.

Mills, Charles W. *The Racial Contract.* Ithaca, NY: Cornell University Press, 1997.

Moody-Adams, Michele M. *Morality, Culture and Philosophy: Fieldwork in Familiar Places.* Cambridge, MA: Harvard University Press, 1997.

Moses, Greg. *Revolution of Conscience: Martin Luther King, Jr., and the Philosophy of Nonviolence.* New York: Guilford Publications, 1998.

Mosley, Albert. *Affirmative Action: Social Justice or Unfair Preference?* Lanham, MD: Rowman & Littlefield, 1996.

Outlaw, Lucius. *On Race and Philosophy.* New York: Routledge, 1996.

Roberts, Rodney C., ed. *Injustice and Rectification.* New York: Peter Lang Publishers, 2002.

Thomas, Laurence. *Vessels of Evil: American Slavery and the Holocaust.* Philadelphia, PA: Temple University Press, 1993.

West, Cornel. *Prophesy Deliverance! An Afro-American Revolutionary Christianity.* Westminster, PA: John Knox Press, 1982.

Yancy, George, ed. *African-American Philosophers, 17 Conversations.* New York: Routledge, 1998.

Zack, Naomi. *Thinking about Race.* Belmont, CA: Thomson Wadsworth, 2006.

### Native American Philosophy

Allen, Paula Gunn. *The Sacred Hoop.* Boston, MA: Beacon Press, 1992.

Cordova, V.F. *How It Is: The Native American Philosophy of V.F. Cordova.* Linda Hogan, Kathleen Dean Moore, Kurt Peters, and Ted Jojoba, eds. Tucson, AZ: University of Arizona Press, 2007.

Cotton, Angela L., and Christa Acampora Crista Davis, eds. *Cultural Sites of Critical Insight: Philosophy, Aesthetics, and African American and Native American Women's Writings.* New York: SUNY Press, 2007.

Waters, Anne. *American Indian Thought: Philosophical Essays.* London: Blackwell, 2003.

Weaver, Jace. *Defending Mother Earth: Native American Perspectives on Environmental Justice.* Maryknoll, NY: Orbis Books, 1996.

### Latin American Philosophy

Alcoff, Linda, and Eduardo Mendieta. *Thinking from the Underside of History: Enrique Dusell's Philosophy of Liberation.* Lanham, MD: Roman & Littlefield, 2000.

Gracia, Jorge J.E., and Elizabeth Millan-Zaibert, eds. *Latin American Philosophy for the 21st Century: The Human Condition, Values, and the Search for Identity.* Buffalo, NY: Prometheus Books, 2003.

Mendieta, Eduardo. *Global Fragments: Critical Theory, Latin America and Globalizations.* New York: SUNY Press, 2007.

Nuccetelli, Susana. *Latin American Thought: Philosophical Problems and Arguments.* Boulder, CO: Westview Press, 2002.

Schutte, Ofelia. *Cultural Identity and Social Liberation in Latin American Thought.* New York: SUNY Press, 1993.

### Other Continental Traditions

### Afro-centrism and African Philosophy

Appiah, K. Anthony. *In My Father's House: Africa in the Philosophy of Culture.* New York: Oxford University Press, 1992.

Asante, Molefi. *The Afrocentric Idea.* Philadelphia, PA: Temple University Press, 1998.

Bernal, Martin. *Black Athena: The Afroasiatic Roots of Classical Civilization.* 3 vols. New Brunswick, NJ: Rutgers University Press, 1987–2006.

Gordon, Lewis R. *Her Majesty's Other Children: Sketches of Racism from a Neocolonial Age.* Lanham, MD: Rowman & Littlefield, 1997.

Gyeke, Kwame. *Tradition and Modernity.* New York: Oxford University Press, 1997.

Eze, Emmanuel, ed. *Postcolonial African Philosophy.* London: Blackwell, 1997.

Hountondji, Paulin J. *African Philosophy: Myth and Reality.* Bloomington, IN: Indiana University Press, 1996.

Mbiti, John. *African Religions and Philosophy.* New York: Doubleday, 1970.

Mosley, Albert, ed. *African Philosophy: Selected Readings.* New York: Prentice Hall, 1995.

Serequeberhan Tsenay, ed. *African Philosophy: The Essential Readings.* New York: Paragon House, 1991.

## Buddhism and Confucianism

Abe, Masao, and Steven Hein. *Zen and Comparative Studies.* Honolulu, HI: University of Hawaii Press, 1997.

Bo Mu, Bo. *Comparative Approaches to Chinese Philosophy.* Farnham, Surrey, UK: Ashgate Publishing, 2003.

Cheng, Chung-Ying. *New Dimensions of Confucian and Neo-Confucian Philosophy.* New York: SUNY Press, 1991.

Ivanhoe, Philip J. *Ethics in the Confucian Tradition: The Thought of Mengzi and Wang Yangming.* Indianapolis, IN: Hackett, 2002.

Keown, Damien. *The Nature of Buddhist Ethics.* Basingstoke, Hampshire, UK: Palgrave Macmillan, 2001.

Li-Hsiang, Lisa Rosenlee, *Confucianism and Women: A Philosophical Interpretation,* Roger T. Ames, ed. New York: SUNY Press, 2006.

Lusthaus, Dan. *Buddhist Phenomenology: A Philosophical Investigation of Yogacara Buddhism.* New York: Routledge, Chapman, & Hall, 1997.

Norden, Bryan W. van. *Confucius and the Analects: New Essays.* New York: Oxford University Press, 2002.

Rosenlee, Li-Hsiang Lisa. *Confucianism and Women: A Philosophical Interpretation.* Roger T. Ames, ed. New York: SUNY Press, 2006.

Shun Kwong-loi, and David B. Wong, *Confucian Ethics: A Comparative Study of Self, Autonomy, and Community,* New York: Cambridge University Press, 2004.

Suzuki, Daisetz Teitaro. *Manuel of Zen Buddhism.* New York: Grove, 1960.

Yao, Xinzhong and Hsin-chung Yao. *An Introduction to Confusianism.* Cambridge University Press, 2000.

## Feminist Philosophy

Afshar, Haleh, ed. *Women and Politics in the Third World*. New York: Routledge, 1996.

Alcoff, Linda and Elizabeth Potter, eds. *Feminist Epistemologies,* New York: Routledge, 1993.

Bartke, Sandra Lee. *Femininity and Domination*. New York: Routledge, 1990.

Butler, Judith. *Gender Trouble: Feminism and the Subversion of Identity*. New York: Routledge, 1990.

Beauvoir, Simone de. *The Second Sex*. New York: Knopf, 1953.

Chodorow, Nancy. *The Reproduction of Mothering*. Berkeley, CA: University of California Press, 1978.

Cixous, Hélène. *The Hélène Cixous Reader*. Susan Sellars and Jacques Derrida, eds. New York: Routledge, 1994.

Daly, Mary. *The Church and the Second Sex*. Boston, MA: Beacon Press, 1986.

Digby, Tom, ed. *Men Doing Feminism*. New York: Routledge, 1998.

Friedan, Betty. *The Feminine Mystique*. New York: W.W. Norton, 1963.

Frye, Marilyn. *The Politics of Reality: Essays in Feminist Theory*. Berkeley, CA: Crossing Press, 1983.

Gilligan, Carol. *In a Different Voice*. Cambridge, MA: Harvard University Press, 1982.

Harding, Sandra G. *Whose Science? Whose Knowledge: Thinking from Women's Lives*. Ithaca, NY: Cornell University Press, 1991.

hooks, bell. *Ain't I a Woman? Black Women and Feminism*. Cambridge, MA: South End Press, 2007.

Heyes, Cressida J. in *Line Drawings: Defining Women through Feminist Practice*. Ithaca, NY: Cornell University Press, 2000.

Hochschild, Arlie Russell, and Anne Machung. *The Second Shift*. New York: Avon Books, 1990.

Irigaray, Luce. *The Forgetting of Air in Martin Heidegger* (Constructs Series). Mary Beth Mader, tr. Austin, TX: University of Texas Press, 1999.

Jagger, Alison M., and Marion Young. *A Companion to Feminist Philosophy*. London: Blackwell, 2000.

Kittay, Eva. *Love's Labor: Essays on Women, Equality and Dependence*. New York: Routledge, 1999.

Kourany, Janet, ed. *The Gender of Science,* Upper Saddle River, NJ: Prentice Hall, 2002.

Kristeva, Julia. *The Kristeva Reader*. Toril Moi, ed. New York: Columbia University Press, 1986.

Lloyd, Genevieve. *The Man of Reason: "Male" and "Female" in Western Philosophy*. New York: Routledge, 1993.

MacKinnon, Catherine (with Andrea Dworkin). *Pornography and Civil Rights: A New Day for Women's Equality*. Minneapolis, MN: Organizing against Pornography, 1988.

Marcus, Ruth Barkan. *Modalities: Philosophical Essays.* New York: Oxford University Press, 1993.

Noddings, Nell. *Caring: A Feminist Approach to Ethics and Moral Education.* Berkeley, CA: University of California Press, 1982.

Pateman, Carole. *The Sexual Contract.* San Francisco, CA: Stanford University Press, 1988.

Ruddick, Sara. *Maternal Thinking: Toward a Politics of Peace.* Boston, MA: Beacon Press, 1990.

Slote, Michael A. *The Ethics of Care and Empathy.* New York: Routledge, 2007.

Strikwerda, Robert, and Larry May, eds. *Rethinking Masculinity: Philosophical Explorations in Light of Feminism.* Lanham, MD: Rowman & Littlefield, 1996.

Shrage, Laurie. Abortion and Social Responsibility: Depolarizing the Debate. New York: Oxford University Press, 2003.

Spelman, Elizabeth V. in *Inessential Woman: Problems of Exclusion in Feminist Thought.* Boston, MA: Beacon Press, 1990.

Weed, Elizabeth, and Naomi Schor, eds. *Feminism Meets Queer Theory.* Bloomington, IN: Indiana University Press, 1997.

Zack, Naomi in *Inclusive Feminism: A Third Wave Theory of Women's Commonality.* Lanham, MD: Rowman & Littlefield, 2005.

## Environmental Philosophy

Benton, Ted. *Natural Relations: Ecology, Animal Rights & Social Justice.* Brooklyn, NY: Verso, 1993.

Bernstein, Jay. *Adorno: Disenchantment and Ethics.* New York: Cambridge University Press, 2001.

Callicott, Baird, and Roger T. Ames. *Nature in Asian Traditions of Thought.* New York: SUNY Press, 1989.

Callicott, J.B. *In Defense of the Land Ethic: Essays in Environmental Philosophy.* New York: SUNY Press, 1989.

Carson, Rachel. *Silent Spring.* New York: Houghton Miflin Books, 2002.

Clark, S.R.L. *The Moral Status of Animals.* Oxford, UK: Clarendon Press, 1977.

Cohen, M.P. *The Pathless Way: John Muir and American Wilderness.* Milwaukee, WI: University of Wisconsin Press, 1984.

Cuomo, Chris. *Feminism and Ecological Communities: An Ethic of Flourishing.* New York: Routledge, 1997.

Dasgupta, Partha. *Human Well-being and the Natural Environment.* New York: Oxford University Press, 2001.

Devall, B., and G. Sessions. *Deep Ecology: Living as if Nature Mattered.* Layton, UT: Gibbs Smith, 1985.

Dobson, A., ed. *Fairness and Futurity: Essays on Environmental Sustainability and Social Justice.* New York: Oxford University Press, 1999.

Gaard, Greta, ed. *Ecofeminism: Women, Animals, Nature.* Philadelphia, PA: Temple University Press, 1993.

Goodin, Robert E. *Green Political Theory.* Cambridge, UK: Polity Press, 1992.

Gore, Al. *An Inconvenient Truth: The Planetary Emergency of Global Warming and What We Can Do about It.* New York: Rodale Press, 2006.

Graham, Harvey. *Animism: Respecting the Living World.* New York: Columbia University Press, 2005.

Hill, Thomas E. "Ideals of Human Virture and Preserving the Natural Environment," in *Ethics,* vol. 5. (1983).

Jamieson, D., ed. *A Companion to Environmental Philosophy.* Malden, MA: Blackwell, 2001.

Leopold, Aldo. *Sand County Almanac.* New York: Ballantine Books, 1949.

Naess, A. *Ecology, Community, Lifestyle.* Cambridge, UK: Cambridge University Press, 1989.

Nash, R. *The Rights of Nature: A History of Environmental Ethics.* Madison, WI: University of Wisconsin Press, 1989.

Plumwood, V. *Environmental Culture.* New York: Routledge, 2002.

Reagan, Tom. *The Case for Animal Rights.* Berkeley, CA: University of California Press, 1983.

Singer, Peter. *Animal Liberation: A New Ethics for Our Treatment of Animals.* London, UK: Jonathan Cape, 1983.

Vogel, S. *Against Nature: The Concept of Nature in Critical Theory.* New York: SUNY Press, 1996.

Warren, K.L., ed. *Ecological Feminism.* New York: Routledge, 1994.

Westra, Laura, and Bill E. Lawson. *Environmental Racism: Confronting Issues of Global Justice.* Lanham, MD: Rowman & Littlefield, 2001.

Zimmerman, M. *Contesting Earth's Future: Radical Ecology and Postmodernity.* Berkeley, CA: University of California Press, 1994.

## Other Trends in New Philosophy

Allen, Richard and Murray Smith, eds. *Film Theory and Philosophy.* New York: Oxford University Press, 1997.

Appiah, Kwame Anthony. *Experiments in Ethics.* Cambridge, MA: Harvard University Press, 2008.

Dennett, Daniel. *Sweet Dreams: Philosophical Obstacles to a Science of Consciousness.* Cambridge, MA: MIT Press, 2005.

Gaarder, Jostein. *Sophie's World: A Novel about the History of Philosophy.* Berkeley, CA: Berkeley Books, 1994.

Higgs, Eric, Andrew Light, and David Strong, eds. *Technology and the Good Life.* Chicago: University of Chicago Press, 2000.

McGinn, Colin. *The Mysterious Flame: Conscious Minds in a Material World.* New York: Basic Books, 1999.

Nichols, Shaun, and Joshua Michael Knobe. *Experimental Philosophy.* New York: Oxford University Press, 2008.

Wartenberg, Thomas E., and Angela Curran, eds. *Philosophy and Film.* Cambridge, MA: Blackwell, 2005.

# Index

Note: (ill.) indicates photos and illustrations.

**469**

# E

early American philosophy.
*See also* New England
transcendentalists; Social
Darwinism; St. Louis
Hegelians
  most influential strains,
  295
  Native Americans,
  296–97
  Sagoewatha, 297
  Tenskwatawa, 296–97
early modern philosophy
  definition of, 119
  epistemological
  rationalism, 119–20
  proponents of, 119
early twentieth century analytic philosophy
  Gödel, Kurt, 338–39
  important themes,
  331–32
  logical atomism, 334
  Tarski, Alfred, 339
  truth-functional logic,
  333–34
Earth, 95–98
Eastern philosophy, 298–99,
  403–4
ecology, 399
economics, 186, 206
Edison, Thomas, 309, 309
  (ill.)
Edmonds, David, 372
education, 147–48, 320
Edwards, John, 148
Edwards, Jonathan, 189–90
  God, 190–91
  lack of mercy, 190–91
  view of God, 190
efficient and final causation,
  137
efficient cause, 36
egoism, 225
egoistic suicide, 252
Eichmann, Adolf, 288
eidetic intuition, 276
eidetic reduction, 276
Eidinow, John, 372
Eightfold Path, 405

Einstein, Albert, 103, 109,
  130, 220, 327, 340
Eisele, Carolyn, 311
Eleatic school, 16–18
Electra complex, 249
eliminative materialism,
  382–83
Eliot, George, 130
Eliot, T. S., 322
elixir of life, 115
Elizabeth I, Queen, 103, 104
Elizabeth of Bohemia,
  Princess, 123–24
Elkaim, Arlette, 268–69
Eloise, 64
Elstob, Elizabeth, 155, 182
Emancipation Proclamation,
  307
embryology, 135 (ill.),
  135–36
emergence, 323
Emerson, Ralph Waldo,
  302–5, 303 (ill.)
  as abolitionist, 304–5
  the *Dial,* 306
  "Divinity School
  Address," 305
  life of, 303
  as New England
  Transcendentalist, 300
  "over-soul," 304
  requirements for a
  scholar, 304
  St. Louis Philosophical
  Society, 299
  transcendentalism
  definition, 303
Emerson, Thomas I., 412
emotion, 141–42, 314
emotivist theory of ethics,
  352–53
Empedocles, 19 (ill.)
  four elements, 13, 18, 22
  Pre-Socratics, 12
empirical ego, 180–81
empirical psychology, 245
empiricism, 77, 84, 110, 159,
  173–74
Enckendorf, Marie-Luise,
  253
encyclopedists, 184

endeavors, 142
Engels, Friedrich, 237–39
Enlightenment period, 155,
  227. *See also* Bentham,
  Jeremy; Berkeley, George;
  Counter-Enlightenment
  figures; Hume, David;
  Kant, Immanuel;
  philosophes; Reid, Thomas;
  Rousseau, Jean-Jacques;
  Wollstonecraft, Mary
  definition of, 157
  effect on United States,
  190
  Enlightenment
  philosophers vs. other
  intellectuals, 158
  pessimists, 158–59
  philosophy, 157
  reason, 158
  Romantics, 158–59
  themes, 157–58
enthusiasm, 150
environmental philosophy
  animal rights, 421–22
  criticism of deep
  ecological and animal
  value views, 421–22
  deep ecology, 419–20
  definition of, 417–18
  domestic animals, 421
  ethics, 422
  feminism, 422
  Jonas, Hans, 271
  Naess, Arne, 419–20
  problems of, 417–18
  racial and international
  studies, 422
  religion issues, 422
  reverence of Earth,
  417–18
  shallow ecology, 419–20
  start of, 419
environmentalism, 399. *See
  also* environmental philos
  ophy
Epictetus, 41–42
Epicurus, 42, 43 (ill.), 80
epicycle, 97
epigenesis, 135
epistemological rationalism,
  119–20

**473**

478